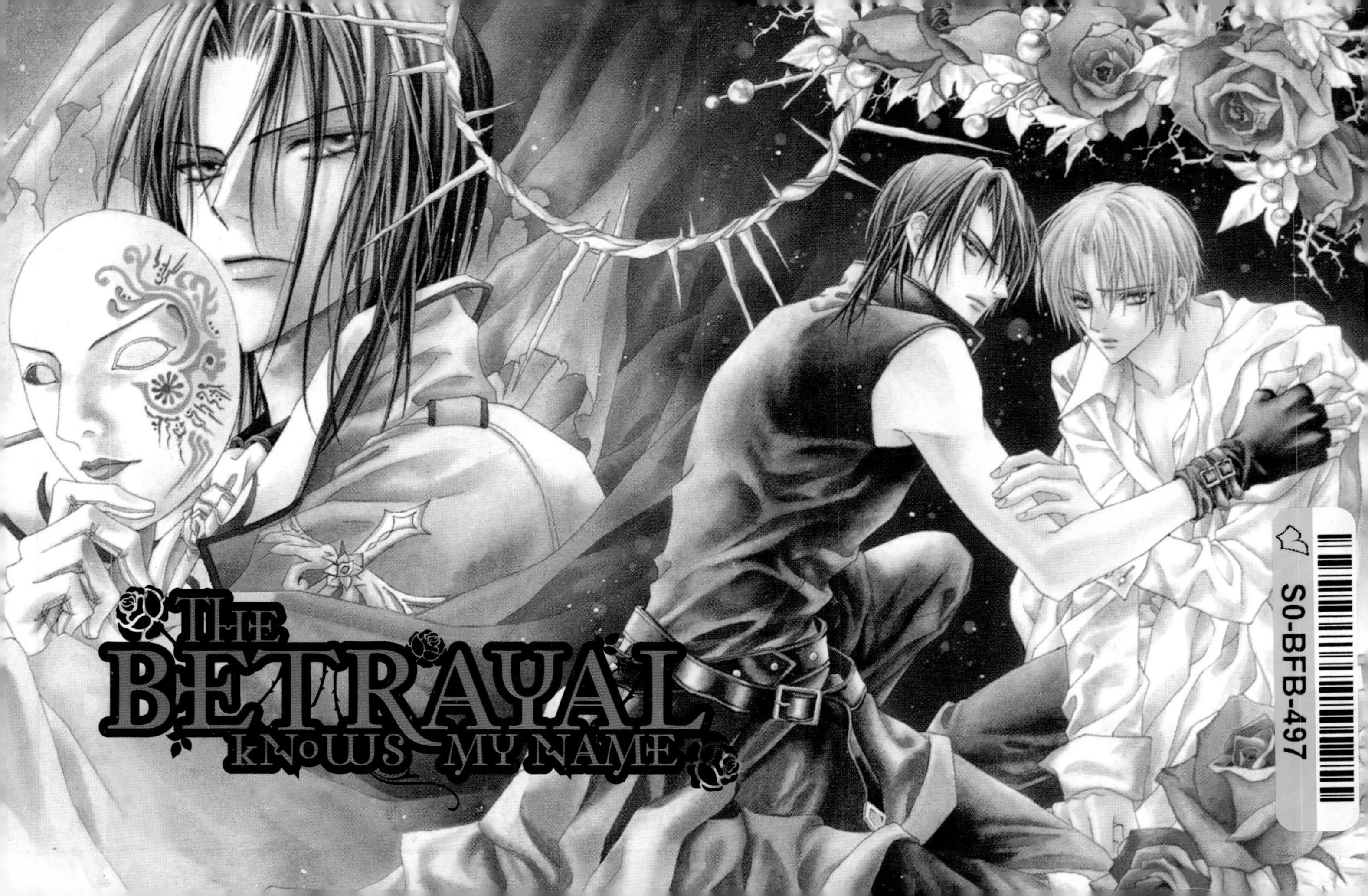
THE
BETRAYAL
KNOWS MY NAME
S0-BFB-497

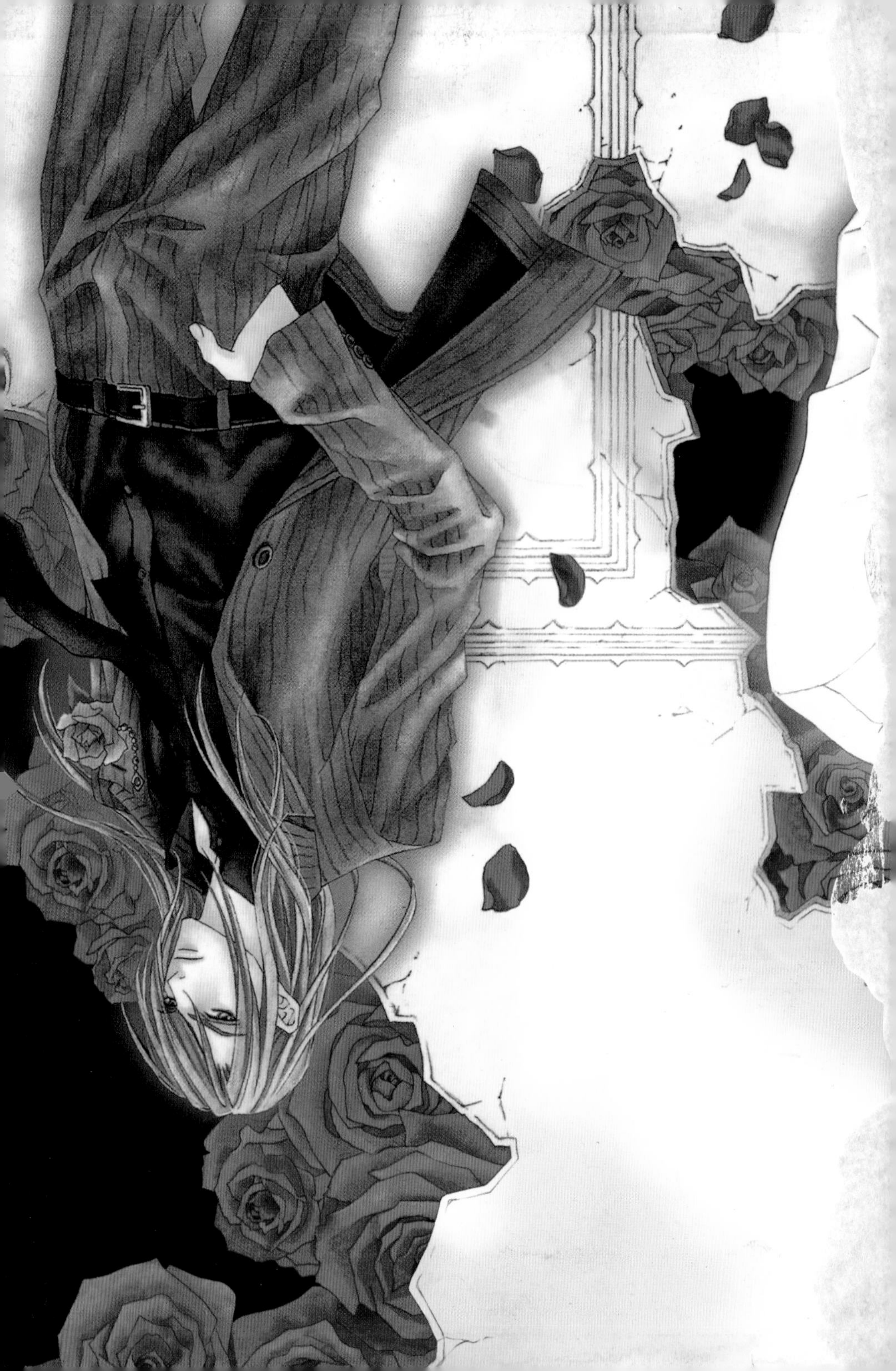

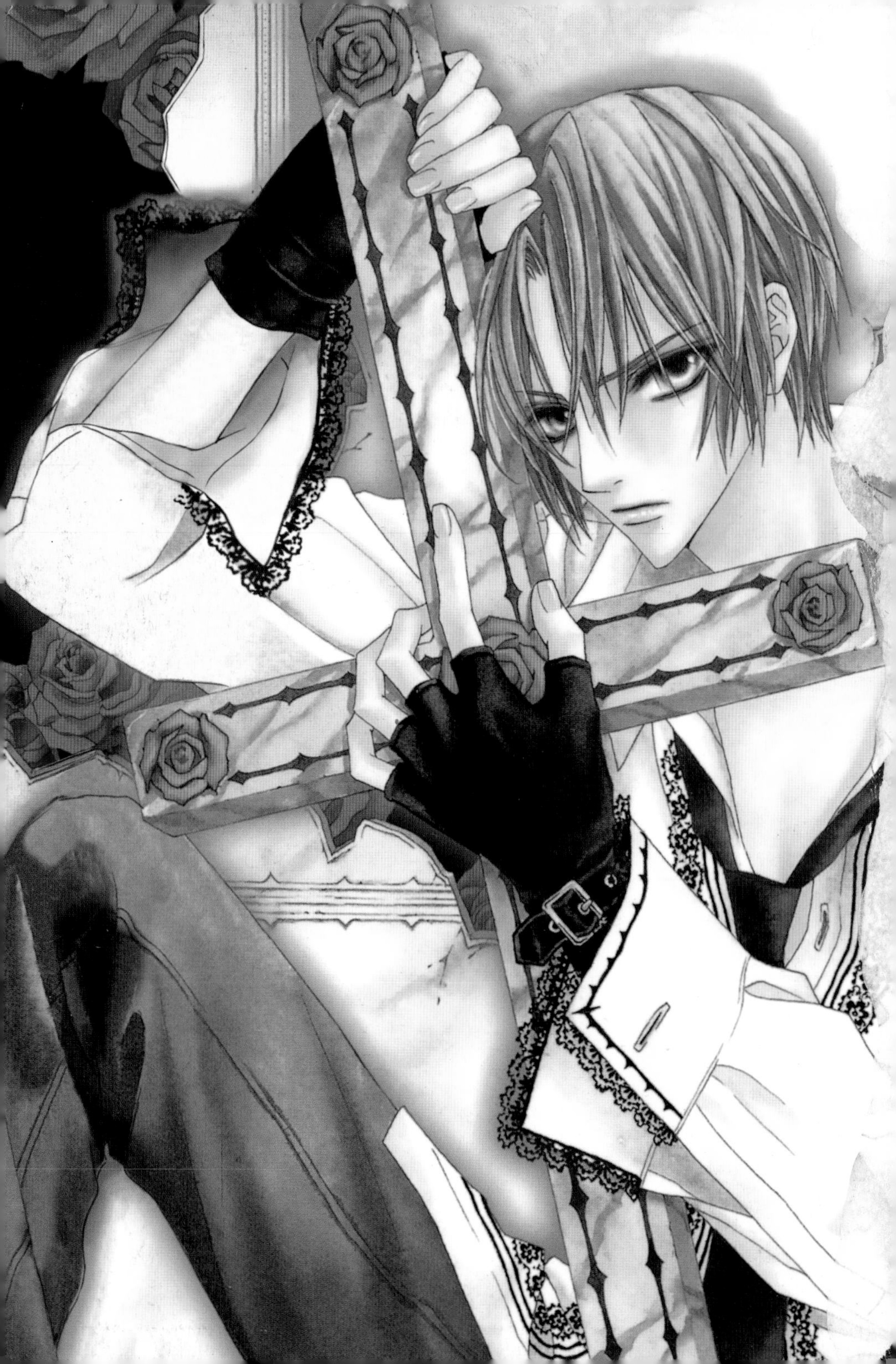

THE BETRAYAL KNOWS MY NAME

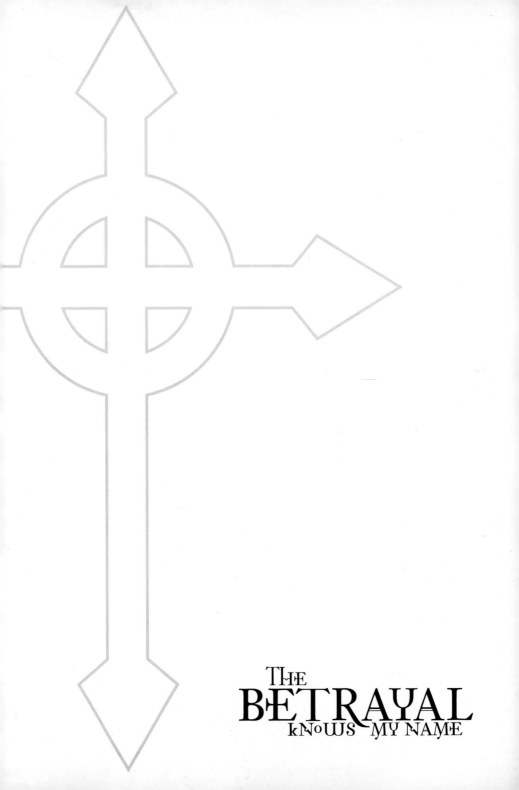

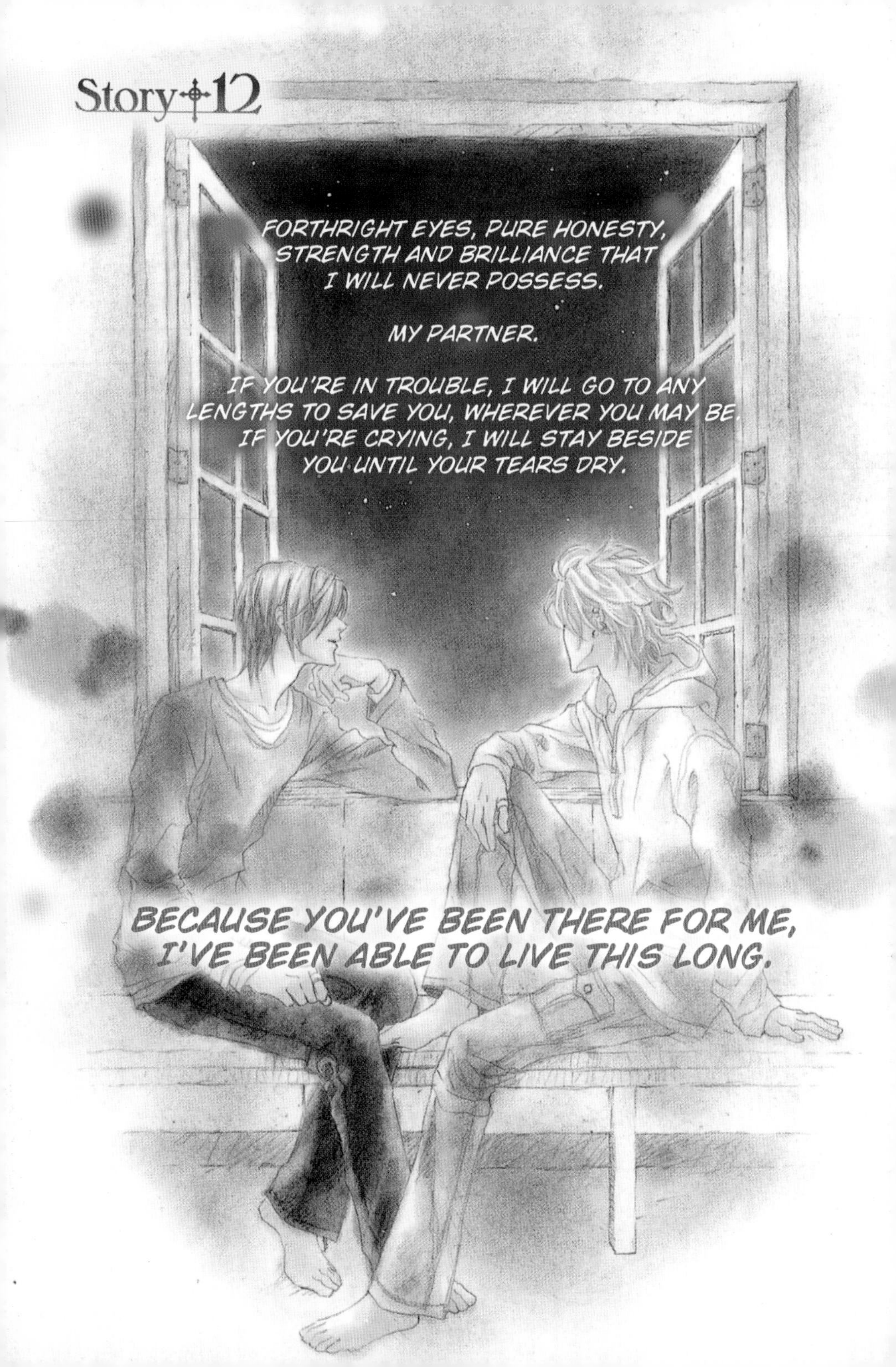
Story 12
FORTHRIGHT EYES, PURE HONESTY, STRENGTH AND BRILLIANCE THAT I WILL NEVER POSSESS.
MY PARTNER.
IF YOU'RE IN TROUBLE, I WILL GO TO ANY LENGTHS TO SAVE YOU, WHEREVER YOU MAY BE. IF YOU'RE CRYING, I WILL STAY BESIDE YOU UNTIL YOUR TEARS DRY.
BECAUSE YOU'VE BEEN THERE FOR ME, I'VE BEEN ABLE TO LIVE THIS LONG.

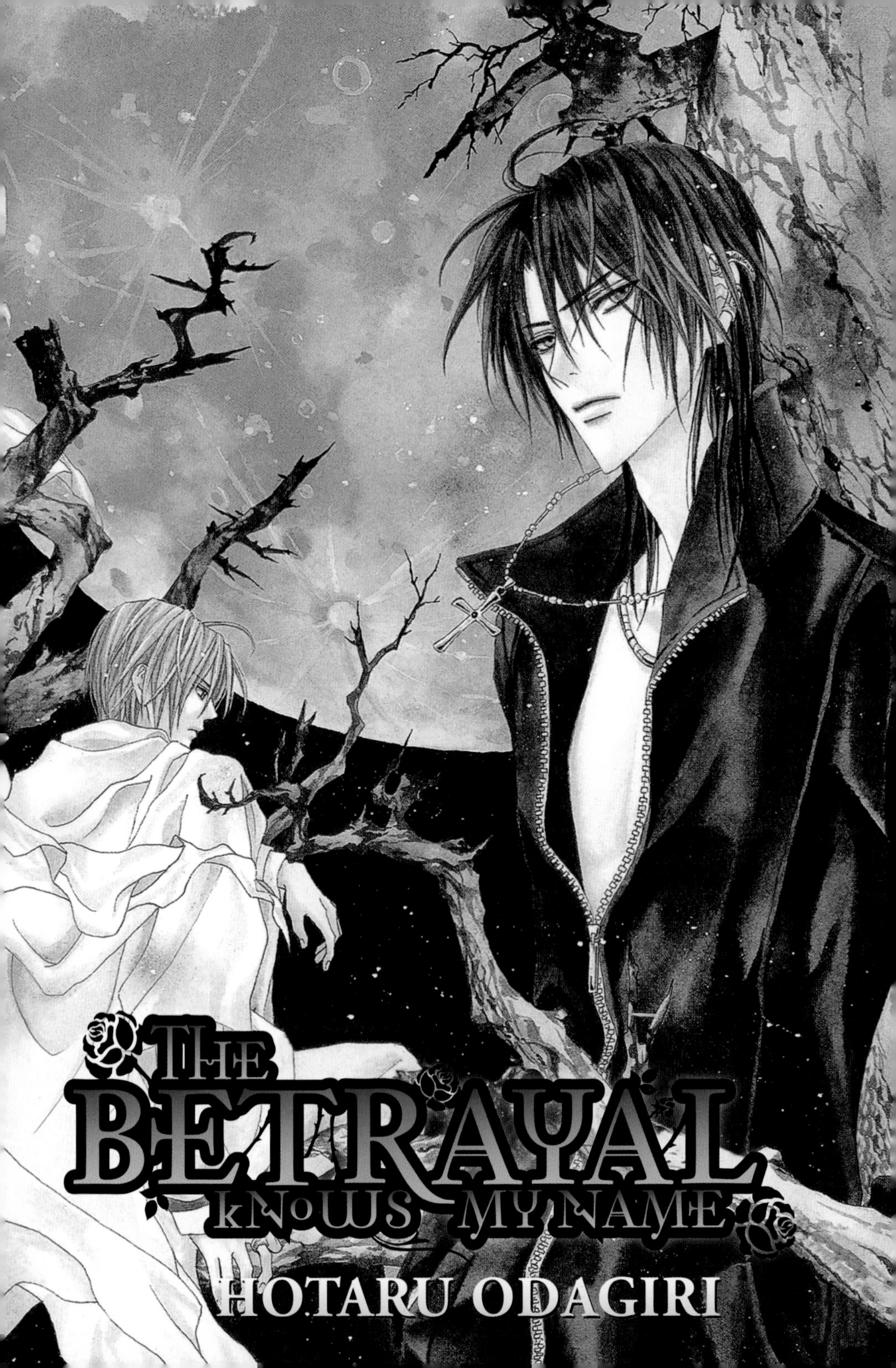
THE BETRAYAL KNOWS MY NAME
HOTARU ODAGIRI

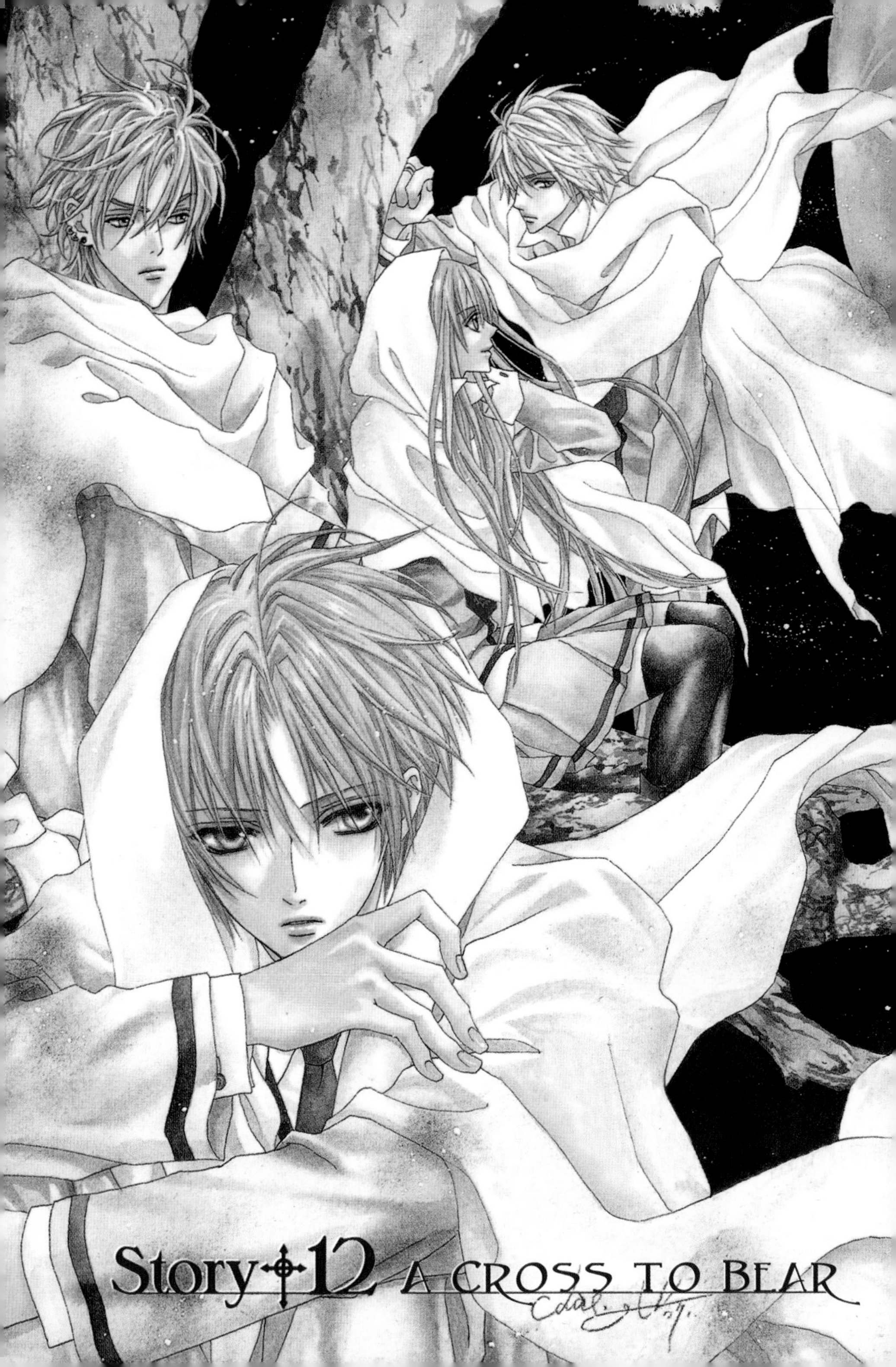
Story 12 A CROSS TO BEAR

2

Contents

CHARACTERS & STORY

The BETRAYAL knows MY NAME

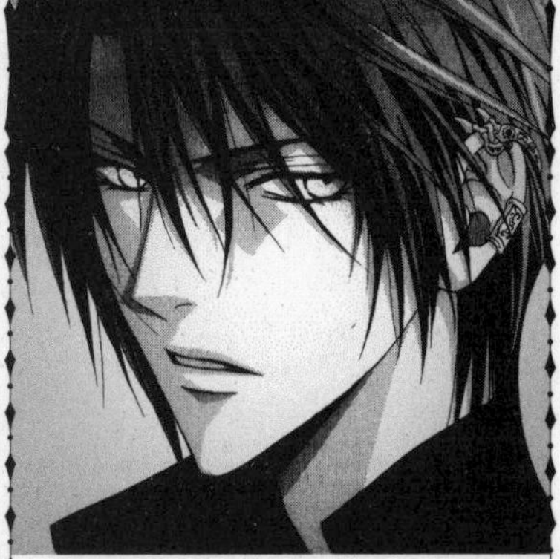

LUKA CROSSZERIA

An Opast profoundly connected with Yuki's previous incarnation. He has been on the Giou (human) side of the recurring war since its last outbreak. He has a double-X mark on his left arm.

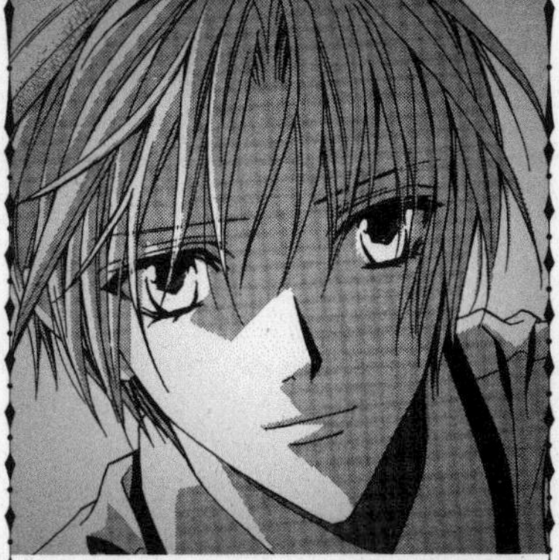

YUKI GIOU

Abandoned outside an orphanage when he was a baby, Yuki grew up thinking himself all alone in the world, but he has been taken in by Takashiro. He has the healing power "Light of God" and sometimes can read people's emotions when he touches them. First-year high school student.

STORY

• For more than a thousand years, the Giou clan and the Duras have been at war. Yuki, the boy who holds the key to that war, has been living in an orphanage, ever seeking out a reason for his own existence.

• Among those waiting at Twilight Hall for Yuki, who arrived after making the decision to fight the Duras, were two Zweilt who don't like Yuki—Hotsuma and Shuusei. Could it be that he did something to them in a previous life? Regardless of his confusion, Yuki transfers into the Mari Izumi Academy, where the other Zweilt go to school.

• Meanwhile, in the city, a man is brutally murdered, and it seems to be the work of a Duras. Takashiro is called in by the police and surmises that since the man was a high school teacher, it may be somehow connected to other developments in recent weeks—incidents of men disappearing, and "Sleeping Beauty Syndrome," in which metropolitan high school girls fall asleep and stay that way.

• With the abilities of Tsukumo and Shuusei, Takashiro is able to ascertain that an Opast is behind the incidents, and orders Yuki and the Zweilt to investigate. And then, Yuki is shocked to hear that Reiga, the overlord of the Duras and the sworn enemy of the Giou, was once one of the Giou clan himself......

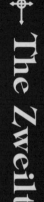

The Zweilt

Those who possess the abilities needed to hunt Duras, and protect Yuki from the Duras that target him. Generally, they work in pairs and are reborn over and over to preserve their abilities.

Tooko Murasame

a.k.a. The One Who Inquires

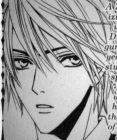

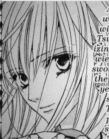

A Zweilt who works in a pair with her brother, Tsukumo, specializing in offense and wielding her greatsword, Eon, against the Duras. Second-year high school student. Like Tsukumo, she possesses the special ability "Ear of God."

Tsukumo Murasame

a.k.a. The One Who Inquires

A Zweilt specializing in defense who releases Duras with his gun, Knell. First-year high school student. Has the special ability "Ear of God," which allows him to "hear" the inner voices of both animals and people.

Hotsuma Renjou

a.k.a. The One Who Burns to Cinders

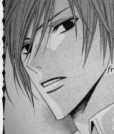

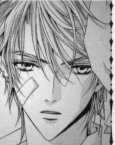

A Zweilt specializing in offense, who has the special ability "Voice of God" and wields a sword called Master Stroke. First-year high school student.

Shuusei Usui

a.k.a. The One Who Sees Through All

A Zweilt specializing in defense, who works in a pair with his childhood friend, Hotsuma. Second-year high school student. Possesses the special ability "Eyes of God."

Takashiro Giou

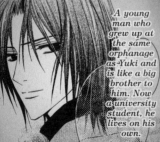

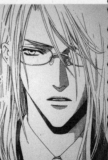

Head of the Giou clan, he possesses all of his memories from the war with the Duras since the Sunset of the Underworld over a thousand years ago. Yuki's brother by a different mother.

Kanata Wakamiya

A young man who grew up at the same orphanage as Yuki and is like a big brother to him. Now a university student, he lives on his own.

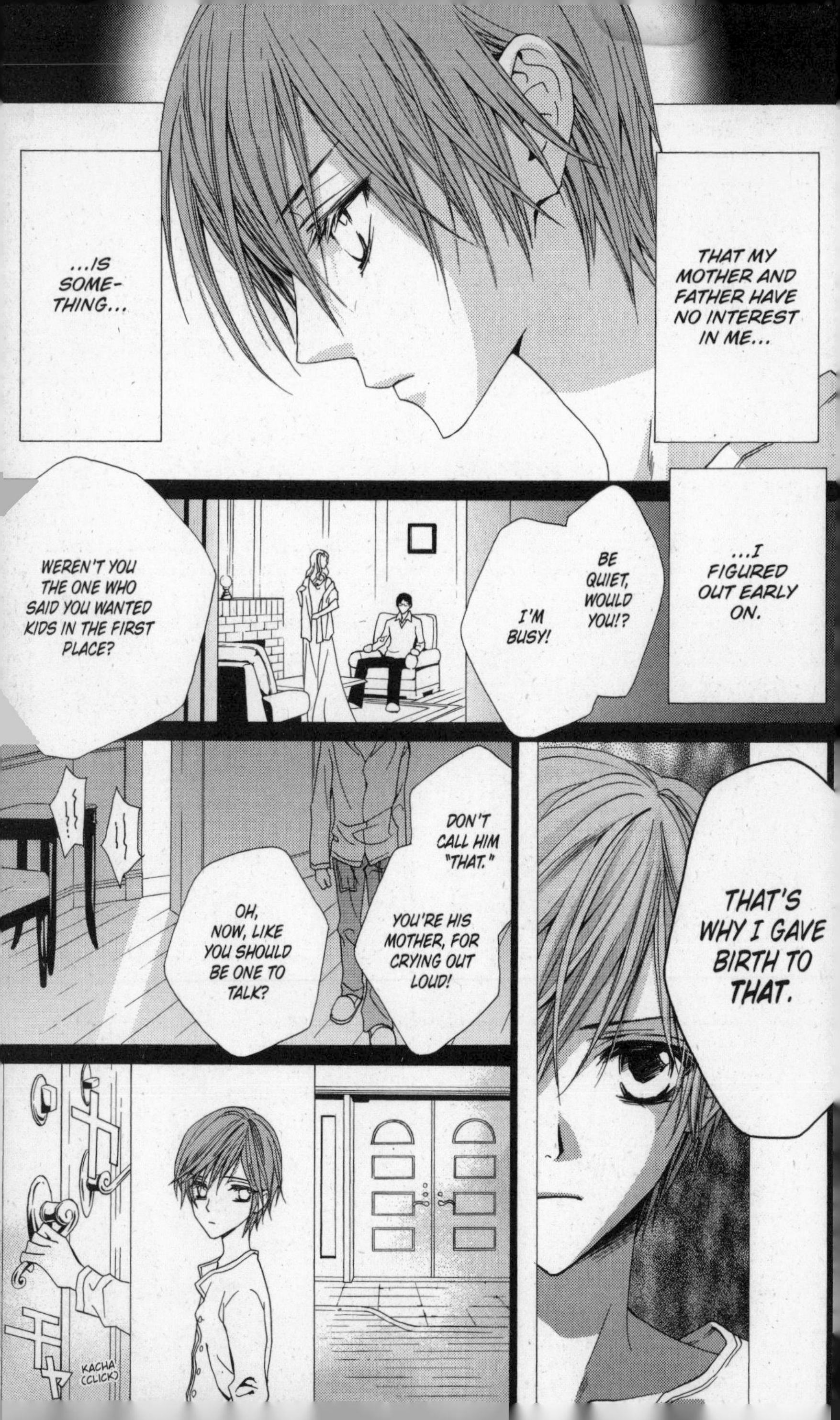
THAT MY MOTHER AND FATHER HAVE NO INTEREST IN ME...
...IS SOME-THING...
...I FIGURED OUT EARLY ON.
BE QUIET, WOULD YOU!?
I'M BUSY!
WEREN'T YOU THE ONE WHO SAID YOU WANTED KIDS IN THE FIRST PLACE?
THAT'S WHY I GAVE BIRTH TO THAT.
DON'T CALL HIM "THAT."
YOU'RE HIS MOTHER, FOR CRYING OUT LOUD!
OH, NOW, LIKE YOU SHOULD BE ONE TO TALK?
KACHA (CLICK)

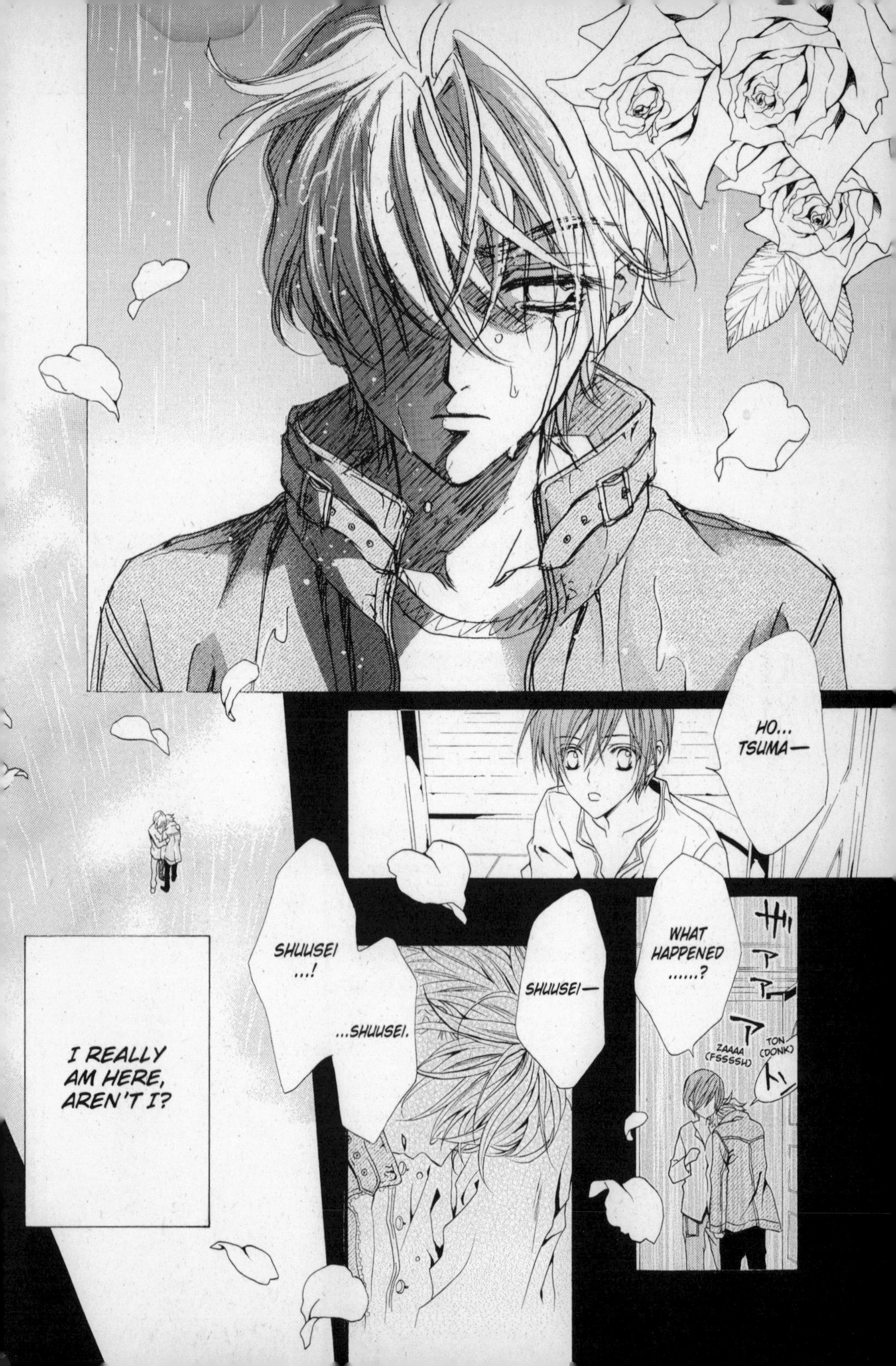
HO... TSUMA—
WHAT HAPPENED ......?
ZAAAA (FSSSSH)
TON (DONK)
SHUUSEI—
SHUUSEI ...!
...SHUUSEI.
I REALLY AM HERE, AREN'T I?

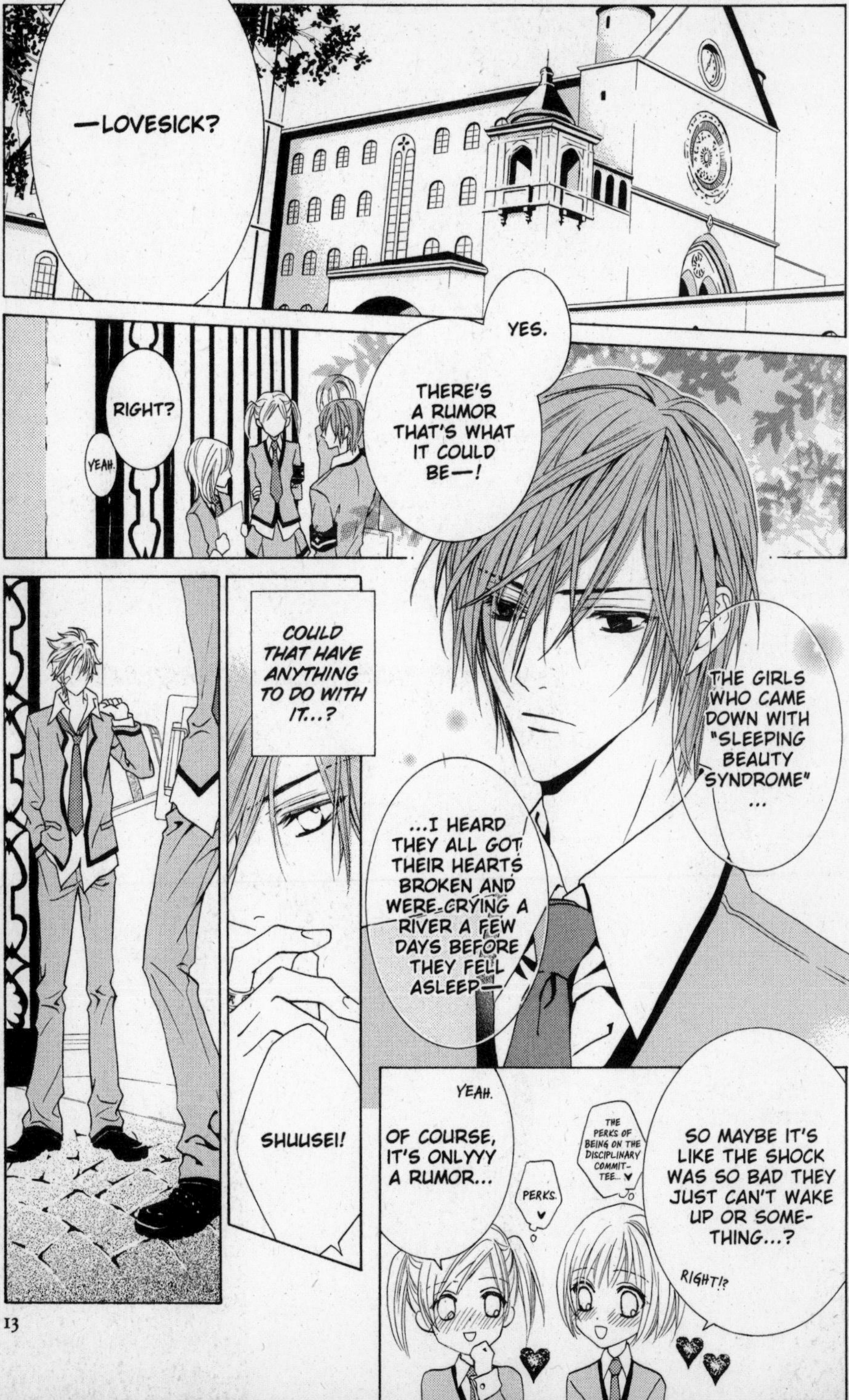
—LOVESICK?
RIGHT?
YEAH.
YES.
THERE'S A RUMOR THAT'S WHAT IT COULD BE—!
THE GIRLS WHO CAME DOWN WITH "SLEEPING BEAUTY SYNDROME"...
...I HEARD THEY ALL GOT THEIR HEARTS BROKEN AND WERE CRYING A RIVER A FEW DAYS BEFORE THEY FELL ASLEEP—
SO MAYBE IT'S LIKE THE SHOCK WAS SO BAD THEY JUST CAN'T WAKE UP OR SOMETHING...?
RIGHT!?
THE PERKS OF BEING ON THE DISCIPLINARY COMMITTEE...♥
PERKS. ♥
YEAH.
OF COURSE, IT'S ONLYYY A RUMOR...
COULD THAT HAVE ANYTHING TO DO WITH IT...?
SHUUSEI!

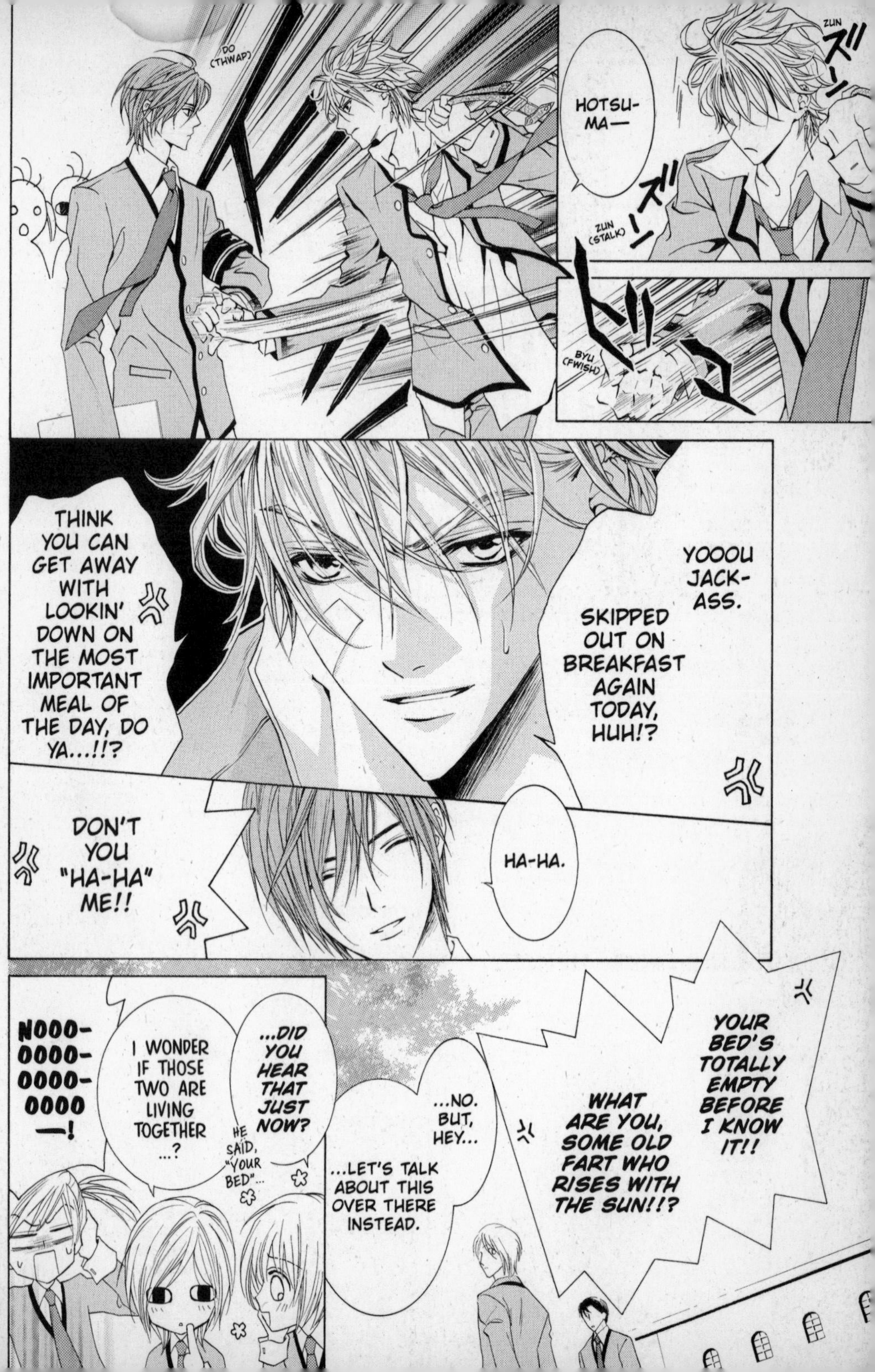
HOTSU-MA—
ZUN
ZUN (STALK)
BYU (FWISH)
DO (THWAP)
YOOOU JACK-ASS.
SKIPPED OUT ON BREAKFAST AGAIN TODAY, HUH!?
THINK YOU CAN GET AWAY WITH LOOKIN' DOWN ON THE MOST IMPORTANT MEAL OF THE DAY, DO YA...!!?
HA-HA.
DON'T YOU "HA-HA" ME!!
YOUR BED'S TOTALLY EMPTY BEFORE I KNOW IT!!
WHAT ARE YOU, SOME OLD FART WHO RISES WITH THE SUN!!?
...NO. BUT, HEY...
...LET'S TALK ABOUT THIS OVER THERE INSTEAD.
...DID YOU HEAR THAT JUST NOW?
HE SAID, "YOUR BED"...
I WONDER IF THOSE TWO ARE LIVING TOGETHER...?
NOOOO-OOOO-OOOO-OOOO—!

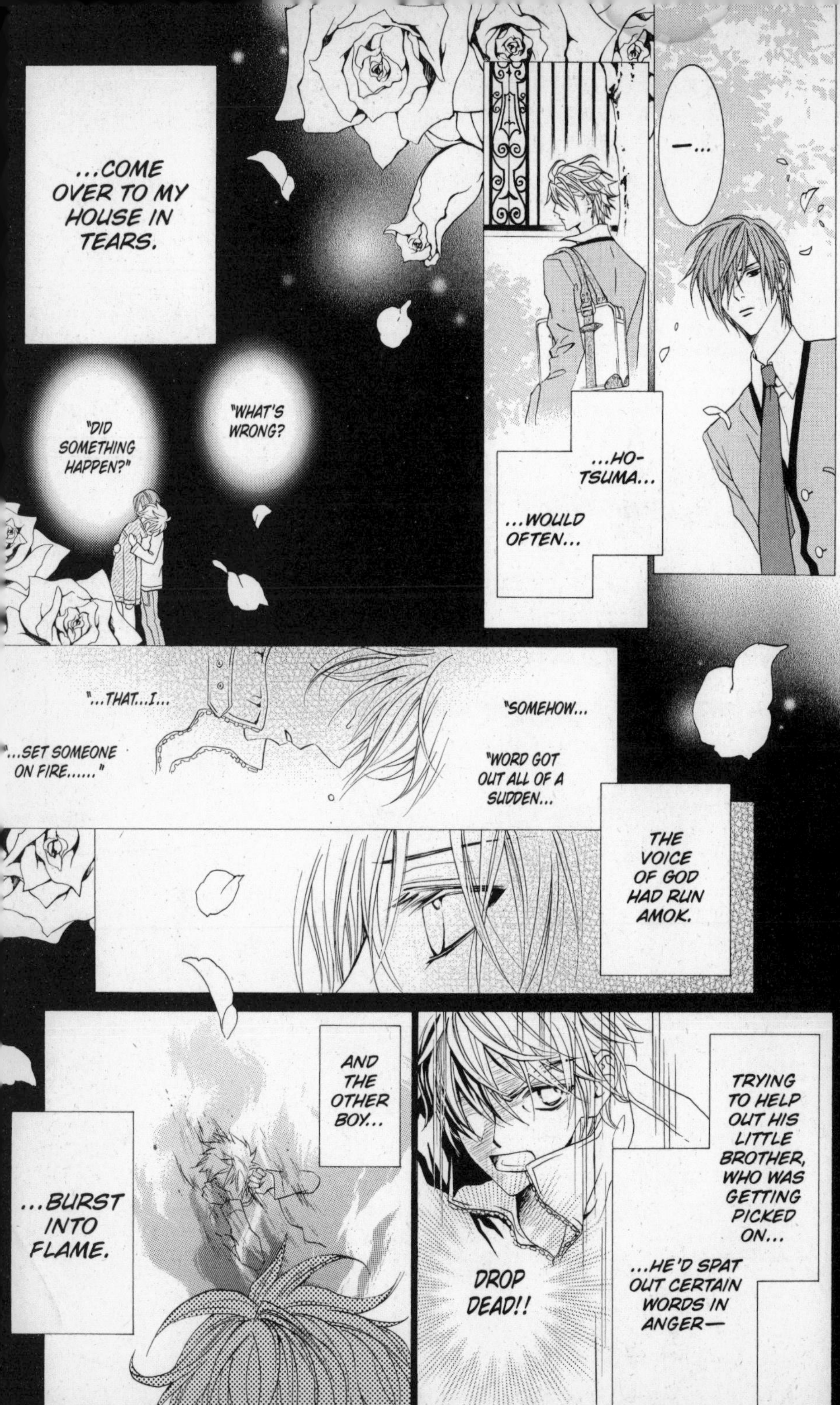
—...
...HO-TSUMA...
...WOULD OFTEN...
...COME OVER TO MY HOUSE IN TEARS.
"WHAT'S WRONG?
"DID SOMETHING HAPPEN?"
"SOMEHOW...
"WORD GOT OUT ALL OF A SUDDEN...
"...THAT...I...
"...SET SOMEONE ON FIRE......"
THE VOICE OF GOD HAD RUN AMOK.
TRYING TO HELP OUT HIS LITTLE BROTHER, WHO WAS GETTING PICKED ON...
...HE'D SPAT OUT CERTAIN WORDS IN ANGER—
DROP DEAD!!
AND THE OTHER BOY...
...BURST INTO FLAME.

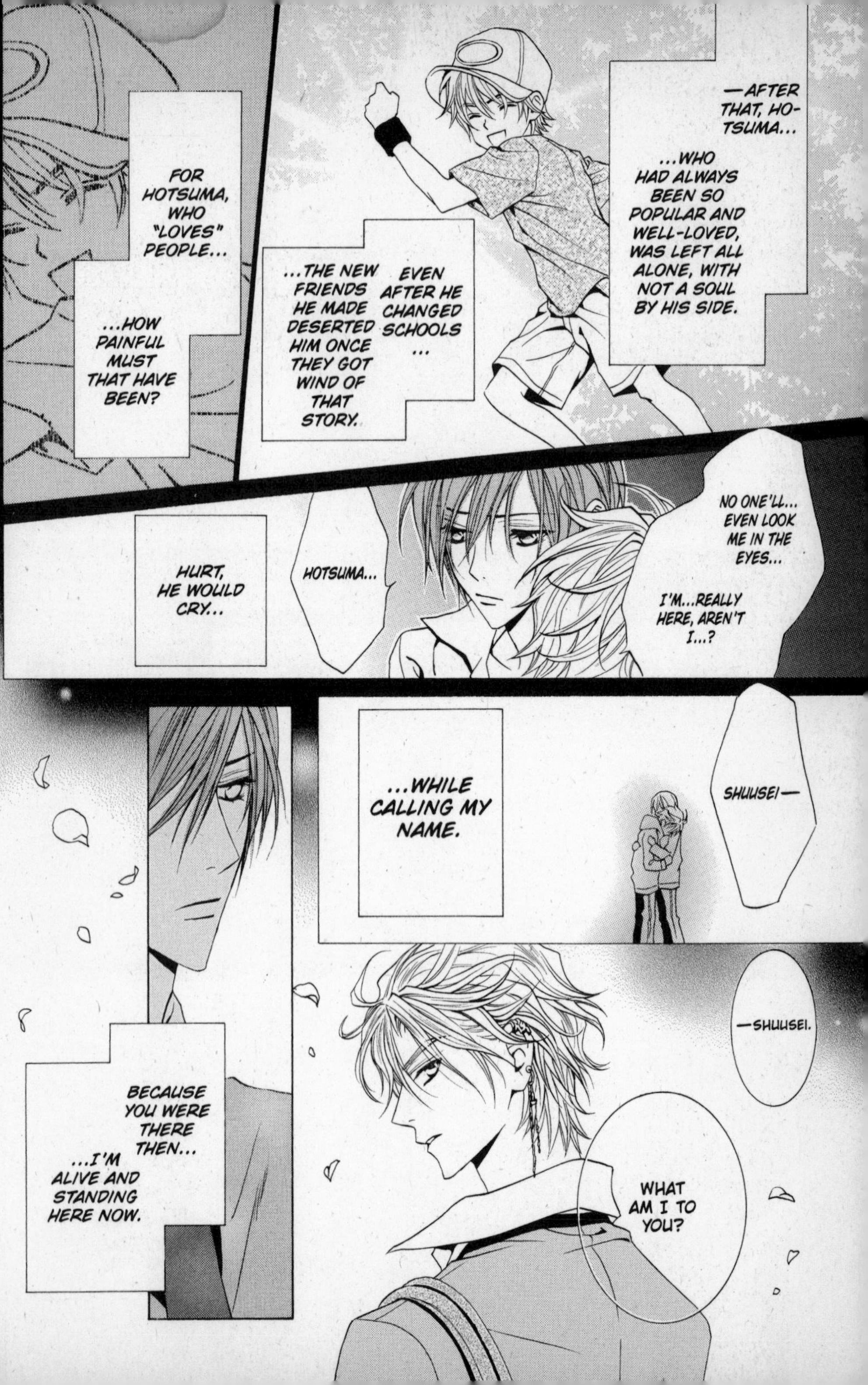
—AFTER THAT, HOTSUMA...
...WHO HAD ALWAYS BEEN SO POPULAR AND WELL-LOVED, WAS LEFT ALL ALONE, WITH NOT A SOUL BY HIS SIDE.
EVEN AFTER HE CHANGED SCHOOLS...
...THE NEW FRIENDS HE MADE DESERTED HIM ONCE THEY GOT WIND OF THAT STORY.
FOR HOTSUMA, WHO "LOVES" PEOPLE...
...HOW PAINFUL MUST THAT HAVE BEEN?
NO ONE'LL... EVEN LOOK ME IN THE EYES...
I'M...REALLY HERE, AREN'T I...?
HOTSUMA...
HURT, HE WOULD CRY...
SHUUSEI—
...WHILE CALLING MY NAME.
—SHUUSEI.
WHAT AM I TO YOU?
BECAUSE YOU WERE THERE THEN...
...I'M ALIVE AND STANDING HERE NOW.

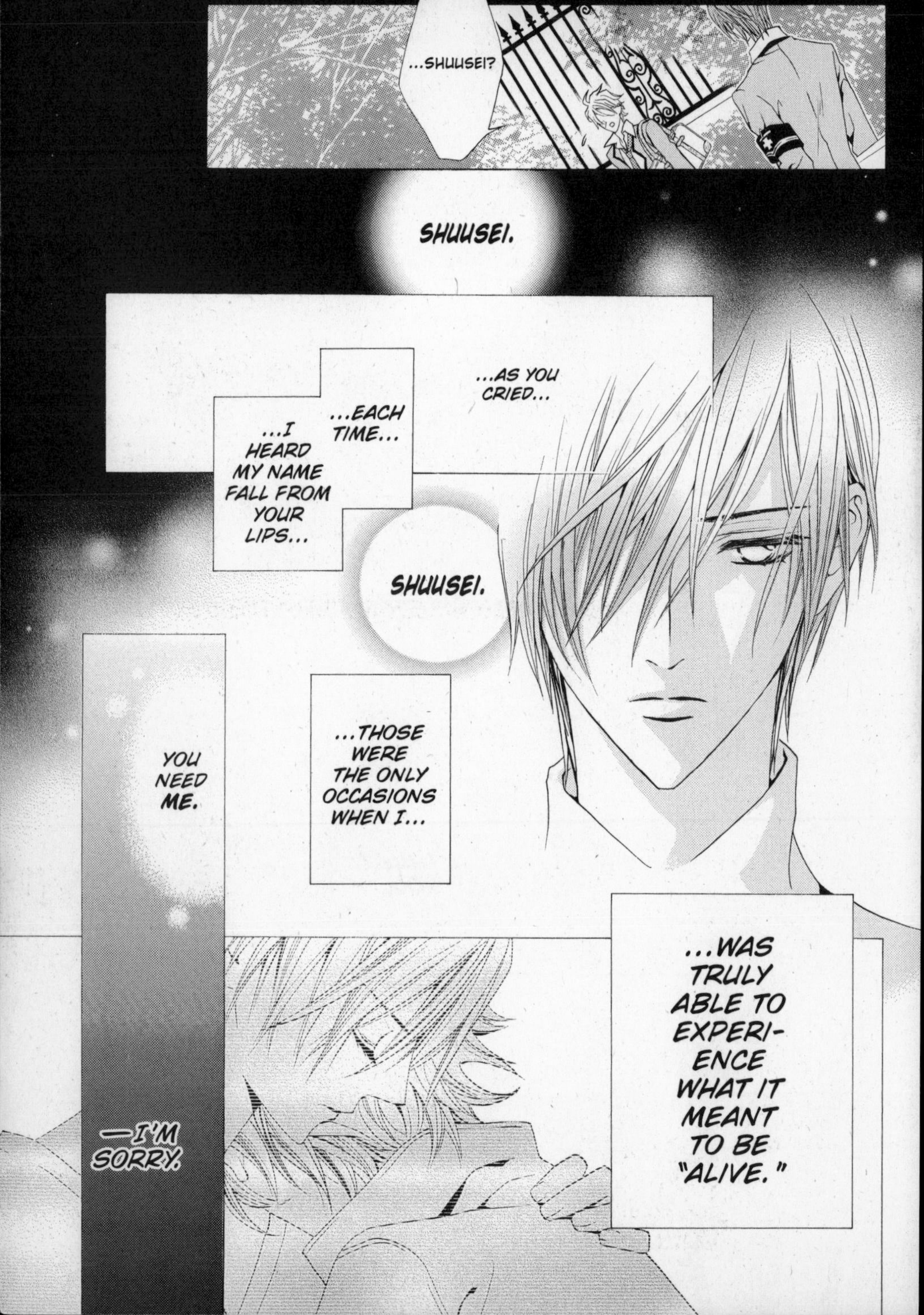
...SHUUSEI?
SHUUSEI.
...AS YOU CRIED...
...EACH TIME...
...I HEARD MY NAME FALL FROM YOUR LIPS...
SHUUSEI.
...THOSE WERE THE ONLY OCCASIONS WHEN I...
...WAS TRULY ABLE TO EXPERIENCE WHAT IT MEANT TO BE "ALIVE."
YOU NEED ME.
—I'M SORRY.

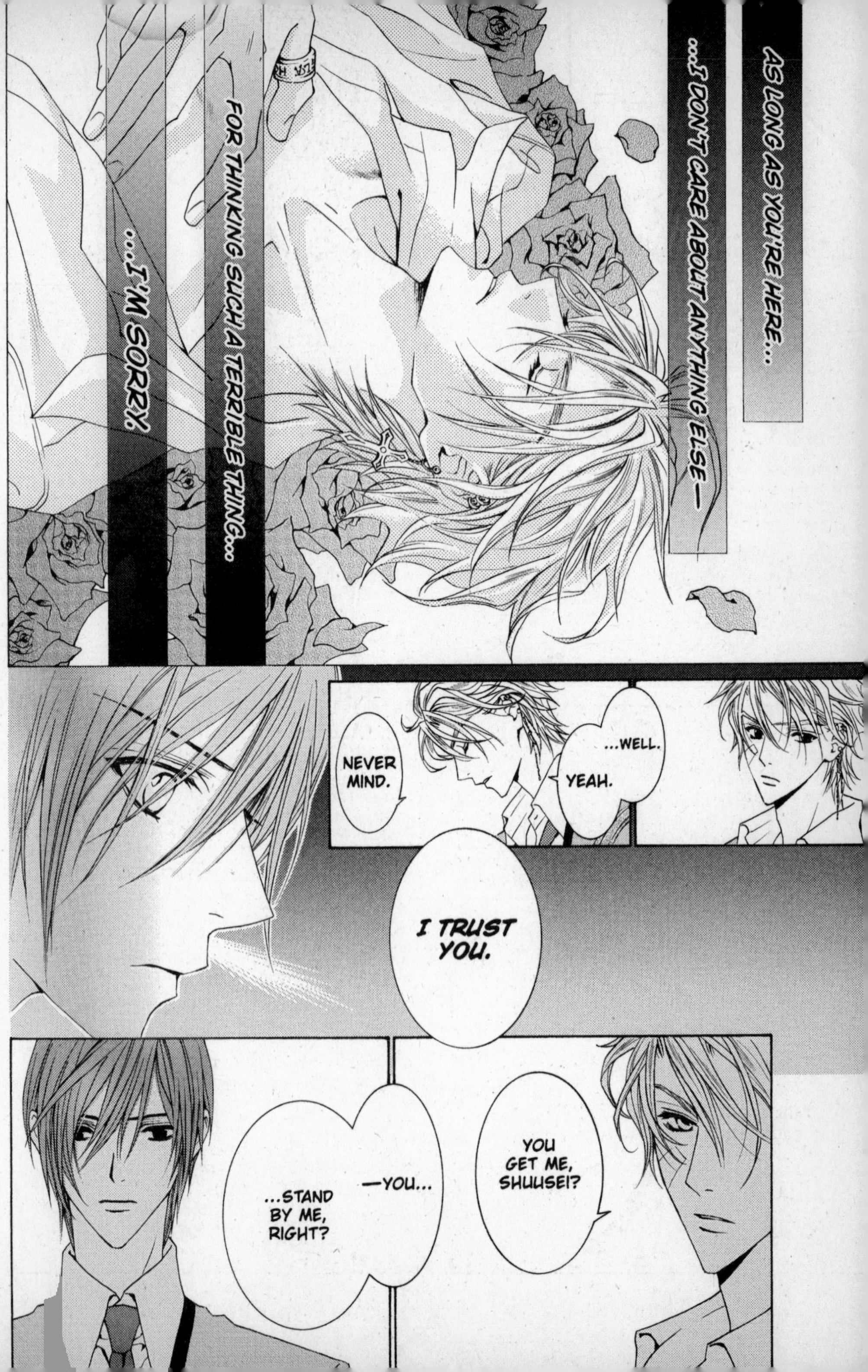
AS LONG AS YOU'RE HERE...
...I DON'T CARE ABOUT ANYTHING ELSE—
FOR THINKING SUCH A TERRIBLE THING...
...I'M SORRY.
...WELL. YEAH.
NEVER MIND.
I TRUST YOU.
YOU GET ME, SHUUSEI?
—YOU...
...STAND BY ME, RIGHT?

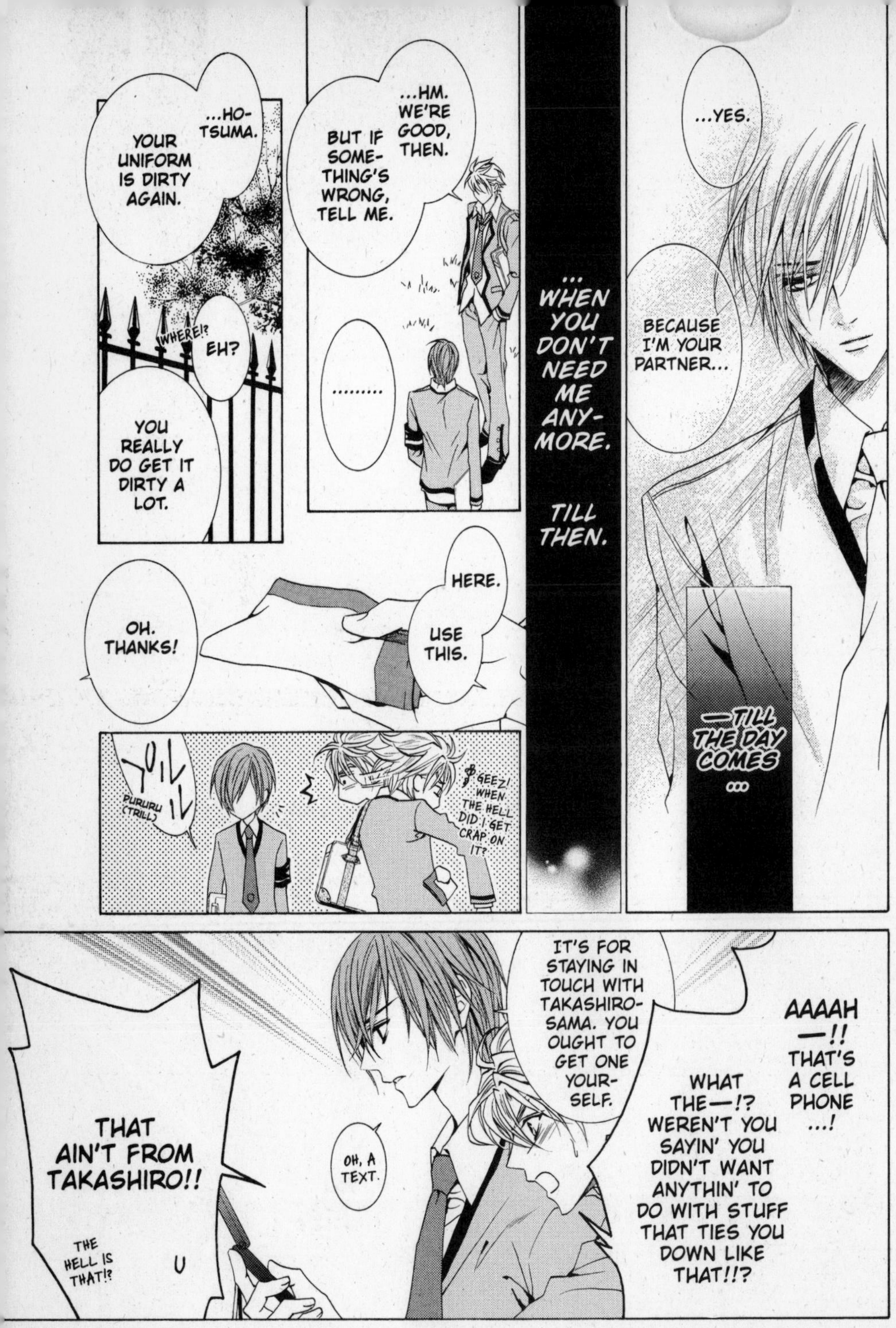

...YES.
BECAUSE I'M YOUR PARTNER...
—TILL THE DAY COMES...
...WHEN YOU DON'T NEED ME ANYMORE.
TILL THEN.
...HM. WE'RE GOOD, THEN.
BUT IF SOMETHING'S WRONG, TELL ME.
....
...HO-TSUMA.
YOUR UNIFORM IS DIRTY AGAIN.
EH?
WHERE!?
YOU REALLY DO GET IT DIRTY A LOT.
HERE.
USE THIS.
OH. THANKS!
GEEZ! WHEN THE HELL DID I GET CRAP ON IT?
PURURU (TRILL)
AAAAH—!! THAT'S A CELL PHONE...!
WHAT THE—!? WEREN'T YOU SAYIN' YOU DIDN'T WANT ANYTHIN' TO DO WITH STUFF THAT TIES YOU DOWN LIKE THAT!!?
IT'S FOR STAYING IN TOUCH WITH TAKASHIRO-SAMA. YOU OUGHT TO GET ONE YOURSELF.
OH, A TEXT.
THAT AIN'T FROM TAKASHIRO!!
THE HELL IS THAT!?

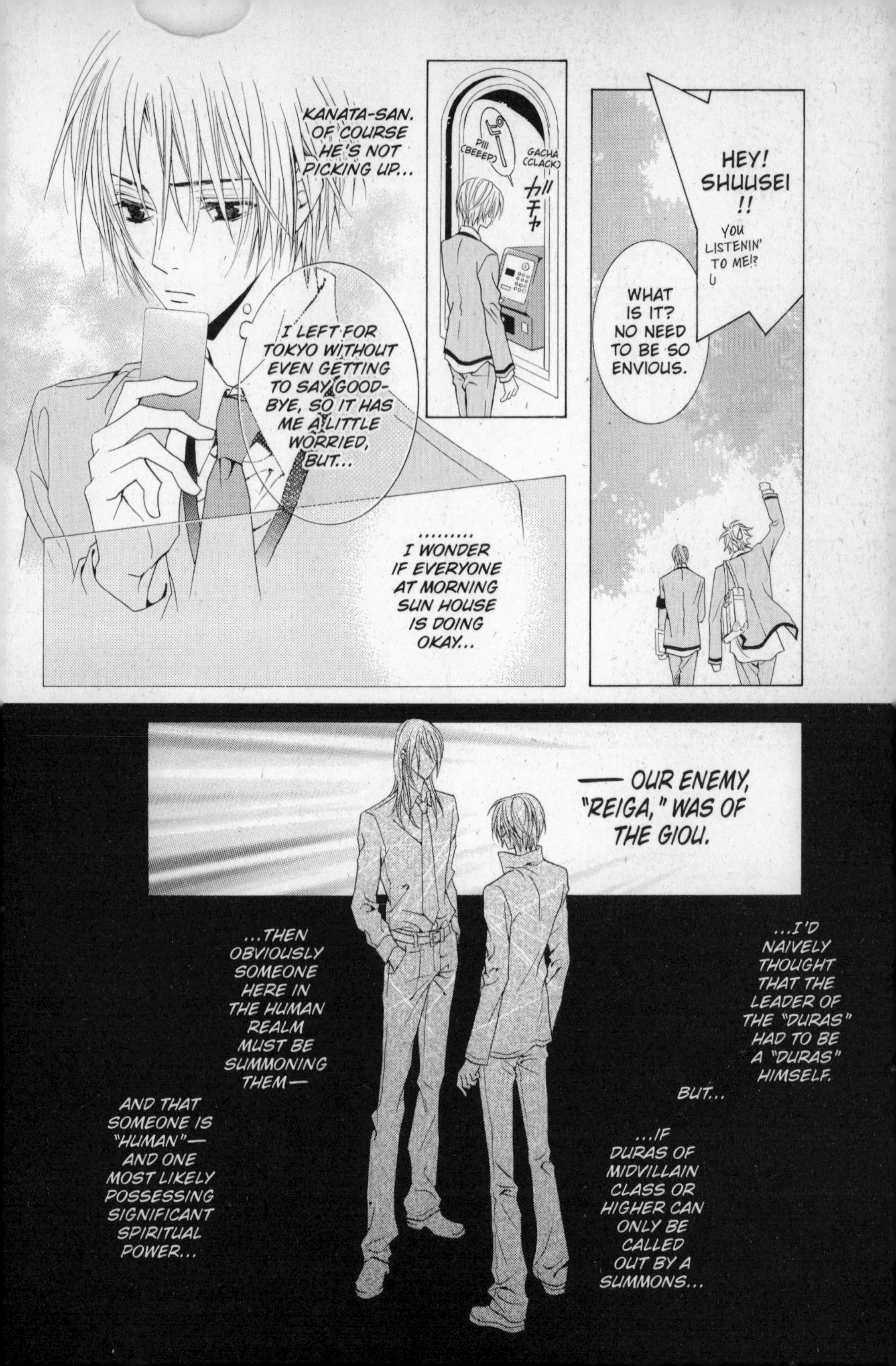
HEY! SHUUSEI !!
YOU LISTENIN' TO ME!?
WHAT IS IT? NO NEED TO BE SO ENVIOUS.
PIII (BEEEP)
GACHA (CLACK)
ガチャ
KANATA-SAN. OF COURSE HE'S NOT PICKING UP...
I LEFT FOR TOKYO WITHOUT EVEN GETTING TO SAY GOOD-BYE, SO IT HAS ME A LITTLE WORRIED, BUT...
.... I WONDER IF EVERYONE AT MORNING SUN HOUSE IS DOING OKAY...
— OUR ENEMY, "REIGA," WAS OF THE GIOU.
...I'D NAIVELY THOUGHT THAT THE LEADER OF THE "DURAS" HAD TO BE A "DURAS" HIMSELF.
BUT...
...IF DURAS OF MIDVILLAIN CLASS OR HIGHER CAN ONLY BE CALLED OUT BY A SUMMONS...
...THEN OBVIOUSLY SOMEONE HERE IN THE HUMAN REALM MUST BE SUMMONING THEM—
AND THAT SOMEONE IS "HUMAN"— AND ONE MOST LIKELY POSSESSING SIGNIFICANT SPIRITUAL POWER...

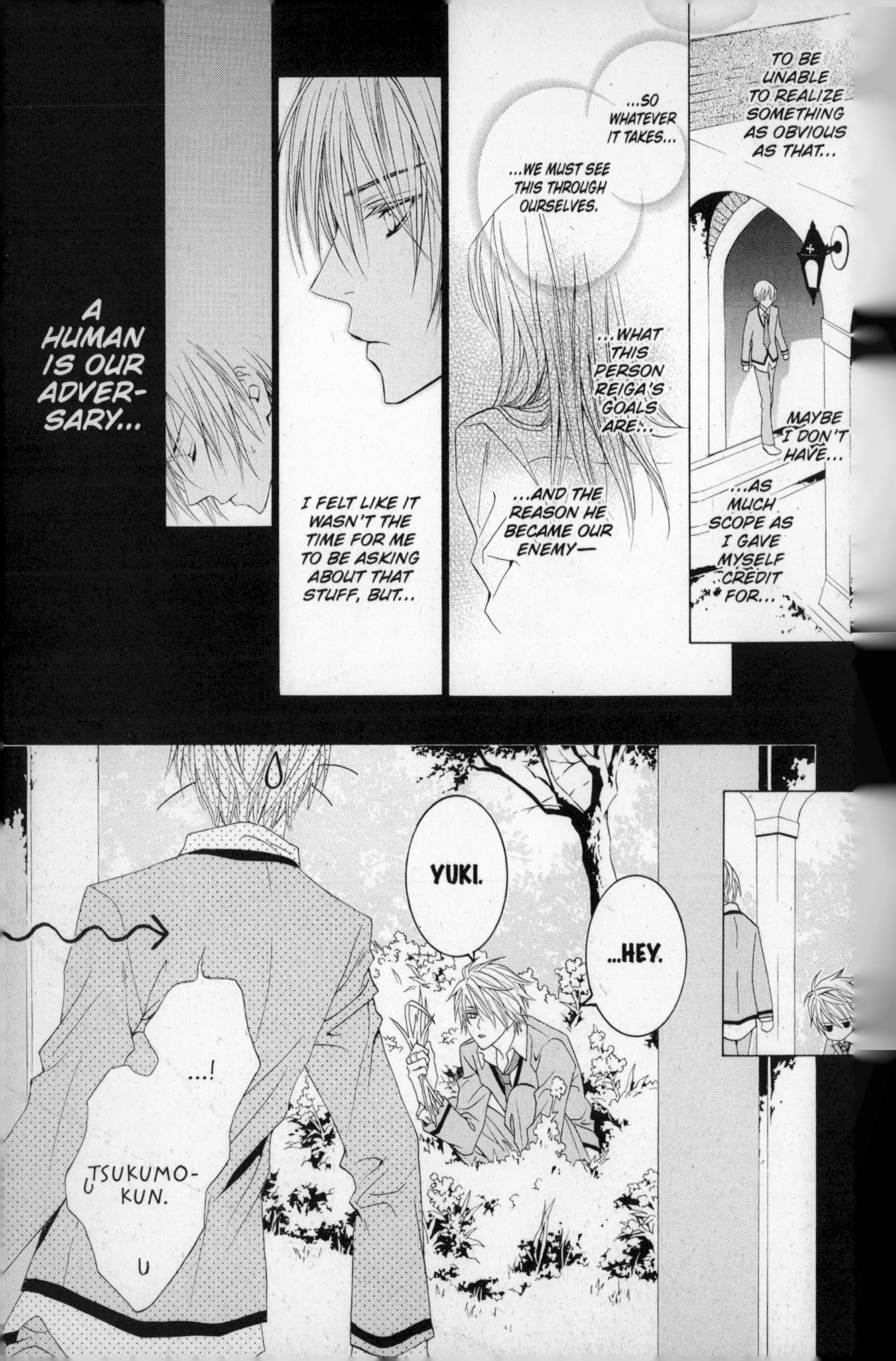
TO BE UNABLE TO REALIZE SOMETHING AS OBVIOUS AS THAT...
MAYBE I DON'T HAVE...
...AS MUCH SCOPE AS I GAVE MYSELF CREDIT FOR...
...SO WHATEVER IT TAKES...
...WE MUST SEE THIS THROUGH OURSELVES.
...WHAT THIS PERSON REIGA'S GOALS ARE...
...AND THE REASON HE BECAME OUR ENEMY—
I FELT LIKE IT WASN'T THE TIME FOR ME TO BE ASKING ABOUT THAT STUFF, BUT...
A HUMAN IS OUR ADVERSARY...
YUKI.
...HEY.
...!
TSUKUMO-KUN.

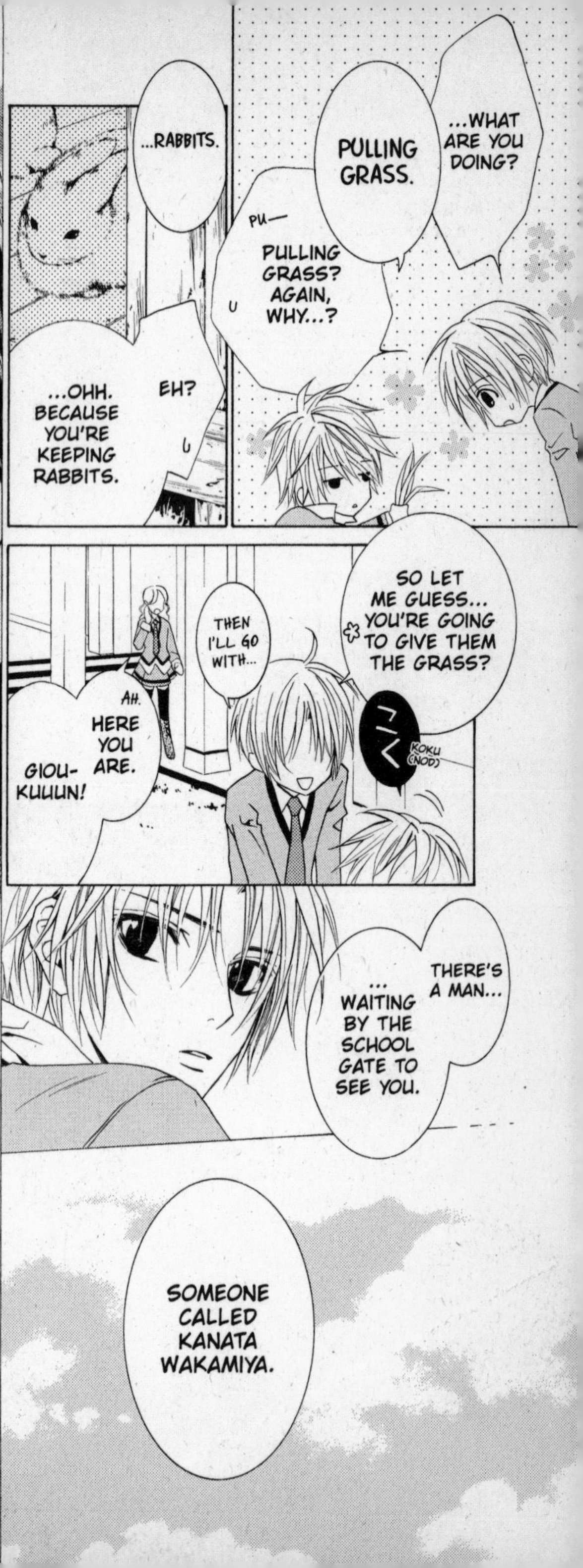
...WHAT ARE YOU DOING?
PULLING GRASS.
PU— PULLING GRASS? AGAIN, WHY...?
...RABBITS.
EH?
...OHH. BECAUSE YOU'RE KEEPING RABBITS.
SO LET ME GUESS... YOU'RE GOING TO GIVE THEM THE GRASS?
KOKU (NOD)
THEN I'LL GO WITH...
AH. HERE YOU ARE. GIOU-KUUUN!
THERE'S A MAN...
... WAITING BY THE SCHOOL GATE TO SEE YOU.
SOMEONE CALLED KANATA WAKAMIYA.
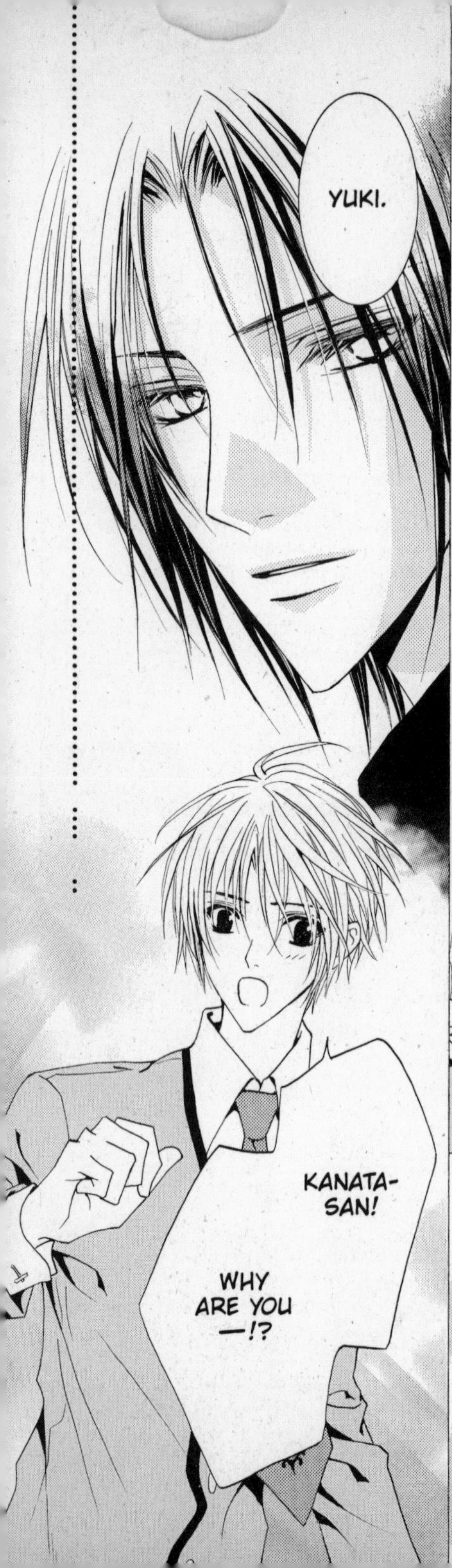
YUKI.
KANATA-SAN!
WHY ARE YOU —!?

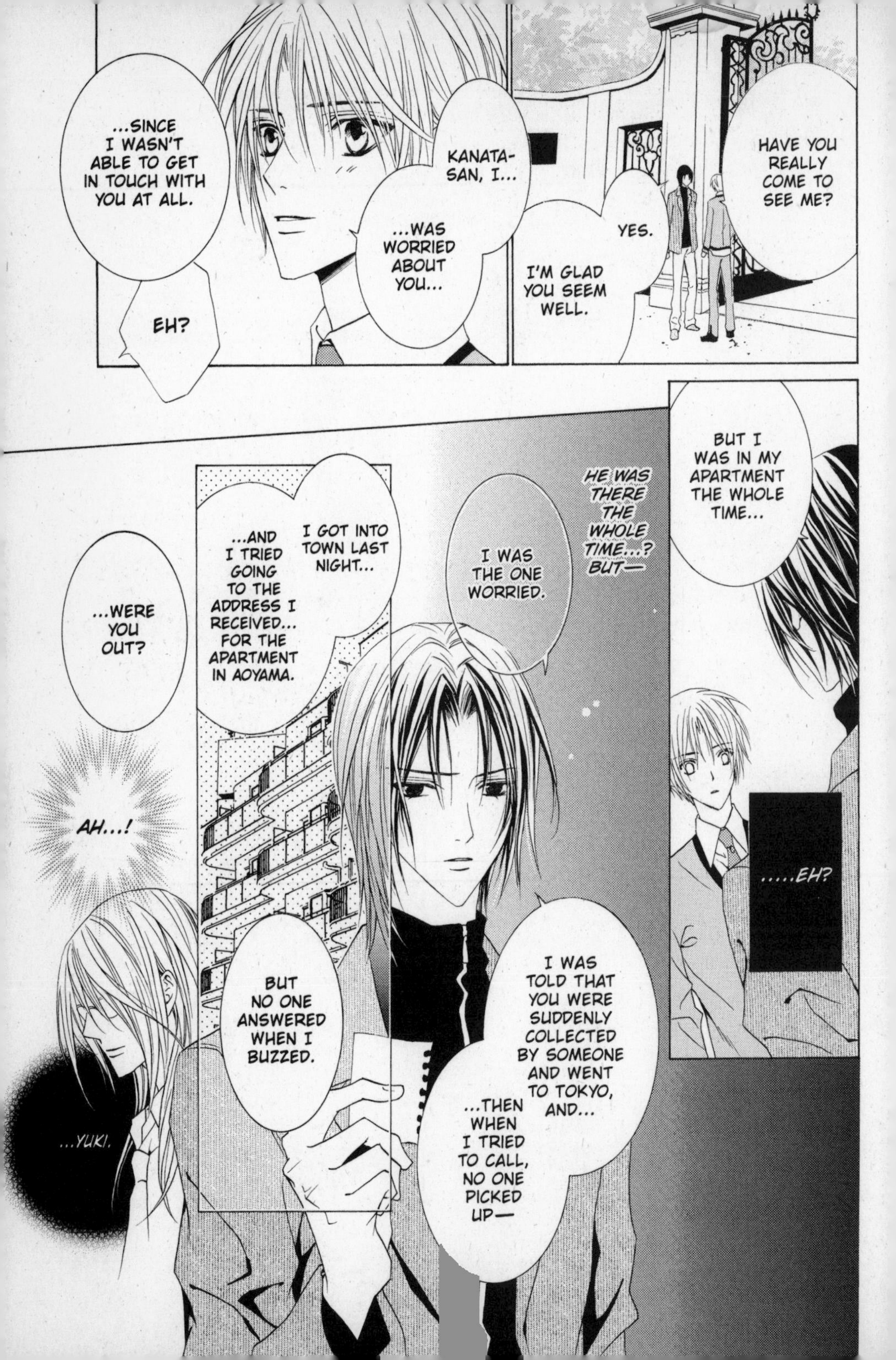
HAVE YOU REALLY COME TO SEE ME?
YES.
I'M GLAD YOU SEEM WELL.
KANATA-SAN, I...
...WAS WORRIED ABOUT YOU...
...SINCE I WASN'T ABLE TO GET IN TOUCH WITH YOU AT ALL.
EH?
BUT I WAS IN MY APARTMENT THE WHOLE TIME...
.....EH?
HE WAS THERE THE WHOLE TIME...? BUT—
I WAS THE ONE WORRIED.
I GOT INTO TOWN LAST NIGHT...
...AND I TRIED GOING TO THE ADDRESS I RECEIVED... FOR THE APARTMENT IN AOYAMA.
BUT NO ONE ANSWERED WHEN I BUZZED.
I WAS TOLD THAT YOU WERE SUDDENLY COLLECTED BY SOMEONE AND WENT TO TOKYO, AND...
...THEN WHEN I TRIED TO CALL, NO ONE PICKED UP—
...WERE YOU OUT?
AH...!
...YUKI.

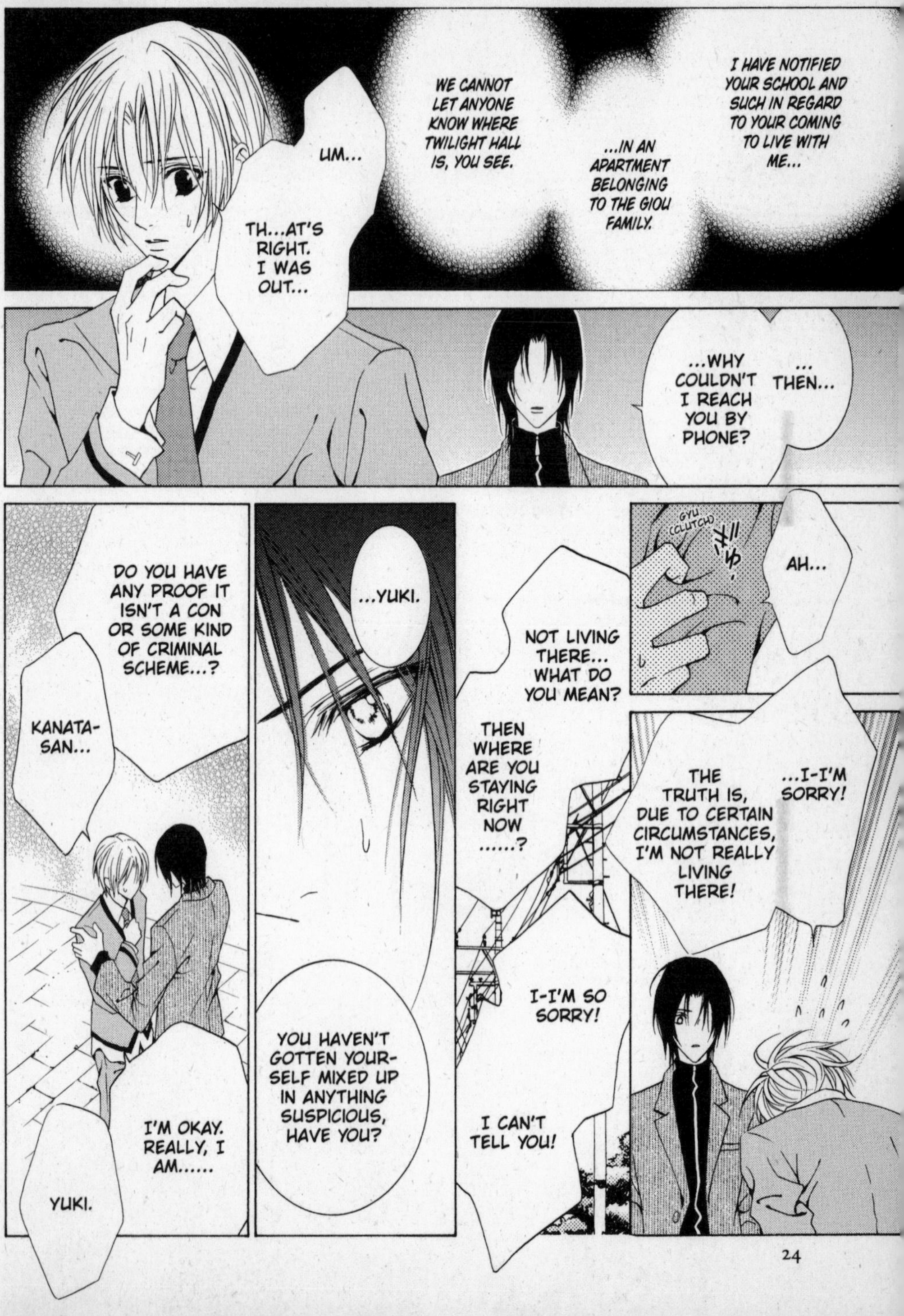
I HAVE NOTIFIED YOUR SCHOOL AND SUCH IN REGARD TO YOUR COMING TO LIVE WITH ME...
...IN AN APARTMENT BELONGING TO THE GIOU FAMILY.
WE CANNOT LET ANYONE KNOW WHERE TWILIGHT HALL IS, YOU SEE.
UM...
TH...AT'S RIGHT. I WAS OUT...
... THEN...
...WHY COULDN'T I REACH YOU BY PHONE?
GYU (CLUTCH)
AH...
...I-I'M SORRY!
THE TRUTH IS, DUE TO CERTAIN CIRCUMSTANCES, I'M NOT REALLY LIVING THERE!
NOT LIVING THERE... WHAT DO YOU MEAN?
THEN WHERE ARE YOU STAYING RIGHT NOW ......?
I-I'M SO SORRY!
I CAN'T TELL YOU!
...YUKI.
YOU HAVEN'T GOTTEN YOURSELF MIXED UP IN ANYTHING SUSPICIOUS, HAVE YOU?
DO YOU HAVE ANY PROOF IT ISN'T A CON OR SOME KIND OF CRIMINAL SCHEME...?
KANATA-SAN...
I'M OKAY. REALLY, I AM......
YUKI.

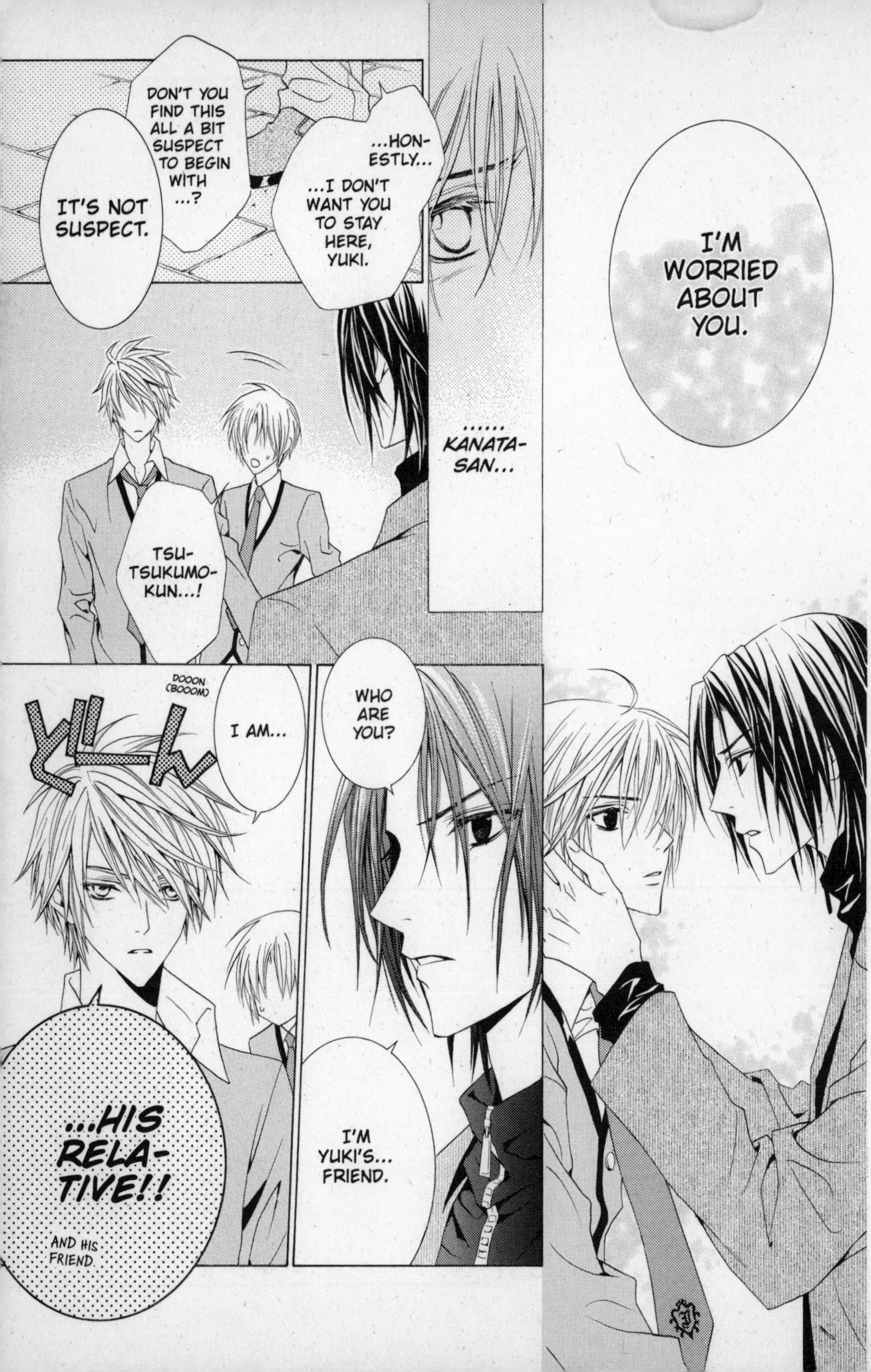
I'M WORRIED ABOUT YOU.
......KANATA-SAN...
...HON-ESTLY...
...I DON'T WANT YOU TO STAY HERE, YUKI.
DON'T YOU FIND THIS ALL A BIT SUSPECT TO BEGIN WITH ...?
IT'S NOT SUSPECT.
TSU-TSUKUMO-KUN...!
WHO ARE YOU?
I'M YUKI'S... FRIEND.
I AM...
DOOON (BOOOM)
...HIS RELA-TIVE!!
AND HIS FRIEND.

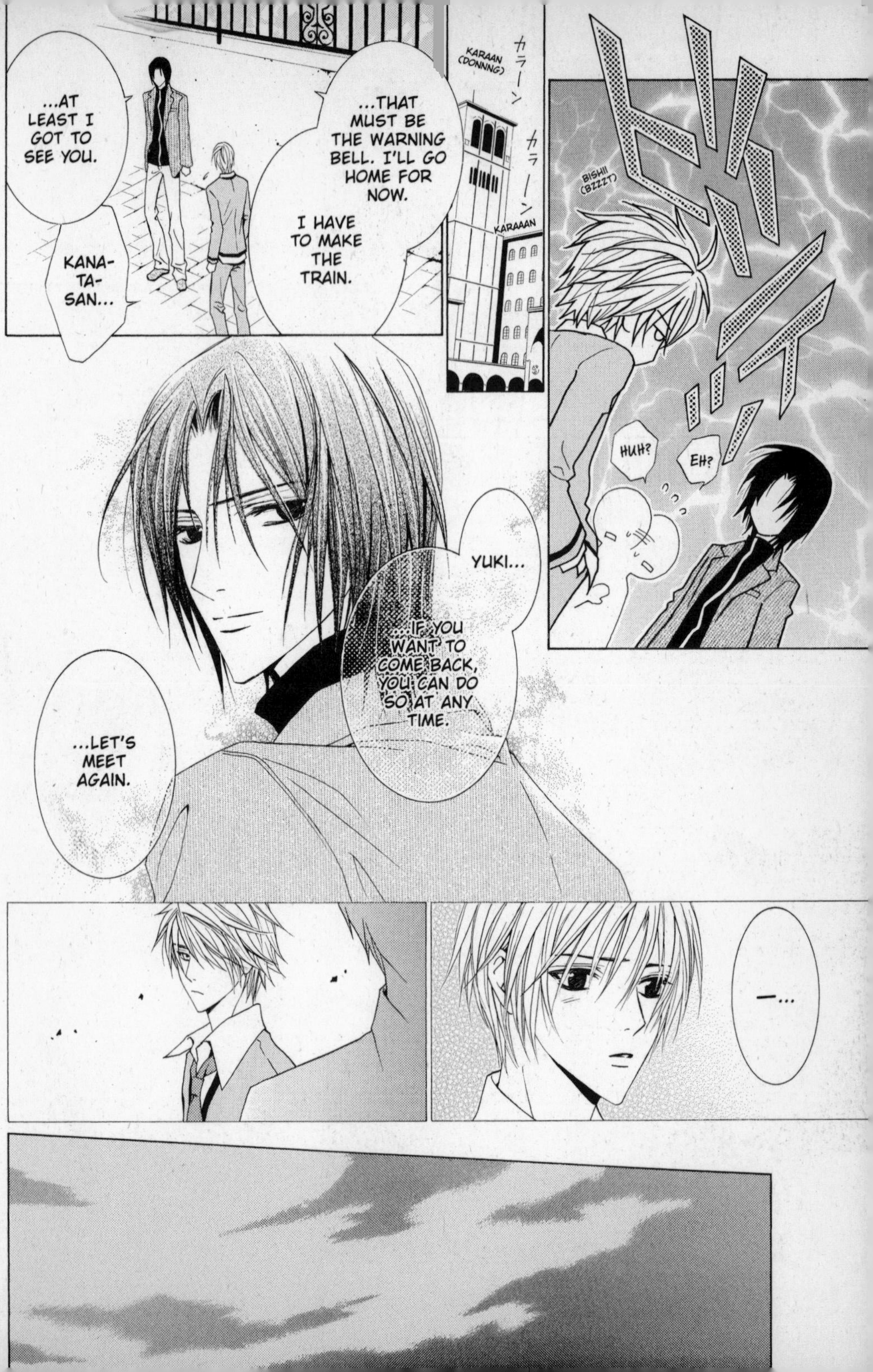
BISHII (BZZZT)
EH?
HUH?
KARAAN (DONNNG)
KARAAAN
...THAT MUST BE THE WARNING BELL. I'LL GO HOME FOR NOW.
I HAVE TO MAKE THE TRAIN.
...AT LEAST I GOT TO SEE YOU.
KANA-TA-SAN...
YUKI...
...IF YOU WANT TO COME BACK, YOU CAN DO SO AT ANY TIME.
...LET'S MEET AGAIN.
—...

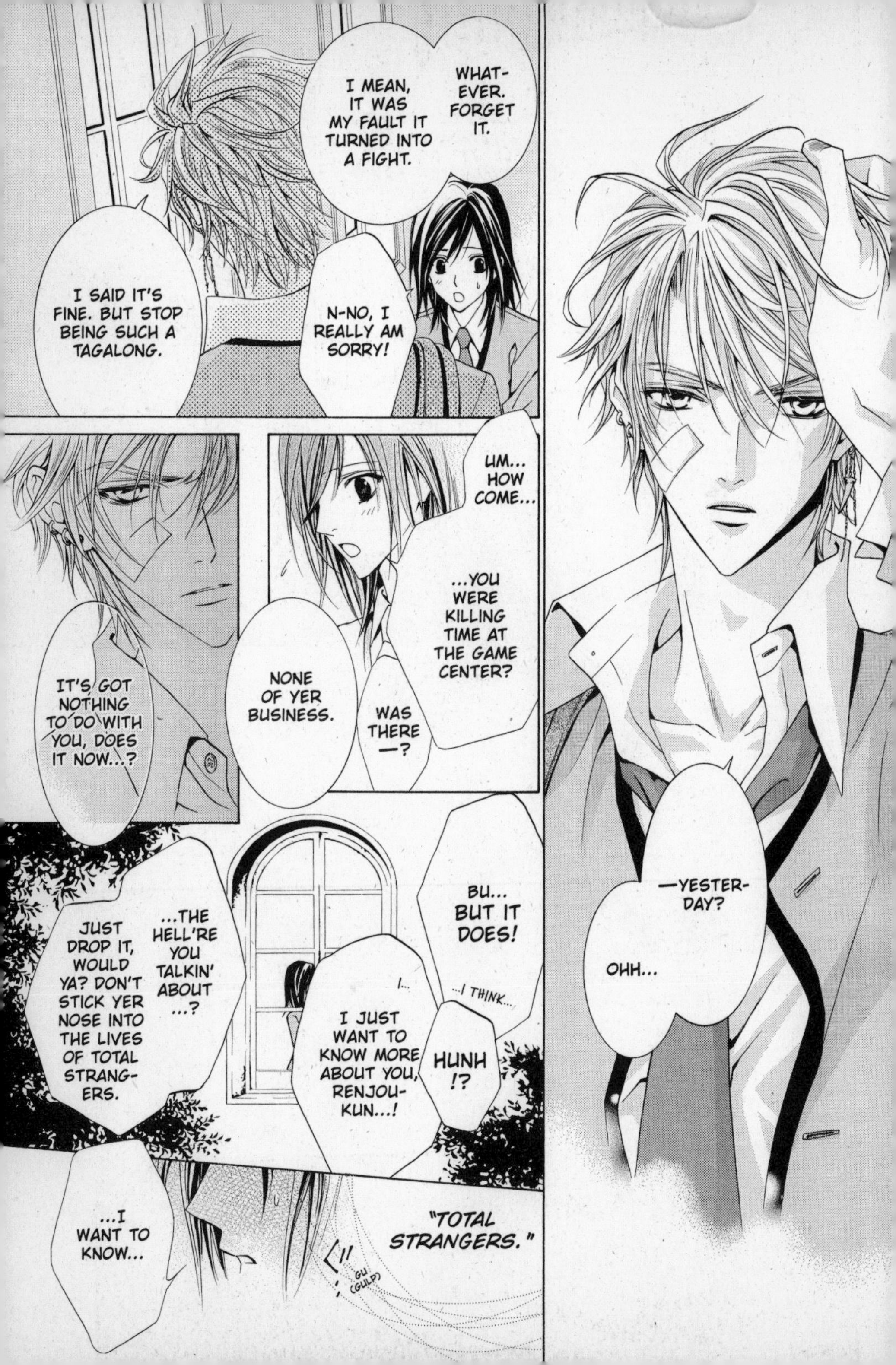
—YESTER-DAY?
OHH...
WHAT-EVER. FORGET IT.
I MEAN, IT WAS MY FAULT IT TURNED INTO A FIGHT.
N-NO, I REALLY AM SORRY!
I SAID IT'S FINE. BUT STOP BEING SUCH A TAGALONG.
UM... HOW COME...
...YOU WERE KILLING TIME AT THE GAME CENTER?
WAS THERE—?
NONE OF YER BUSINESS.
IT'S GOT NOTHING TO DO WITH YOU, DOES IT NOW...?
BU... BUT IT DOES!
...I THINK...
I...
I JUST WANT TO KNOW MORE ABOUT YOU, RENJOU-KUN...!
HUNH!?
...THE HELL'RE YOU TALKIN' ABOUT...?
JUST DROP IT, WOULD YA? DON'T STICK YER NOSE INTO THE LIVES OF TOTAL STRANGERS.
"TOTAL STRANGERS."
!!
GU (GULP)
...I WANT TO KNOW...

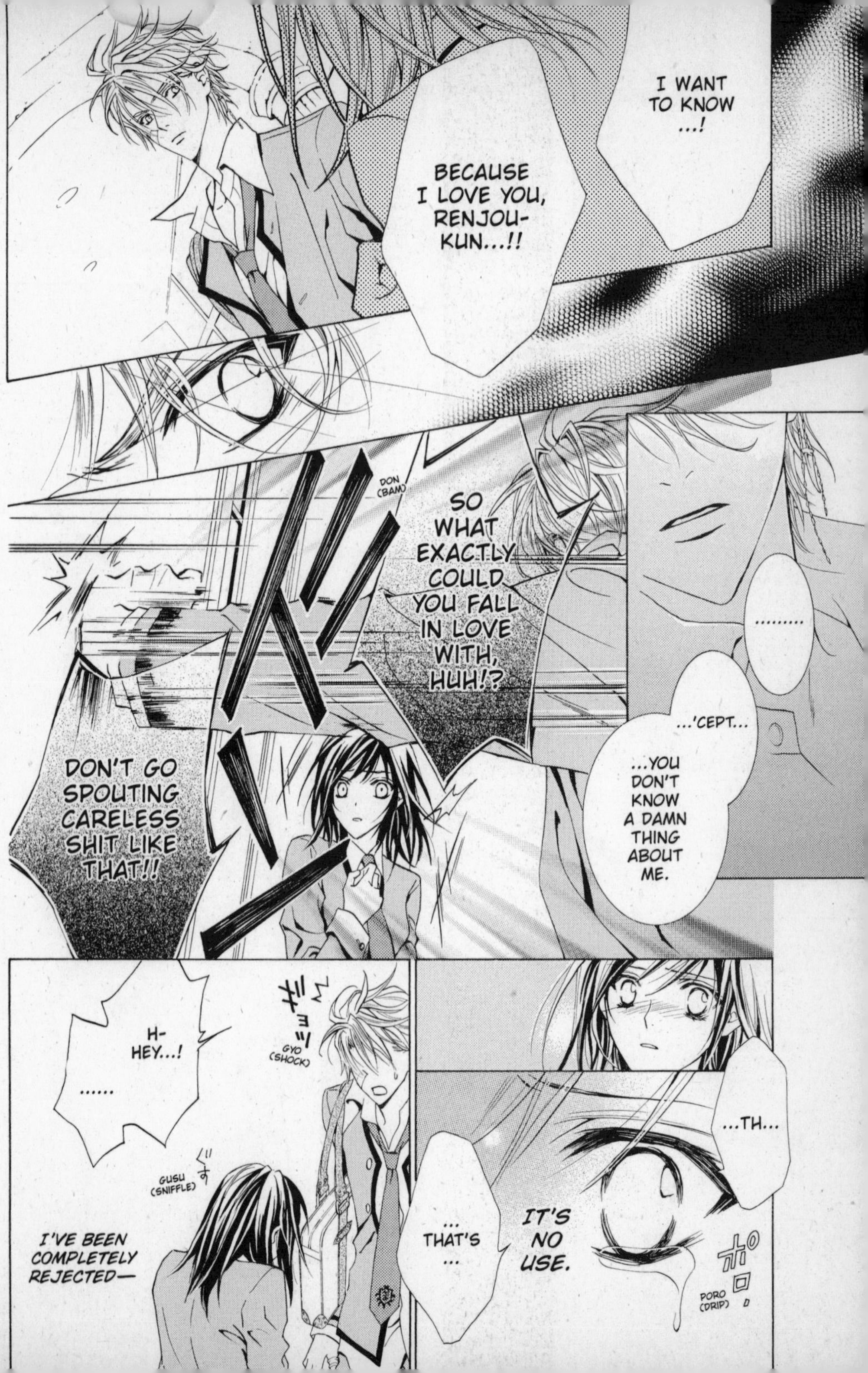

I WANT TO KNOW ...!
BECAUSE I LOVE YOU, RENJOU-KUN...!!
....
...'CEPT...
...YOU DON'T KNOW A DAMN THING ABOUT ME.
DON (BAM)
SO WHAT EXACTLY COULD YOU FALL IN LOVE WITH, HUH!?
DON'T GO SPOUTING CARELESS SHIT LIKE THAT!!
...TH...
... THAT'S ...
IT'S NO USE.
ポロ
PORO (DRIP)
ギョッ
GYO (SHOCK)
H-HEY...!
......
ぐす
GUSU (SNIFFLE)
I'VE BEEN COMPLETELY REJECTED—

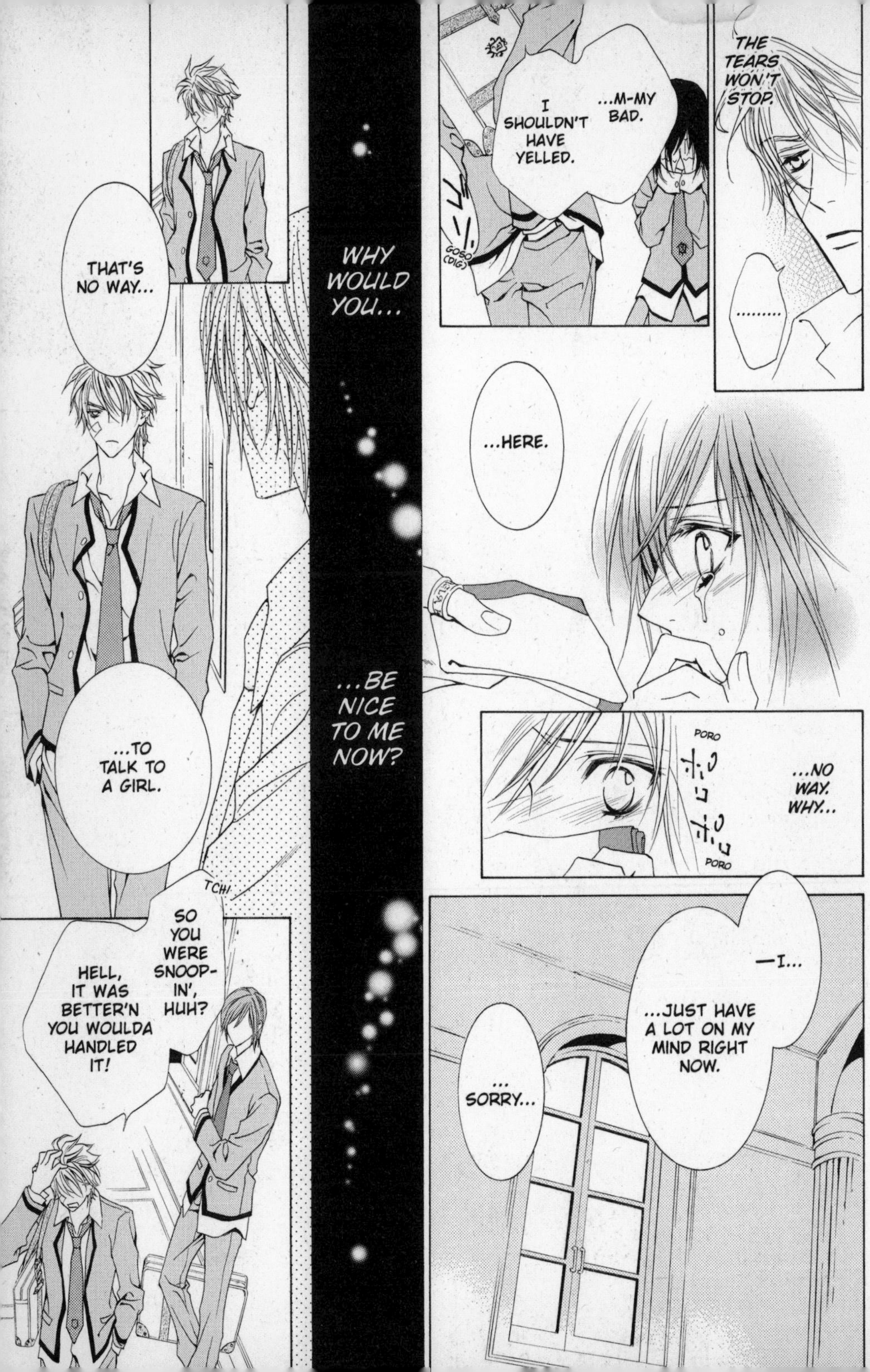
THE TEARS WON'T STOP.
....
...M-MY BAD.
I SHOULDN'T HAVE YELLED.
GOSO (DIG)
...HERE.
...NO WAY. WHY...
PORO
PORO
—I...
...JUST HAVE A LOT ON MY MIND RIGHT NOW.
... SORRY...
WHY WOULD YOU...
...BE NICE TO ME NOW?
THAT'S NO WAY...
...TO TALK TO A GIRL.
TCH!
SO YOU WERE SNOOP-IN', HUH?
HELL, IT WAS BETTER'N YOU WOULDA HANDLED IT!

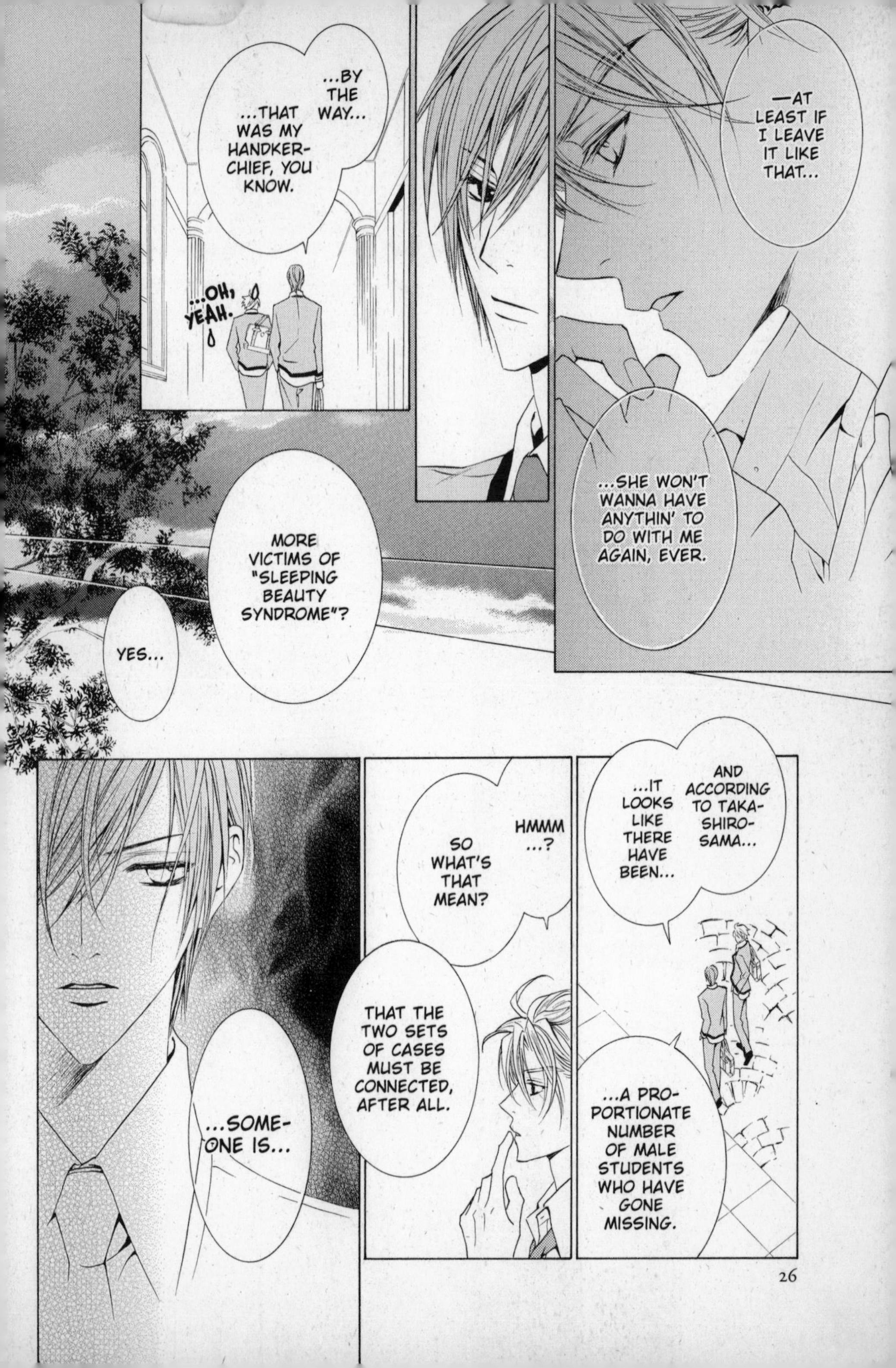
—AT LEAST IF I LEAVE IT LIKE THAT...
...SHE WON'T WANNA HAVE ANYTHIN' TO DO WITH ME AGAIN, EVER.
...BY THE WAY...
...THAT WAS MY HANDKERCHIEF, YOU KNOW.
...OH, YEAH.
MORE VICTIMS OF "SLEEPING BEAUTY SYNDROME"?
YES...
AND ACCORDING TO TAKASHIRO-SAMA...
...IT LOOKS LIKE THERE HAVE BEEN...
...A PROPORTIONATE NUMBER OF MALE STUDENTS WHO HAVE GONE MISSING.
HMMM...?
SO WHAT'S THAT MEAN?
THAT THE TWO SETS OF CASES MUST BE CONNECTED, AFTER ALL.
...SOMEONE IS...

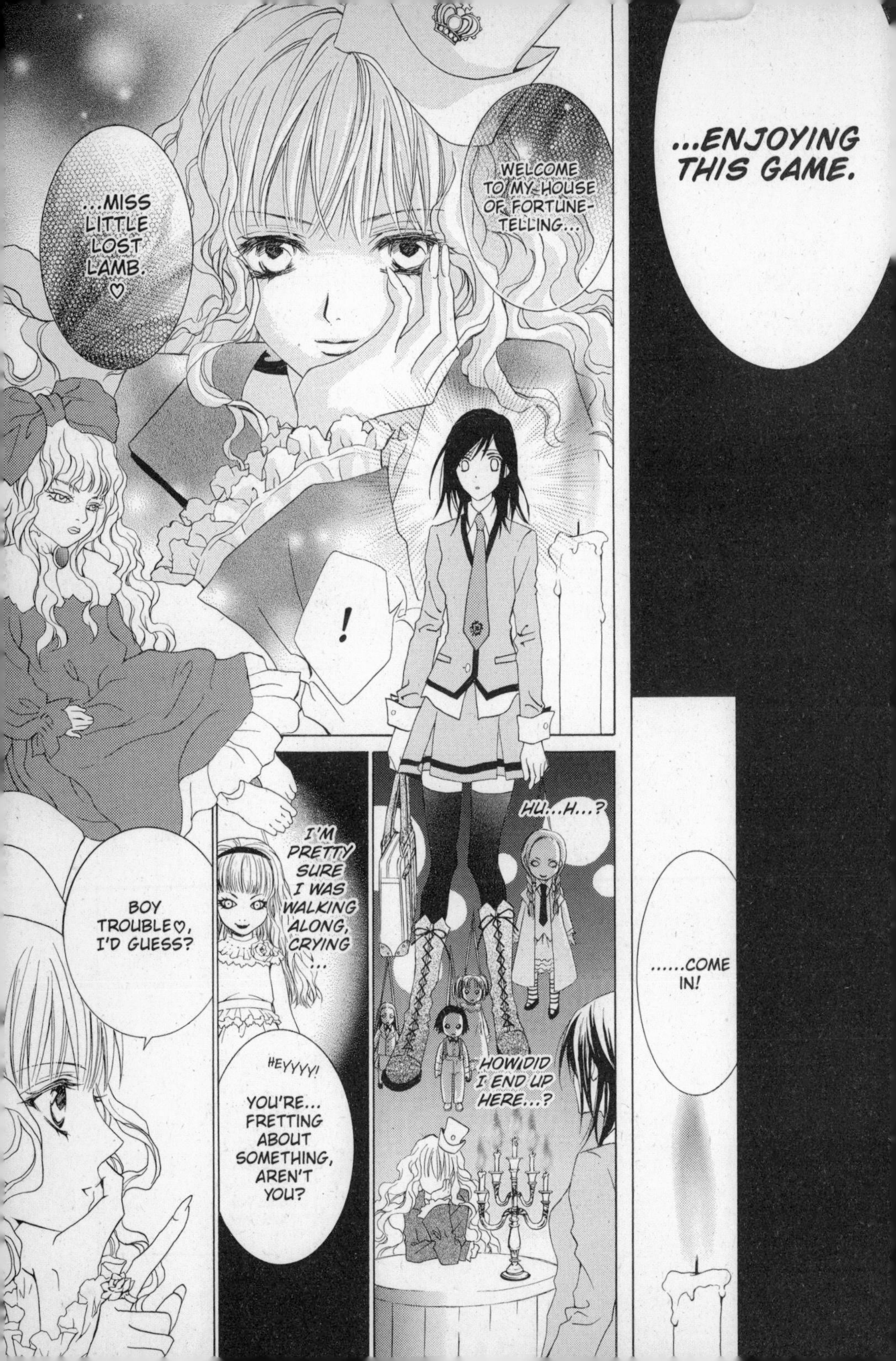
...ENJOYING THIS GAME.
......COME IN!
WELCOME TO MY HOUSE OF FORTUNE-TELLING...
...MISS LITTLE LOST LAMB. ♡
!
HU...H...?
I'M PRETTY SURE I WAS WALKING ALONG, CRYING...
HOW DID I END UP HERE...?
HEYYYY!
YOU'RE... FRETTING ABOUT SOMETHING, AREN'T YOU?
BOY TROUBLE♡, I'D GUESS?

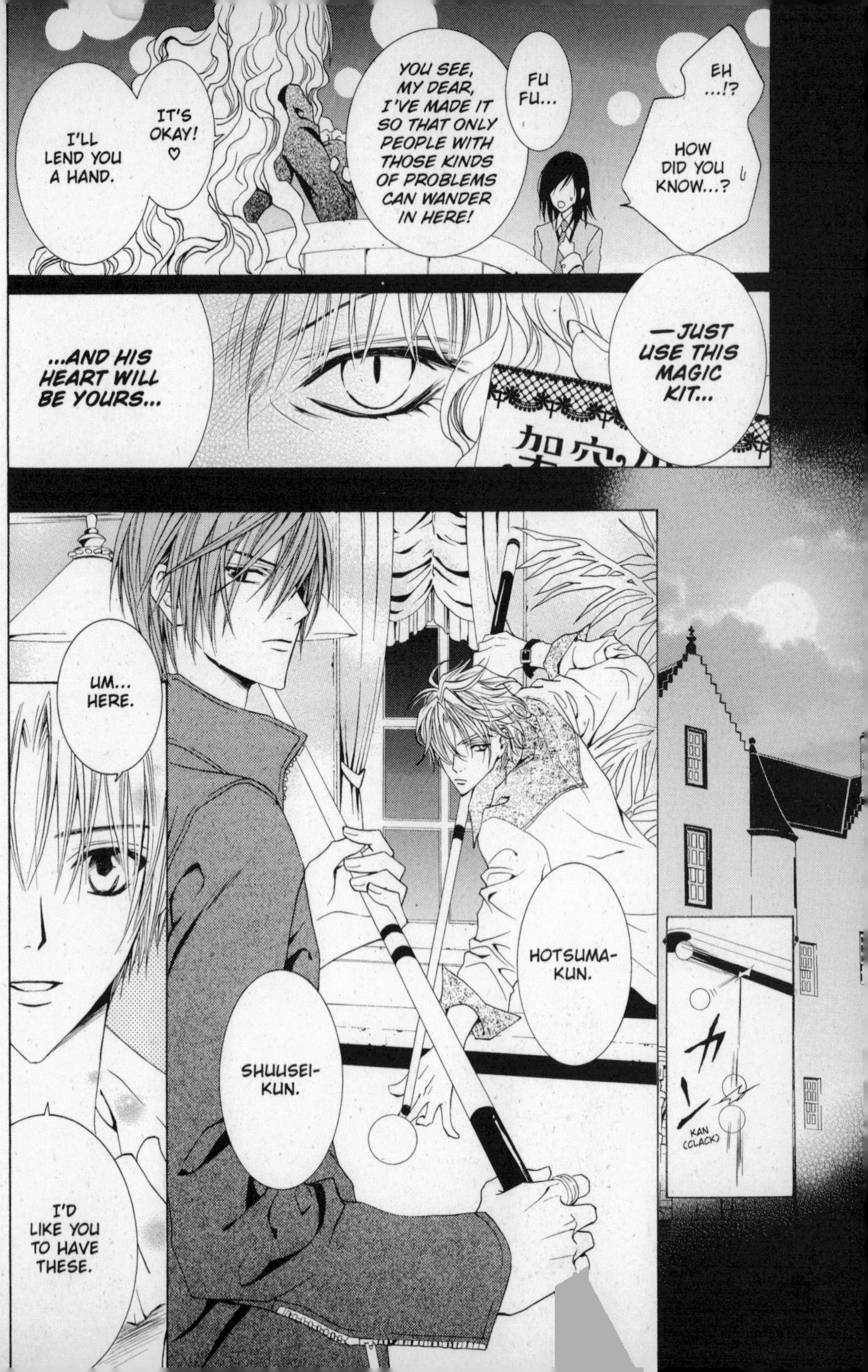
EH ...!?
HOW DID YOU KNOW...?
FU FU...
YOU SEE, MY DEAR, I'VE MADE IT SO THAT ONLY PEOPLE WITH THOSE KINDS OF PROBLEMS CAN WANDER IN HERE!
IT'S OKAY! ♡
I'LL LEND YOU A HAND.
—JUST USE THIS MAGIC KIT...
...AND HIS HEART WILL BE YOURS...
KAN (CLACK)
HOTSUMA-KUN.
SHUUSEI-KUN.
UM... HERE.
I'D LIKE YOU TO HAVE THESE.

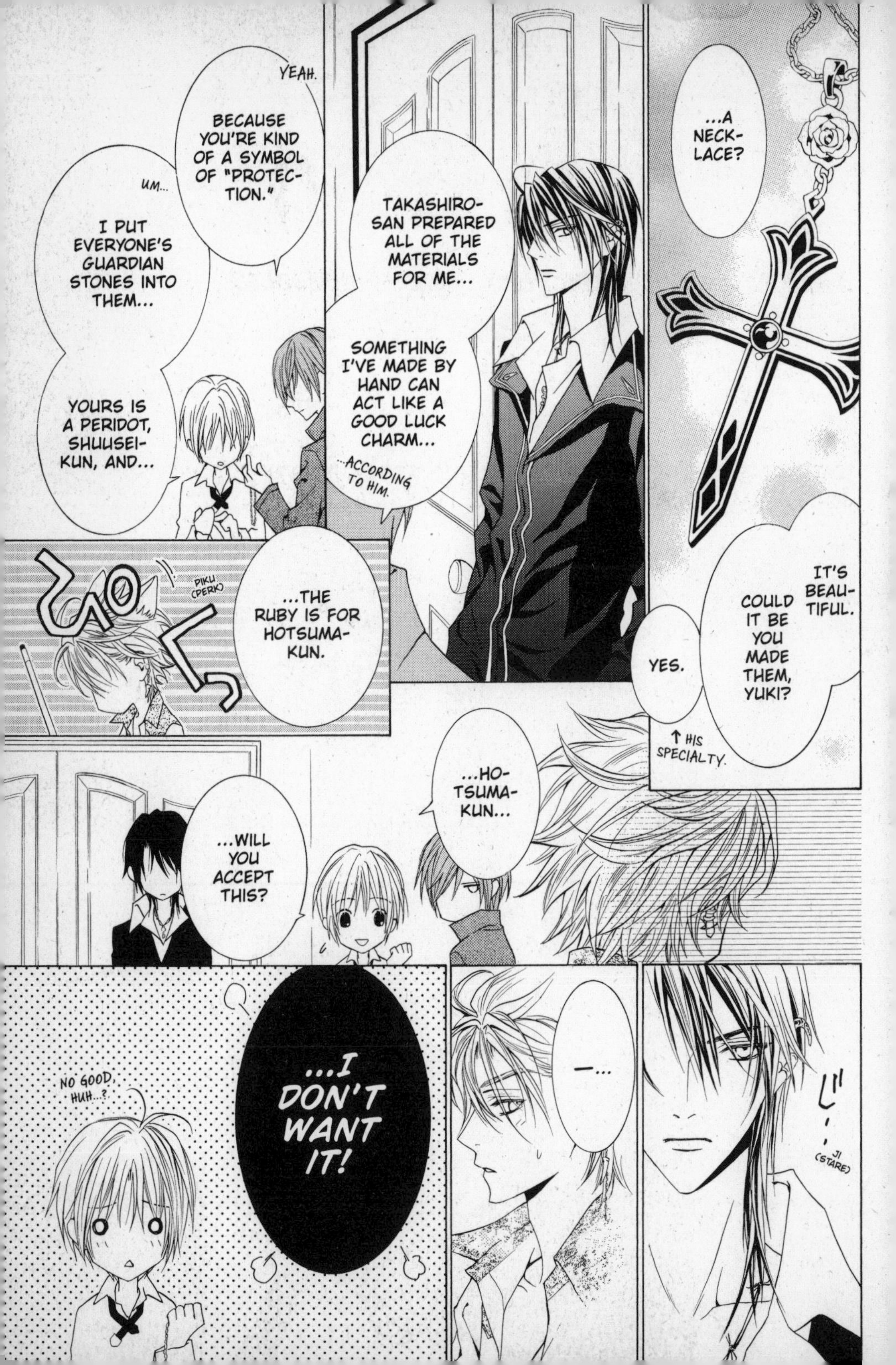
...A NECKLACE?
IT'S BEAUTIFUL.
COULD IT BE YOU MADE THEM, YUKI?
YES.
↑ HIS SPECIALTY.
TAKASHIRO-SAN PREPARED ALL OF THE MATERIALS FOR ME...
SOMETHING I'VE MADE BY HAND CAN ACT LIKE A GOOD LUCK CHARM...
...ACCORDING TO HIM.
YEAH.
BECAUSE YOU'RE KIND OF A SYMBOL OF "PROTECTION."
UM...
I PUT EVERYONE'S GUARDIAN STONES INTO THEM...
YOURS IS A PERIDOT, SHUUSEI-KUN, AND...
...THE RUBY IS FOR HOTSUMA-KUN.
PIKU (PERK)
...HOTSUMA-KUN...
...WILL YOU ACCEPT THIS?
JI (STARE)
—...
...I DON'T WANT IT!
NO GOOD, HUH...?

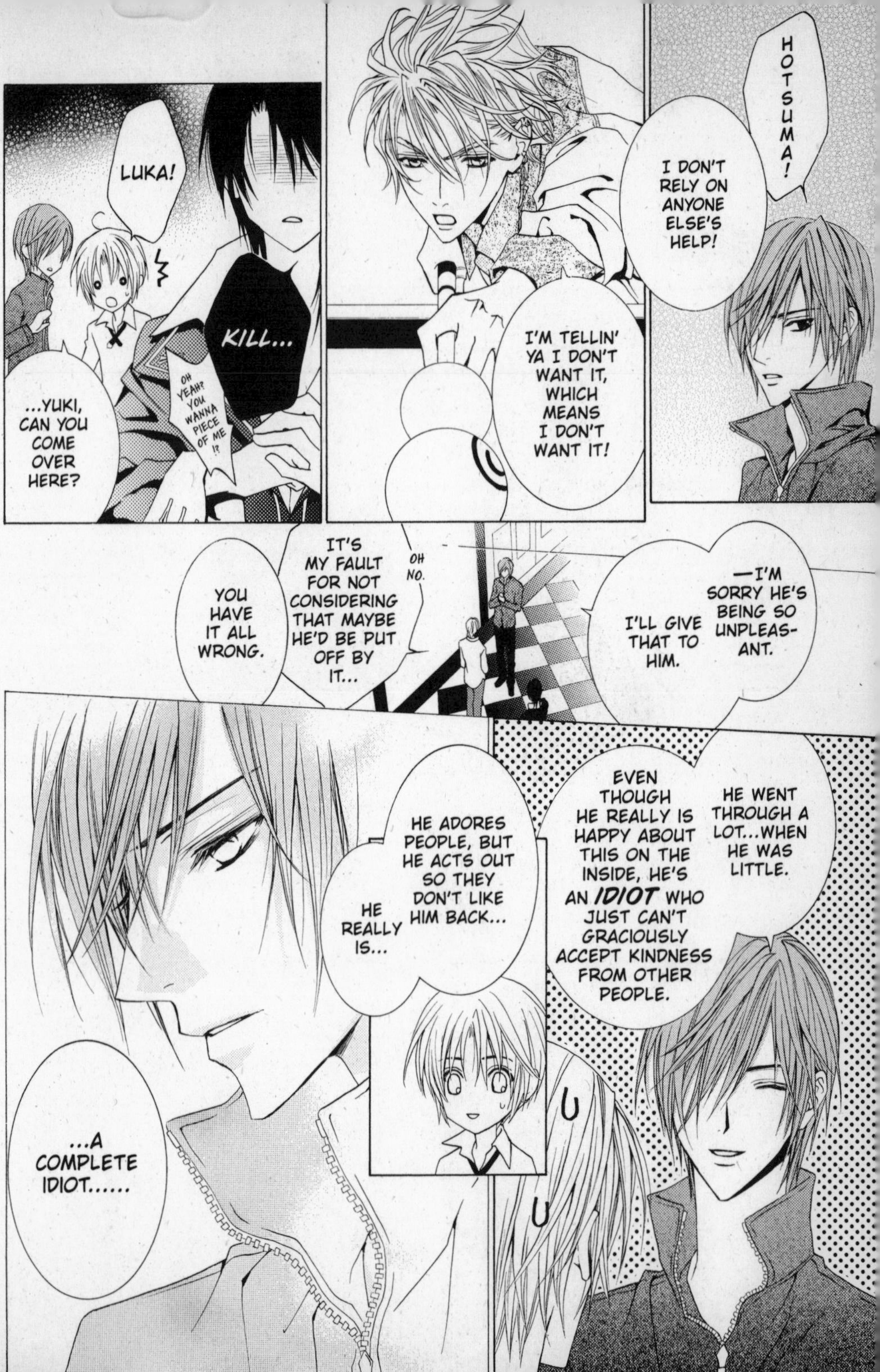
HOTSUMA!
I DON'T RELY ON ANYONE ELSE'S HELP!
I'M TELLIN' YA I DON'T WANT IT, WHICH MEANS I DON'T WANT IT!
LUKA!
KILL...
OH YEAH? YOU WANNA PIECE OF ME!?
...YUKI, CAN YOU COME OVER HERE?
—I'M SORRY HE'S BEING SO UNPLEASANT.
I'LL GIVE THAT TO HIM.
OH NO.
IT'S MY FAULT FOR NOT CONSIDERING THAT MAYBE HE'D BE PUT OFF BY IT...
YOU HAVE IT ALL WRONG.
HE WENT THROUGH A LOT...WHEN HE WAS LITTLE.
EVEN THOUGH HE REALLY IS HAPPY ABOUT THIS ON THE INSIDE, HE'S AN IDIOT WHO JUST CAN'T GRACIOUSLY ACCEPT KINDNESS FROM OTHER PEOPLE.
HE ADORES PEOPLE, BUT HE ACTS OUT SO THEY DON'T LIKE HIM BACK...
HE REALLY IS...
...A COMPLETE IDIOT......

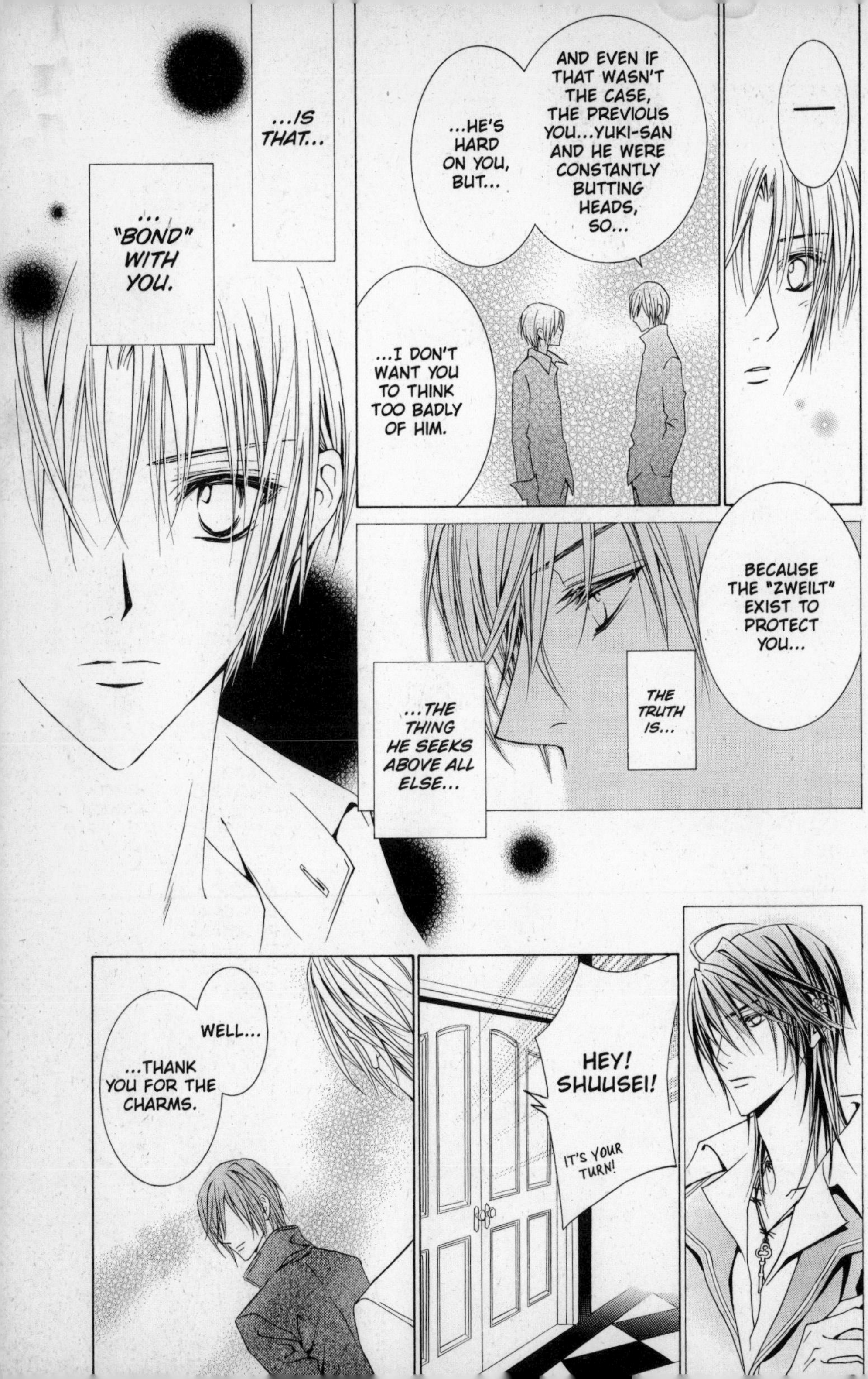
—
...HE'S HARD ON YOU, BUT...
AND EVEN IF THAT WASN'T THE CASE, THE PREVIOUS YOU...YUKI-SAN AND HE WERE CONSTANTLY BUTTING HEADS, SO...
...I DON'T WANT YOU TO THINK TOO BADLY OF HIM.
BECAUSE THE "ZWEILT" EXIST TO PROTECT YOU...
THE TRUTH IS...
...THE THING HE SEEKS ABOVE ALL ELSE...
...IS THAT...
... "BOND" WITH YOU.
HEY! SHUUSEI!
IT'S YOUR TURN!
WELL...
...THANK YOU FOR THE CHARMS.

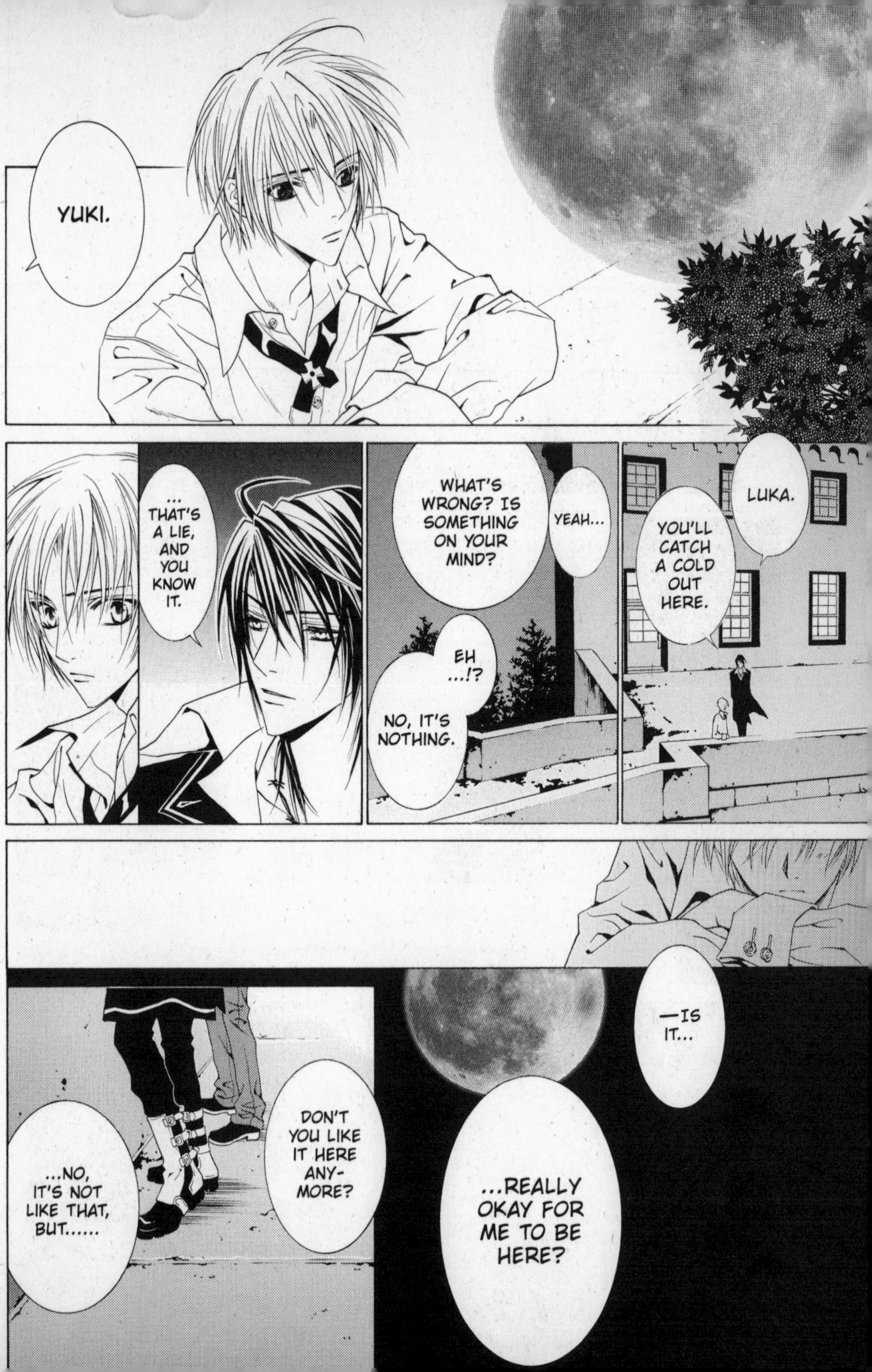
YUKI.
LUKA.
YOU'LL CATCH A COLD OUT HERE.
YEAH...
WHAT'S WRONG? IS SOMETHING ON YOUR MIND?
EH ...!?
NO, IT'S NOTHING.
... THAT'S A LIE, AND YOU KNOW IT.
—IS IT...
...REALLY OKAY FOR ME TO BE HERE?
DON'T YOU LIKE IT HERE ANY-MORE?
...NO, IT'S NOT LIKE THAT, BUT......

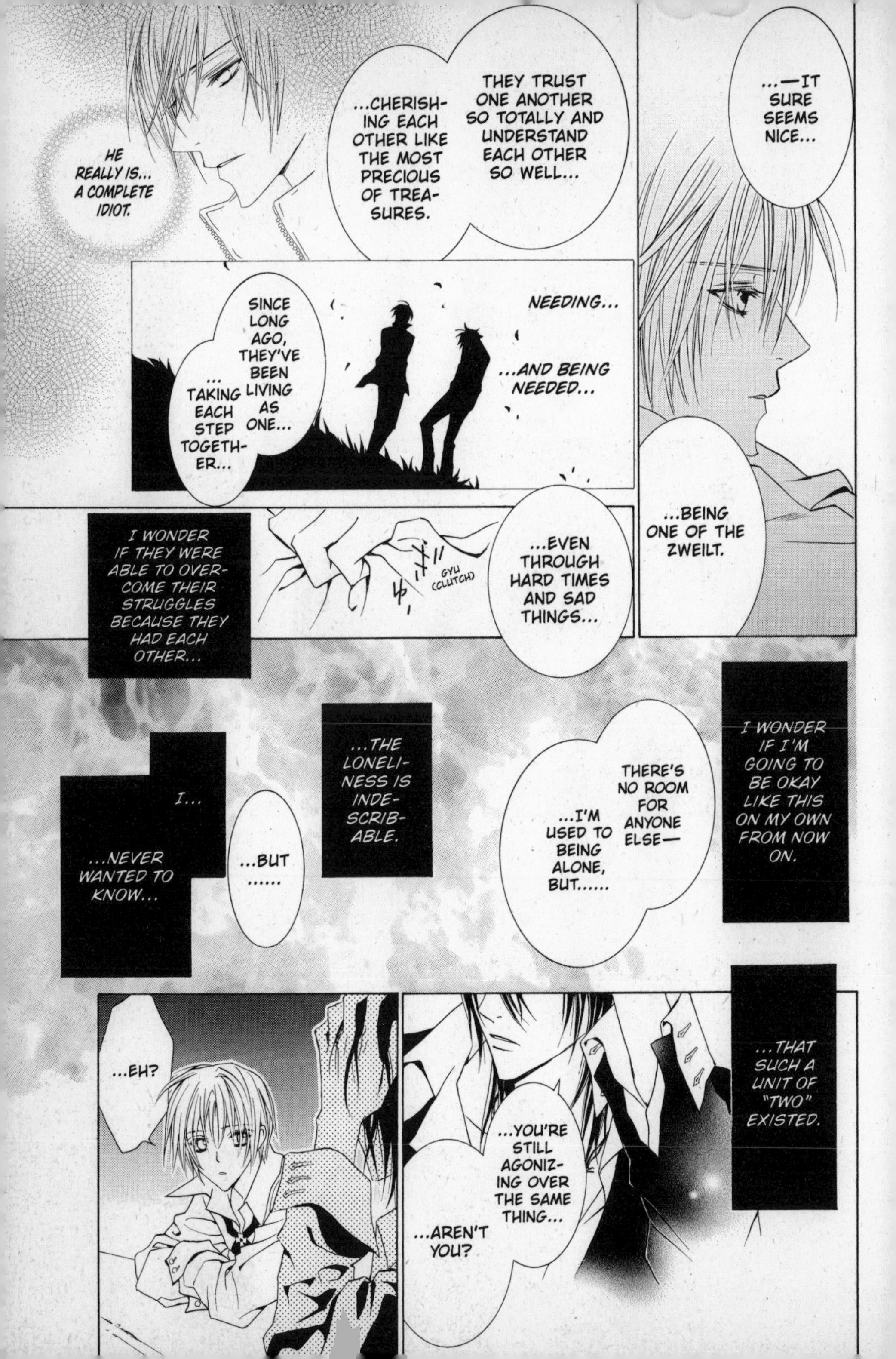
...—IT SURE SEEMS NICE...
...BEING ONE OF THE ZWEILT.
THEY TRUST ONE ANOTHER SO TOTALLY AND UNDERSTAND EACH OTHER SO WELL...
...CHERISHING EACH OTHER LIKE THE MOST PRECIOUS OF TREASURES.
HE REALLY IS... A COMPLETE IDIOT.
NEEDING...
...AND BEING NEEDED...
SINCE LONG AGO, THEY'VE BEEN LIVING AS ONE...
...TAKING EACH STEP TOGETHER...
...EVEN THROUGH HARD TIMES AND SAD THINGS...
GYU (CLUTCH)
I WONDER IF THEY WERE ABLE TO OVERCOME THEIR STRUGGLES BECAUSE THEY HAD EACH OTHER...
I WONDER IF I'M GOING TO BE OKAY LIKE THIS ON MY OWN FROM NOW ON.
THERE'S NO ROOM FOR ANYONE ELSE—
...I'M USED TO BEING ALONE, BUT......
...THE LONELINESS IS INDESCRIBABLE.
...BUT ......
I...
...NEVER WANTED TO KNOW...
...THAT SUCH A UNIT OF "TWO" EXISTED.
...YOU'RE STILL AGONIZING OVER THE SAME THING...
...AREN'T YOU?
...EH?

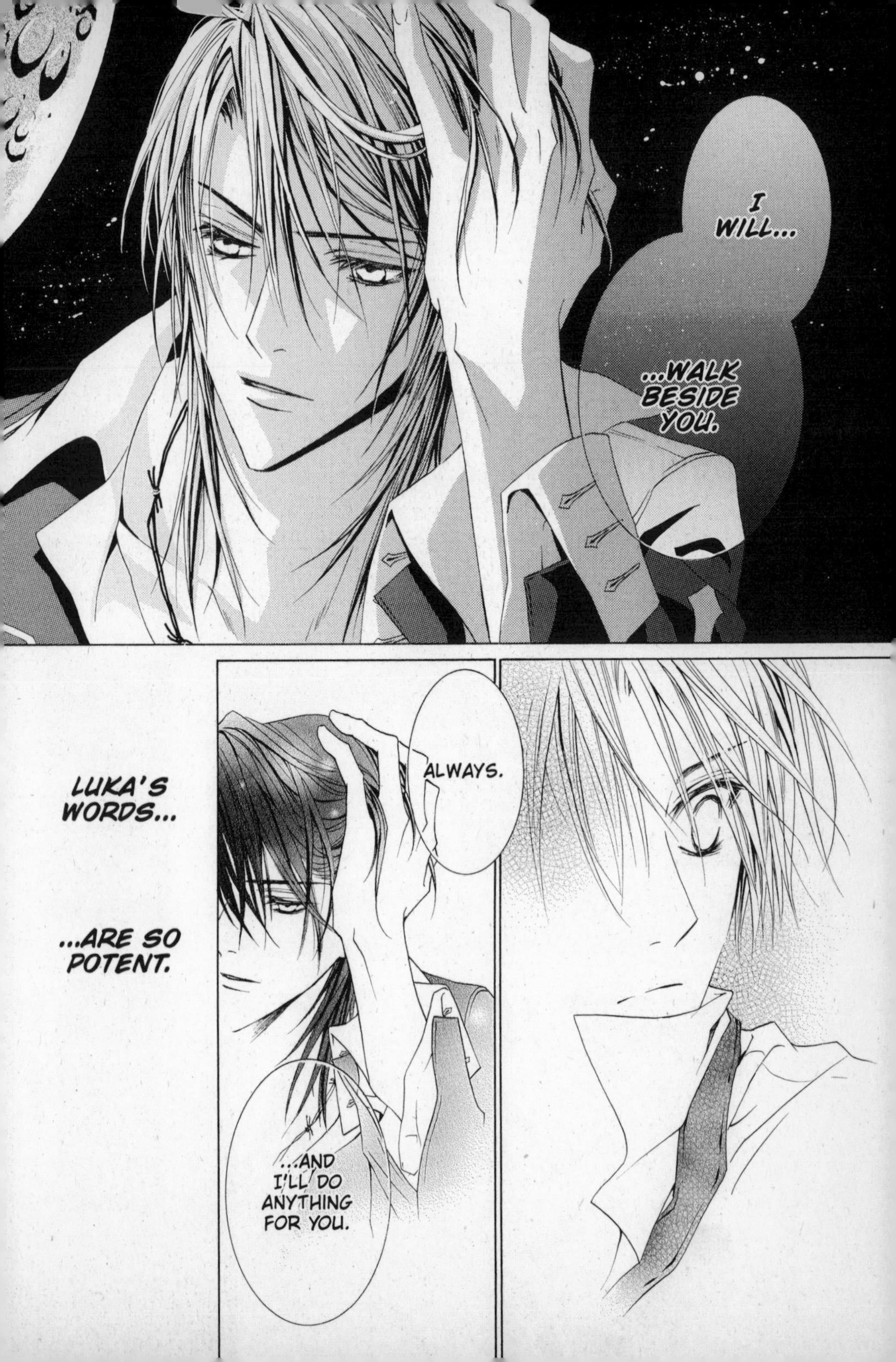
I WILL...
...WALK BESIDE YOU.
ALWAYS.
...AND I'LL DO ANYTHING FOR YOU.
LUKA'S WORDS...
...ARE SO POTENT.

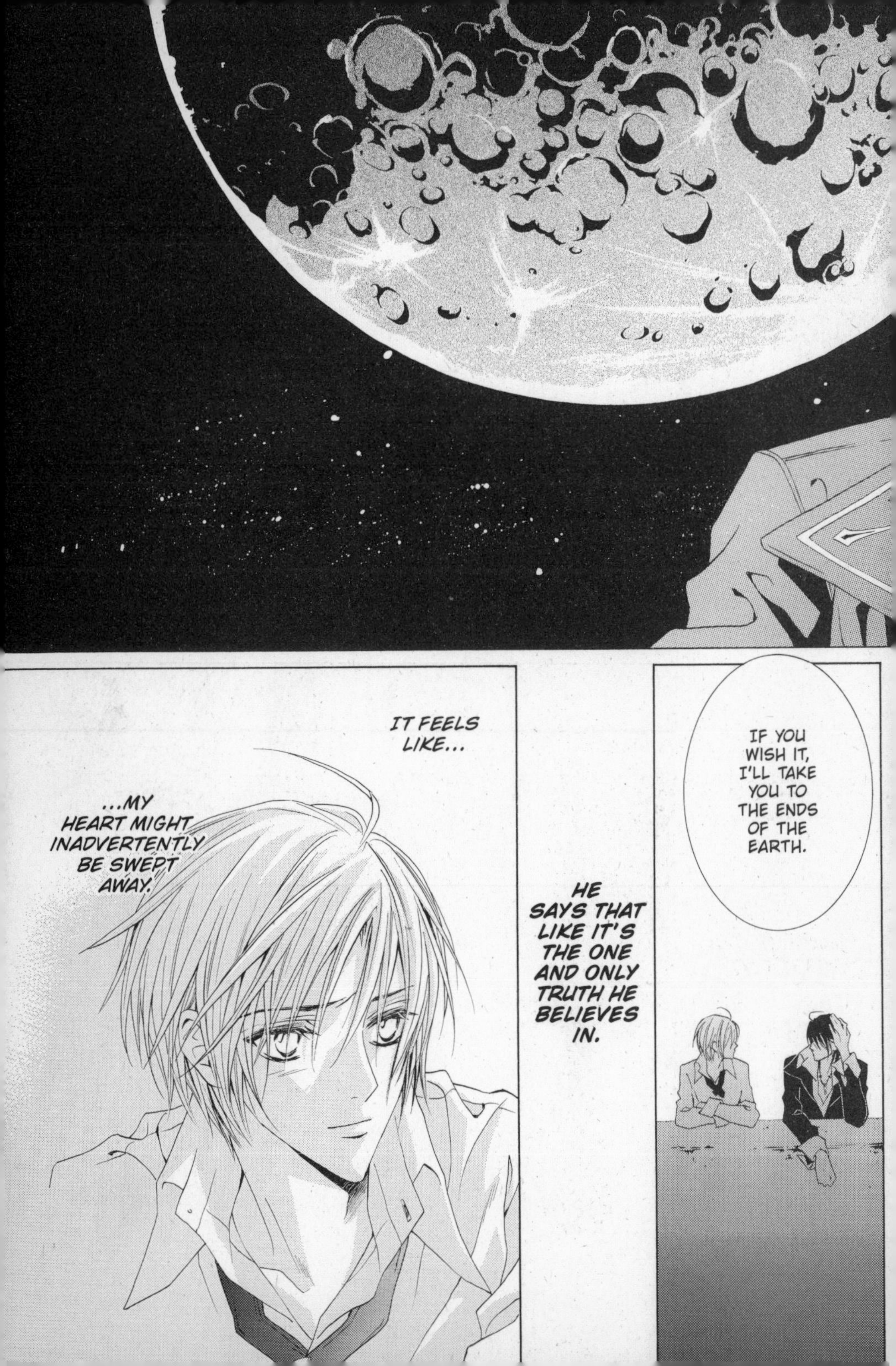
IF YOU WISH IT, I'LL TAKE YOU TO THE ENDS OF THE EARTH.
HE SAYS THAT LIKE IT'S THE ONE AND ONLY TRUTH HE BELIEVES IN.
IT FEELS LIKE...
...MY HEART MIGHT INADVERTENTLY BE SWEPT AWAY.

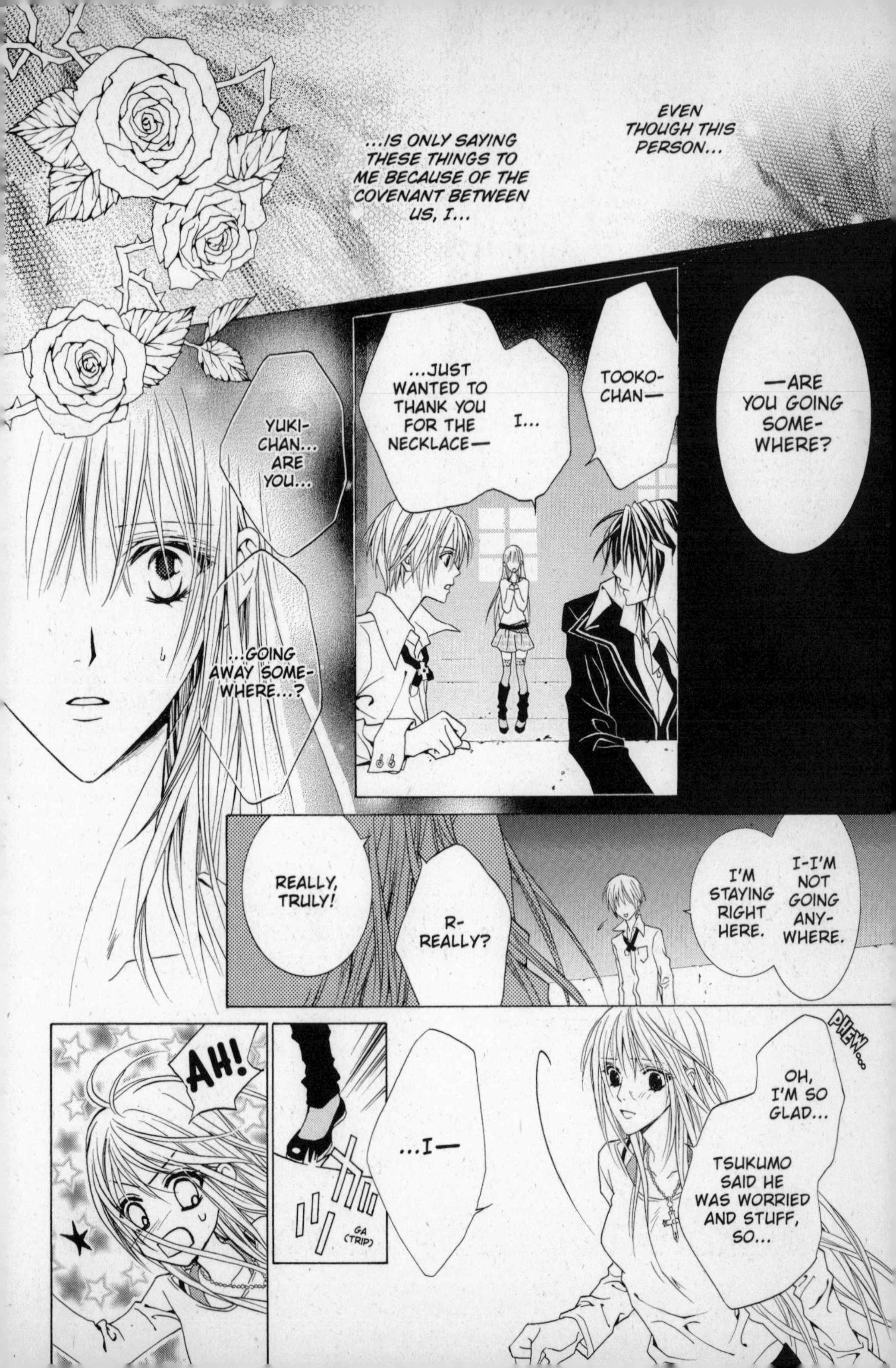
EVEN THOUGH THIS PERSON...
...IS ONLY SAYING THESE THINGS TO ME BECAUSE OF THE COVENANT BETWEEN US, I...
—ARE YOU GOING SOMEWHERE?
TOOKO-CHAN—
I...
...JUST WANTED TO THANK YOU FOR THE NECKLACE—
I-I'M NOT GOING ANYWHERE.
I'M STAYING RIGHT HERE.
R-REALLY?
REALLY, TRULY!
YUKI-CHAN... ARE YOU...
...GOING AWAY SOMEWHERE...?
PHEW...
OH, I'M SO GLAD...
TSUKUMO SAID HE WAS WORRIED AND STUFF, SO...
...I—
GA (TRIP)
AH!

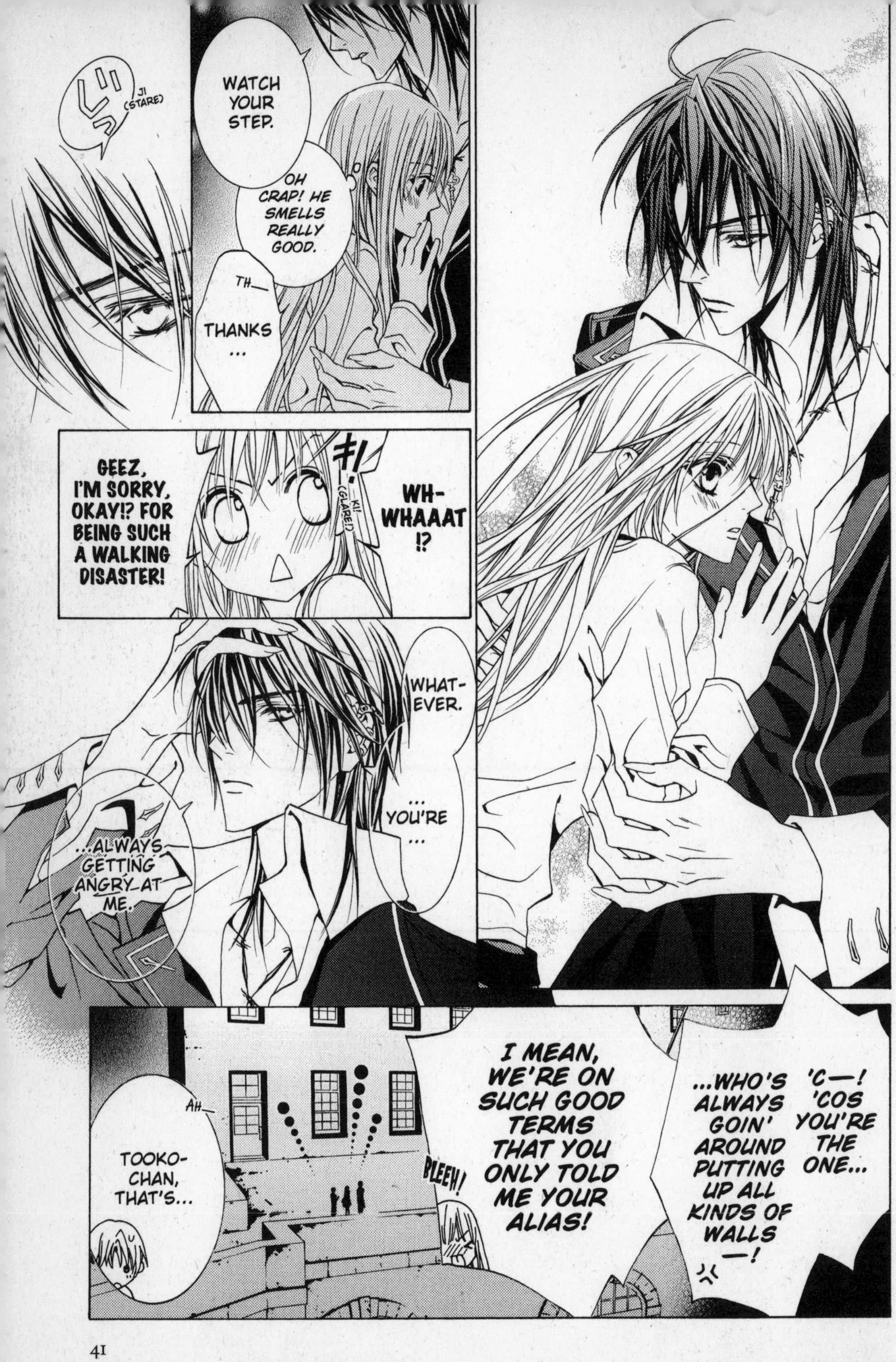
WATCH YOUR STEP.
OH CRAP! HE SMELLS REALLY GOOD.
TH— THANKS ...
JI (STARE)
WH- WHAAAT !?
KI! (GLARE!)
GEEZ, I'M SORRY, OKAY!? FOR BEING SUCH A WALKING DISASTER!
WHAT- EVER.
... YOU'RE ...
...ALWAYS GETTING ANGRY AT ME.
'C—! 'COS YOU'RE THE ONE...
...WHO'S ALWAYS GOIN' AROUND PUTTING UP ALL KINDS OF WALLS —!
I MEAN, WE'RE ON SUCH GOOD TERMS THAT YOU ONLY TOLD ME YOUR ALIAS!
BLEEH!
AH—
TOOKO- CHAN, THAT'S...

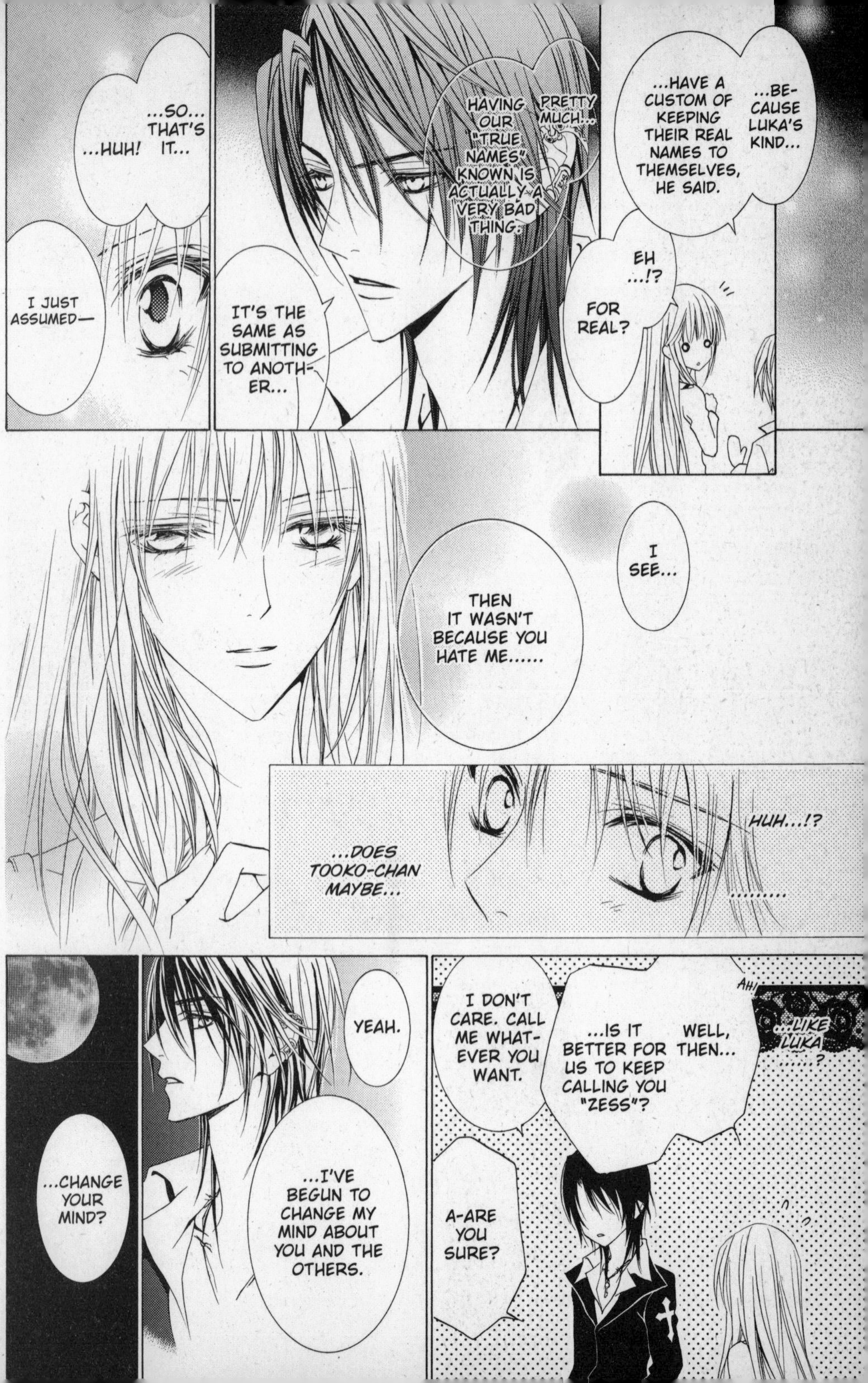
...BECAUSE LUKA'S KIND...
...HAVE A CUSTOM OF KEEPING THEIR REAL NAMES TO THEMSELVES, HE SAID.
EH ...!? FOR REAL?
PRETTY MUCH...
HAVING OUR "TRUE NAMES" KNOWN IS ACTUALLY A VERY BAD THING.
IT'S THE SAME AS SUBMITTING TO ANOTHER...
...SO... THAT'S IT...
...HUH!
I JUST ASSUMED—
I SEE...
THEN IT WASN'T BECAUSE YOU HATE ME......
HUH...!?
....
...DOES TOOKO-CHAN MAYBE...
AH!
...LIKE LUKA......?
WELL, THEN...
...IS IT BETTER FOR US TO KEEP CALLING YOU "ZESS"?
I DON'T CARE. CALL ME WHATEVER YOU WANT.
A-ARE YOU SURE?
YEAH.
...I'VE BEGUN TO CHANGE MY MIND ABOUT YOU AND THE OTHERS.
...CHANGE YOUR MIND?

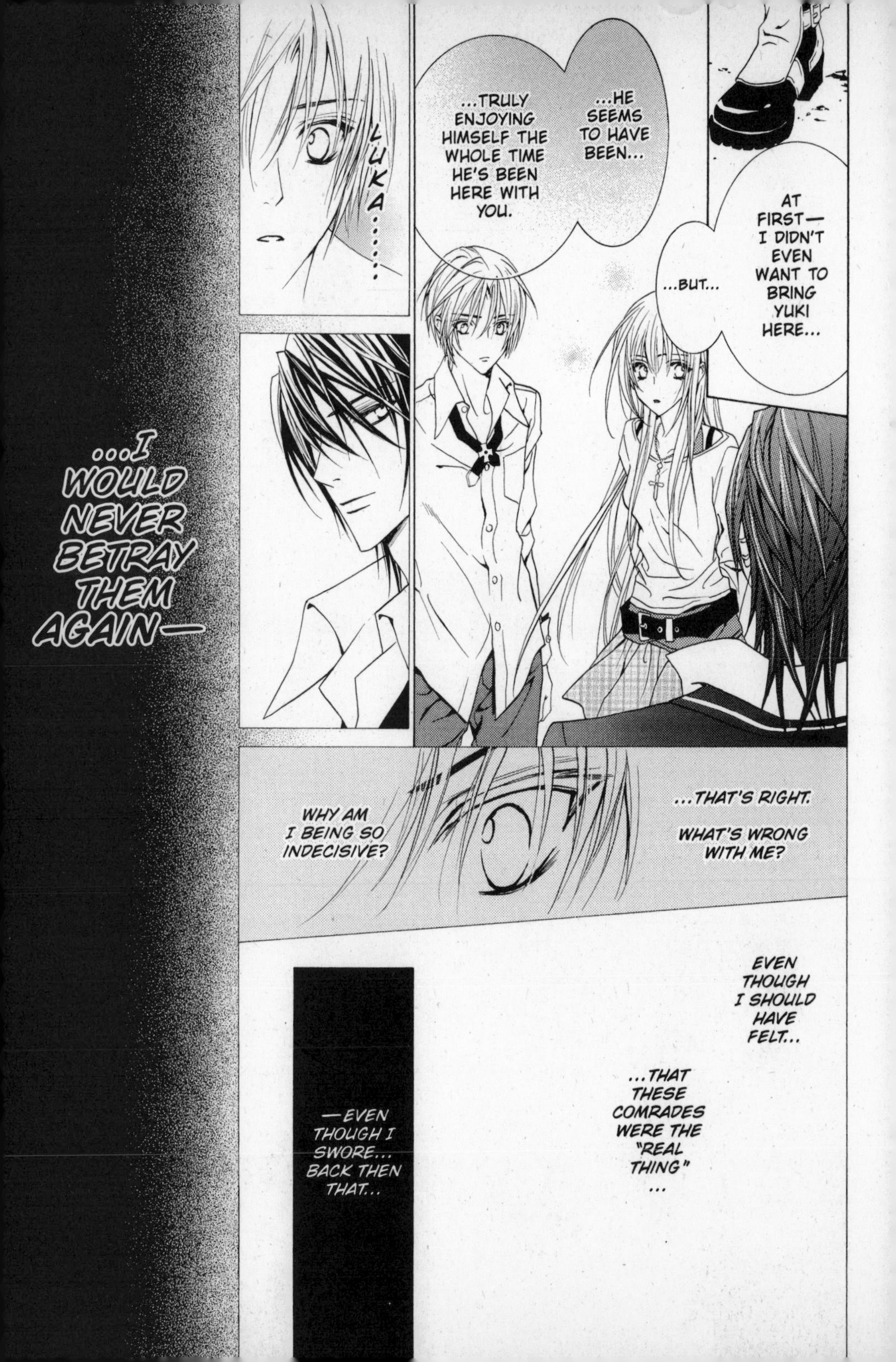

AT FIRST— I DIDN'T EVEN WANT TO BRING YUKI HERE...
...BUT...
...HE SEEMS TO HAVE BEEN...
...TRULY ENJOYING HIMSELF THE WHOLE TIME HE'S BEEN HERE WITH YOU.
LUKA......
...I WOULD NEVER BETRAY THEM AGAIN—
...THAT'S RIGHT.
WHAT'S WRONG WITH ME?
WHY AM I BEING SO INDECISIVE?
EVEN THOUGH I SHOULD HAVE FELT...
...THAT THESE COMRADES WERE THE "REAL THING"...
—EVEN THOUGH I SWORE... BACK THEN THAT...

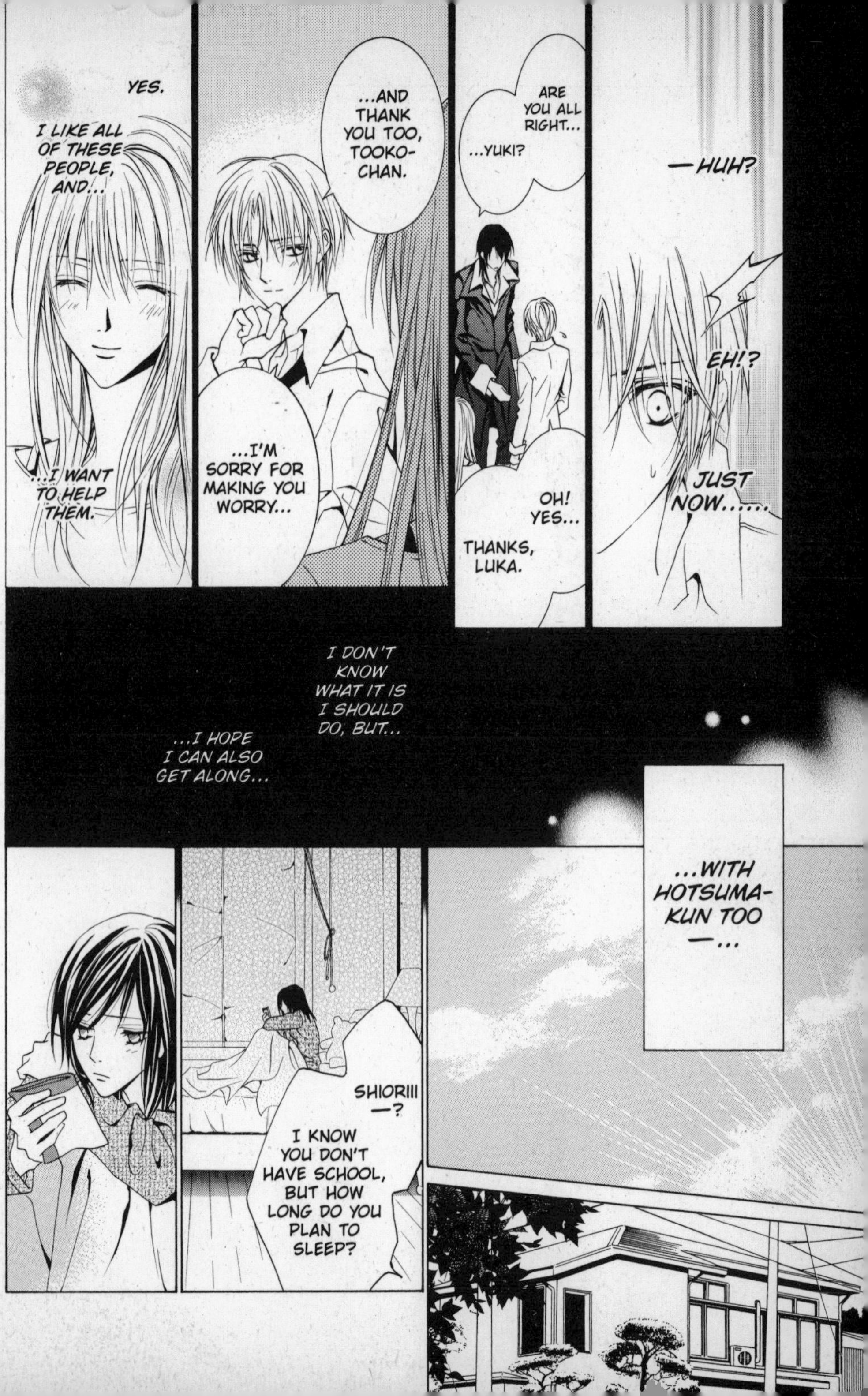
—HUH?
EH!?
JUST NOW......
ARE YOU ALL RIGHT...
...YUKI?
OH! YES...
THANKS, LUKA.
...AND THANK YOU TOO, TOOKO-CHAN.
...I'M SORRY FOR MAKING YOU WORRY...
YES.
I LIKE ALL OF THESE PEOPLE, AND...
...I WANT TO HELP THEM.
I DON'T KNOW WHAT IT IS I SHOULD DO, BUT...
...I HOPE I CAN ALSO GET ALONG...
...WITH HOTSUMA-KUN TOO —...
SHIORIII —?
I KNOW YOU DON'T HAVE SCHOOL, BUT HOW LONG DO YOU PLAN TO SLEEP?

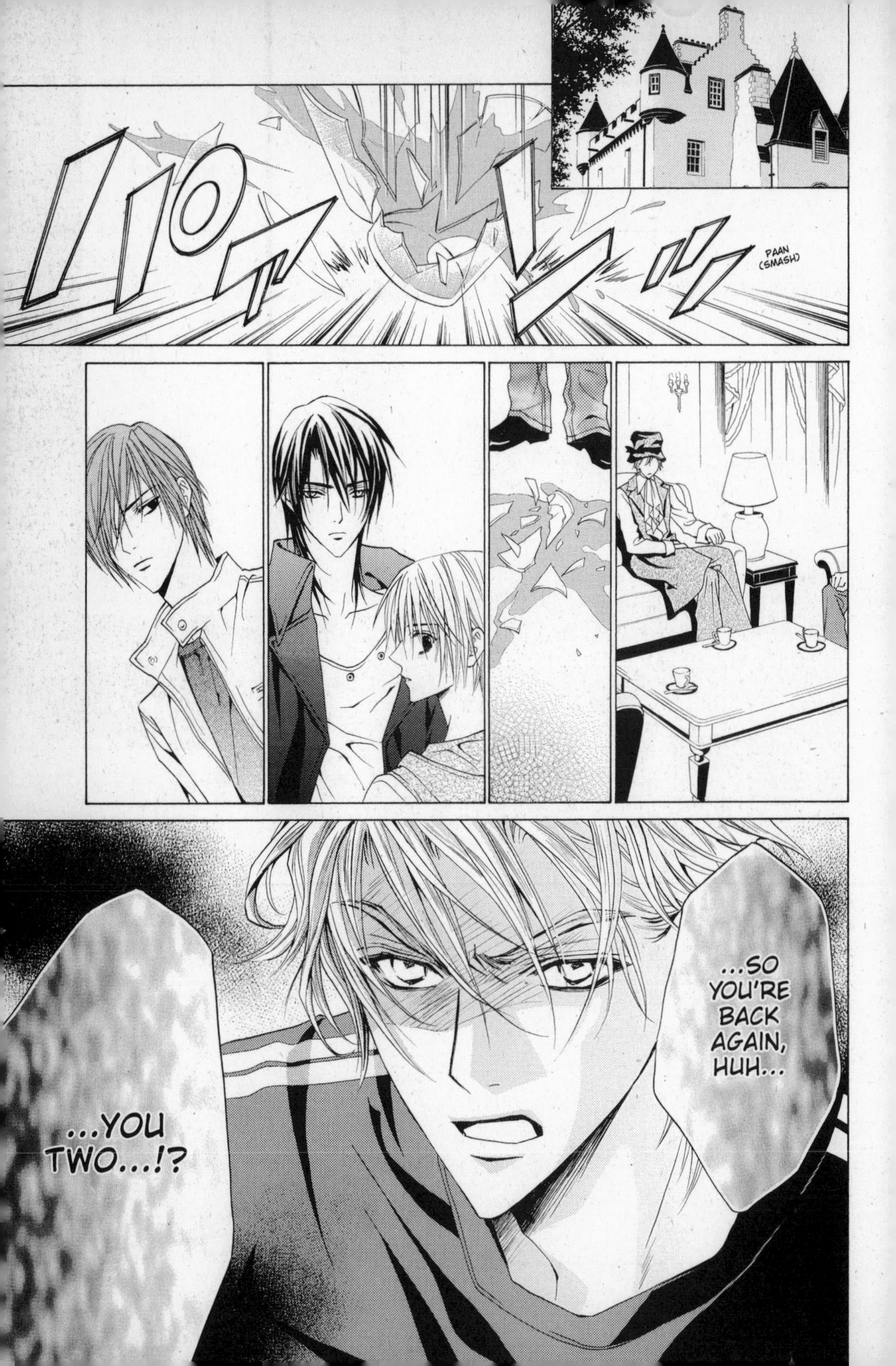
PAAN (SMASH)
...SO YOU'RE BACK AGAIN, HUH...
...YOU TWO...!?

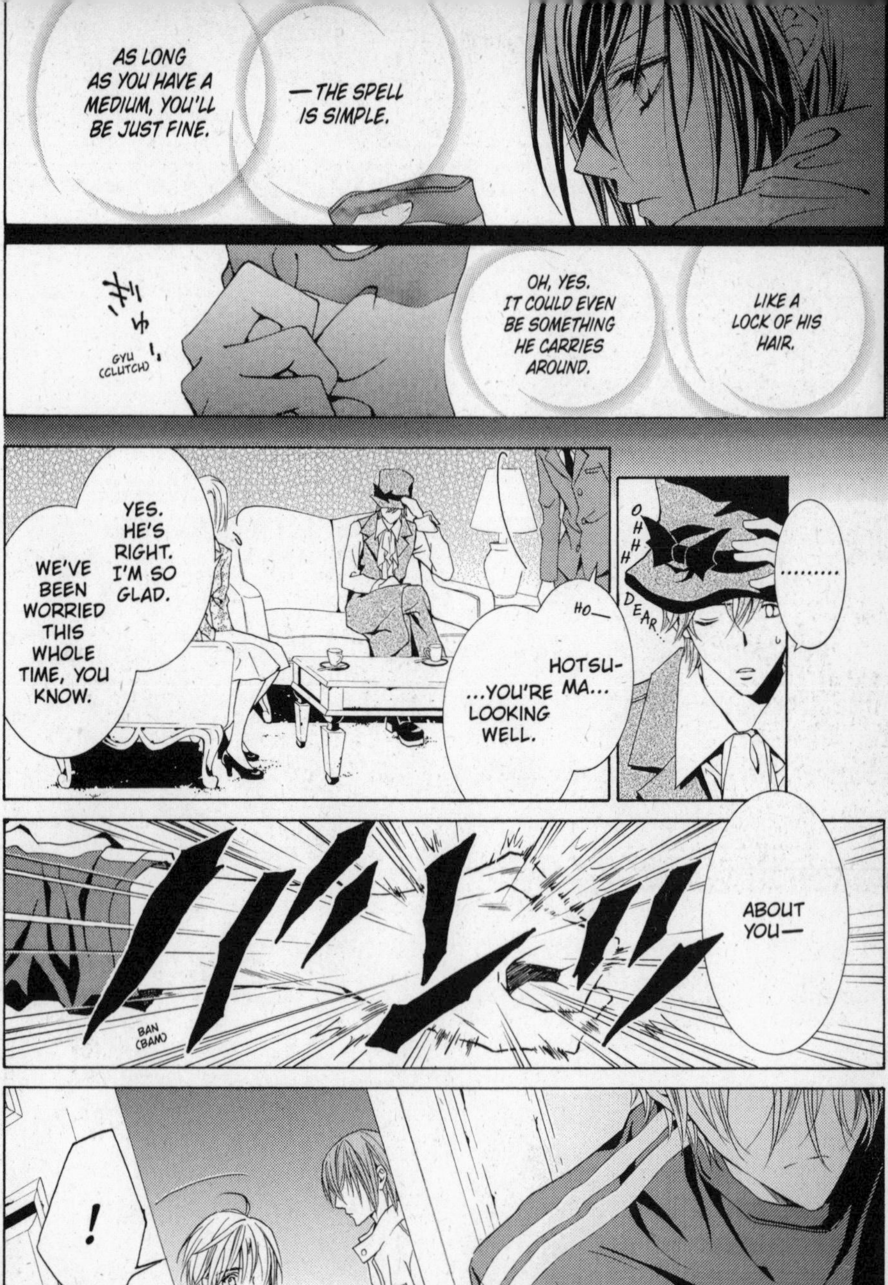
—THE SPELL IS SIMPLE.
AS LONG AS YOU HAVE A MEDIUM, YOU'LL BE JUST FINE.
LIKE A LOCK OF HIS HAIR.
OH, YES. IT COULD EVEN BE SOMETHING HE CARRIES AROUND.
ぎゅ
GYU (CLUTCH)
....
OHHH DEAR...
HO—
HOTSU-MA... ...YOU'RE LOOKING WELL.
YES. HE'S RIGHT. I'M SO GLAD.
WE'VE BEEN WORRIED THIS WHOLE TIME, YOU KNOW.
ABOUT YOU—
BAN (BAM)
!

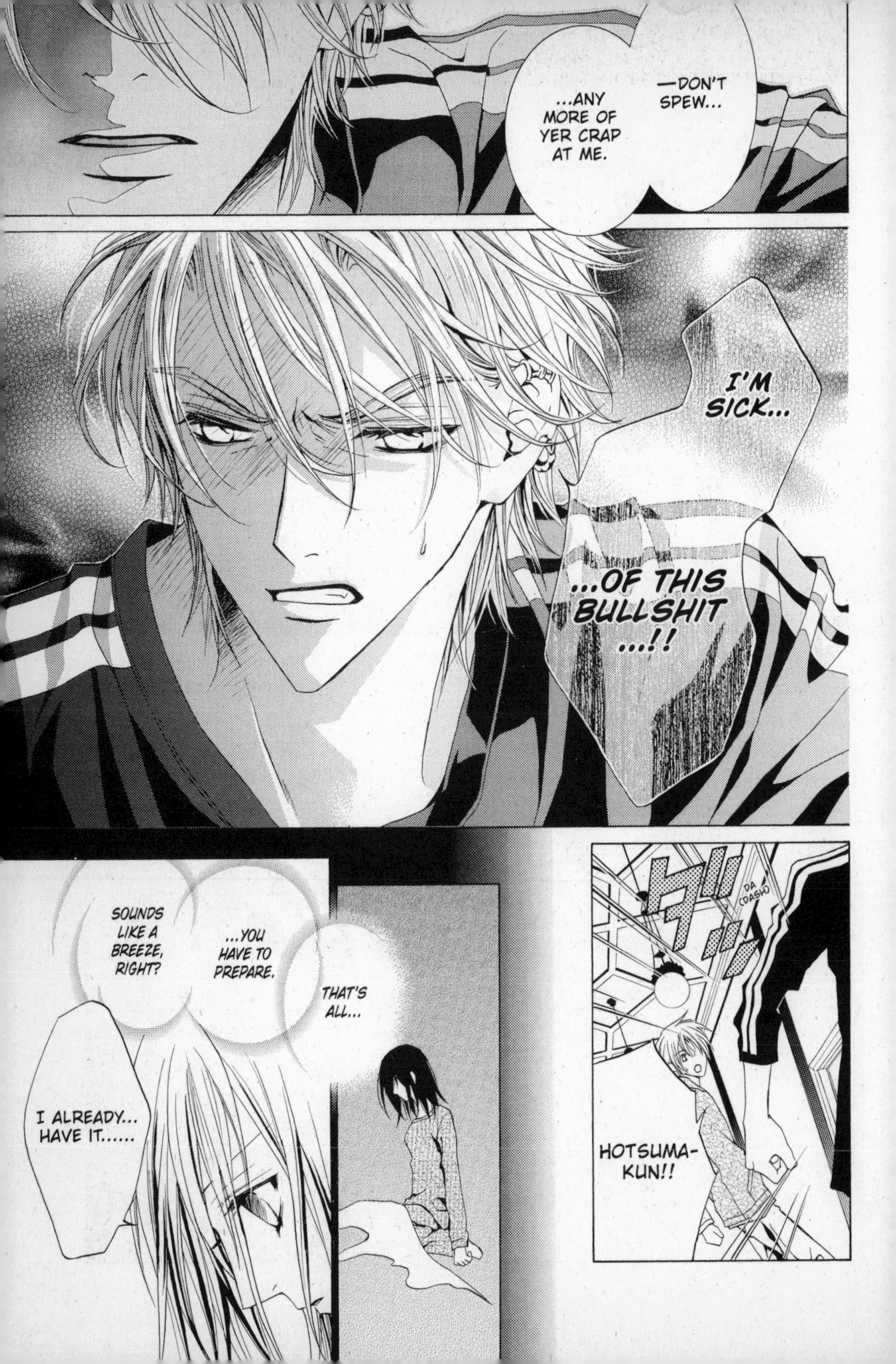
—DON'T SPEW...
...ANY MORE OF YER CRAP AT ME.
I'M SICK...
...OF THIS BULLSHIT ...!!
DA (DASH)
HOTSUMA-KUN!!
THAT'S ALL...
...YOU HAVE TO PREPARE.
SOUNDS LIKE A BREEZE, RIGHT?
I ALREADY... HAVE IT......

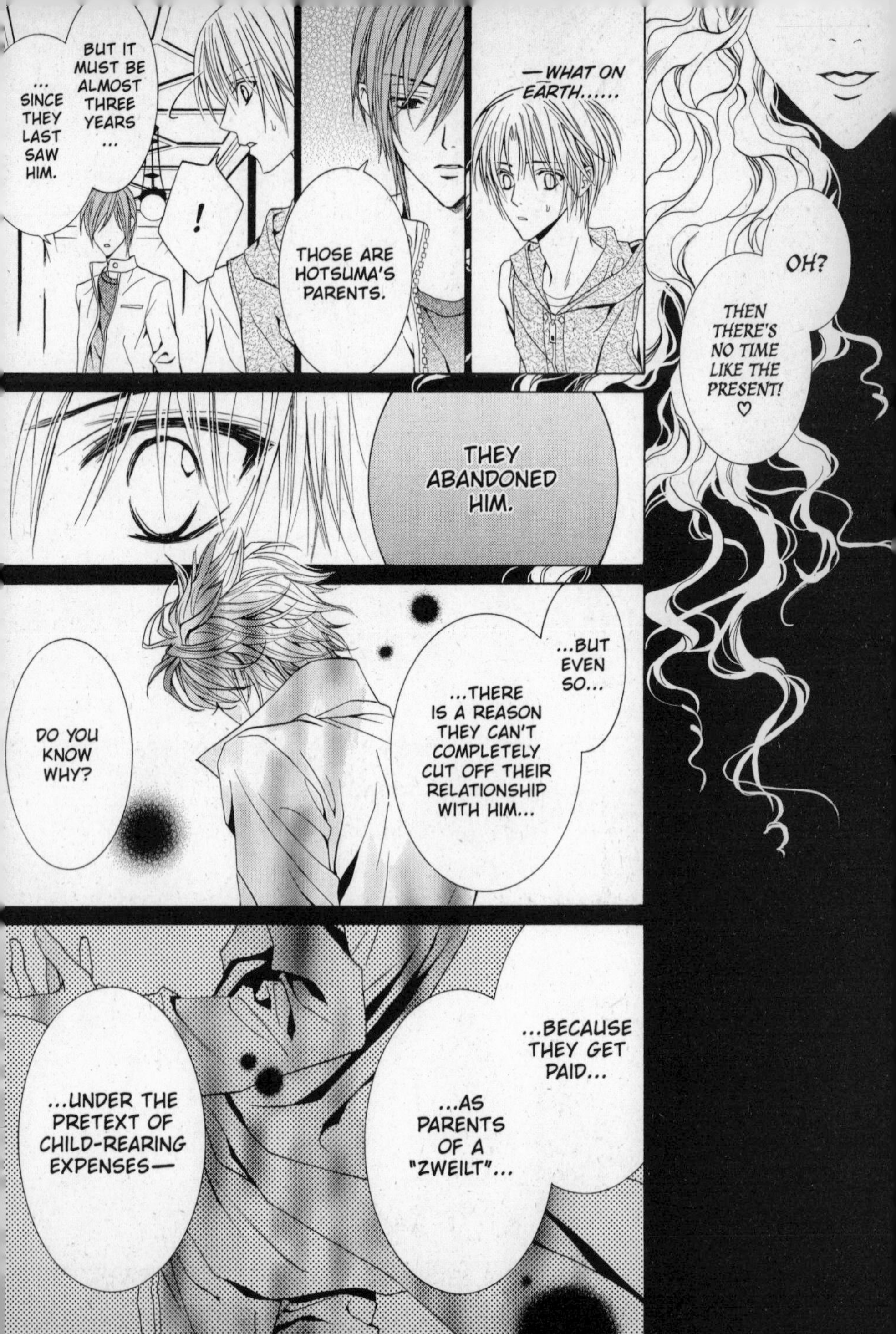
OH?
THEN THERE'S NO TIME LIKE THE PRESENT! ♡
—WHAT ON EARTH......
THOSE ARE HOTSUMA'S PARENTS.
!
BUT IT MUST BE ALMOST THREE YEARS...
...SINCE THEY LAST SAW HIM.
THEY ABANDONED HIM.
...BUT EVEN SO...
...THERE IS A REASON THEY CAN'T COMPLETELY CUT OFF THEIR RELATIONSHIP WITH HIM...
DO YOU KNOW WHY?
...BECAUSE THEY GET PAID...
...AS PARENTS OF A "ZWEILT"...
...UNDER THE PRETEXT OF CHILD-REARING EXPENSES—

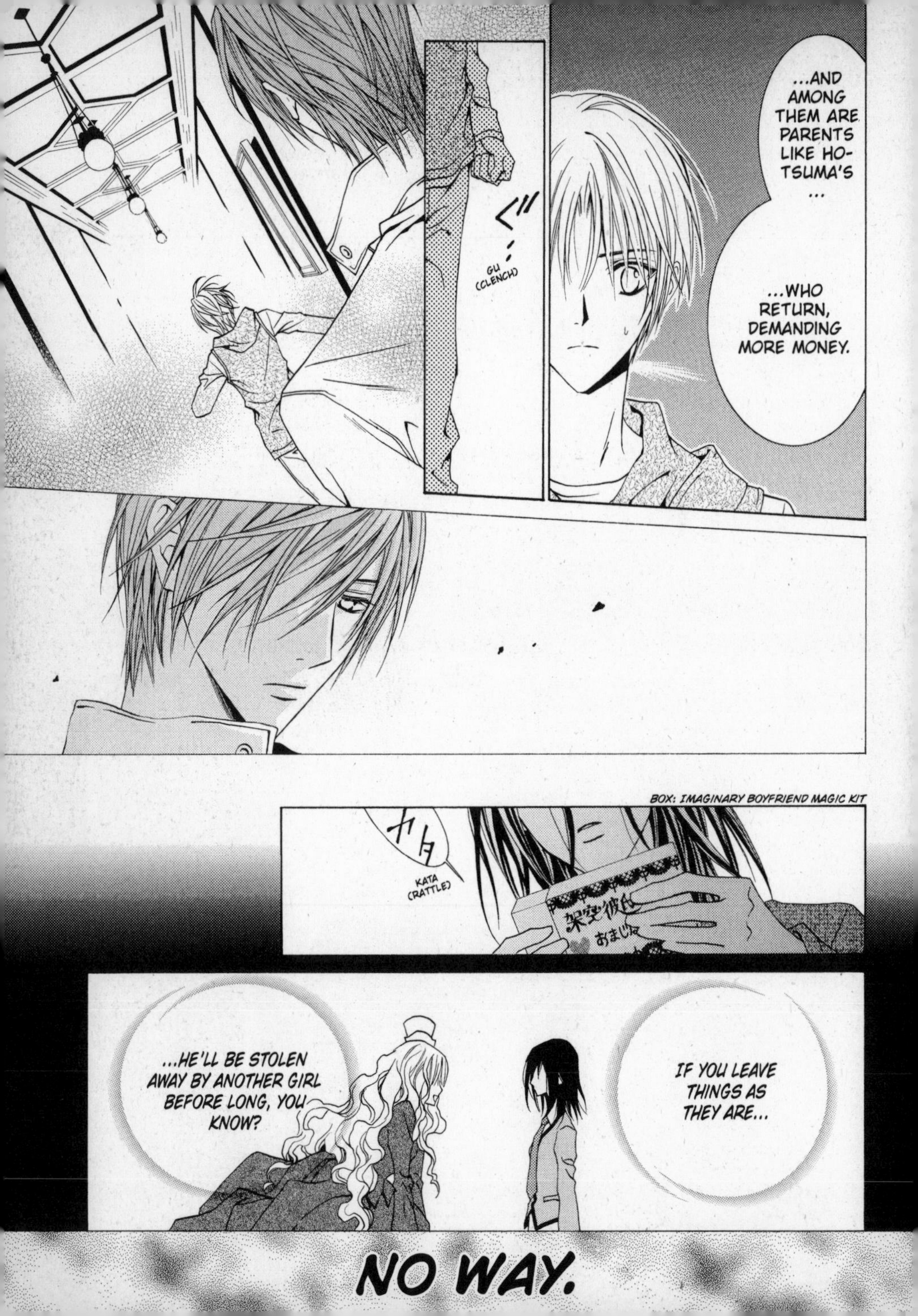
...AND AMONG THEM ARE PARENTS LIKE HO-TSUMA'S ...
...WHO RETURN, DEMANDING MORE MONEY.
ぐ
GU (CLENCH)
BOX: IMAGINARY BOYFRIEND MAGIC KIT
カタ
KATA (RATTLE)
架空彼氏
IF YOU LEAVE THINGS AS THEY ARE...
...HE'LL BE STOLEN AWAY BY ANOTHER GIRL BEFORE LONG, YOU KNOW?
NO WAY.

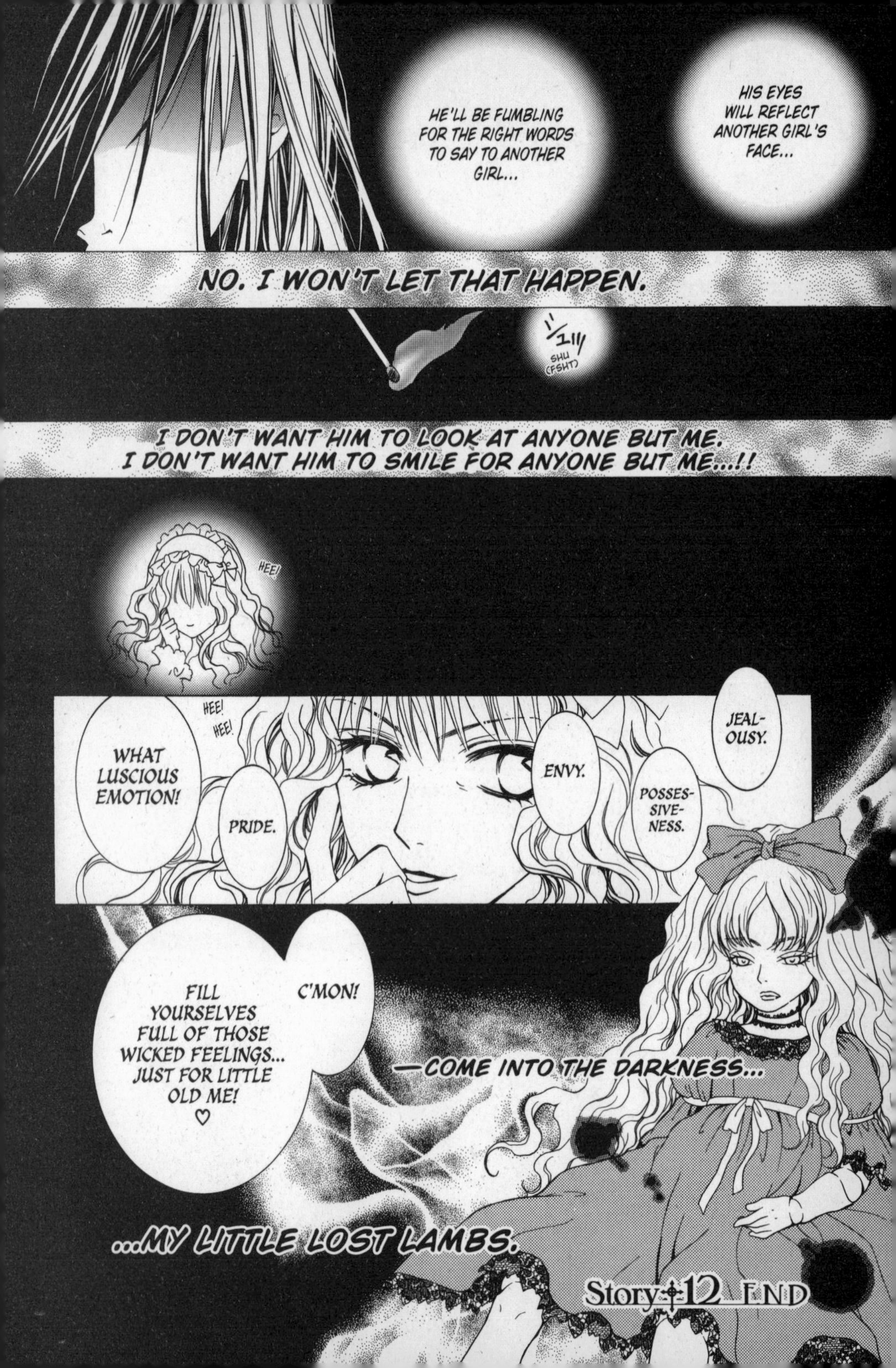
HIS EYES WILL REFLECT ANOTHER GIRL'S FACE...
HE'LL BE FUMBLING FOR THE RIGHT WORDS TO SAY TO ANOTHER GIRL...
NO. I WON'T LET THAT HAPPEN.
SHU (FSHT)
I DON'T WANT HIM TO LOOK AT ANYONE BUT ME.
I DON'T WANT HIM TO SMILE FOR ANYONE BUT ME...!!
HEE!
JEAL-OUSY.
POSSES-SIVE-NESS.
ENVY.
PRIDE.
WHAT LUSCIOUS EMOTION!
HEE! HEE!
C'MON!
FILL YOURSELVES FULL OF THOSE WICKED FEELINGS... JUST FOR LITTLE OLD ME! ♡
—COME INTO THE DARKNESS...
...MY LITTLE LOST LAMBS.
Story 12 END

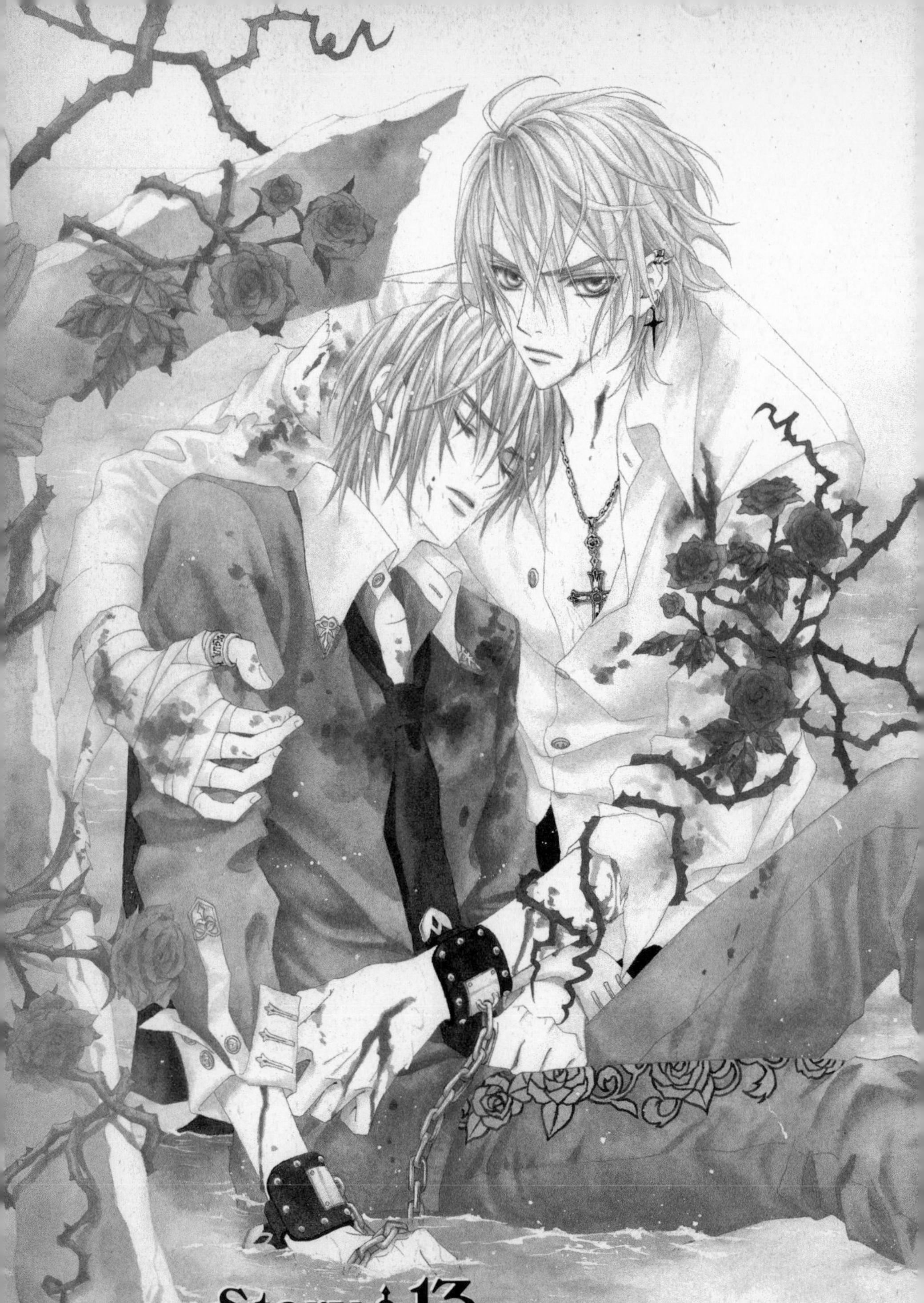

Story 13 Scarlet Darkness

The Betrayal Knows My Name

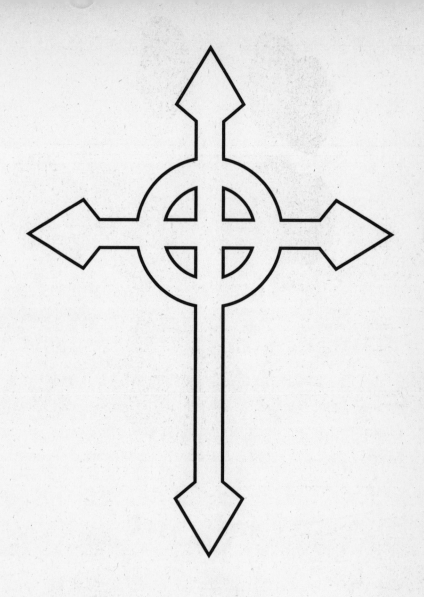

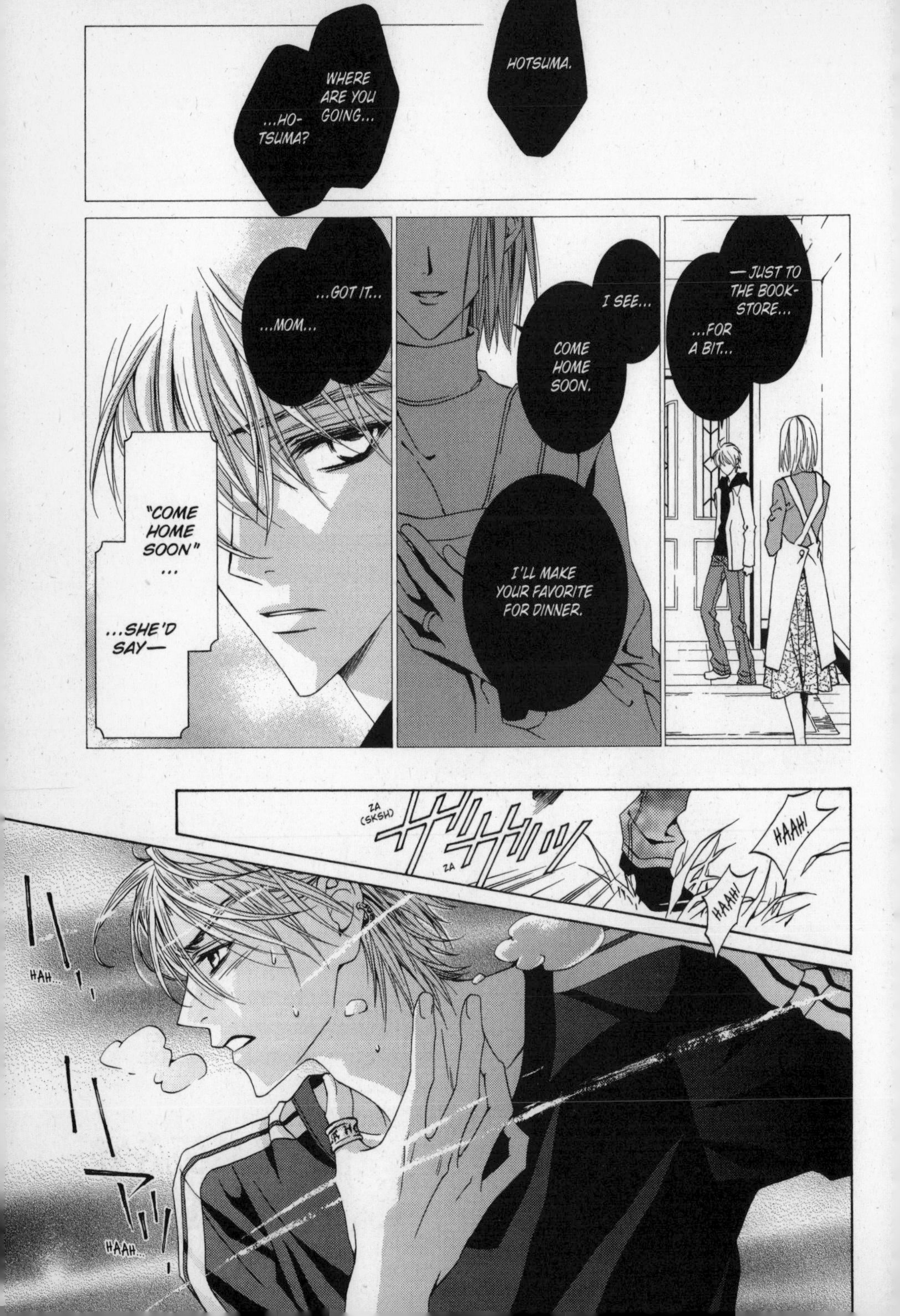
HOTSUMA.
WHERE ARE YOU GOING...
...HO-TSUMA?
—JUST TO THE BOOK-STORE...
...FOR A BIT...
I SEE...
COME HOME SOON.
I'LL MAKE YOUR FAVORITE FOR DINNER.
...GOT IT...
...MOM...
"COME HOME SOON" ...
...SHE'D SAY—
HAAH!
HAAH!
ZA (SKSH)
ZA
HAH...
HAAH...

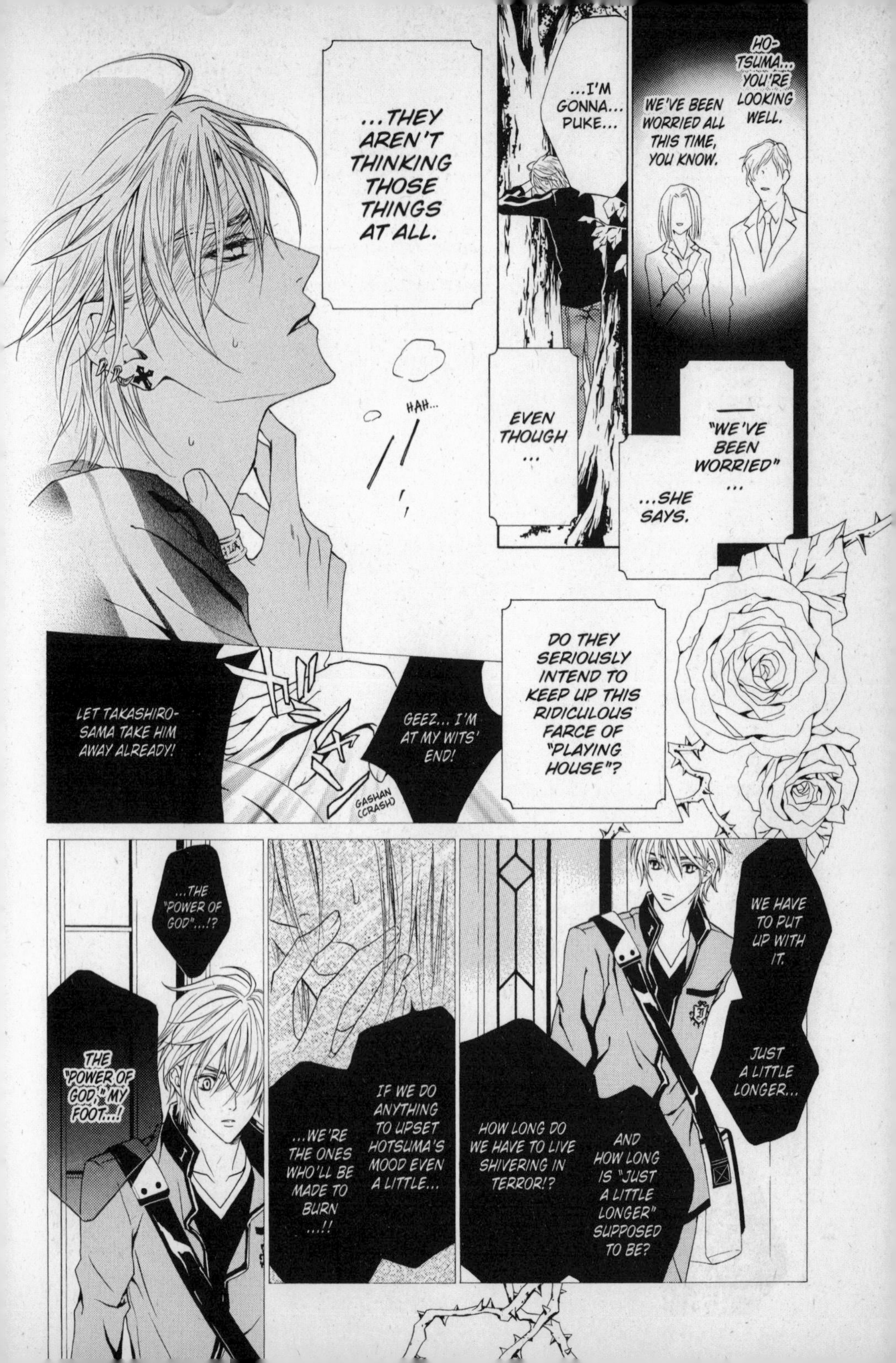
HO-TSUMA... YOU'RE LOOKING WELL.
WE'VE BEEN WORRIED ALL THIS TIME, YOU KNOW.
—"WE'VE BEEN WORRIED" ...
...SHE SAYS.
...I'M GONNA... PUKE...
EVEN THOUGH ...
...THEY AREN'T THINKING THOSE THINGS AT ALL.
HAH...
DO THEY SERIOUSLY INTEND TO KEEP UP THIS RIDICULOUS FARCE OF "PLAYING HOUSE"?
GEEZ... I'M AT MY WITS' END!
GASHAN (CRASH)
LET TAKASHIRO-SAMA TAKE HIM AWAY ALREADY!
WE HAVE TO PUT UP WITH IT.
JUST A LITTLE LONGER...
AND HOW LONG IS "JUST A LITTLE LONGER" SUPPOSED TO BE?
HOW LONG DO WE HAVE TO LIVE SHIVERING IN TERROR!?
IF WE DO ANYTHING TO UPSET HOTSUMA'S MOOD EVEN A LITTLE...
...WE'RE THE ONES WHO'LL BE MADE TO BURN ...!!
...THE "POWER OF GOD"...!?
THE "POWER OF GOD," MY FOOT...!

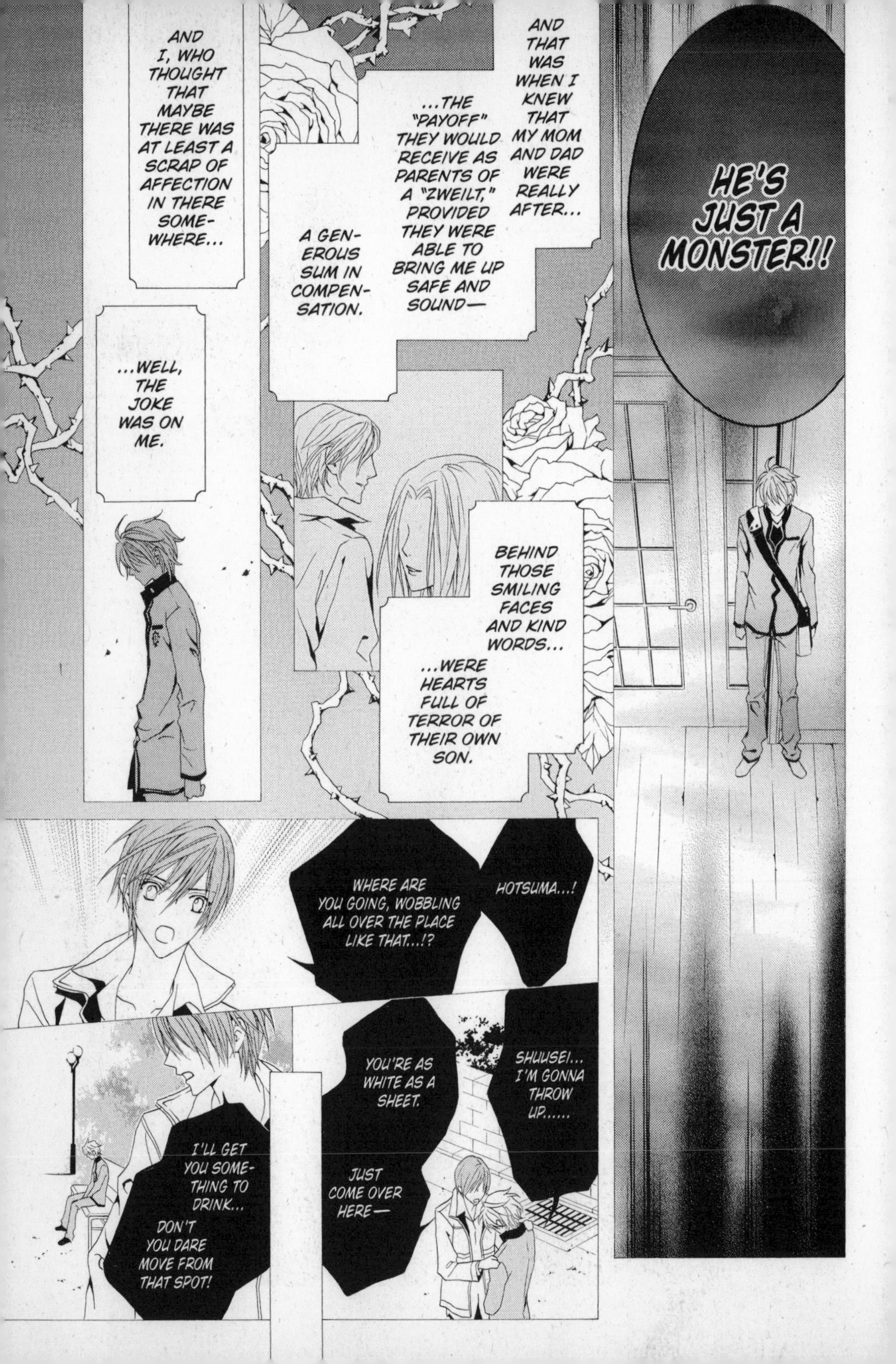
HE'S JUST A MONSTER!!
AND THAT WAS WHEN I KNEW THAT MY MOM AND DAD WERE REALLY AFTER...
...THE "PAYOFF" THEY WOULD RECEIVE AS PARENTS OF A "ZWEILT," PROVIDED THEY WERE ABLE TO BRING ME UP SAFE AND SOUND—
A GENEROUS SUM IN COMPENSATION.
AND I, WHO THOUGHT THAT MAYBE THERE WAS AT LEAST A SCRAP OF AFFECTION IN THERE SOMEWHERE...
...WELL, THE JOKE WAS ON ME.
BEHIND THOSE SMILING FACES AND KIND WORDS...
...WERE HEARTS FULL OF TERROR OF THEIR OWN SON.
HOTSUMA...!
WHERE ARE YOU GOING, WOBBLING ALL OVER THE PLACE LIKE THAT...!?
SHUUSEI... I'M GONNA THROW UP.....
YOU'RE AS WHITE AS A SHEET.
JUST COME OVER HERE—
I'LL GET YOU SOMETHING TO DRINK...
DON'T YOU DARE MOVE FROM THAT SPOT!

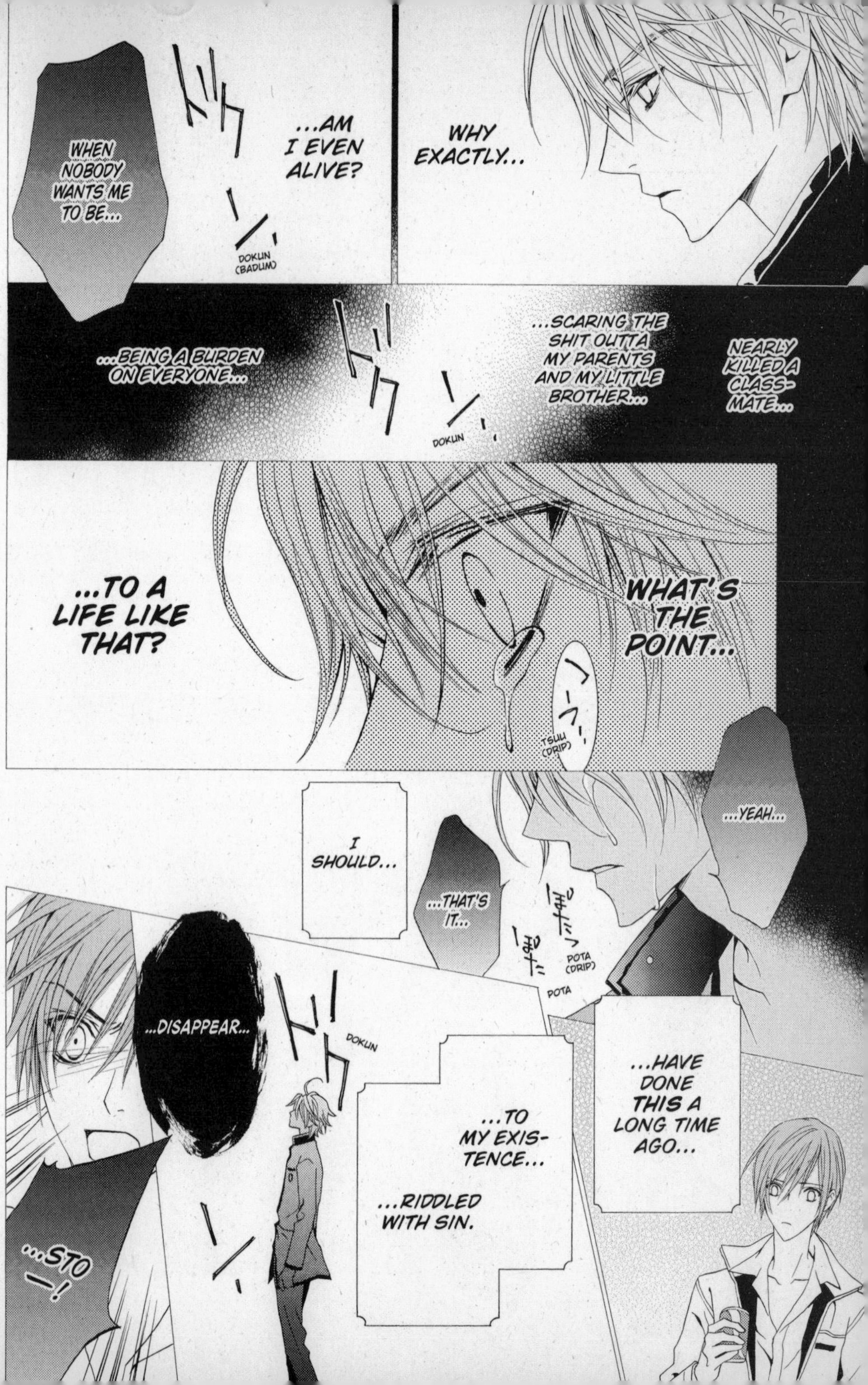
WHY EXACTLY...
...AM I EVEN ALIVE?
WHEN NOBODY WANTS ME TO BE...
DOKUN (BADUM)
NEARLY KILLED A CLASS-MATE...
...SCARING THE SHIT OUTTA MY PARENTS AND MY LITTLE BROTHER...
DOKUN
...BEING A BURDEN ON EVERYONE...
WHAT'S THE POINT...
TSUU (DRIP)
...TO A LIFE LIKE THAT?
...YEAH...
POTA (DRIP)
POTA
I SHOULD...
...THAT'S IT...
...HAVE DONE THIS A LONG TIME AGO...
...TO MY EXISTENCE...
...RIDDLED WITH SIN.
DOKUN
...DISAPPEAR...
...STO—!

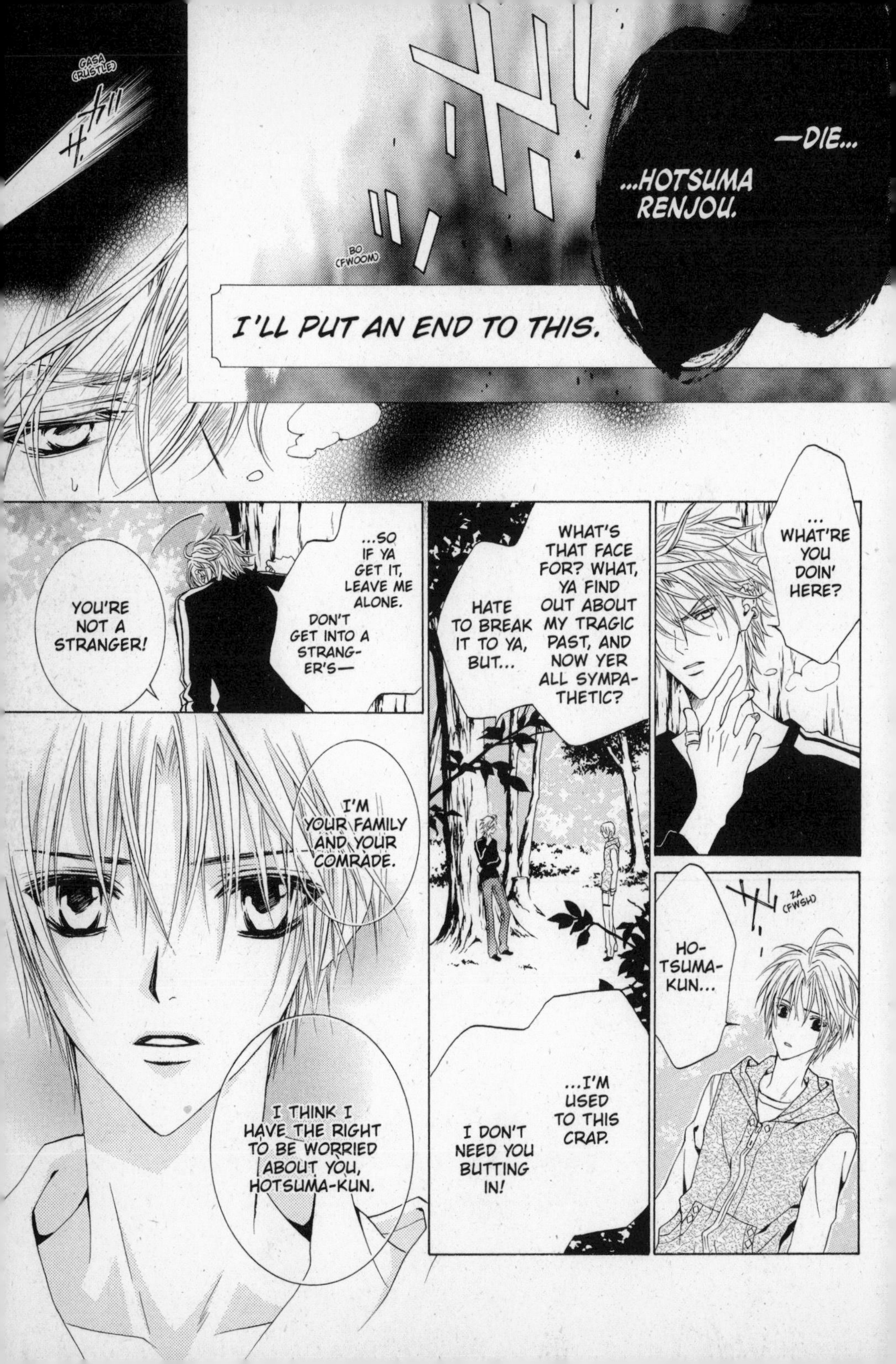
—DIE...
...HOTSUMA RENJOU.
BO (FWOOM)
I'LL PUT AN END TO THIS.
GASA (RUSTLE)
... WHAT'RE YOU DOIN' HERE?
ZA (FWSH)
HO-TSUMA-KUN...
WHAT'S THAT FACE FOR? WHAT, YA FIND OUT ABOUT MY TRAGIC PAST, AND NOW YER ALL SYMPA-THETIC?
HATE TO BREAK IT TO YA, BUT...
...I'M USED TO THIS CRAP.
I DON'T NEED YOU BUTTING IN!
...SO IF YA GET IT, LEAVE ME ALONE.
DON'T GET INTO A STRANG-ER'S—
YOU'RE NOT A STRANGER!
I'M YOUR FAMILY AND YOUR COMRADE.
I THINK I HAVE THE RIGHT TO BE WORRIED ABOUT YOU, HOTSUMA-KUN.

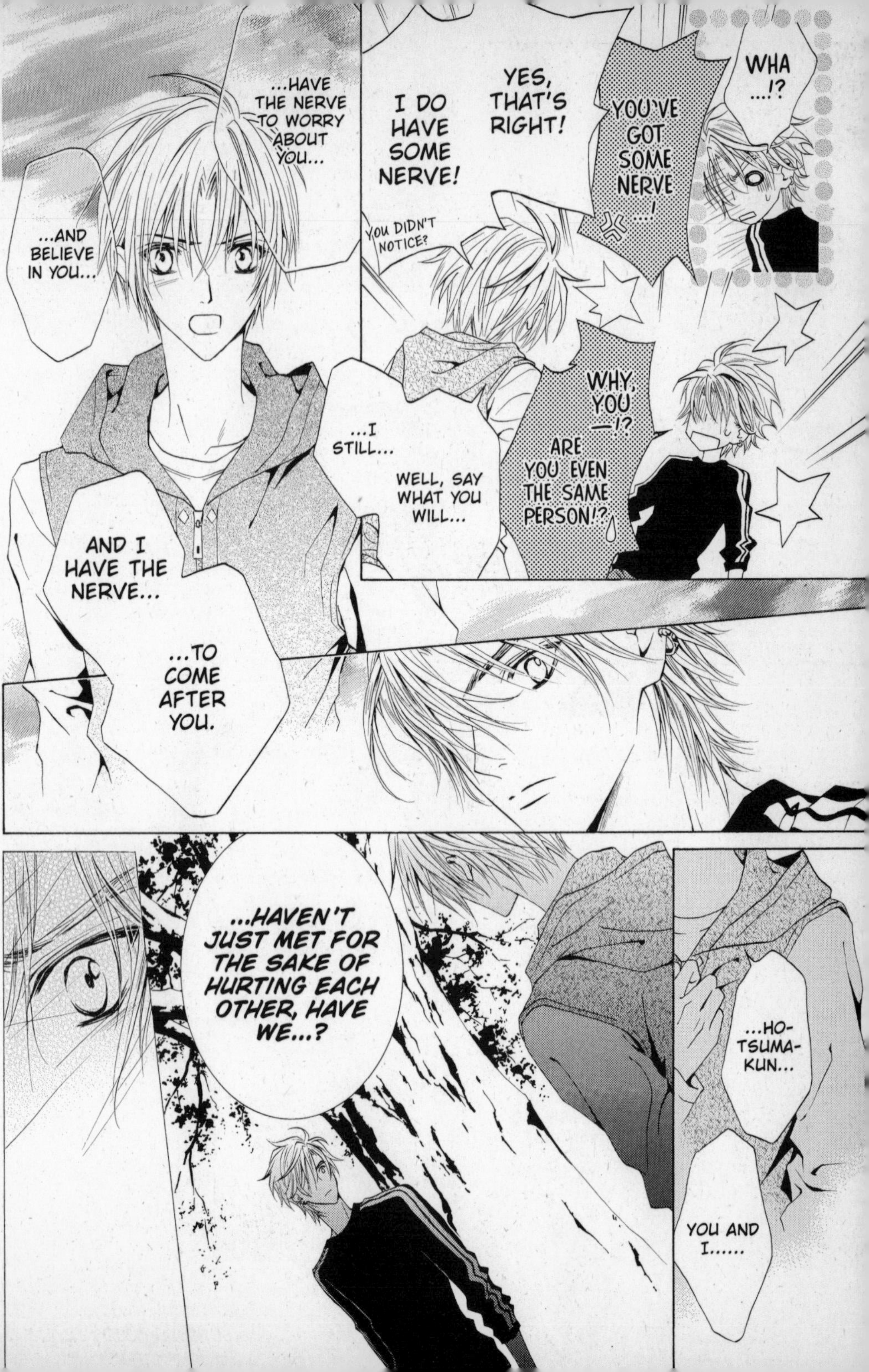
WHA ...!?
YOU'VE GOT SOME NERVE ...!
YES, THAT'S RIGHT!
I DO HAVE SOME NERVE!
YOU DIDN'T NOTICE?
WHY, YOU —!?
ARE YOU EVEN THE SAME PERSON!?
WELL, SAY WHAT YOU WILL...
...I STILL...
...HAVE THE NERVE TO WORRY ABOUT YOU...
...AND BELIEVE IN YOU...
AND I HAVE THE NERVE...
...TO COME AFTER YOU.
...HO-TSUMA-KUN...
YOU AND I......
...HAVEN'T JUST MET FOR THE SAKE OF HURTING EACH OTHER, HAVE WE...?

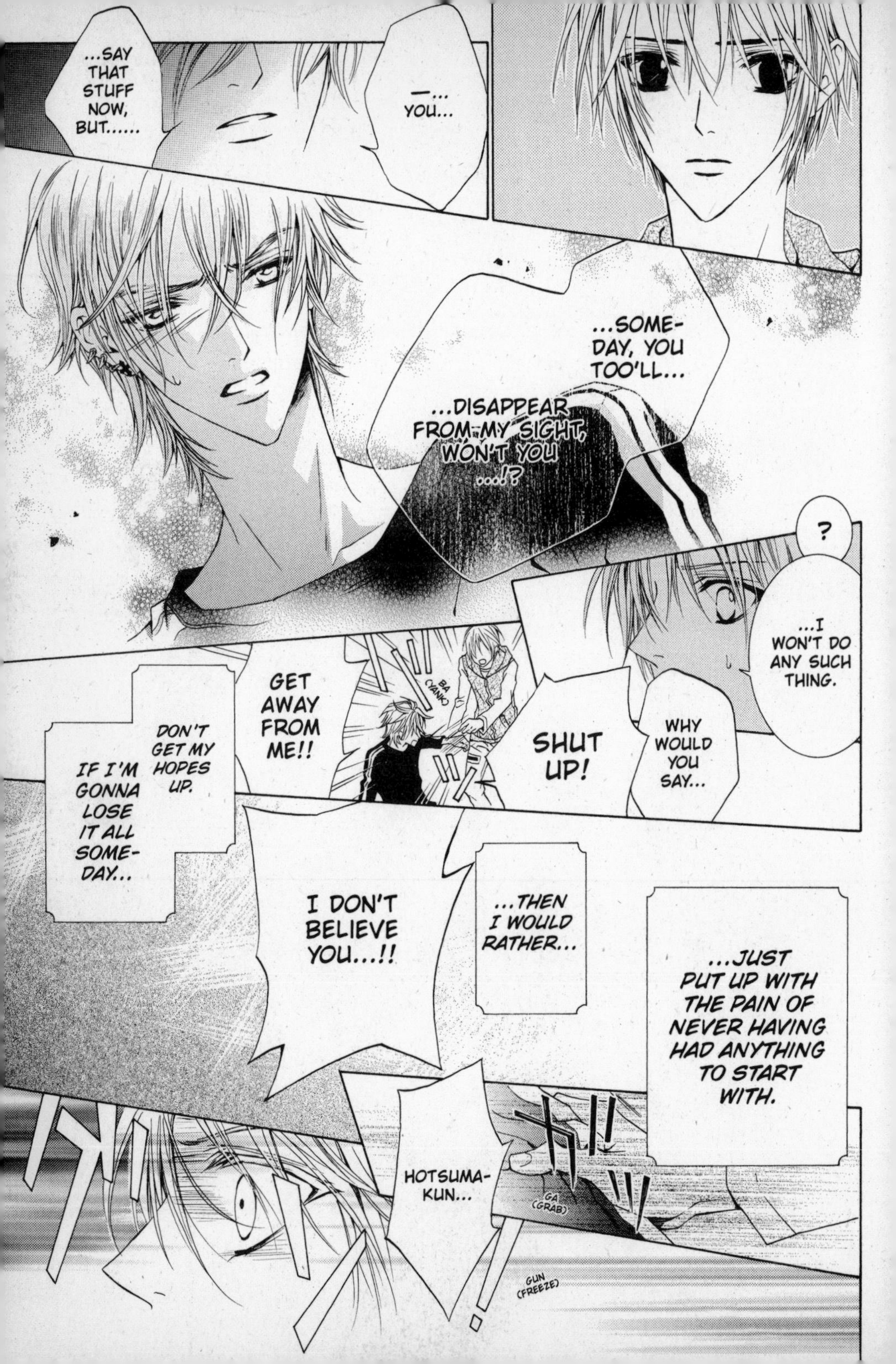
—...
YOU...
...SAY THAT STUFF NOW, BUT......
...SOME-DAY, YOU TOO'LL...
...DISAPPEAR FROM MY SIGHT, WON'T YOU ...!?
?
...I WON'T DO ANY SUCH THING.
WHY WOULD YOU SAY...
SHUT UP!
BA (YANK)
GET AWAY FROM ME!!
DON'T GET MY HOPES UP.
IF I'M GONNA LOSE IT ALL SOME-DAY...
I DON'T BELIEVE YOU...!!
...THEN I WOULD RATHER...
...JUST PUT UP WITH THE PAIN OF NEVER HAVING HAD ANYTHING TO START WITH.
GA (GRAB)
HOTSUMA-KUN...
GUN (FREEZE)

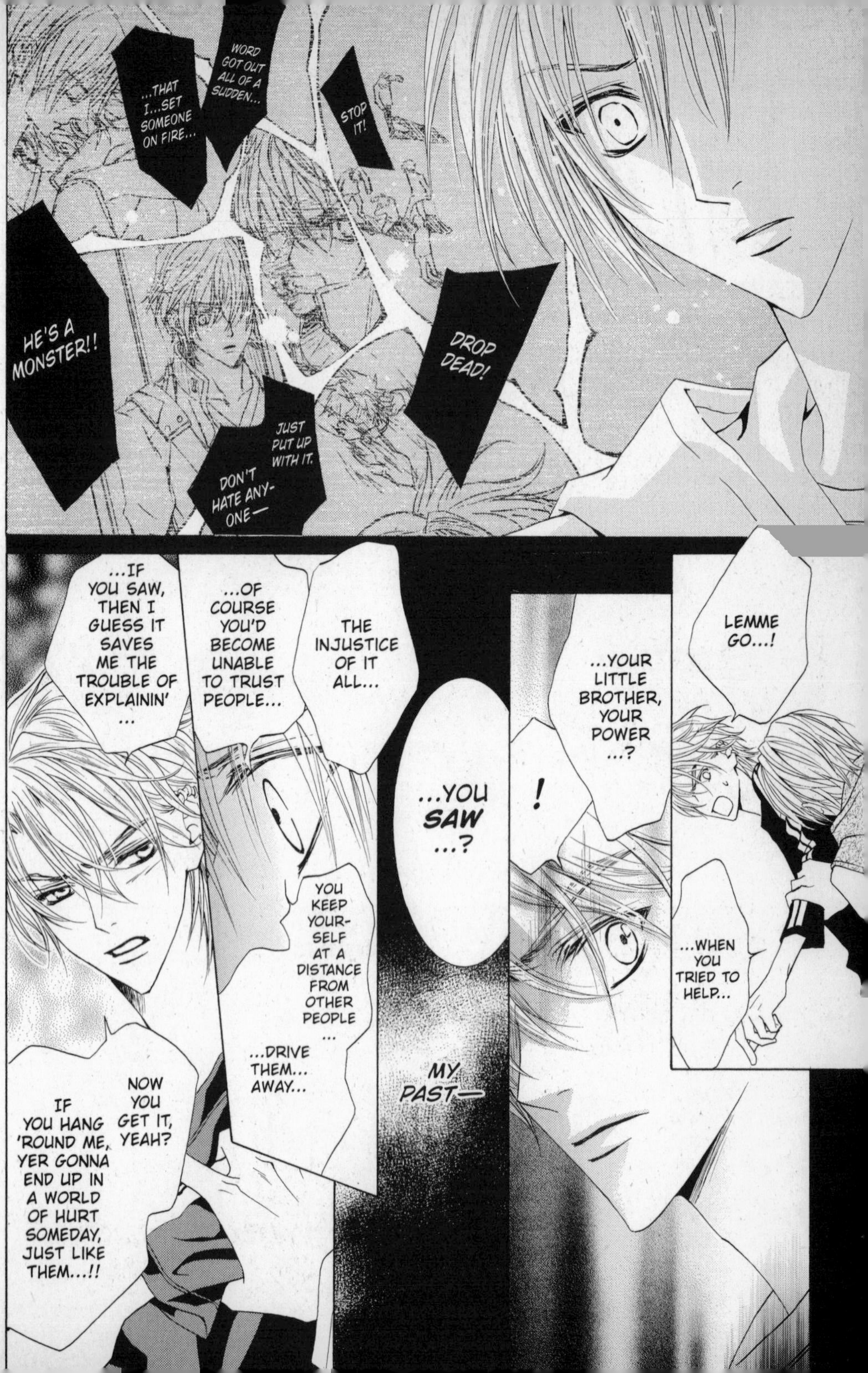
STOP IT!
WORD GOT OUT ALL OF A SUDDEN...
...THAT I...SET SOMEONE ON FIRE...
DROP DEAD!
JUST PUT UP WITH IT.
DON'T HATE ANY-ONE—
HE'S A MONSTER!!
LEMME GO...!
...YOUR LITTLE BROTHER, YOUR POWER...?
...WHEN YOU TRIED TO HELP...
!
...YOU SAW...?
MY PAST—
THE INJUSTICE OF IT ALL...
...OF COURSE YOU'D BECOME UNABLE TO TRUST PEOPLE...
...IF YOU SAW, THEN I GUESS IT SAVES ME THE TROUBLE OF EXPLAININ'...
YOU KEEP YOUR-SELF AT A DISTANCE FROM OTHER PEOPLE...
...DRIVE THEM... AWAY...
NOW YOU GET IT, YEAH?
IF YOU HANG 'ROUND ME, YER GONNA END UP IN A WORLD OF HURT SOMEDAY, JUST LIKE THEM...!!

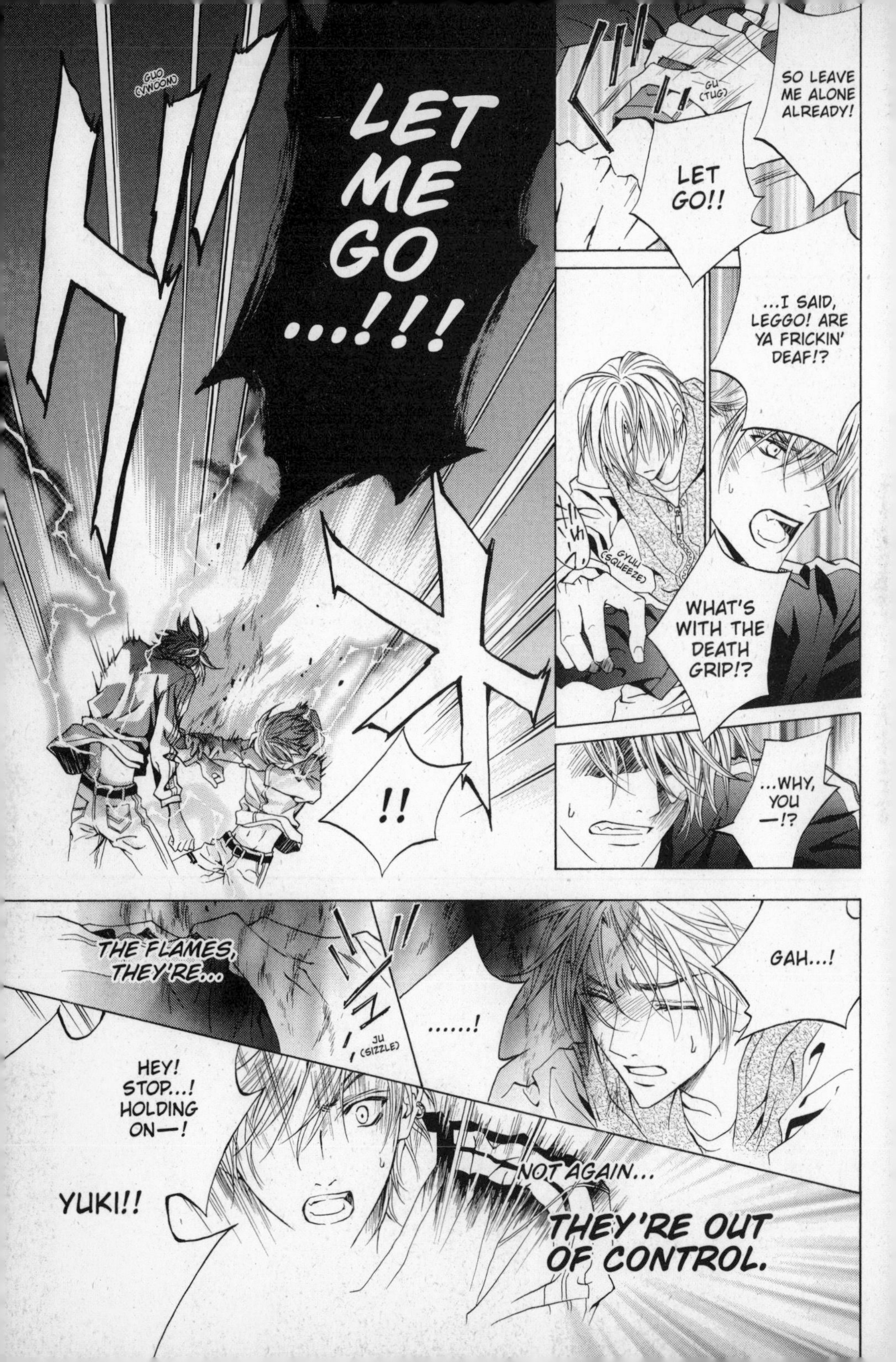
SO LEAVE ME ALONE ALREADY!
GU (TUG)
LET GO!!
...I SAID, LEGGO! ARE YA FRICKIN' DEAF!?
GYUU (SQUEEZE)
WHAT'S WITH THE DEATH GRIP!?
...WHY, YOU—!?
GUO (VWOOM)
LET ME GO...!!!
!!
GAH...!
......!
JU (SIZZLE)
THE FLAMES, THEY'RE...
HEY! STOP...! HOLDING ON—!
YUKI!!
NOT AGAIN...
THEY'RE OUT OF CONTROL.

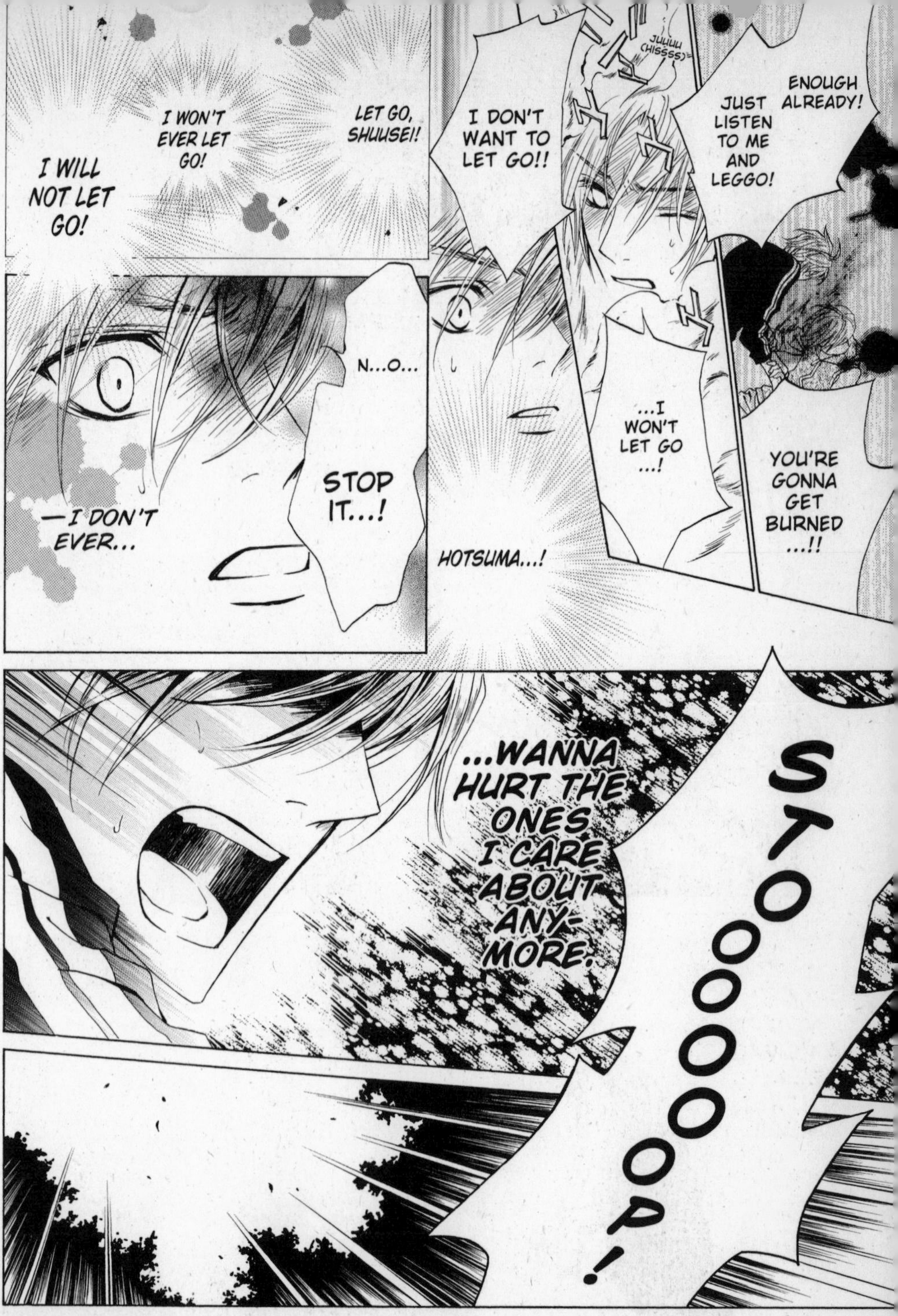
ENOUGH ALREADY!
JUST LISTEN TO ME AND LEGGO!
YOU'RE GONNA GET BURNED ...!!
JUUUU (HISSSS)
I DON'T WANT TO LET GO!!
...I WON'T LET GO ...!
LET GO, SHUUSEI!
I WON'T EVER LET GO!
I WILL NOT LET GO!
N...O...
STOP IT...!
HOTSUMA...!
—I DON'T EVER...
...WANNA HURT THE ONES I CARE ABOUT ANY-MORE.
STOOOOOOOP!

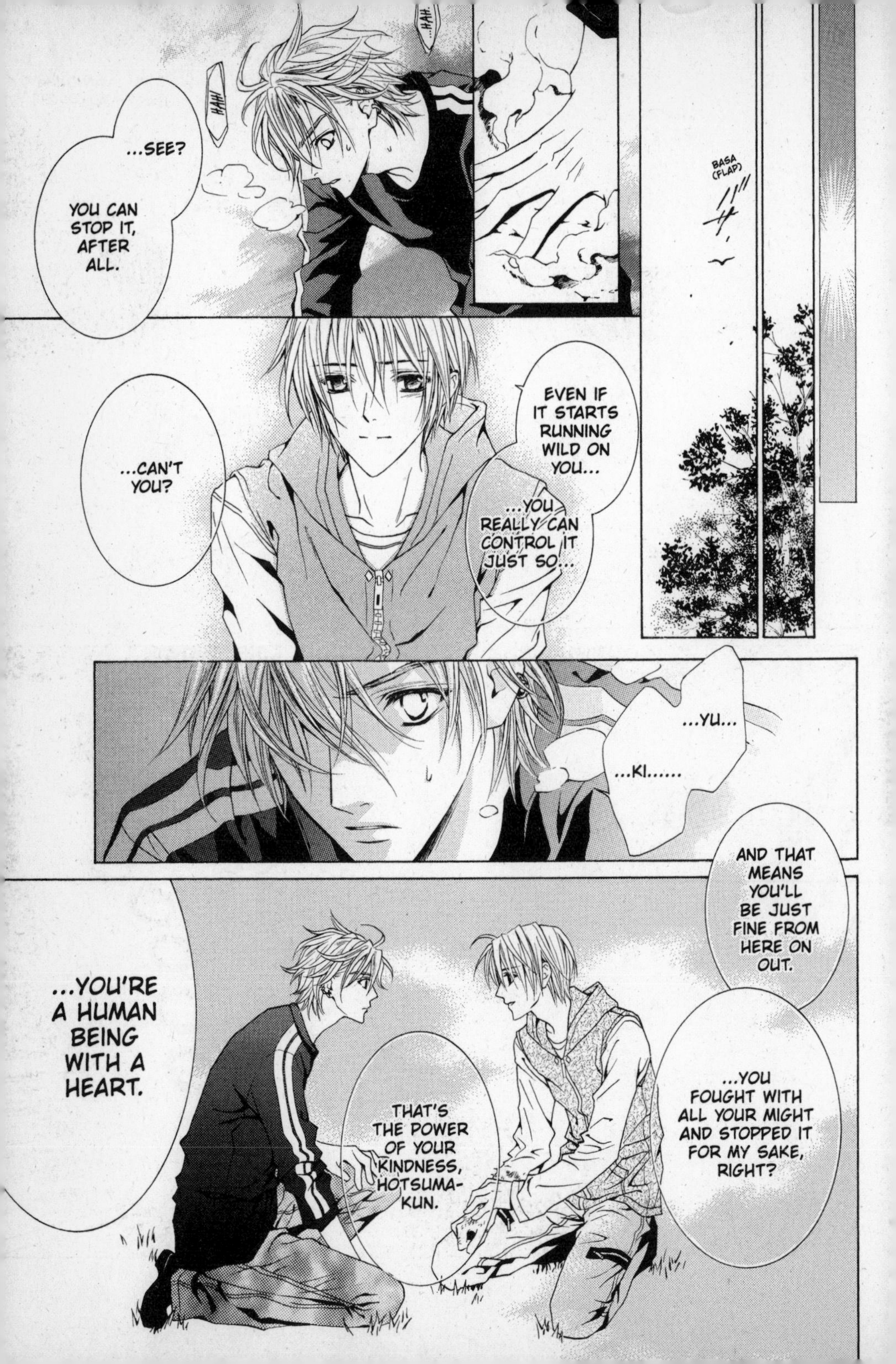
BASA (FLAP)
...HAH
HAH!
...SEE?
YOU CAN STOP IT, AFTER ALL.
EVEN IF IT STARTS RUNNING WILD ON YOU...
...YOU REALLY CAN CONTROL IT JUST SO...
...CAN'T YOU?
...YU...
...KI......
AND THAT MEANS YOU'LL BE JUST FINE FROM HERE ON OUT.
...YOU FOUGHT WITH ALL YOUR MIGHT AND STOPPED IT FOR MY SAKE, RIGHT?
THAT'S THE POWER OF YOUR KINDNESS, HOTSUMA-KUN.
...YOU'RE A HUMAN BEING WITH A HEART.

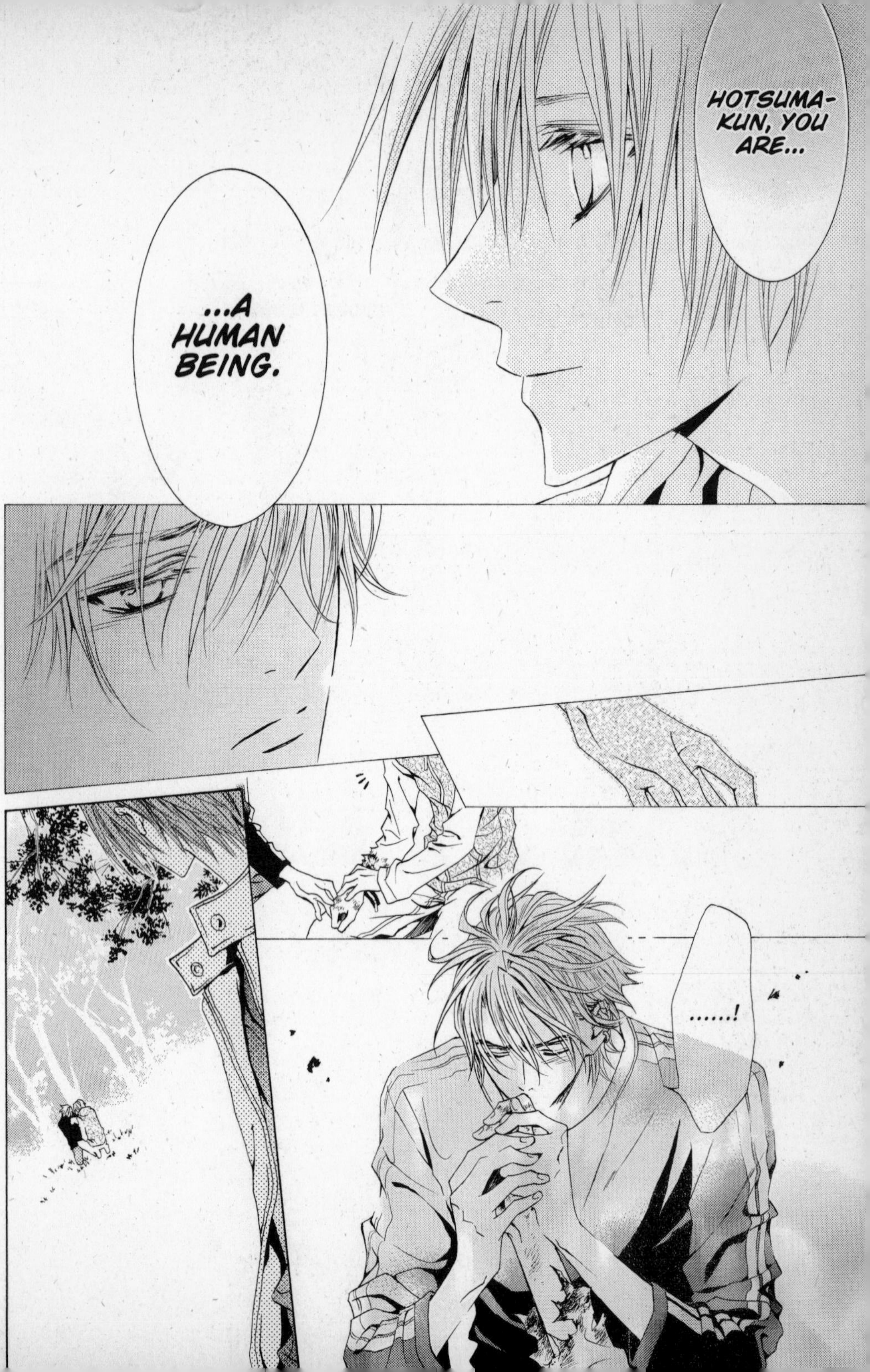
HOTSUMA-KUN, YOU ARE...
...A HUMAN BEING.
......!

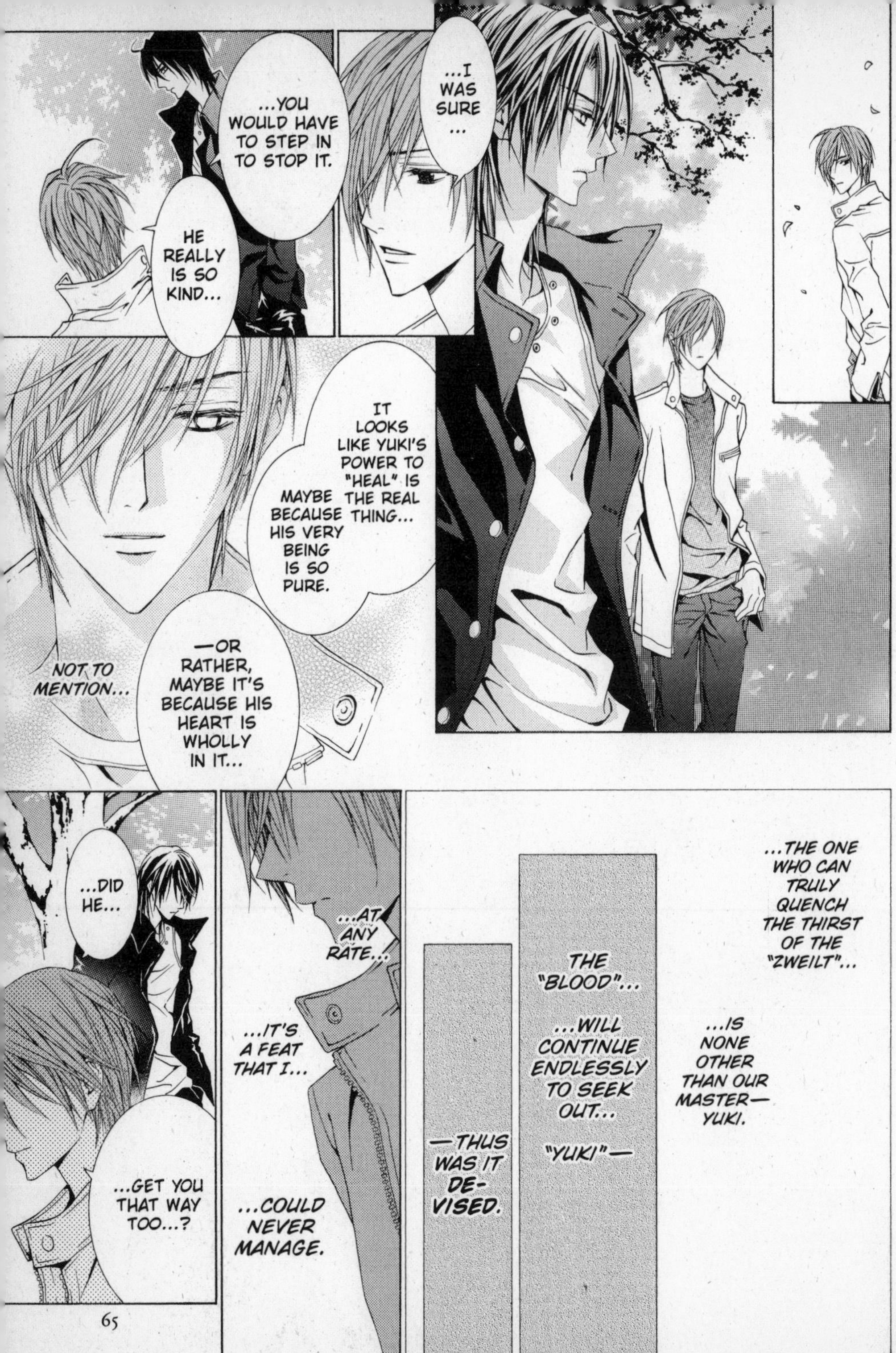
...I WAS SURE...
...YOU WOULD HAVE TO STEP IN TO STOP IT.
HE REALLY IS SO KIND...
IT LOOKS LIKE YUKI'S POWER TO "HEAL" IS THE REAL THING...
MAYBE BECAUSE HIS VERY BEING IS SO PURE.
—OR RATHER, MAYBE IT'S BECAUSE HIS HEART IS WHOLLY IN IT...
NOT TO MENTION...
...THE ONE WHO CAN TRULY QUENCH THE THIRST OF THE "ZWEILT"...
...IS NONE OTHER THAN OUR MASTER—YUKI.
THE "BLOOD"...
...WILL CONTINUE ENDLESSLY TO SEEK OUT...
"YUKI"—
—THUS WAS IT DE-VISED.
...AT ANY RATE...
...IT'S A FEAT THAT I...
...COULD NEVER MANAGE.
...DID HE...
...GET YOU THAT WAY TOO...?

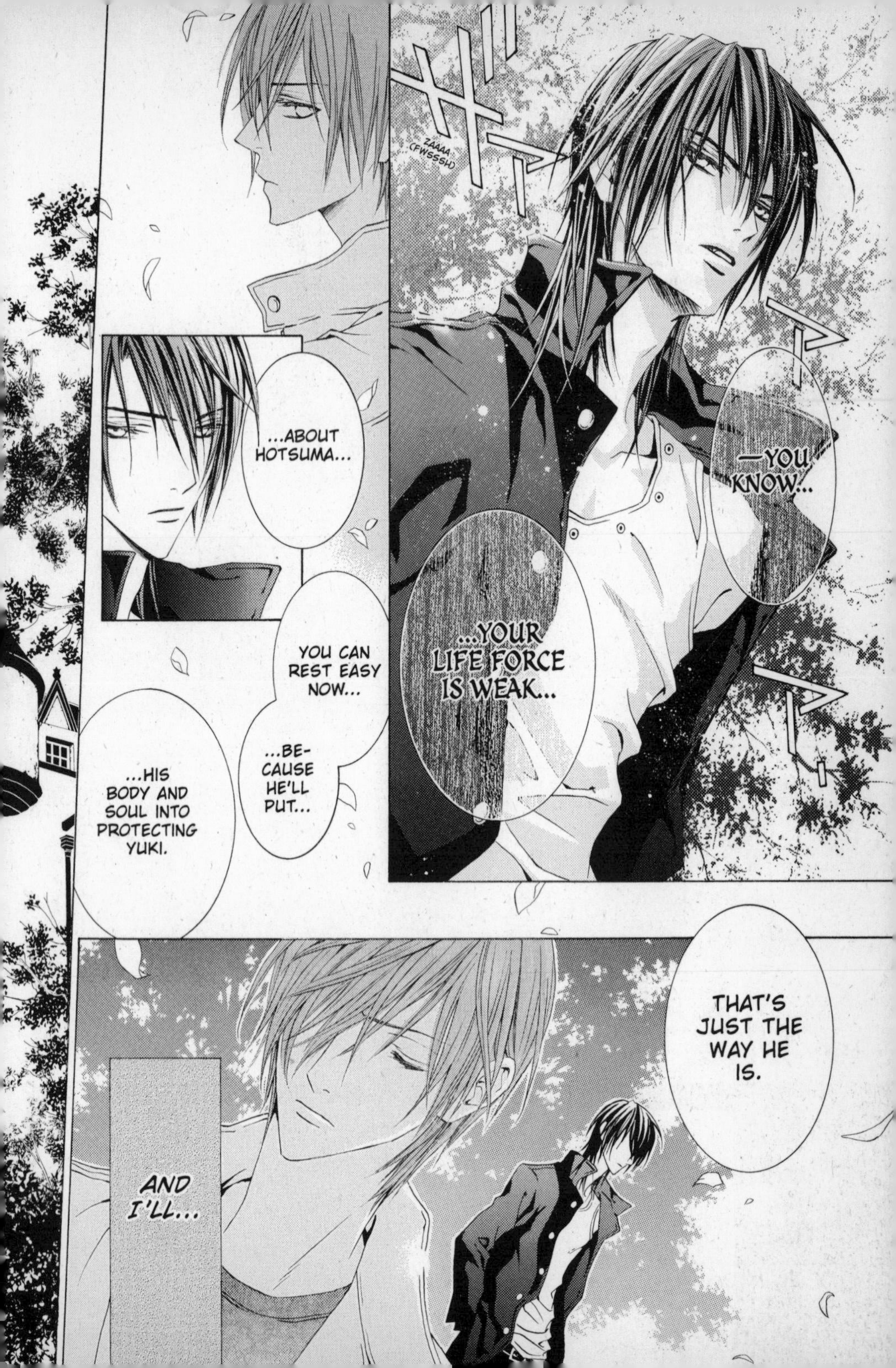
ZAAAA (FWSSSH)
—YOU KNOW...
...YOUR LIFE FORCE IS WEAK...
...ABOUT HOTSUMA...
YOU CAN REST EASY NOW...
...BE-CAUSE HE'LL PUT...
...HIS BODY AND SOUL INTO PROTECTING YUKI.
THAT'S JUST THE WAY HE IS.
AND I'LL...

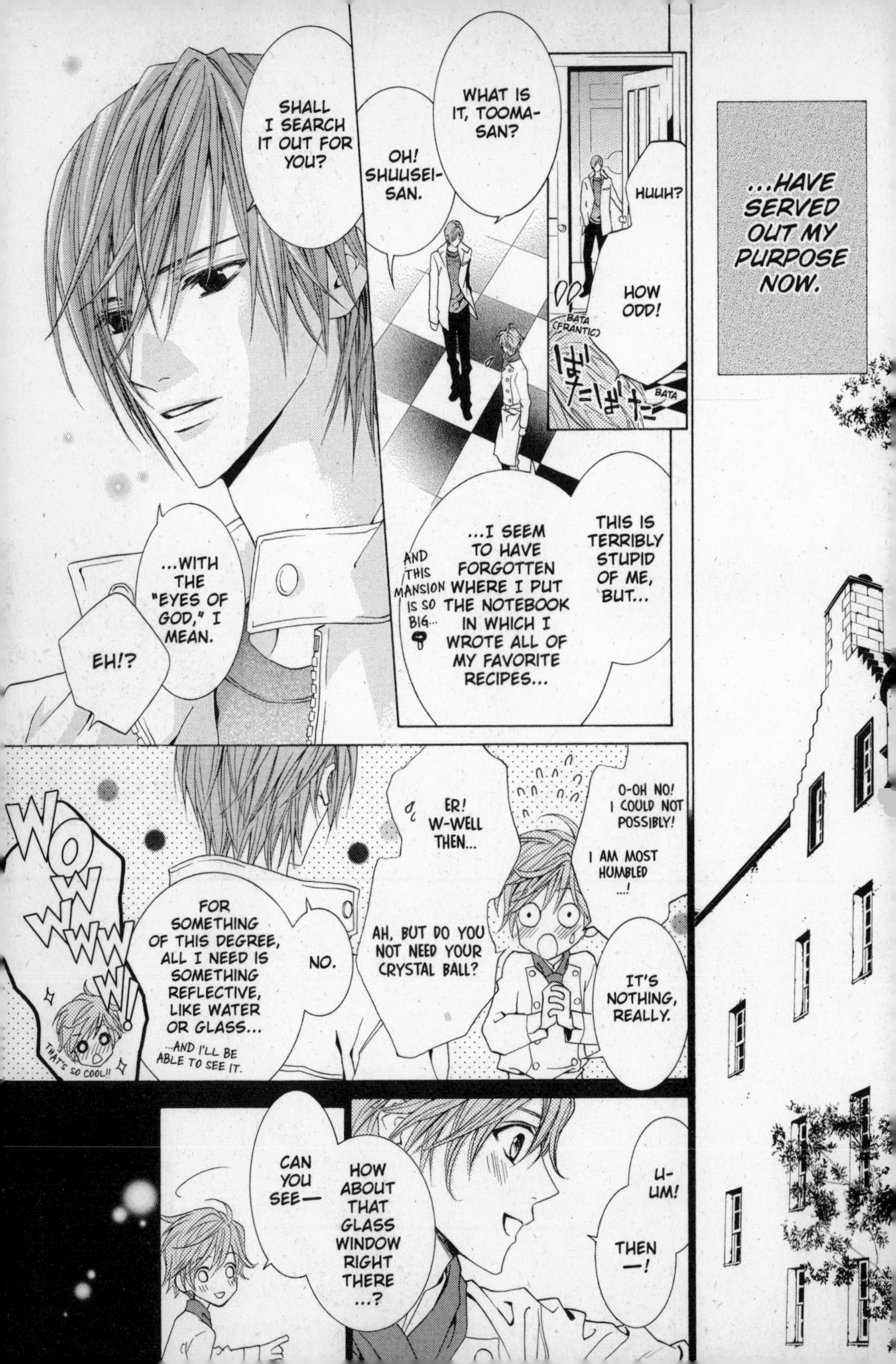
...HAVE SERVED OUT MY PURPOSE NOW.
HUUH?
HOW ODD!
BATA (FRANTIC)
BATA
WHAT IS IT, TOOMA-SAN?
OH! SHUUSEI-SAN.
THIS IS TERRIBLY STUPID OF ME, BUT...
...I SEEM TO HAVE FORGOTTEN WHERE I PUT THE NOTEBOOK IN WHICH I WROTE ALL OF MY FAVORITE RECIPES...
AND THIS MANSION IS SO BIG...
SHALL I SEARCH IT OUT FOR YOU?
...WITH THE "EYES OF GOD," I MEAN.
EH!?
O-OH NO! I COULD NOT POSSIBLY!
I AM MOST HUMBLED ...!
IT'S NOTHING, REALLY.
ER! W-WELL THEN...
AH, BUT DO YOU NOT NEED YOUR CRYSTAL BALL?
NO.
FOR SOMETHING OF THIS DEGREE, ALL I NEED IS SOMETHING REFLECTIVE, LIKE WATER OR GLASS...
...AND I'LL BE ABLE TO SEE IT.
WOWWWWWW!
THAT'S SO COOL!!
U-UM!
THEN—!
HOW ABOUT THAT GLASS WINDOW RIGHT THERE...?
CAN YOU SEE—

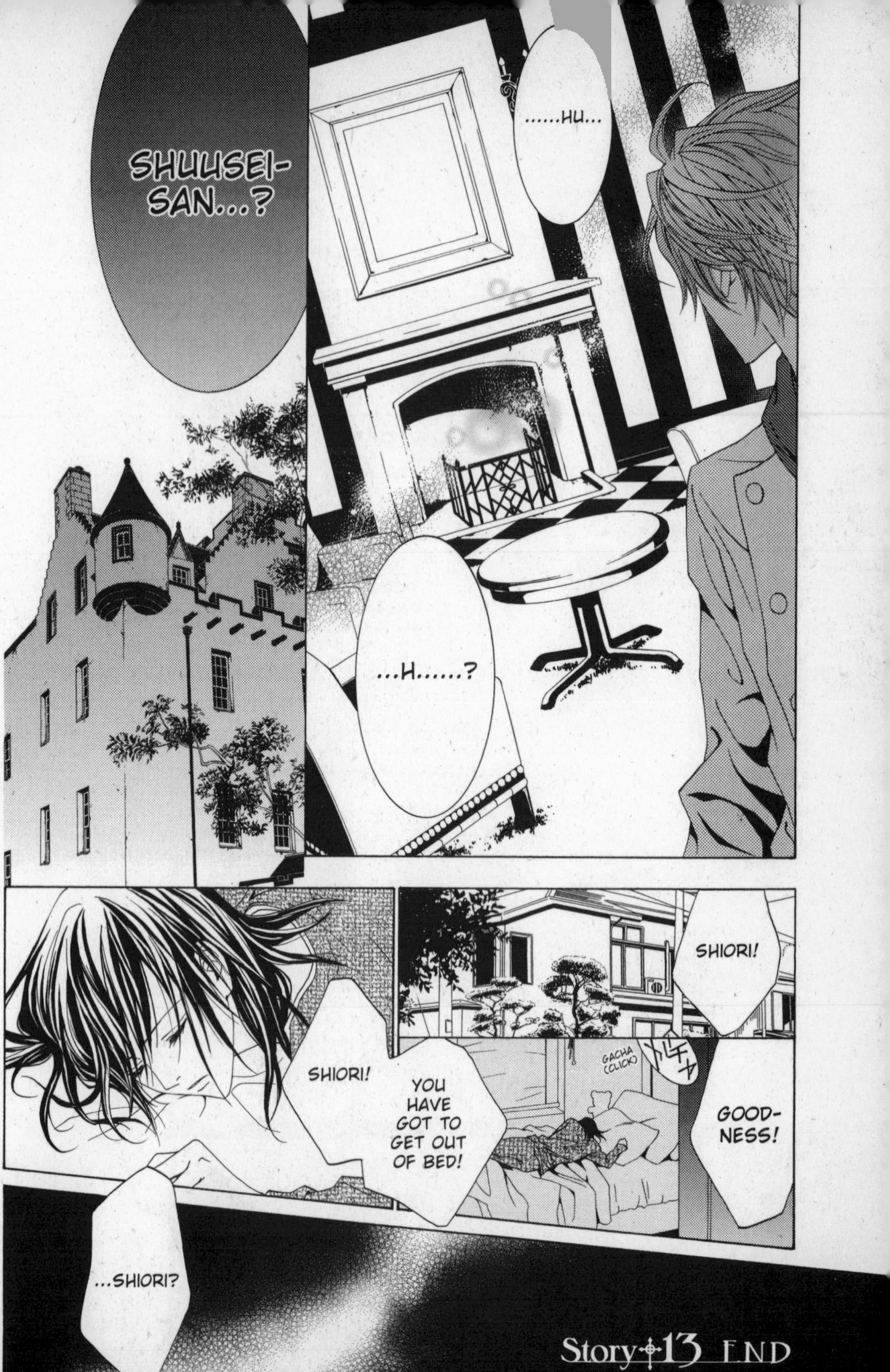
......HU...
...H......?
SHUUSEI-SAN...?
SHIORI!
GOODNESS!
GACHA (CLICK)
SHIORI!
YOU HAVE GOT TO GET OUT OF BED!
...SHIORI?
Story 13 END

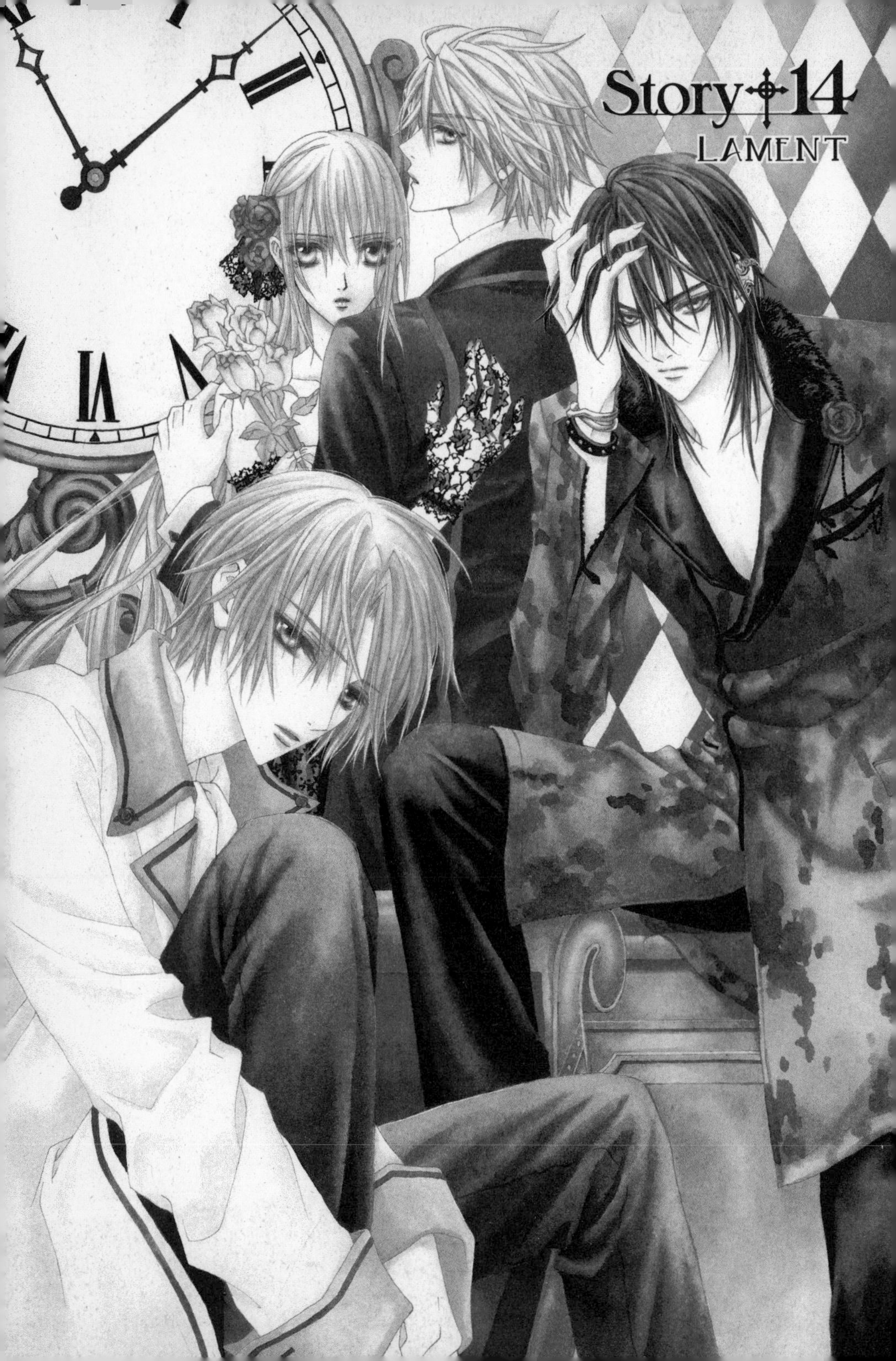
Story 14
LAMENT

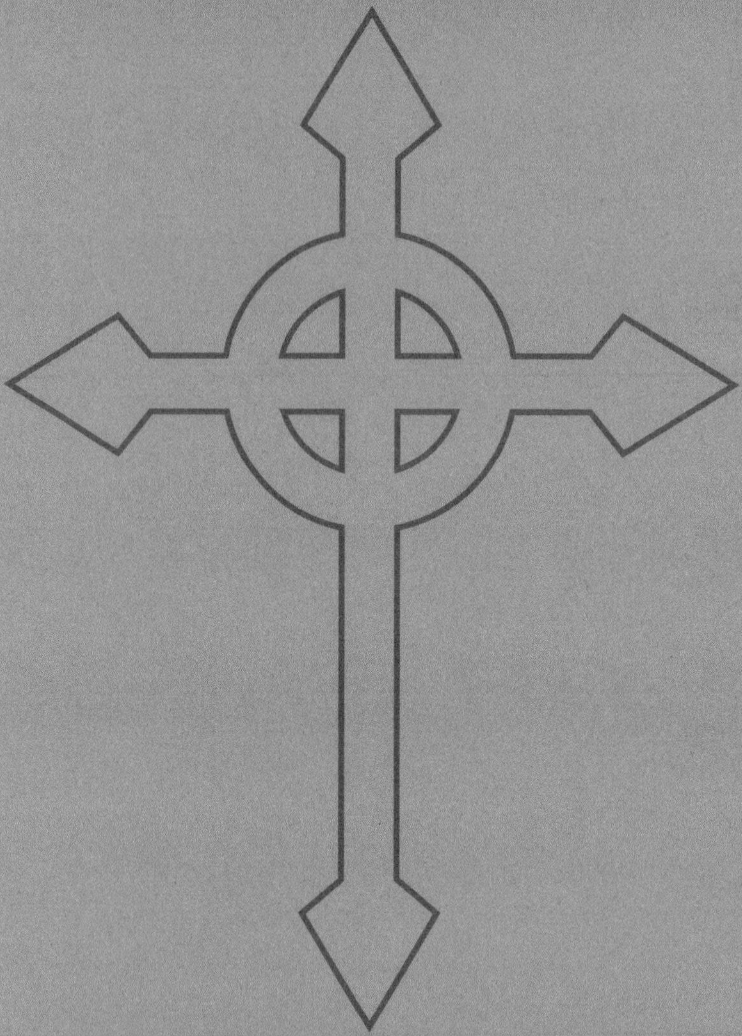

The Betrayal Knows My Name

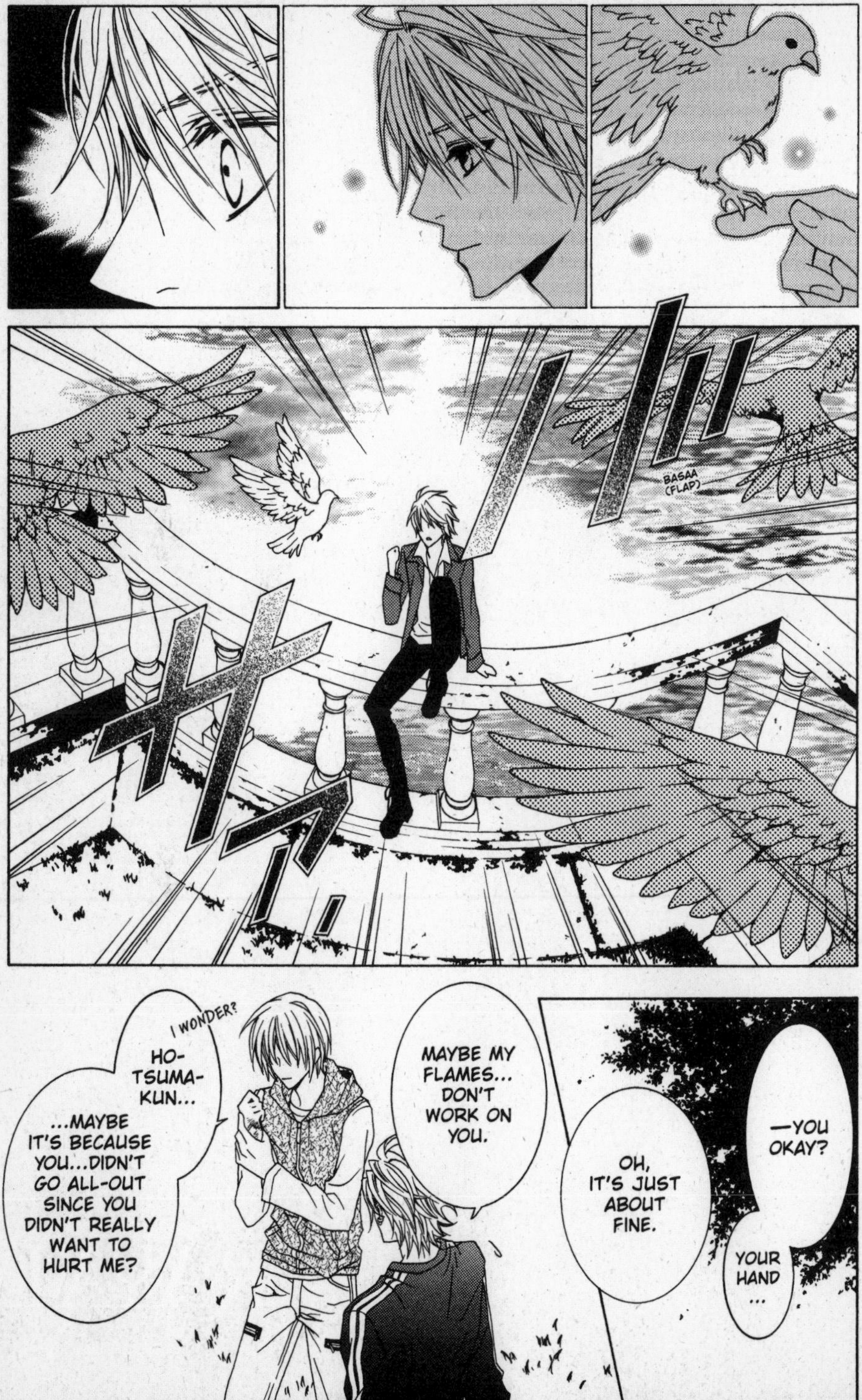
BASAA (FLAP)
—YOU OKAY?
YOUR HAND ...
OH, IT'S JUST ABOUT FINE.
MAYBE MY FLAMES... DON'T WORK ON YOU.
HO-TSUMA-KUN...
...MAYBE IT'S BECAUSE YOU...DIDN'T GO ALL-OUT SINCE YOU DIDN'T REALLY WANT TO HURT ME?
I WONDER?

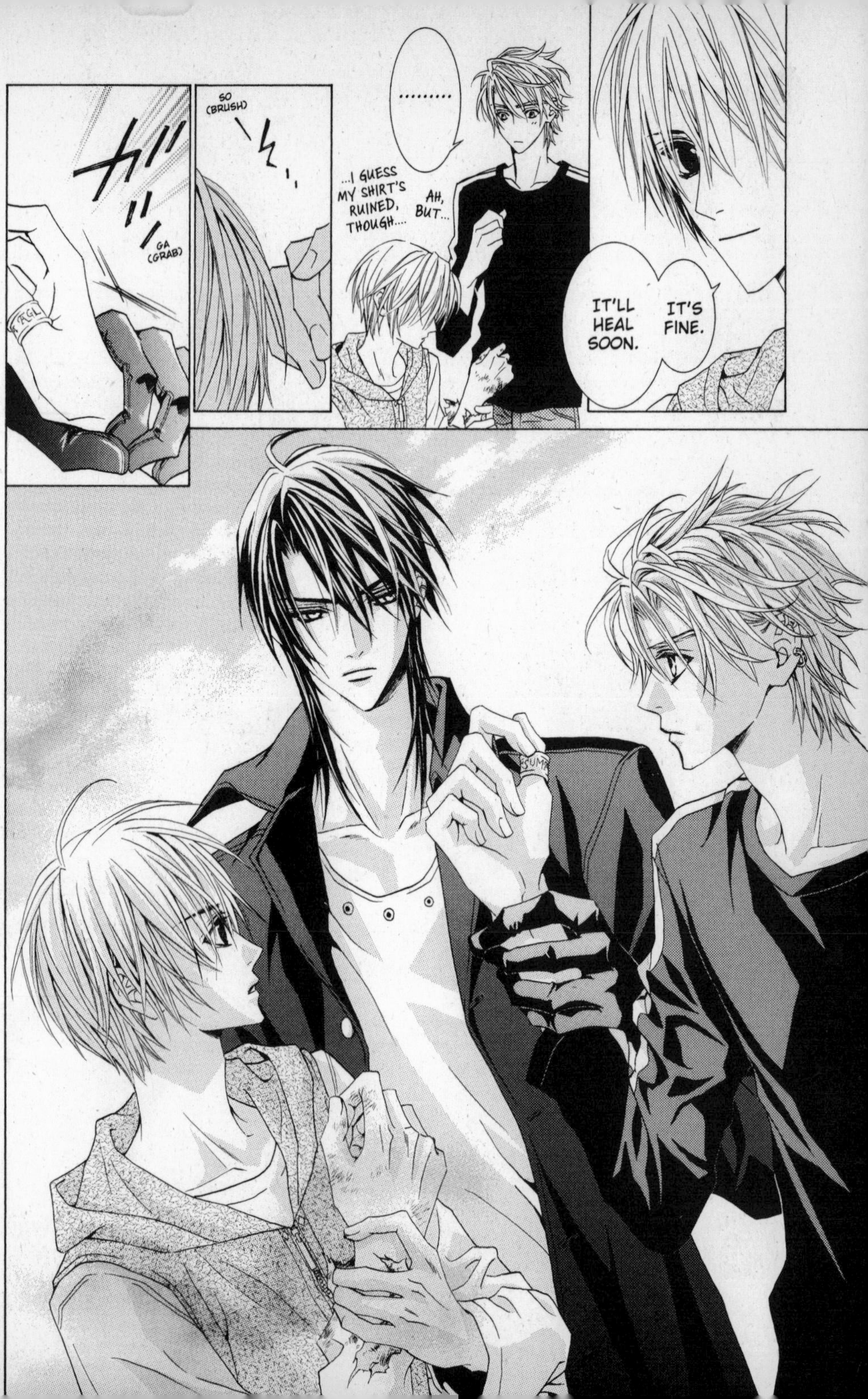
IT'S FINE.
IT'LL HEAL SOON.
....
AH, BUT...
...I GUESS MY SHIRT'S RUINED, THOUGH....
SO (BRUSH)
GA (GRAB)

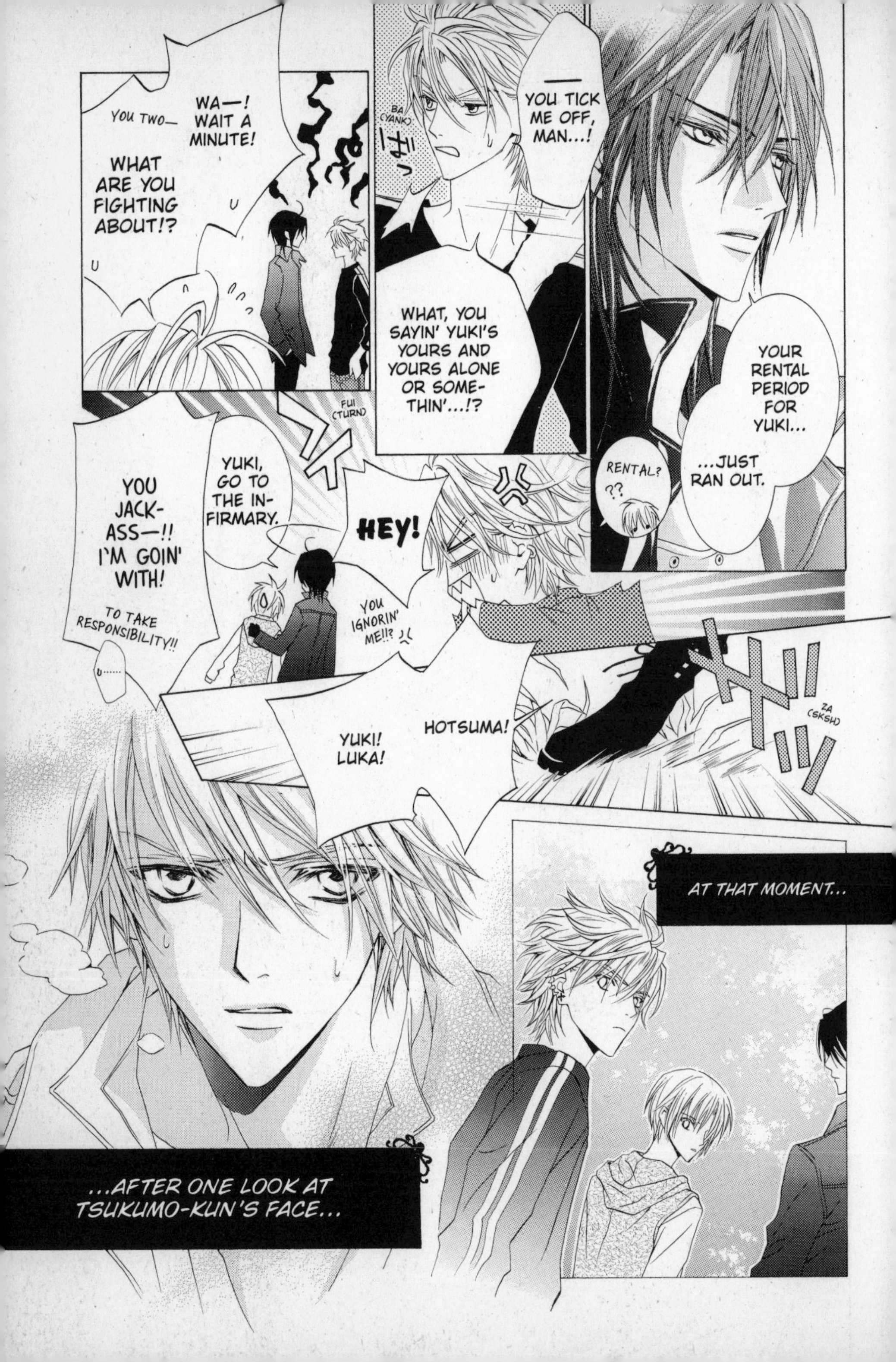
YOUR RENTAL PERIOD FOR YUKI...
...JUST RAN OUT.
RENTAL? ??
—YOU TICK ME OFF, MAN...!
BA (YANK)
WHAT, YOU SAYIN' YUKI'S YOURS AND YOURS ALONE OR SOMETHIN'...!?
WA—! WAIT A MINUTE!
YOU TWO—
WHAT ARE YOU FIGHTING ABOUT!?
ZA (SKSH)
HEY!
YOU IGNORIN' ME!!?
FUI (TURN)
YUKI, GO TO THE INFIRMARY.
YOU JACKASS—!! I'M GOIN' WITH!
TO TAKE RESPONSIBILITY!!
U......
AT THAT MOMENT...
HOTSUMA!
YUKI! LUKA!
...AFTER ONE LOOK AT TSUKUMO-KUN'S FACE...

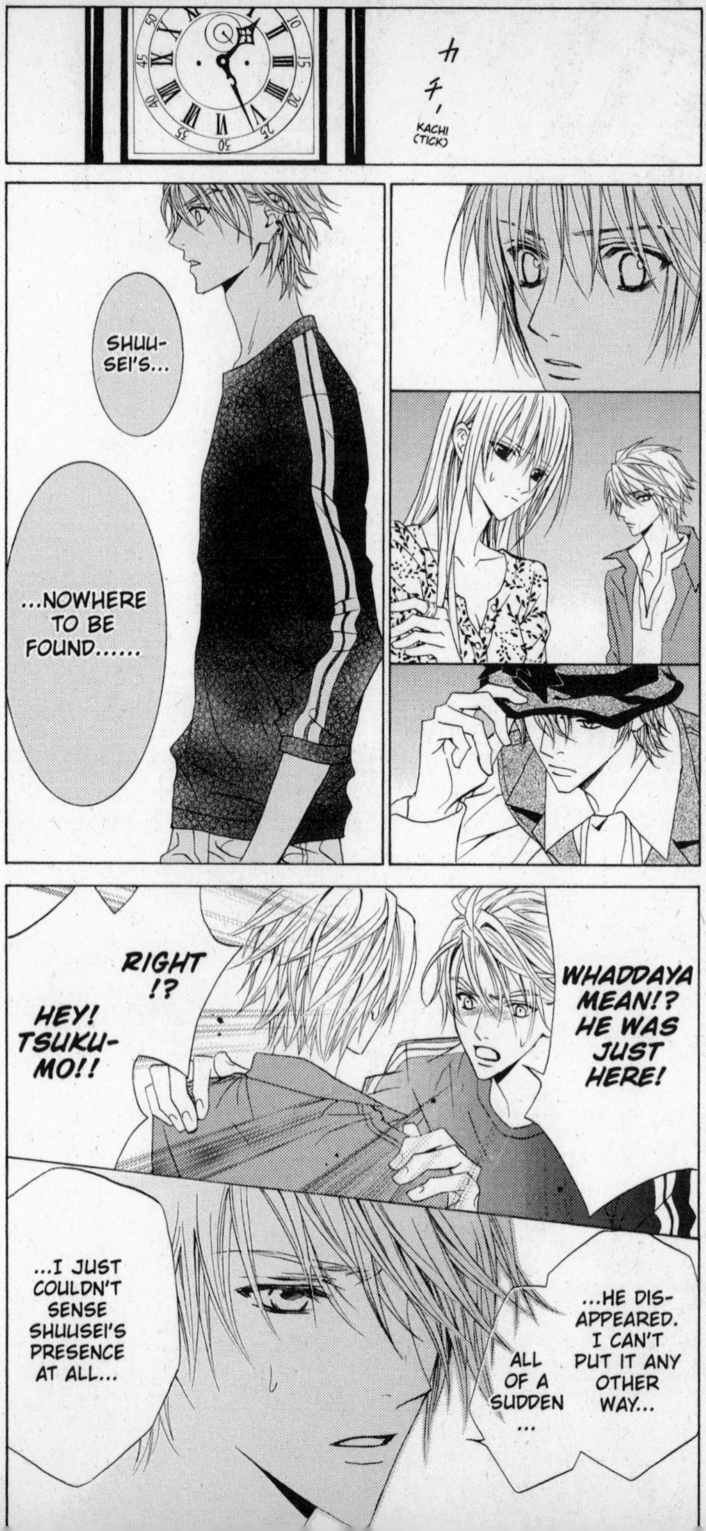
カチ
KACHI (TICK)
SHUU-SEI'S...
...NOWHERE TO BE FOUND......
WHADDAYA MEAN!? HE WAS JUST HERE!
RIGHT !?
HEY! TSUKU-MO!!
...HE DIS-APPEARED. I CAN'T PUT IT ANY OTHER WAY...
ALL OF A SUDDEN ...
...I JUST COULDN'T SENSE SHUUSEI'S PRESENCE AT ALL...

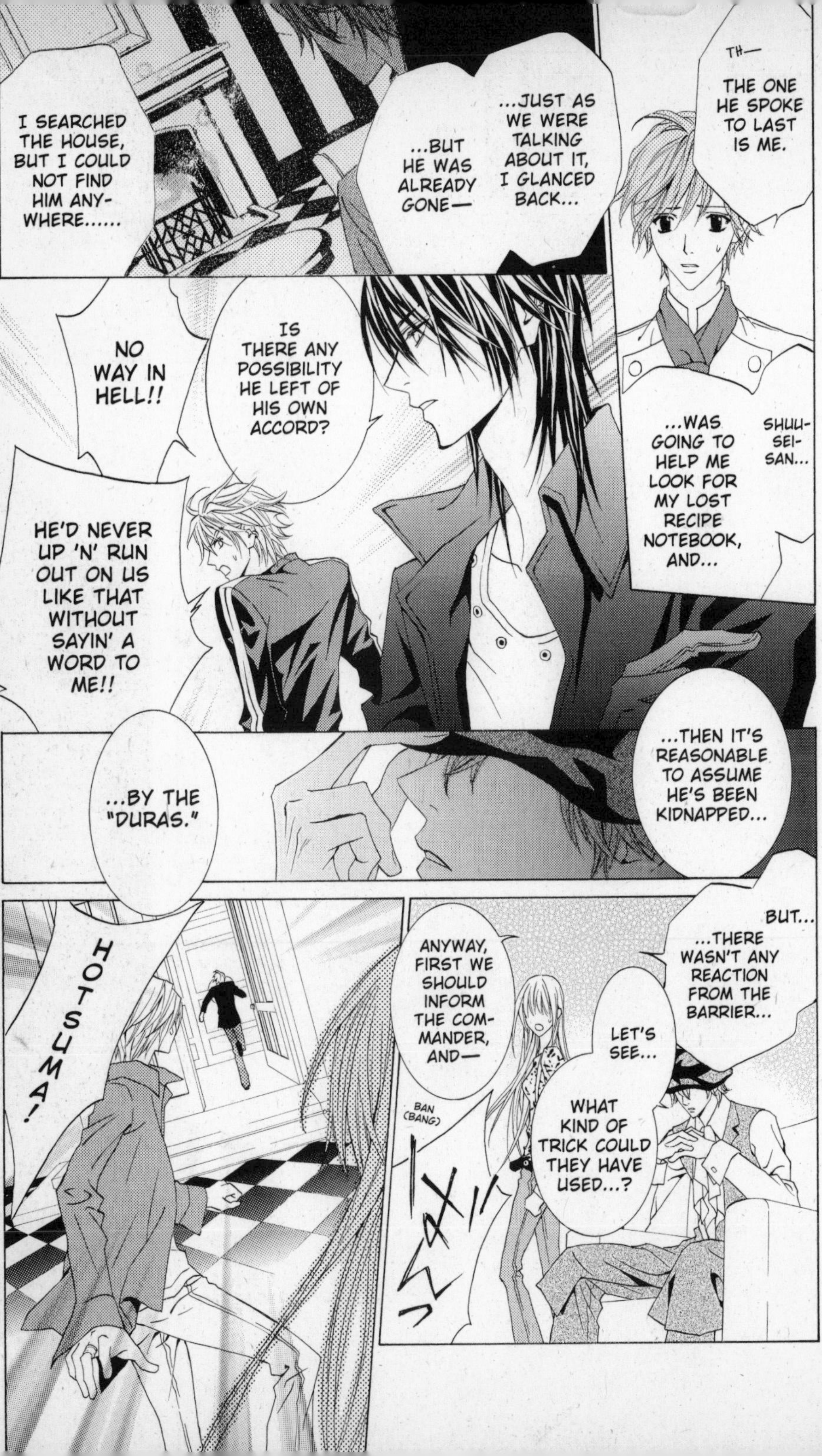
TH—
THE ONE HE SPOKE TO LAST IS ME.
SHUU-SEI-SAN...
...WAS GOING TO HELP ME LOOK FOR MY LOST RECIPE NOTEBOOK, AND...
...JUST AS WE WERE TALKING ABOUT IT, I GLANCED BACK...
...BUT HE WAS ALREADY GONE—
I SEARCHED THE HOUSE, BUT I COULD NOT FIND HIM ANY-WHERE......
IS THERE ANY POSSIBILITY HE LEFT OF HIS OWN ACCORD?
NO WAY IN HELL!!
HE'D NEVER UP 'N' RUN OUT ON US LIKE THAT WITHOUT SAYIN' A WORD TO ME!!
...THEN IT'S REASONABLE TO ASSUME HE'S BEEN KIDNAPPED...
...BY THE "DURAS."
BUT...
...THERE WASN'T ANY REACTION FROM THE BARRIER...
LET'S SEE...
WHAT KIND OF TRICK COULD THEY HAVE USED...?
ANYWAY, FIRST WE SHOULD INFORM THE COM-MANDER, AND—
BAN (BANG)
HOTSUMA!

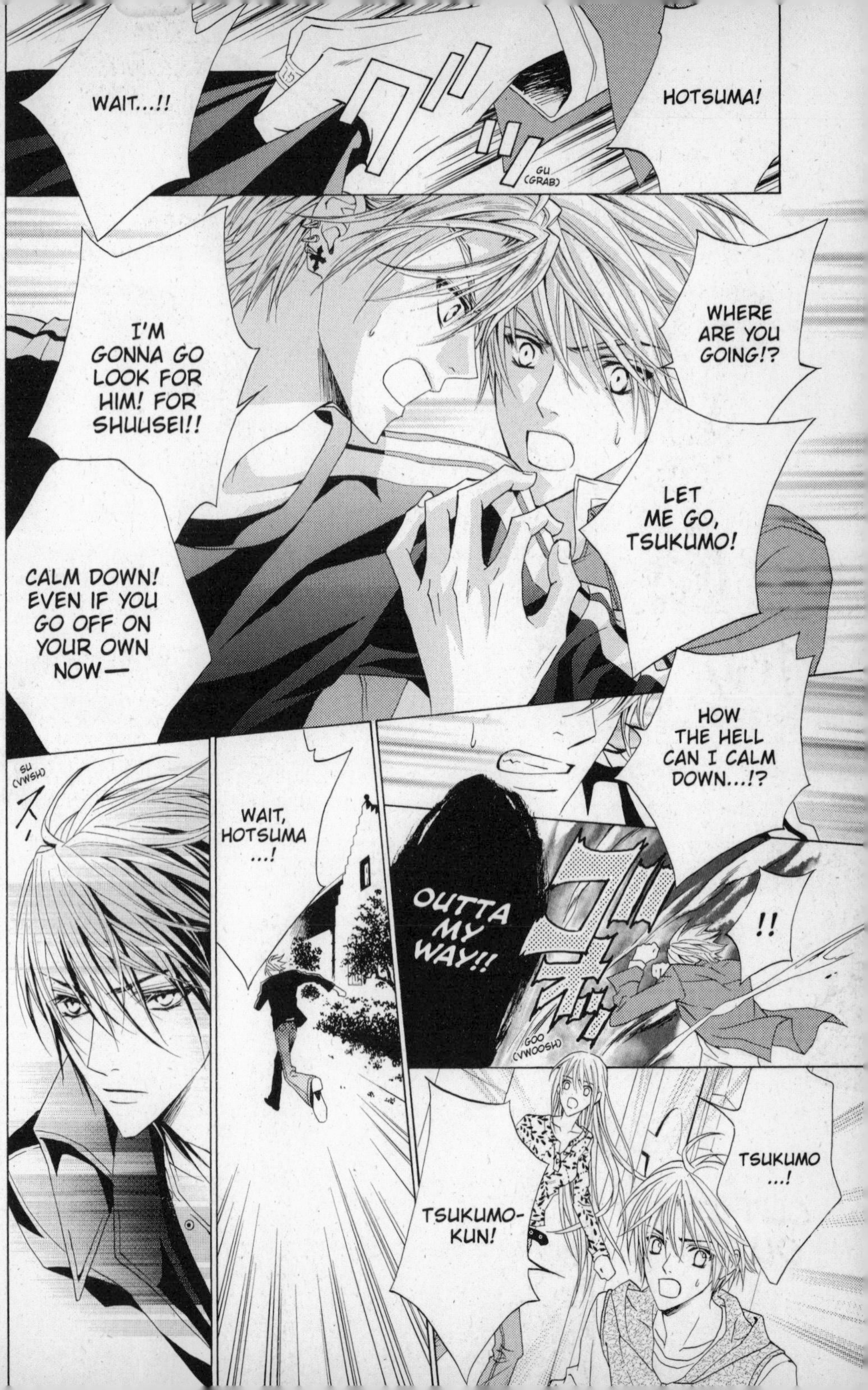
HOTSUMA!
GU (GRAB)
WAIT...!!
WHERE ARE YOU GOING!?
I'M GONNA GO LOOK FOR HIM! FOR SHUUSEI!!
LET ME GO, TSUKUMO!
CALM DOWN! EVEN IF YOU GO OFF ON YOUR OWN NOW—
HOW THE HELL CAN I CALM DOWN...!?
!!
OUTTA MY WAY!!
GOO (VWOOSH)
TSUKUMO ...!
TSUKUMO-KUN!
WAIT, HOTSUMA ...!
SU (VWSH)

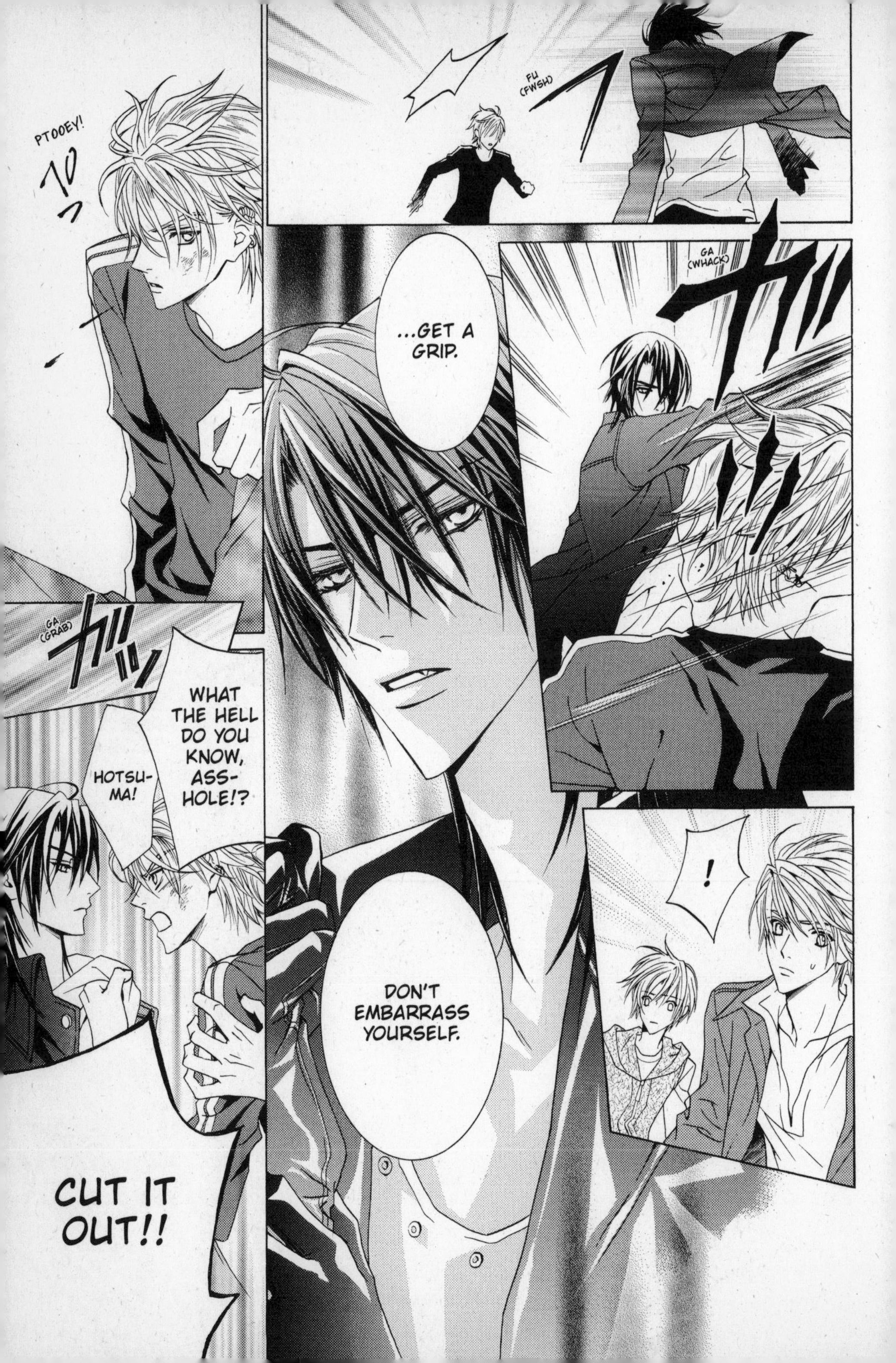

FU (FWSH)
GA (WHACK)
!
...GET A GRIP.
DON'T EMBARRASS YOURSELF.
PTOOEY!
GA (GRAB)
WHAT THE HELL DO YOU KNOW, ASS-HOLE!?
HOTSU-MA!
CUT IT OUT!!

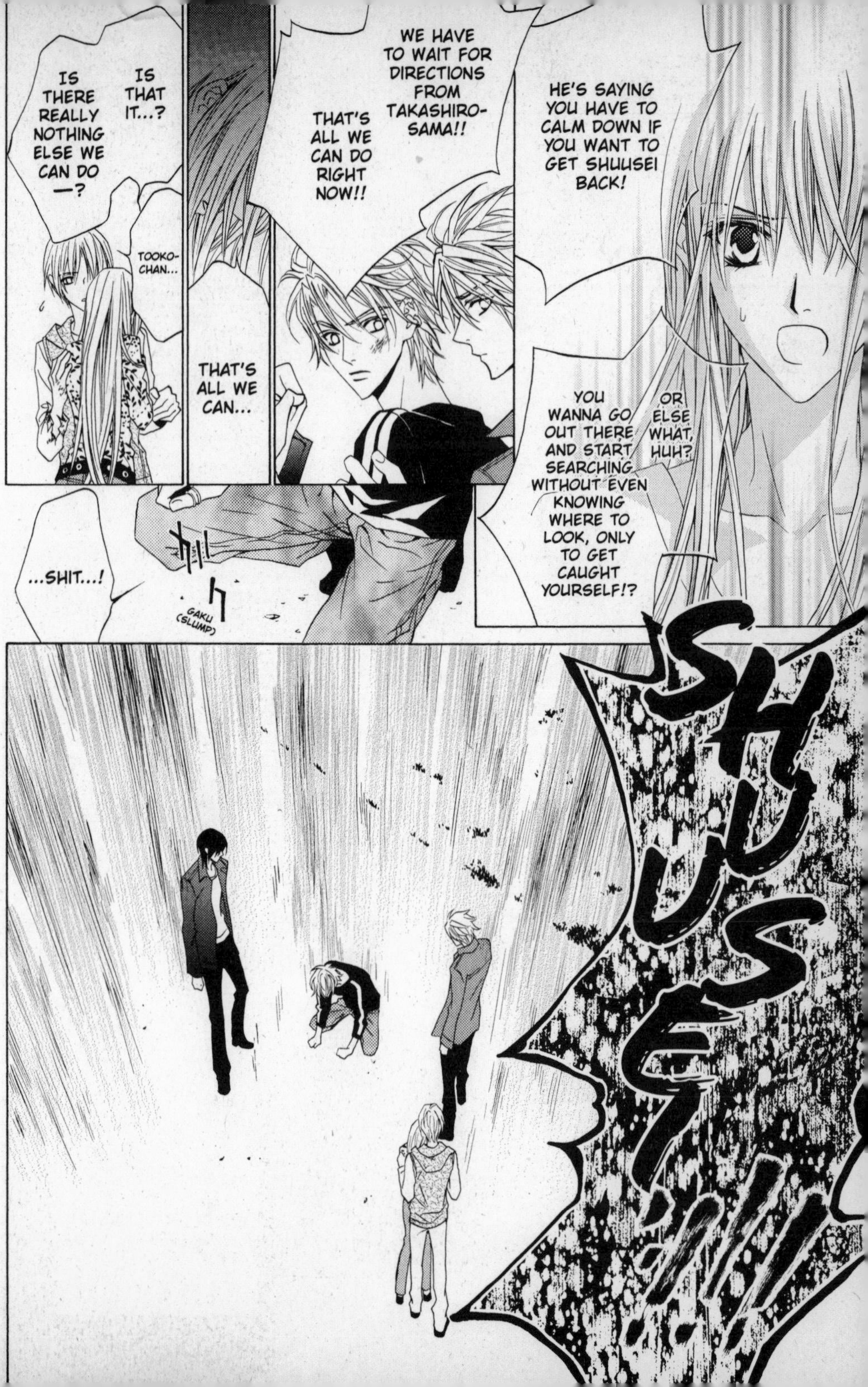
HE'S SAYING YOU HAVE TO CALM DOWN IF YOU WANT TO GET SHUUSEI BACK!
OR ELSE WHAT, HUH?
YOU WANNA GO OUT THERE AND START SEARCHING WITHOUT EVEN KNOWING WHERE TO LOOK, ONLY TO GET CAUGHT YOURSELF!?
WE HAVE TO WAIT FOR DIRECTIONS FROM TAKASHIRO-SAMA!!
THAT'S ALL WE CAN DO RIGHT NOW!!
THAT'S ALL WE CAN...
IS THAT IT...?
IS THERE REALLY NOTHING ELSE WE CAN DO—?
TOOKO-CHAN...
...SHIT...!
GAKU (SLUMP)
SHUUSEI!!!

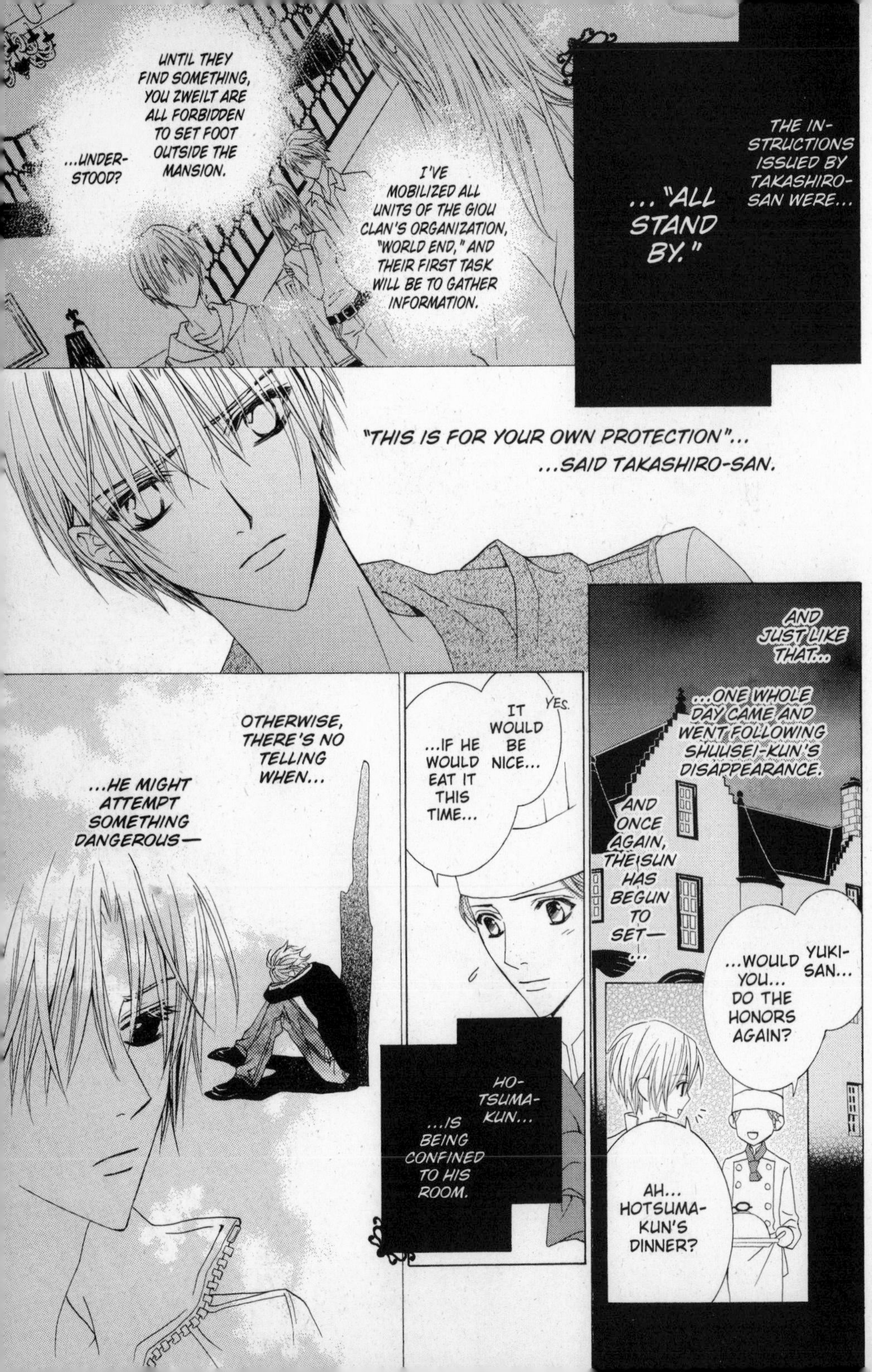

THE IN-STRUCTIONS ISSUED BY TAKASHIRO-SAN WERE...
..."ALL STAND BY."
I'VE MOBILIZED ALL UNITS OF THE GIOU CLAN'S ORGANIZATION, "WORLD END," AND THEIR FIRST TASK WILL BE TO GATHER INFORMATION.
UNTIL THEY FIND SOMETHING, YOU ZWEILT ARE ALL FORBIDDEN TO SET FOOT OUTSIDE THE MANSION.
...UNDER-STOOD?
"THIS IS FOR YOUR OWN PROTECTION"...
...SAID TAKASHIRO-SAN.
AND JUST LIKE THAT...
...ONE WHOLE DAY CAME AND WENT FOLLOWING SHUUSEI-KUN'S DISAPPEARANCE.
AND ONCE AGAIN, THE SUN HAS BEGUN TO SET—...
YUKI-SAN...
...WOULD YOU... DO THE HONORS AGAIN?
AH... HOTSUMA-KUN'S DINNER?
YES.
IT WOULD BE NICE...
...IF HE WOULD EAT IT THIS TIME...
HO-TSUMA-KUN...
...IS BEING CONFINED TO HIS ROOM.
OTHERWISE, THERE'S NO TELLING WHEN...
...HE MIGHT ATTEMPT SOMETHING DANGEROUS—

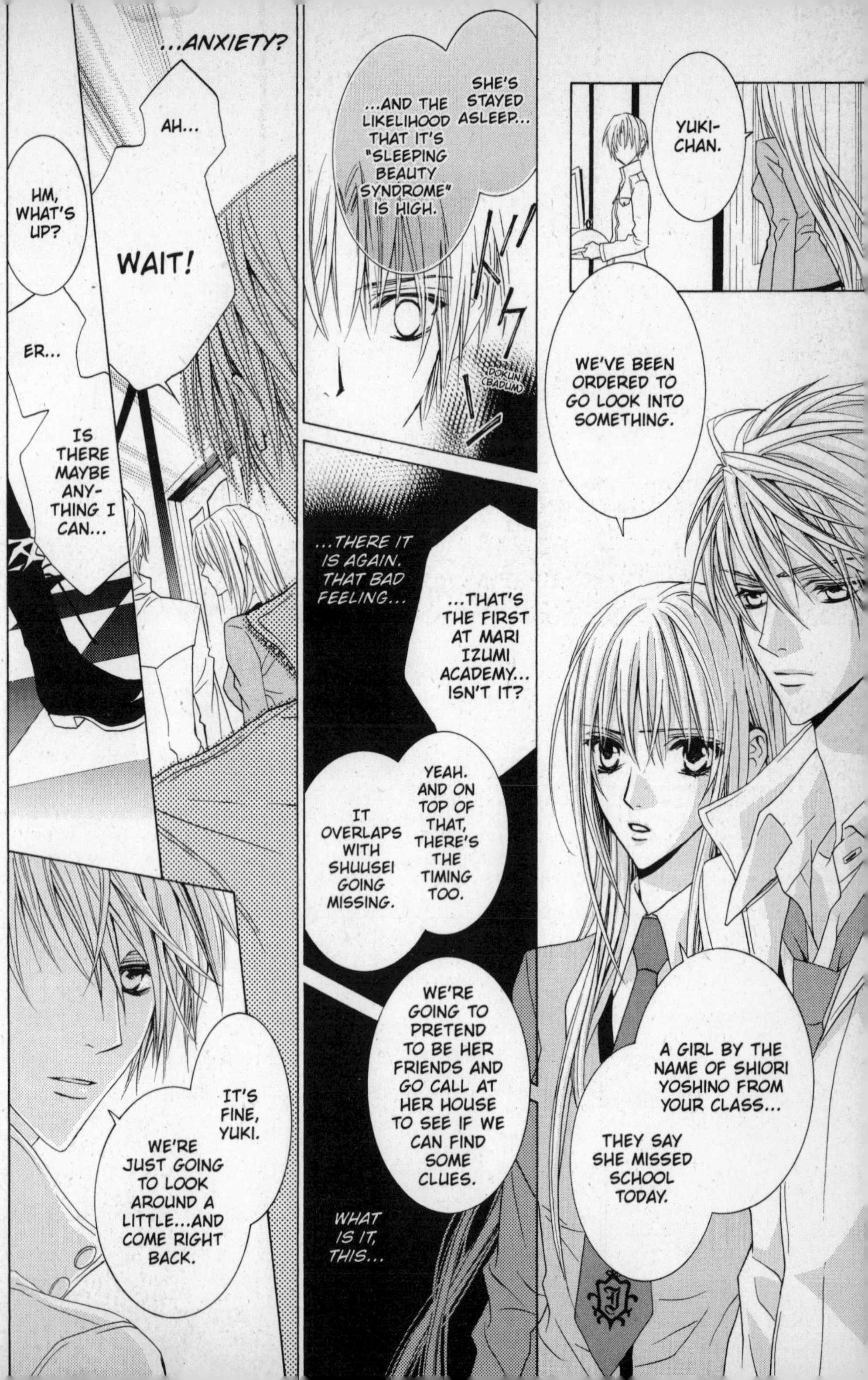
YUKI-CHAN.
WE'VE BEEN ORDERED TO GO LOOK INTO SOMETHING.
A GIRL BY THE NAME OF SHIORI YOSHINO FROM YOUR CLASS...
THEY SAY SHE MISSED SCHOOL TODAY.
SHE'S STAYED ASLEEP...
...AND THE LIKELIHOOD THAT IT'S "SLEEPING BEAUTY SYNDROME" IS HIGH.
DOKUN (BADUM)
...THAT'S THE FIRST AT MARI IZUMI ACADEMY... ISN'T IT?
...THERE IT IS AGAIN. THAT BAD FEELING...
YEAH. AND ON TOP OF THAT, THERE'S THE TIMING TOO.
IT OVERLAPS WITH SHUUSEI GOING MISSING.
WE'RE GOING TO PRETEND TO BE HER FRIENDS AND GO CALL AT HER HOUSE TO SEE IF WE CAN FIND SOME CLUES.
WHAT IS IT, THIS...
...ANXIETY?
AH...
WAIT!
HM, WHAT'S UP?
ER...
IS THERE MAYBE ANYTHING I CAN...
IT'S FINE, YUKI.
WE'RE JUST GOING TO LOOK AROUND A LITTLE...AND COME RIGHT BACK.

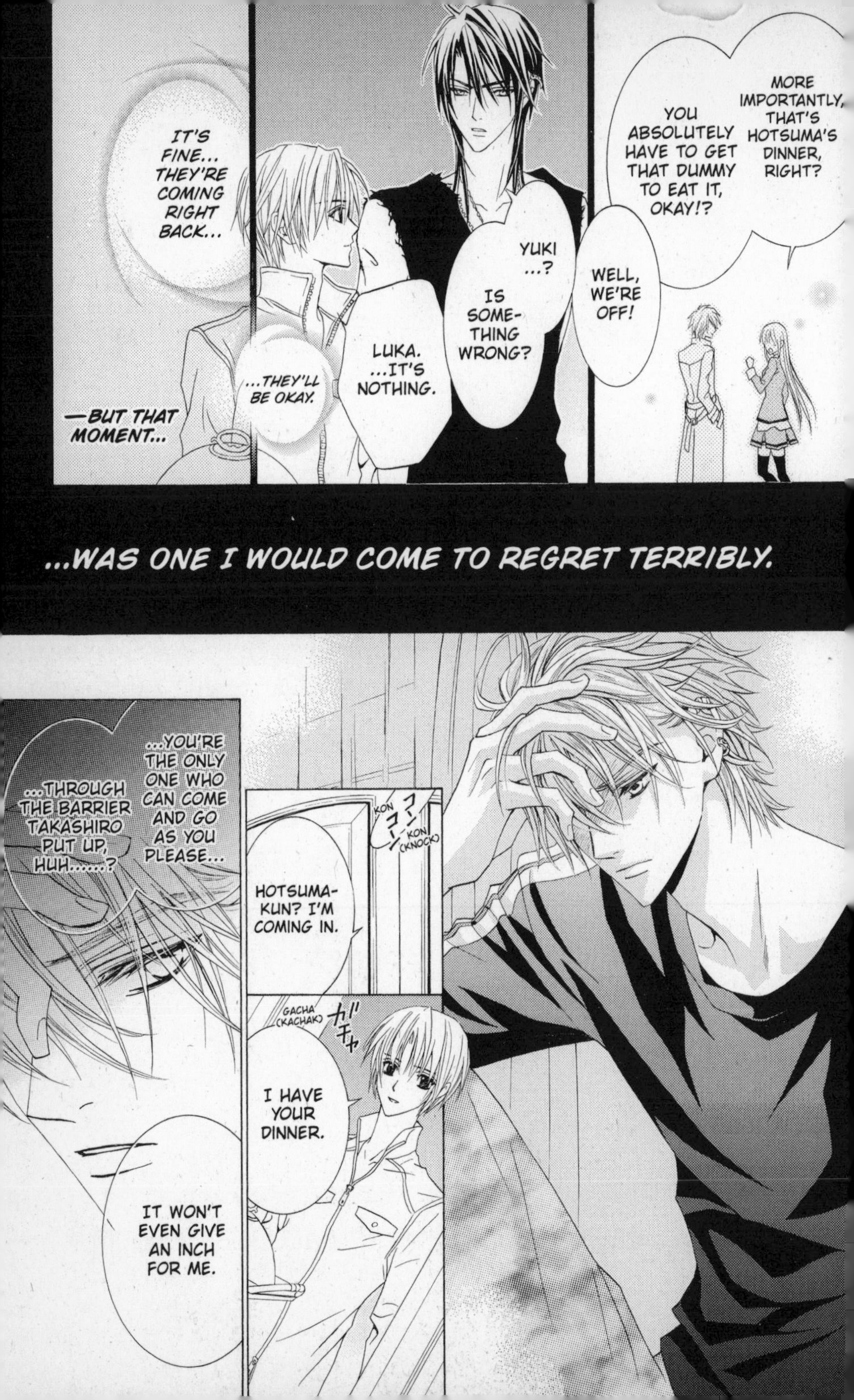
MORE IMPORTANTLY, THAT'S HOTSUMA'S DINNER, RIGHT?
YOU ABSOLUTELY HAVE TO GET THAT DUMMY TO EAT IT, OKAY!?
WELL, WE'RE OFF!
YUKI ...? IS SOMETHING WRONG?
LUKA. ...IT'S NOTHING.
...THEY'LL BE OKAY.
IT'S FINE... THEY'RE COMING RIGHT BACK...
—BUT THAT MOMENT...
...WAS ONE I WOULD COME TO REGRET TERRIBLY.
KON KON (KNOCK)
HOTSUMA-KUN? I'M COMING IN.
GACHA (KACHAK)
I HAVE YOUR DINNER.
...YOU'RE THE ONLY ONE WHO CAN COME AND GO AS YOU PLEASE...
...THROUGH THE BARRIER TAKASHIRO PUT UP, HUH......?
IT WON'T EVEN GIVE AN INCH FOR ME.

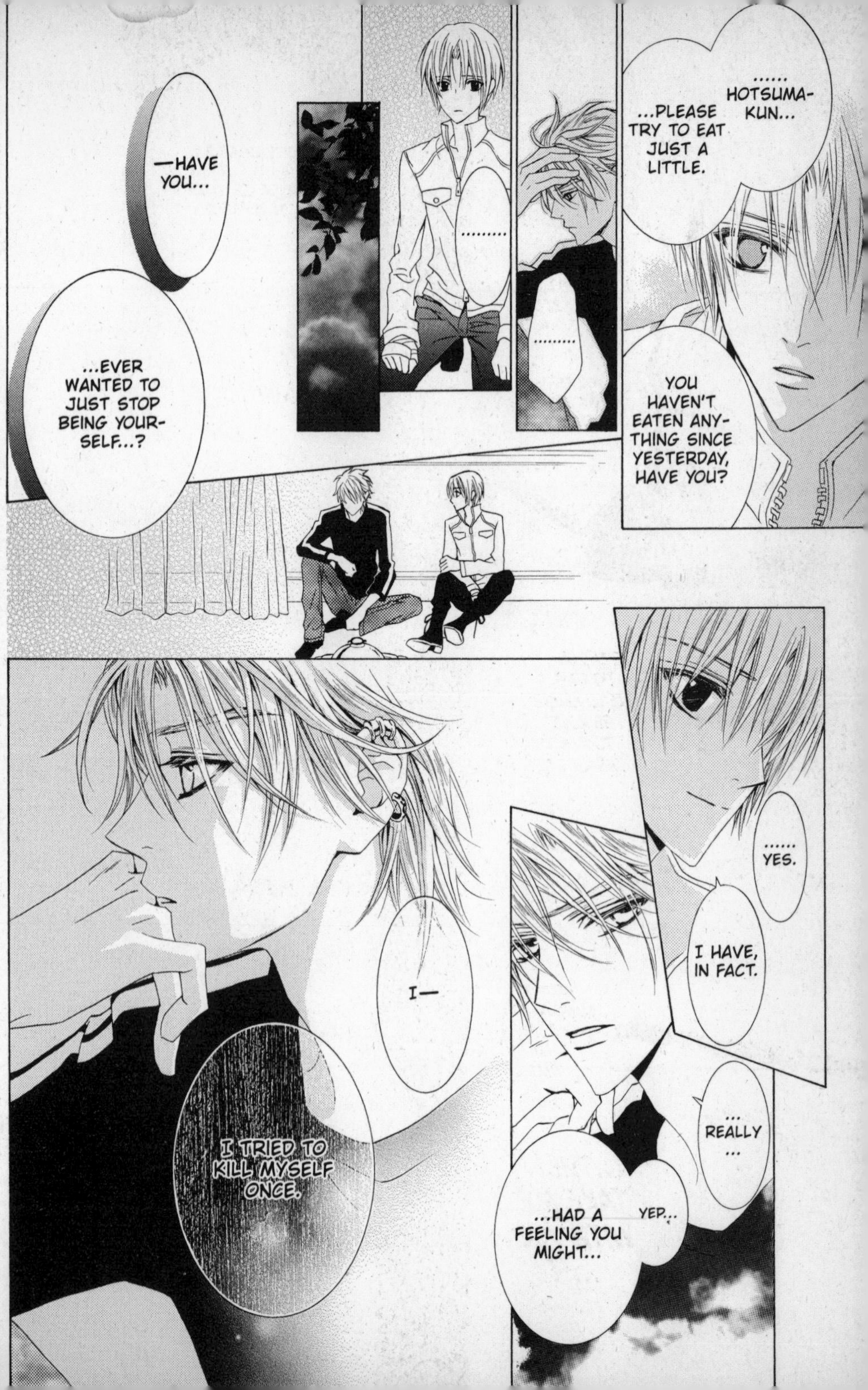
......HOTSUMA-KUN...
...PLEASE TRY TO EAT JUST A LITTLE.
YOU HAVEN'T EATEN ANYTHING SINCE YESTERDAY, HAVE YOU?
....
....
—HAVE YOU...
...EVER WANTED TO JUST STOP BEING YOURSELF...?
......YES.
I HAVE, IN FACT.
...REALLY...
YEP...
...HAD A FEELING YOU MIGHT...
I—
I TRIED TO KILL MYSELF ONCE.

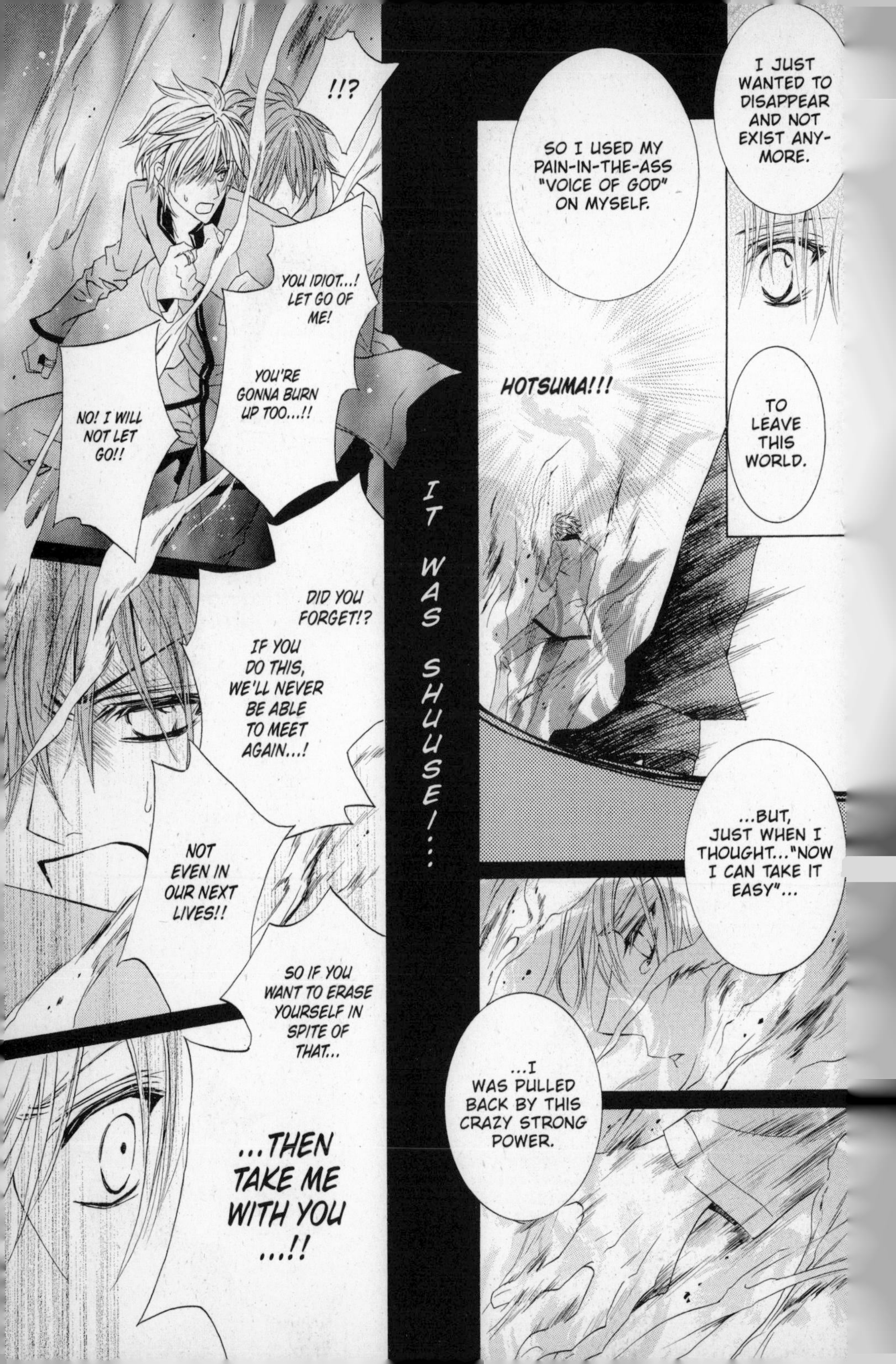
I JUST WANTED TO DISAPPEAR AND NOT EXIST ANY-MORE.
TO LEAVE THIS WORLD.
SO I USED MY PAIN-IN-THE-ASS "VOICE OF GOD" ON MYSELF.
HOTSUMA!!!
...BUT, JUST WHEN I THOUGHT..."NOW I CAN TAKE IT EASY"...
...I WAS PULLED BACK BY THIS CRAZY STRONG POWER.
IT WAS SHUUSE!...
!!?
YOU IDIOT...! LET GO OF ME!
YOU'RE GONNA BURN UP TOO...!!
NO! I WILL NOT LET GO!!
DID YOU FORGET!?
IF YOU DO THIS, WE'LL NEVER BE ABLE TO MEET AGAIN...!
NOT EVEN IN OUR NEXT LIVES!!
SO IF YOU WANT TO ERASE YOURSELF IN SPITE OF THAT...
...THEN TAKE ME WITH YOU ...!!

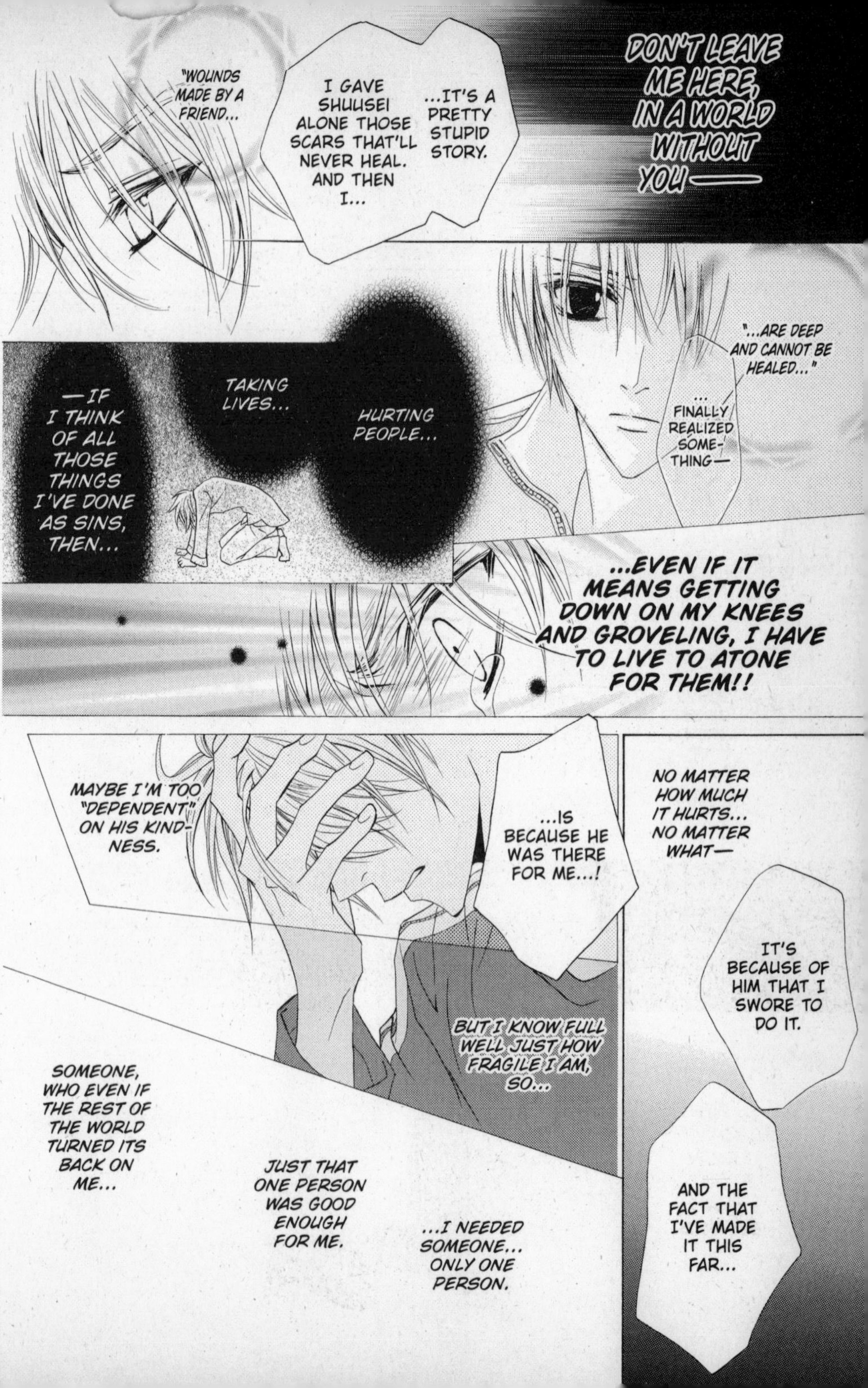
DON'T LEAVE ME HERE, IN A WORLD WITHOUT YOU—
I GAVE SHUUSEI ALONE THOSE SCARS THAT'LL NEVER HEAL. AND THEN I...
...IT'S A PRETTY STUPID STORY.
"WOUNDS MADE BY A FRIEND...
"...ARE DEEP AND CANNOT BE HEALED..."
...FINALLY REALIZED SOME-THING—
HURTING PEOPLE...
TAKING LIVES...
—IF I THINK OF ALL THOSE THINGS I'VE DONE AS SINS, THEN...
...EVEN IF IT MEANS GETTING DOWN ON MY KNEES AND GROVELING, I HAVE TO LIVE TO ATONE FOR THEM!!
NO MATTER HOW MUCH IT HURTS... NO MATTER WHAT—
IT'S BECAUSE OF HIM THAT I SWORE TO DO IT.
AND THE FACT THAT I'VE MADE IT THIS FAR...
...IS BECAUSE HE WAS THERE FOR ME...!
MAYBE I'M TOO "DEPENDENT" ON HIS KIND-NESS.
BUT I KNOW FULL WELL JUST HOW FRAGILE I AM, SO...
...I NEEDED SOMEONE... ONLY ONE PERSON.
JUST THAT ONE PERSON WAS GOOD ENOUGH FOR ME.
SOMEONE, WHO EVEN IF THE REST OF THE WORLD TURNED ITS BACK ON ME...

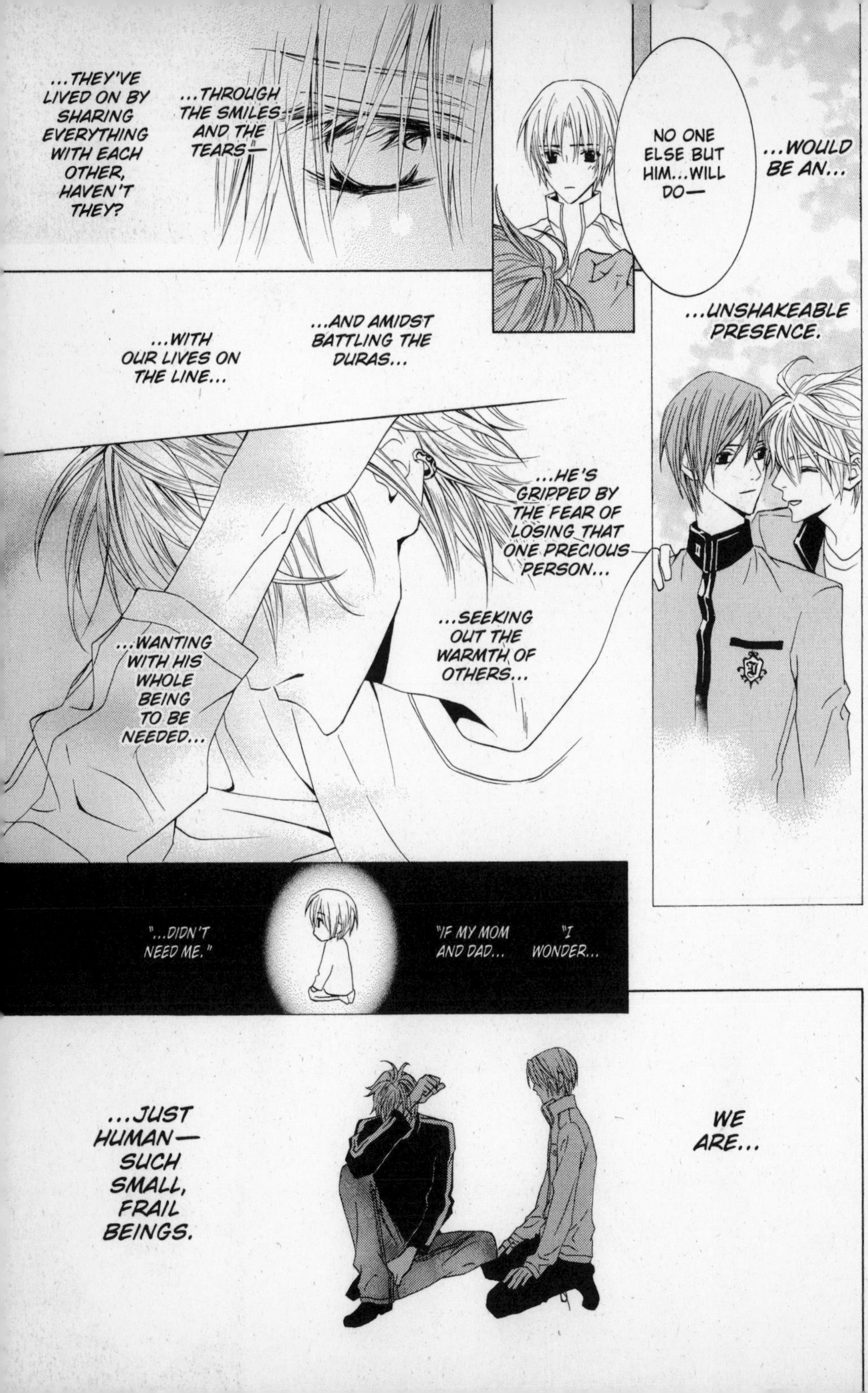
...WOULD BE AN...
...UNSHAKEABLE PRESENCE.
NO ONE ELSE BUT HIM...WILL DO—
...THROUGH THE SMILES AND THE TEARS—
...THEY'VE LIVED ON BY SHARING EVERYTHING WITH EACH OTHER, HAVEN'T THEY?
...AND AMIDST BATTLING THE DURAS...
...WITH OUR LIVES ON THE LINE...
...HE'S GRIPPED BY THE FEAR OF LOSING THAT ONE PRECIOUS PERSON...
...SEEKING OUT THE WARMTH OF OTHERS...
...WANTING WITH HIS WHOLE BEING TO BE NEEDED...
"I WONDER...
"IF MY MOM AND DAD...
"...DIDN'T NEED ME."
WE ARE...
...JUST HUMAN—SUCH SMALL, FRAIL BEINGS.

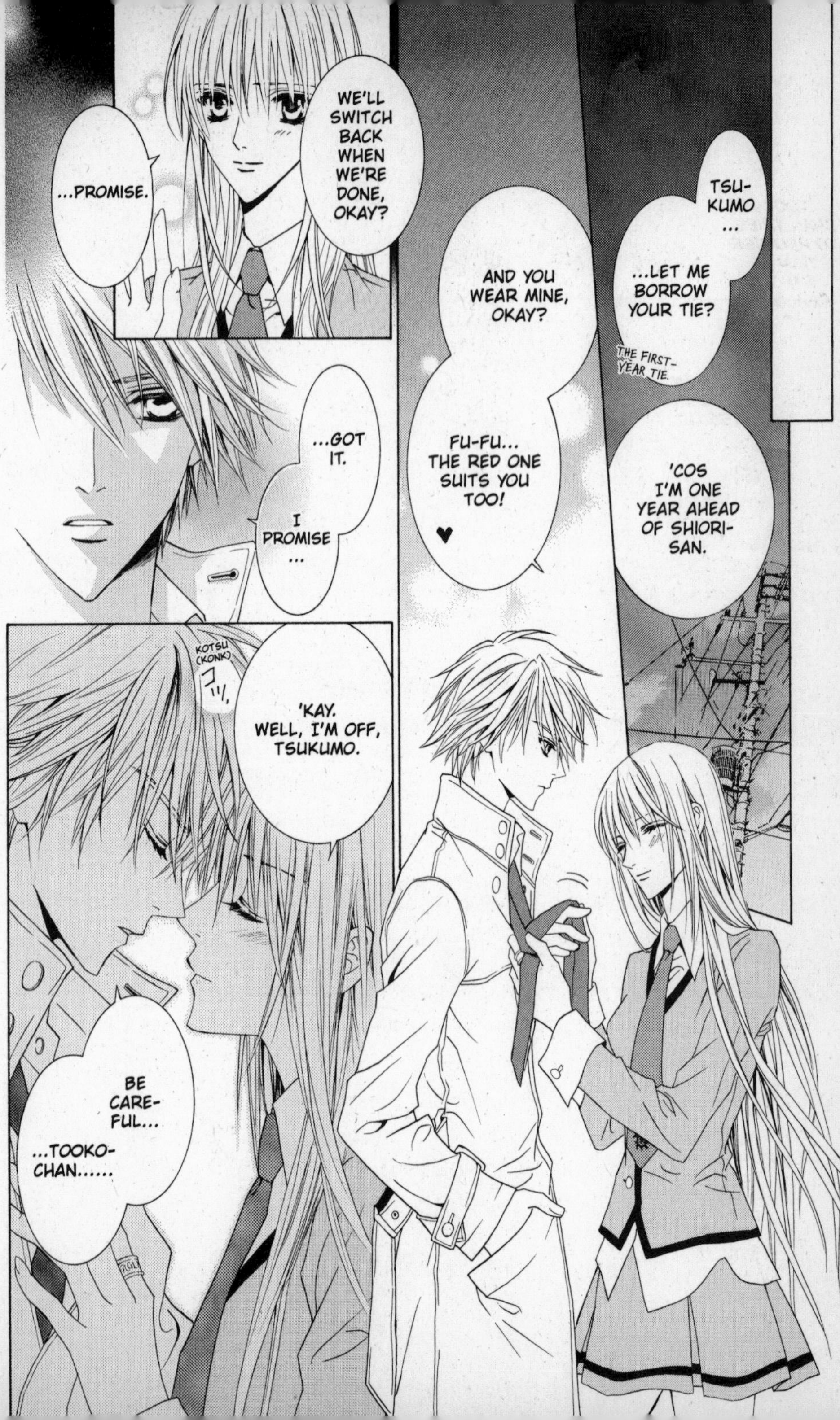
TSU-KUMO...
...LET ME BORROW YOUR TIE?
THE FIRST-YEAR TIE.
'COS I'M ONE YEAR AHEAD OF SHIORI-SAN.
AND YOU WEAR MINE, OKAY?
FU-FU... THE RED ONE SUITS YOU TOO! ♥
WE'LL SWITCH BACK WHEN WE'RE DONE, OKAY?
...PROMISE.
...GOT IT.
I PROMISE...
'KAY. WELL, I'M OFF, TSUKUMO.
KOTSU (KONK)
BE CARE-FUL...
...TOOKO-CHAN......

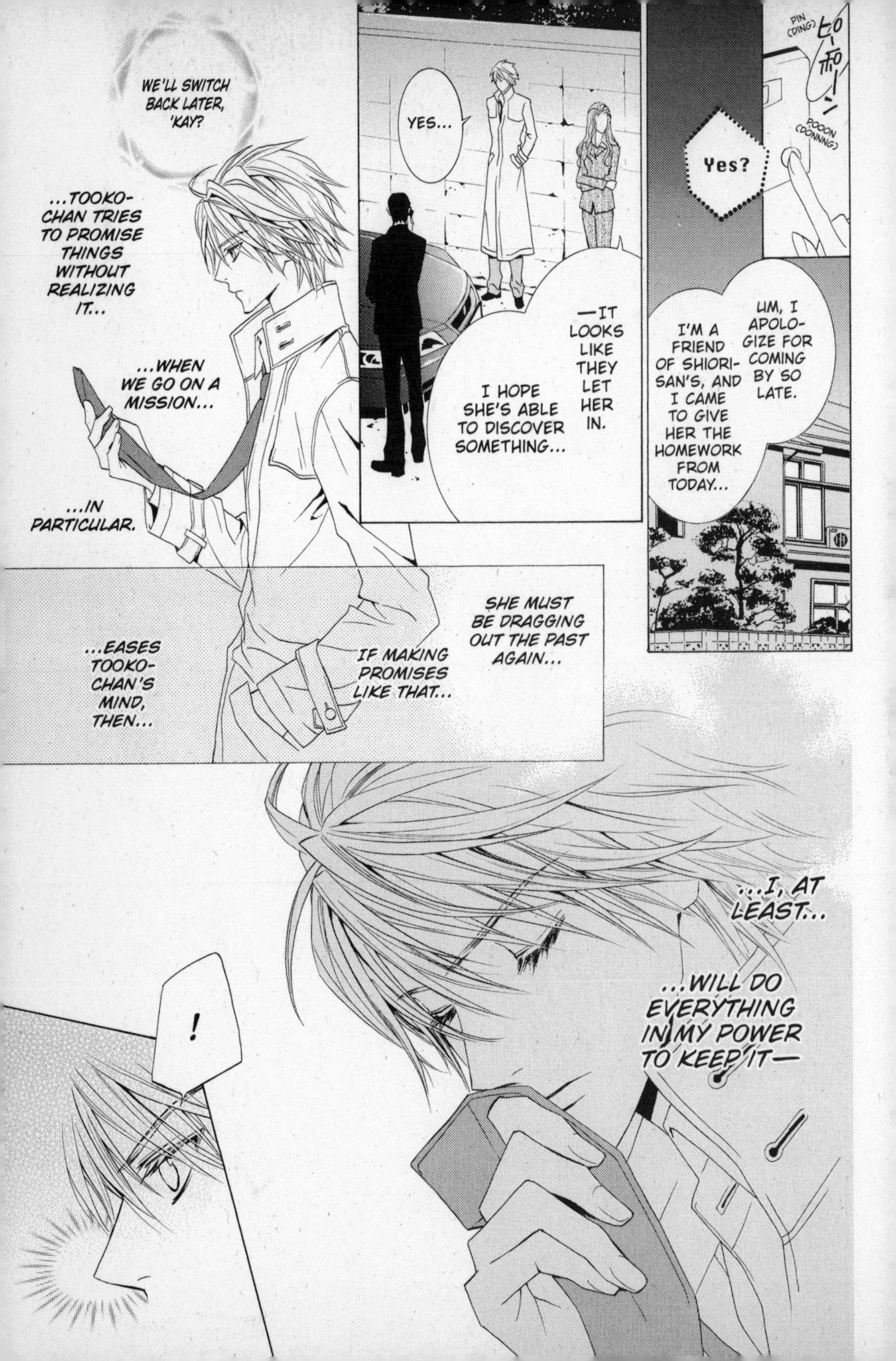
PIN (DING)
POOON (DONNNG)
Yes?
UM, I APOLOGIZE FOR COMING BY SO LATE.
I'M A FRIEND OF SHIORI-SAN'S, AND I CAME TO GIVE HER THE HOMEWORK FROM TODAY...
YES...
—IT LOOKS LIKE THEY LET HER IN.
I HOPE SHE'S ABLE TO DISCOVER SOMETHING...
WE'LL SWITCH BACK LATER, 'KAY?
...TOOKO-CHAN TRIES TO PROMISE THINGS WITHOUT REALIZING IT...
...WHEN WE GO ON A MISSION...
...IN PARTICULAR.
SHE MUST BE DRAGGING OUT THE PAST AGAIN...
IF MAKING PROMISES LIKE THAT...
...EASES TOOKO-CHAN'S MIND, THEN...
...I, AT LEAST...
...WILL DO EVERYTHING IN MY POWER TO KEEP IT—
!

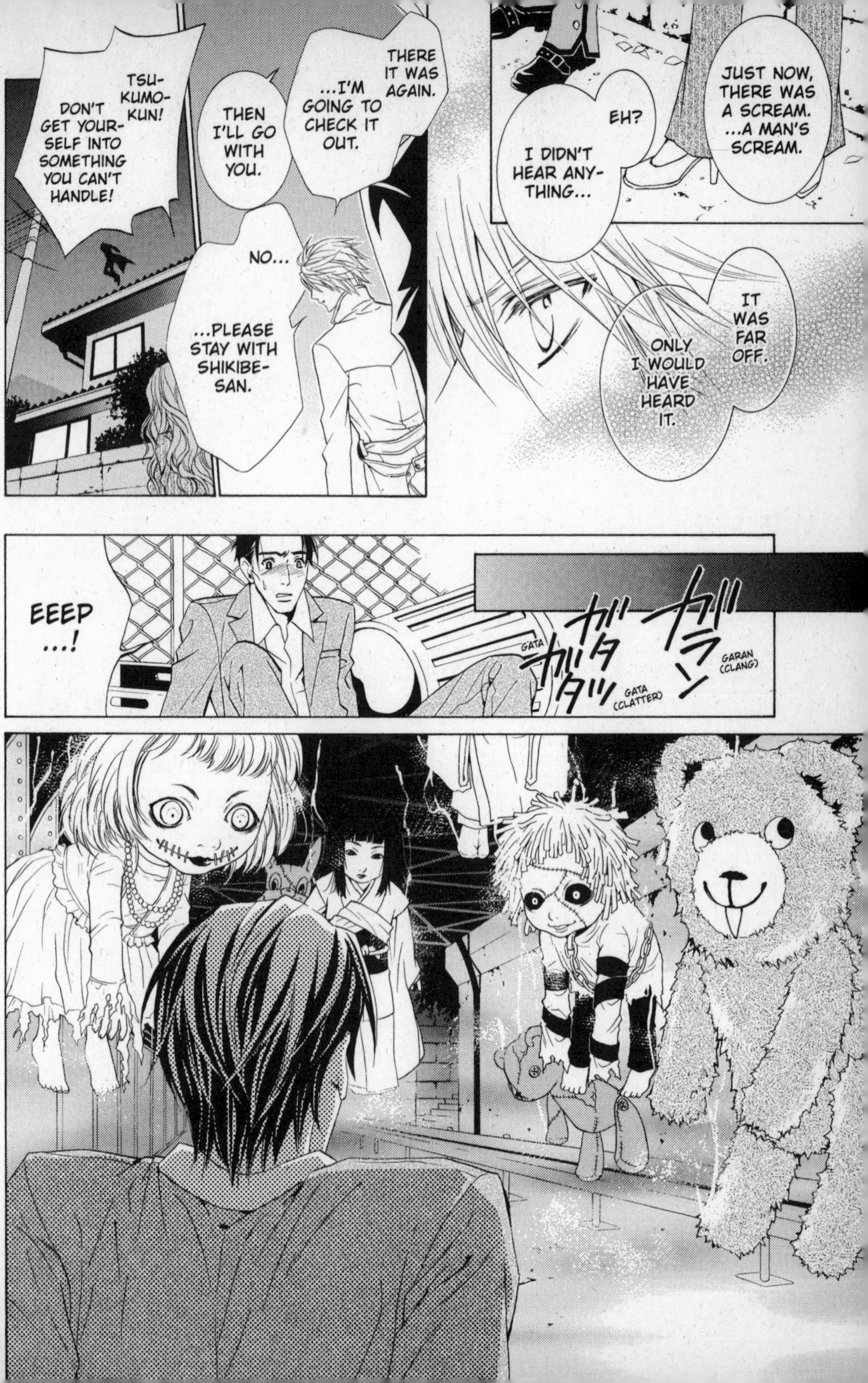
JUST NOW, THERE WAS A SCREAM. ...A MAN'S SCREAM.
EH?
I DIDN'T HEAR ANYTHING...
IT WAS FAR OFF.
ONLY I WOULD HAVE HEARD IT.
THERE IT WAS AGAIN.
...I'M GOING TO CHECK IT OUT.
THEN I'LL GO WITH YOU.
TSUKUMO-KUN!
DON'T GET YOURSELF INTO SOMETHING YOU CAN'T HANDLE!
NO...
...PLEASE STAY WITH SHIKIBE-SAN.
ガラン
GARAN (CLANG)
ガタ
GATA
ガタッ
GATA (CLATTER)
EEEP ...!

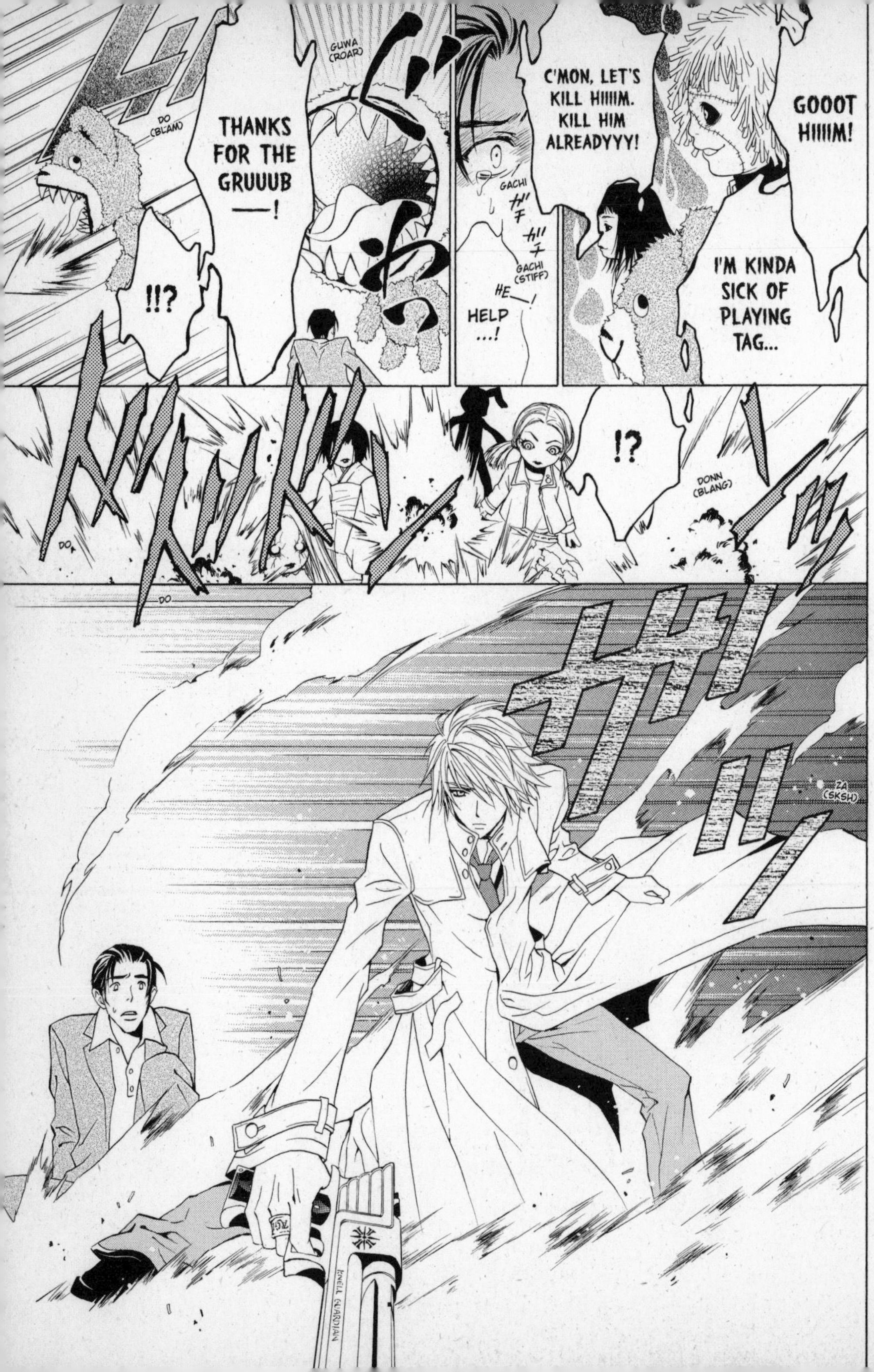
GOOOT HIIIIM!
I'M KINDA SICK OF PLAYING TAG...
C'MON, LET'S KILL HIIIIM. KILL HIM ALREADYYY!
GACHI
GACHI (STIFF)
HE—!
HELP ...!
GUWA (ROAR)
THANKS FOR THE GRUUUB —!
DO (BLAM)
!!?
DONN (BLANG)
!?
DO
DO
ZA (SKSH)
KNELL GUARDIAN

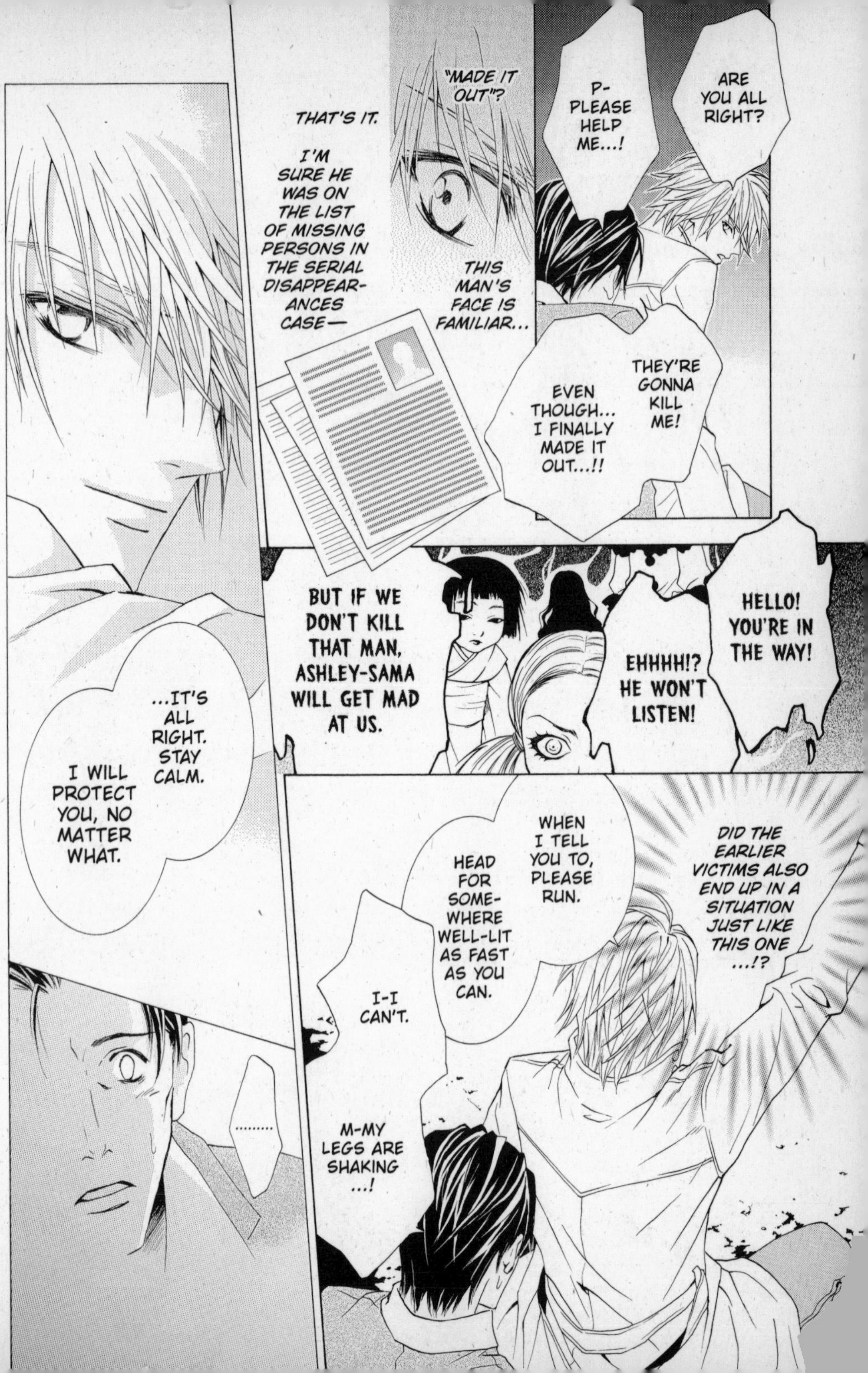
ARE YOU ALL RIGHT?
P-PLEASE HELP ME...!
THEY'RE GONNA KILL ME!
EVEN THOUGH... I FINALLY MADE IT OUT...!!
"MADE IT 'OUT'"?
THIS MAN'S FACE IS FAMILIAR...
THAT'S IT.
I'M SURE HE WAS ON THE LIST OF MISSING PERSONS IN THE SERIAL DISAPPEARANCES CASE—
...IT'S ALL RIGHT. STAY CALM.
I WILL PROTECT YOU, NO MATTER WHAT.
HELLO! YOU'RE IN THE WAY!
EHHHH!? HE WON'T LISTEN!
BUT IF WE DON'T KILL THAT MAN, ASHLEY-SAMA WILL GET MAD AT US.
DID THE EARLIER VICTIMS ALSO END UP IN A SITUATION JUST LIKE THIS ONE ...!?
WHEN I TELL YOU TO, PLEASE RUN.
HEAD FOR SOMEWHERE WELL-LIT AS FAST AS YOU CAN.
I-I CAN'T.
M-MY LEGS ARE SHAKING ...!
....

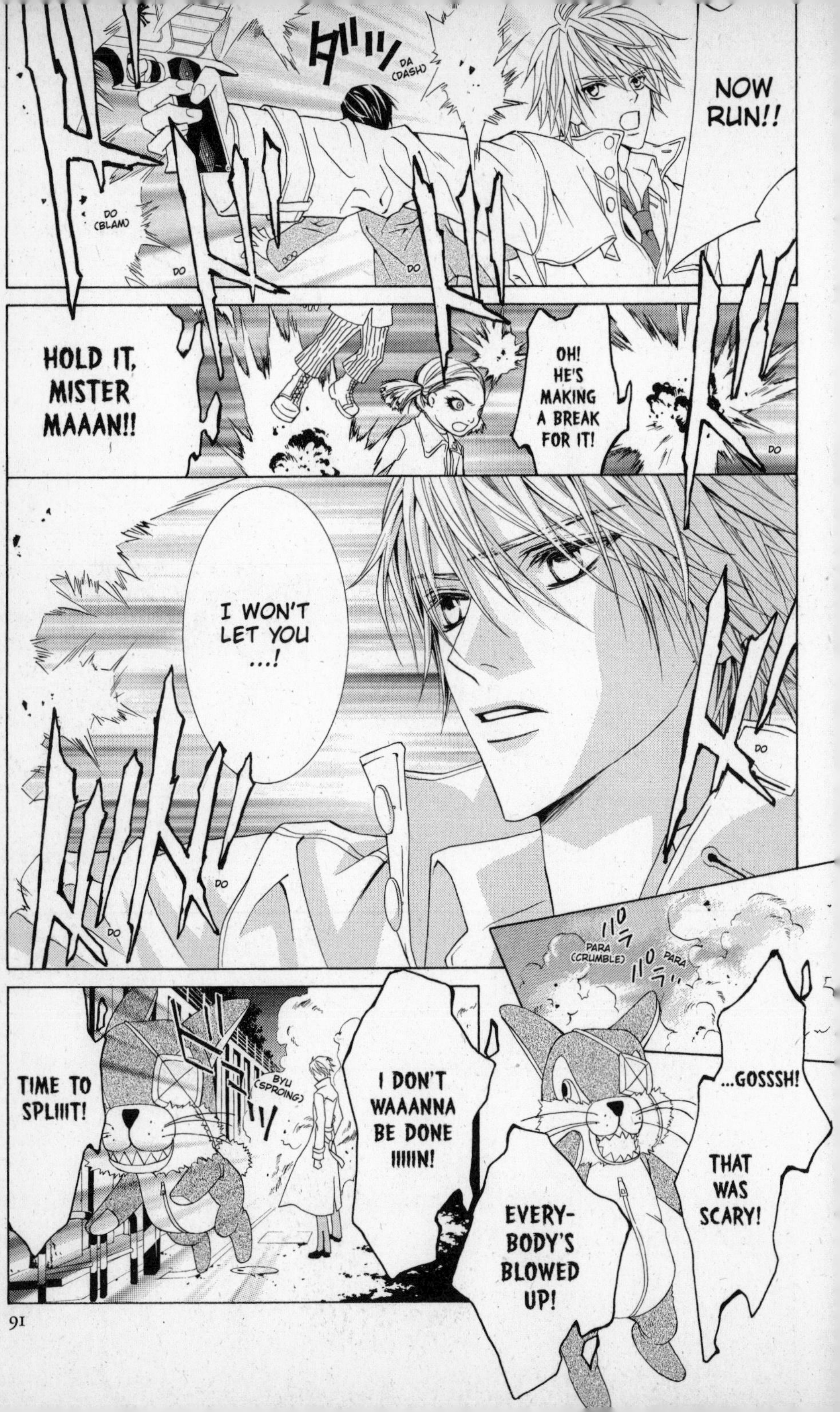
NOW RUN!!
DA (DASH)
DO (BLAM)
DO
DO
DO
OH! HE'S MAKING A BREAK FOR IT!
HOLD IT, MISTER MAAAN!!
DO
I WON'T LET YOU ...!
DO
DO
PARA (CRUMBLE)
PARA
...GOSSSH!
THAT WAS SCARY!
EVERY-BODY'S BLOWED UP!
I DON'T WAAANNA BE DONE IIIIIIN!
BYU (SPROING)
TIME TO SPLIIIT!

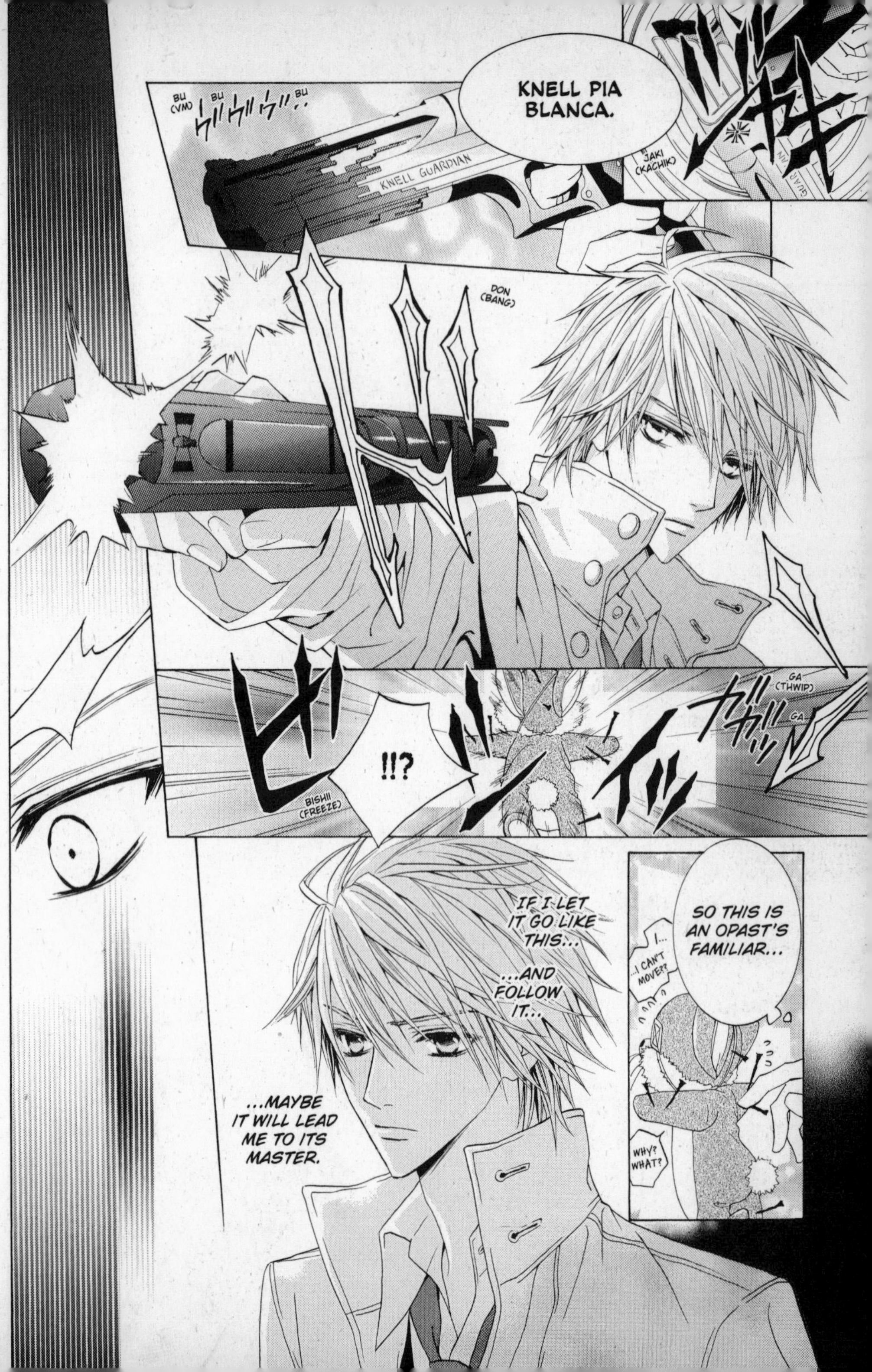

JAKI (KACHIK)
KNELL PIA BLANCA.
BU (VM) BU BU
KNELL GUARDIAN
DON (BANG)
GA (THWIP) GA
!!?
BISHII (FREEZE)
SO THIS IS AN OPAST'S FAMILIAR...
I... ...I CAN'T MOVE?!
WHY? WHAT?
IF I LET IT GO LIKE THIS...
...AND FOLLOW IT...
...MAYBE IT WILL LEAD ME TO ITS MASTER.

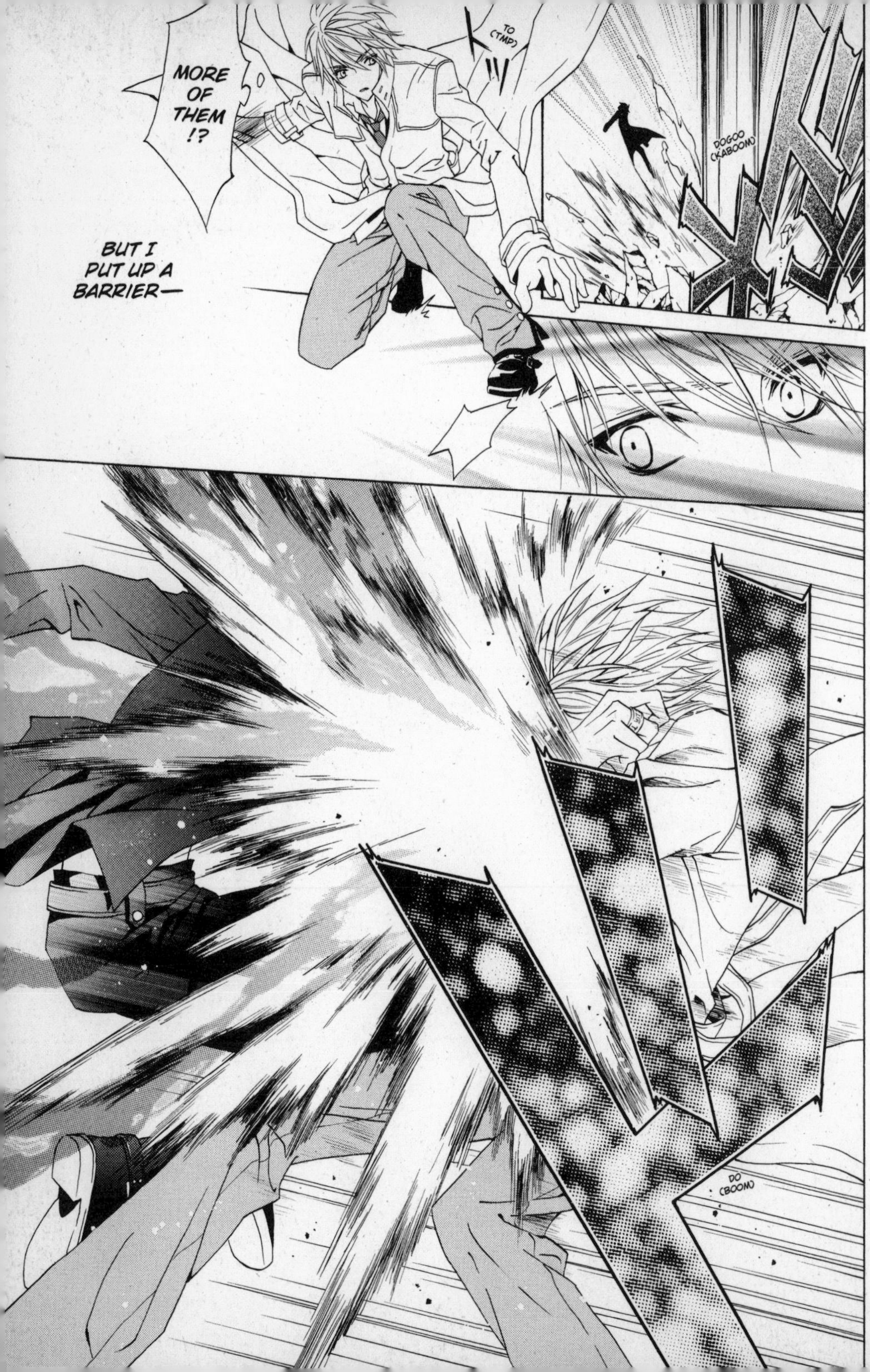
DOGOO (KABOOM)
TO (TMP)
MORE OF THEM !?
BUT I PUT UP A BARRIER—
DO (BOOM)

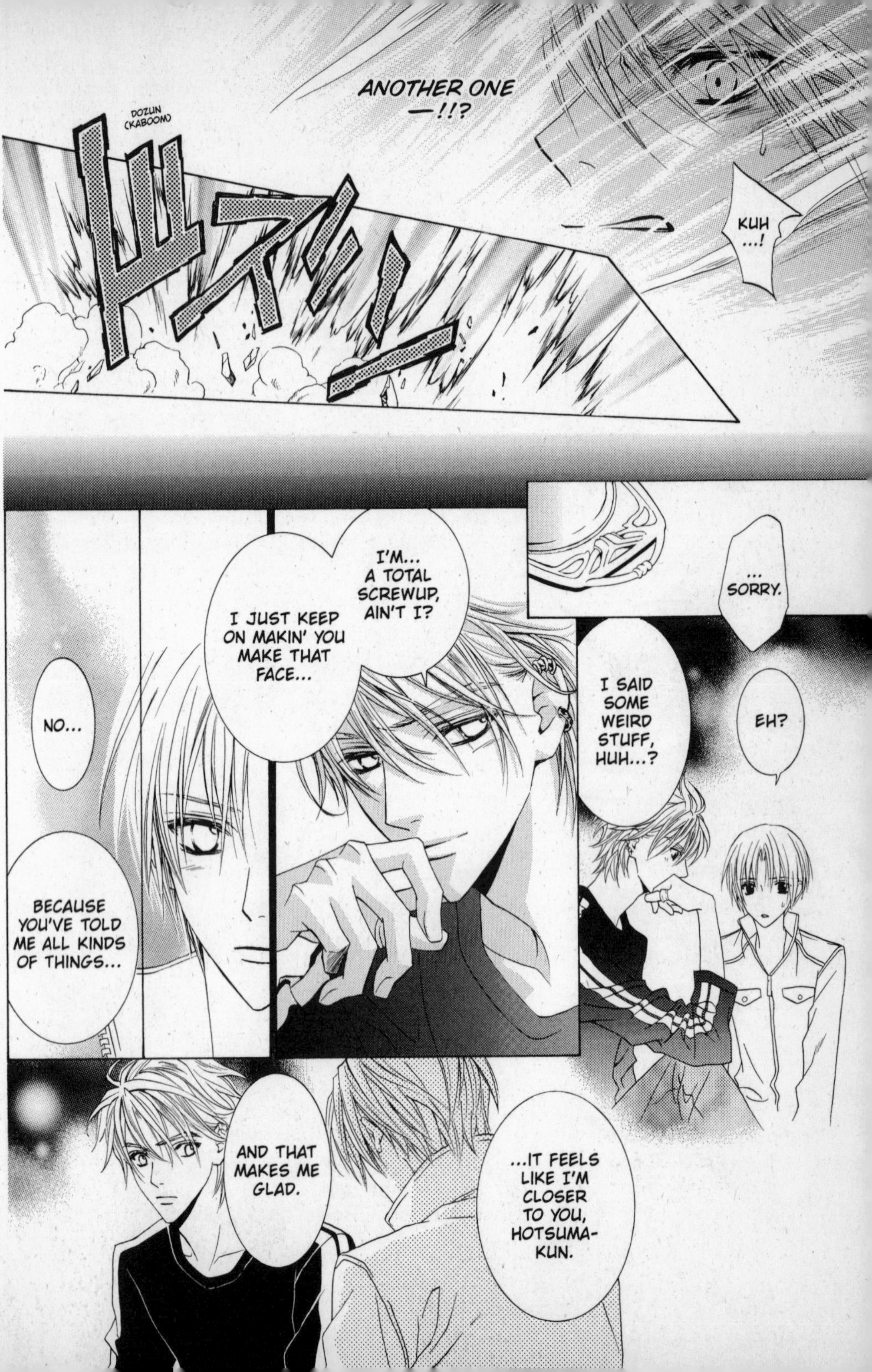
ANOTHER ONE —!!?
KUH ...!
DOZUN (KABOOM)
... SORRY.
EH?
I SAID SOME WEIRD STUFF, HUH...?
I'M... A TOTAL SCREWUP, AIN'T I?
I JUST KEEP ON MAKIN' YOU MAKE THAT FACE...
NO...
BECAUSE YOU'VE TOLD ME ALL KINDS OF THINGS...
...IT FEELS LIKE I'M CLOSER TO YOU, HOTSUMA-KUN.
AND THAT MAKES ME GLAD.

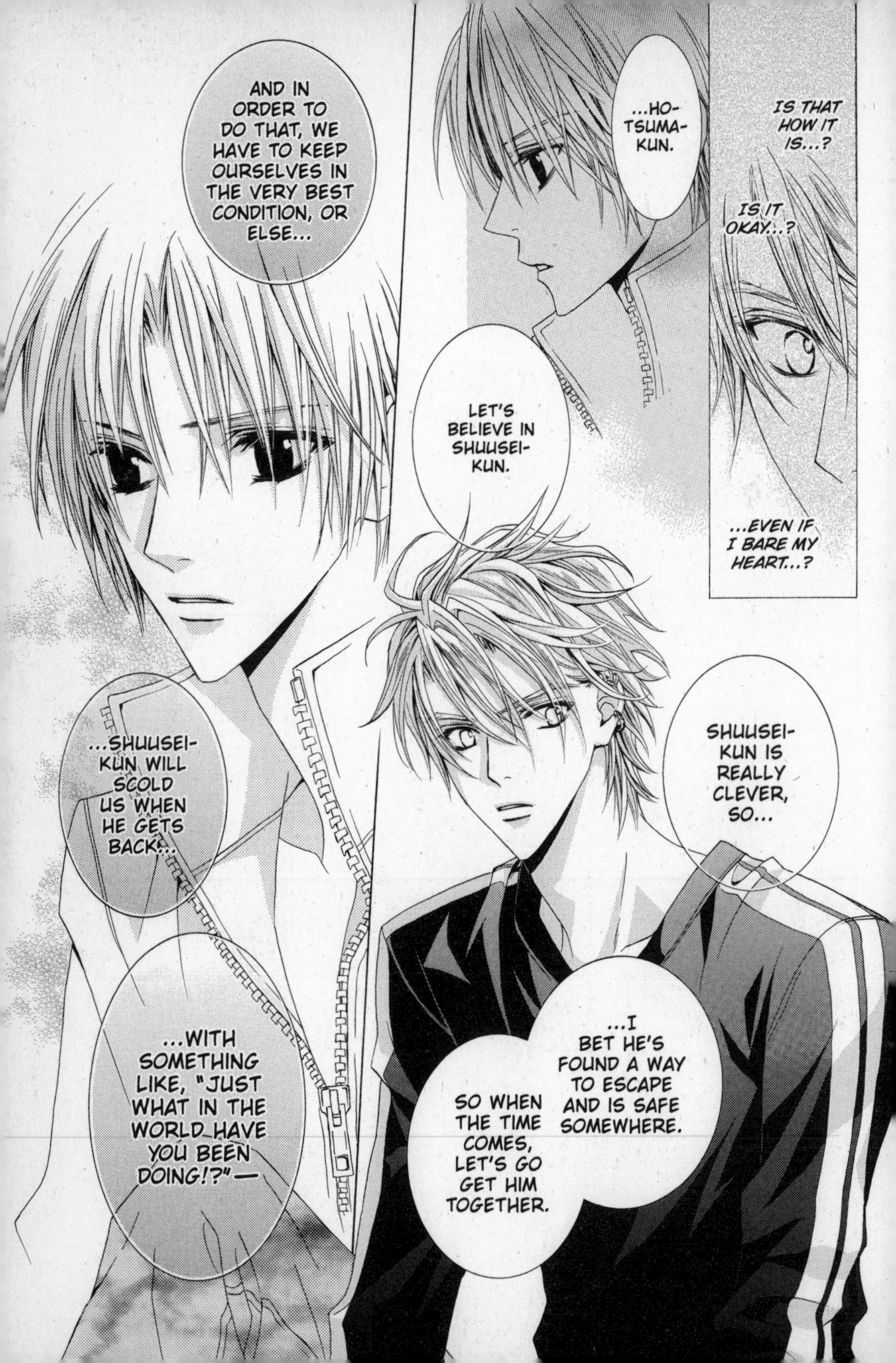
IS THAT HOW IT IS...?
IS IT OKAY...?
...EVEN IF I BARE MY HEART...?
...HO-TSUMA-KUN.
LET'S BELIEVE IN SHUUSEI-KUN.
SHUUSEI-KUN IS REALLY CLEVER, SO...
...I BET HE'S FOUND A WAY TO ESCAPE AND IS SAFE SOMEWHERE.
SO WHEN THE TIME COMES, LET'S GO GET HIM TOGETHER.
AND IN ORDER TO DO THAT, WE HAVE TO KEEP OURSELVES IN THE VERY BEST CONDITION, OR ELSE...
...SHUUSEI-KUN WILL SCOLD US WHEN HE GETS BACK...
...WITH SOMETHING LIKE, "JUST WHAT IN THE WORLD HAVE YOU BEEN DOING!?"—

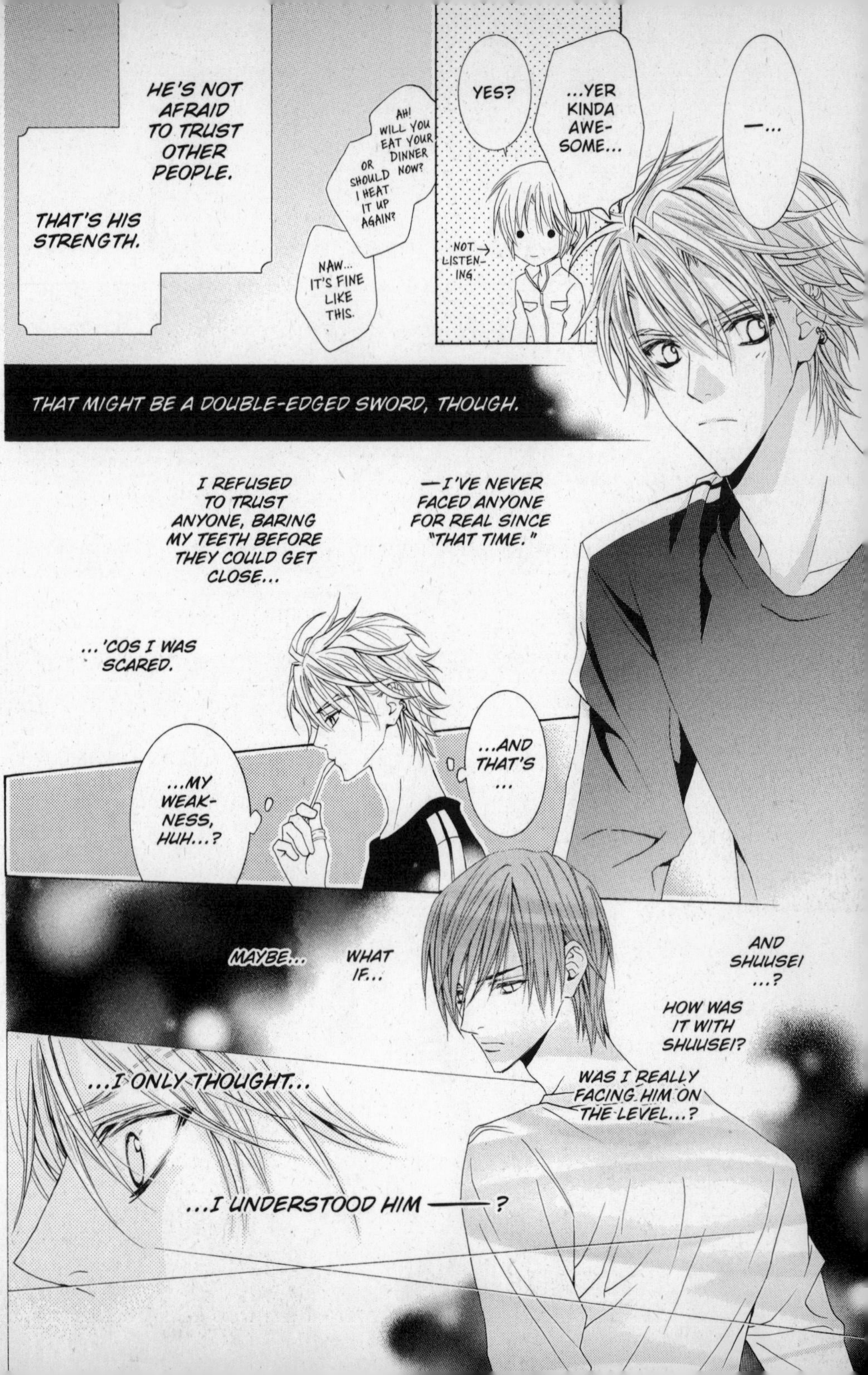
—...
...YER KINDA AWE-SOME...
YES?
NOT LISTENING
AH! WILL YOU EAT YOUR DINNER NOW? OR SHOULD I HEAT IT UP AGAIN?
NAW... IT'S FINE LIKE THIS.
HE'S NOT AFRAID TO TRUST OTHER PEOPLE.
THAT'S HIS STRENGTH.
THAT MIGHT BE A DOUBLE-EDGED SWORD, THOUGH.
—I'VE NEVER FACED ANYONE FOR REAL SINCE "THAT TIME."
I REFUSED TO TRUST ANYONE, BARING MY TEETH BEFORE THEY COULD GET CLOSE...
...'COS I WAS SCARED.
...AND THAT'S ...
...MY WEAK-NESS, HUH...?
AND SHUUSEI ...?
HOW WAS IT WITH SHUUSEI?
WAS I REALLY FACING HIM ON THE LEVEL...?
WHAT IF...
MAYBE...
...I ONLY THOUGHT...
...I UNDERSTOOD HIM —— ?

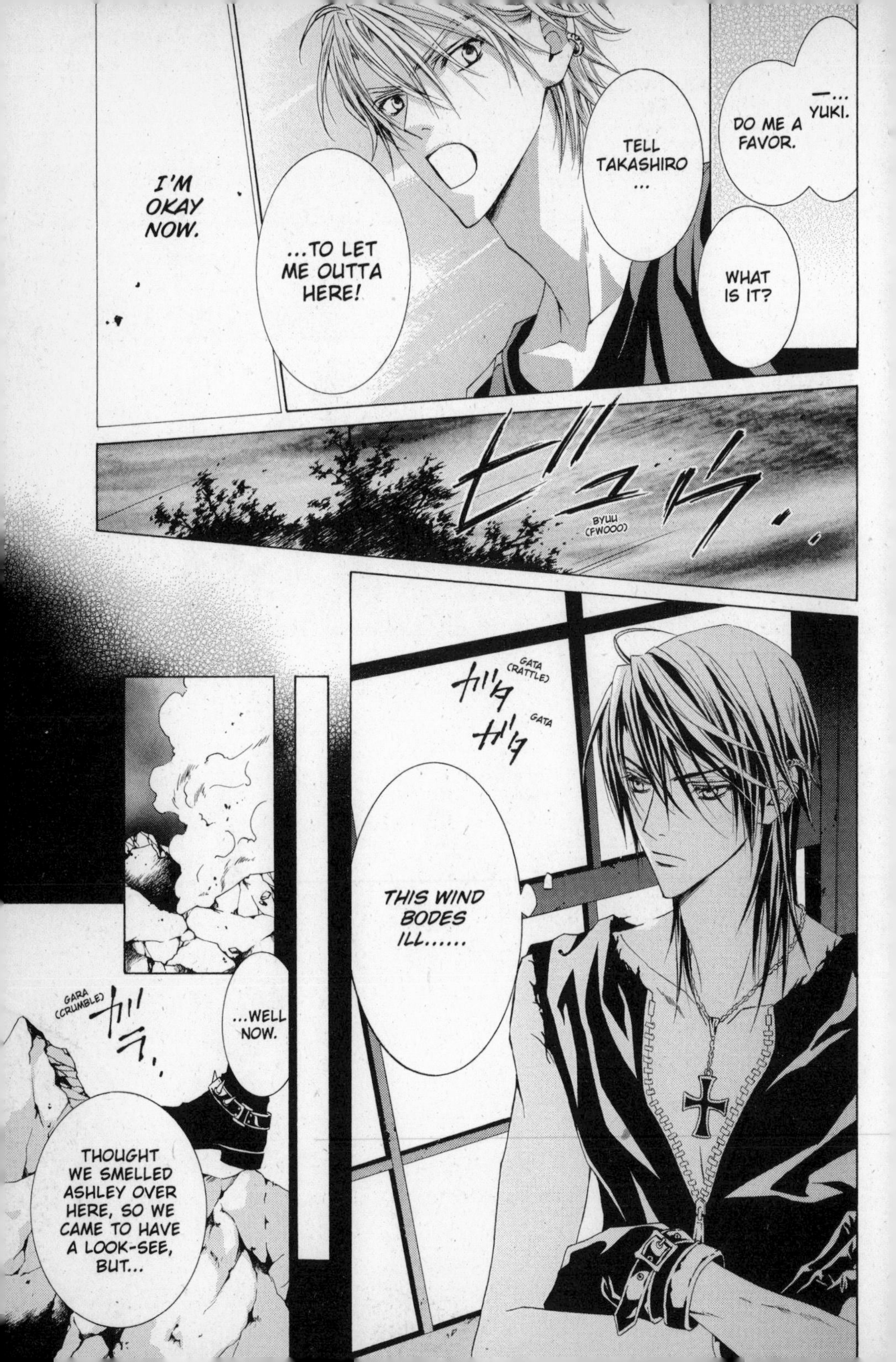
—... YUKI.
DO ME A FAVOR.
WHAT IS IT?
TELL TAKASHIRO ...
...TO LET ME OUTTA HERE!
I'M OKAY NOW.
BYUU (FWOOO)
GATA (RATTLE)
GATA
THIS WIND BODES ILL......
GARA (CRUMBLE)
...WELL NOW.
THOUGHT WE SMELLED ASHLEY OVER HERE, SO WE CAME TO HAVE A LOOK-SEE, BUT...

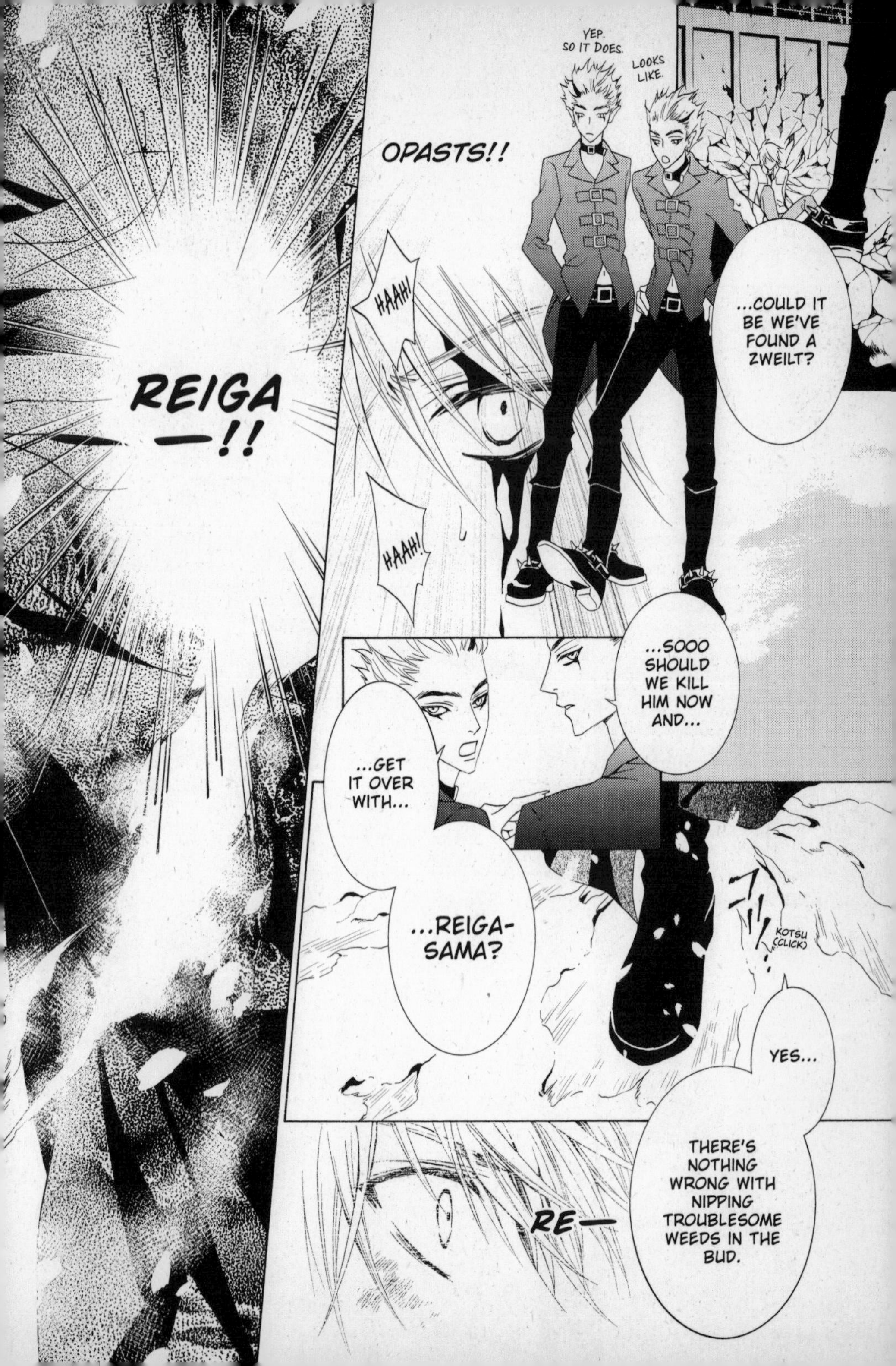
...COULD IT BE WE'VE FOUND A ZWEILT?
LOOKS LIKE.
YEP. SO IT DOES.
OPASTS!!
HAAH!
HAAH!
...SOOO SHOULD WE KILL HIM NOW AND...
...GET IT OVER WITH...
...REIGA-SAMA?
KOTSU (CLICK)
YES...
THERE'S NOTHING WRONG WITH NIPPING TROUBLESOME WEEDS IN THE BUD.
RE—
REIGA —!!

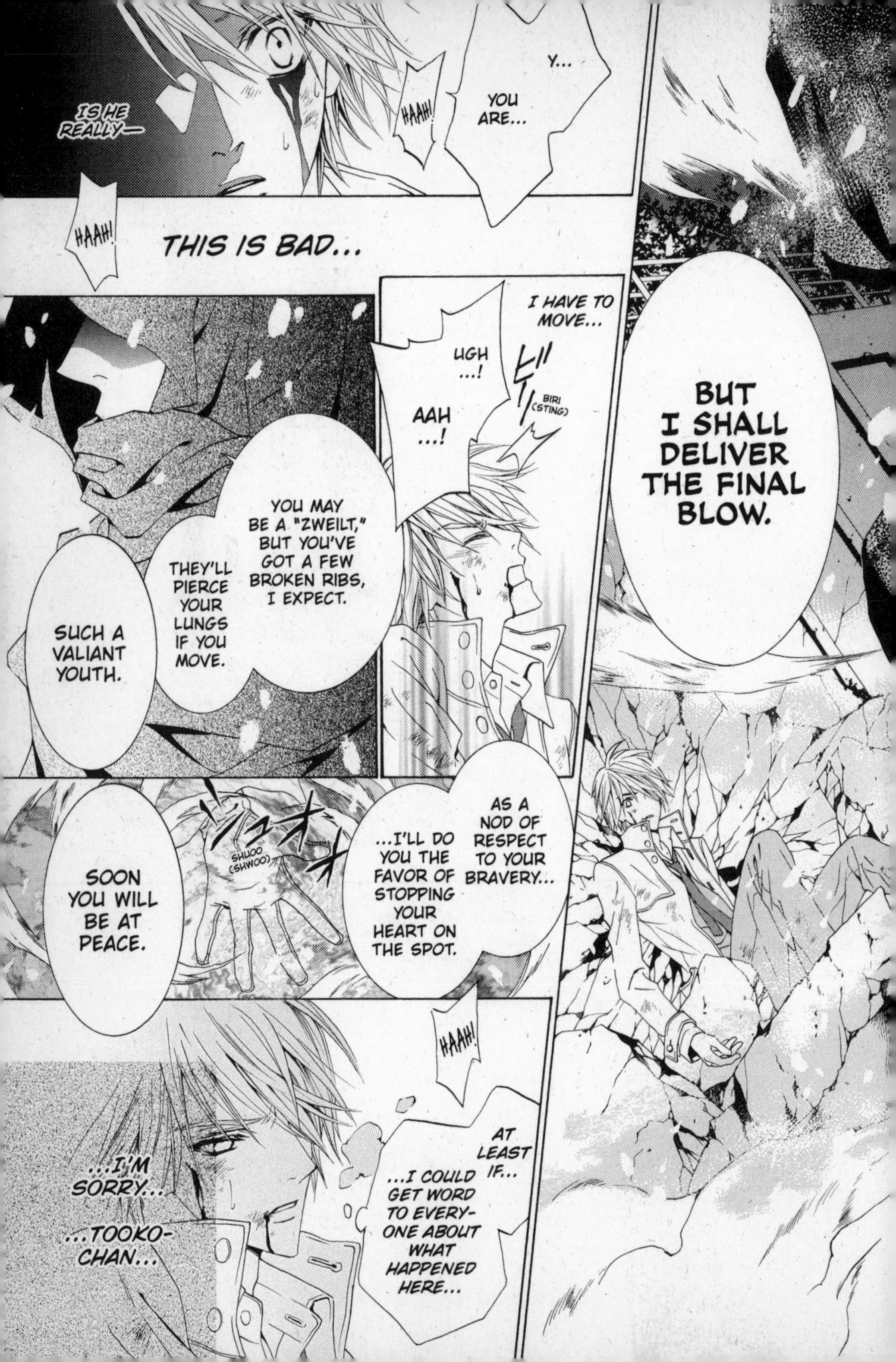
BUT I SHALL DELIVER THE FINAL BLOW.
Y...
YOU ARE...
HAAH!
IS HE REALLY—
HAAH!
THIS IS BAD...
I HAVE TO MOVE...
UGH ...!
BIRI (STING)
AAH ...!
YOU MAY BE A "ZWEILT," BUT YOU'VE GOT A FEW BROKEN RIBS, I EXPECT.
THEY'LL PIERCE YOUR LUNGS IF YOU MOVE.
SUCH A VALIANT YOUTH.
AS A NOD OF RESPECT TO YOUR BRAVERY...
...I'LL DO YOU THE FAVOR OF STOPPING YOUR HEART ON THE SPOT.
SHUOO (SHWOO)
SOON YOU WILL BE AT PEACE.
HAAH!
AT LEAST IF...
...I COULD GET WORD TO EVERY-ONE ABOUT WHAT HAPPENED HERE...
...I'M SORRY...
...TOOKO-CHAN...

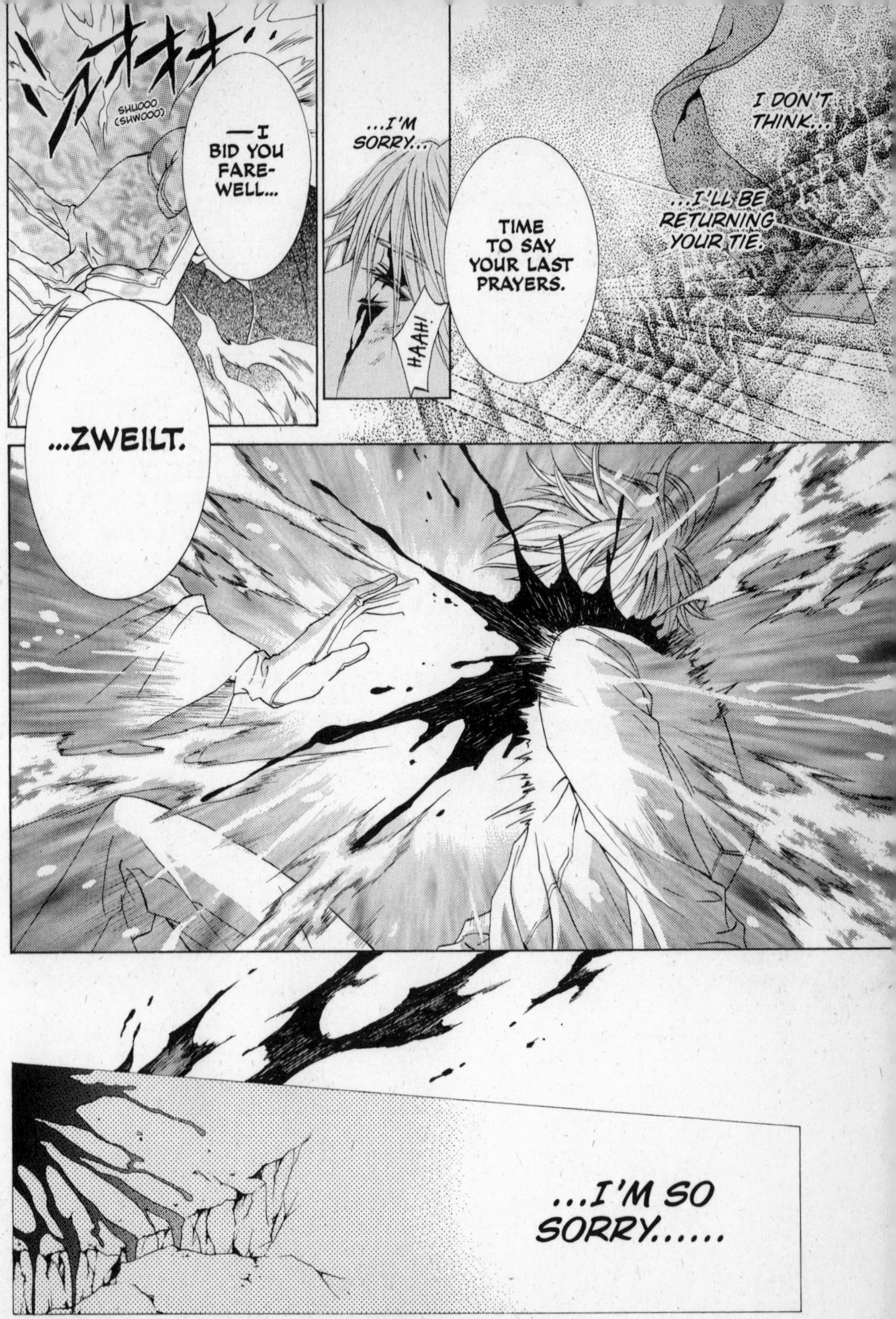
I DON'T THINK...
...I'LL BE RETURNING YOUR TIE.
...I'M SORRY...
TIME TO SAY YOUR LAST PRAYERS.
HAAH!
SHUOOO (SHWOOO)
—I BID YOU FARE-WELL...
...ZWEILT.
...I'M SO SORRY......

Story 14 END

Story 15
THAT WHICH IS FLEETING, STRONG, AND NOBLE

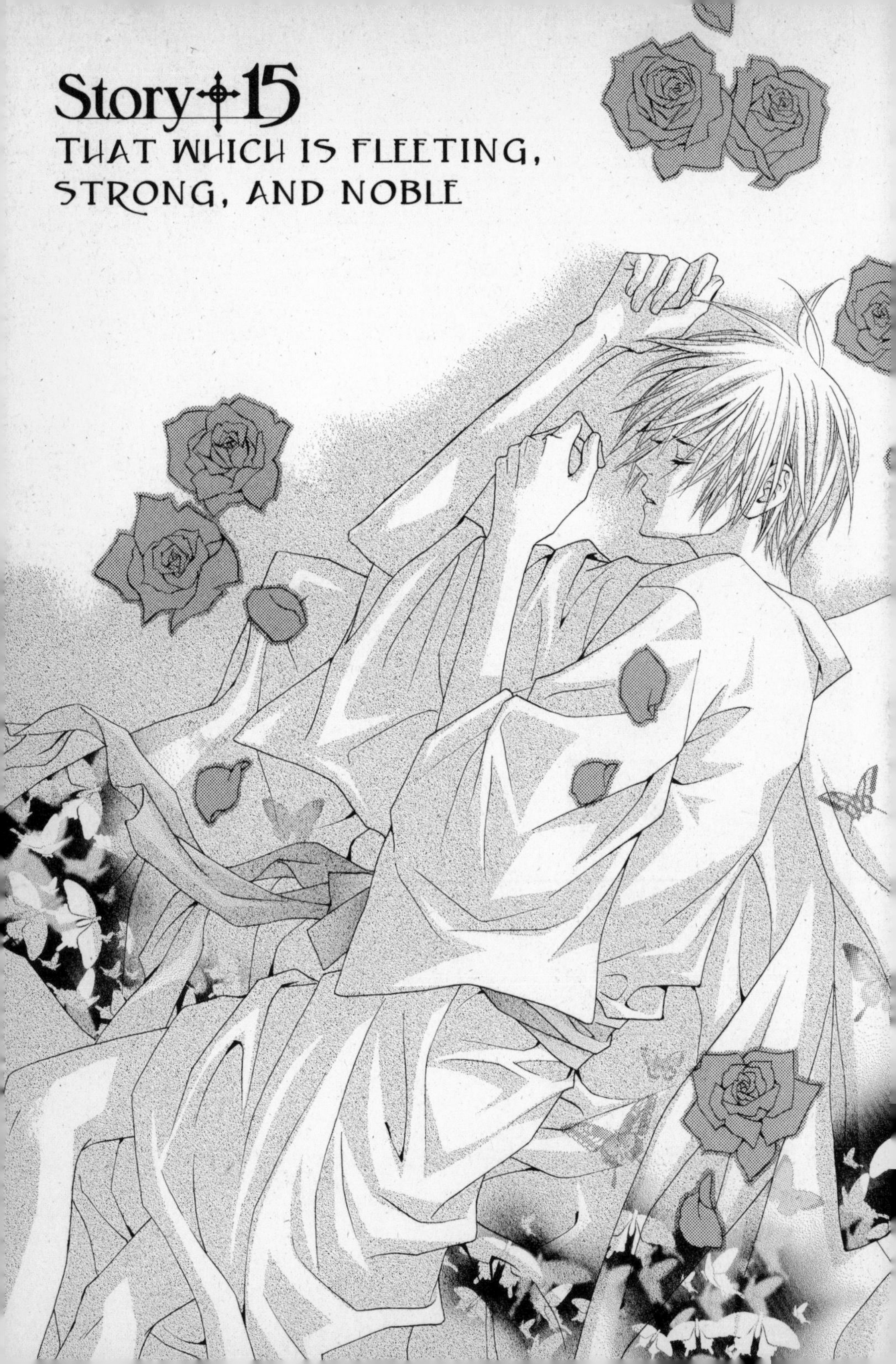

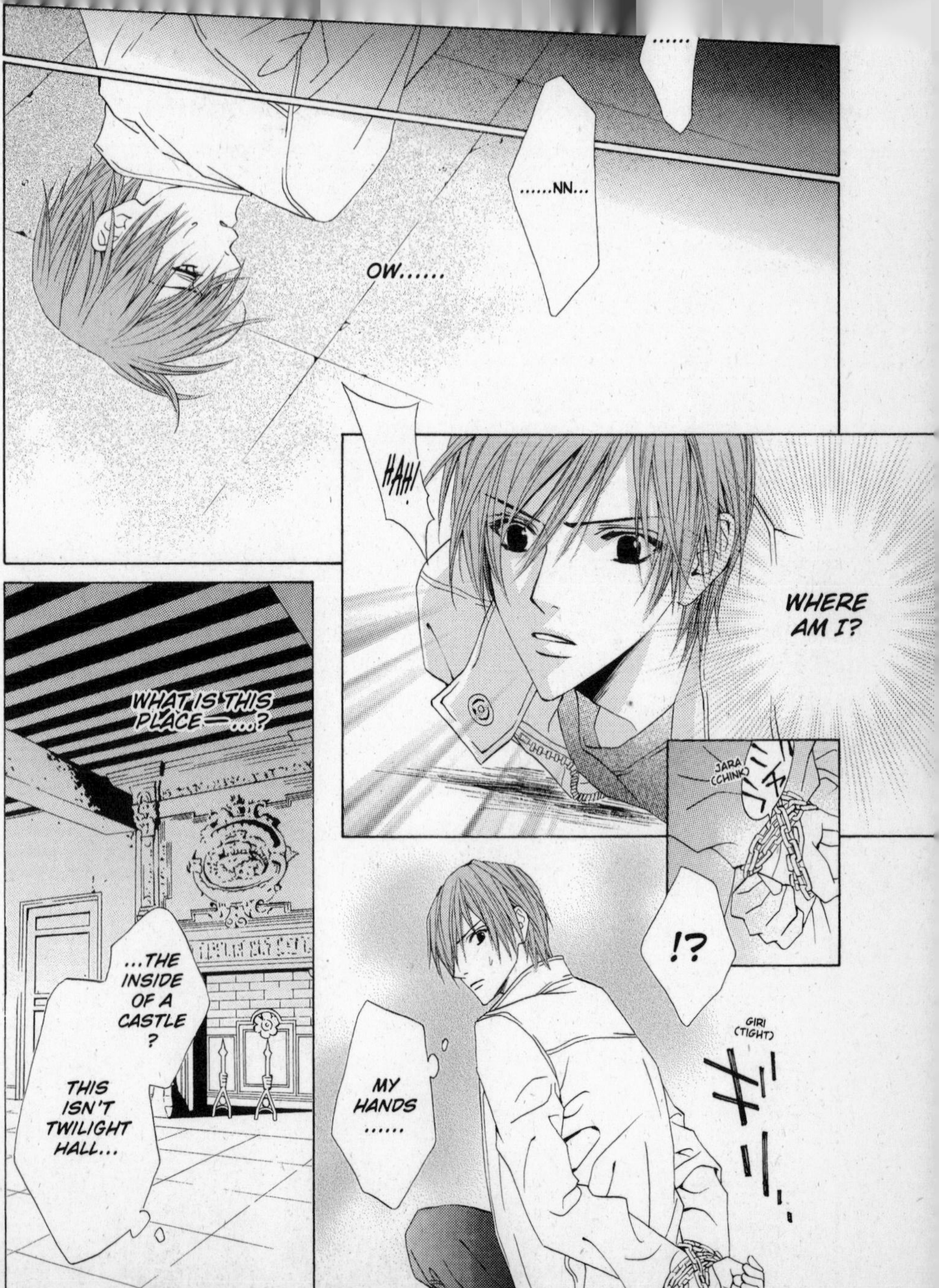
......
......NN...
OW......
HAH!
WHERE AM I?
JARA (CHINK)
!?
GIRI (TIGHT)
MY HANDS ......
WHAT IS THIS PLACE—...?
...THE INSIDE OF A CASTLE ?
THIS ISN'T TWILIGHT HALL...

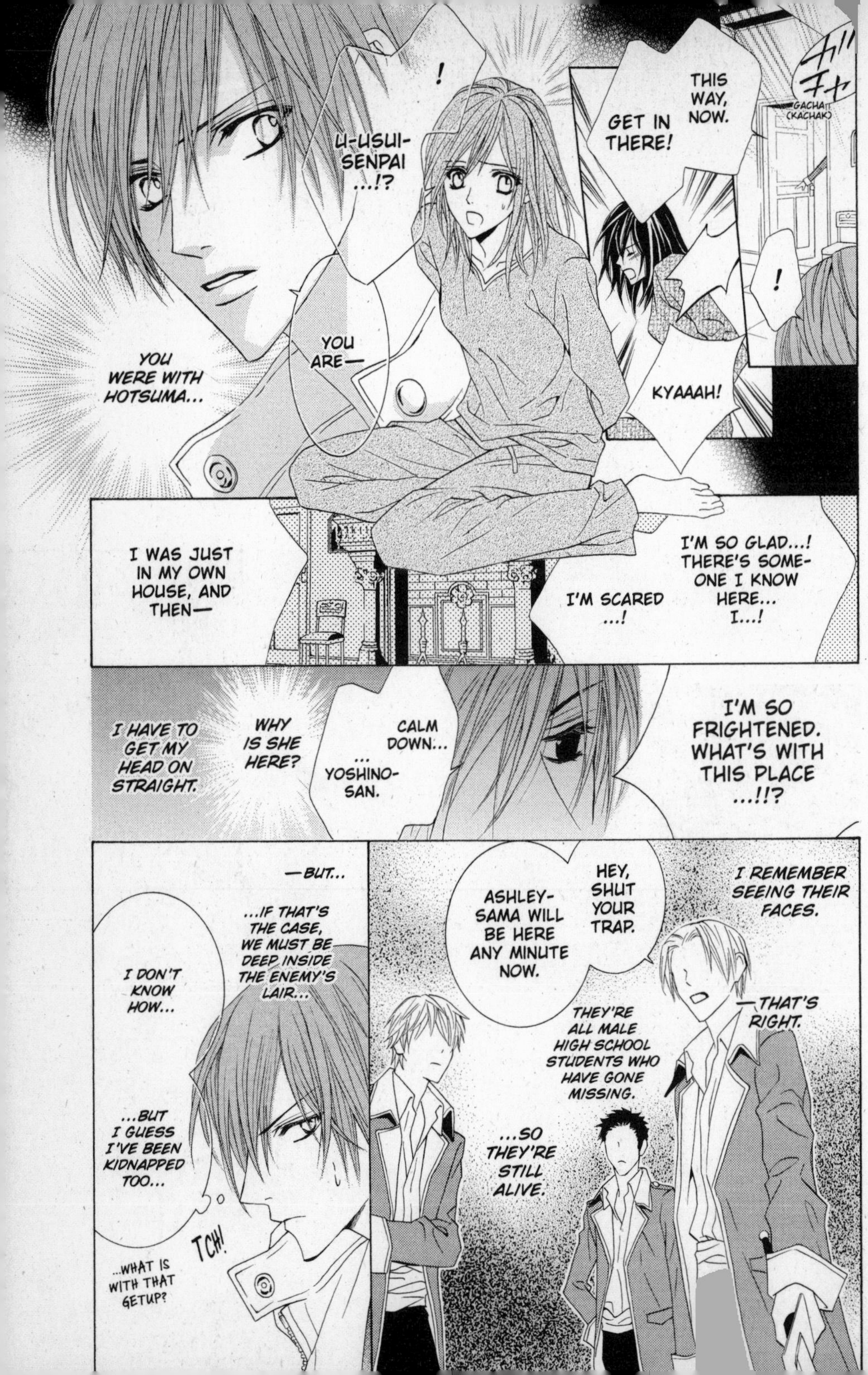
ガチャ
GACHA (KACHAK)
THIS WAY, NOW.
GET IN THERE!
!
KYAAAH!
!
U-USUI-SENPAI ...!?
YOU ARE—
YOU WERE WITH HOTSUMA...
I'M SO GLAD...! THERE'S SOME-ONE I KNOW HERE... I...!
I'M SCARED ...!
I WAS JUST IN MY OWN HOUSE, AND THEN—
I'M SO FRIGHTENED. WHAT'S WITH THIS PLACE ...!!?
CALM DOWN... ... YOSHINO-SAN.
WHY IS SHE HERE?
I HAVE TO GET MY HEAD ON STRAIGHT.
I REMEMBER SEEING THEIR FACES.
HEY, SHUT YOUR TRAP.
ASHLEY-SAMA WILL BE HERE ANY MINUTE NOW.
—THAT'S RIGHT.
THEY'RE ALL MALE HIGH SCHOOL STUDENTS WHO HAVE GONE MISSING.
...SO THEY'RE STILL ALIVE.
—BUT...
...IF THAT'S THE CASE, WE MUST BE DEEP INSIDE THE ENEMY'S LAIR...
I DON'T KNOW HOW...
...BUT I GUESS I'VE BEEN KIDNAPPED TOO...
TCH!
...WHAT IS WITH THAT GETUP?

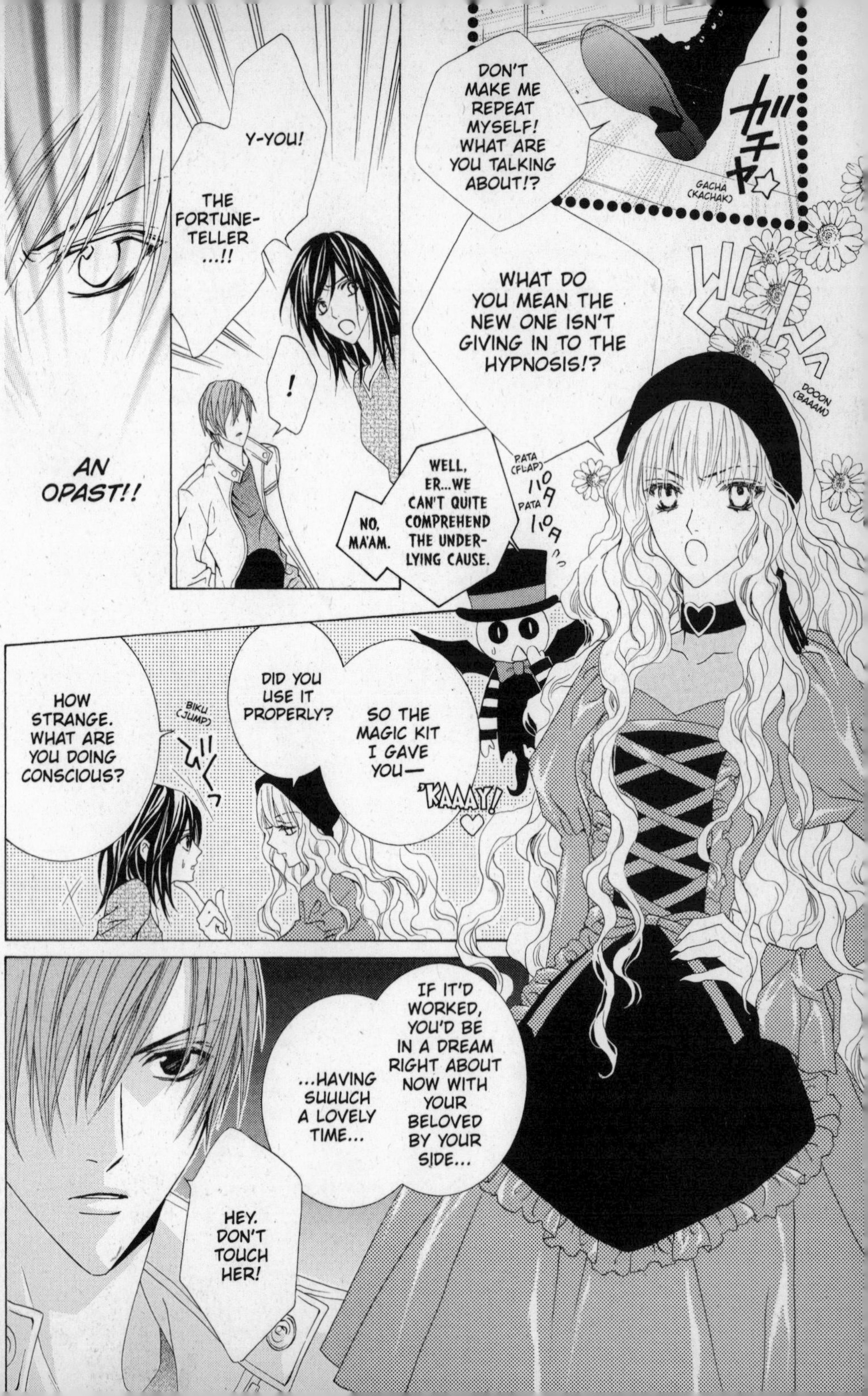
GACHA (KACHAK)
DON'T MAKE ME REPEAT MYSELF! WHAT ARE YOU TALKING ABOUT!?
WHAT DO YOU MEAN THE NEW ONE ISN'T GIVING IN TO THE HYPNOSIS!?
DOOON (BAAAM)
PATA (FLAP) PATA
NO, MA'AM.
WELL, ER...WE CAN'T QUITE COMPREHEND THE UNDER-LYING CAUSE.
Y-YOU!
THE FORTUNE-TELLER ...!!
!
AN OPAST!!
SO THE MAGIC KIT I GAVE YOU—
'KAAAY!
DID YOU USE IT PROPERLY?
BIKU (JUMP)
HOW STRANGE. WHAT ARE YOU DOING CONSCIOUS?
IF IT'D WORKED, YOU'D BE IN A DREAM RIGHT ABOUT NOW WITH YOUR BELOVED BY YOUR SIDE...
...HAVING SUUUCH A LOVELY TIME...
HEY. DON'T TOUCH HER!

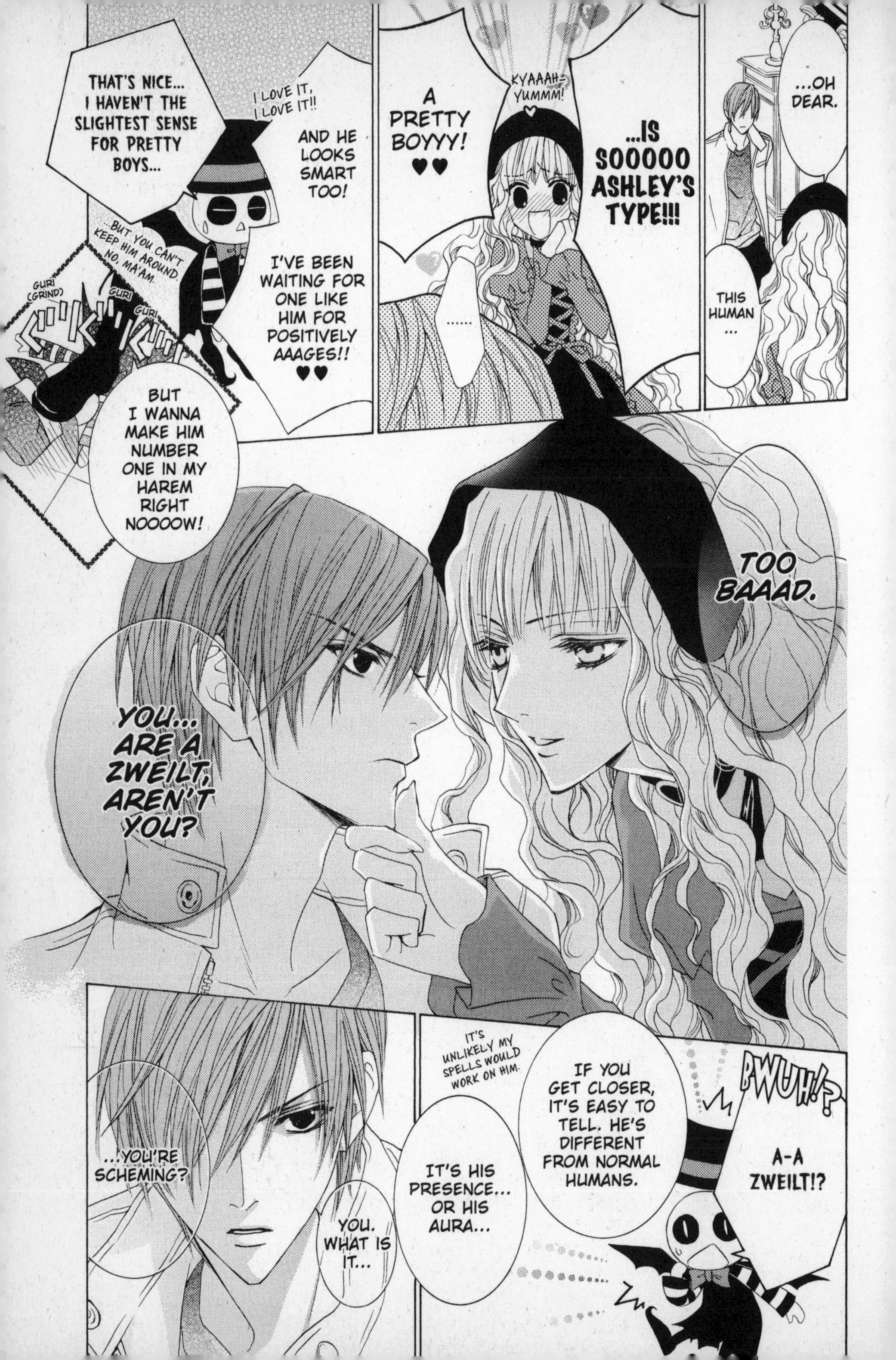

...OH DEAR.
THIS HUMAN ...
KYAAAH- YUMMM!
A PRETTY BOYYY! ♥♥
...IS SOOOOO ASHLEY'S TYPE!!!
......
THAT'S NICE... I HAVEN'T THE SLIGHTEST SENSE FOR PRETTY BOYS...
I LOVE IT, I LOVE IT!!
AND HE LOOKS SMART TOO!
I'VE BEEN WAITING FOR ONE LIKE HIM FOR POSITIVELY AAAGES!! ♥♥
...BUT YOU CAN'T KEEP HIM AROUND. NO, MA'AM.
GURI (GRIND) GURI GURI
BUT I WANNA MAKE HIM NUMBER ONE IN MY HAREM RIGHT NOOOOW!
TOO BAAAD.
YOU... ARE A ZWEILT, AREN'T YOU?
PWUH!?
A-A ZWEILT!?
IF YOU GET CLOSER, IT'S EASY TO TELL. HE'S DIFFERENT FROM NORMAL HUMANS.
IT'S UNLIKELY MY SPELLS WOULD WORK ON HIM.
IT'S HIS PRESENCE... OR HIS AURA...
YOU. WHAT IS IT...
...YOU'RE SCHEMING?

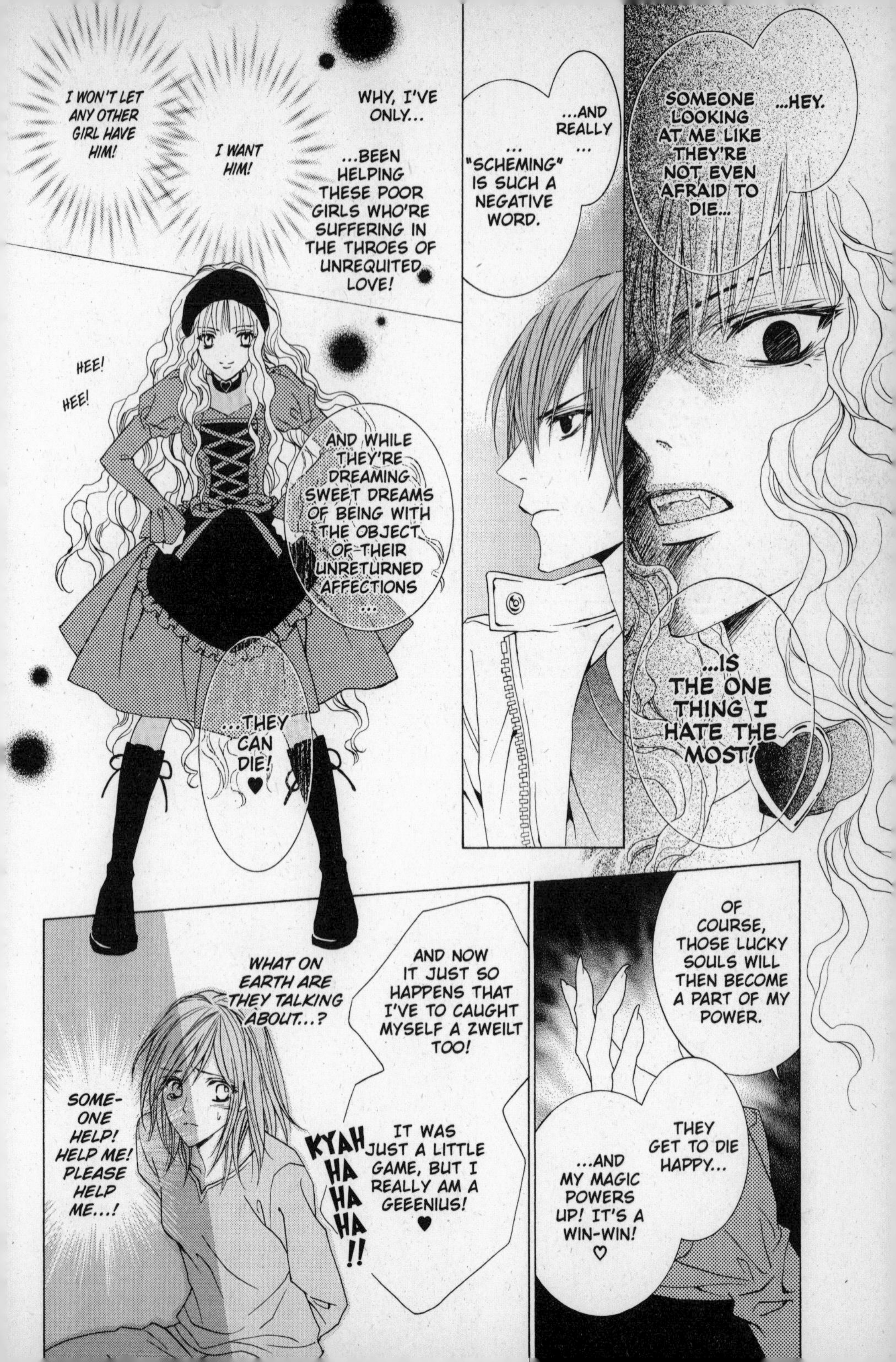
...HEY.
SOMEONE LOOKING AT ME LIKE THEY'RE NOT EVEN AFRAID TO DIE...
...IS THE ONE THING I HATE THE MOST!
...AND REALLY ...
... "SCHEMING" IS SUCH A NEGATIVE WORD.
WHY, I'VE ONLY...
...BEEN HELPING THESE POOR GIRLS WHO'RE SUFFERING IN THE THROES OF UNREQUITED LOVE!
I WANT HIM!
I WON'T LET ANY OTHER GIRL HAVE HIM!
AND WHILE THEY'RE DREAMING SWEET DREAMS OF BEING WITH THE OBJECT OF THEIR UNRETURNED AFFECTIONS ...
...THEY CAN DIE! ♥
HEE! HEE!
OF COURSE, THOSE LUCKY SOULS WILL THEN BECOME A PART OF MY POWER.
THEY GET TO DIE HAPPY...
...AND MY MAGIC POWERS UP! IT'S A WIN-WIN! ♡
AND NOW IT JUST SO HAPPENS THAT I'VE TO CAUGHT MYSELF A ZWEILT TOO!
WHAT ON EARTH ARE THEY TALKING ABOUT...?
IT WAS JUST A LITTLE GAME, BUT I REALLY AM A GEEENIUS! ♥
KYAH HA HA HA HA!!
SOME-ONE HELP! HELP ME! PLEASE HELP ME...!

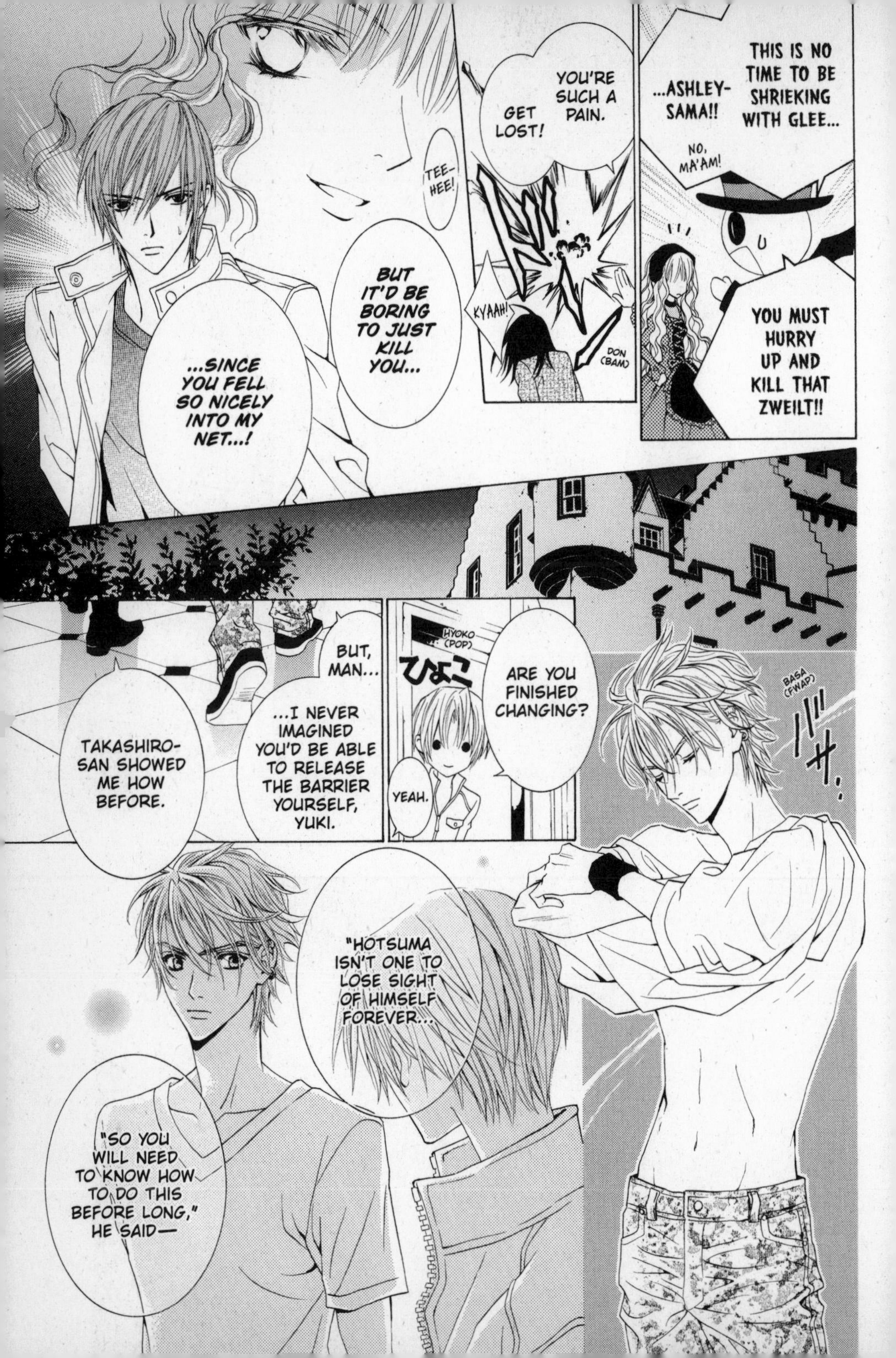
THIS IS NO TIME TO BE SHRIEKING WITH GLEE...
...ASHLEY-SAMA!!
NO, MA'AM!
YOU MUST HURRY UP AND KILL THAT ZWEILT!!
YOU'RE SUCH A PAIN.
GET LOST!
KYAAH!
DON (BAM)
TEE-HEE!
BUT IT'D BE BORING TO JUST KILL YOU...
...SINCE YOU FELL SO NICELY INTO MY NET...!
HYOKO (POP)
ひょこ
ARE YOU FINISHED CHANGING?
YEAH.
BASA (FWAP)
バサ
BUT, MAN...
...I NEVER IMAGINED YOU'D BE ABLE TO RELEASE THE BARRIER YOURSELF, YUKI.
TAKASHIRO-SAN SHOWED ME HOW BEFORE.
"HOTSUMA ISN'T ONE TO LOSE SIGHT OF HIMSELF FOREVER...
"SO YOU WILL NEED TO KNOW HOW TO DO THIS BEFORE LONG," HE SAID—

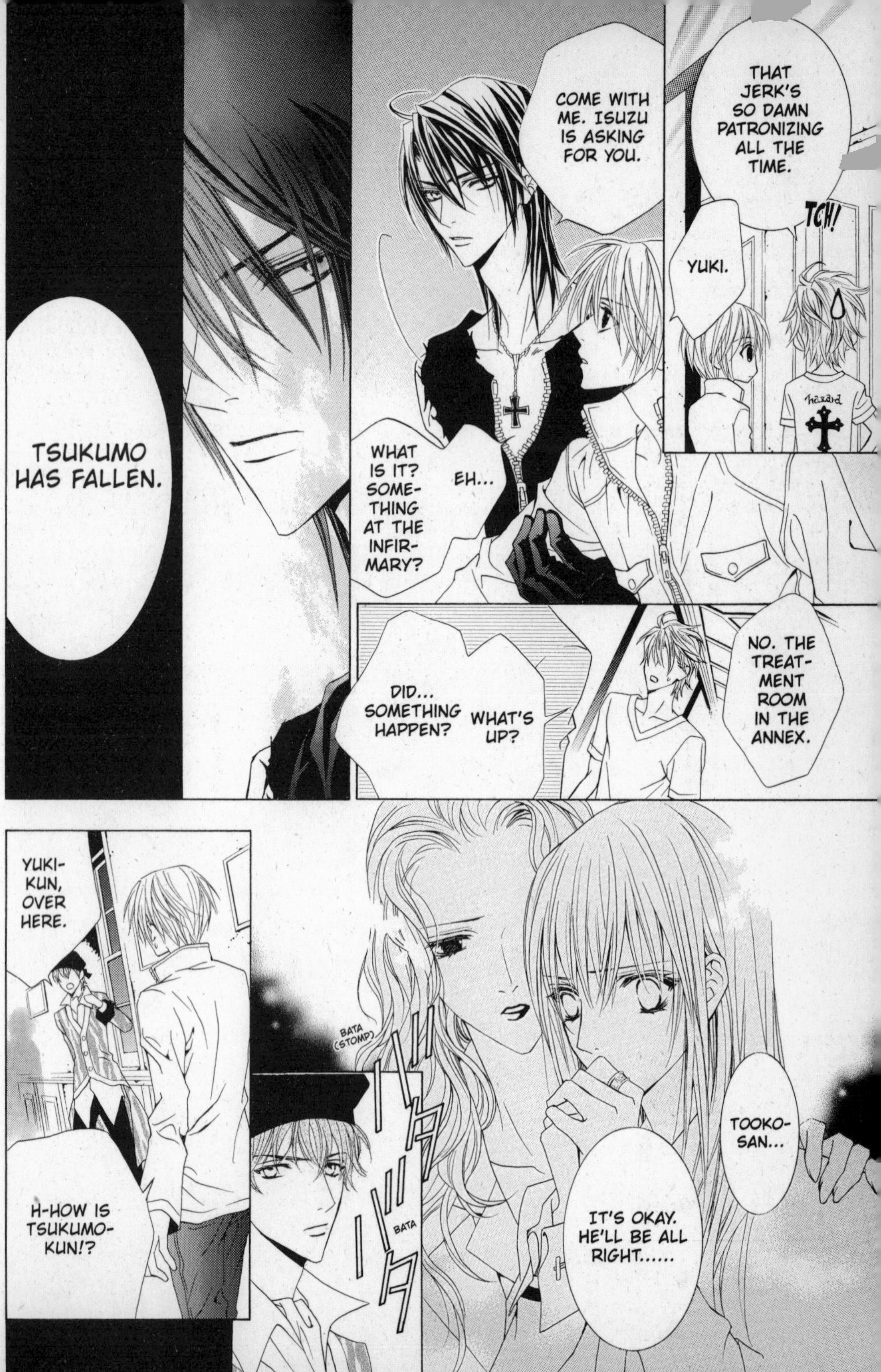
THAT JERK'S SO DAMN PATRONIZING ALL THE TIME.
TCH!
YUKI.
COME WITH ME. ISUZU IS ASKING FOR YOU.
EH...
WHAT IS IT? SOMETHING AT THE INFIRMARY?
NO. THE TREATMENT ROOM IN THE ANNEX.
WHAT'S UP?
DID... SOMETHING HAPPEN?
TSUKUMO HAS FALLEN.
TOOKO-SAN...
IT'S OKAY. HE'LL BE ALL RIGHT......
BATA (STOMP)
BATA
YUKI-KUN, OVER HERE.
H-HOW IS TSUKUMO-KUN!?

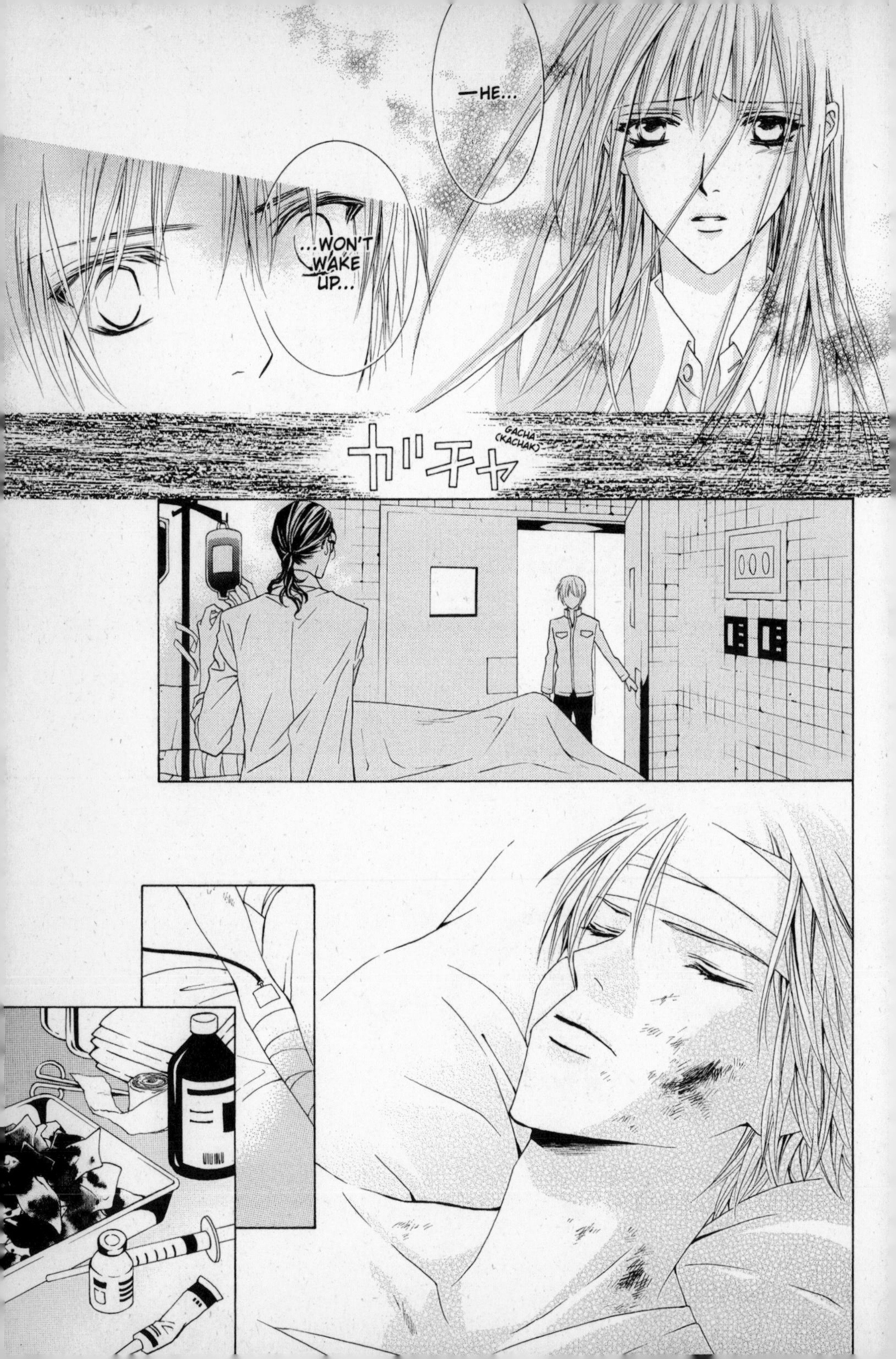
—HE...
...WON'T WAKE UP...
カチャ
GACHA (KACHAK)

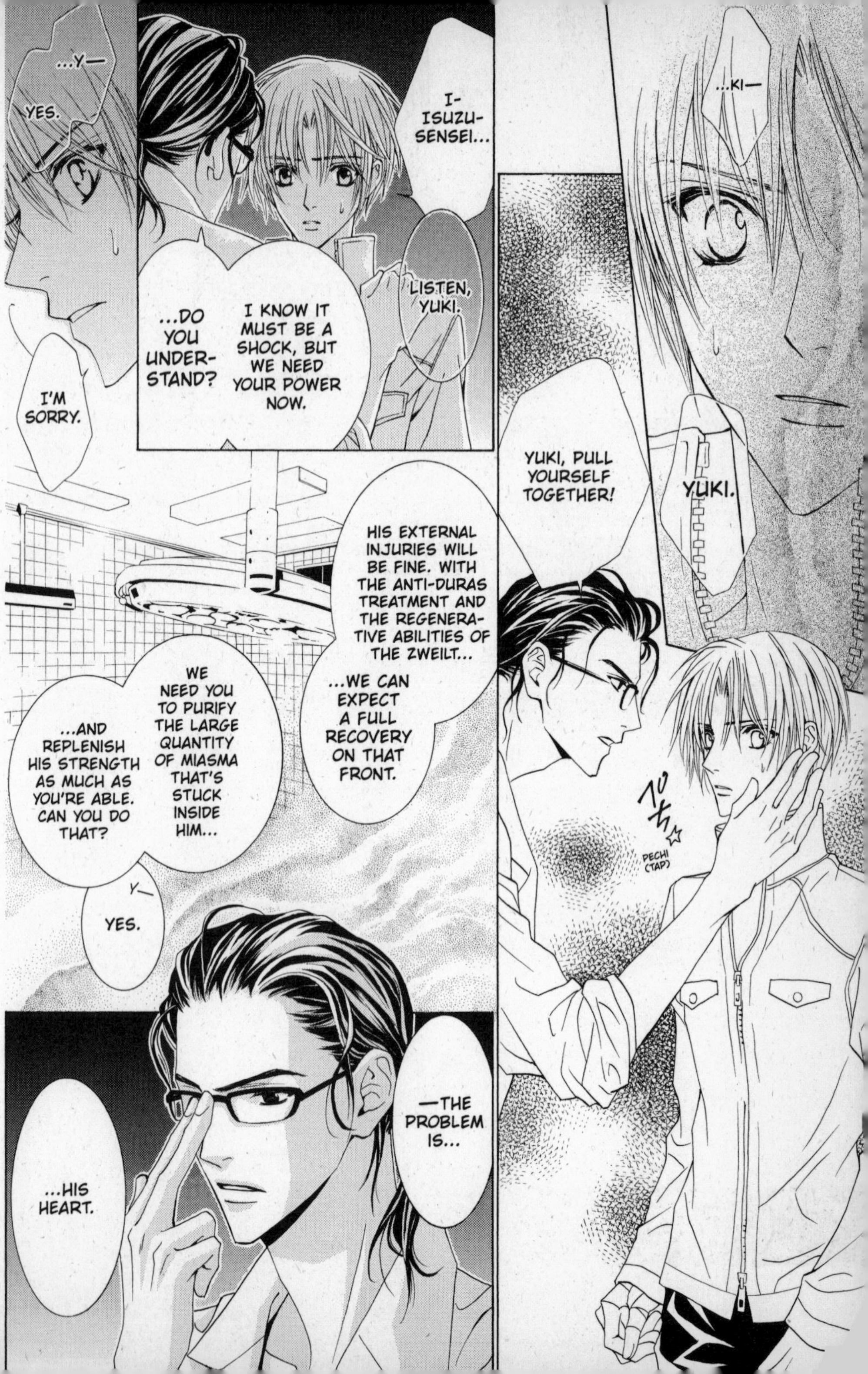
...KI—
YUKI.
YUKI, PULL YOURSELF TOGETHER!
PECHI (TAP)
I- ISUZU-SENSEI...
LISTEN, YUKI.
I KNOW IT MUST BE A SHOCK, BUT WE NEED YOUR POWER NOW.
...DO YOU UNDERSTAND?
...Y— YES.
I'M SORRY.
HIS EXTERNAL INJURIES WILL BE FINE. WITH THE ANTI-DURAS TREATMENT AND THE REGENERATIVE ABILITIES OF THE ZWEILT...
...WE CAN EXPECT A FULL RECOVERY ON THAT FRONT.
WE NEED YOU TO PURIFY THE LARGE QUANTITY OF MIASMA THAT'S STUCK INSIDE HIM...
...AND REPLENISH HIS STRENGTH AS MUCH AS YOU'RE ABLE. CAN YOU DO THAT?
Y— YES.
—THE PROBLEM IS...
...HIS HEART.

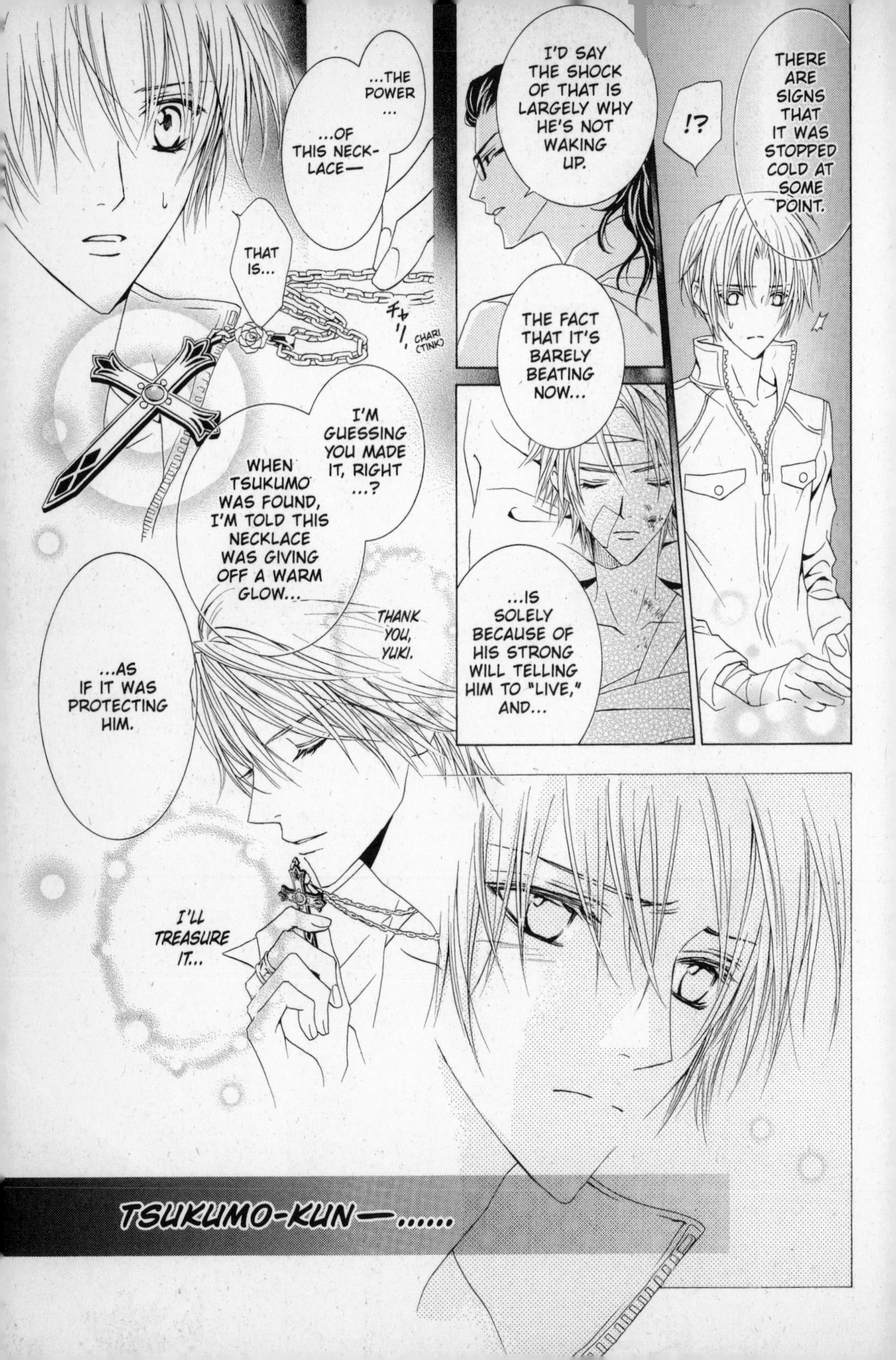
THERE ARE SIGNS THAT IT WAS STOPPED COLD AT SOME POINT.
!?
I'D SAY THE SHOCK OF THAT IS LARGELY WHY HE'S NOT WAKING UP.
THE FACT THAT IT'S BARELY BEATING NOW...
...IS SOLELY BECAUSE OF HIS STRONG WILL TELLING HIM TO "LIVE," AND...
...THE POWER...
...OF THIS NECK-LACE—
THAT IS...
CHARI (TINK)
I'M GUESSING YOU MADE IT, RIGHT...?
WHEN TSUKUMO WAS FOUND, I'M TOLD THIS NECKLACE WAS GIVING OFF A WARM GLOW...
...AS IF IT WAS PROTECTING HIM.
THANK YOU, YUKI.
I'LL TREASURE IT...
TSUKUMO-KUN—......

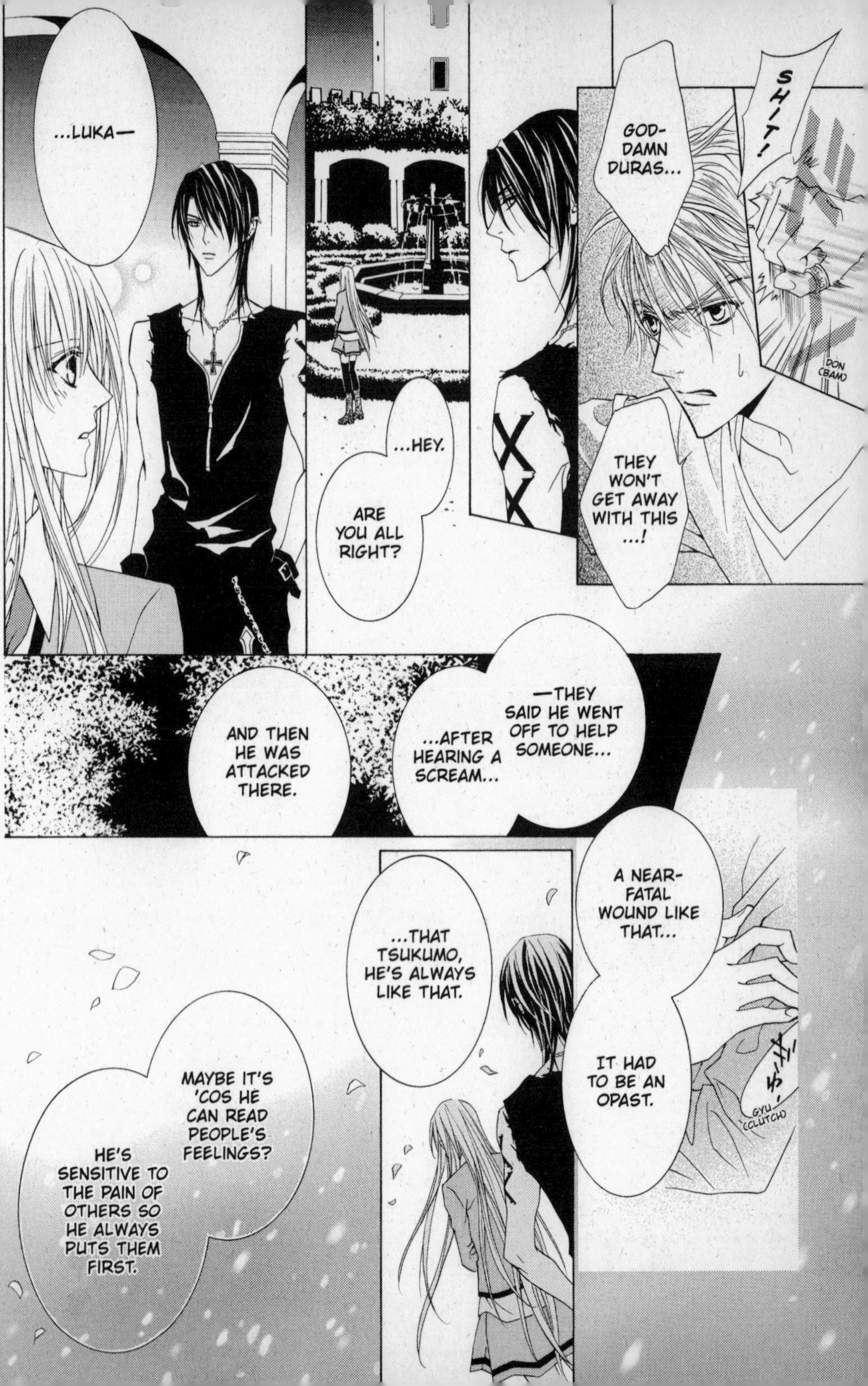
SHIT!
DON (BAM)
GOD-DAMN DURAS...
THEY WON'T GET AWAY WITH THIS...!
...HEY.
ARE YOU ALL RIGHT?
...LUKA—
—THEY SAID HE WENT OFF TO HELP SOMEONE...
...AFTER HEARING A SCREAM...
AND THEN HE WAS ATTACKED THERE.
A NEAR-FATAL WOUND LIKE THAT...
IT HAD TO BE AN OPAST.
GYU (CLUTCH)
...THAT TSUKUMO, HE'S ALWAYS LIKE THAT.
MAYBE IT'S 'COS HE CAN READ PEOPLE'S FEELINGS?
HE'S SENSITIVE TO THE PAIN OF OTHERS SO HE ALWAYS PUTS THEM FIRST.

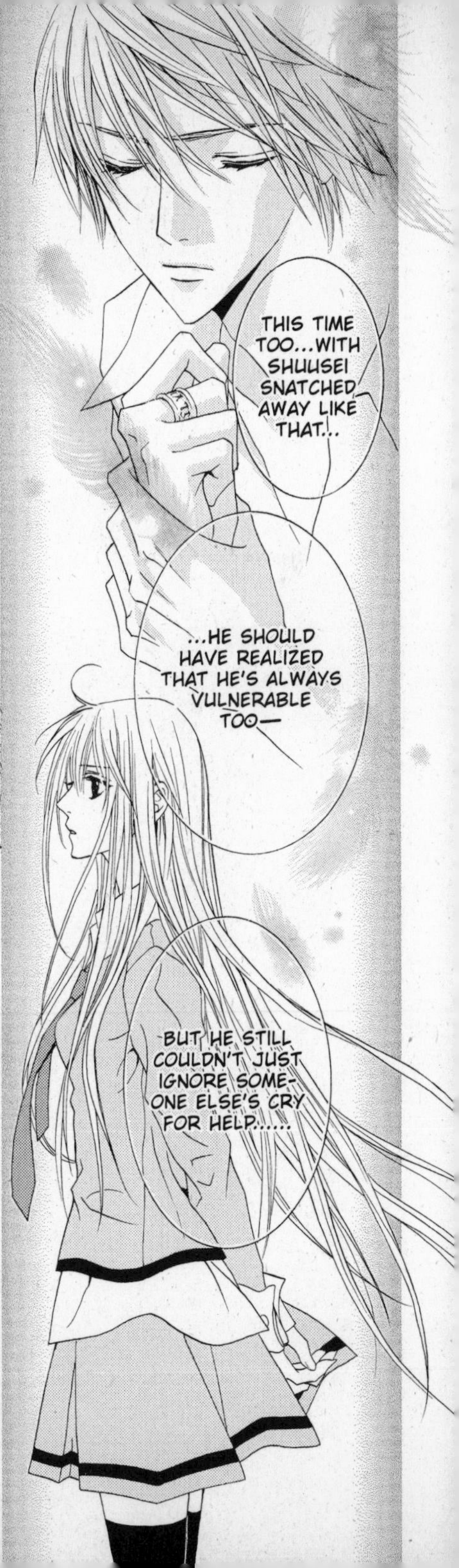
THIS TIME TOO...WITH SHUUSEI SNATCHED AWAY LIKE THAT...
...HE SHOULD HAVE REALIZED THAT HE'S ALWAYS VULNERABLE TOO—
BUT HE STILL COULDN'T JUST IGNORE SOME-ONE ELSE'S CRY FOR HELP......

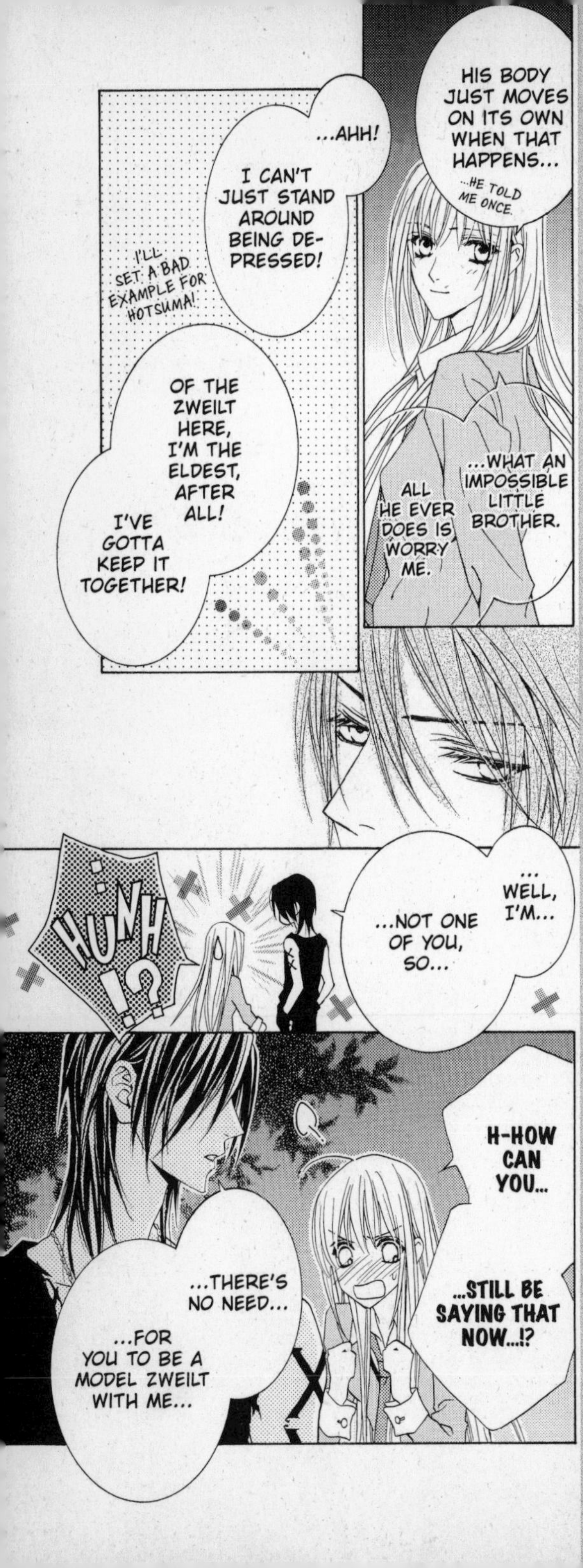
HIS BODY JUST MOVES ON ITS OWN WHEN THAT HAPPENS...
...HE TOLD ME ONCE.
...WHAT AN IMPOSSIBLE LITTLE BROTHER.
ALL HE EVER DOES IS WORRY ME.
...AHH!
I CAN'T JUST STAND AROUND BEING DE-PRESSED!
I'LL SET A BAD EXAMPLE FOR HOTSUMA!
OF THE ZWEILT HERE, I'M THE ELDEST, AFTER ALL!
I'VE GOTTA KEEP IT TOGETHER!
... WELL, I'M...
...NOT ONE OF YOU, SO...
HUNH !?
H-HOW CAN YOU...
...STILL BE SAYING THAT NOW...!?
...THERE'S NO NEED...
...FOR YOU TO BE A MODEL ZWEILT WITH ME...

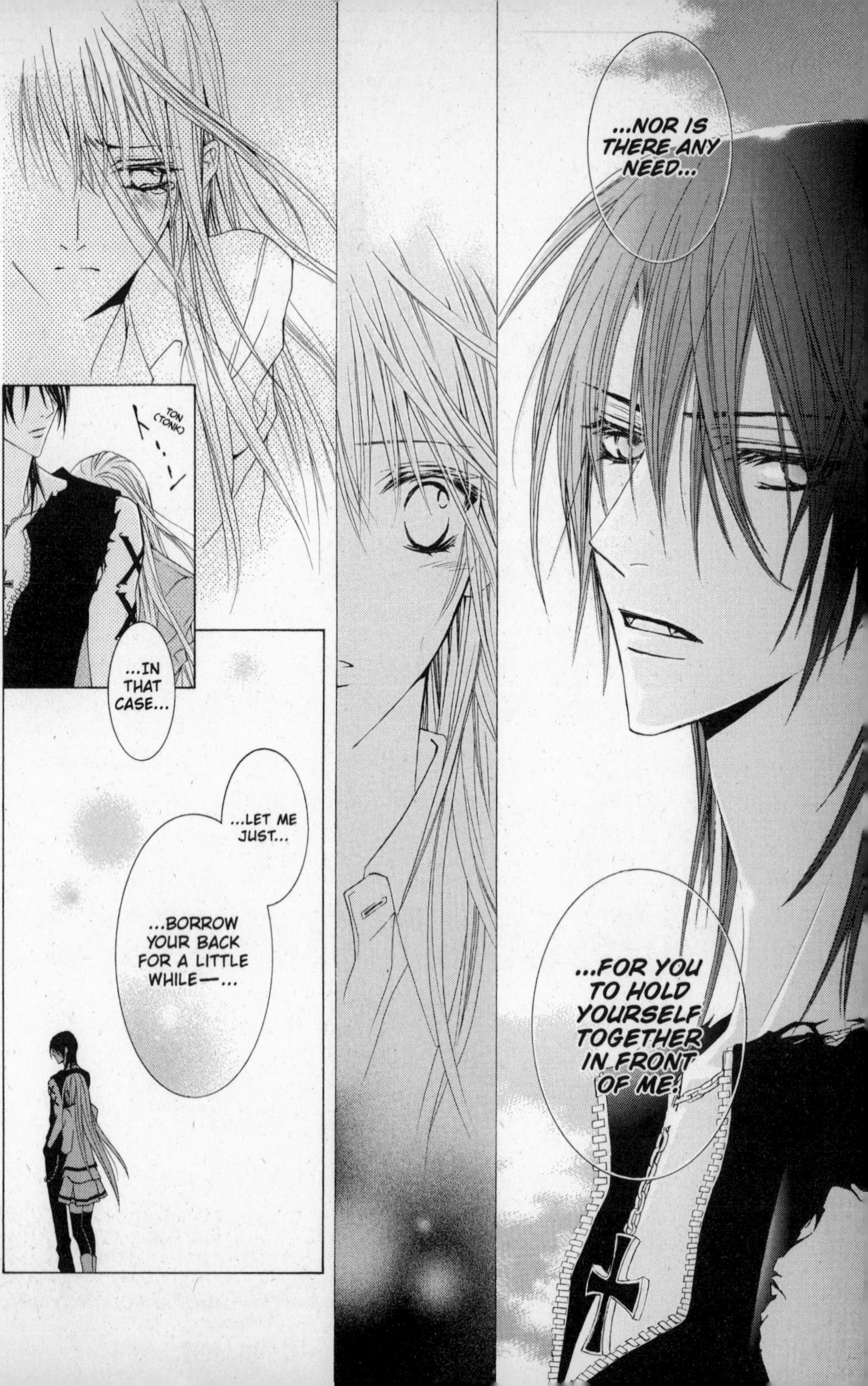
...NOR IS THERE ANY NEED...
...FOR YOU TO HOLD YOURSELF TOGETHER IN FRONT OF ME!
TON (TONK)
...IN THAT CASE...
...LET ME JUST...
...BORROW YOUR BACK FOR A LITTLE WHILE—...

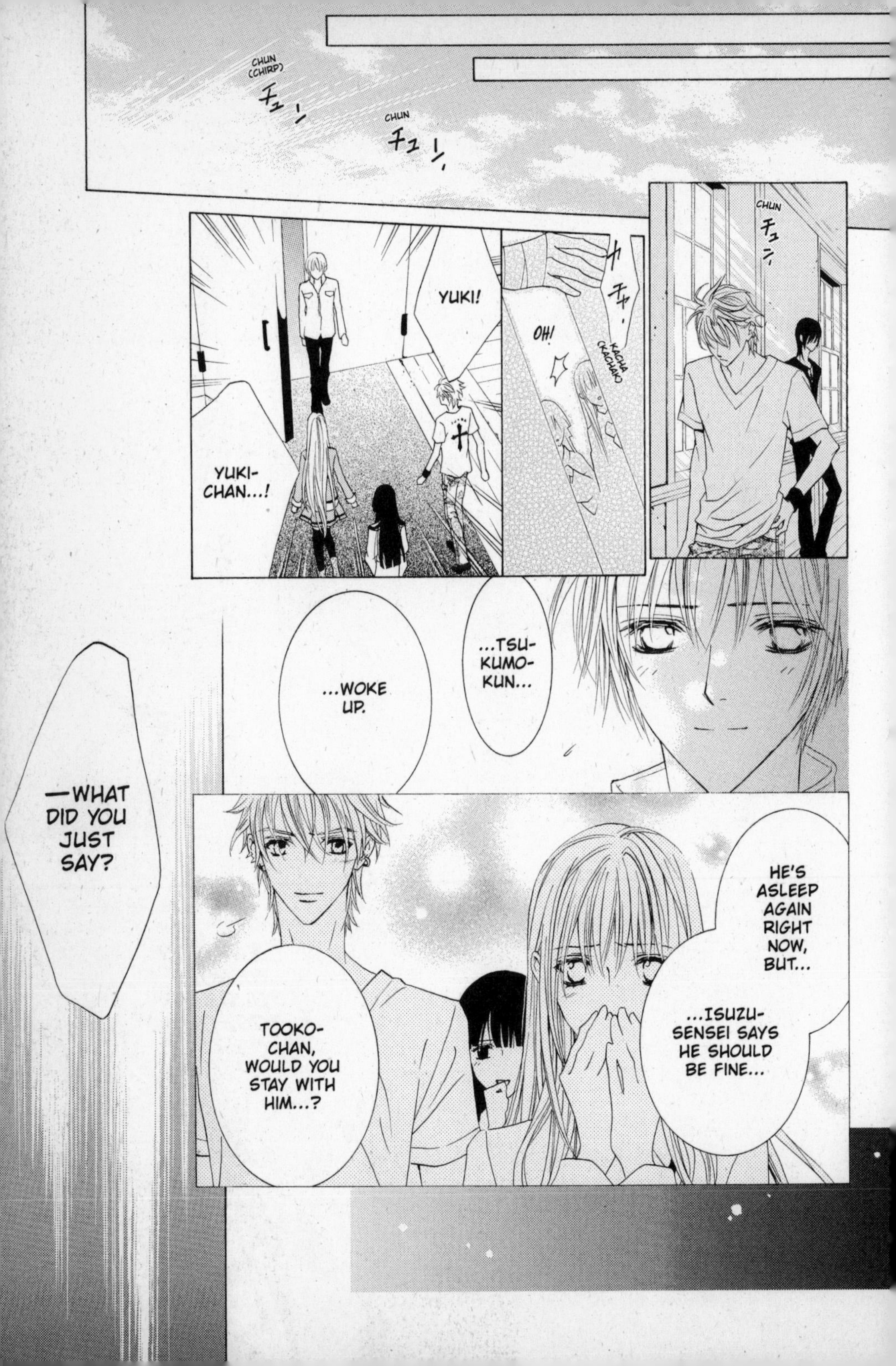
CHUN (CHIRP)
チュン
CHUN
チュン
CHUN
チュン
KACHA (KACHAN)
ガチャ
OH!
YUKI!
YUKI-CHAN...!
...TSU-KUMO-KUN...
...WOKE UP.
HE'S ASLEEP AGAIN RIGHT NOW, BUT...
...ISUZU-SENSEI SAYS HE SHOULD BE FINE...
TOOKO-CHAN, WOULD YOU STAY WITH HIM...?
—WHAT DID YOU JUST SAY?

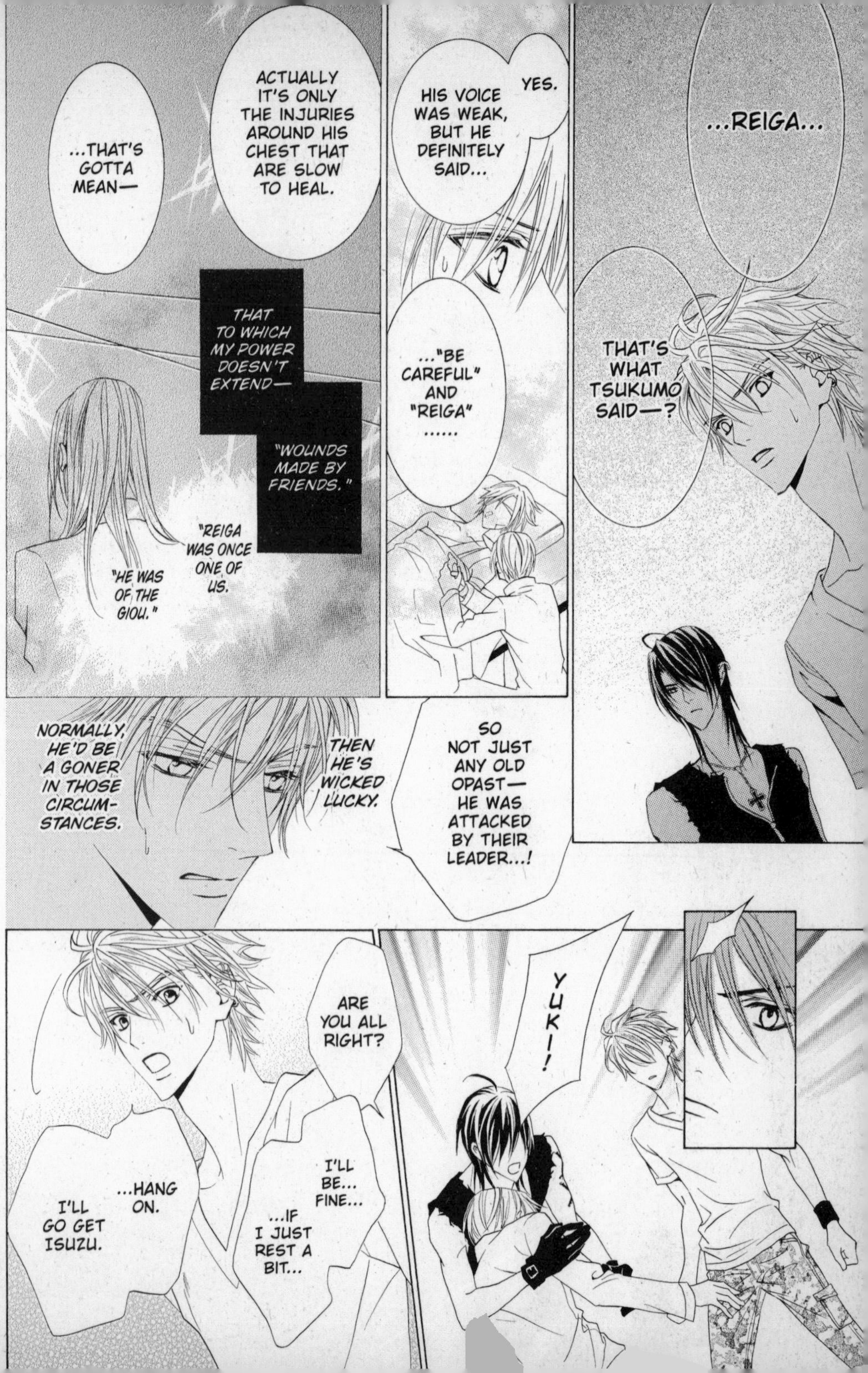

...REIGA...
THAT'S WHAT TSUKUMO SAID—?
YES.
HIS VOICE WAS WEAK, BUT HE DEFINITELY SAID...
..."BE CAREFUL" AND "REIGA" ......
ACTUALLY IT'S ONLY THE INJURIES AROUND HIS CHEST THAT ARE SLOW TO HEAL.
...THAT'S GOTTA MEAN—
THAT TO WHICH MY POWER DOESN'T EXTEND—
"WOUNDS MADE BY FRIENDS."
"REIGA WAS ONCE ONE OF US.
"HE WAS OF THE GIOU."
SO NOT JUST ANY OLD OPAST—HE WAS ATTACKED BY THEIR LEADER...!
THEN HE'S WICKED LUCKY.
NORMALLY, HE'D BE A GONER IN THOSE CIRCUM-STANCES.
YUKI!
ARE YOU ALL RIGHT?
I'LL BE... FINE...
...IF I JUST REST A BIT...
...HANG ON.
I'LL GO GET ISUZU.

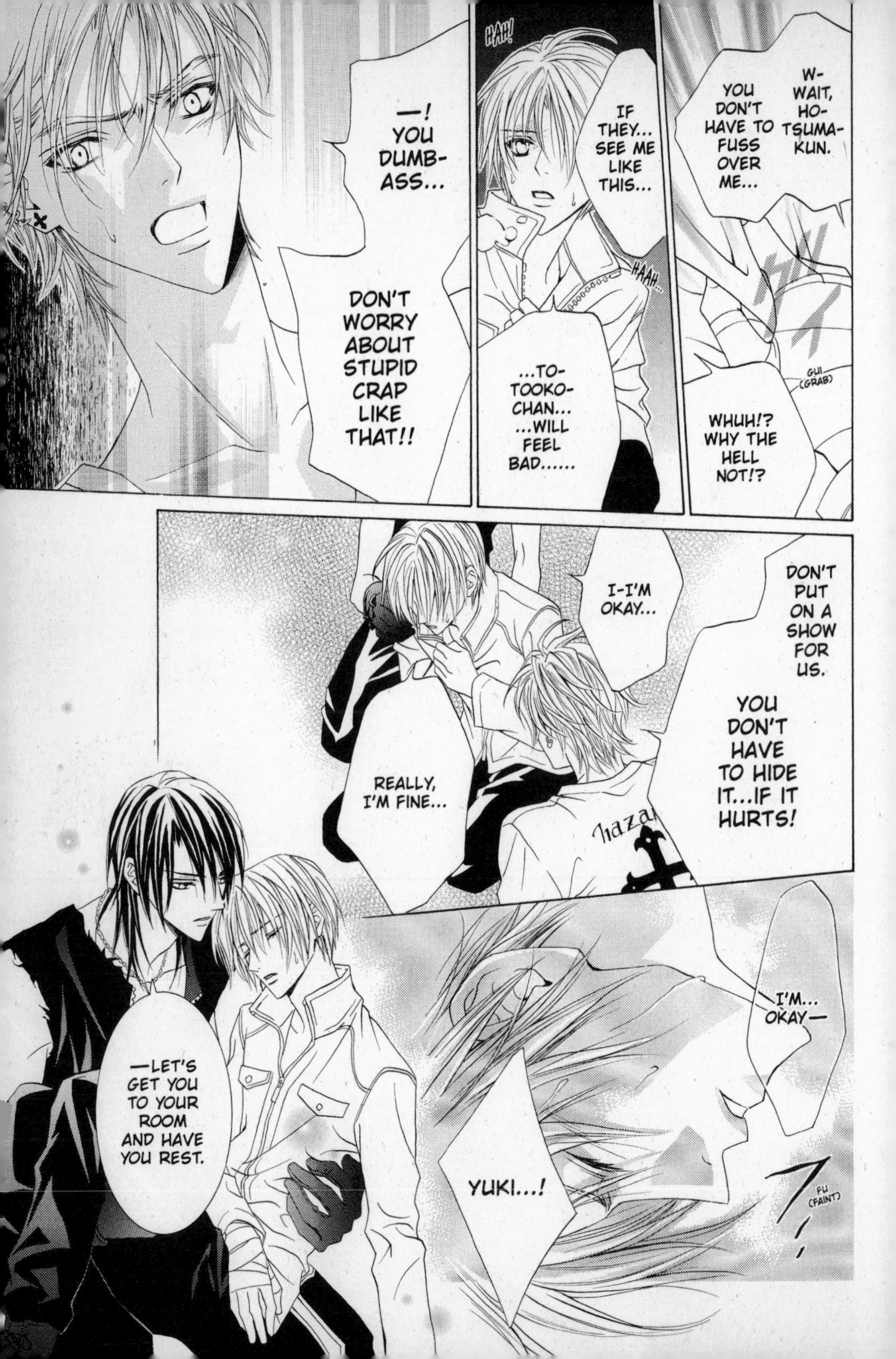
W-WAIT, HO-TSUMA-KUN.
YOU DON'T HAVE TO FUSS OVER ME...
GUI (GRAB)
WHUH!? WHY THE HELL NOT!?
HAH!
IF THEY... SEE ME LIKE THIS...
HAAH...
...TO-TOOKO-CHAN... ...WILL FEEL BAD......
—! YOU DUMB-ASS...
DON'T WORRY ABOUT STUPID CRAP LIKE THAT!!
DON'T PUT ON A SHOW FOR US.
YOU DON'T HAVE TO HIDE IT...IF IT HURTS!
I-I'M OKAY...
REALLY, I'M FINE...
I'M... OKAY—
FU (FAINT)
YUKI...!
—LET'S GET YOU TO YOUR ROOM AND HAVE YOU REST.

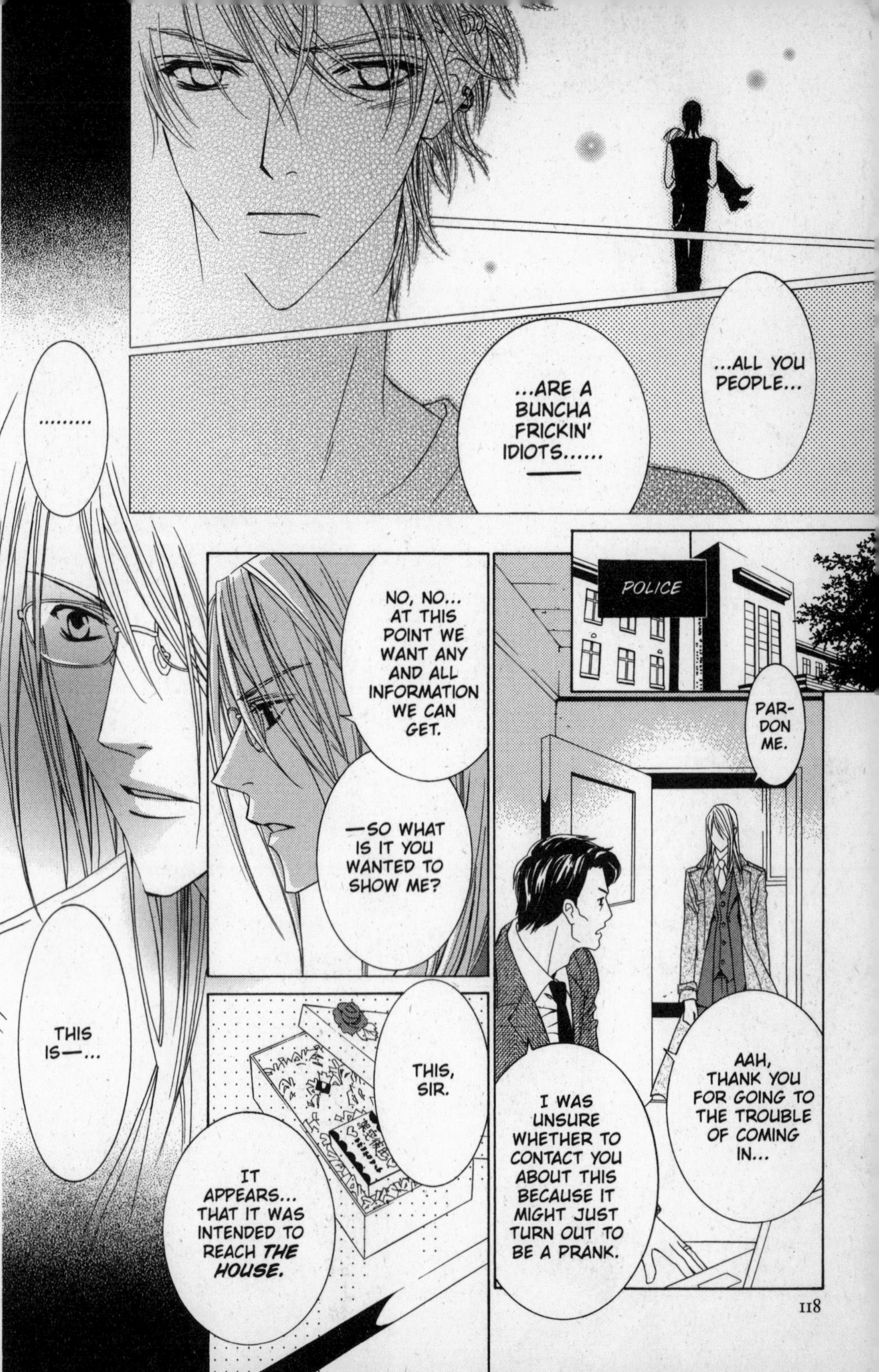
...ALL YOU PEOPLE...
...ARE A BUNCHA FRICKIN' IDIOTS......
....
PAR-DON ME.
AAH, THANK YOU FOR GOING TO THE TROUBLE OF COMING IN...
I WAS UNSURE WHETHER TO CONTACT YOU ABOUT THIS BECAUSE IT MIGHT JUST TURN OUT TO BE A PRANK.
POLICE
NO, NO... AT THIS POINT WE WANT ANY AND ALL INFORMATION WE CAN GET.
—SO WHAT IS IT YOU WANTED TO SHOW ME?
THIS, SIR.
IT APPEARS... THAT IT WAS INTENDED TO REACH *THE HOUSE.*
THIS IS—...

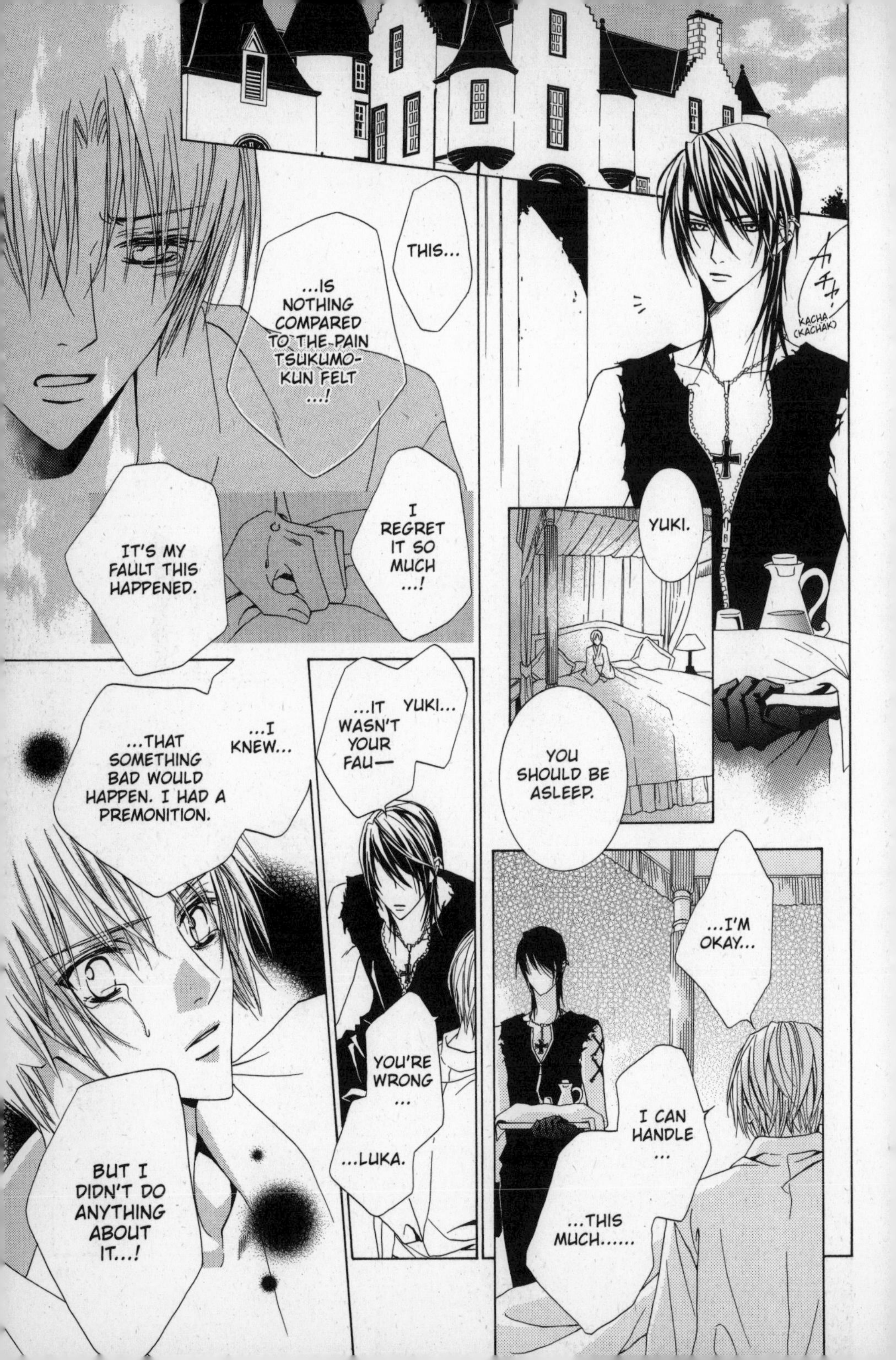

KACHA (KACHAK)
YUKI.
YOU SHOULD BE ASLEEP.
...I'M OKAY...
I CAN HANDLE ...
...THIS MUCH......
THIS...
...IS NOTHING COMPARED TO THE PAIN TSUKUMO-KUN FELT ...!
I REGRET IT SO MUCH ...!
IT'S MY FAULT THIS HAPPENED.
YUKI...
...IT WASN'T YOUR FAU—
YOU'RE WRONG ...
...LUKA.
...I KNEW...
...THAT SOMETHING BAD WOULD HAPPEN. I HAD A PREMONITION.
BUT I DIDN'T DO ANYTHING ABOUT IT...!

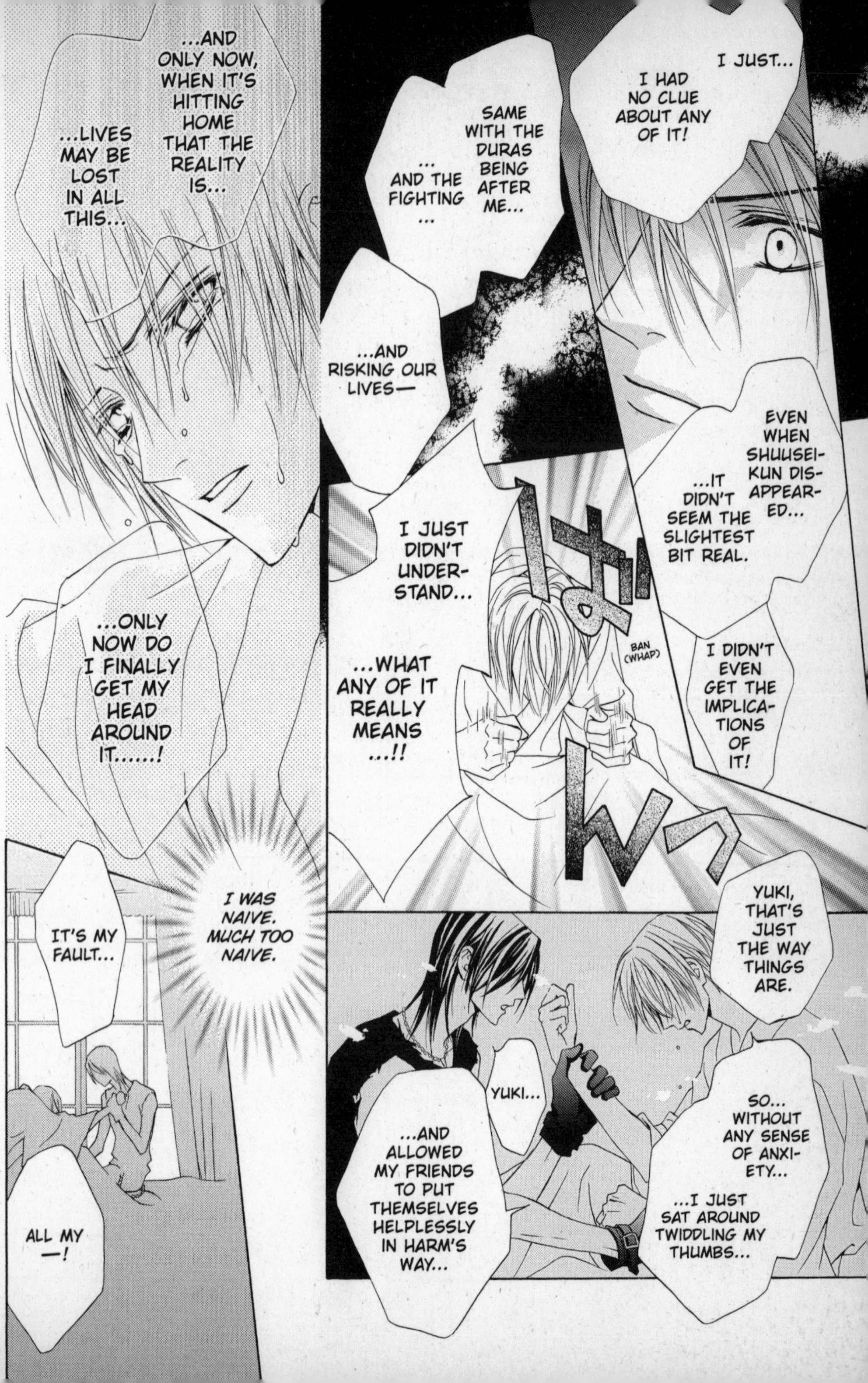
I JUST...
I HAD NO CLUE ABOUT ANY OF IT!
SAME WITH THE DURAS BEING AFTER ME...
...AND THE FIGHTING...
...AND RISKING OUR LIVES—
EVEN WHEN SHUUSEI-KUN DIS-APPEAR-ED...
...IT DIDN'T SEEM THE SLIGHTEST BIT REAL.
I DIDN'T EVEN GET THE IMPLICA-TIONS OF IT!
BAN (WHAP)
I JUST DIDN'T UNDER-STAND...
...WHAT ANY OF IT REALLY MEANS...!!
YUKI, THAT'S JUST THE WAY THINGS ARE.
SO... WITHOUT ANY SENSE OF ANXI-ETY...
...I JUST SAT AROUND TWIDDLING MY THUMBS...
YUKI...
...AND ALLOWED MY FRIENDS TO PUT THEMSELVES HELPLESSLY IN HARM'S WAY...
...AND ONLY NOW, WHEN IT'S HITTING HOME THAT THE REALITY IS...
...LIVES MAY BE LOST IN ALL THIS...
...ONLY NOW DO I FINALLY GET MY HEAD AROUND IT......!
I WAS NAIVE. MUCH TOO NAIVE.
IT'S MY FAULT...
ALL MY —!

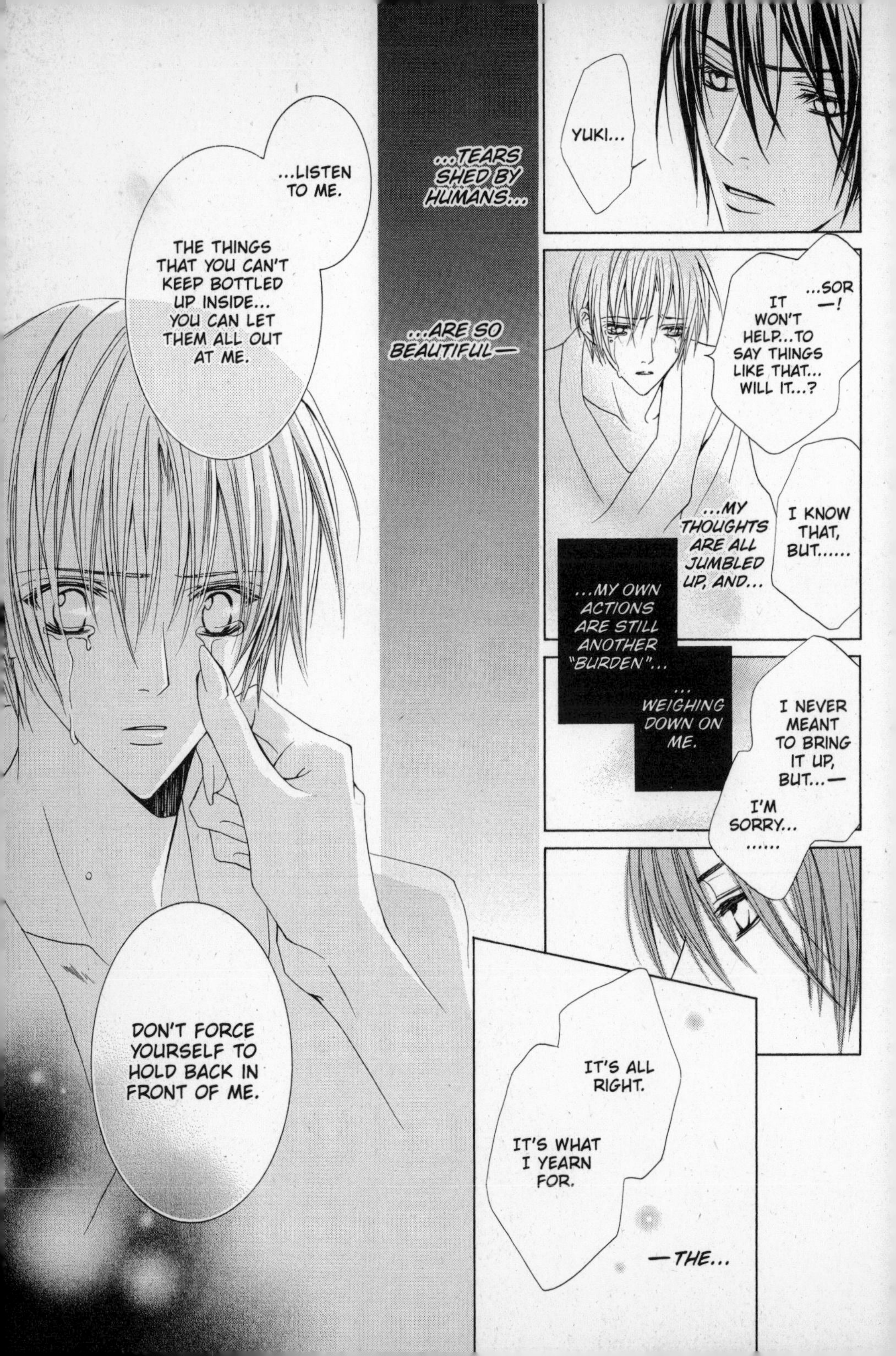
YUKI...
...SOR—!
IT WON'T HELP...TO SAY THINGS LIKE THAT... WILL IT...?
I KNOW THAT, BUT......
...MY THOUGHTS ARE ALL JUMBLED UP, AND...
...MY OWN ACTIONS ARE STILL ANOTHER "BURDEN"...
...WEIGHING DOWN ON ME.
I NEVER MEANT TO BRING IT UP, BUT...—
I'M SORRY... ......
IT'S ALL RIGHT.
IT'S WHAT I YEARN FOR.
—THE...
...TEARS SHED BY HUMANS...
...ARE SO BEAUTIFUL—
...LISTEN TO ME.
THE THINGS THAT YOU CAN'T KEEP BOTTLED UP INSIDE... YOU CAN LET THEM ALL OUT AT ME.
DON'T FORCE YOURSELF TO HOLD BACK IN FRONT OF ME.

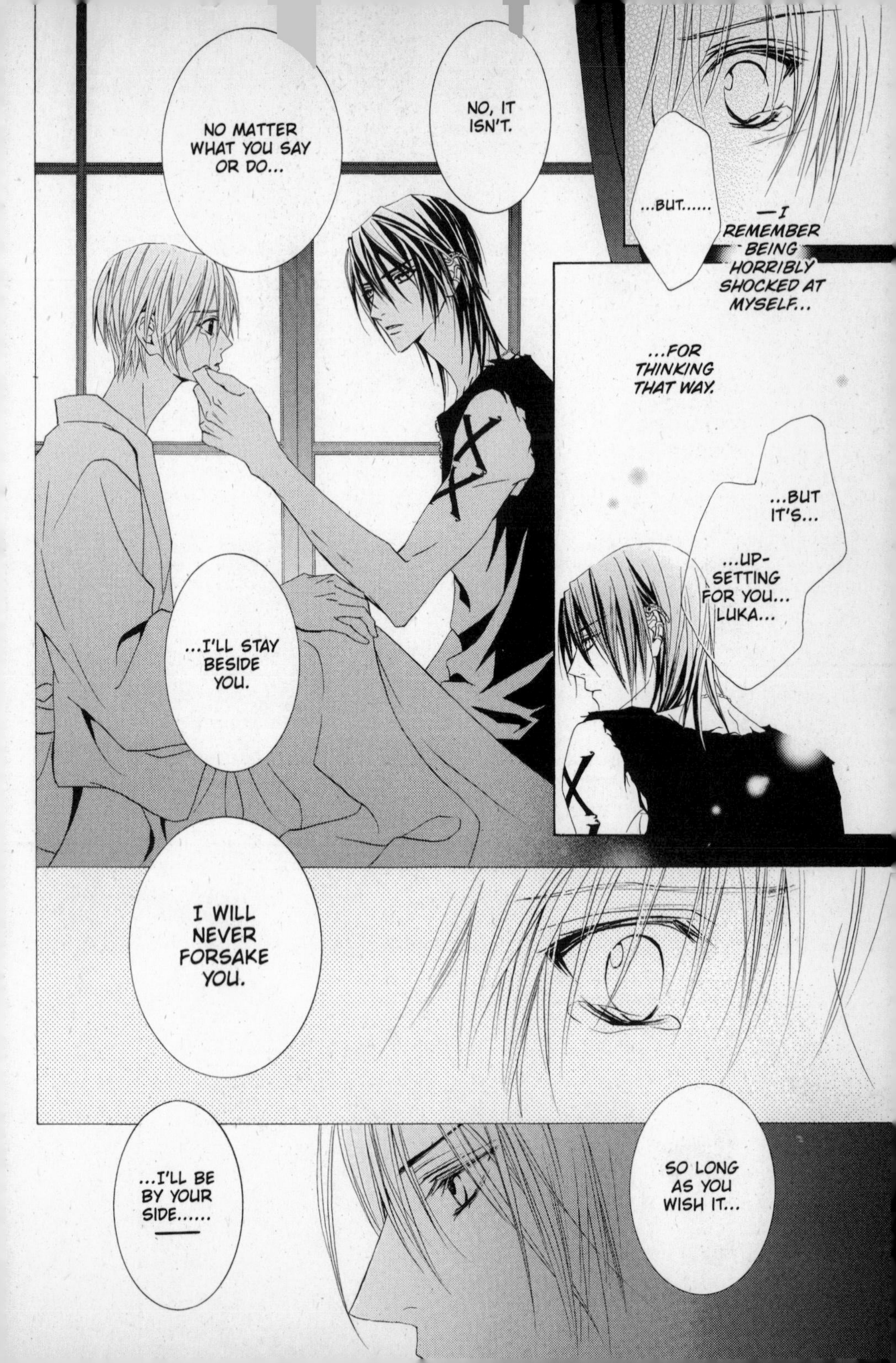
...BUT......
—I REMEMBER BEING HORRIBLY SHOCKED AT MYSELF...
...FOR THINKING THAT WAY.
...BUT IT'S...
...UP-SETTING FOR YOU... LUKA...
NO, IT ISN'T.
NO MATTER WHAT YOU SAY OR DO...
...I'LL STAY BESIDE YOU.
I WILL NEVER FORSAKE YOU.
SO LONG AS YOU WISH IT...
...I'LL BE BY YOUR SIDE......—

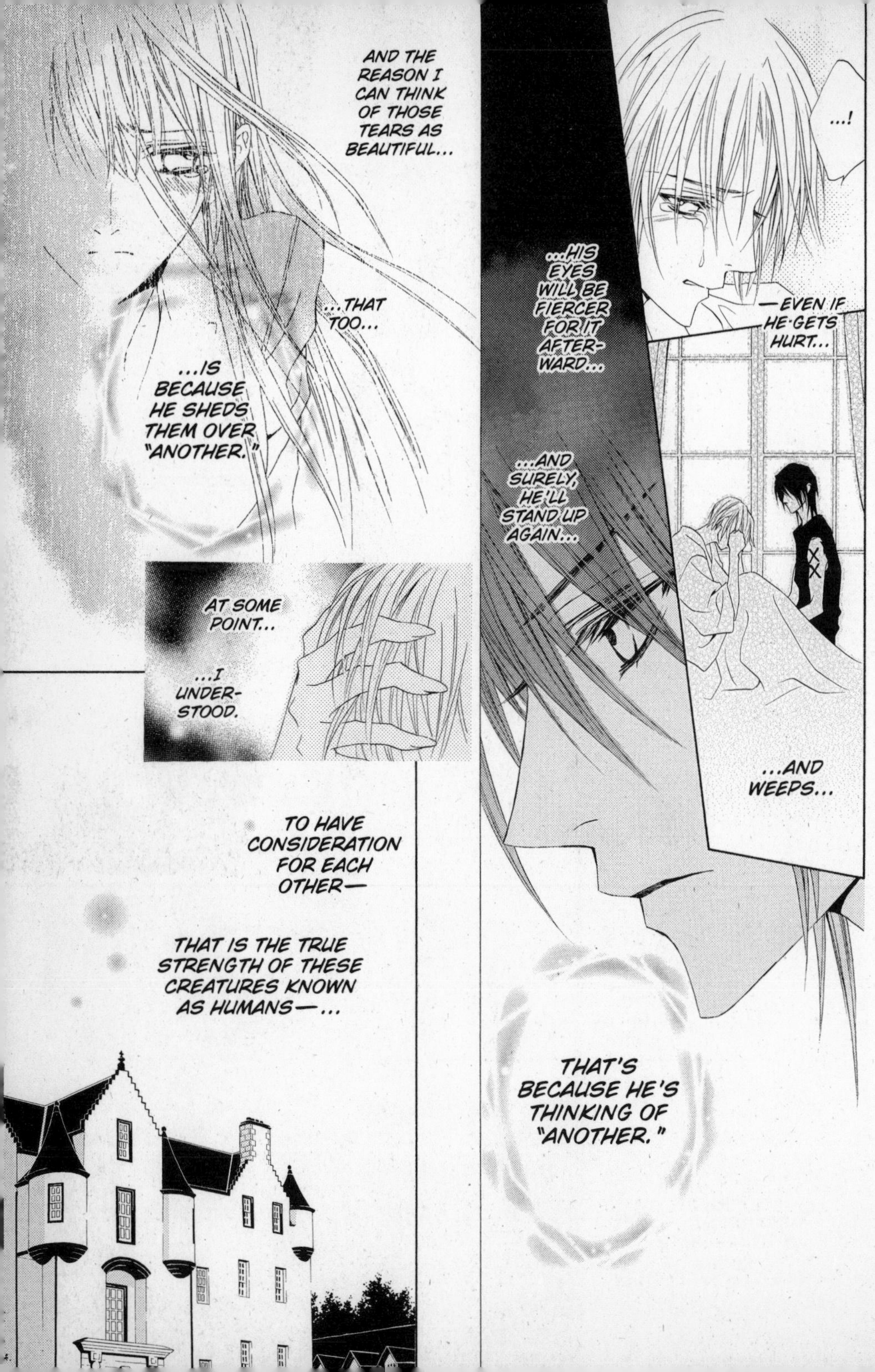
...!
—EVEN IF HE·GETS HURT...
...AND WEEPS...
...HIS EYES WILL BE FIERCER FOR IT AFTER-WARD...
...AND SURELY, HE'LL STAND UP AGAIN...
THAT'S BECAUSE HE'S THINKING OF "ANOTHER."
AND THE REASON I CAN THINK OF THOSE TEARS AS BEAUTIFUL...
...THAT TOO...
...IS BECAUSE HE SHEDS THEM OVER "ANOTHER."
AT SOME POINT...
...I UNDER-STOOD.
TO HAVE CONSIDERATION FOR EACH OTHER—
THAT IS THE TRUE STRENGTH OF THESE CREATURES KNOWN AS HUMANS—...

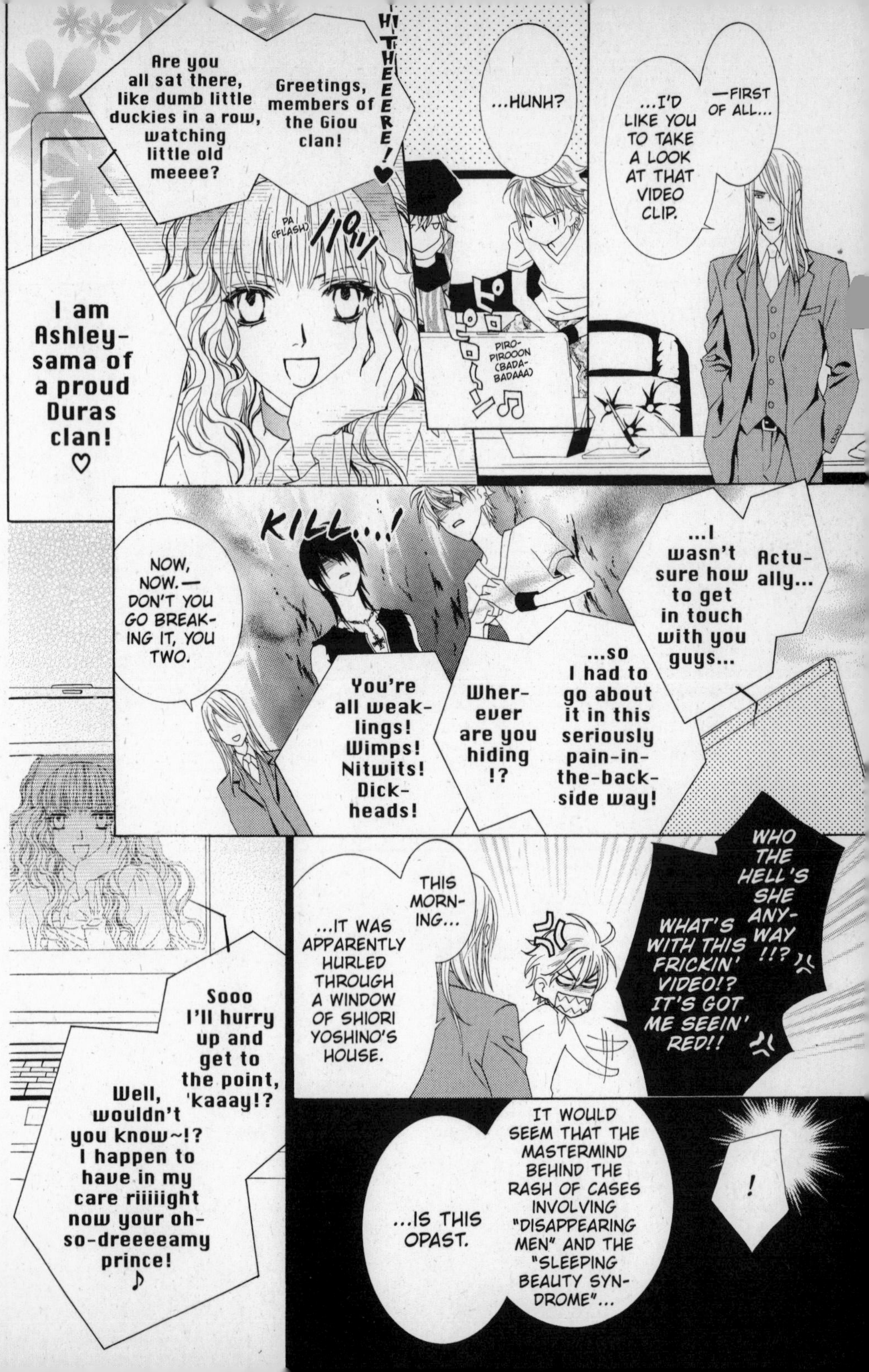
—FIRST OF ALL...
...I'D LIKE YOU TO TAKE A LOOK AT THAT VIDEO CLIP.
...HUNH?
PIRO-PIROOON (BADA-BADAAA)
HI THEEEERE!♥
Greetings, members of the Giou clan!
Are you all sat there, like dumb little duckies in a row, watching little old meeee?
PA (FLASH)
I am Ashley-sama of a proud Duras clan! ♡
Actually...
...I wasn't sure how to get in touch with you guys...
...so I had to go about it in this seriously pain-in-the-backside way!
Wherever are you hiding!?
You're all weaklings! Wimps! Nitwits! Dickheads!
KILL...!
NOW, NOW.— DON'T YOU GO BREAKING IT, YOU TWO.
WHO THE HELL'S SHE ANYWAY!!?
WHAT'S WITH THIS FRICKIN' VIDEO!? IT'S GOT ME SEEIN' RED!!
THIS MORNING...
...IT WAS APPARENTLY HURLED THROUGH A WINDOW OF SHIORI YOSHINO'S HOUSE.
!
IT WOULD SEEM THAT THE MASTERMIND BEHIND THE RASH OF CASES INVOLVING "DISAPPEARING MEN" AND THE "SLEEPING BEAUTY SYNDROME"...
...IS THIS OPAST.
Sooo I'll hurry up and get to the point, 'kaaay!?
Well, wouldn't you know~!? I happen to have in my care riiiiight now your oh-so-dreeeeamy prince! ♪

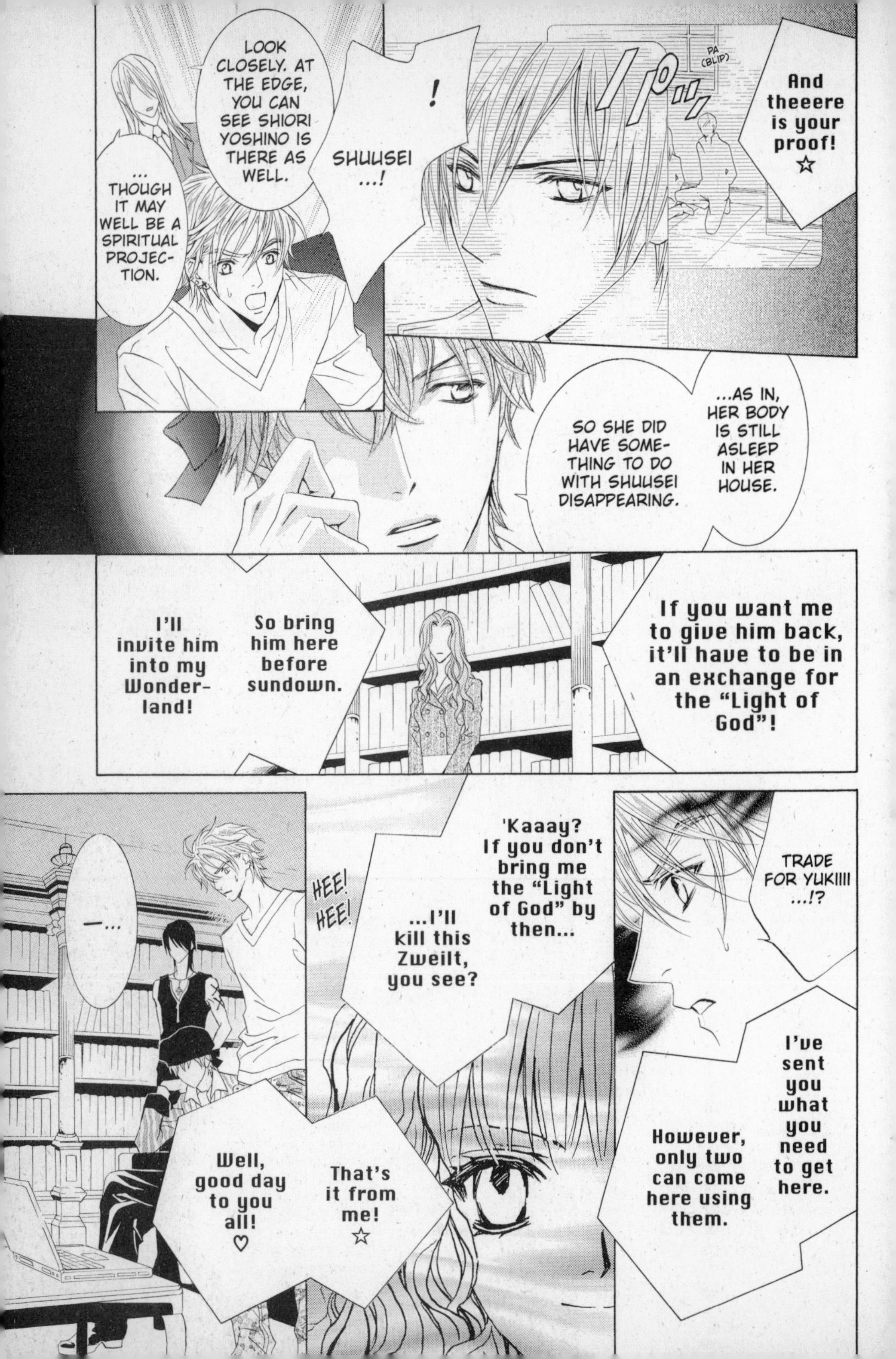
And theeere is your proof! ☆
PA (BLIP)
!
SHUUSEI ...!
LOOK CLOSELY. AT THE EDGE, YOU CAN SEE SHIORI YOSHINO IS THERE AS WELL.
... THOUGH IT MAY WELL BE A SPIRITUAL PROJEC-TION.
...AS IN, HER BODY IS STILL ASLEEP IN HER HOUSE.
SO SHE DID HAVE SOME-THING TO DO WITH SHUUSEI DISAPPEARING.
If you want me to give him back, it'll have to be in an exchange for the "Light of God"!
So bring him here before sundown.
I'll invite him into my Wonder-land!
TRADE FOR YUKIIII ...!?
I've sent you what you need to get here.
However, only two can come here using them.
'Kaaay? If you don't bring me the "Light of God" by then...
...I'll kill this Zweilt, you see?
HEE! HEE!
That's it from me! ☆
Well, good day to you all! ♡
—...

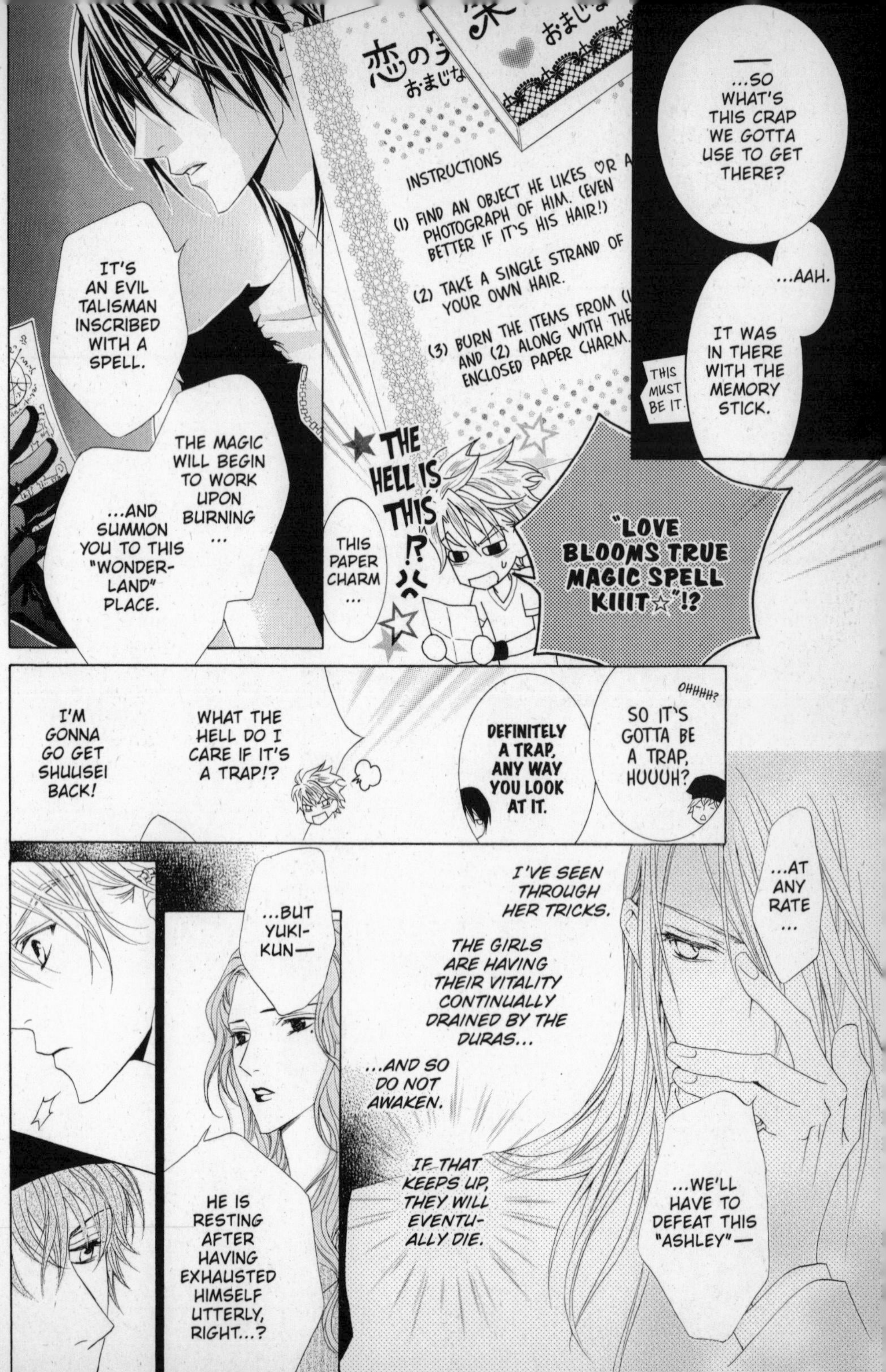
—
...SO WHAT'S THIS CRAP WE GOTTA USE TO GET THERE?
...AAH.
IT WAS IN THERE WITH THE MEMORY STICK.
THIS MUST BE IT.
恋の
おまじな
INSTRUCTIONS
(1) FIND AN OBJECT HE LIKES ♡R A PHOTOGRAPH OF HIM. (EVEN BETTER IF IT'S HIS HAIR!)
(2) TAKE A SINGLE STRAND OF YOUR OWN HAIR.
(3) BURN THE ITEMS FROM (AND (2) ALONG WITH THE ENCLOSED PAPER CHARM.
"LOVE BLOOMS TRUE MAGIC SPELL KIIIT☆"!?
THE HELL IS THIS!?
THIS PAPER CHARM...
IT'S AN EVIL TALISMAN INSCRIBED WITH A SPELL.
THE MAGIC WILL BEGIN TO WORK UPON BURNING...
...AND SUMMON YOU TO THIS "WONDER-LAND" PLACE.
OHHHH?
SO IT'S GOTTA BE A TRAP, HUUUH?
DEFINITELY A TRAP, ANY WAY YOU LOOK AT IT.
WHAT THE HELL DO I CARE IF IT'S A TRAP!?
I'M GONNA GO GET SHUUSEI BACK!
...AT ANY RATE...
I'VE SEEN THROUGH HER TRICKS.
...WE'LL HAVE TO DEFEAT THIS "ASHLEY"—
THE GIRLS ARE HAVING THEIR VITALITY CONTINUALLY DRAINED BY THE DURAS...
...AND SO DO NOT AWAKEN.
IF THAT KEEPS UP, THEY WILL EVENTU-ALLY DIE.
...BUT YUKI-KUN—
HE IS RESTING AFTER HAVING EXHAUSTED HIMSELF UTTERLY, RIGHT...?

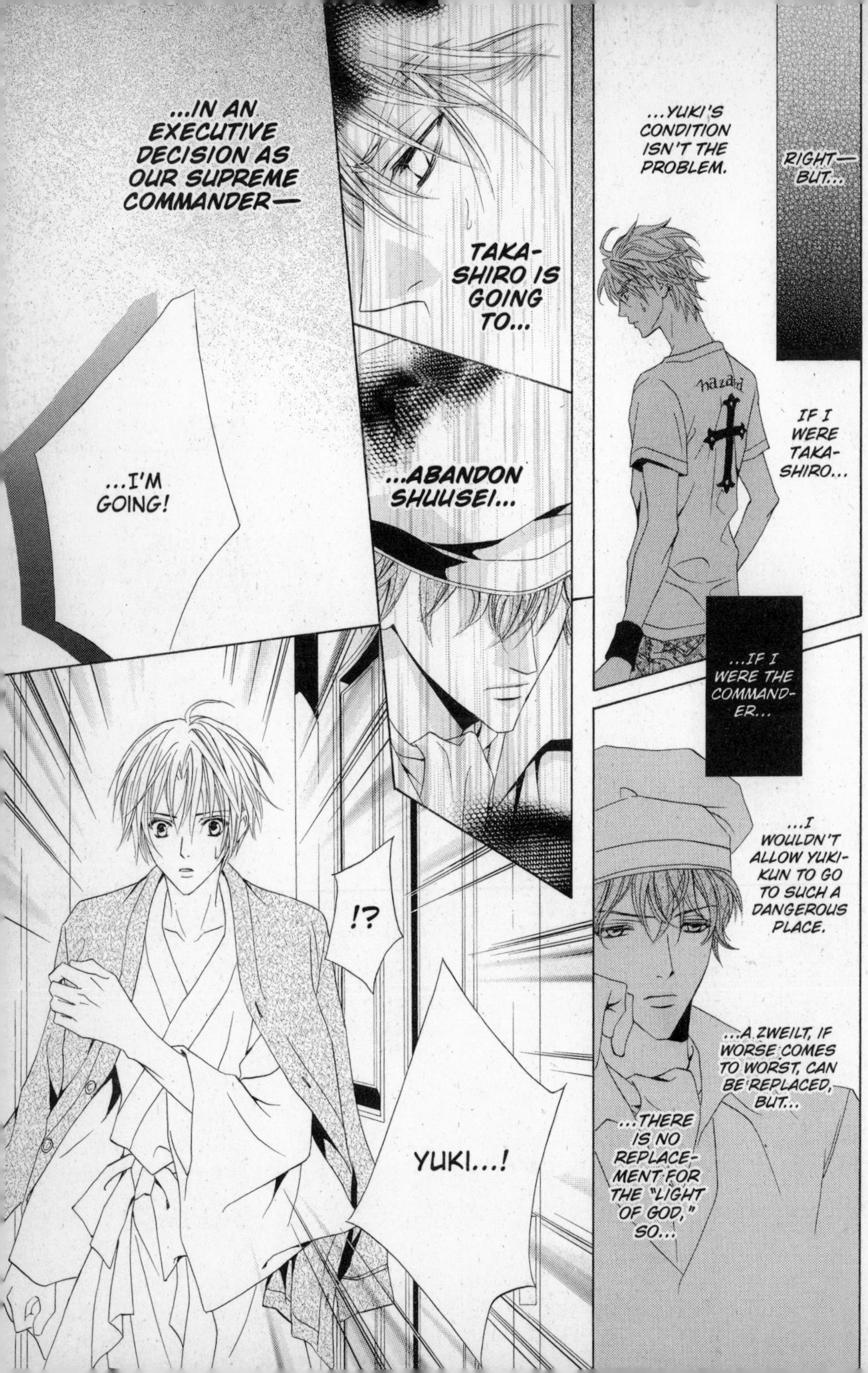

RIGHT— BUT...
...YUKI'S CONDITION ISN'T THE PROBLEM.
IF I WERE TAKA-SHIRO...
...IF I WERE THE COMMAND-ER...
...I WOULDN'T ALLOW YUKI-KUN TO GO TO SUCH A DANGEROUS PLACE.
...A ZWEILT, IF WORSE COMES TO WORST, CAN BE REPLACED, BUT...
...THERE IS NO REPLACE-MENT FOR THE "LIGHT OF GOD," SO...
TAKA-SHIRO IS GOING TO...
...ABANDON SHUUSEI...
...IN AN EXECUTIVE DECISION AS OUR SUPREME COMMANDER—
...I'M GOING!
!?
YUKI...!

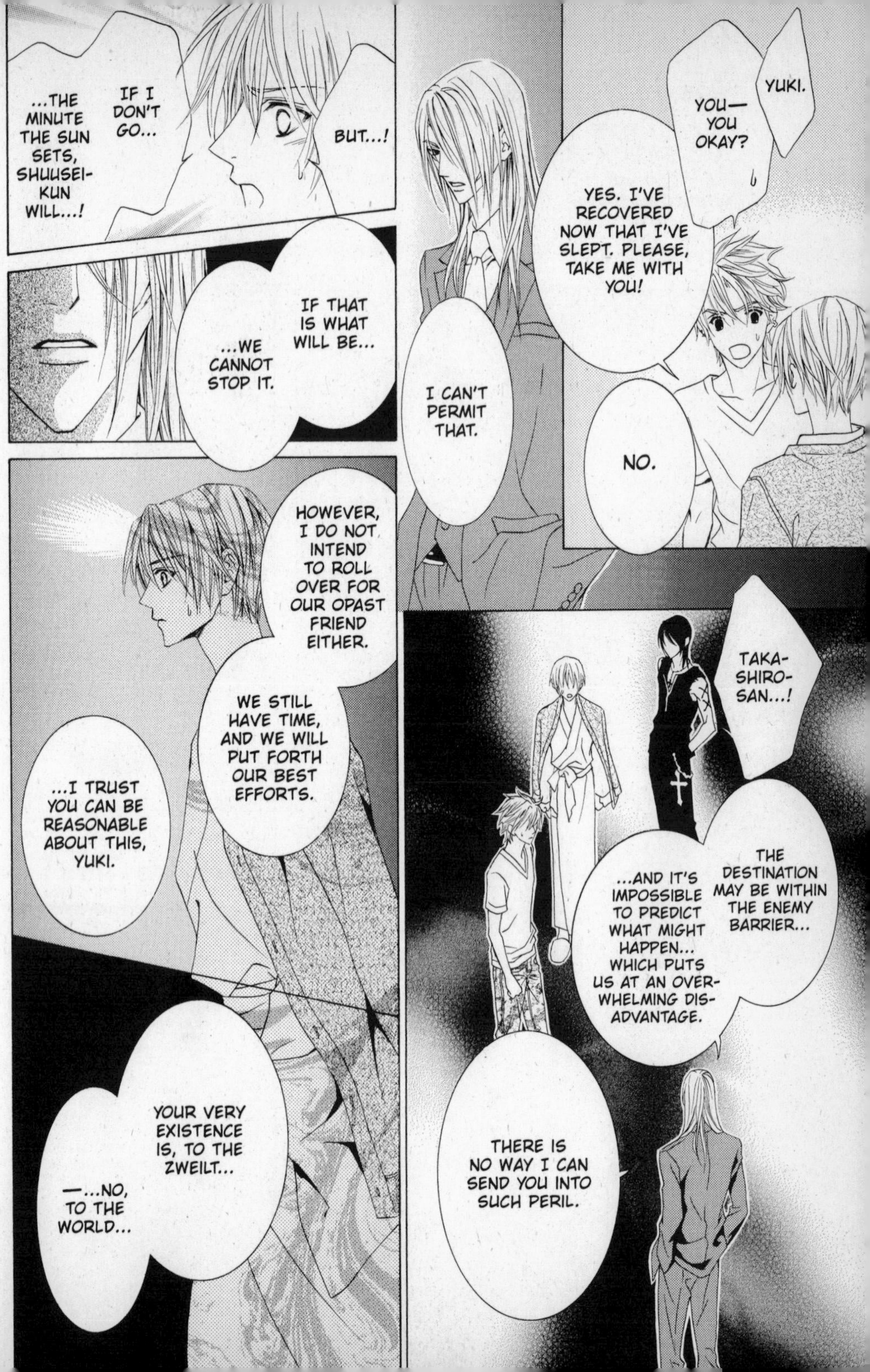
YUKI.
YOU— YOU OKAY?
YES. I'VE RECOVERED NOW THAT I'VE SLEPT. PLEASE, TAKE ME WITH YOU!
NO.
I CAN'T PERMIT THAT.
TAKA-SHIRO-SAN...!
THE DESTINATION MAY BE WITHIN THE ENEMY BARRIER...
...AND IT'S IMPOSSIBLE TO PREDICT WHAT MIGHT HAPPEN... WHICH PUTS US AT AN OVER-WHELMING DIS-ADVANTAGE.
THERE IS NO WAY I CAN SEND YOU INTO SUCH PERIL.
BUT...!
IF I DON'T GO...
...THE MINUTE THE SUN SETS, SHUUSEI-KUN WILL...!
IF THAT IS WHAT WILL BE...
...WE CANNOT STOP IT.
HOWEVER, I DO NOT INTEND TO ROLL OVER FOR OUR OPAST FRIEND EITHER.
WE STILL HAVE TIME, AND WE WILL PUT FORTH OUR BEST EFFORTS.
...I TRUST YOU CAN BE REASONABLE ABOUT THIS, YUKI.
YOUR VERY EXISTENCE IS, TO THE ZWEILT...
—...NO, TO THE WORLD...

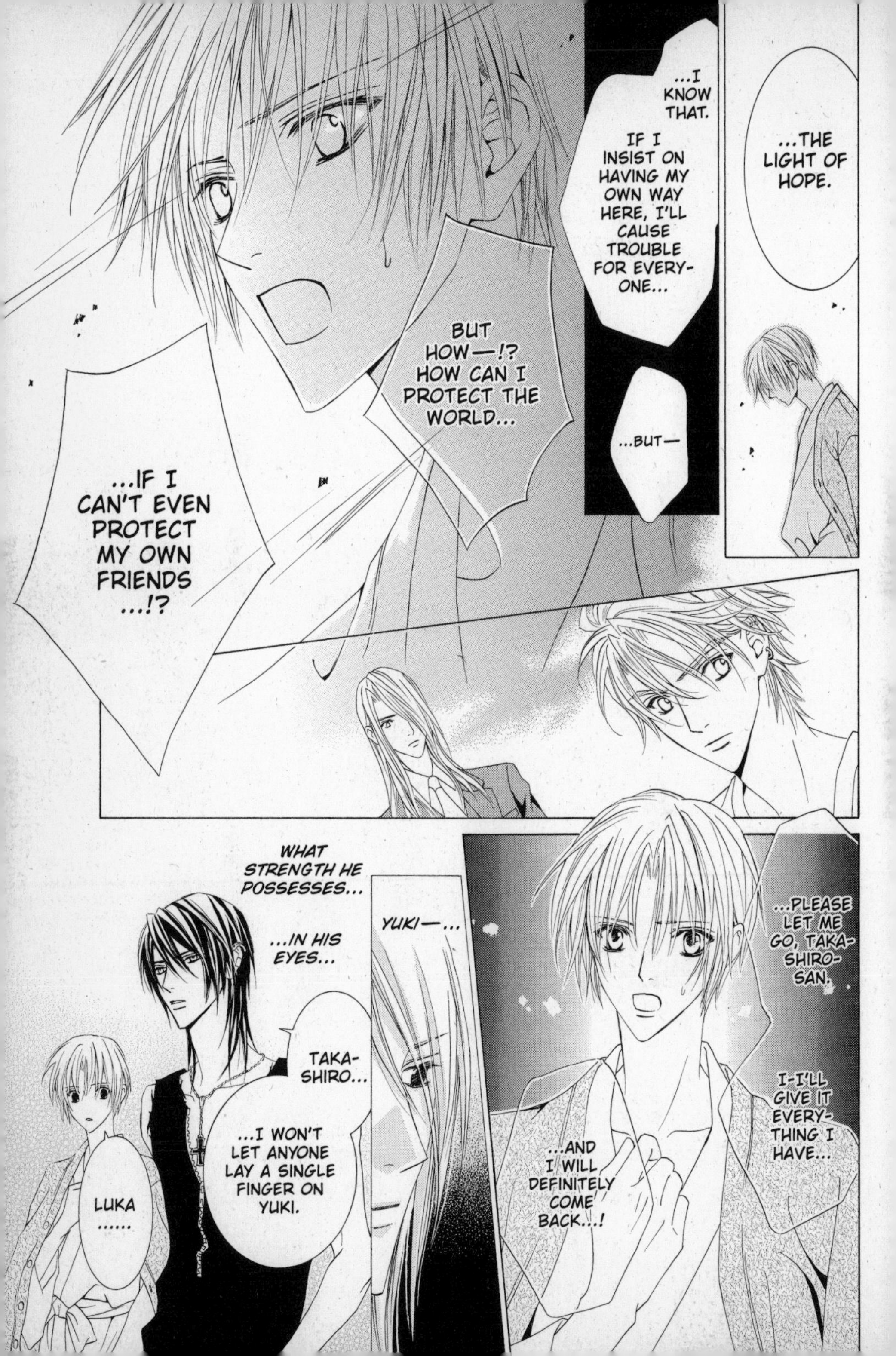
...THE LIGHT OF HOPE.
...I KNOW THAT.
IF I INSIST ON HAVING MY OWN WAY HERE, I'LL CAUSE TROUBLE FOR EVERY-ONE...
...BUT—
BUT HOW—!? HOW CAN I PROTECT THE WORLD...
...IF I CAN'T EVEN PROTECT MY OWN FRIENDS ...!?
...PLEASE LET ME GO, TAKA-SHIRO-SAN.
I-I'LL GIVE IT EVERY-THING I HAVE...
...AND I WILL DEFINITELY COME BACK...!
YUKI—...
WHAT STRENGTH HE POSSESSES...
...IN HIS EYES...
TAKA-SHIRO...
...I WON'T LET ANYONE LAY A SINGLE FINGER ON YUKI.
LUKA ......

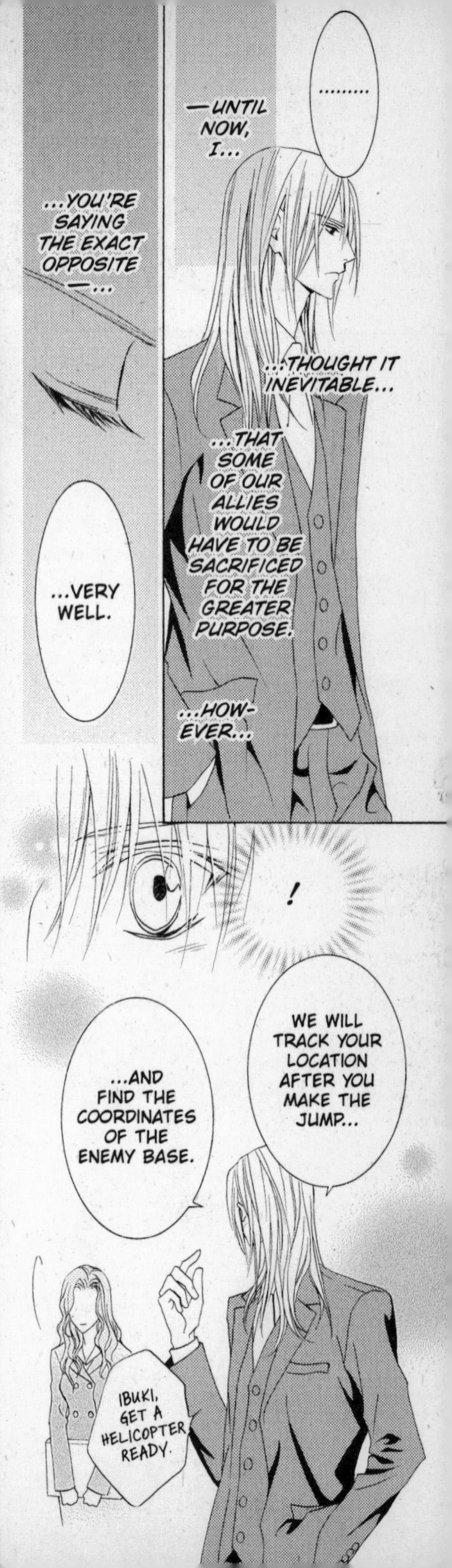
....
—UNTIL NOW, I...
...THOUGHT IT INEVITABLE...
...THAT SOME OF OUR ALLIES WOULD HAVE TO BE SACRIFICED FOR THE GREATER PURPOSE.
...HOW-EVER...
...YOU'RE SAYING THE EXACT OPPOSITE —...
...VERY WELL.
!
WE WILL TRACK YOUR LOCATION AFTER YOU MAKE THE JUMP...
...AND FIND THE COORDINATES OF THE ENEMY BASE.
IBUKI, GET A HELICOPTER READY.
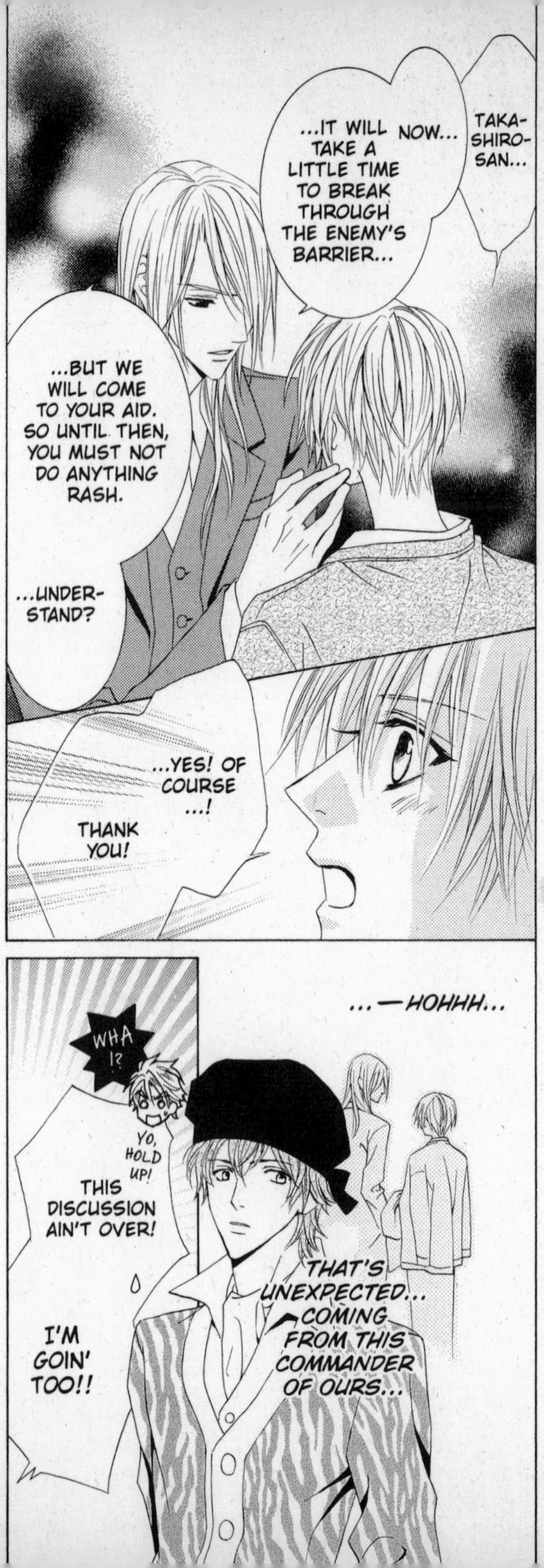
TAKA-SHIRO-SAN...
NOW...
...IT WILL TAKE A LITTLE TIME TO BREAK THROUGH THE ENEMY'S BARRIER...
...BUT WE WILL COME TO YOUR AID. SO UNTIL THEN, YOU MUST NOT DO ANYTHING RASH.
...UNDER-STAND?
...YES! OF COURSE ...!
THANK YOU!
...—HOHHH...
WHA !?
THAT'S UNEXPECTED... COMING FROM THIS COMMANDER OF OURS...
YO, HOLD UP!
THIS DISCUSSION AIN'T OVER!
I'M GOIN' TOO!!

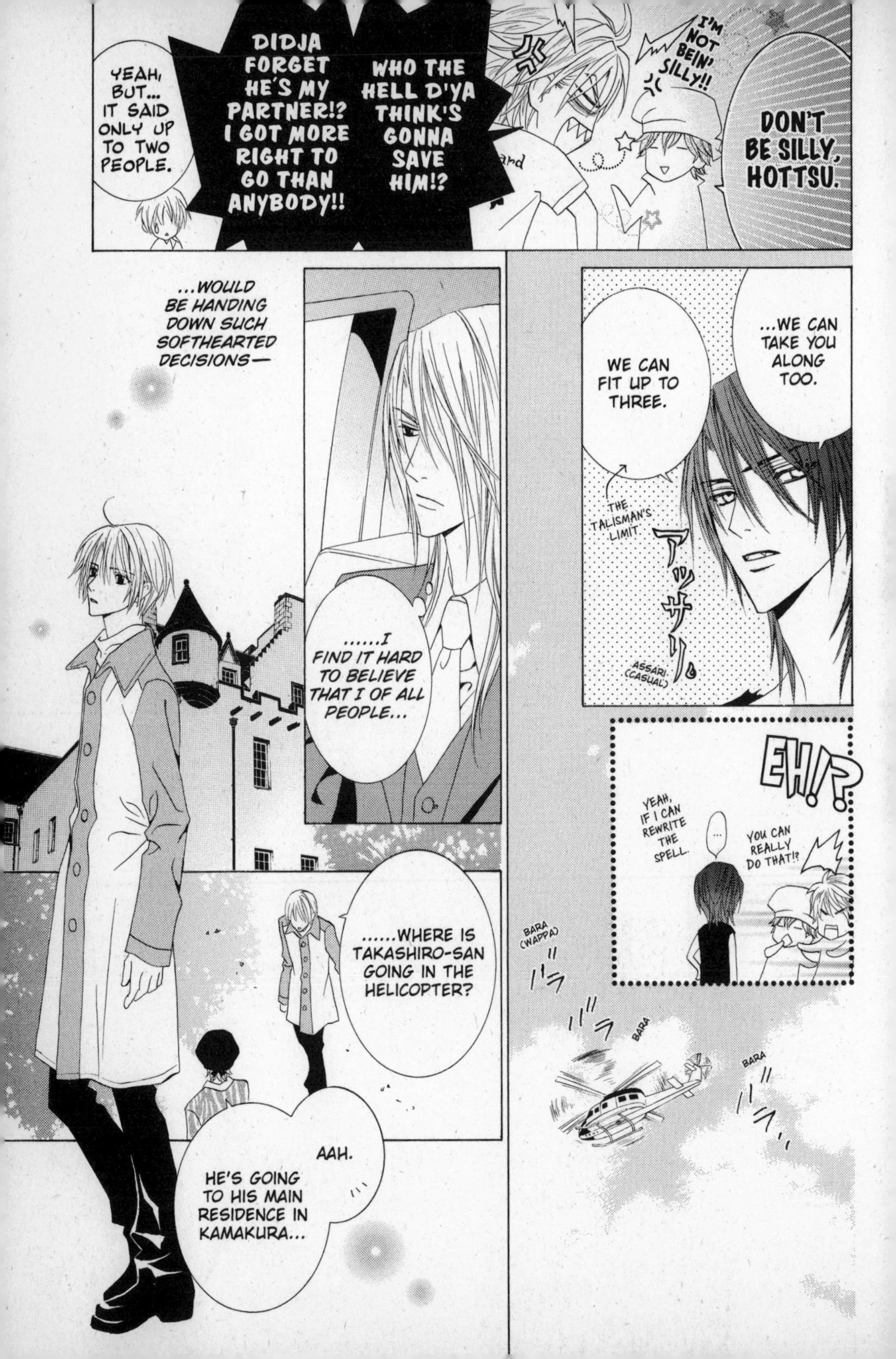
DON'T BE SILLY, HOTTSU.
I'M NOT BEIN' SILLY!!
WHO THE HELL D'YA THINK'S GONNA SAVE HIM!?
DIDJA FORGET HE'S MY PARTNER!? I GOT MORE RIGHT TO GO THAN ANYBODY!!
YEAH, BUT... IT SAID ONLY UP TO TWO PEOPLE.
...WE CAN TAKE YOU ALONG TOO.
WE CAN FIT UP TO THREE.
THE TALISMAN'S LIMIT
アッサリ
ASSARI (CASUAL)
EH!?
YOU CAN REALLY DO THAT!?
...
YEAH, IF I CAN REWRITE THE SPELL.
BARA (WAPPA)
バラ
BARA
BARA
......I FIND IT HARD TO BELIEVE THAT I OF ALL PEOPLE...
...WOULD BE HANDING DOWN SUCH SOFTHEARTED DECISIONS—
......WHERE IS TAKASHIRO-SAN GOING IN THE HELICOPTER?
AAH.
HE'S GOING TO HIS MAIN RESIDENCE IN KAMAKURA...

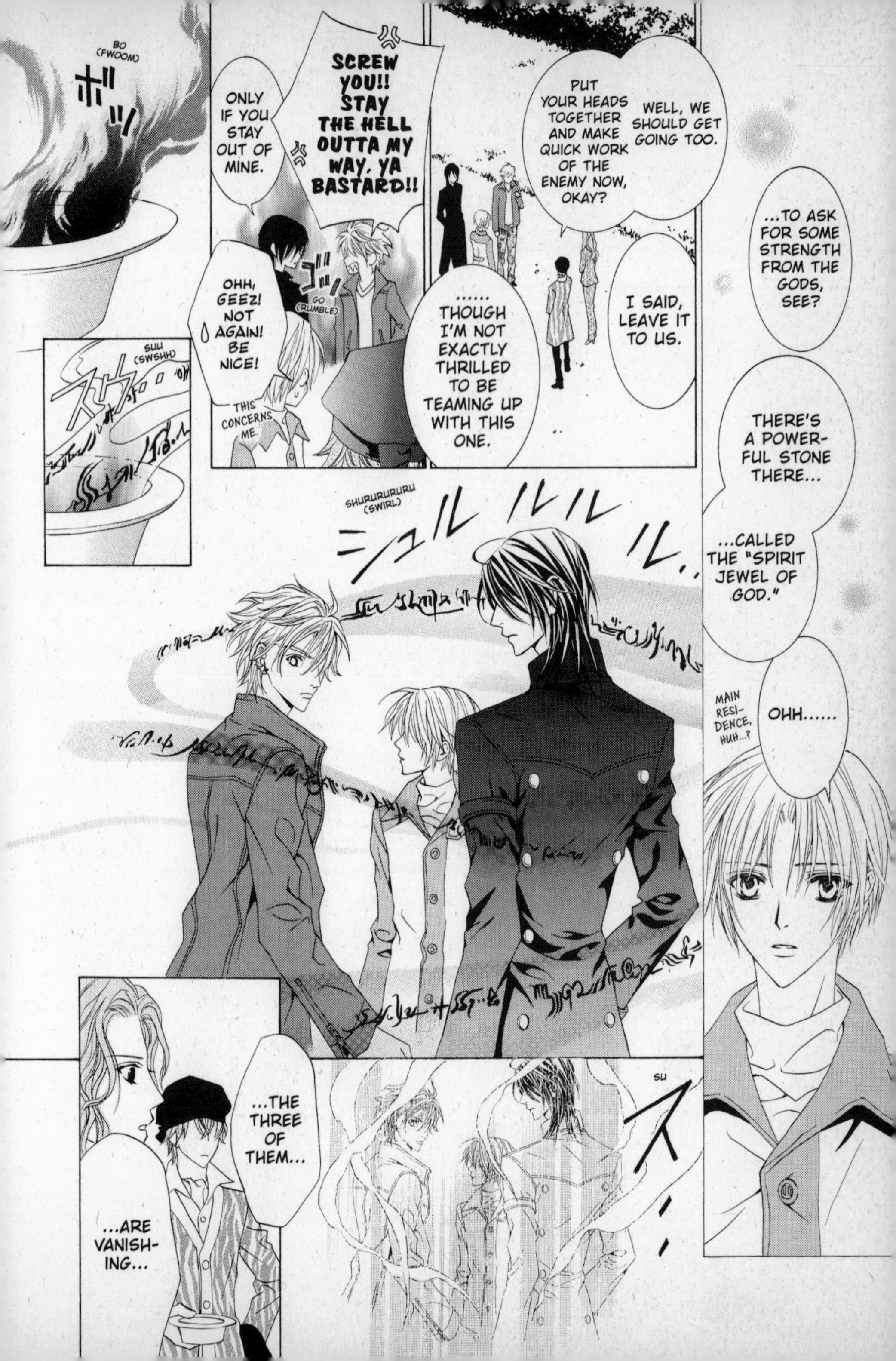

...TO ASK FOR SOME STRENGTH FROM THE GODS, SEE?
THERE'S A POWERFUL STONE THERE...
...CALLED THE "SPIRIT JEWEL OF GOD."
OHH......
MAIN RESIDENCE, HUH...?
WELL, WE SHOULD GET GOING TOO.
PUT YOUR HEADS TOGETHER AND MAKE QUICK WORK OF THE ENEMY NOW, OKAY?
I SAID, LEAVE IT TO US.
SCREW YOU!! STAY THE HELL OUTTA MY WAY, YA BASTARD!!
ONLY IF YOU STAY OUT OF MINE.
GO (RUMBLE)
......THOUGH I'M NOT EXACTLY THRILLED TO BE TEAMING UP WITH THIS ONE.
OHH, GEEZ! NOT AGAIN! BE NICE!
THIS CONCERNS ME.
BO (FWOOM)
SUU (SWSHH)
SHURURURURU (SWIRL)
SU
...THE THREE OF THEM...
...ARE VANISHING...

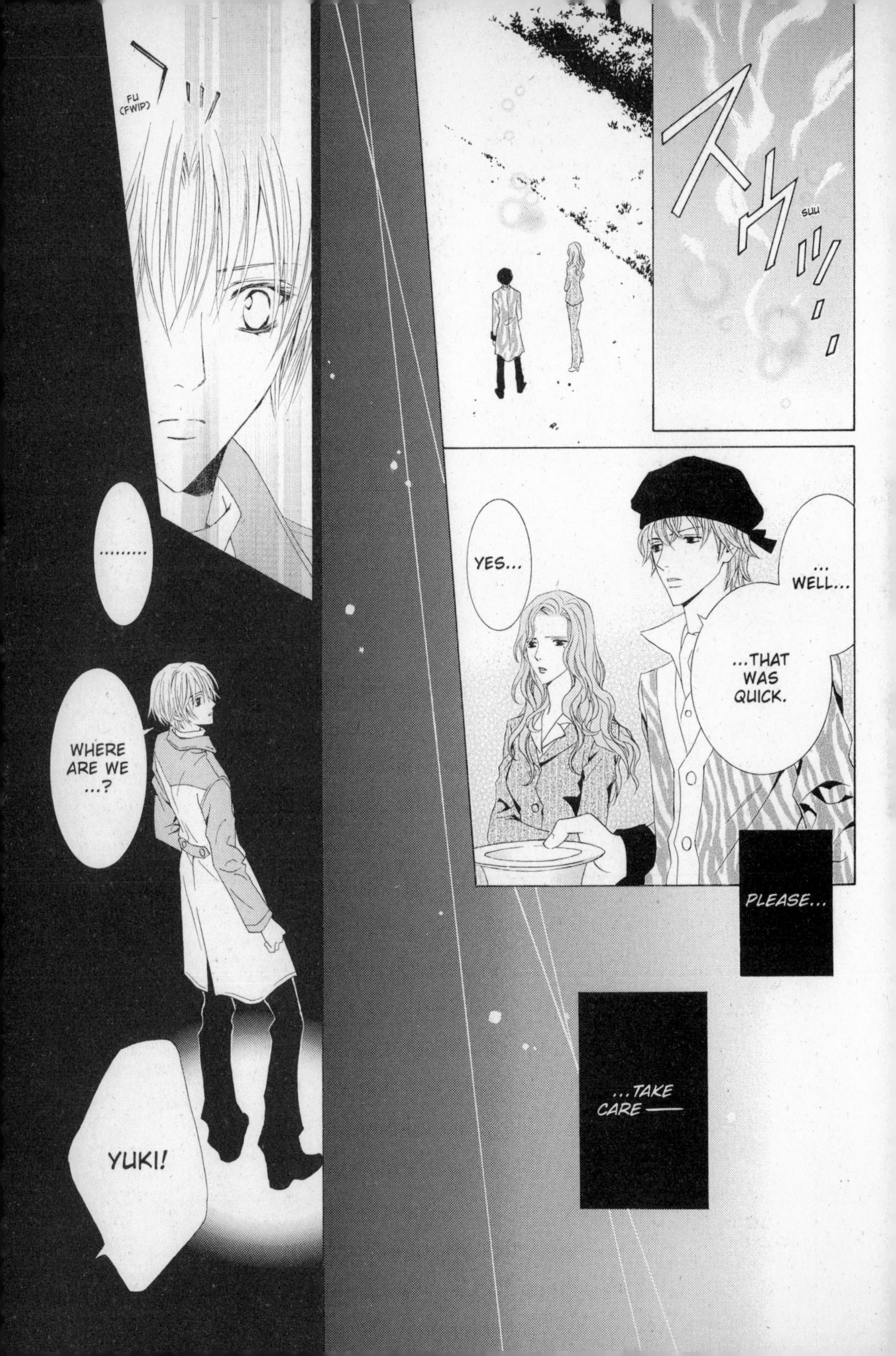
SUU
... WELL...
...THAT WAS QUICK.
YES...
PLEASE...
...TAKE CARE—
FU (FWIP)
....
WHERE ARE WE ...?
YUKI!

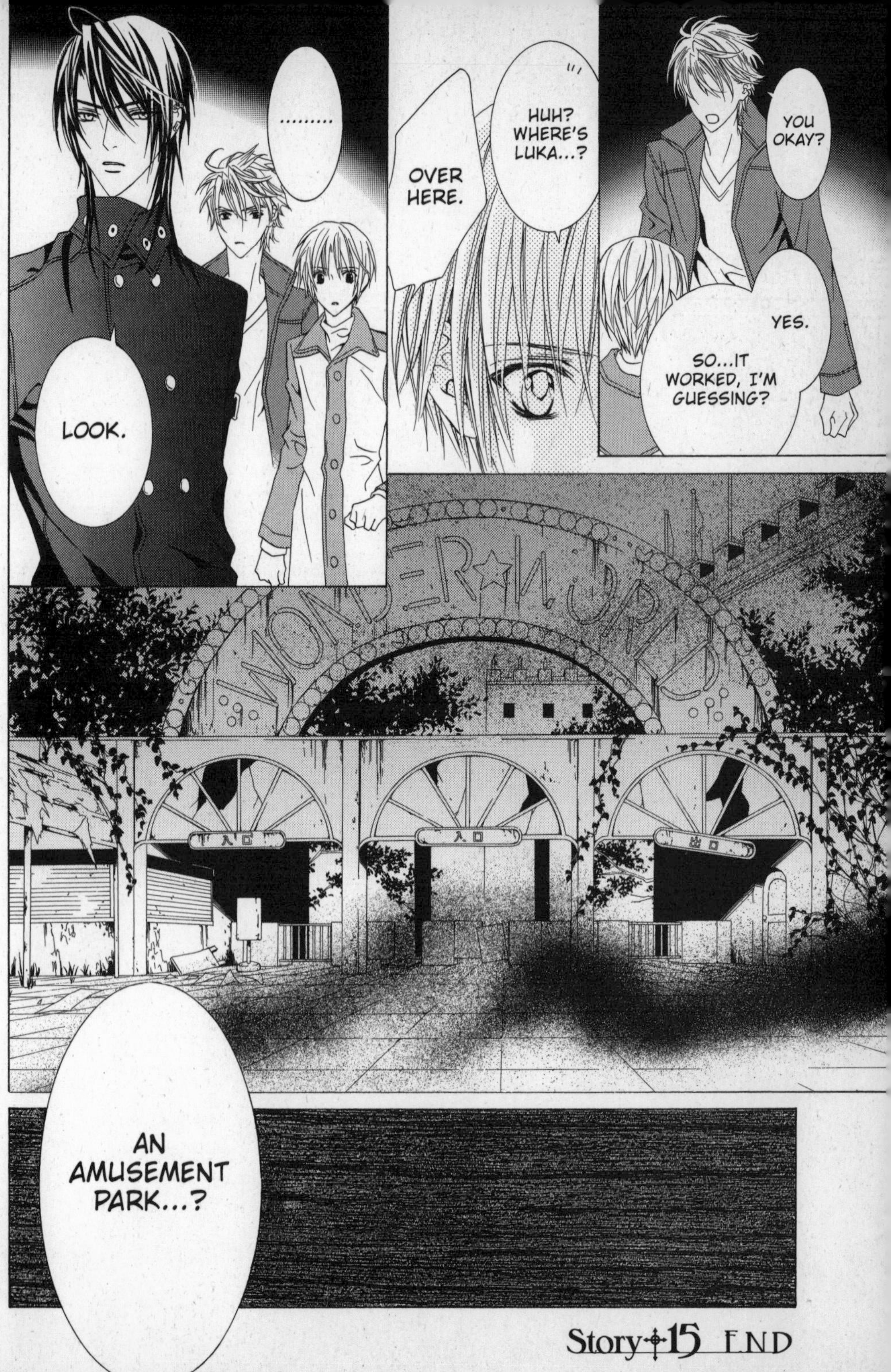
YOU OKAY?
YES.
SO...IT WORKED, I'M GUESSING?
HUH? WHERE'S LUKA...?
OVER HERE.
....
LOOK.
AN AMUSEMENT PARK...?

Story 15 END

Story ✝ 16
DANCING MARIONETTE

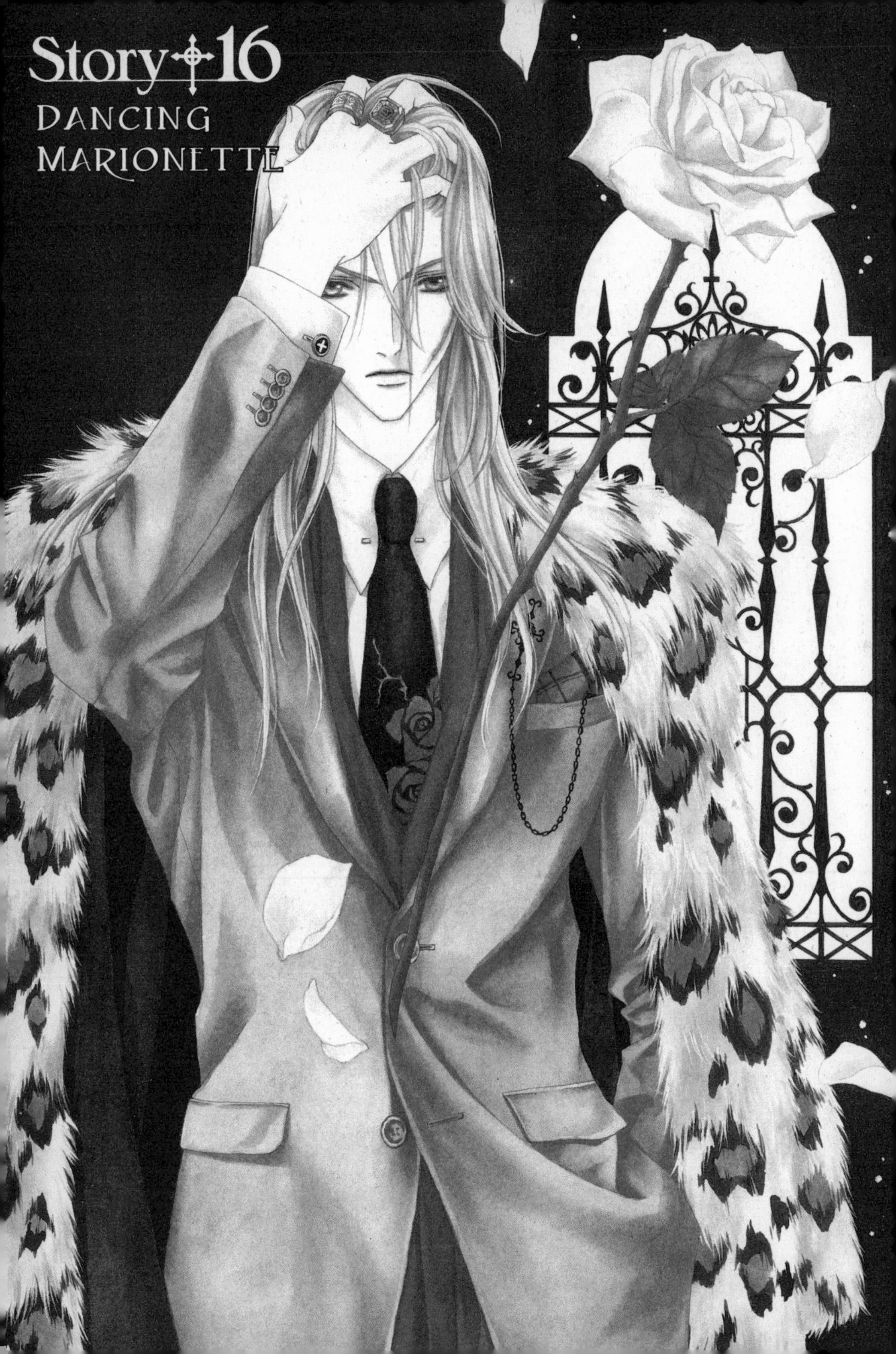

▶HELLO EVERYONE, ODAGIRI HERE. THANK YOU FOR READING VOLUME 3! ☆ ...I CAN'T HELP BUT THINK IT MYSTERIOUS THAT THIS STORY IS STILL GOING ON (OMG). THERE ARE PEOPLE WHO READ IT AND TELL ME THEY LIKE IT, BUT EVERY TIME I HEAR THAT, I END UP WONDERING IF THEY'RE JUST CRAZY LIKE ME... (HEY, THAT'S RUDE!) BUT THAT'S BECAUSE I'M CRAZY (LOL).
NOT QUITE OBSCURE, BUT NOT QUITE MAINSTREAM EITHER... JUST CAN'T GET WITH THE REST OF THE WORLD SOMEHOW... THAT'S ME (SADNESS). THERE ARE EVEN THOSE OF YOU WHO HAVE STUCK WITH ME FROM MY OTHER WORKS, AND I CAN'T SAY ANYTHING BUT THANK YOU SO MUCH...!
▶HOWEVER...THIS URABOKU BUSINESS...I GUESS IT'S BECAUSE OF THE SUBJECT MATTER, BUT IT JUST DRAINS ALL MY PHYSICAL AND MENTAL STAMINA...REALLY RUTHLESSLY. WHILE I'M GRATEFUL THAT THE SERIES IS CONTINUING, RECENTLY IT HIT HOME THAT THE LONGER IT GOES ON, THE WORSE 'N' WORSE THINGS'RE GONNA GIT (MY JAPANESE IS WEIRD). I DON'T HAVE MUCH STAMINA TO BE-GIN WITH, AND THE OTHER DAY MY CHIROPRACTOR TOLD ME, "YOU AREN'T REALLY BUILT FOR LABOR-INTENSIVE WORK LIKE DRAWING MANGA." (SADNESS) ...NEVERTHELESS, ABOUT THE ONLY THING I CAN DO IS MAKE THE EFFORT TO MOVE THINGS FORWARD. AT TIMES LIKE THESE, WHEN THE GOING GETS A LITTLE TOUGH, YOUR LET-TERS AND POSTCARDS AND COMMENTS ENCOURAGE ME SO MUCH. SOME PEOPLE EVEN DRAW ME PICTURES OR SEND ME PRESENTS AND LITTLE SOUVENIRS...
SOMETHING THAT REALLY ENTERTAINED ME THE OTHER DAY WAS A LETTER THAT OPENED UP IN 3-D, LIKE A POP-UP PICTURE BOOK!! IT WAS HANDMADE, AND IT LOOKED LIKE IT TOOK A WHOLE LOT OF TIME... IT REALLY TRULY WARMED MY HEART! ♪ OH, ABOUT THE REPLY, THOUGH, I HAVEN'T BEEN ABLE TO GET IT OUT YET (...I HAVEN'T HAD ANY EXTENDED TIME OFF...) ...I'M SORRY, I BEG YOUR PATIENCE (TEARS). THE REASON I'M ALWAYS SAYING "REPLY! REPLY!" IS BECAUSE HOWEVER MUCH I THINK "THANK YOU" IN MY HEART, THAT WON'T BE ENOUGH TO COMMUNICATE IT. IF I DON'T MAKE THE EFFORT TO TURN IT INTO WORDS OR AC-TIONS, THAT SENTIMENT MIGHT AS WELL NOT EXIST TO THE OTHER PERSON, YOU KNOW... THAT'S HOW I ALWAYS FEEL. IN WHATEVER FORM I CAN, I WANT TO BE ABLE TO SHOW MY GRATITUDE... BUT JUST GOING OFF ABOUT IDEALS IS EASY, HUH? (TEARS) THIS TIME AT LEAST I TRIED TO MAKE IT COUNT AND WORKED HARD ON THIS DRAWING (!).
DID ANYONE ENJOY IT, EVEN A LITTLE? BEFORE, I WAS REALLY HAPPY TO FIND OUT THAT THERE WERE ACTUALLY PEOPLE WHO ENJOYED THE "OFF-SHOT CARDS" THAT WERE INCLUDED IN THE FIRST EDITION ONLY AND THAT A LOT OF PEOPLE LOOK FORWARD TO THESE DOODLES! ♪

LUKA'S TIME OFF:
IT SEEMS LIKE HE'S BEEN TOLD SOME THINGS HE DOESN'T NEED TO KNOW BY TACHIBANA AND ISUZU-SENSEI... (LOL)
POOR THING......

▼ I DID THESE ILLUSTRATIONS FOR A MUG PROMO GIVEAWAY IN ASUKA EARLIER. IT'S FUN TO DO IMAGES LIKE THESE! ☆

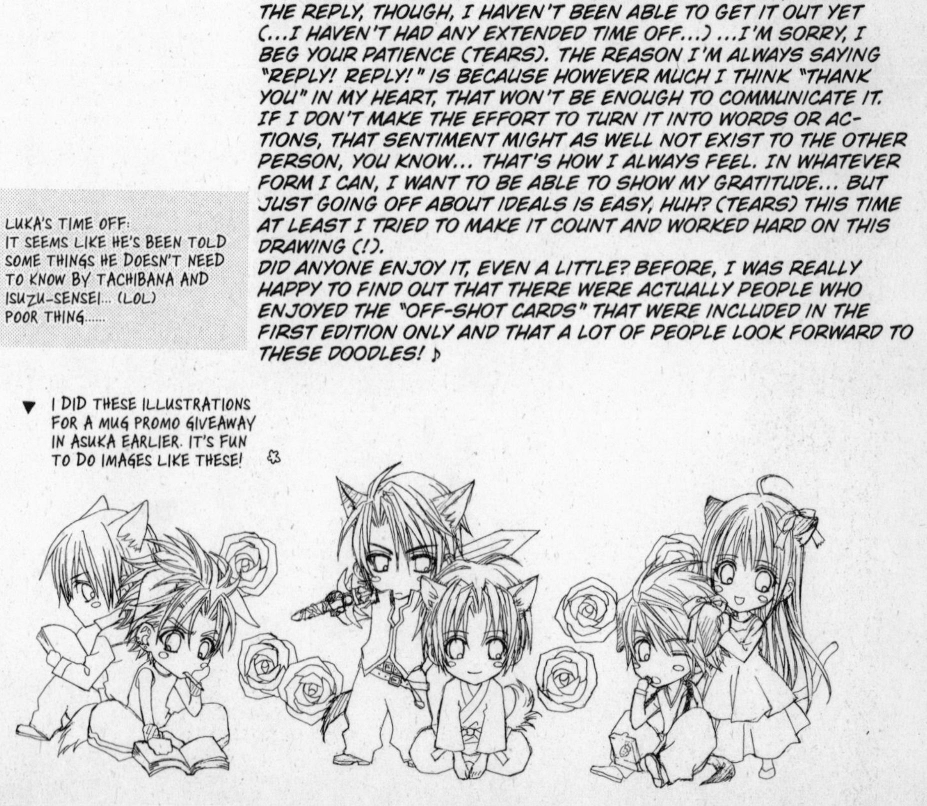

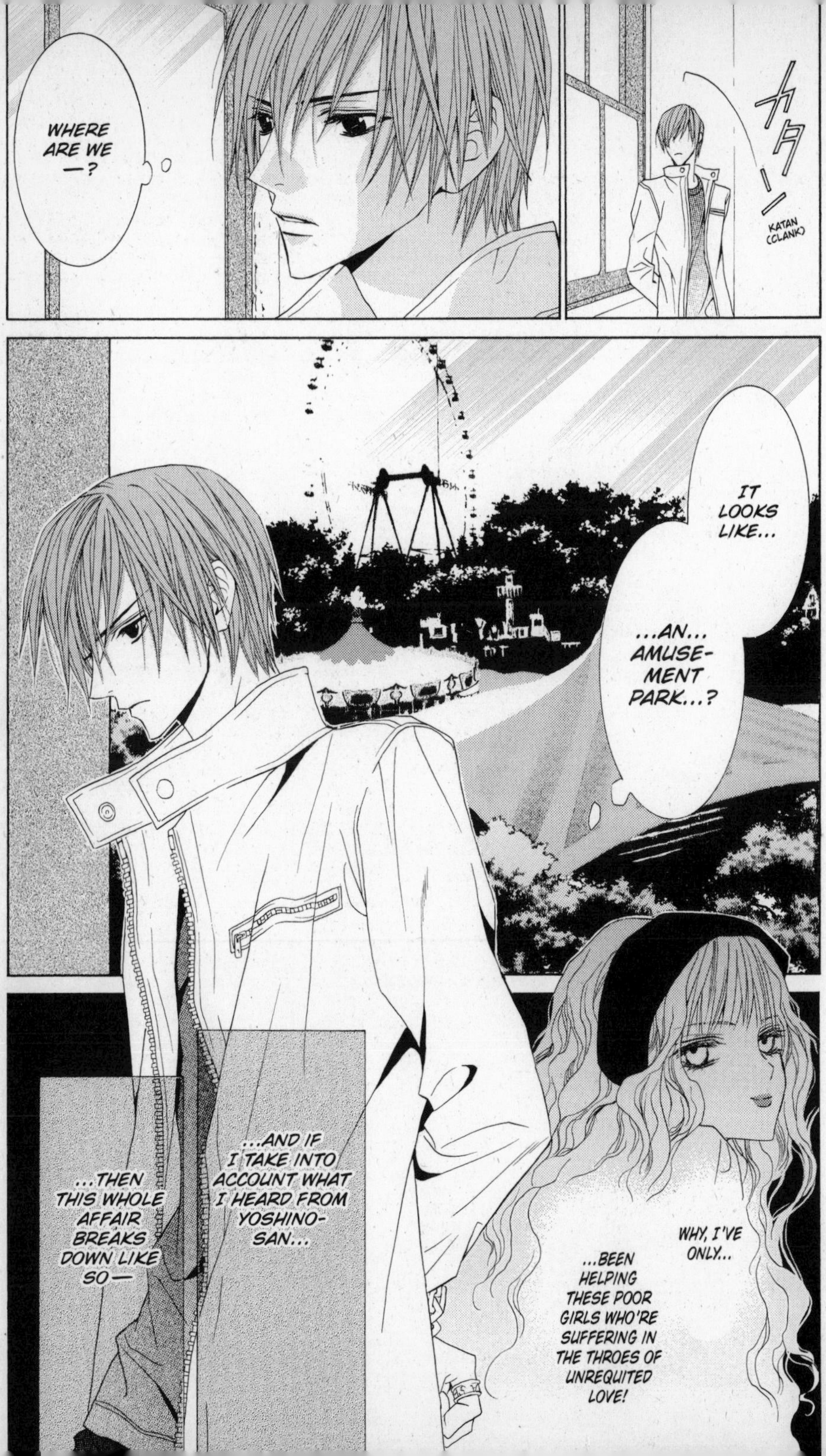
カタン
KATAN (CLANK)
WHERE ARE WE —?
IT LOOKS LIKE...
...AN... AMUSEMENT PARK...?
WHY, I'VE ONLY...
...BEEN HELPING THESE POOR GIRLS WHO'RE SUFFERING IN THE THROES OF UNREQUITED LOVE!
...AND IF I TAKE INTO ACCOUNT WHAT I HEARD FROM YOSHINO-SAN...
...THEN THIS WHOLE AFFAIR BREAKS DOWN LIKE SO—

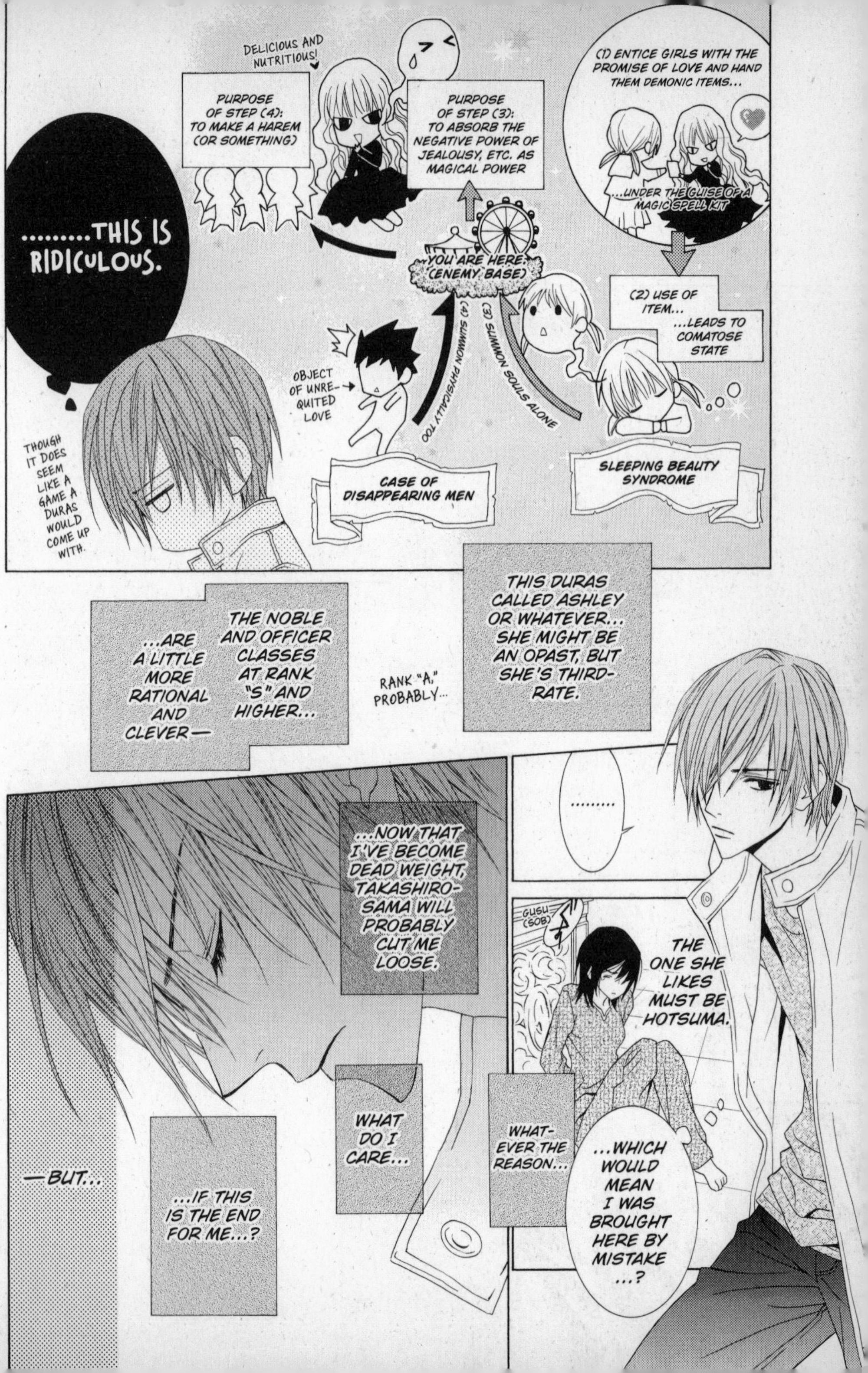
(1) ENTICE GIRLS WITH THE PROMISE OF LOVE AND HAND THEM DEMONIC ITEMS...
...UNDER THE GUISE OF A MAGIC SPELL KIT
(2) USE OF ITEM... ...LEADS TO COMATOSE STATE
SLEEPING BEAUTY SYNDROME
(3) SUMMON SOULS ALONE
PURPOSE OF STEP (3): TO ABSORB THE NEGATIVE POWER OF JEALOUSY, ETC. AS MAGICAL POWER
YOU ARE HERE. (ENEMY BASE)
DELICIOUS AND NUTRITIOUS!
PURPOSE OF STEP (4): TO MAKE A HAREM (OR SOMETHING)
(4) SUMMON PHYSICALLY TOO
OBJECT OF UNREQUITED LOVE
CASE OF DISAPPEARING MEN
.........THIS IS RIDICULOUS.
THOUGH IT DOES SEEM LIKE A GAME A DURAS WOULD COME UP WITH.
THIS DURAS CALLED ASHLEY OR WHATEVER... SHE MIGHT BE AN OPAST, BUT SHE'S THIRD-RATE.
RANK "A," PROBABLY...
THE NOBLE AND OFFICER CLASSES AT RANK "S" AND HIGHER...
...ARE A LITTLE MORE RATIONAL AND CLEVER—
....
GUSU (SOB)
THE ONE SHE LIKES MUST BE HOTSUMA.
...WHICH WOULD MEAN I WAS BROUGHT HERE BY MISTAKE...?
WHATEVER THE REASON...
...NOW THAT I'VE BECOME DEAD WEIGHT, TAKASHIRO-SAMA WILL PROBABLY CUT ME LOOSE.
WHAT DO I CARE...
...IF THIS IS THE END FOR ME...?
—BUT...

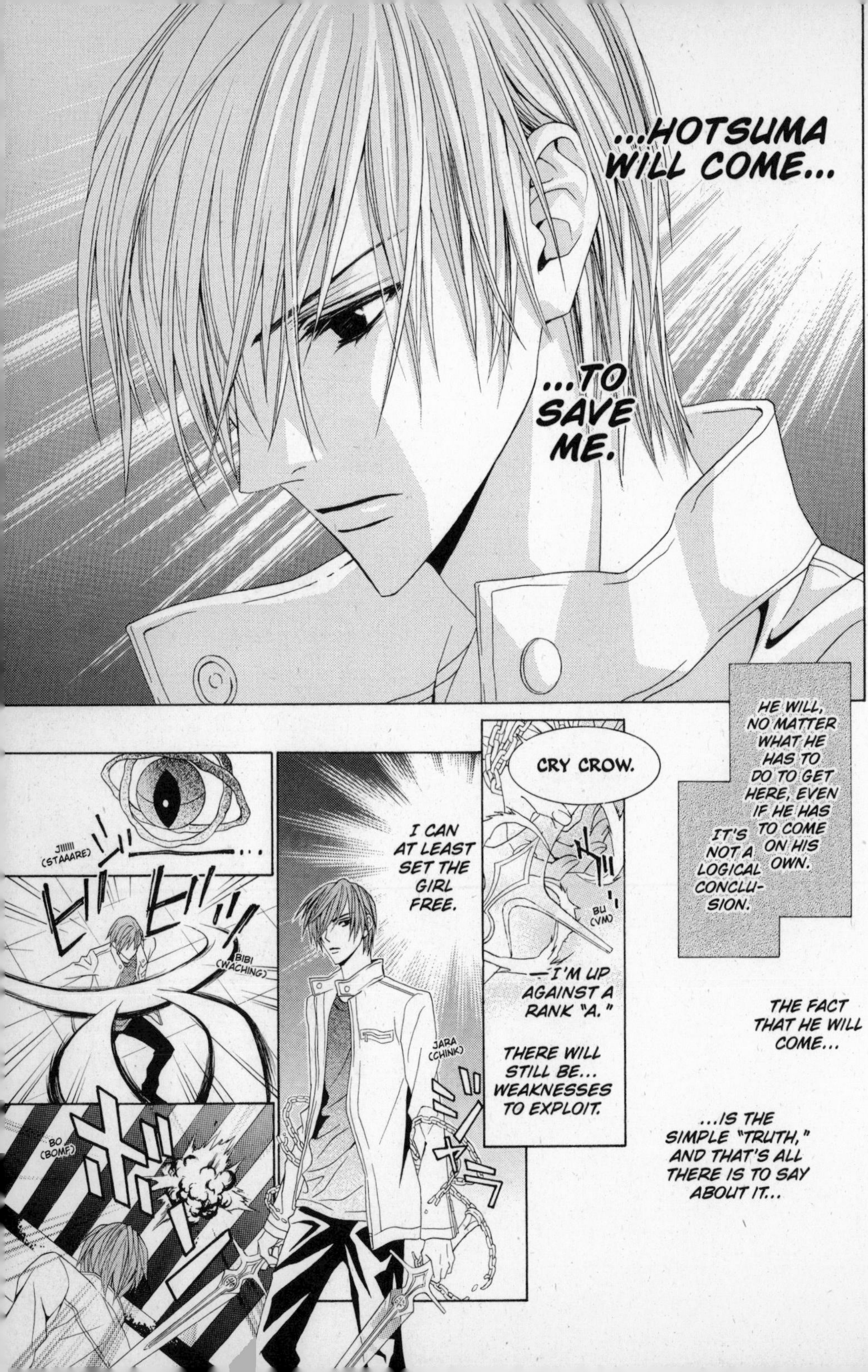
...HOTSUMA WILL COME...
...TO SAVE ME.
HE WILL, NO MATTER WHAT HE HAS TO DO TO GET HERE, EVEN IF HE HAS TO COME ON HIS OWN.
IT'S NOT A LOGICAL CONCLUSION.
THE FACT THAT HE WILL COME...
...IS THE SIMPLE "TRUTH," AND THAT'S ALL THERE IS TO SAY ABOUT IT...
CRY CROW.
BU (VM)
—I'M UP AGAINST A RANK "A."
THERE WILL STILL BE... WEAKNESSES TO EXPLOIT.
I CAN AT LEAST SET THE GIRL FREE.
JARA (CHINK)
JIIIIII (STAAARE)
BIBI (WACHING)
BO (BOMF)

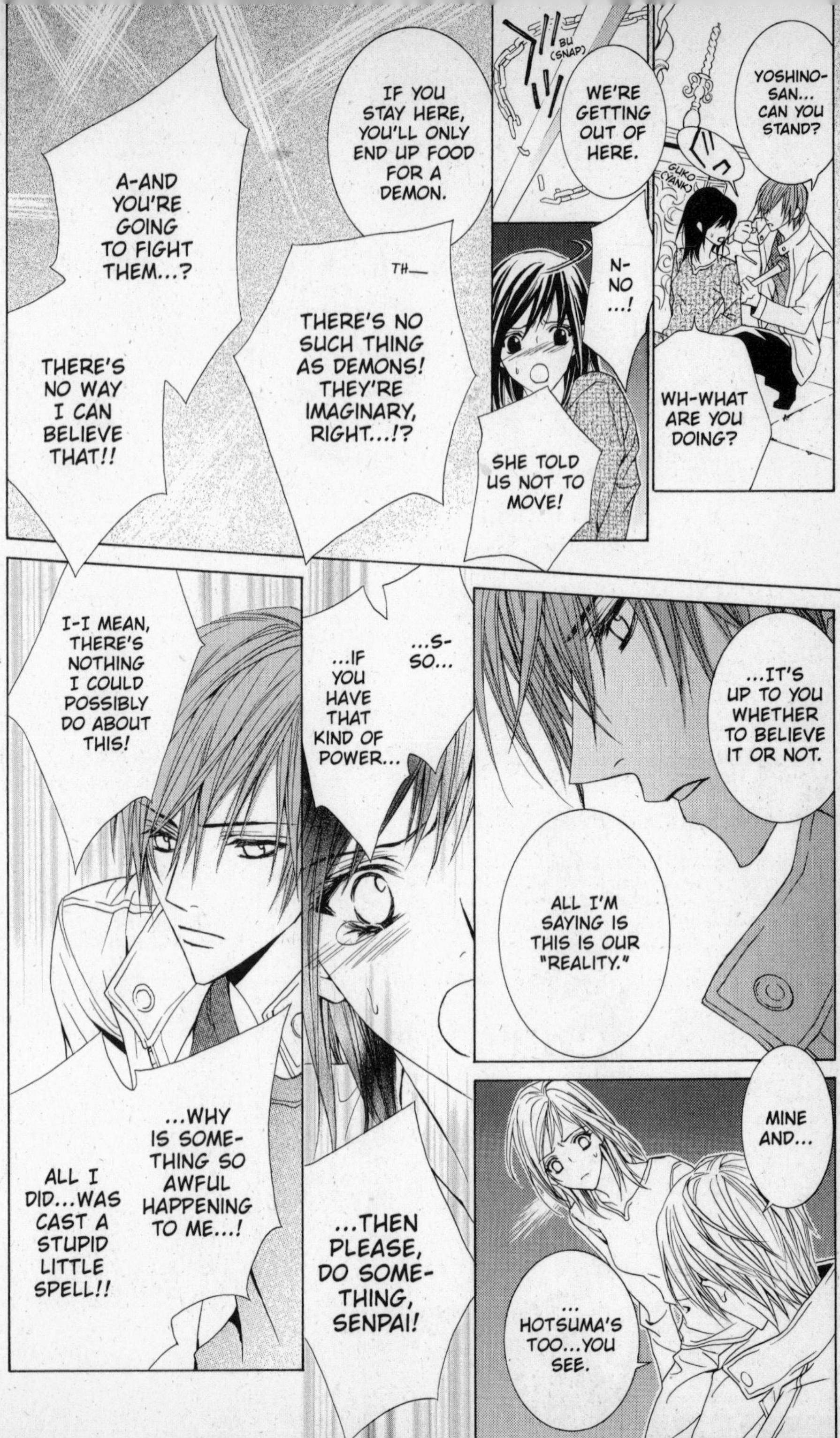
YOSHINO-SAN... CAN YOU STAND?
GUKO (YANK)
WH-WHAT ARE YOU DOING?
BU (SNAP)
WE'RE GETTING OUT OF HERE.
N-NO ...!
SHE TOLD US NOT TO MOVE!
IF YOU STAY HERE, YOU'LL ONLY END UP FOOD FOR A DEMON.
TH—
THERE'S NO SUCH THING AS DEMONS! THEY'RE IMAGINARY, RIGHT...!?
A-AND YOU'RE GOING TO FIGHT THEM...?
THERE'S NO WAY I CAN BELIEVE THAT!!
...IT'S UP TO YOU WHETHER TO BELIEVE IT OR NOT.
ALL I'M SAYING IS THIS IS OUR "REALITY."
MINE AND...
... HOTSUMA'S TOO...YOU SEE.
...S-SO...
...IF YOU HAVE THAT KIND OF POWER...
...THEN PLEASE, DO SOME-THING, SENPAI!
I-I MEAN, THERE'S NOTHING I COULD POSSIBLY DO ABOUT THIS!
...WHY IS SOME-THING SO AWFUL HAPPENING TO ME...!
ALL I DID...WAS CAST A STUPID LITTLE SPELL!!

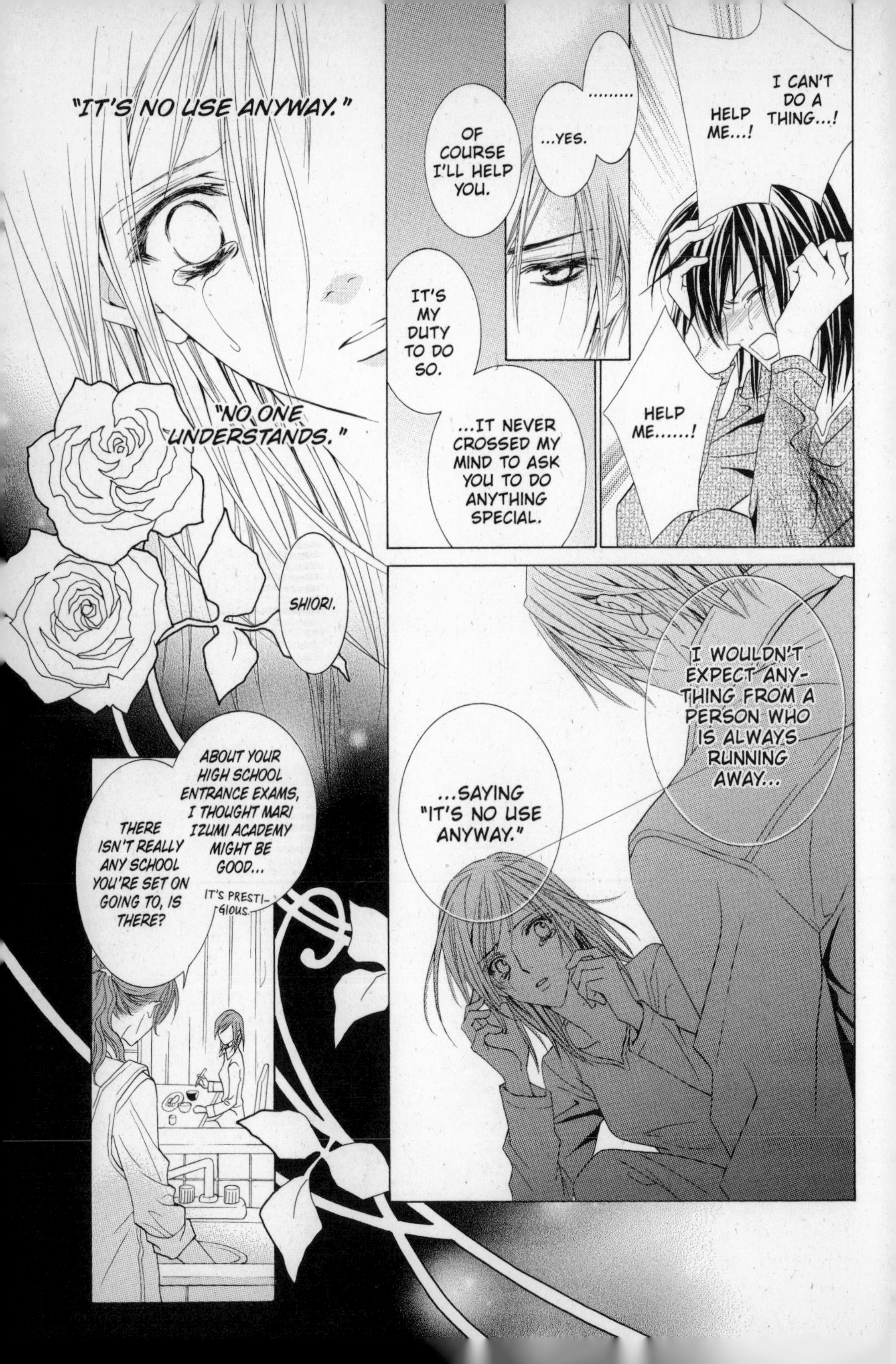
I CAN'T DO A THING...!
HELP ME...!
HELP ME......!
....
...YES.
OF COURSE I'LL HELP YOU.
IT'S MY DUTY TO DO SO.
...IT NEVER CROSSED MY MIND TO ASK YOU TO DO ANYTHING SPECIAL.
I WOULDN'T EXPECT ANYTHING FROM A PERSON WHO IS ALWAYS RUNNING AWAY...
...SAYING "IT'S NO USE ANYWAY."
"IT'S NO USE ANYWAY."
"NO ONE UNDERSTANDS."
SHIORI.
ABOUT YOUR HIGH SCHOOL ENTRANCE EXAMS, I THOUGHT MARI IZUMI ACADEMY MIGHT BE GOOD...
IT'S PRESTIGIOUS.
THERE ISN'T REALLY ANY SCHOOL YOU'RE SET ON GOING TO, IS THERE?

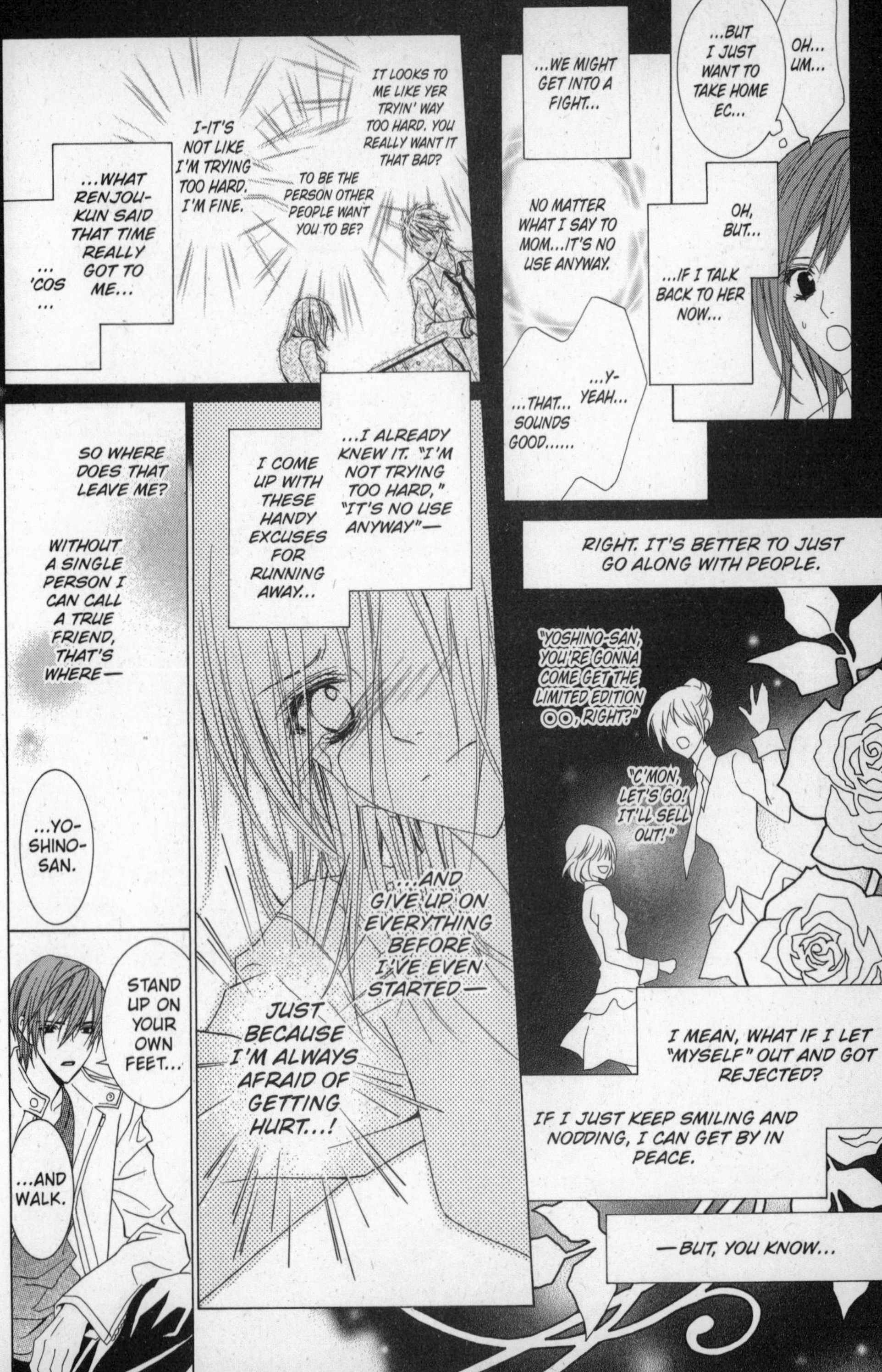
OH... UM...
...BUT I JUST WANT TO TAKE HOME EC...
OH, BUT...
...IF I TALK BACK TO HER NOW...
...WE MIGHT GET INTO A FIGHT...
NO MATTER WHAT I SAY TO MOM...IT'S NO USE ANYWAY.
...Y-YEAH...
...THAT... SOUNDS GOOD......
IT LOOKS TO ME LIKE YER TRYIN' WAY TOO HARD. YOU REALLY WANT IT THAT BAD?
TO BE THE PERSON OTHER PEOPLE WANT YOU TO BE?
I-IT'S NOT LIKE I'M TRYING TOO HARD. I'M FINE.
...WHAT RENJOU-KUN SAID THAT TIME REALLY GOT TO ME...
...'COS...
RIGHT. IT'S BETTER TO JUST GO ALONG WITH PEOPLE.
"YOSHINO-SAN, YOU'RE GONNA COME GET THE LIMITED EDITION ○○, RIGHT?"
"C'MON, LET'S GO! IT'LL SELL OUT!"
I MEAN, WHAT IF I LET "MYSELF" OUT AND GOT REJECTED?
IF I JUST KEEP SMILING AND NODDING, I CAN GET BY IN PEACE.
—BUT, YOU KNOW...
...I ALREADY KNEW IT. "I'M NOT TRYING TOO HARD," "IT'S NO USE ANYWAY"—
I COME UP WITH THESE HANDY EXCUSES FOR RUNNING AWAY...
...AND GIVE UP ON EVERYTHING BEFORE I'VE EVEN STARTED—
JUST BECAUSE I'M ALWAYS AFRAID OF GETTING HURT...!
SO WHERE DOES THAT LEAVE ME?
WITHOUT A SINGLE PERSON I CAN CALL A TRUE FRIEND, THAT'S WHERE—
...YO-SHINO-SAN.
STAND UP ON YOUR OWN FEET...
...AND WALK.

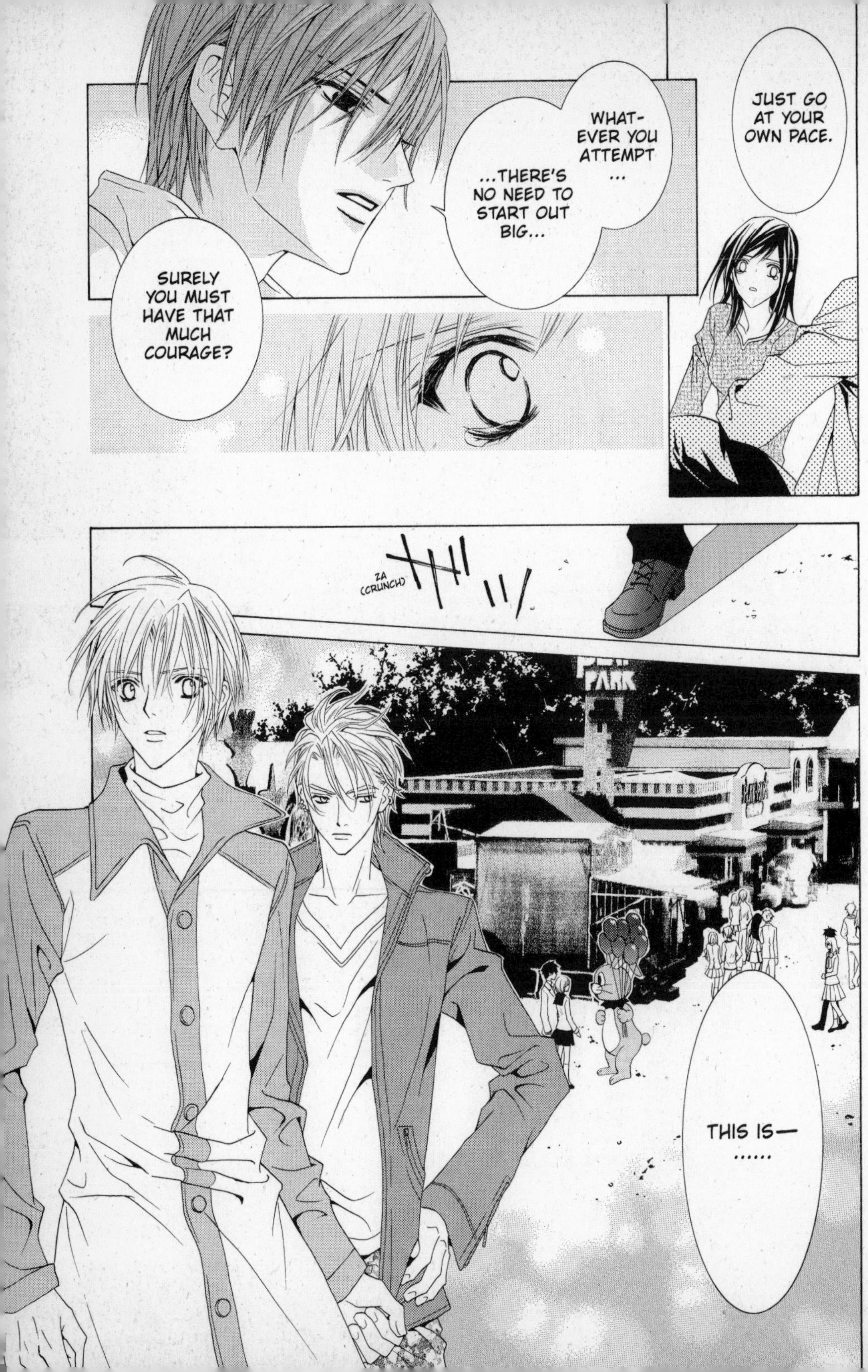
JUST GO AT YOUR OWN PACE.
WHAT-EVER YOU ATTEMPT ...
...THERE'S NO NEED TO START OUT BIG...
SURELY YOU MUST HAVE THAT MUCH COURAGE?
ZA (CRUNCH)
PARK
THIS IS— ......

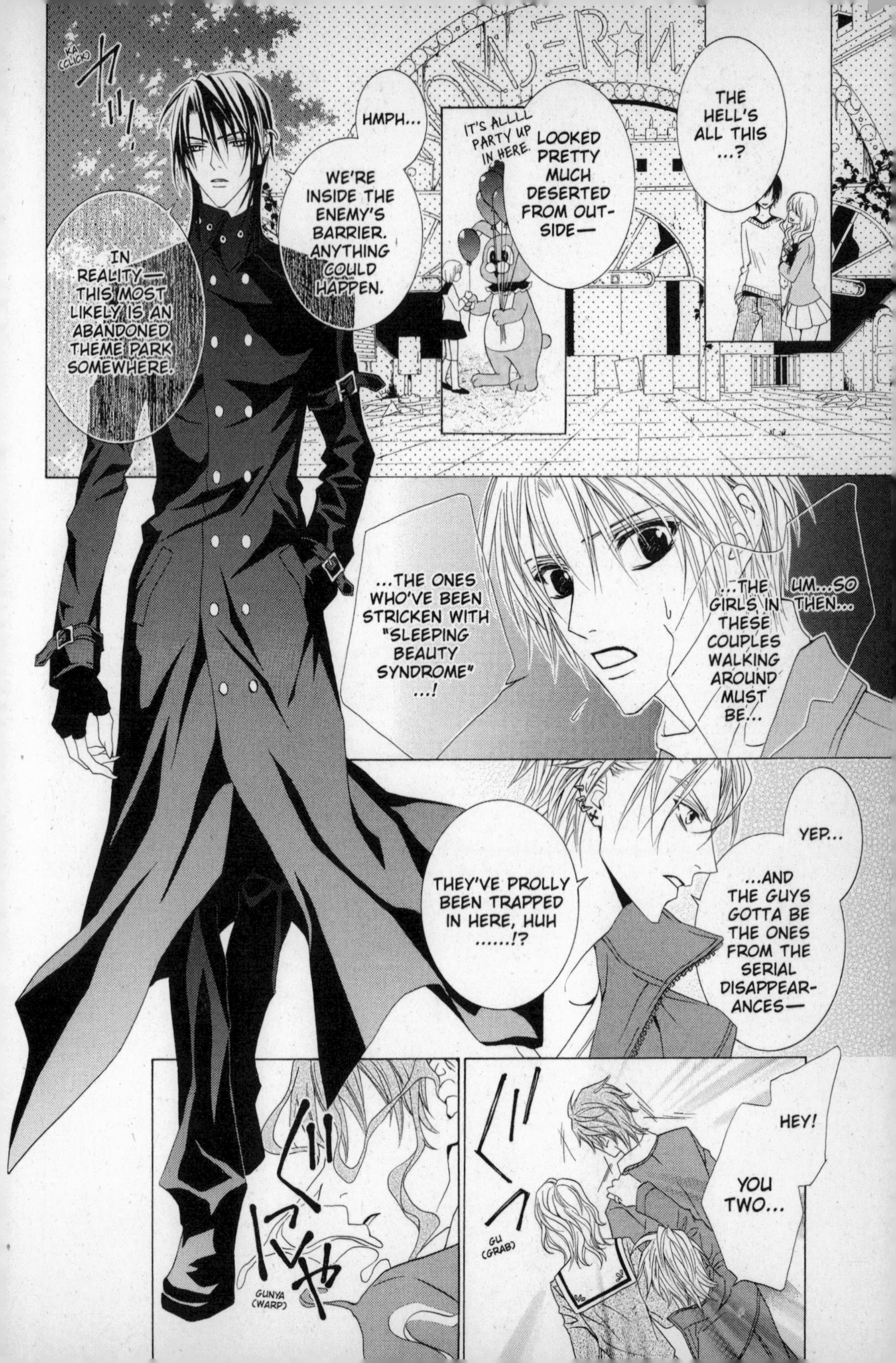
THE HELL'S ALL THIS ...?
IT'S ALLLL PARTY UP IN HERE.
LOOKED PRETTY MUCH DESERTED FROM OUT-SIDE—
KA (CLICK)
HMPH...
WE'RE INSIDE THE ENEMY'S BARRIER. ANYTHING COULD HAPPEN.
IN REALITY— THIS MOST LIKELY IS AN ABANDONED THEME PARK SOMEWHERE.
UM...SO THEN...
...THE GIRLS IN THESE COUPLES WALKING AROUND MUST BE...
...THE ONES WHO'VE BEEN STRICKEN WITH "SLEEPING BEAUTY SYNDROME" ...!
YEP...
...AND THE GUYS GOTTA BE THE ONES FROM THE SERIAL DISAPPEAR-ANCES—
THEY'VE PROLLY BEEN TRAPPED IN HERE, HUH ......!?
HEY!
YOU TWO...
GU (GRAB)
GUNYA (WARP)

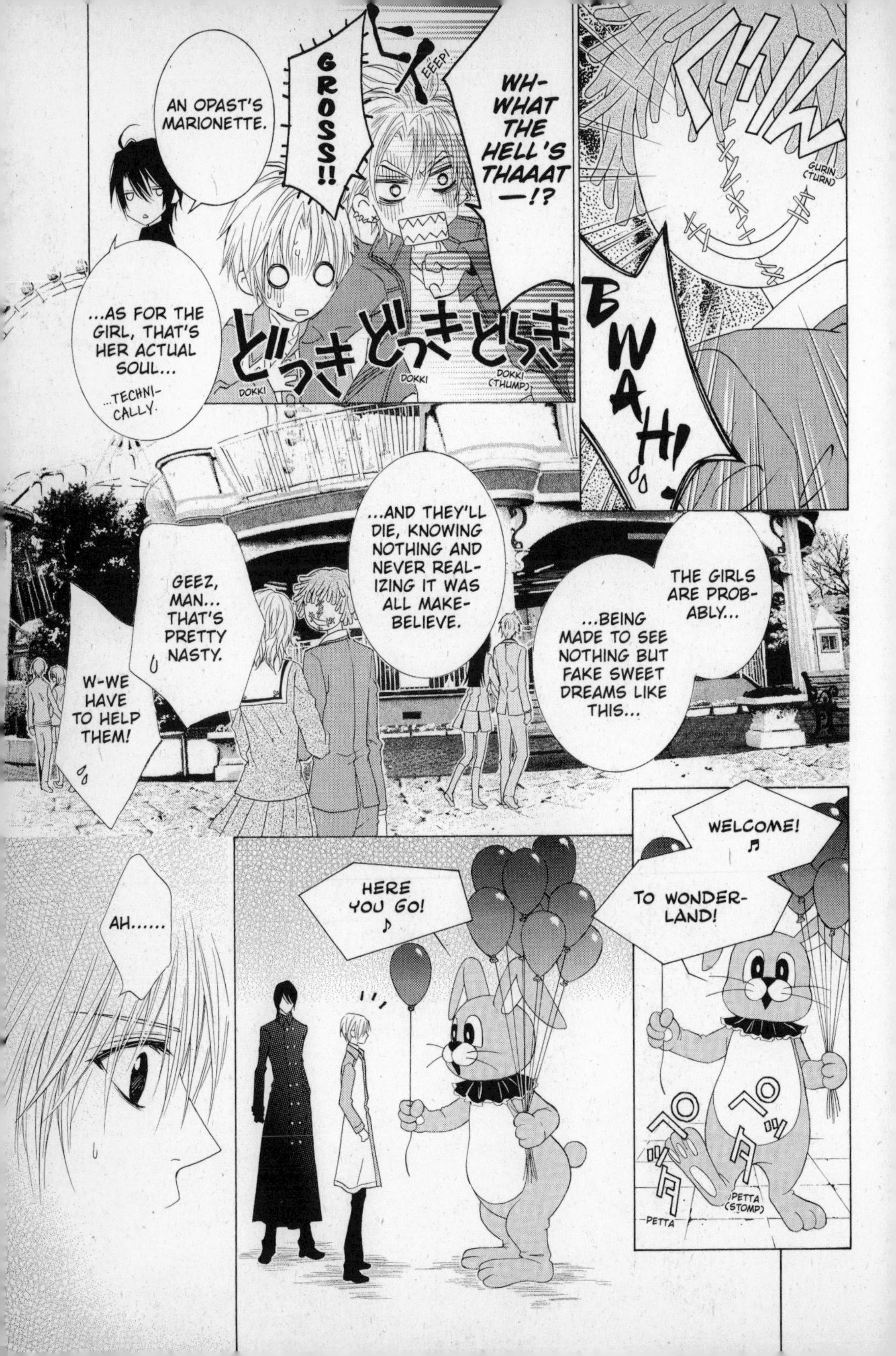
GURIN (TURN)
BWAH!
WH-WHAT THE HELL'S THAAAT—!?
EEEP!
GROSS!!
AN OPAST'S MARIONETTE.
DOKKI (THUMP)
DOKKI
DOKKI
...AS FOR THE GIRL, THAT'S HER ACTUAL SOUL...
...TECHNI-CALLY.
THE GIRLS ARE PROB-ABLY...
...BEING MADE TO SEE NOTHING BUT FAKE SWEET DREAMS LIKE THIS...
...AND THEY'LL DIE, KNOWING NOTHING AND NEVER REAL-IZING IT WAS ALL MAKE-BELIEVE.
GEEZ, MAN... THAT'S PRETTY NASTY.
W-WE HAVE TO HELP THEM!
WELCOME! ♪
TO WONDER-LAND!
PETTA (STOMP)
PETTA
HERE YOU GO! ♪
AH......

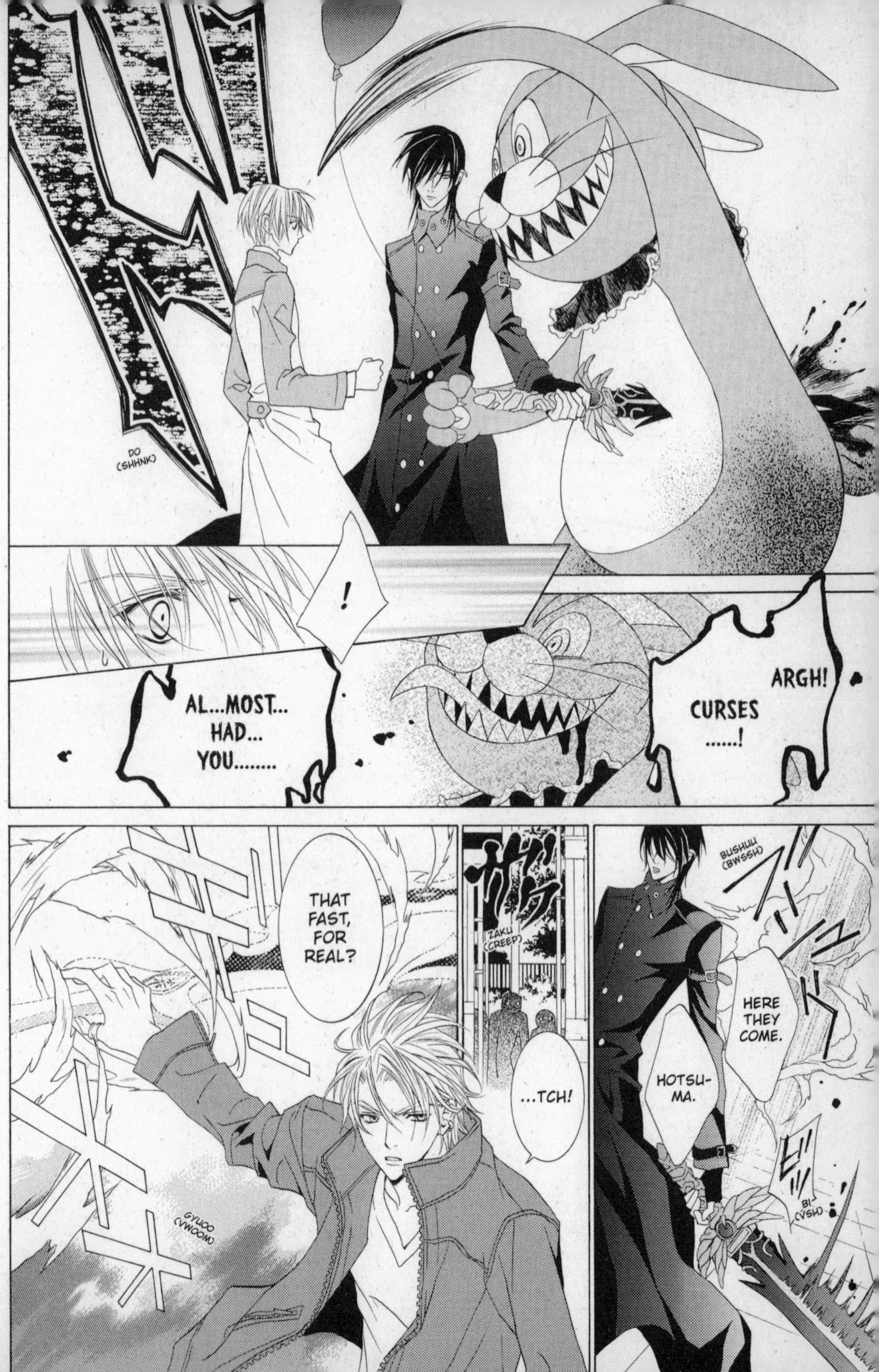

DO (SHHNK)
!
ARGH! CURSES ......!
AL...MOST... HAD... YOU........
BUSHUU (BWSSH)
HERE THEY COME.
HOTSU-MA.
BI (VSH)
ZAKU (CREEP)
...TCH!
THAT FAST, FOR REAL?
GYUOO (VWOOM)

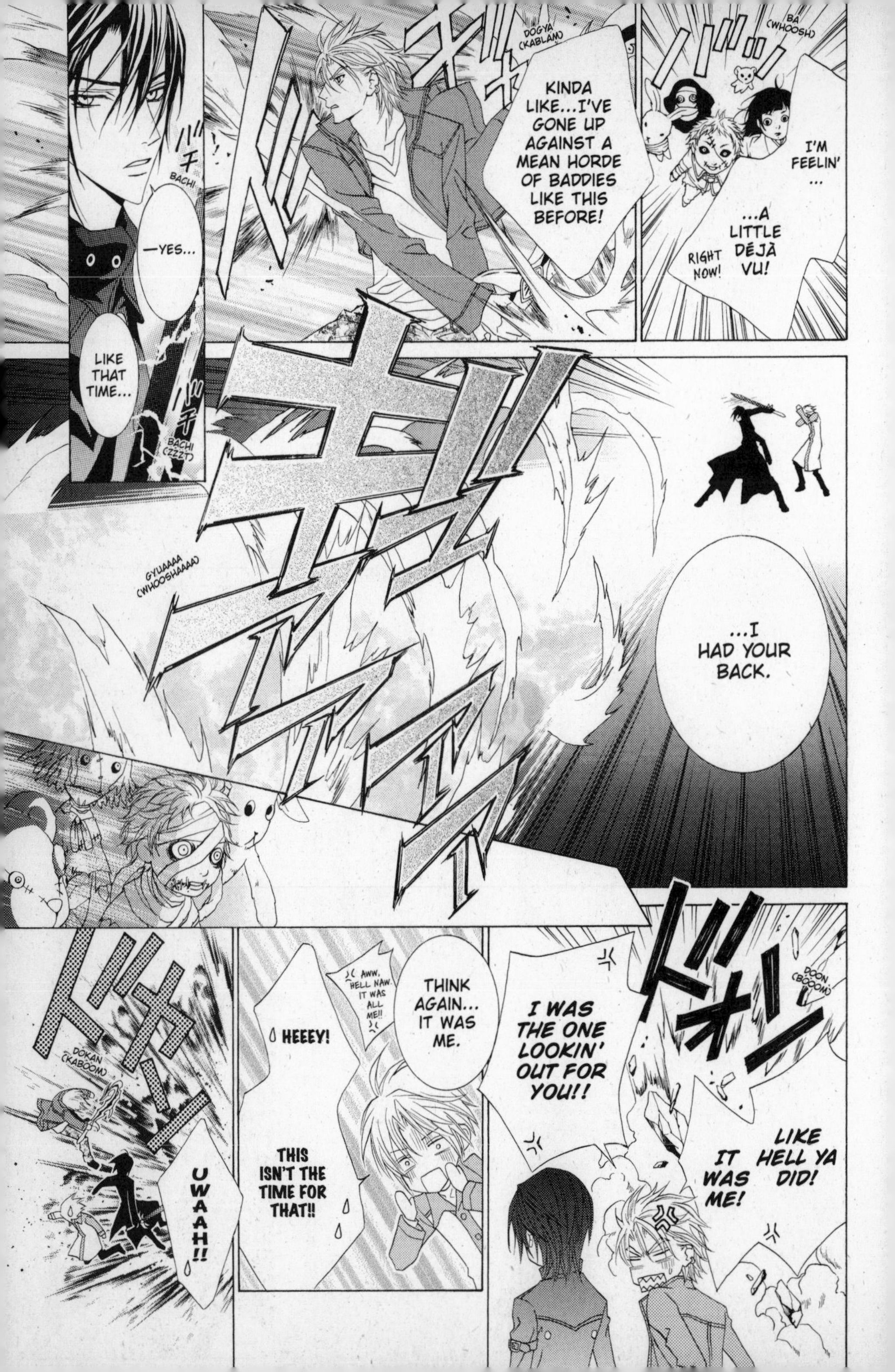
BA (WHOOSH)
I'M FEELIN'...
...A LITTLE DÉJÀ VU!
RIGHT NOW!
DOGYA (KABLAM)
KINDA LIKE...I'VE GONE UP AGAINST A MEAN HORDE OF BADDIES LIKE THIS BEFORE!
BACHI
—YES...
LIKE THAT TIME...
BACHI (ZZZT)
...I HAD YOUR BACK.
GYUAAAA (WHOOSHAAAA)
DOON (BOOOM)
I WAS THE ONE LOOKIN' OUT FOR YOU!!
LIKE HELL YA DID!
IT WAS ME!
THINK AGAIN... IT WAS ME.
AWW, HELL NAW. IT WAS ALL ME!!
HEEEY!
THIS ISN'T THE TIME FOR THAT!!
DOKAN (KABOOM)
UWAAAH!!

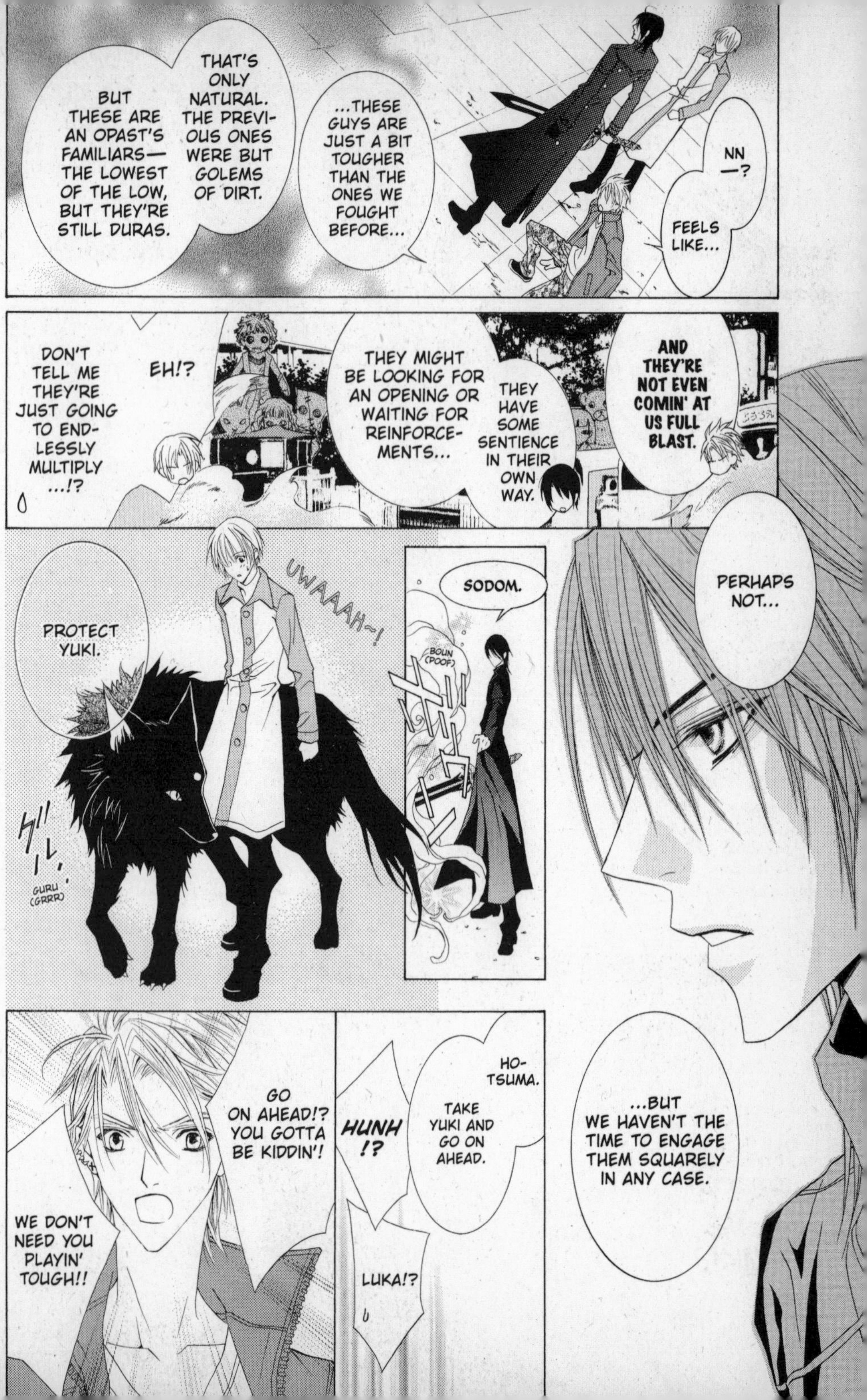
NN—?
FEELS LIKE...
...THESE GUYS ARE JUST A BIT TOUGHER THAN THE ONES WE FOUGHT BEFORE...
THAT'S ONLY NATURAL. THE PREVIOUS ONES WERE BUT GOLEMS OF DIRT.
BUT THESE ARE AN OPAST'S FAMILIARS—THE LOWEST OF THE LOW, BUT THEY'RE STILL DURAS.
AND THEY'RE NOT EVEN COMIN' AT US FULL BLAST.
THEY HAVE SOME SENTIENCE IN THEIR OWN WAY.
THEY MIGHT BE LOOKING FOR AN OPENING OR WAITING FOR REINFORCE-MENTS...
EH!?
DON'T TELL ME THEY'RE JUST GOING TO END-LESSLY MULTIPLY ...!?
PERHAPS NOT...
...BUT WE HAVEN'T THE TIME TO ENGAGE THEM SQUARELY IN ANY CASE.
SODOM.
BOUN (POOF)
UWAAAH~!
PROTECT YUKI.
GURU (GRRR)
HO-TSUMA.
TAKE YUKI AND GO ON AHEAD.
HUNH!?
LUKA!?
GO ON AHEAD!? YOU GOTTA BE KIDDIN'!
WE DON'T NEED YOU PLAYIN' TOUGH!!

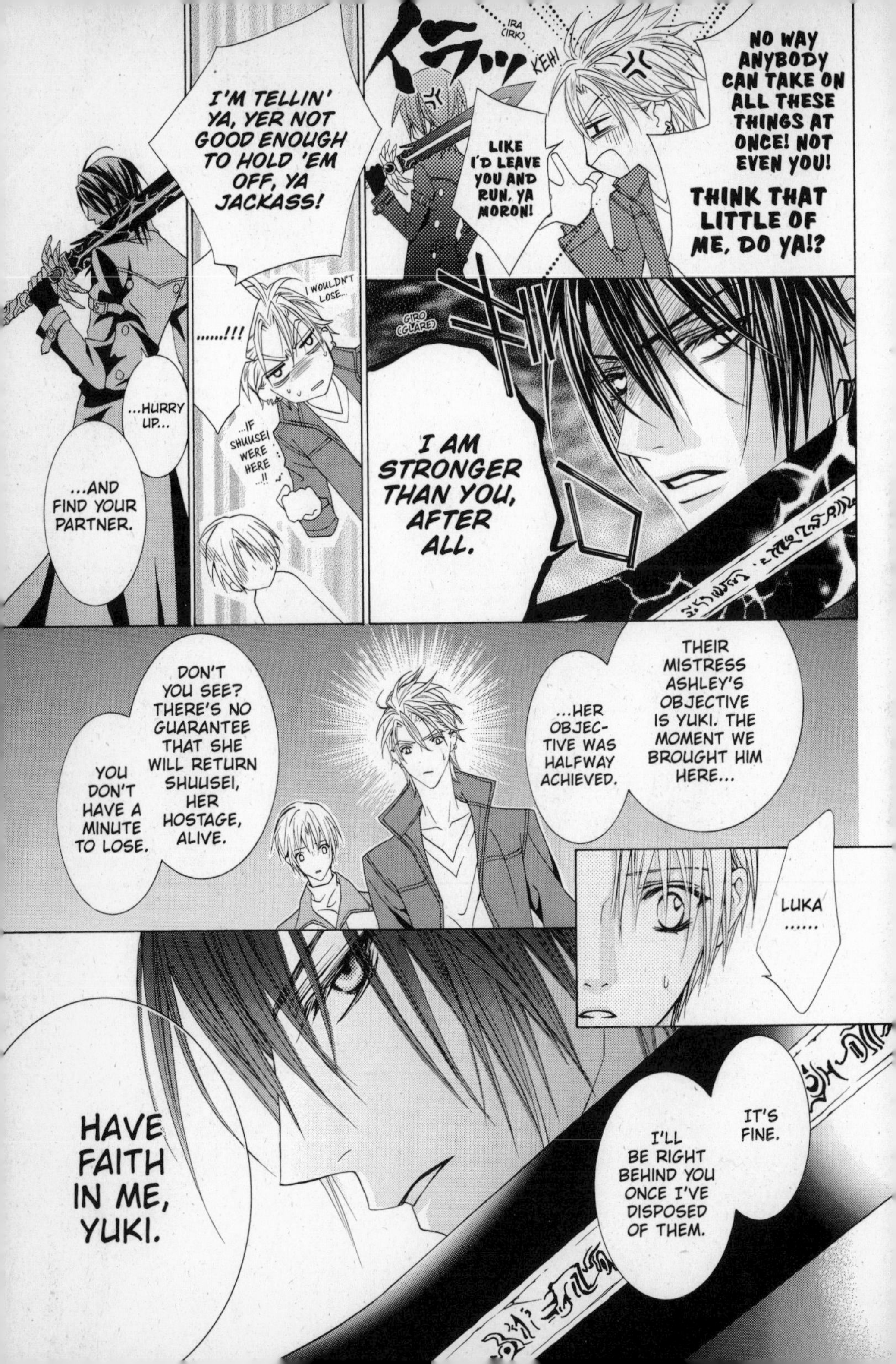
NO WAY ANYBODY CAN TAKE ON ALL THESE THINGS AT ONCE! NOT EVEN YOU!
IRA (IRK)
KEH!
LIKE I'D LEAVE YOU AND RUN, YA MORON!
THINK THAT LITTLE OF ME, DO YA!?
GIRO (GLARE)
I AM STRONGER THAN YOU, AFTER ALL.
I'M TELLIN' YA, YER NOT GOOD ENOUGH TO HOLD 'EM OFF, YA JACKASS!
I WOULDN'T LOSE...
......!!!
...IF SHUUSEI WERE HERE ...!!
...HURRY UP...
...AND FIND YOUR PARTNER.
THEIR MISTRESS ASHLEY'S OBJECTIVE IS YUKI. THE MOMENT WE BROUGHT HIM HERE...
...HER OBJECTIVE WAS HALFWAY ACHIEVED.
DON'T YOU SEE? THERE'S NO GUARANTEE THAT SHE WILL RETURN SHUUSEI, HER HOSTAGE, ALIVE.
YOU DON'T HAVE A MINUTE TO LOSE.
LUKA ......
IT'S FINE.
I'LL BE RIGHT BEHIND YOU ONCE I'VE DISPOSED OF THEM.
HAVE FAITH IN ME, YUKI.

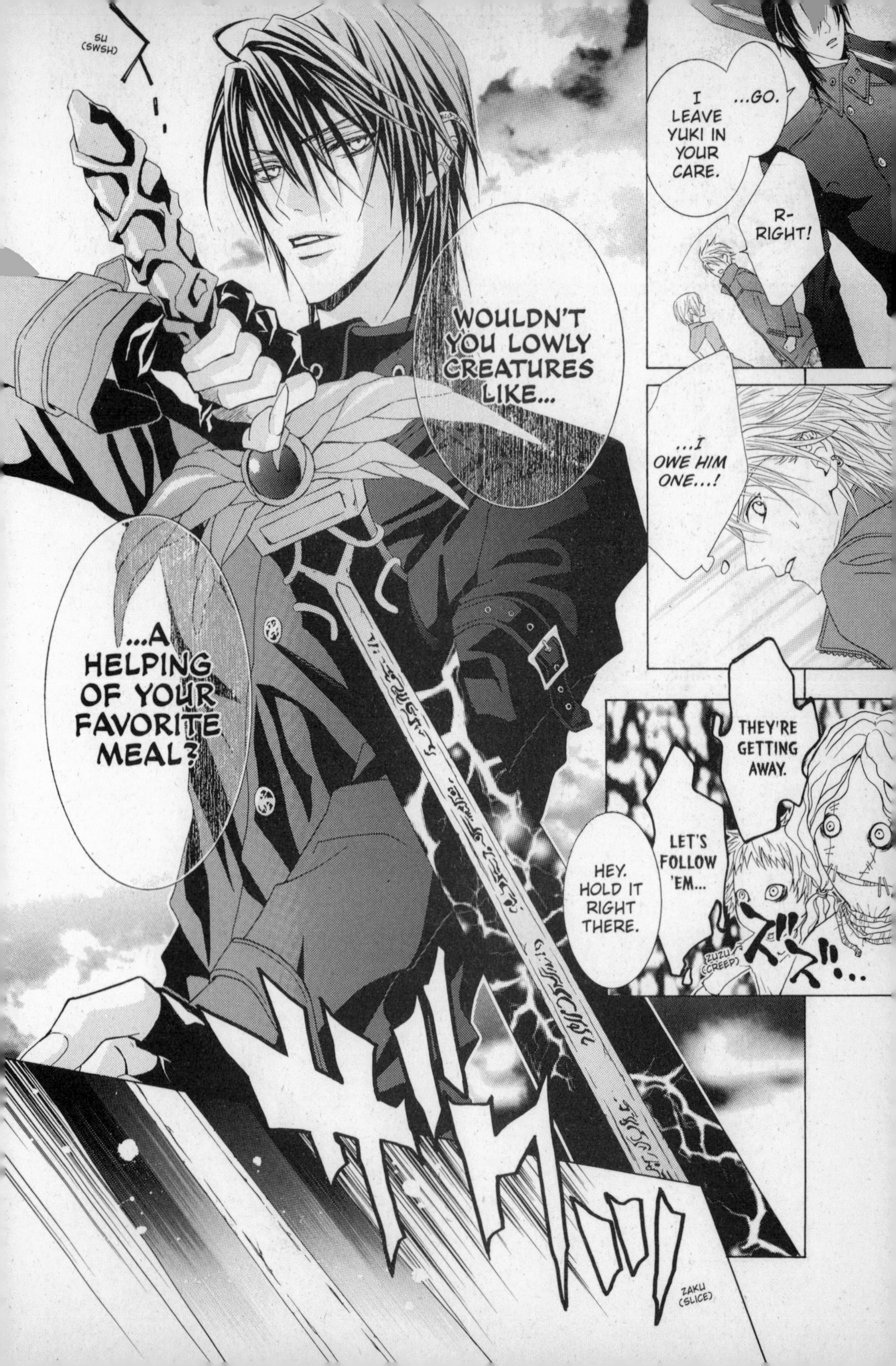
...GO.
I LEAVE YUKI IN YOUR CARE.
R-RIGHT!
...I OWE HIM ONE...!
THEY'RE GETTING AWAY.
LET'S FOLLOW 'EM...
ZUZU (CREEP)
HEY. HOLD IT RIGHT THERE.
SU (SWSH)
WOULDN'T YOU LOWLY CREATURES LIKE...
...A HELPING OF YOUR FAVORITE MEAL?
ZAKU (SLICE)

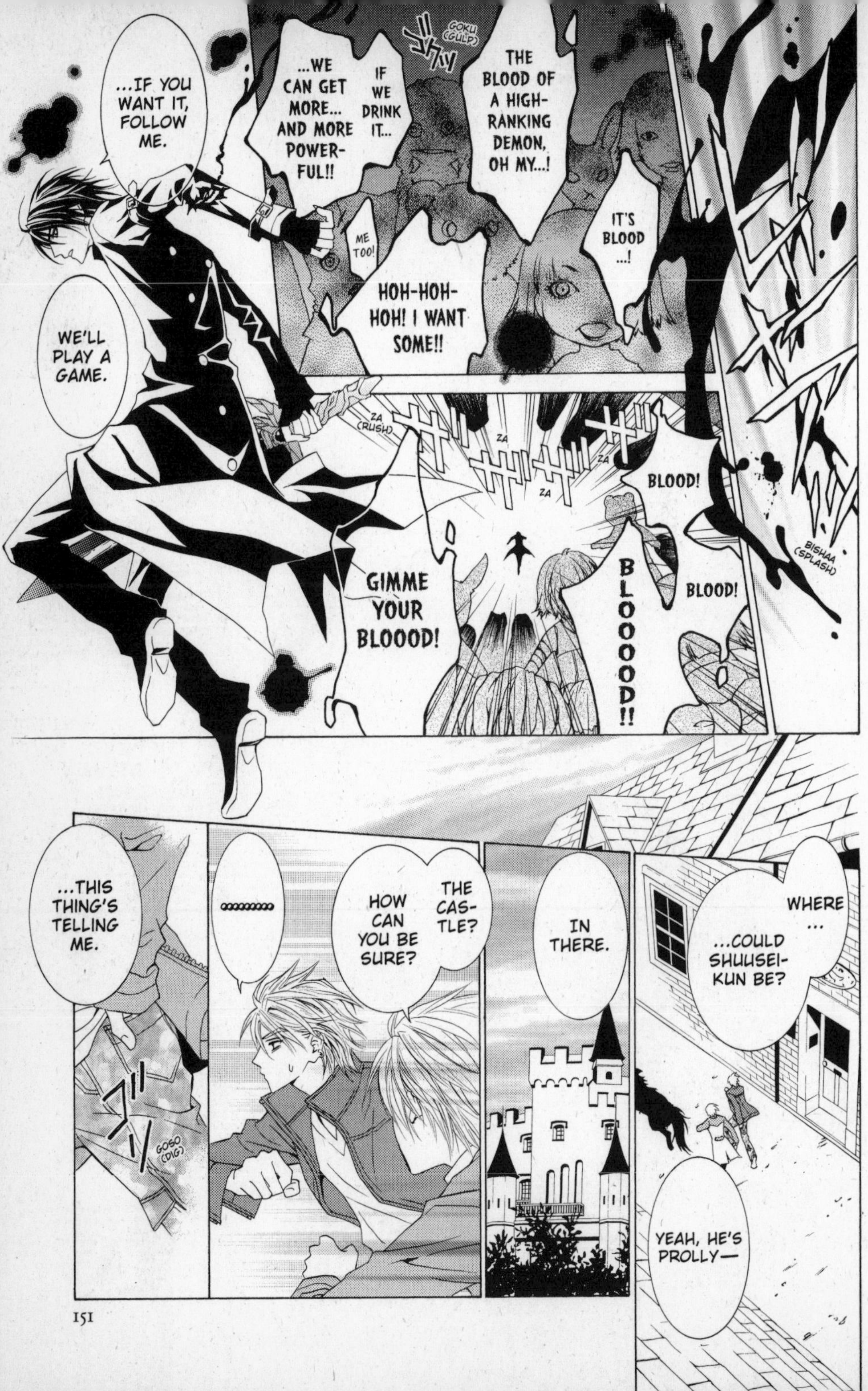
BISHAA (SPLASH)
IT'S BLOOD ...!
THE BLOOD OF A HIGH-RANKING DEMON, OH MY...!
GOKU (GULP)
IF WE DRINK IT...
...WE CAN GET MORE... AND MORE POWERFUL!!
ME TOO!
HOH-HOH-HOH! I WANT SOME!!
BLOOD!
BLOOD!
ZA
ZA
ZA
BLOOOOOD!!
ZA (RUSH)
GIMME YOUR BLOOOD!
...IF YOU WANT IT, FOLLOW ME.
WE'LL PLAY A GAME.
WHERE ...
...COULD SHUUSEI-KUN BE?
YEAH, HE'S PROLLY—
IN THERE.
THE CASTLE?
HOW CAN YOU BE SURE?
....
...THIS THING'S TELLING ME.
GOSO (DIG)

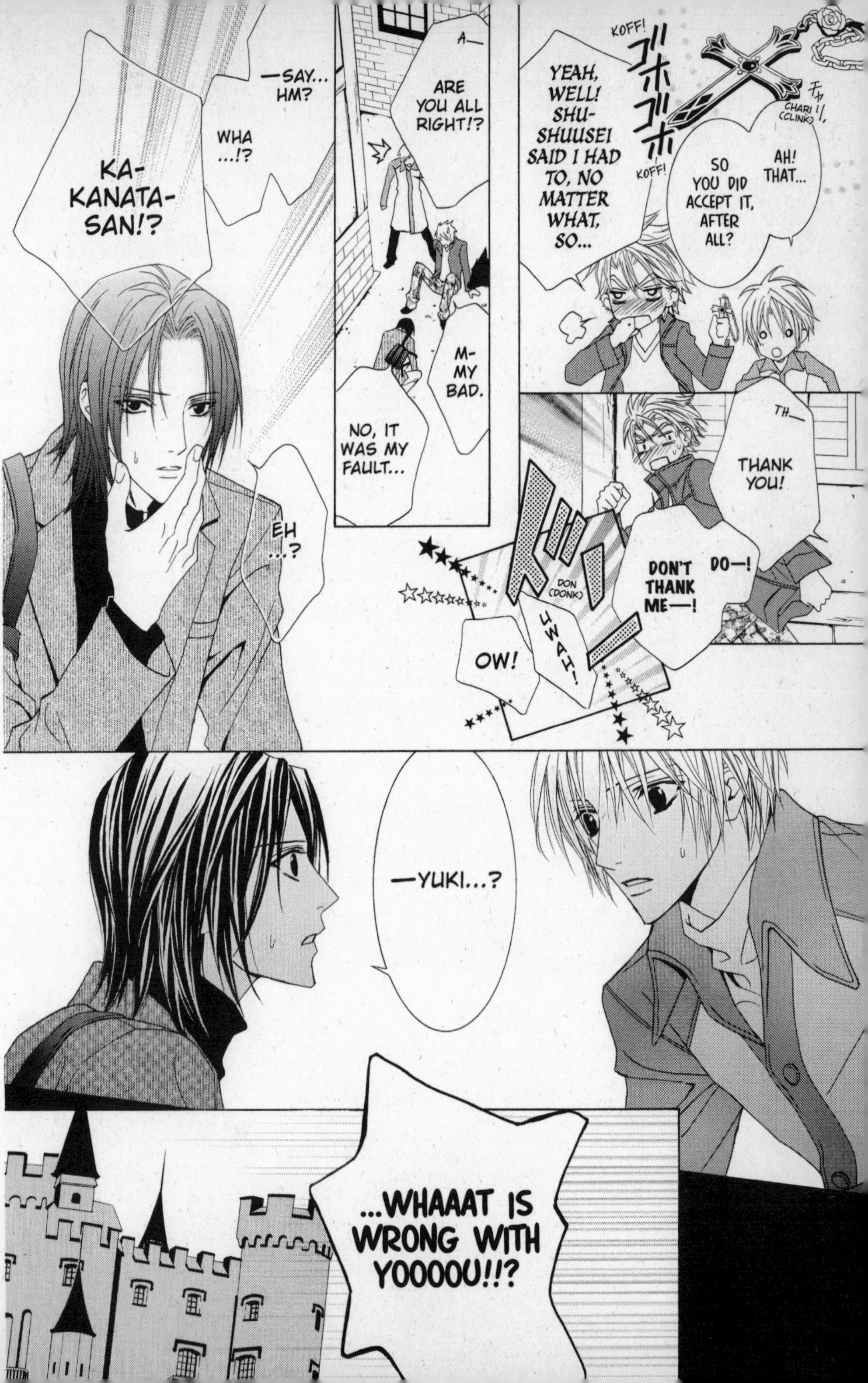
チャリ
CHARI (CLINK)
AH! THAT...
SO YOU DID ACCEPT IT, AFTER ALL?
ゴホゴホ
KOFF!
KOFF!
YEAH, WELL! SHU-SHUUSEI SAID I HAD TO, NO MATTER WHAT, SO...
TH—
THANK YOU!
DO—!
DON'T THANK ME—!
DON (DONK)
UWAH!
OW!
A—
ARE YOU ALL RIGHT!?
M-MY BAD.
NO, IT WAS MY FAULT...
—SAY... HM?
WHA ...!?
KA-KANATA-SAN!?
EH ...?
—YUKI...?
...WHAAAT IS WRONG WITH YOOOOU!!?

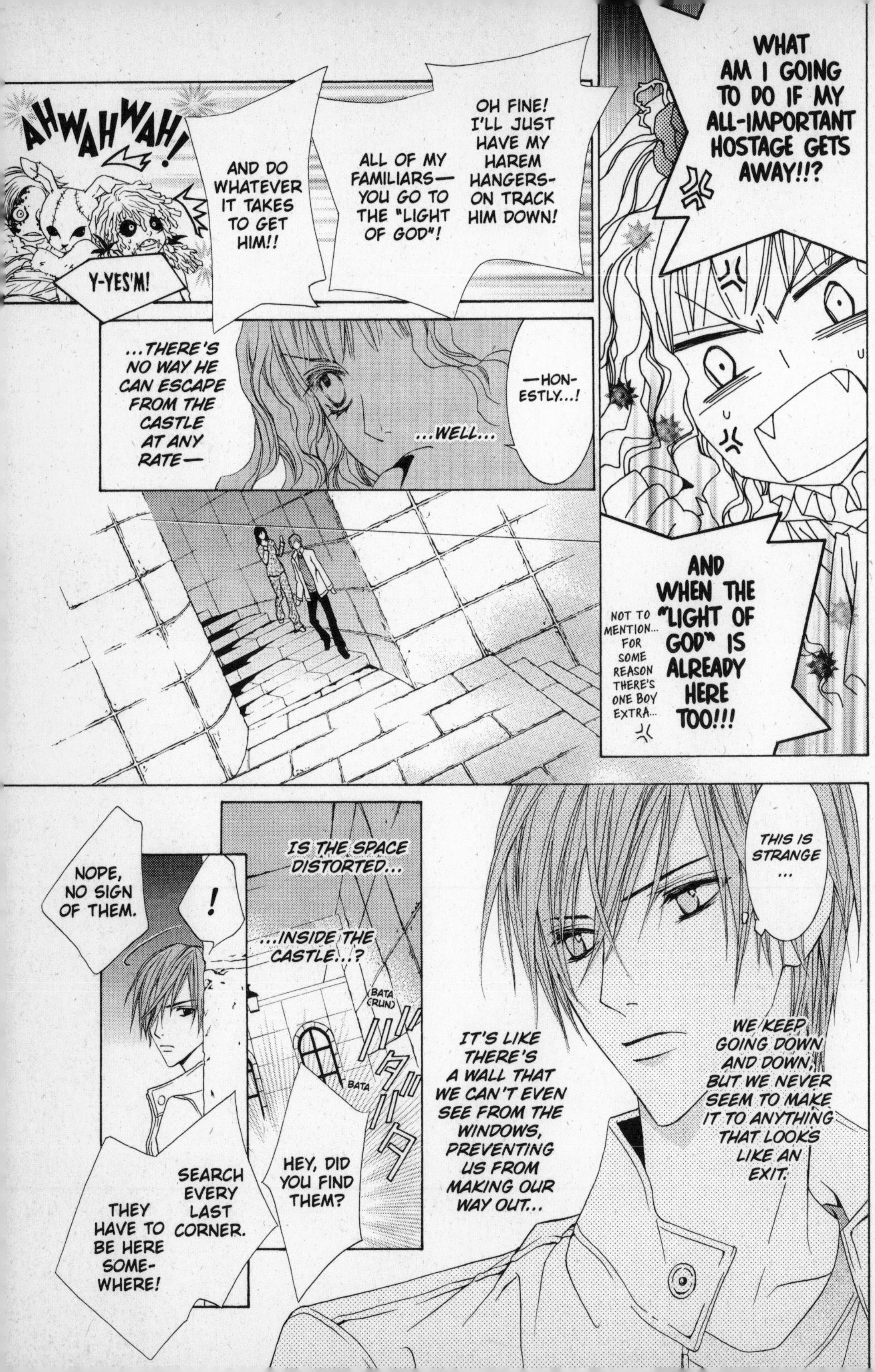
WHAT AM I GOING TO DO IF MY ALL-IMPORTANT HOSTAGE GETS AWAY!!?
AND WHEN THE "LIGHT OF GOD" IS ALREADY HERE TOO!!!
NOT TO MENTION... FOR SOME REASON THERE'S ONE BOY EXTRA...
OH FINE! I'LL JUST HAVE MY HAREM HANGERS-ON TRACK HIM DOWN!
ALL OF MY FAMILIARS— YOU GO TO THE "LIGHT OF GOD"!
AND DO WHATEVER IT TAKES TO GET HIM!!
AHWAHWAH!
Y-YES'M!
—HON-ESTLY...!
...WELL...
...THERE'S NO WAY HE CAN ESCAPE FROM THE CASTLE AT ANY RATE—
THIS IS STRANGE ...
WE KEEP GOING DOWN AND DOWN, BUT WE NEVER SEEM TO MAKE IT TO ANYTHING THAT LOOKS LIKE AN EXIT.
IT'S LIKE THERE'S A WALL THAT WE CAN'T EVEN SEE FROM THE WINDOWS, PREVENTING US FROM MAKING OUR WAY OUT...
IS THE SPACE DISTORTED...
...INSIDE THE CASTLE...?
BATA
BATA
HEY, DID YOU FIND THEM?
!
NOPE, NO SIGN OF THEM.
SEARCH EVERY LAST CORNER.
THEY HAVE TO BE HERE SOMEWHERE!

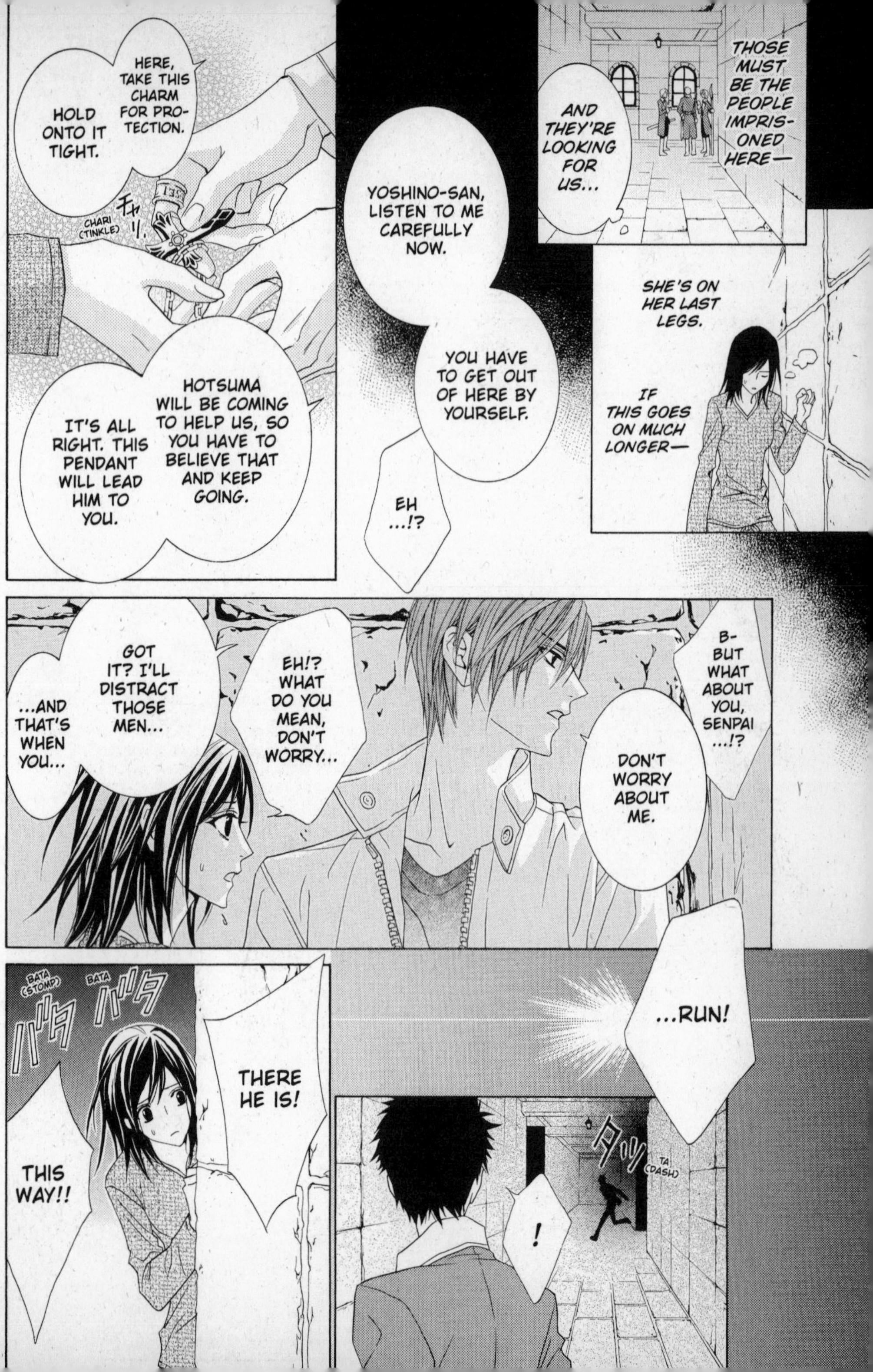
THOSE MUST BE THE PEOPLE IMPRISONED HERE—
AND THEY'RE LOOKING FOR US...
SHE'S ON HER LAST LEGS.
IF THIS GOES ON MUCH LONGER—
YOSHINO-SAN, LISTEN TO ME CAREFULLY NOW.
YOU HAVE TO GET OUT OF HERE BY YOURSELF.
EH ...!?
HERE, TAKE THIS CHARM FOR PROTECTION.
HOLD ONTO IT TIGHT.
CHARI (TINKLE)
HOTSUMA WILL BE COMING TO HELP US, SO YOU HAVE TO BELIEVE THAT AND KEEP GOING.
IT'S ALL RIGHT. THIS PENDANT WILL LEAD HIM TO YOU.
B-BUT WHAT ABOUT YOU, SENPAI...!?
DON'T WORRY ABOUT ME.
EH!? WHAT DO YOU MEAN, DON'T WORRY...
GOT IT? I'LL DISTRACT THOSE MEN...
...AND THAT'S WHEN YOU...
...RUN!
TA (DASH)
!
THERE HE IS!
BATA (STOMP) BATA
THIS WAY!!

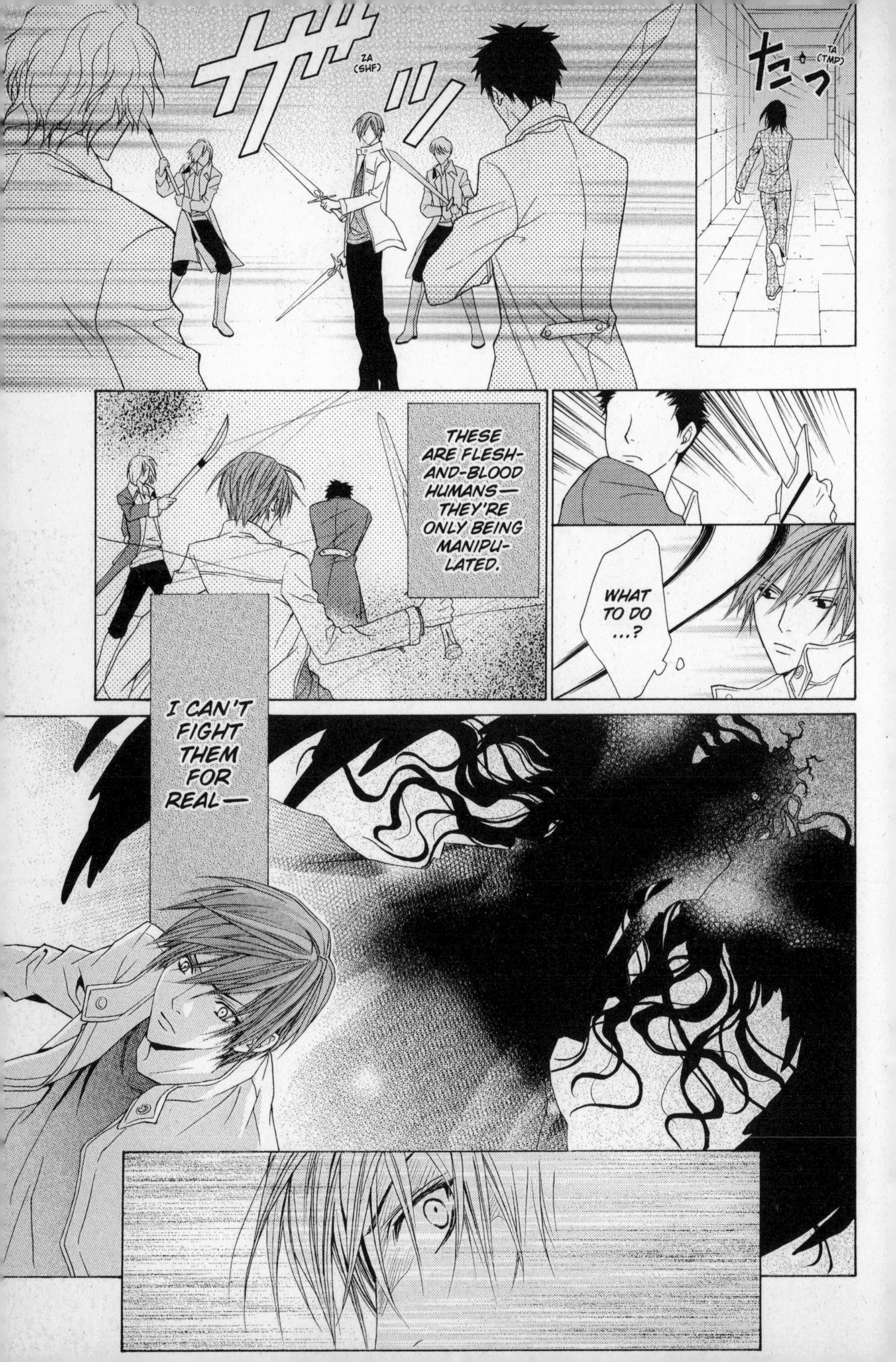
たっ
TA (TMP)
ZA (SHF)
WHAT TO DO ...?
THESE ARE FLESH-AND-BLOOD HUMANS—THEY'RE ONLY BEING MANIPULATED.
I CAN'T FIGHT THEM FOR REAL—

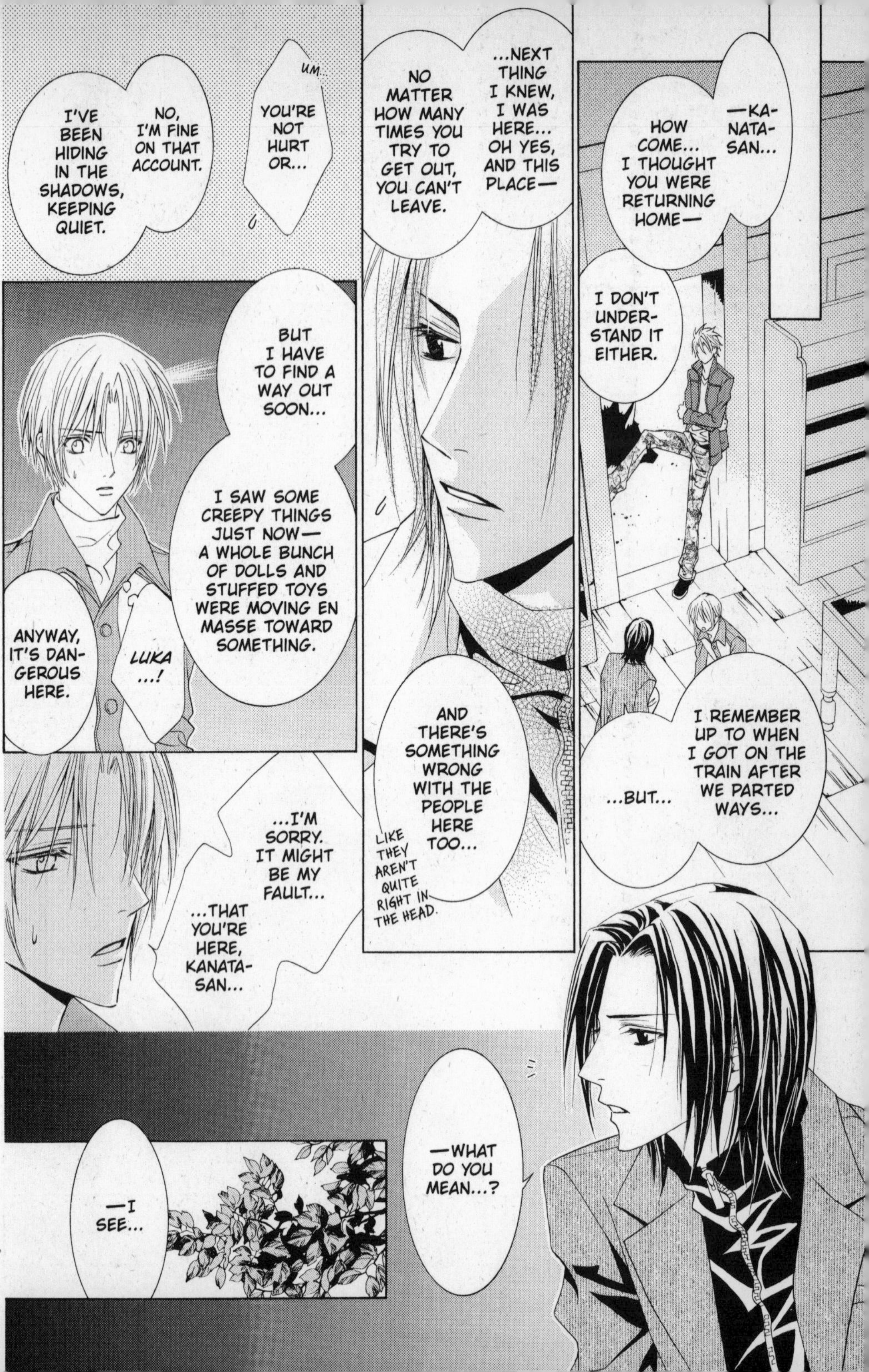
—KA-NATA-SAN...
HOW COME... I THOUGHT YOU WERE RETURNING HOME—
I DON'T UNDER-STAND IT EITHER.
I REMEMBER UP TO WHEN I GOT ON THE TRAIN AFTER WE PARTED WAYS...
...BUT...
...NEXT THING I KNEW, I WAS HERE... OH YES, AND THIS PLACE—
NO MATTER HOW MANY TIMES YOU TRY TO GET OUT, YOU CAN'T LEAVE.
AND THERE'S SOMETHING WRONG WITH THE PEOPLE HERE TOO...
LIKE THEY AREN'T QUITE RIGHT IN THE HEAD.
UM...
YOU'RE NOT HURT OR...
NO, I'M FINE ON THAT ACCOUNT.
I'VE BEEN HIDING IN THE SHADOWS, KEEPING QUIET.
BUT I HAVE TO FIND A WAY OUT SOON...
I SAW SOME CREEPY THINGS JUST NOW—A WHOLE BUNCH OF DOLLS AND STUFFED TOYS WERE MOVING EN MASSE TOWARD SOMETHING.
LUKA ...!
ANYWAY, IT'S DAN-GEROUS HERE.
...I'M SORRY. IT MIGHT BE MY FAULT...
...THAT YOU'RE HERE, KANATA-SAN...
—WHAT DO YOU MEAN...?
—I SEE...

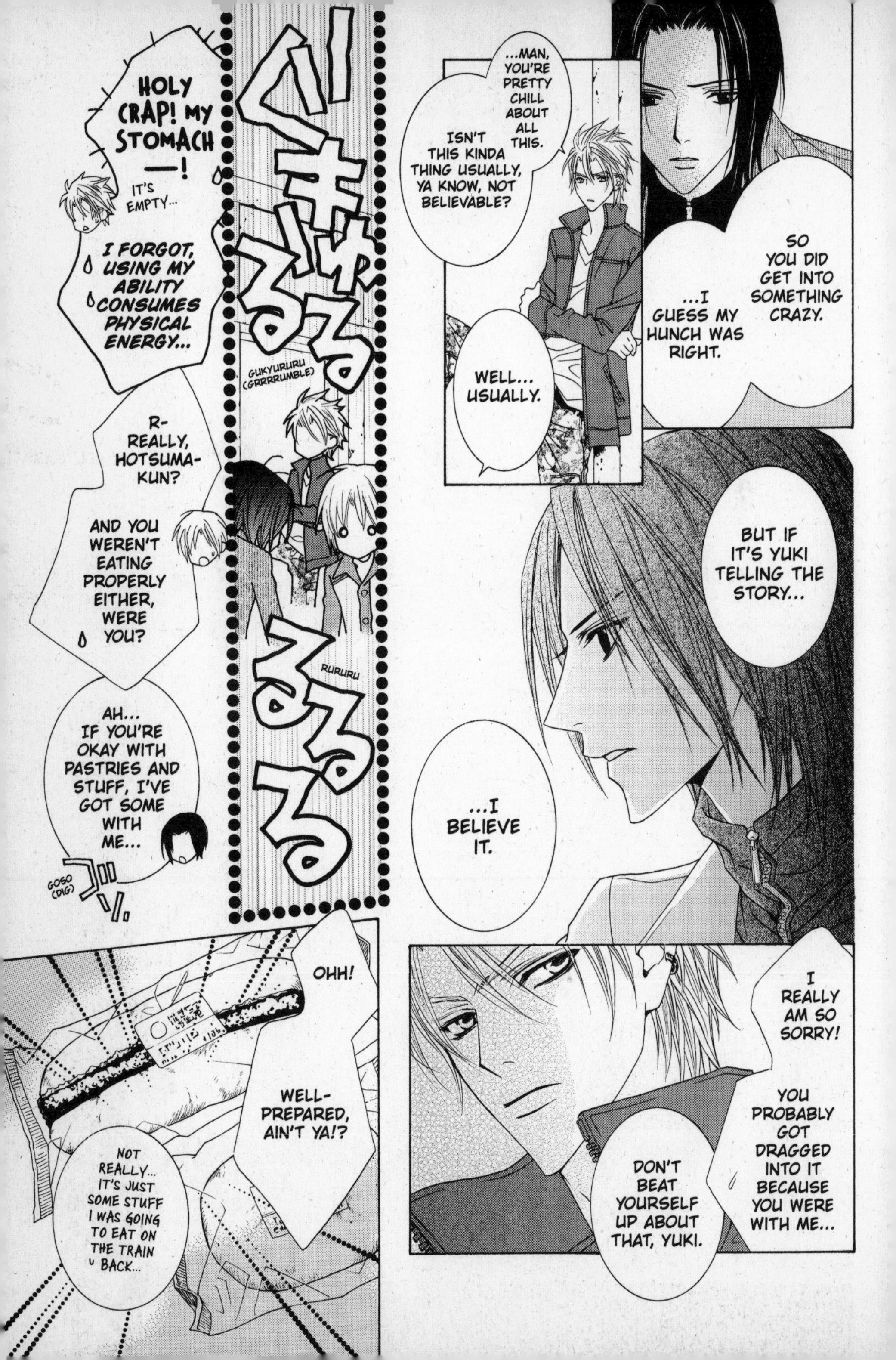
SO YOU DID GET INTO SOMETHING CRAZY.
...I GUESS MY HUNCH WAS RIGHT.
...MAN, YOU'RE PRETTY CHILL ABOUT ALL THIS.
ISN'T THIS KINDA THING USUALLY, YA KNOW, NOT BELIEVABLE?
WELL... USUALLY.
BUT IF IT'S YUKI TELLING THE STORY...
...I BELIEVE IT.
I REALLY AM SO SORRY!
YOU PROBABLY GOT DRAGGED INTO IT BECAUSE YOU WERE WITH ME...
DON'T BEAT YOURSELF UP ABOUT THAT, YUKI.
HOLY CRAP! MY STOMACH—!
IT'S EMPTY...
I FORGOT, USING MY ABILITY CONSUMES PHYSICAL ENERGY...
GUKYURURU (GRRRRUMBLE)
RURURU
R-REALLY, HOTSUMA-KUN?
AND YOU WEREN'T EATING PROPERLY EITHER, WERE YOU?
AH... IF YOU'RE OKAY WITH PASTRIES AND STUFF, I'VE GOT SOME WITH ME...
GOSO (DIG)
OHH!
WELL-PREPARED, AIN'T YA!?
NOT REALLY... IT'S JUST SOME STUFF I WAS GOING TO EAT ON THE TRAIN BACK...

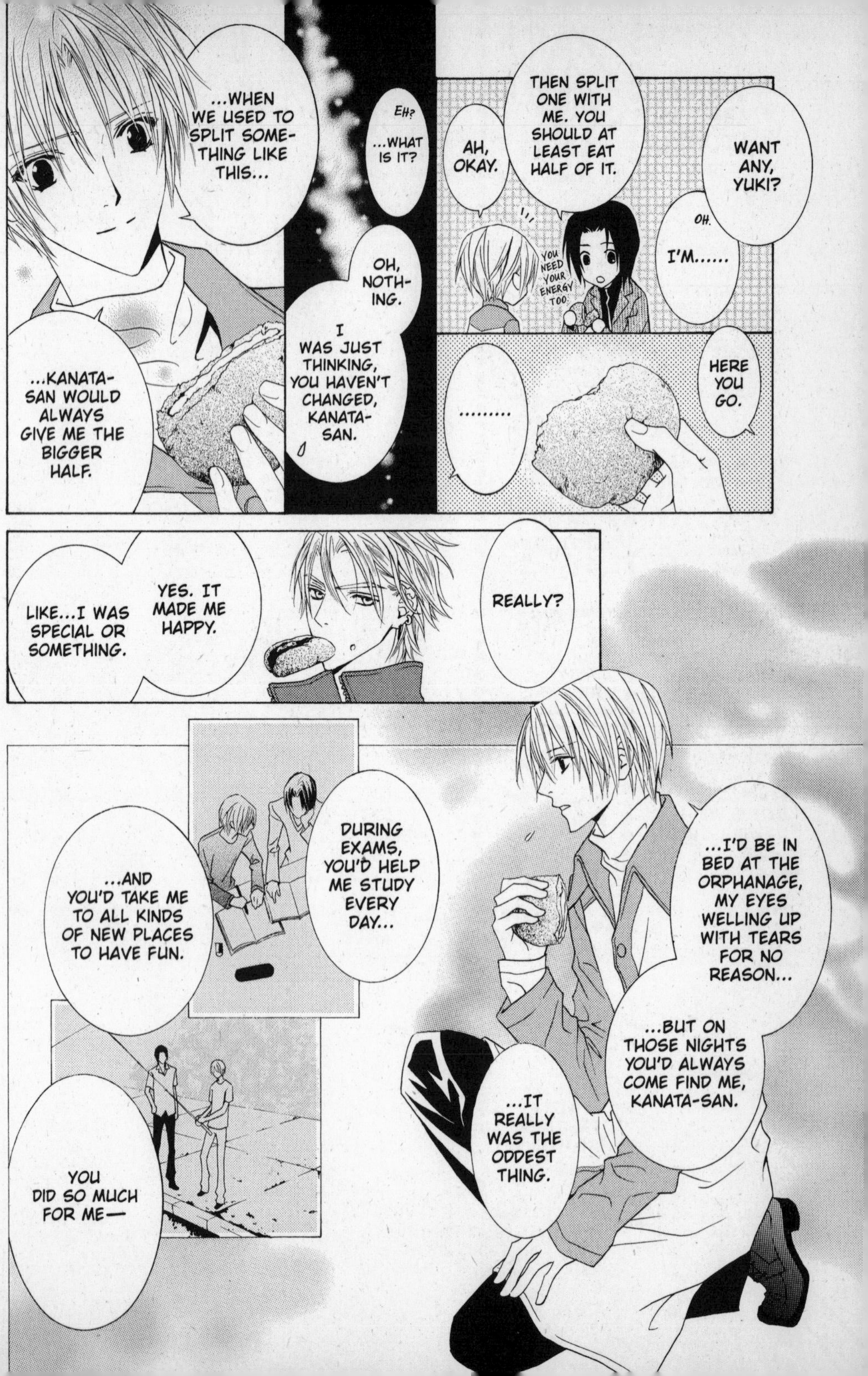
WANT ANY, YUKI?
OH.
I'M......
THEN SPLIT ONE WITH ME. YOU SHOULD AT LEAST EAT HALF OF IT.
YOU NEED YOUR ENERGY TOO.
AH, OKAY.
HERE YOU GO.
....
EH?
...WHAT IS IT?
OH, NOTHING.
I WAS JUST THINKING, YOU HAVEN'T CHANGED, KANATA-SAN.
...WHEN WE USED TO SPLIT SOMETHING LIKE THIS...
...KANATA-SAN WOULD ALWAYS GIVE ME THE BIGGER HALF.
REALLY?
YES. IT MADE ME HAPPY.
LIKE...I WAS SPECIAL OR SOMETHING.
...I'D BE IN BED AT THE ORPHANAGE, MY EYES WELLING UP WITH TEARS FOR NO REASON...
...BUT ON THOSE NIGHTS YOU'D ALWAYS COME FIND ME, KANATA-SAN.
...IT REALLY WAS THE ODDEST THING.
DURING EXAMS, YOU'D HELP ME STUDY EVERY DAY...
...AND YOU'D TAKE ME TO ALL KINDS OF NEW PLACES TO HAVE FUN.
YOU DID SO MUCH FOR ME—

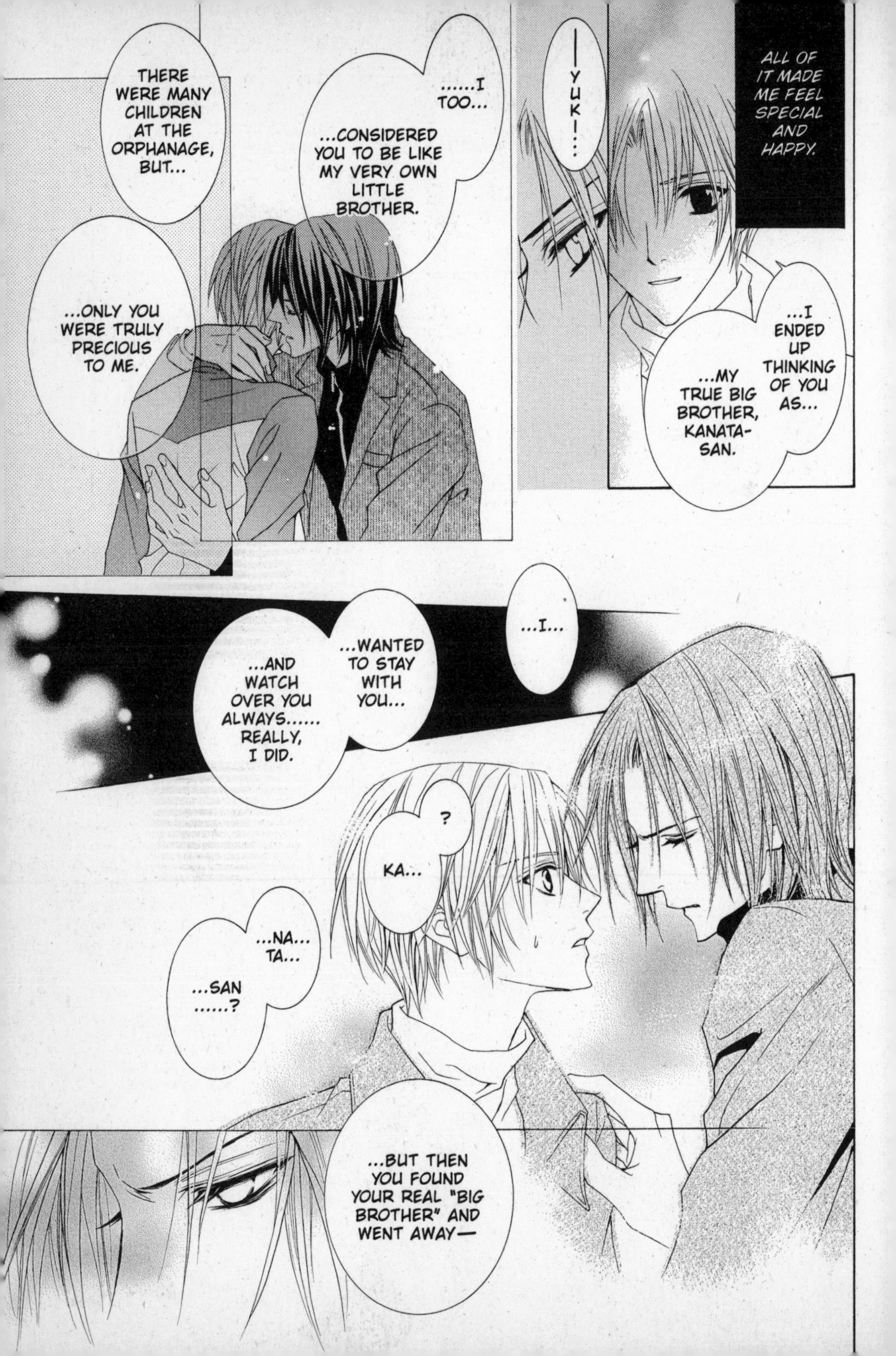
ALL OF IT MADE ME FEEL SPECIAL AND HAPPY.
—YUKI...
...I ENDED UP THINKING OF YOU AS...
...MY TRUE BIG BROTHER, KANATA-SAN.
......I TOO...
...CONSIDERED YOU TO BE LIKE MY VERY OWN LITTLE BROTHER.
THERE WERE MANY CHILDREN AT THE ORPHANAGE, BUT...
...ONLY YOU WERE TRULY PRECIOUS TO ME.
...I...
...WANTED TO STAY WITH YOU...
...AND WATCH OVER YOU ALWAYS...... REALLY, I DID.
?
KA...
...NA... TA...
...SAN ......?
...BUT THEN YOU FOUND YOUR REAL "BIG BROTHER" AND WENT AWAY—

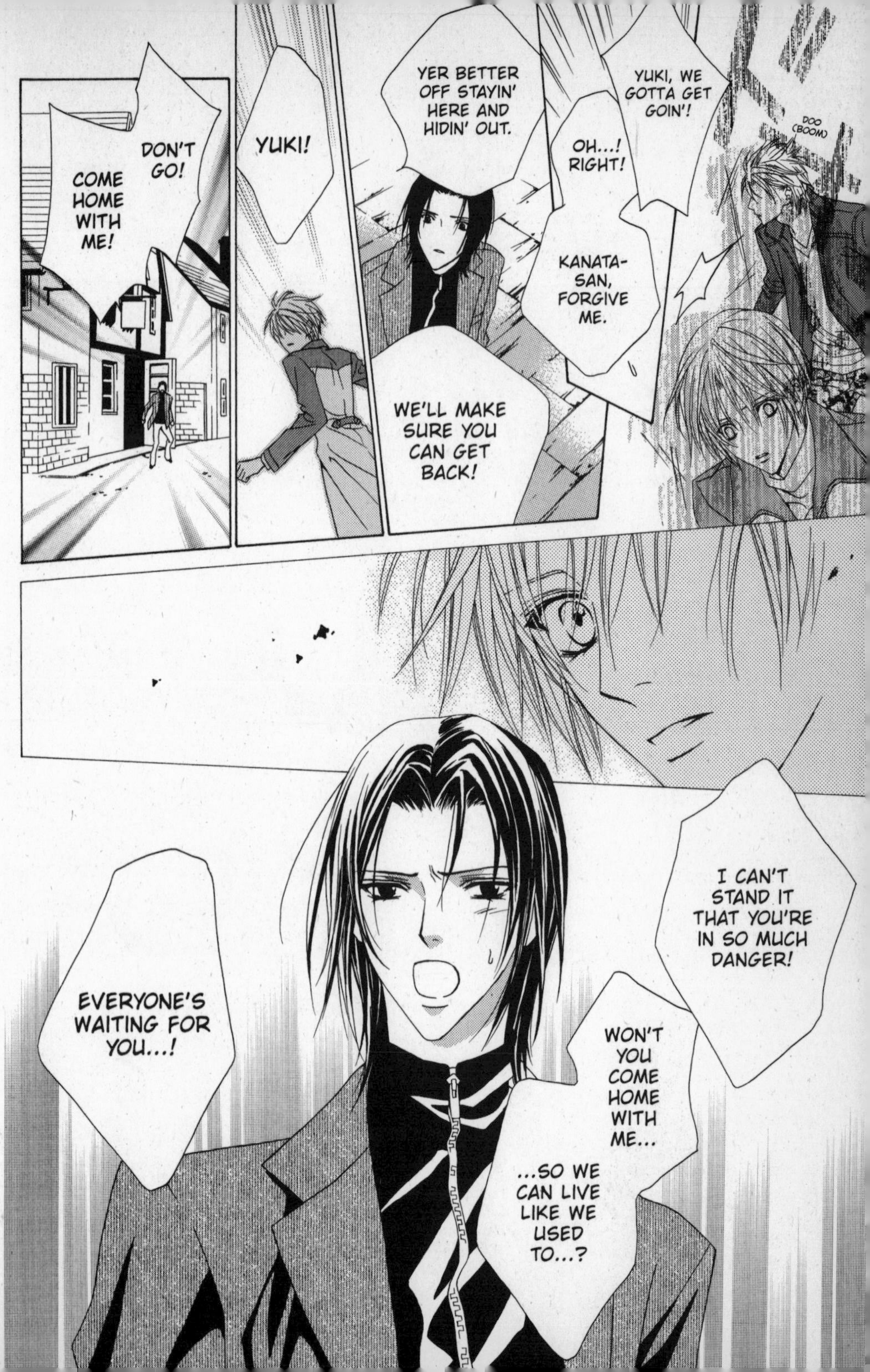
DOO (BOOM)
YUKI, WE GOTTA GET GOIN'!
OH...! RIGHT!
KANATA-SAN, FORGIVE ME.
YER BETTER OFF STAYIN' HERE AND HIDIN' OUT.
WE'LL MAKE SURE YOU CAN GET BACK!
YUKI!
DON'T GO!
COME HOME WITH ME!
I CAN'T STAND IT THAT YOU'RE IN SO MUCH DANGER!
WON'T YOU COME HOME WITH ME...
...SO WE CAN LIVE LIKE WE USED TO...?
EVERYONE'S WAITING FOR YOU...!

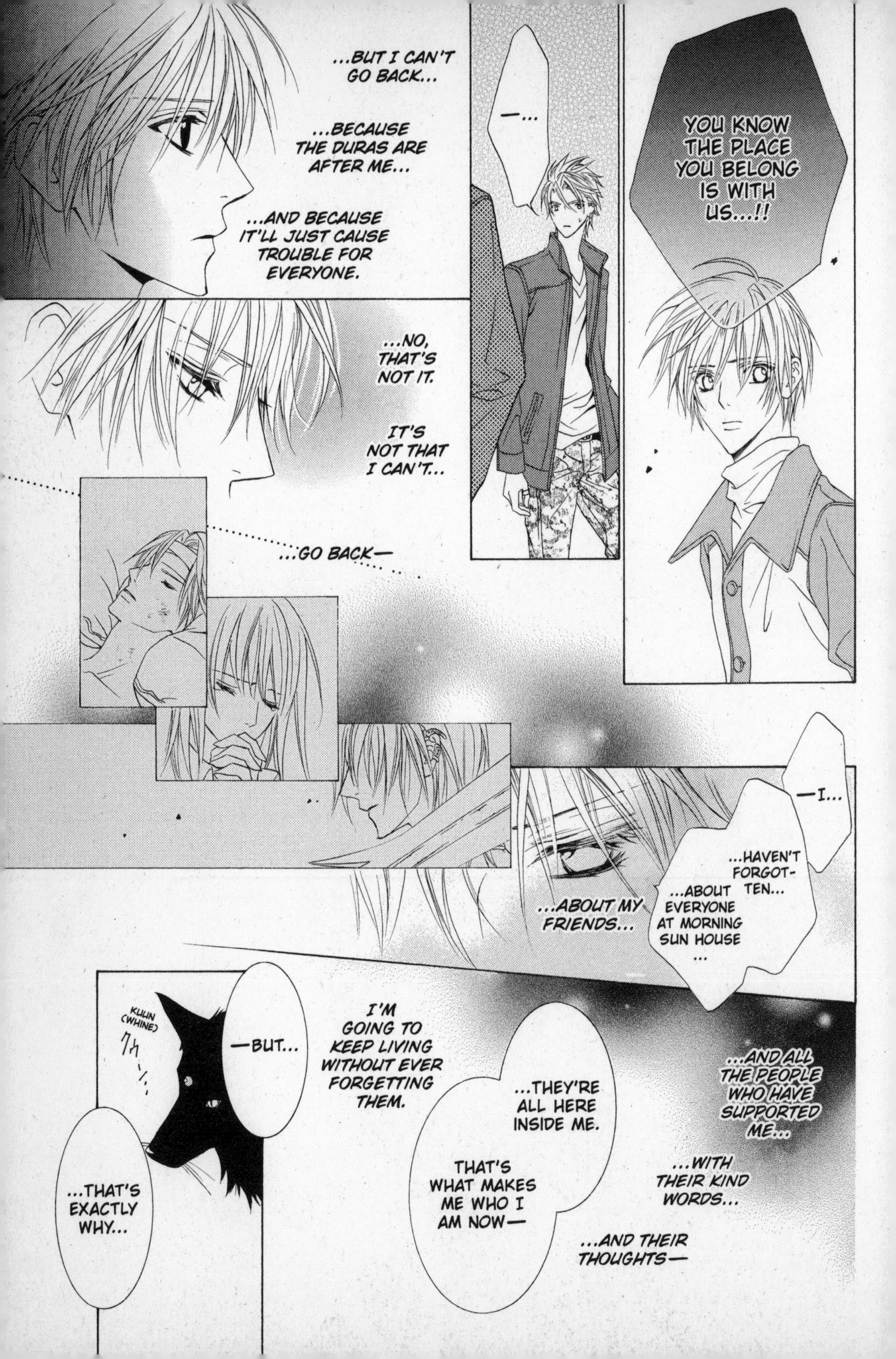
YOU KNOW THE PLACE YOU BELONG IS WITH US...!!
—...
...BUT I CAN'T GO BACK...
...BECAUSE THE DURAS ARE AFTER ME...
...AND BECAUSE IT'LL JUST CAUSE TROUBLE FOR EVERYONE.
...NO, THAT'S NOT IT.
IT'S NOT THAT I CAN'T...
...GO BACK—
—I...
...HAVEN'T FORGOTTEN...
...ABOUT EVERYONE AT MORNING SUN HOUSE...
...ABOUT MY FRIENDS...
...AND ALL THE PEOPLE WHO HAVE SUPPORTED ME...
...WITH THEIR KIND WORDS...
...AND THEIR THOUGHTS—
...THEY'RE ALL HERE INSIDE ME.
THAT'S WHAT MAKES ME WHO I AM NOW—
I'M GOING TO KEEP LIVING WITHOUT EVER FORGETTING THEM.
—BUT...
KUUN (WHINE)
...THAT'S EXACTLY WHY...

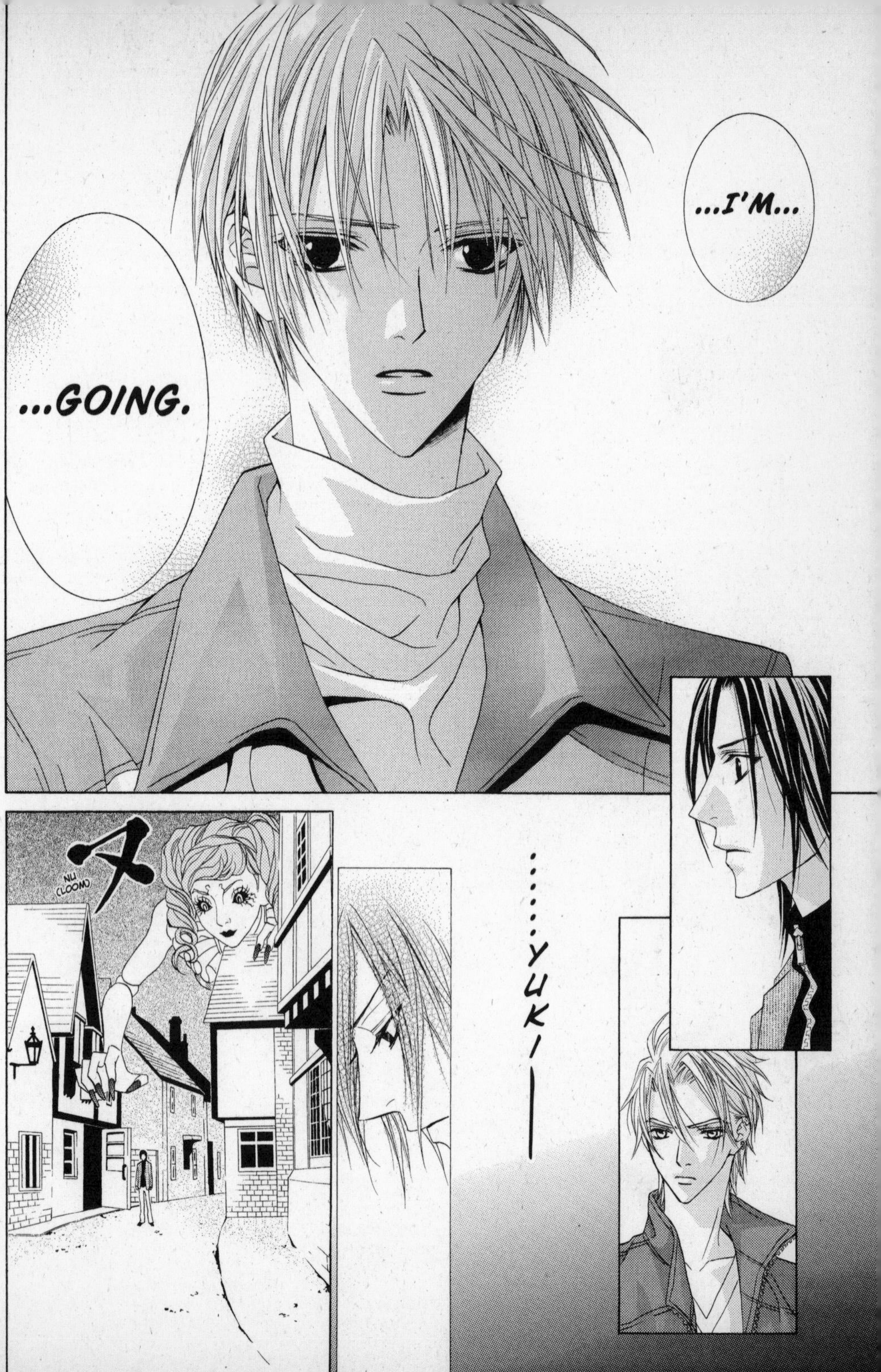
...I'M...
...GOING.
....YUKI—
NU
(LOOM)

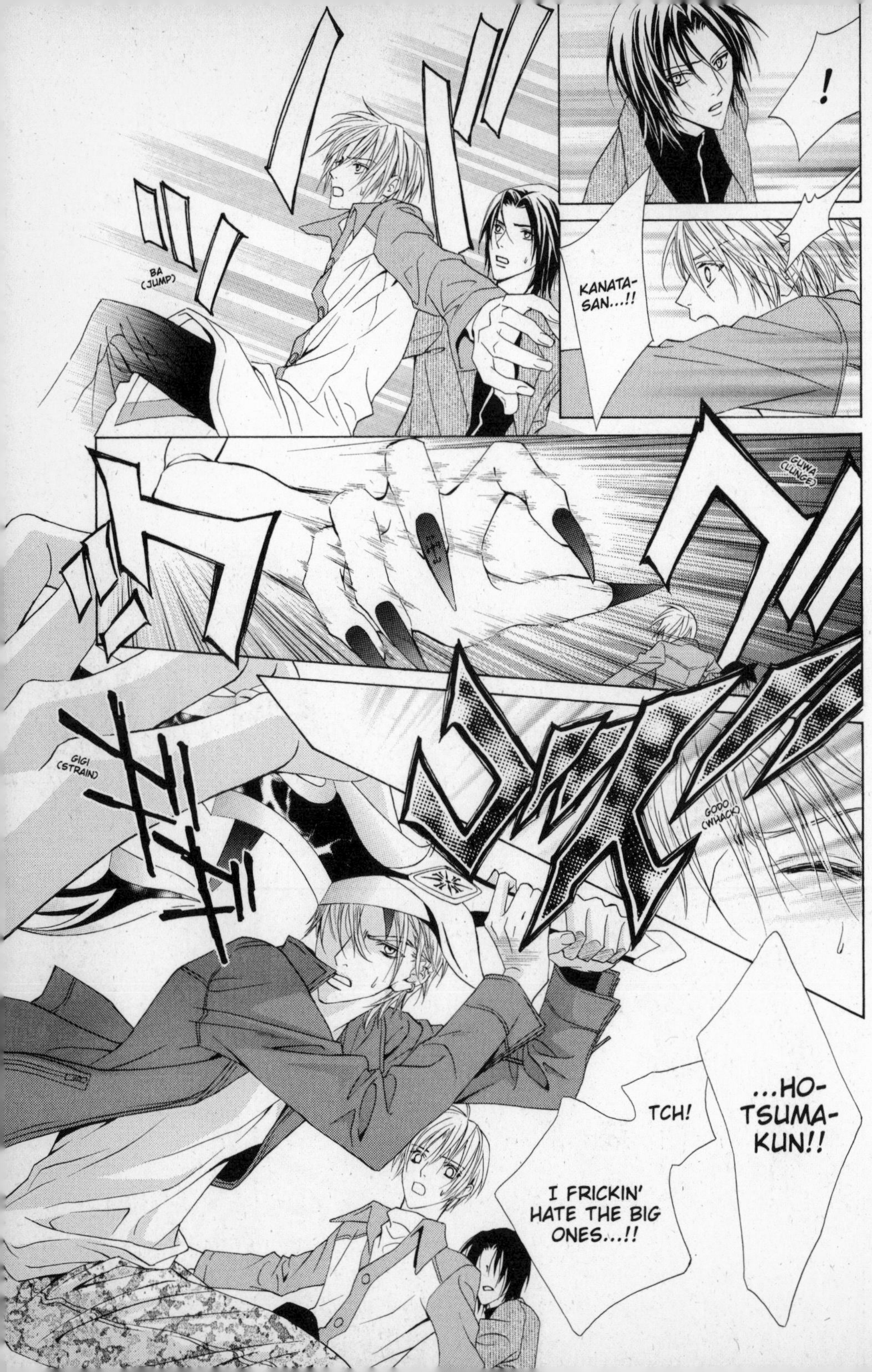
!
KANATA-SAN...!!
BA (JUMP)
GUWA (LUNGE)
GODO (WHACK)
GIGI (STRAIN)
...HO-TSUMA-KUN!!
TCH!
I FRICKIN' HATE THE BIG ONES...!!

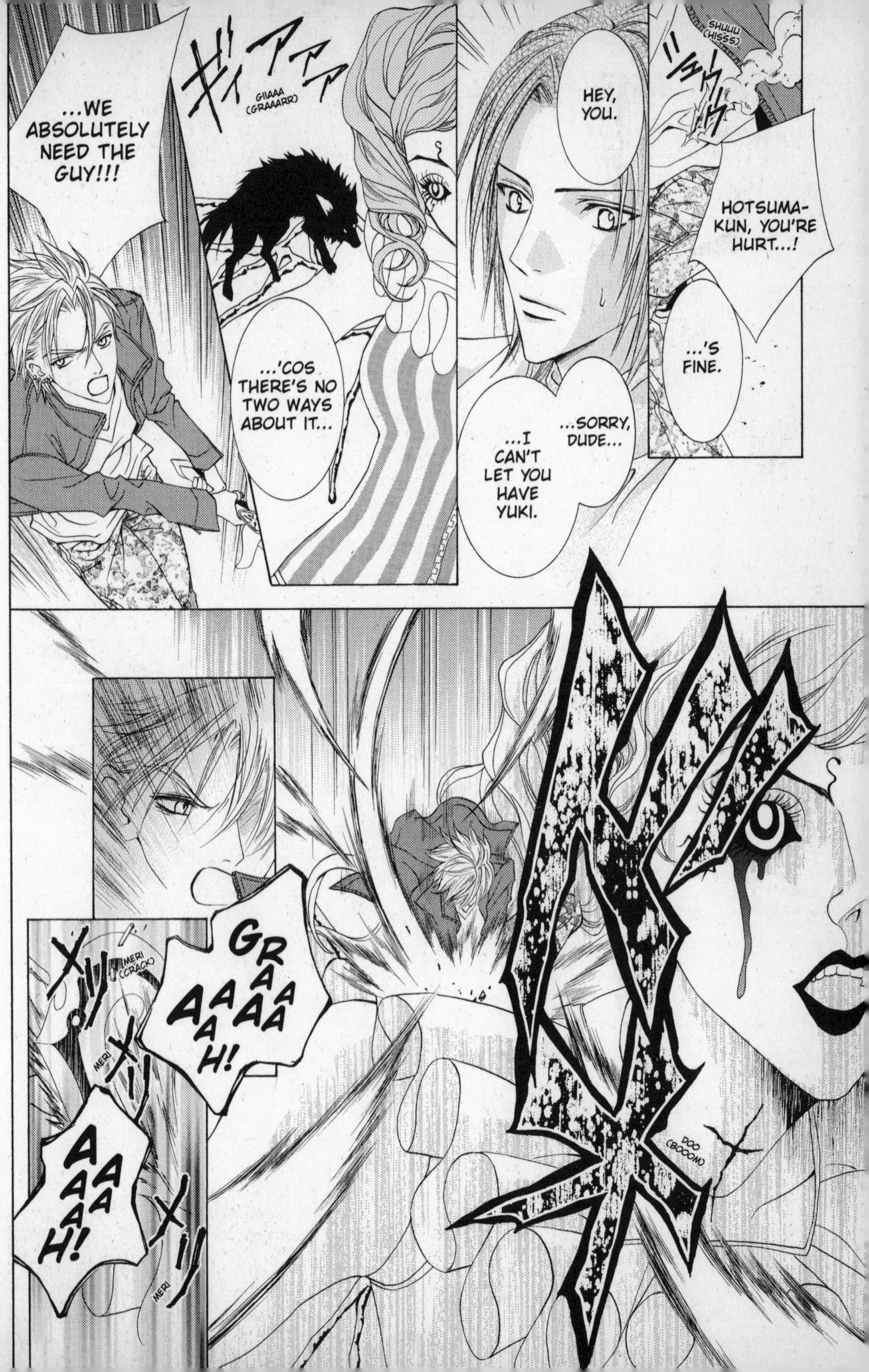

SHUUU (HISSS)
HOTSUMA-KUN, YOU'RE HURT...!
...'S FINE.
HEY, YOU.
...SORRY, DUDE...
...I CAN'T LET YOU HAVE YUKI.
GIIAAA (GRAAARR)
...'COS THERE'S NO TWO WAYS ABOUT IT...
...WE ABSOLUTELY NEED THE GUY!!!
DOO (BOOOM)
GRAAAAAAAAH!
MERI (CRACK)
MERI
AAAAAH!
MERI

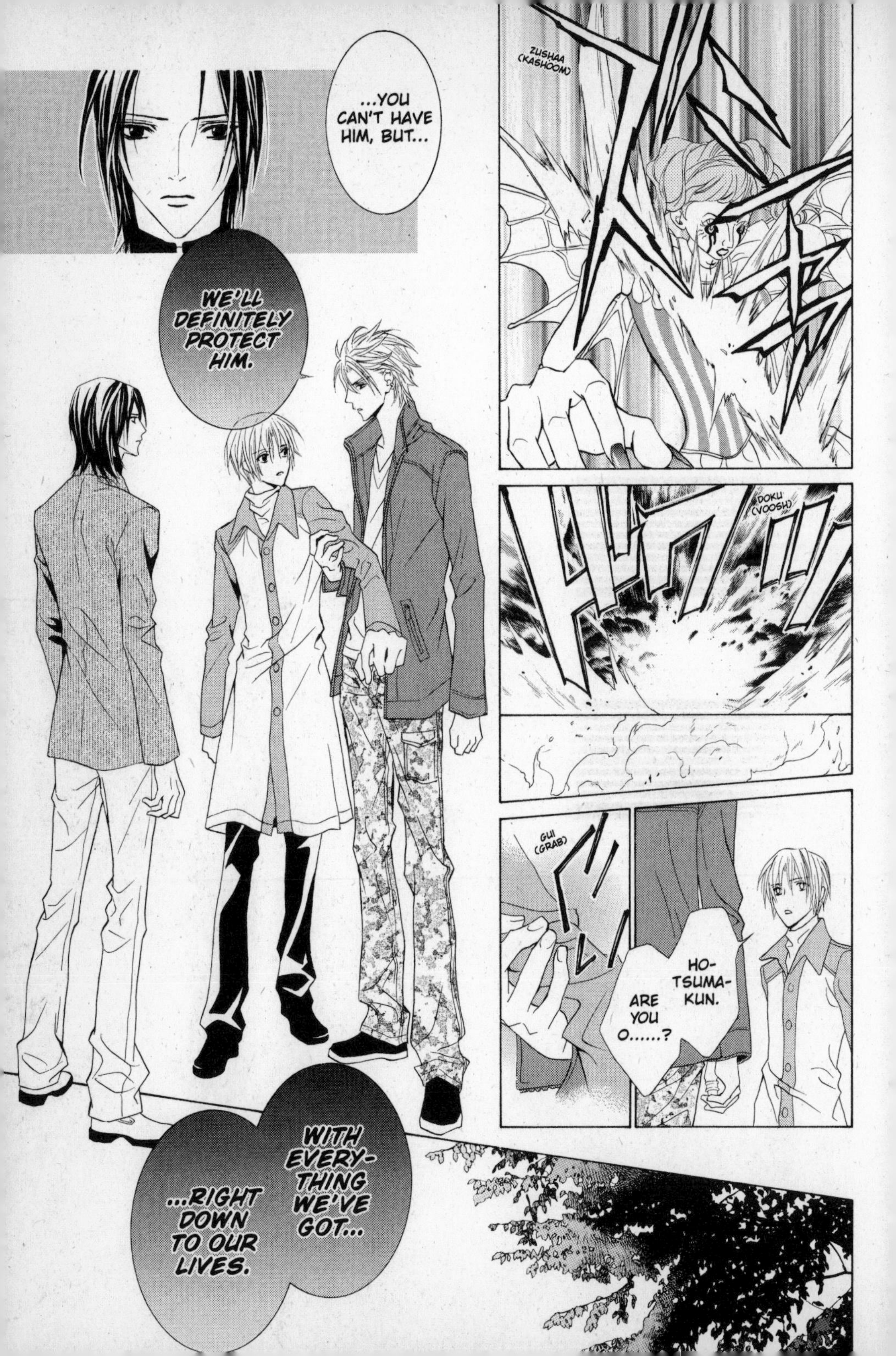
ZUSHAA (KASHOOM)
DOKU (VOOSH)
GUI (GRAB)
HO-TSUMA-KUN.
ARE YOU O......?
...YOU CAN'T HAVE HIM, BUT...
WE'LL DEFINITELY PROTECT HIM.
WITH EVERY-THING WE'VE GOT...
...RIGHT DOWN TO OUR LIVES.

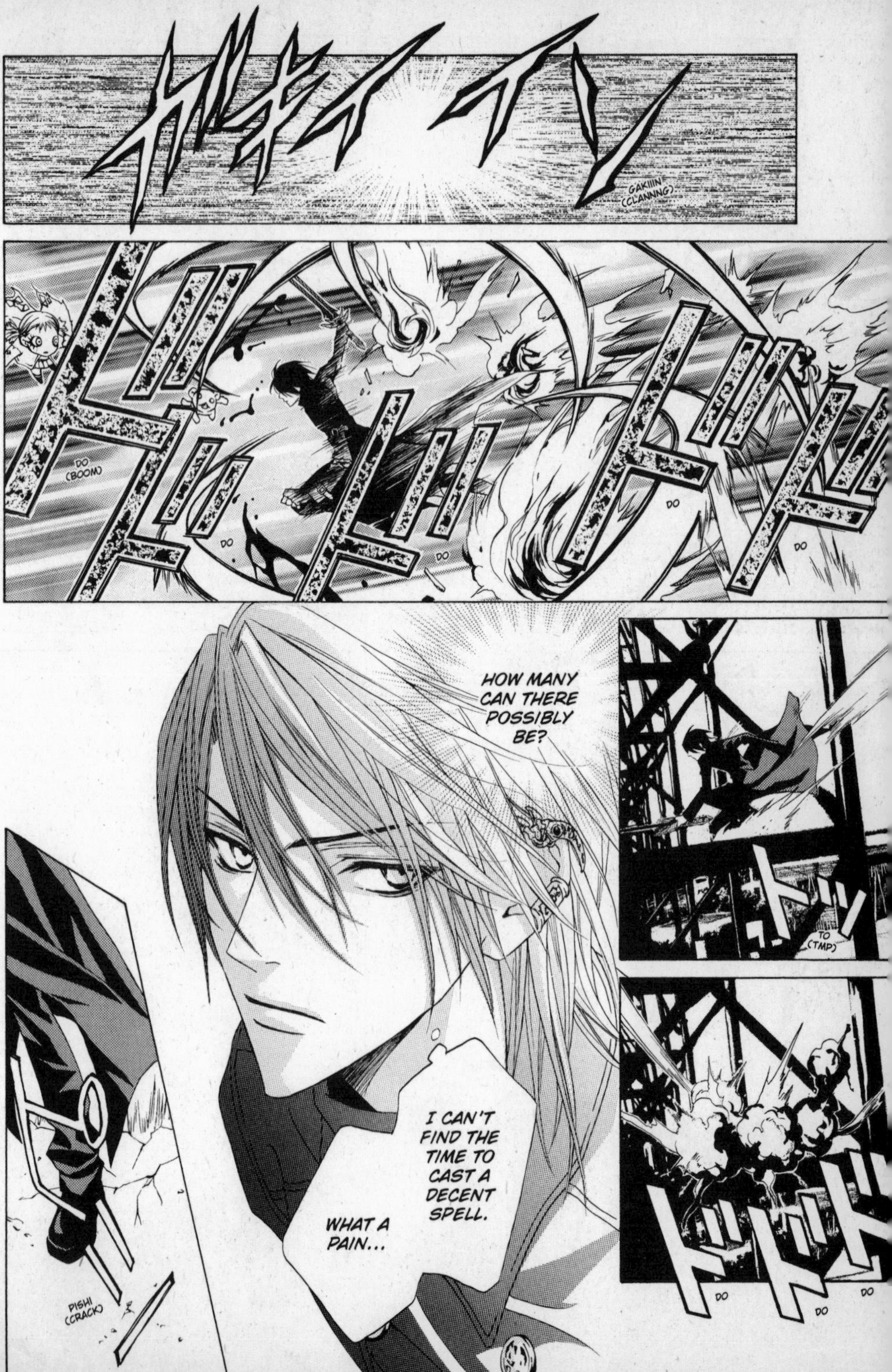
GAKIIN (CLANNNG)
DO
DO
DO
DO
DO (BOOM)
TO (TMP)
DO
DO
DO
HOW MANY CAN THERE POSSIBLY BE?
I CAN'T FIND THE TIME TO CAST A DECENT SPELL.
WHAT A PAIN...
PISHI (CRACK)

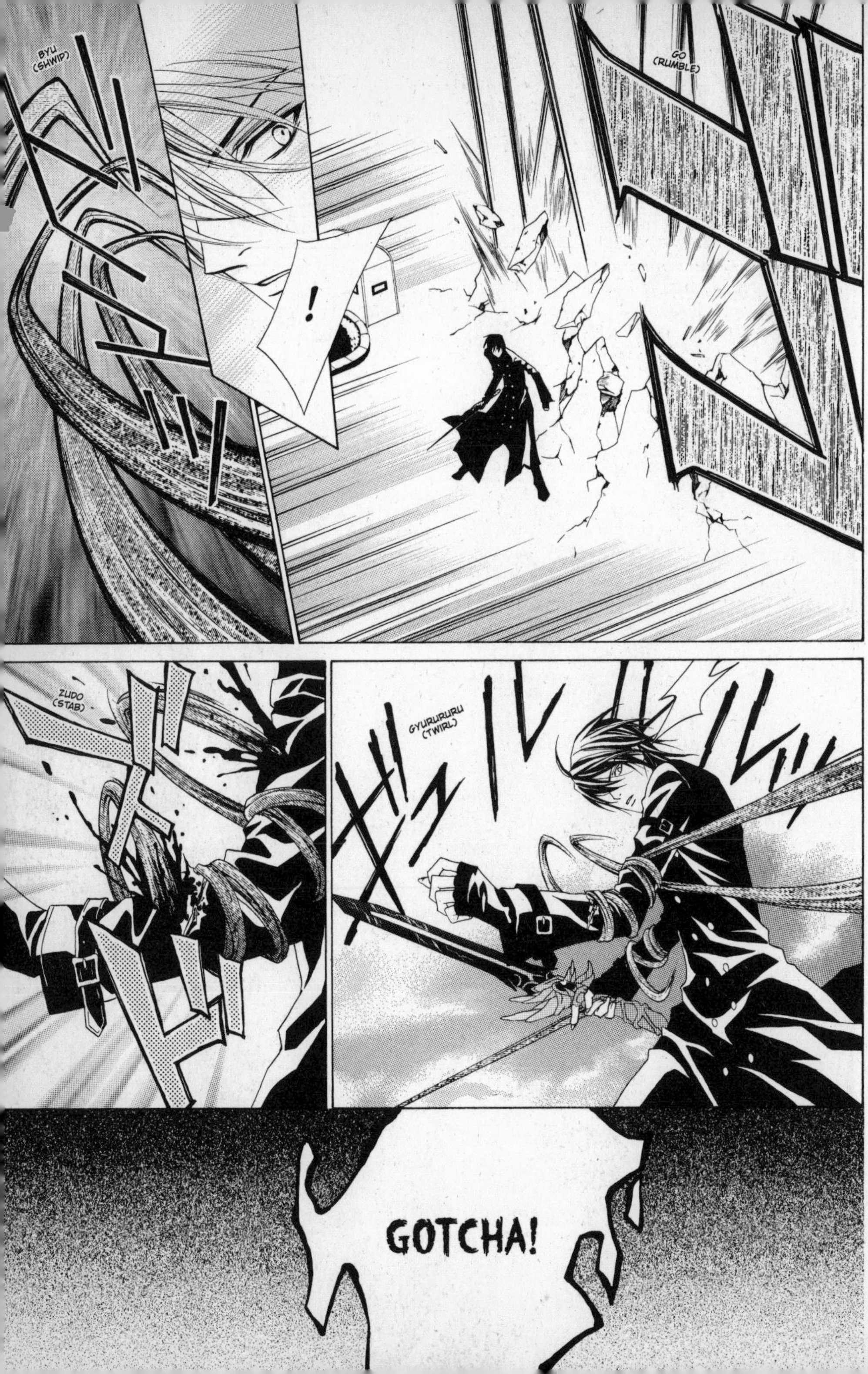
GO (RUMBLE)
!
BYU (SHWIP)
GYURURURU (TWIRL)
ZUDO (STAB)
GOTCHA!

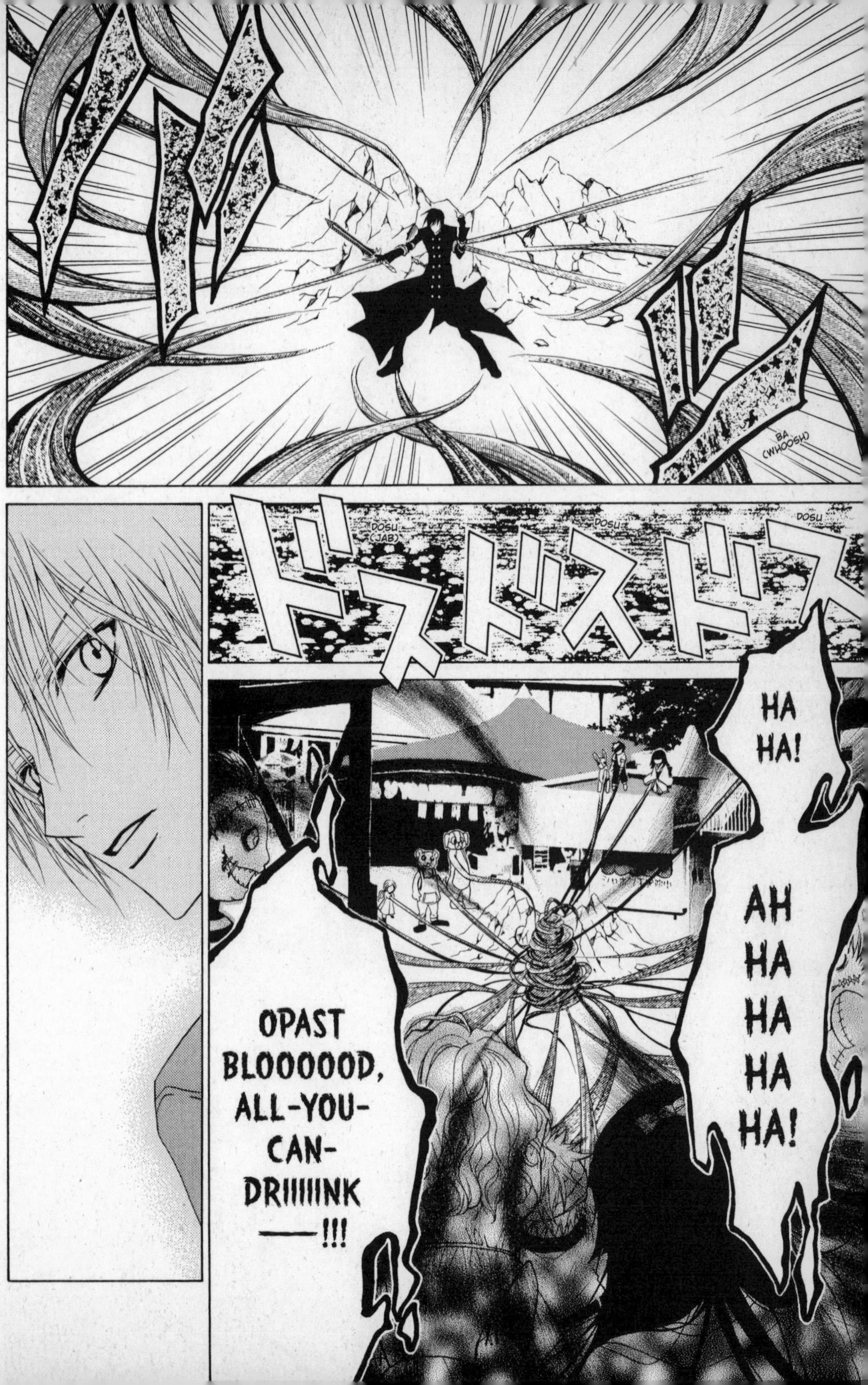
BA
(WHOOSH)
ドスドスドス
DOSU
(JAB)
DOSU
DOSU
HA HA!
AH HA HA HA HA HA!
OPAST BLOOOOOD, ALL-YOU-CAN-DRIIIIINK——!!!

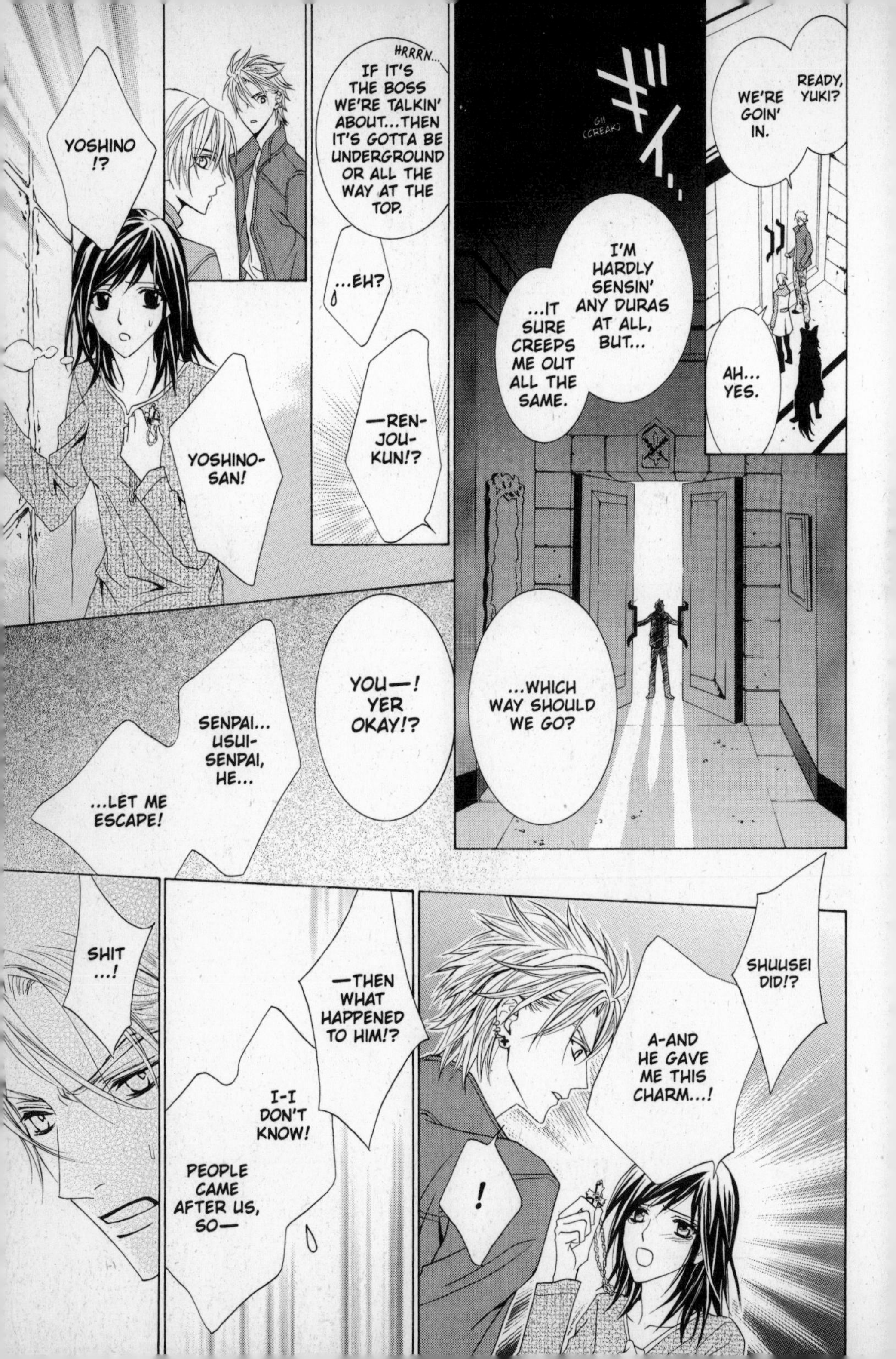

READY, YUKI?
WE'RE GOIN' IN.
AH... YES.
ギィ..
GII (CREAK)
I'M HARDLY SENSIN' ANY DURAS AT ALL, BUT...
...IT SURE CREEPS ME OUT ALL THE SAME.
...WHICH WAY SHOULD WE GO?
HRRRN...
IF IT'S THE BOSS WE'RE TALKIN' ABOUT...THEN IT'S GOTTA BE UNDERGROUND OR ALL THE WAY AT THE TOP.
...EH?
—REN-JOU-KUN!?
YOSHINO !?
YOSHINO-SAN!
YOU—! YER OKAY!?
SENPAI... USUI-SENPAI, HE...
...LET ME ESCAPE!
SHUUSEI DID!?
A-AND HE GAVE ME THIS CHARM...!
!
—THEN WHAT HAPPENED TO HIM!?
I-I DON'T KNOW!
PEOPLE CAME AFTER US, SO—
SHIT ...!

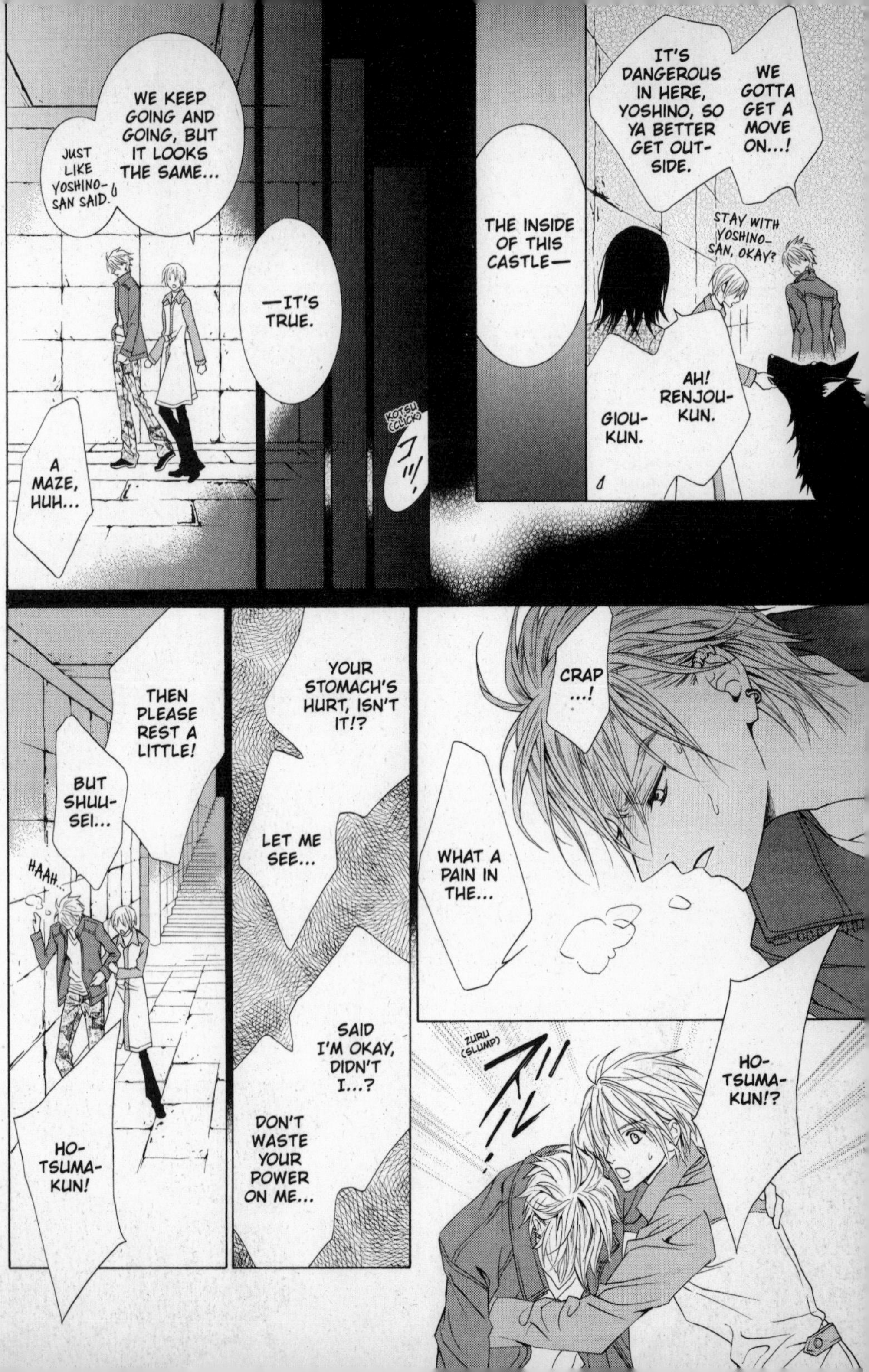

WE GOTTA GET A MOVE ON...!
IT'S DANGEROUS IN HERE, YOSHINO, SO YA BETTER GET OUTSIDE.
STAY WITH YOSHINO-SAN, OKAY?
AH! RENJOU-KUN.
GIOU-KUN.
THE INSIDE OF THIS CASTLE—
—IT'S TRUE.
KOTSU (CLICK)
WE KEEP GOING AND GOING, BUT IT LOOKS THE SAME...
JUST LIKE YOSHINO-SAN SAID.
A MAZE, HUH...
CRAP...!
WHAT A PAIN IN THE...
HOTSUMA-KUN!?
ZURU (SLUMP)
YOUR STOMACH'S HURT, ISN'T IT!?
LET ME SEE...
SAID I'M OKAY, DIDN'T I...?
DON'T WASTE YOUR POWER ON ME...
THEN PLEASE REST A LITTLE!
BUT SHUUSEI...
HAAH...
HOTSUMA-KUN!

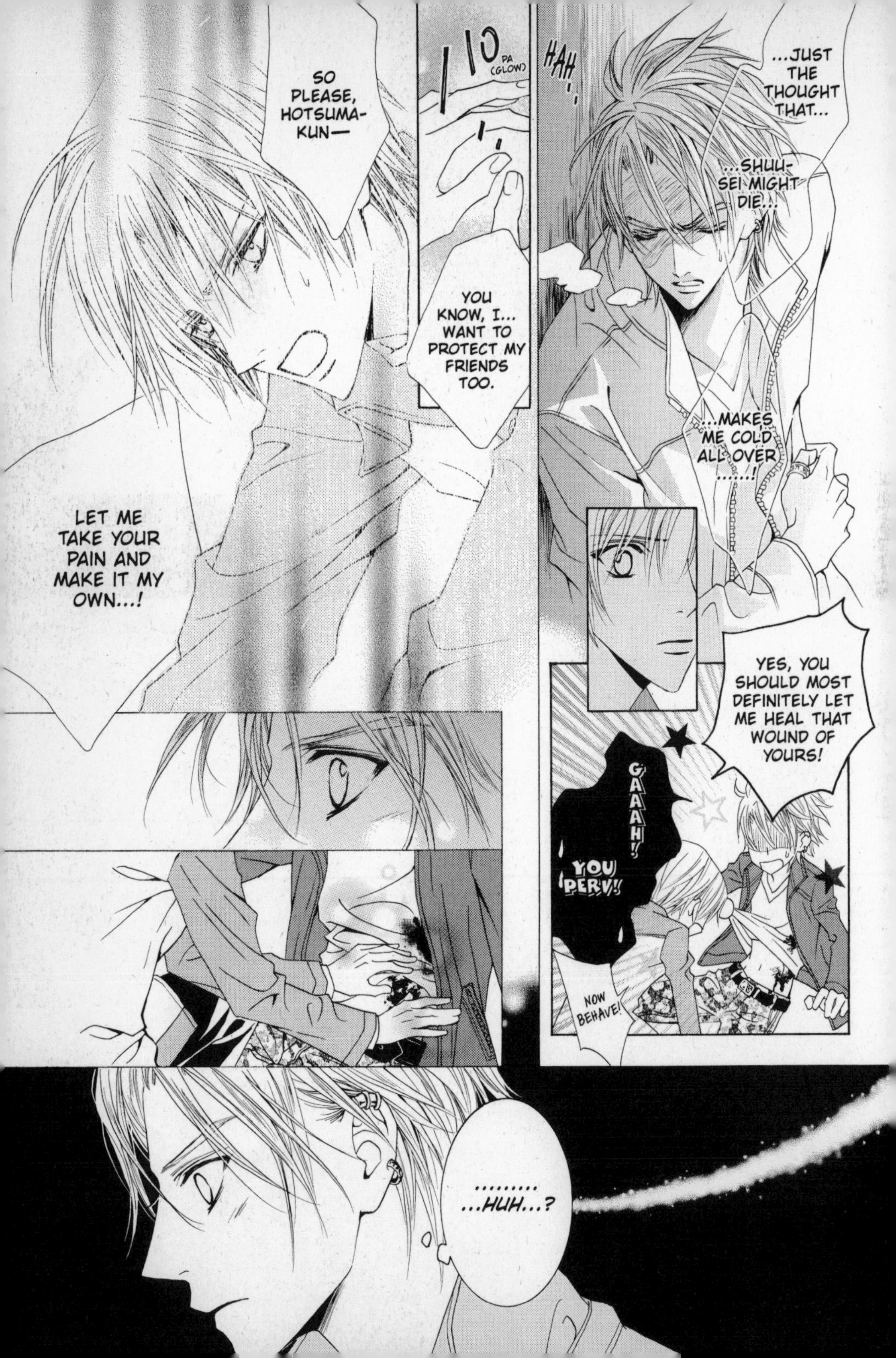

HAH
...JUST THE THOUGHT THAT...
...SHUU-SEI MIGHT DIE...
...MAKES ME COLD ALL OVER ......!
PA (GLOW)
YOU KNOW, I... WANT TO PROTECT MY FRIENDS TOO.
SO PLEASE, HOTSUMA-KUN—
LET ME TAKE YOUR PAIN AND MAKE IT MY OWN...!
YES, YOU SHOULD MOST DEFINITELY LET ME HEAL THAT WOUND OF YOURS!
GAAAH!
YOU PERV!!
NOW BEHAVE!
....
...HUH...?

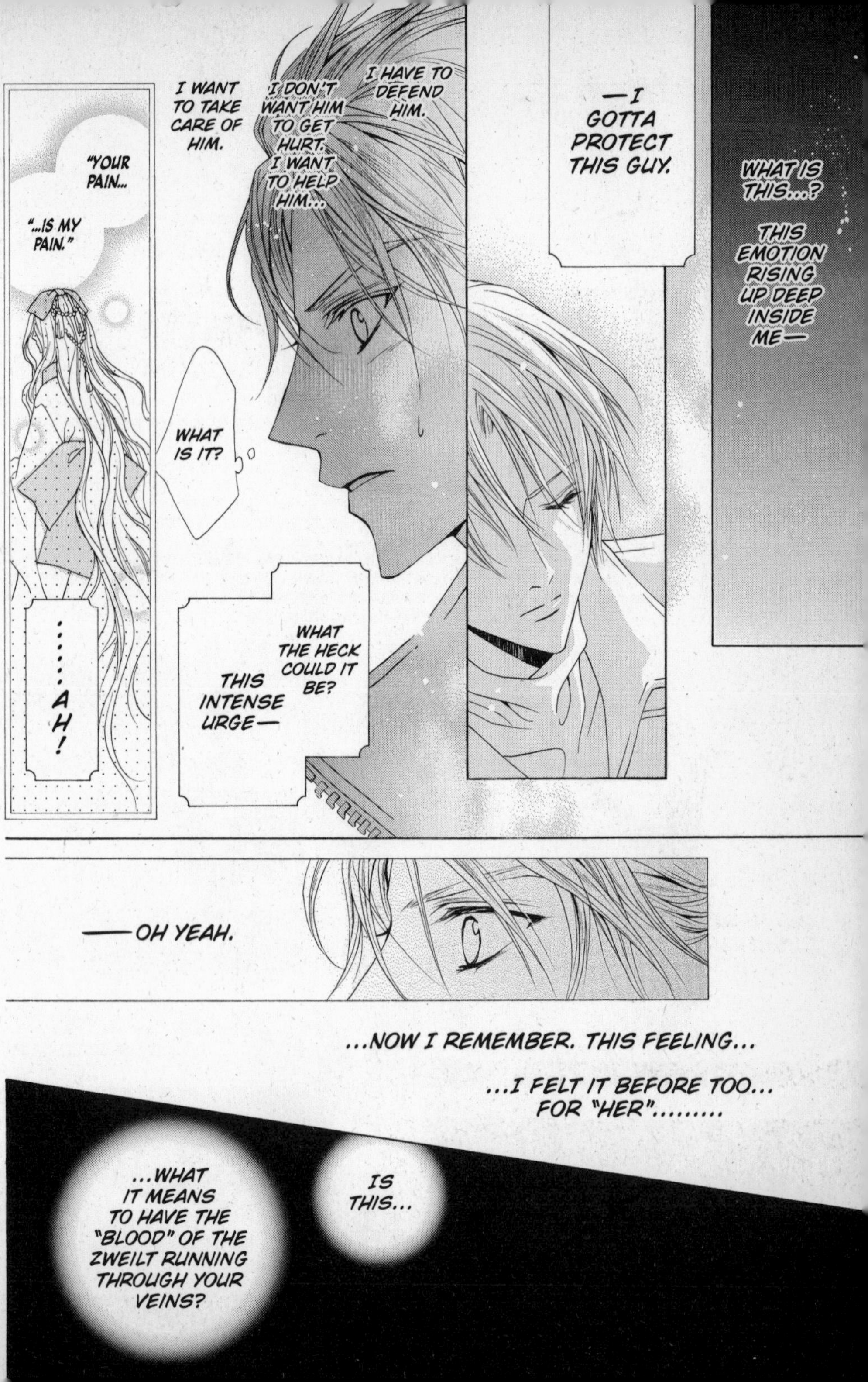
WHAT IS THIS...? THIS EMOTION RISING UP DEEP INSIDE ME—
—I GOTTA PROTECT THIS GUY.
I HAVE TO DEFEND HIM.
I DON'T WANT HIM TO GET HURT. I WANT TO HELP HIM...
I WANT TO TAKE CARE OF HIM.
WHAT IS IT?
WHAT THE HECK COULD IT BE?
THIS INTENSE URGE—
"YOUR PAIN...
"...IS MY PAIN."
......AH!
—OH YEAH.
...NOW I REMEMBER. THIS FEELING...
...I FELT IT BEFORE TOO... FOR "HER"........
IS THIS...
...WHAT IT MEANS TO HAVE THE "BLOOD" OF THE ZWEILT RUNNING THROUGH YOUR VEINS?

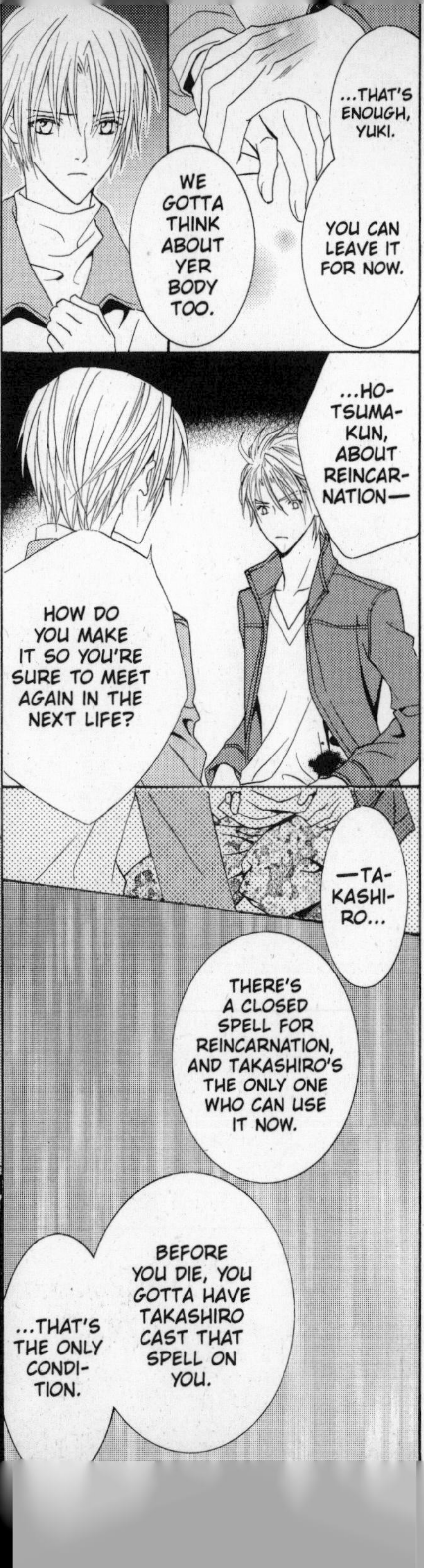
...THAT'S ENOUGH, YUKI.
YOU CAN LEAVE IT FOR NOW.
WE GOTTA THINK ABOUT YER BODY TOO.
...HO-TSUMA-KUN, ABOUT REINCAR-NATION—
HOW DO YOU MAKE IT SO YOU'RE SURE TO MEET AGAIN IN THE NEXT LIFE?
—TA-KASHI-RO...
THERE'S A CLOSED SPELL FOR REINCARNATION, AND TAKASHIRO'S THE ONLY ONE WHO CAN USE IT NOW.
BEFORE YOU DIE, YOU GOTTA HAVE TAKASHIRO CAST THAT SPELL ON YOU.
...THAT'S THE ONLY CONDITION.
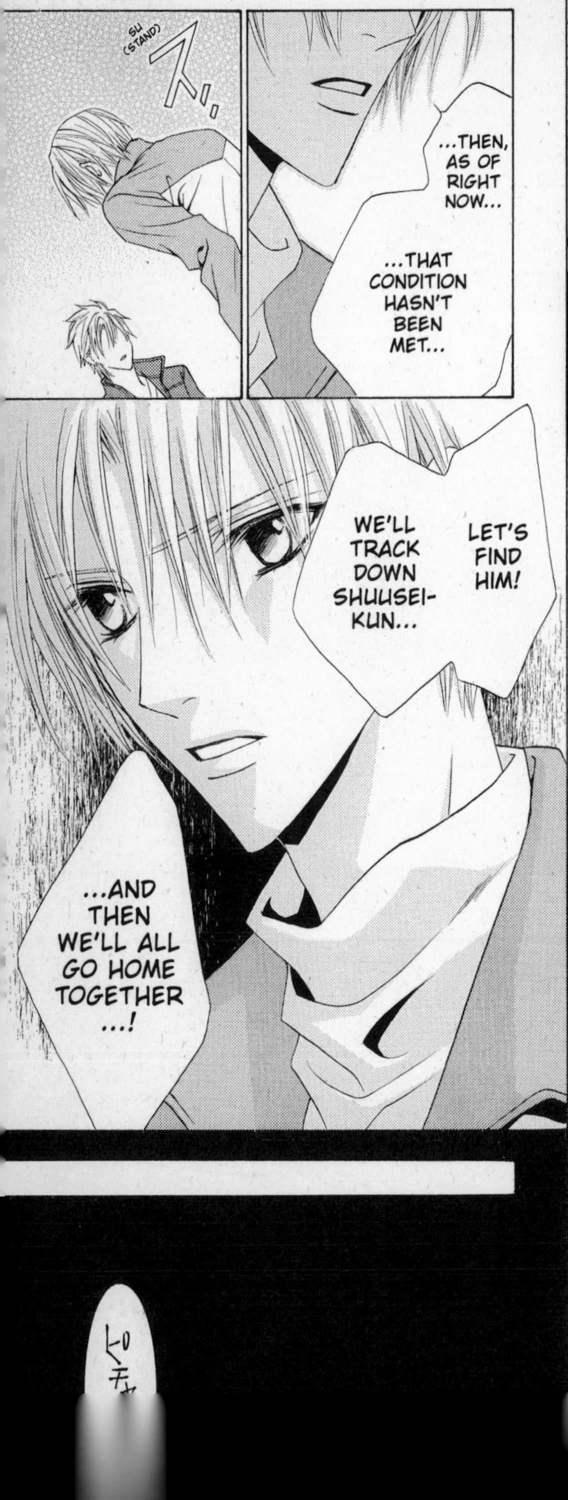
...THEN, AS OF RIGHT NOW...
...THAT CONDITION HASN'T BEEN MET...
SU (STAND)
LET'S FIND HIM!
WE'LL TRACK DOWN SHUUSEI-KUN...
...AND THEN WE'LL ALL GO HOME TOGETHER...!

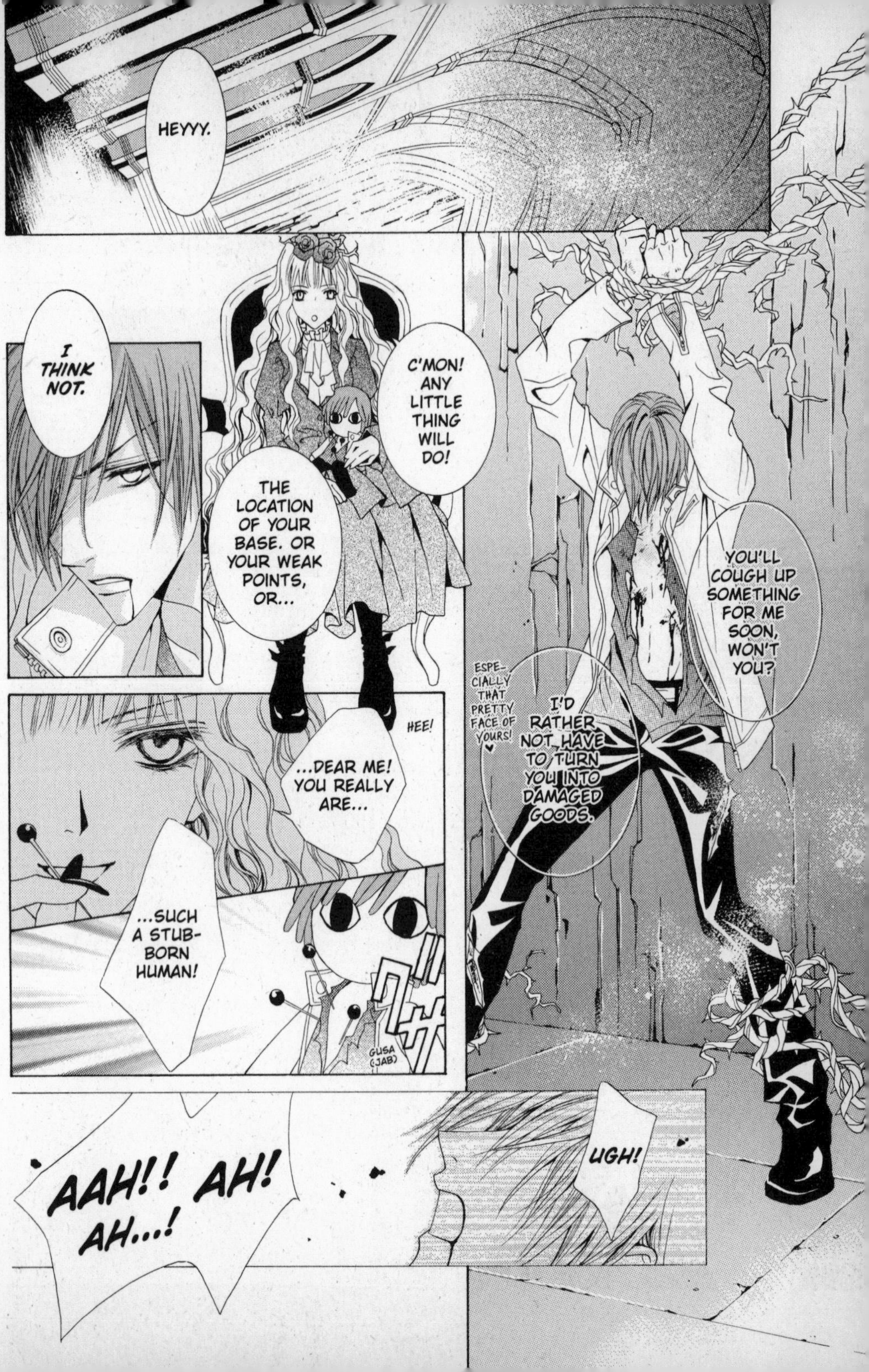
HEYYY.
YOU'LL COUGH UP SOMETHING FOR ME SOON, WON'T YOU?
I'D RATHER NOT HAVE TO TURN YOU INTO DAMAGED GOODS.
ESPECIALLY THAT PRETTY FACE OF YOURS! ♥
C'MON! ANY LITTLE THING WILL DO!
THE LOCATION OF YOUR BASE. OR YOUR WEAK POINTS, OR...
I THINK NOT.
HEE!
...DEAR ME! YOU REALLY ARE...
...SUCH A STUBBORN HUMAN!
GUSA (JAB)
UGH!
AAH!! AH! AH...!

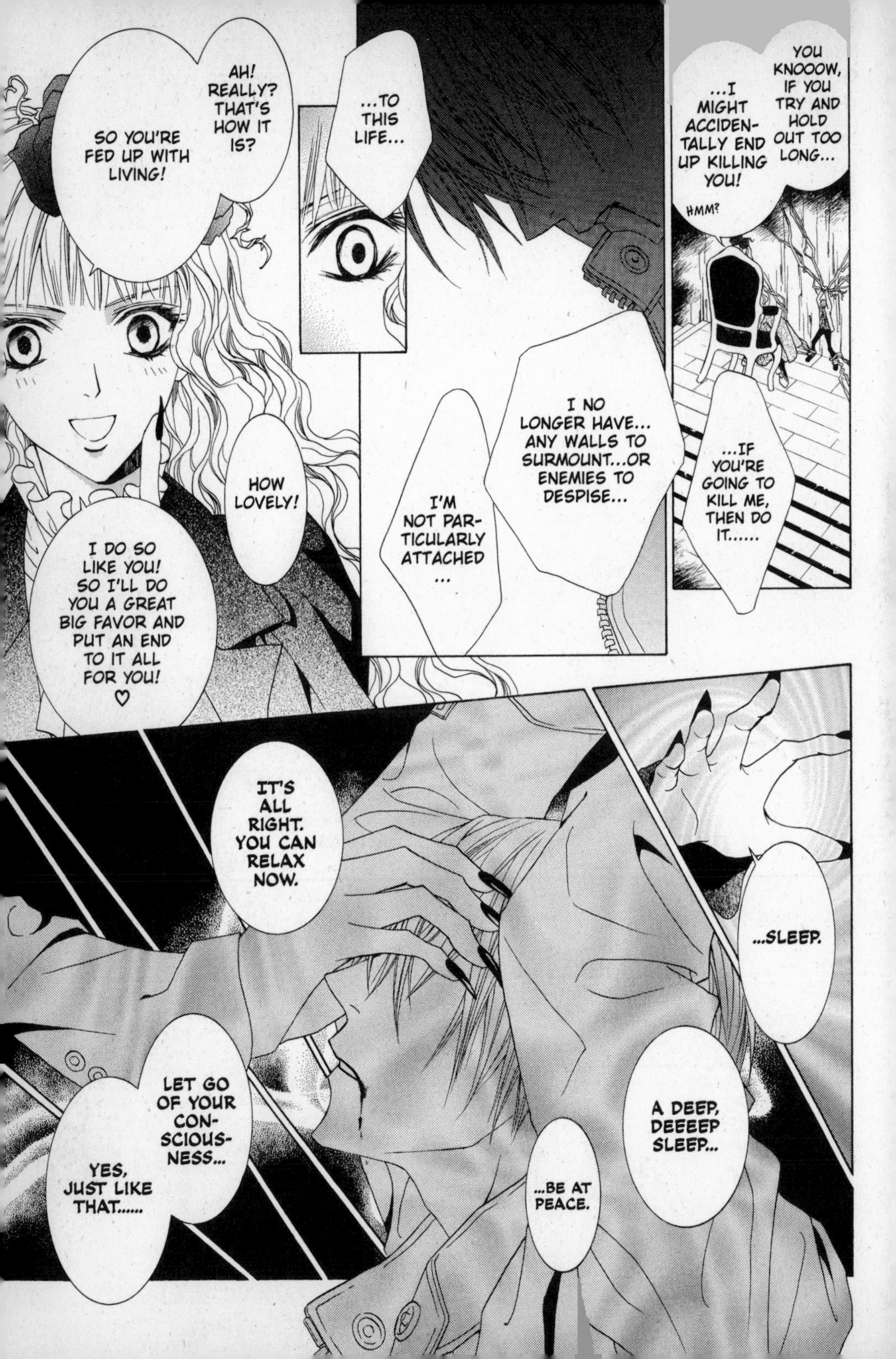
YOU KNOOOW, IF YOU TRY AND HOLD OUT TOO LONG...
...I MIGHT ACCIDENTALLY END UP KILLING YOU!
HMM?
...IF YOU'RE GOING TO KILL ME, THEN DO IT......
I NO LONGER HAVE... ANY WALLS TO SURMOUNT...OR ENEMIES TO DESPISE...
I'M NOT PARTICULARLY ATTACHED ...
...TO THIS LIFE...
AH! REALLY? THAT'S HOW IT IS?
SO YOU'RE FED UP WITH LIVING!
HOW LOVELY!
I DO SO LIKE YOU! SO I'LL DO YOU A GREAT BIG FAVOR AND PUT AN END TO IT ALL FOR YOU! ♡
...SLEEP.
A DEEP, DEEEEP SLEEP...
...BE AT PEACE.
IT'S ALL RIGHT. YOU CAN RELAX NOW.
LET GO OF YOUR CONSCIOUSNESS...
YES, JUST LIKE THAT......

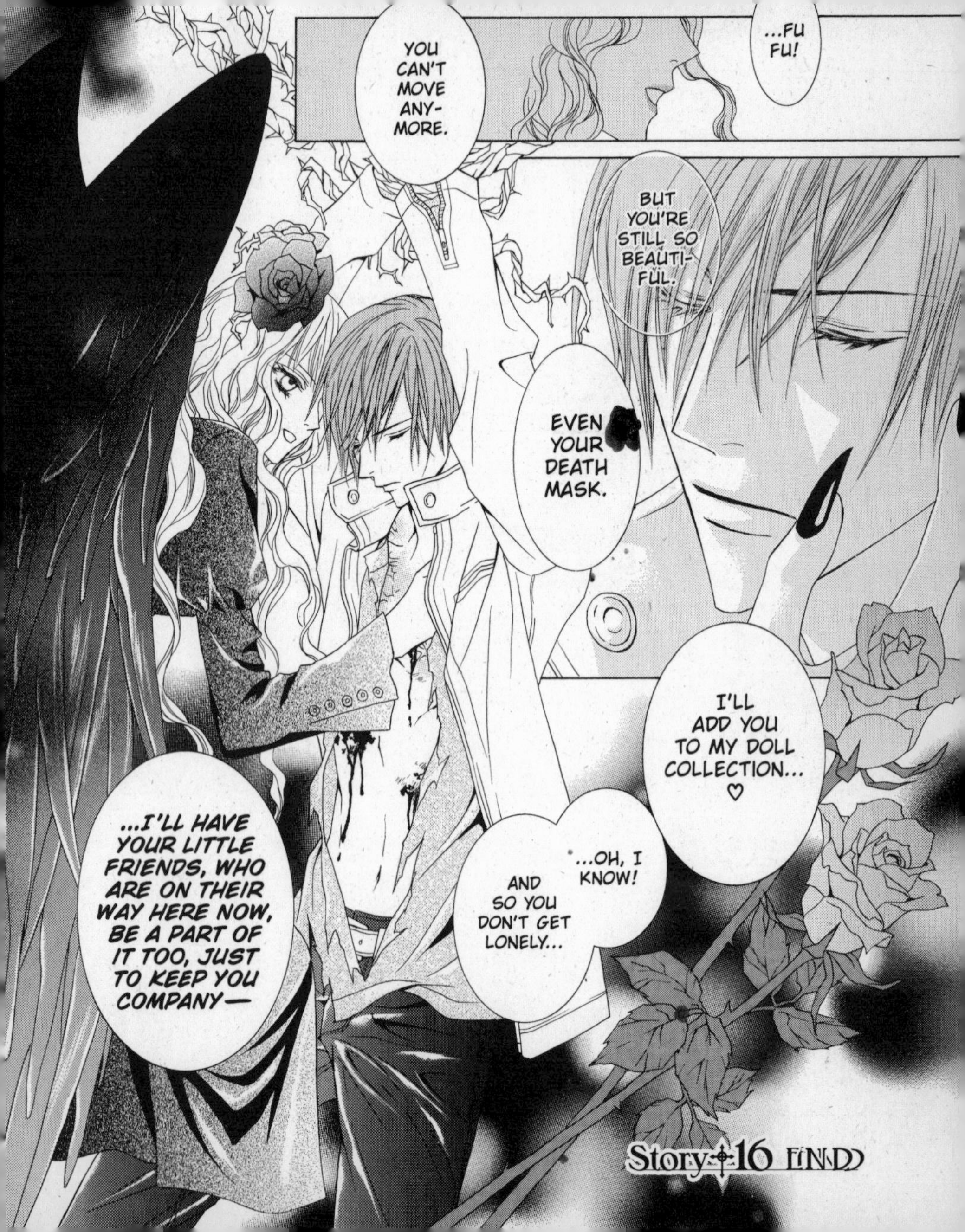
...FU FU!
YOU CAN'T MOVE ANYMORE.
BUT YOU'RE STILL SO BEAUTIFUL.
EVEN YOUR DEATH MASK.
I'LL ADD YOU TO MY DOLL COLLECTION... ♡
...OH, I KNOW!
AND SO YOU DON'T GET LONELY...
...I'LL HAVE YOUR LITTLE FRIENDS, WHO ARE ON THEIR WAY HERE NOW, BE A PART OF IT TOO, JUST TO KEEP YOU COMPANY—
Story 16 END

Extra ✝ Tell me a secret about your partner

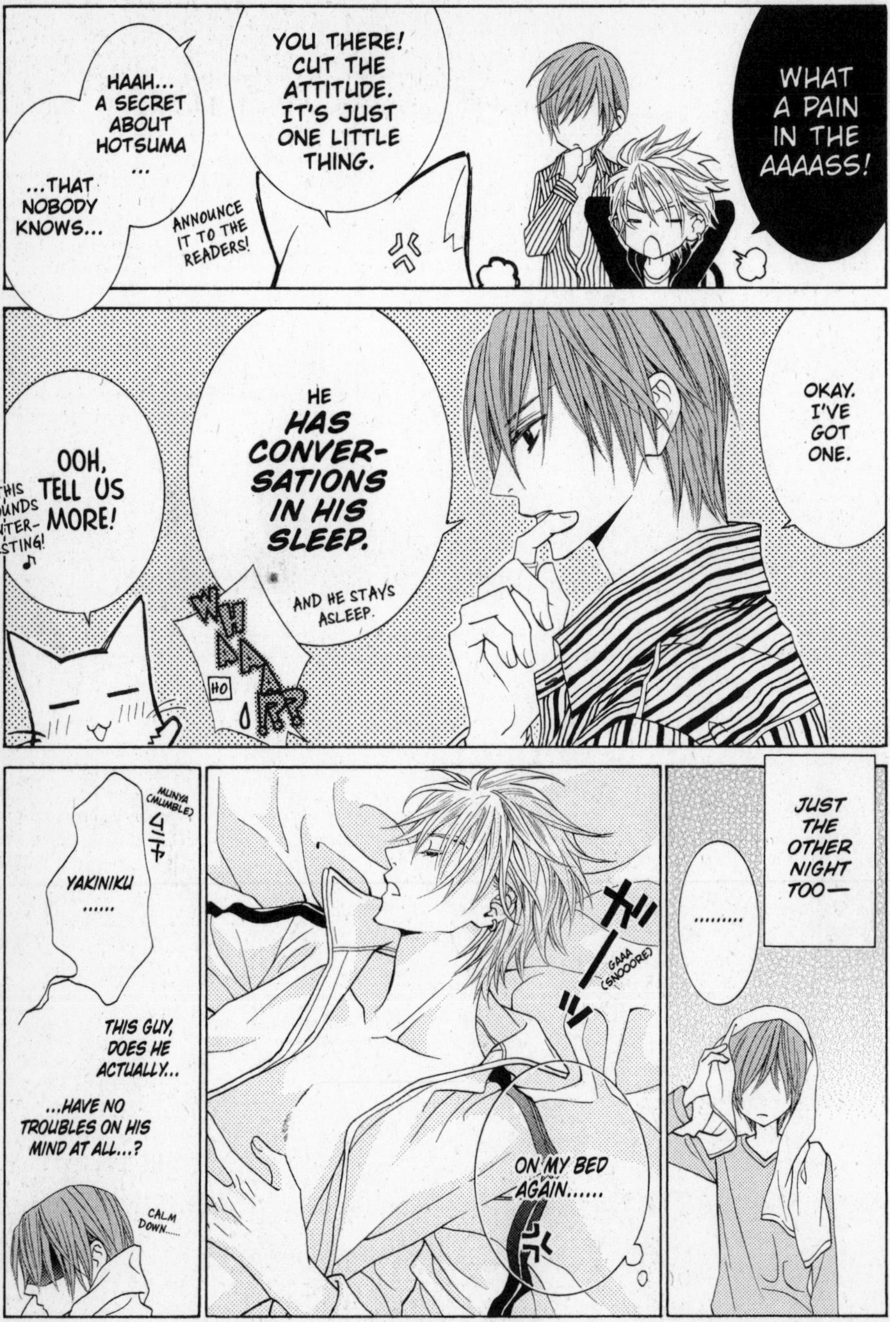
WHAT A PAIN IN THE AAAASS!
YOU THERE! CUT THE ATTITUDE. IT'S JUST ONE LITTLE THING.
ANNOUNCE IT TO THE READERS!
HAAH... A SECRET ABOUT HOTSUMA ...
...THAT NOBODY KNOWS...
OKAY. I'VE GOT ONE.
HE HAS CONVERSATIONS IN HIS SLEEP.
AND HE STAYS ASLEEP.
OOH, TELL US MORE!
THIS SOUNDS INTERESTING! ♪
JUST THE OTHER NIGHT TOO—
....
GAAA (SNOOORE)
ON MY BED AGAIN......
MUNYA (MUMBLE)
YAKINIKU ......
THIS GUY, DOES HE ACTUALLY...
...HAVE NO TROUBLES ON HIS MIND AT ALL...?
CALM DOWN......

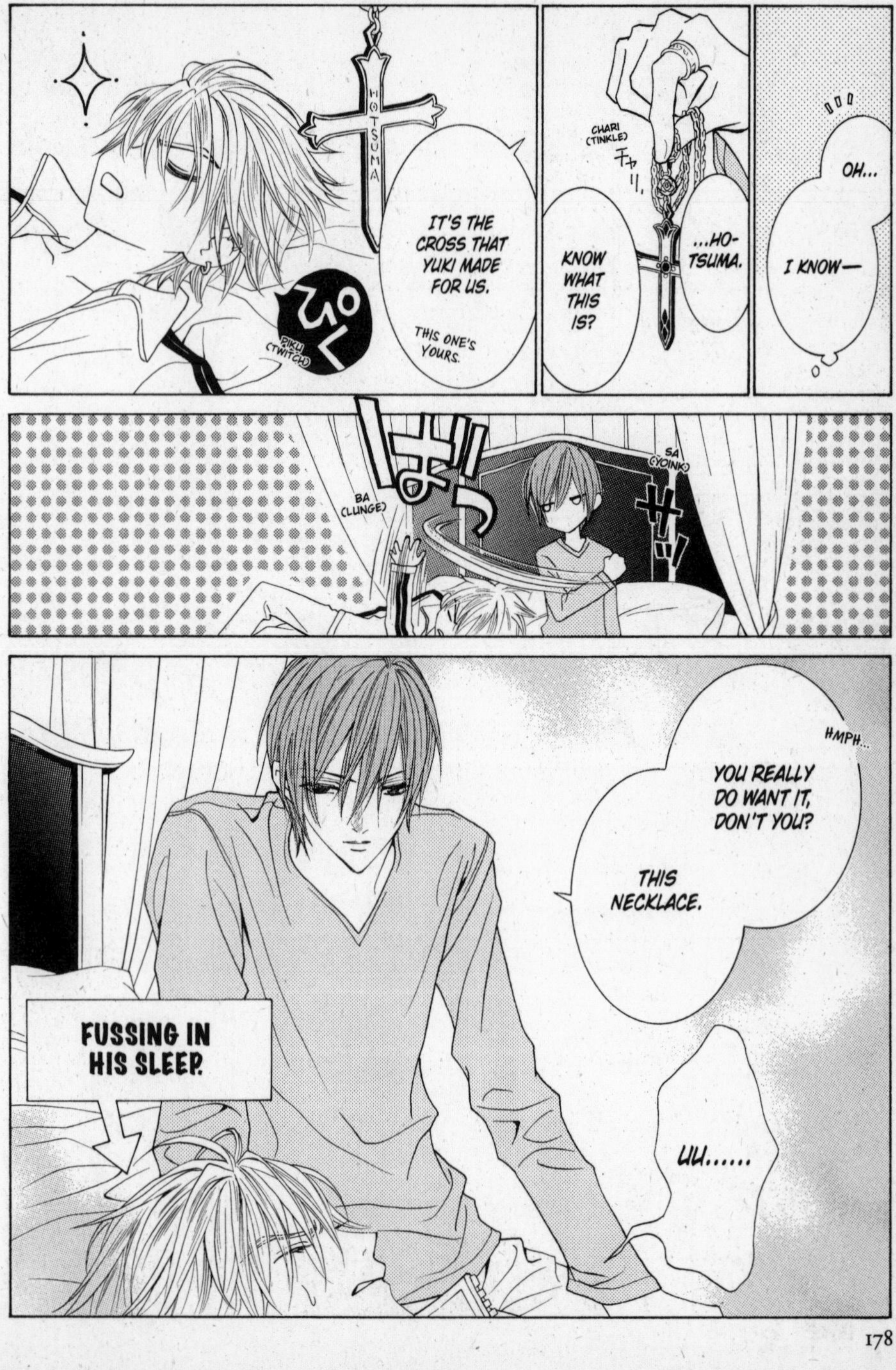
OH...
I KNOW—
...HO-TSUMA.
KNOW WHAT THIS IS?
CHARI (TINKLE)
HOTSUMA
IT'S THE CROSS THAT YUKI MADE FOR US.
THIS ONE'S YOURS.
PIKU (TWITCH)
SA (YOINK)
BA (LUNGE)
HMPH...
YOU REALLY DO WANT IT, DON'T YOU?
THIS NECKLACE.
UU......
FUSSING IN HIS SLEEP.

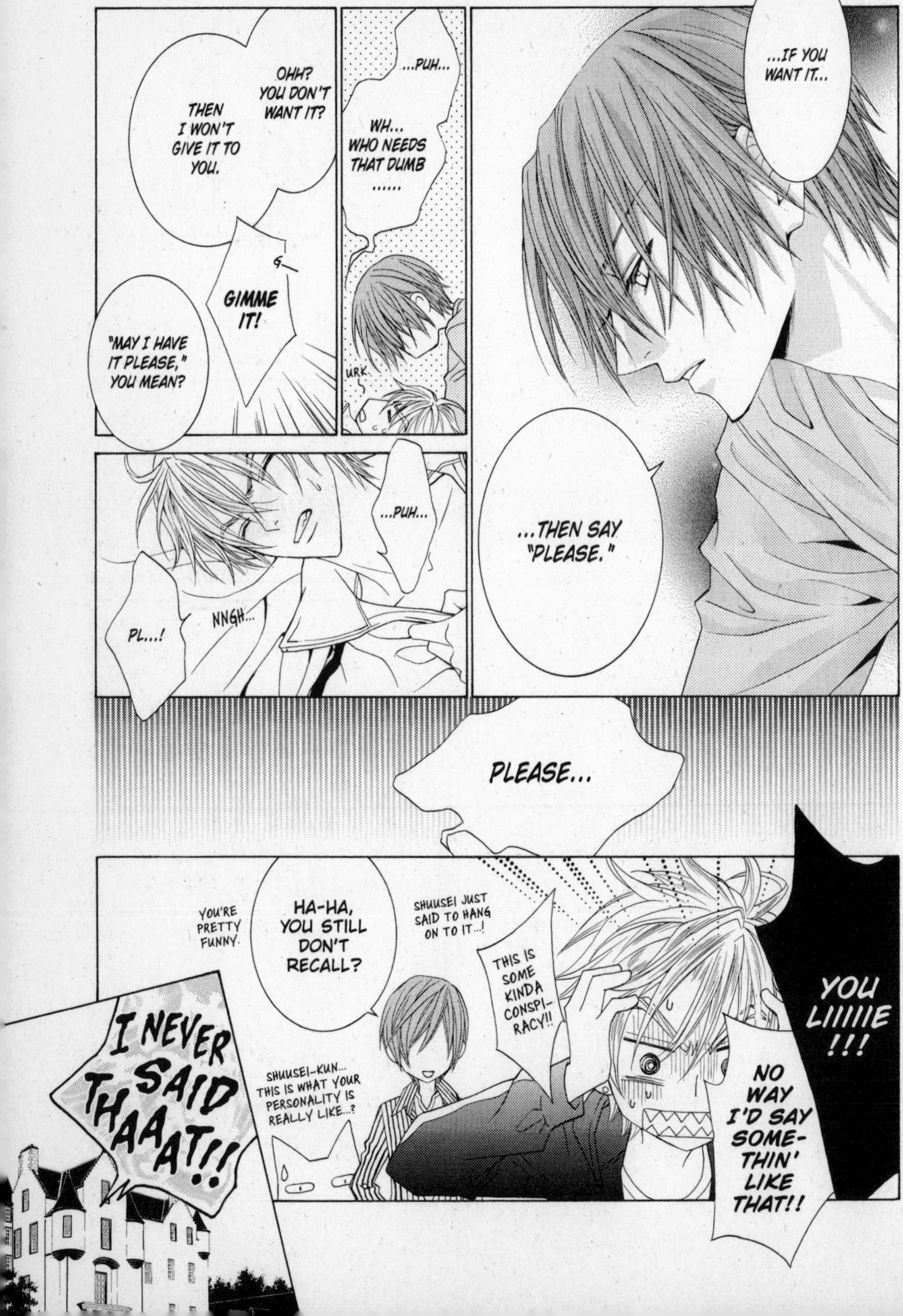
...IF YOU WANT IT...
...THEN SAY "PLEASE."
...PUH...
WH... WHO NEEDS THAT DUMB ......
URK
OHH? YOU DON'T WANT IT?
THEN I WON'T GIVE IT TO YOU.
G—
GIMME IT!
"MAY I HAVE IT PLEASE," YOU MEAN?
...PUH...
NNGH...
PL...!
PLEASE...
YOU LIIIIIE!!!
NO WAY I'D SAY SOME-THIN' LIKE THAT!!
SHUUSEI JUST SAID TO HANG ON TO IT...!
THIS IS SOME KINDA CONSPI-RACY!!
HA-HA, YOU STILL DON'T RECALL?
YOU'RE PRETTY FUNNY.
SHUUSEI-KUN... THIS IS WHAT YOUR PERSONALITY IS REALLY LIKE...?
I NEVER SAID THAAAT!!

▸THIS IS LAST MINUTE, BUT... I THINK IT WAS ADVERTISED IN THE PREVIOUS VOLUME, BUT THEY MADE A DRAMA CD OF URABOKU. IS IT OKAY TO MAKE SOMETHING LIKE THAT OUT OF THIS THING I'M WRITING BY THE SEAT OF MY PANTS...? I'M THINKING AND GETTING ALL TIMID, WHILE ALL THE GROWN-UPS AROUND ME ARE WORKING SO HARD, THERE WILL BE A WHOLE CD DONE BY THE TIME THIS VOLUME COMES OUT. BUT WE'LL BE ABLE TO LISTEN TO YUKI AND LUKA'S CONVERSATIONS! PLEASE TRY AND CHECK IT OUT~♪

▸THEY LET ME SIT IN ON THE RECORDING THE OTHER DAY. I WAS AFRAID THAT HEARING THE LINES I WROTE SPOKEN ALOUD WOULD BE SOME LIGHT TORTURE, AND I WENT IN TOTALLY PALE, BUT I WAS BLOWN AWAY! THE VOICE ACTORS REALLY PUT THEIR HEARTS INTO IT AND I WAS SO IMPRESSED—EVEN THOUGH I WROTE THE THING MYSELF, BY THE END IT WAS REALLY HITTING HOME... AND I WAS FLIPPING OUT, LIKE, THESE ARE THE PROS! WOW! SERIOUS ACTORS!! EVERYONE HAD SUCH WONDERFUL VOICES THAT MY HEART WAS POUNDING (OKAY, AND AMAZING LOOKS TOO...) AND IT FELT LIKE I WAS UNDER A SPELL! ♪

▸AND THE WAY THE STAFF WORKED WAS AMAZING—THEY ALL MOVED SO SWIFTLY AND SMARTLY, IT WAS TERRIBLY DAZZLING TO SOMEONE LIKE ME WHO'S ALWAYS DELIBERATING. AND THEY'RE ALL SUCH GOOD PEOPLE. I WANTED TO THANK THEM DIRECTLY IF I COULD, BUT SOMETIMES PEOPLE LOOKED SO BUSY THAT I DIDN'T WANT TO BOTHER THEM WITH IT, SO I'LL TAKE SOME SPACE HERE TO SHOW MY GRATITUDE...! TO THE VOICE ACTORS WHO AGREED TO TAKE THE JOB DESPITE THEIR BUSY SCHEDULES, AND TO EVERYONE ELSE WHO WORKED ON IT—THANK YOU SO MUCH!

▸WORK WAS PRETTY ROUGH UNTIL THE SCRIPT WAS DONE~ (THEY PUT TOGETHER A NICELY BALANCED SCRIPT FROM THE STUFF I SCRIBBLED OUT.) THERE WERE ONLY TWO VOLUMES OUT, SO I HAD TO EXPLAIN A LOT OF THINGS I HADN'T WRITTEN YET. (N-SAMA, THANKS FOR PUTTING THAT PLOT POINT IN!) AND THEN I THOUGHT...I HAVE TO GET TO IT FASTER... I ALSO WROTE A BONUS TRACK WHERE TEAM HOTTSU & SHUUSEI SHOW UP TOO! ♪ HOW SHOULD I SAY THIS... EVEN THOUGH THEY'RE EXTRAS, I ENDED UP WRITING SOME LINES THAT REALLY GET AT THE CORE OF THE ZWEILT, SO IF YOU WANT TO BE A HARDCORE URABOKU FAN YOU SHOULD PROBABLY PICK IT UP... (IF I DO SAY SO MYSELF!) AND THEN I HAD TO USE THE CHANCE TO TRY HAVING THE CHARACTERS SAY SOME ATYPICAL EMBARRASSING LINES (LOL).

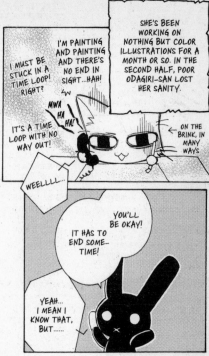

SHE'S BEEN WORKING ON NOTHING BUT COLOR ILLUSTRATIONS FOR A MONTH OR SO. IN THE SECOND HALF, POOR ODAGIRI-SAN LOST HER SANITY.
I'M PAINTING AND PAINTING AND THERE'S NO END IN SIGHT...HAH!
I MUST BE STUCK IN A TIME LOOP! RIGHT?
ON THE BRINK, IN MANY WAYS
MWA HA HA!
IT'S A TIME LOOP WITH NO WAY OUT!
WEELLLL...
YOU'LL BE OKAY!
IT HAS TO END SOME-TIME!
YEAH... I MEAN I KNOW THAT, BUT......
...AS SOON AS I FINISH THIS I'LL HAVE TO GET BACK TO MY REAL WORK ON THE SERIES...
SO MUCH INKING, I'M GONNA DIE...
TENOSY-NOVITIS.
OH, YEAH, THAT'S TRUE. SO BASICALLY...
ALL THAT'LL HAPPEN IS THAT YOUR TIME LOOP WILL TURN INTO "HELL," RIGHT?
THE USUAL.
I DON'T WANT TO HEAR THAT FROM YOU!
BLACK RABBIT OF DOOM!!

↑ ACTUALLY, DESPITE SCENES LIKE THIS, WE GET ALONG PRETTY WELL... (LOL) BUT REALLY, I SPEND ALL DAY EVERY DAY DRAWING MANGA, SO IT'S KIND OF SAD. BUT I CAN'T WRITE ABOUT ANYTHING MUCH BESIDES WORK...||||!

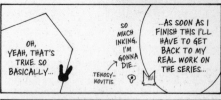

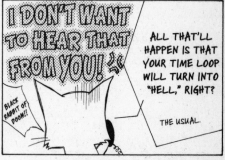

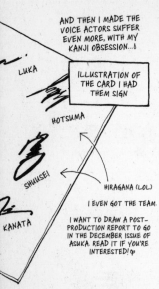

AND THEN I MADE THE VOICE ACTORS SUFFER EVEN MORE, WITH MY KANJI OBSESSION...♪
LUKA
ILLUSTRATION OF THE CARD I HAD THEM SIGN
HOTSUMA
SHUUSEI
HIRAGANA (LOL)
I EVEN GOT THE TEAM.
KANATA
I WANT TO DRAW A POST-PRODUCTION REPORT TO GO IN THE DECEMBER ISSUE OF ASUKA. READ IT IF YOU'RE INTERESTED! ♡

[CONTINUED]▼
IT WAS KIND OF IN THE SPIRIT OF MISCHIEF (HEY!), BUT THE SCENE OF THE RECORDING DEALT SOME CRITICAL DAMAGE...(TO ME). ALL THE VOICE ACTORS, OF COURSE, PERFORMED WITHOUT A HITCH...BUT EVEN IF IT IS THEIR JOB, IT'S STILL AMAZING. ...SO, HAVE I MADE YOU WANT TO LISTEN TO IT YET? (LOL) IF YOU DO GET A CHANCE TO HEAR IT, PLEASE LET ME KNOW YOUR THOUGHTS.

▶SO HERE IN VOLUME 3, THE FOCUS IS ON TEAM HOTSUMA & SHUUSEI...AND LUKA HARDLY SHOWS UP AT ALL. NOT BECAUSE LUKA'S SUCH A PAIN TO DRAW, OR BECAUSE I'M TRYING THE SOULS OF THE LUKA FANS...PROBABLY NOT. (THEN WHY?) BIT BY BIT HE'LL GET BACK IN THE GAME! THERE WERE A FEW BOLD YOUNG LADIES WHO TOLD ME THEY WOULDN'T HAVE MINDED GIVING LUKA AN EYEFUL IN THE "SUDDENLY! BATHTIME!" SCENE IN VOLUME 2, SO THAT WAS FUN (LOL).
HOTSUMA IS GETTING CALLED TSUNDERE. ...YEAHHH, I GUESS YOU WOULD CALL THAT TSUNDERE (I HAD NO IDEA AS I WROTE HIM). SHUUSEI-KUN IS MORE MYSTERIOUS AND FOR SOME REASON QUITE A FEW NAME HIM AS THEIR FAVORITE. I'M SORRY IF I MAKE EVERYONE DISILLUSIONED WITH HIM IN THIS VOLUME! (CRIES) AFTER I'VE GOTTEN PEOPLE SAYING HE'S "MYSTERIOUS" AND EVERYTHING... THERE ARE ALSO MORE THAN A FEW OPINIONS TO THE TUNE OF "PUT SOME MORE GIRLS IN IT!" ♡ ...I WILL!! (DEFINITIVE DECLARATION!) ACTUALLY THERE ARE STILL MORE ZWEILT TO APPEAR~~ GIRLS. I AM LATE INTRODUCING THE NEW CHARACTERS (PATHETIC). BUT I DO LOVE DRAWING PRETTY GIRLS, SO THE FUN WILL SOON BEGIN! ♡ HEH-HEH... IN ALL HONESTY, THERE ARE TIMES WHEN I'VE WISHED I MADE YUKI A GIRL, BUT WHEN I LISTENED TO HOSHI-SAN'S YUKI, THERE I WAS THINKING ANEW, "I WAS RIGHT TO MAKE HIM A BOY! A BOY!!" A MAIN CHARACTER GIVING IT HIS ALL... I'M SO GLAD... ♪

Extra ✝ TELL ME A SECRET ABOUT YOUR PARTNER (CONT'D)

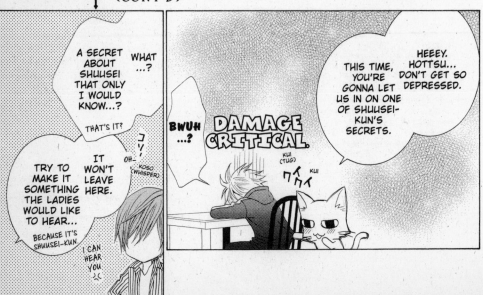

HEEEY. HOTTSU... DON'T GET SO DEPRESSED.
THIS TIME, YOU'RE GONNA LET US IN ON ONE OF SHUUSEI-KUN'S SECRETS.
BWUH ...?
DAMAGE CRITICAL
KUI (TUG)
KUI
WHAT ...?
A SECRET ABOUT SHUUSEI THAT ONLY I WOULD KNOW...?
THAT'S IT?
OH-
KOSO (WHISPER)
IT WON'T LEAVE HERE.
TRY TO MAKE IT SOMETHING THE LADIES WOULD LIKE TO HEAR...
BECAUSE IT'S SHUUSEI-KUN.
I CAN HEAR YOU

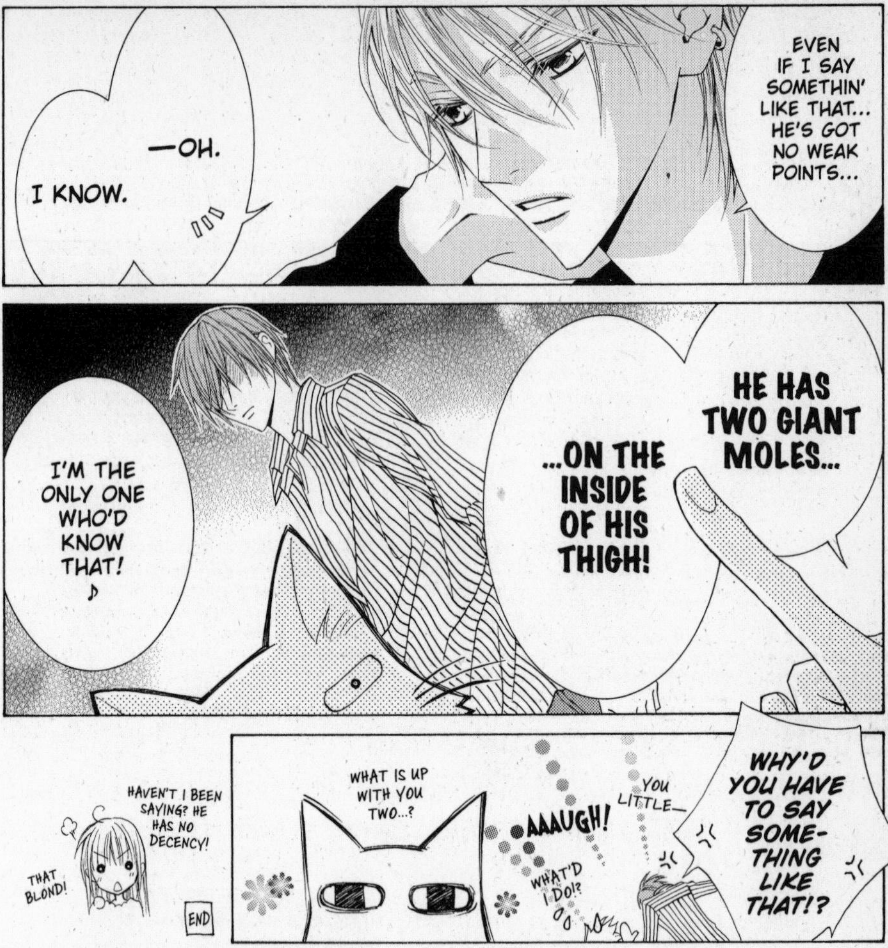
EVEN IF I SAY SOMETHIN' LIKE THAT... HE'S GOT NO WEAK POINTS...
—OH.
I KNOW.
HE HAS TWO GIANT MOLES...
...ON THE INSIDE OF HIS THIGH!
I'M THE ONLY ONE WHO'D KNOW THAT! ♪
WHY'D YOU HAVE TO SAY SOME-THING LIKE THAT!?
YOU LITTLE—
AAAUGH!
WHAT'D I DO!?
WHAT IS UP WITH YOU TWO...?
HAVEN'T I BEEN SAYING? HE HAS NO DECENCY!
THAT BLOND!
END

THANK YOU FOR READING SO FAR. I'D LIKE TO HEAR YOUR THOUGHTS, SO PLEASE LET ME KNOW IF YOU HAVE ANY OPINIONS OR REQUESTS. AND KEEP READING TO SEE WHAT HAPPENS TO YUKI AND THE OTHERS! SEE YOU AGAIN IN VOLUME 4!

➔ SPECIAL THANKS
K-SAN
A. FUJISAKI, H. MATSUO, K. O., E. Y., Y. SUZUKI ... AND ALL THE STAFF

➔ SEND LETTERS TO:
GEKKAN ASUKA EDITING DEPARTMENT C/O HOTARU ODAGIRI
KADOKAWA SHOTEN KK
102-8078

EDITOR～S-KAWA-SAN～..THANK YOU FOR ALWAYS BEING ON MY CASE!～

➔ TO BE CONTINUED.

ALL THE STUDENTS TAKING ENTRANCE EXAMS WILL PROBABLY BE AT THE FINAL STRETCH WHEN THIS VOLUME COMES OUT, RIGHT? I'M EVEN RECEIVING LETTERS FROM THE TEST-TAKERS... IT MUST BE SO MUCH ANXIETY AND PRESSURE. LIVING EACH DAY ALWAYS COMES WITH SOME AMOUNT OF ANXIETY, BUT WHEN I FEEL THAT WAY, AFTER I'VE STRUGGLED AND KICKED AND SCREAMED, I END UP THINKING, "WELL, I'VE DONE WHAT I COULD; WHAT WILL BE WILL BE!"

↖ ESPECIALLY BEFORE A DEADLINE (LOL)

IT'S OKAY. LET'S ALL CARRY OUR BURDENS LIGHTLY AND GIVE IT OUR BEST!

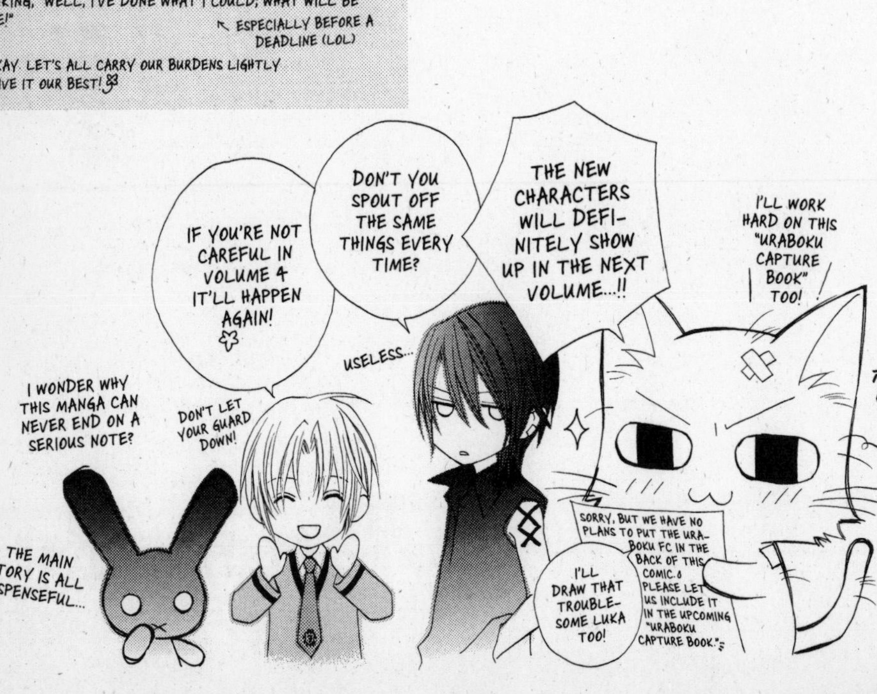
I'LL WORK HARD ON THIS "URABOKU CAPTURE BOOK" TOO!
THE NEW CHARACTERS WILL DEFINITELY SHOW UP IN THE NEXT VOLUME...!!
ボロッ
BORO (DOINK)
DON'T YOU SPOUT OFF THE SAME THINGS EVERY TIME?
USELESS...
IF YOU'RE NOT CAREFUL IN VOLUME 4 IT'LL HAPPEN AGAIN!
SORRY, BUT WE HAVE NO PLANS TO PUT THE URABOKU FC IN THE BACK OF THIS COMIC. PLEASE LET US INCLUDE IT IN THE UPCOMING "URABOKU CAPTURE BOOK."
I'LL DRAW THAT TROUBLESOME LUKA TOO!
DON'T LET YOUR GUARD DOWN!
I WONDER WHY THIS MANGA CAN NEVER END ON A SERIOUS NOTE?
THE MAIN STORY IS ALL SUSPENSEFUL...

The Betrayal Knows My Name

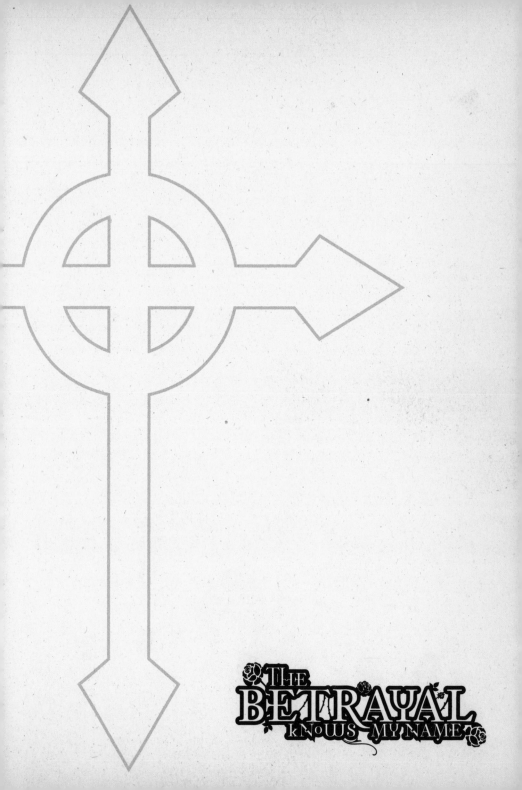

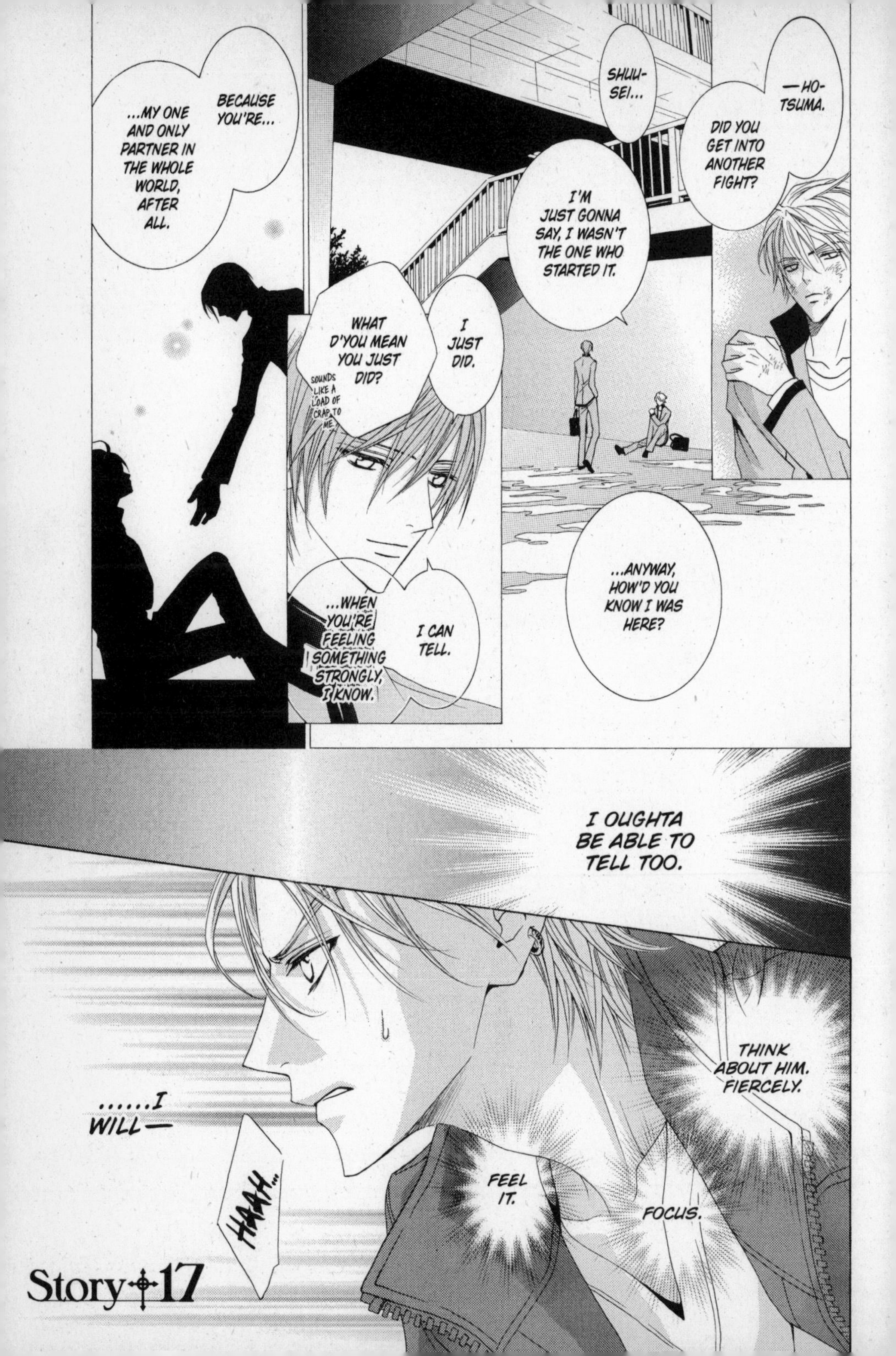

—HO-TSUMA.
DID YOU GET INTO ANOTHER FIGHT?
SHUU-SEI...
I'M JUST GONNA SAY, I WASN'T THE ONE WHO STARTED IT.
...ANYWAY, HOW'D YOU KNOW I WAS HERE?
I JUST DID.
WHAT D'YOU MEAN YOU JUST DID?
SOUNDS LIKE A LOAD OF CRAP TO ME.
I CAN TELL.
...WHEN YOU'RE FEELING SOMETHING STRONGLY, I KNOW.
BECAUSE YOU'RE...
...MY ONE AND ONLY PARTNER IN THE WHOLE WORLD, AFTER ALL.
I OUGHTA BE ABLE TO TELL TOO.
THINK ABOUT HIM. FIERCELY.
FOCUS.
FEEL IT.
......I WILL—
HAAH...

Story 17

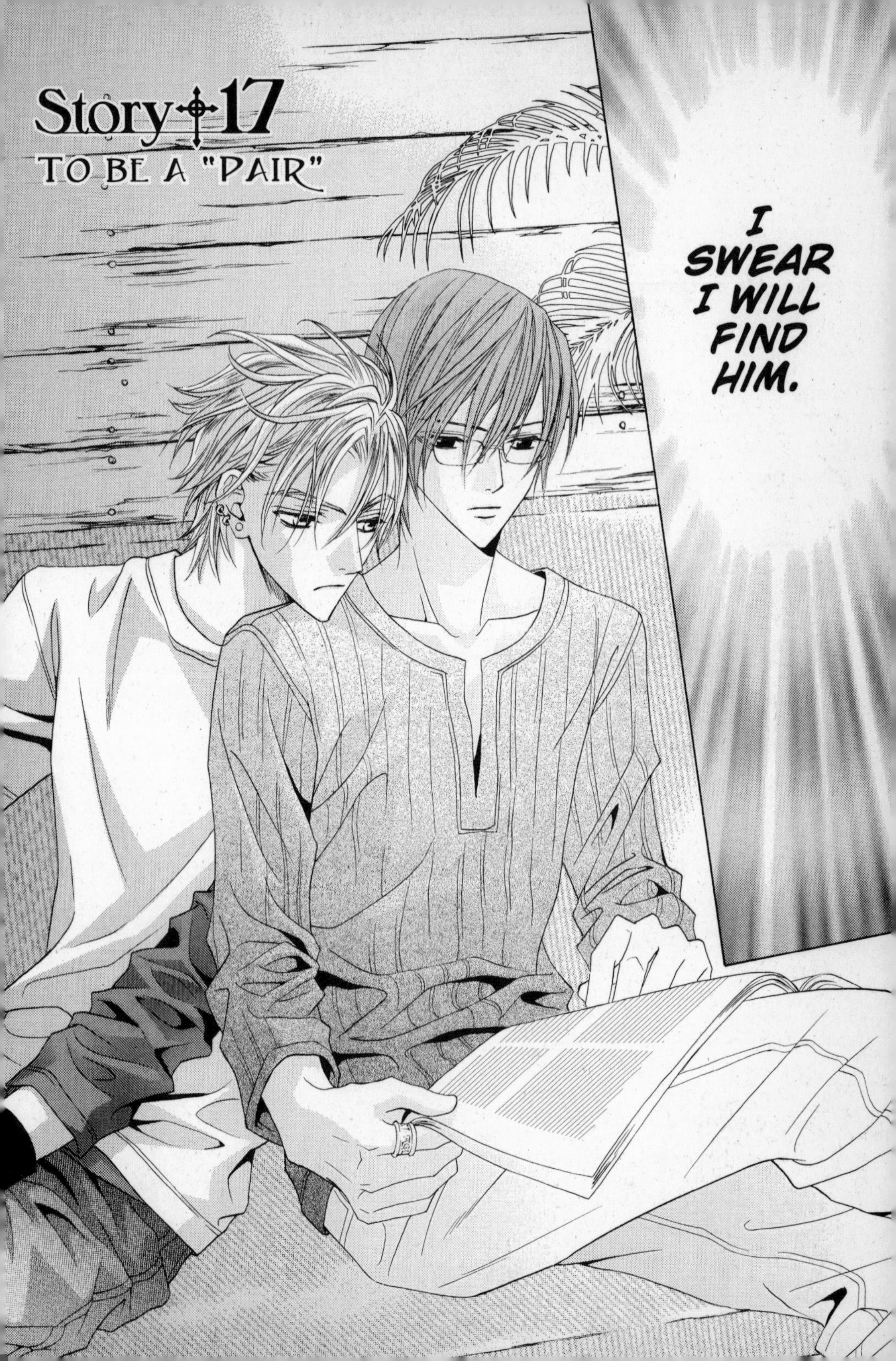
Story 17
TO BE A "PAIR"
I SWEAR I WILL FIND HIM.

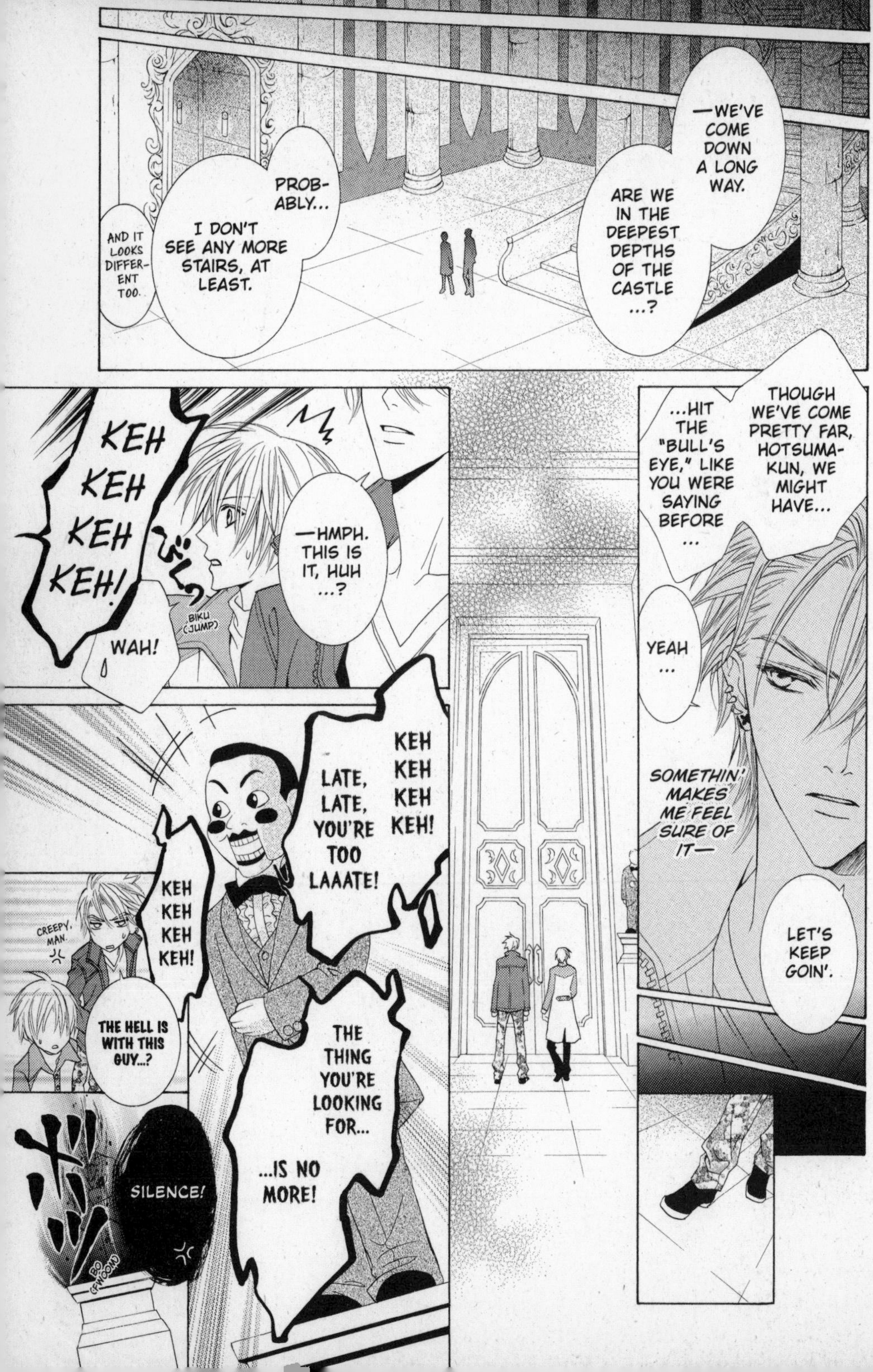
—WE'VE COME DOWN A LONG WAY.
ARE WE IN THE DEEPEST DEPTHS OF THE CASTLE ...?
PROB-ABLY... I DON'T SEE ANY MORE STAIRS, AT LEAST.
AND IT LOOKS DIFFER-ENT TOO.
THOUGH WE'VE COME PRETTY FAR, HOTSUMA-KUN, WE MIGHT HAVE...
...HIT THE "BULL'S EYE," LIKE YOU WERE SAYING BEFORE ...
YEAH ...
SOMETHIN' MAKES ME FEEL SURE OF IT—
LET'S KEEP GOIN'.
—HMPH. THIS IS IT, HUH ...?
KEH KEH KEH KEH!
BIKU (JUMP)
WAH!
KEH KEH KEH KEH!
LATE, LATE, YOU'RE TOO LAAATE!
KEH KEH KEH KEH!
CREEPY, MAN.
THE HELL IS WITH THIS GUY...?
THE THING YOU'RE LOOKING FOR...
...IS NO MORE!
SILENCE!
BO (FWOOM)

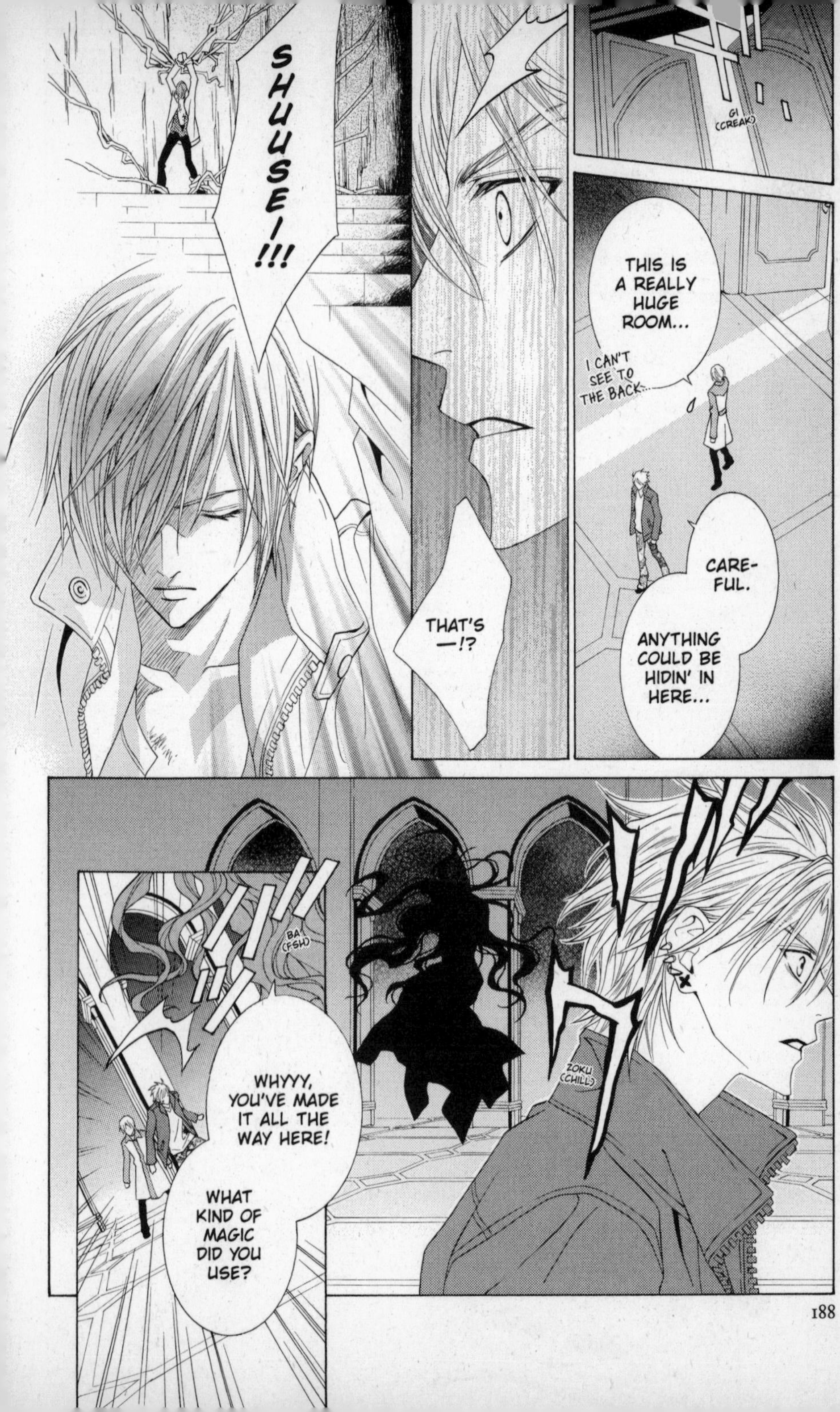
GI (CREAK)
THIS IS A REALLY HUGE ROOM...
I CAN'T SEE TO THE BACK...
CAREFUL.
ANYTHING COULD BE HIDIN' IN HERE...
THAT'S —!?
SHUUSEI!!!
ZOKU (CHILL)
BA (FSH)
WHYYY, YOU'VE MADE IT ALL THE WAY HERE!
WHAT KIND OF MAGIC DID YOU USE?

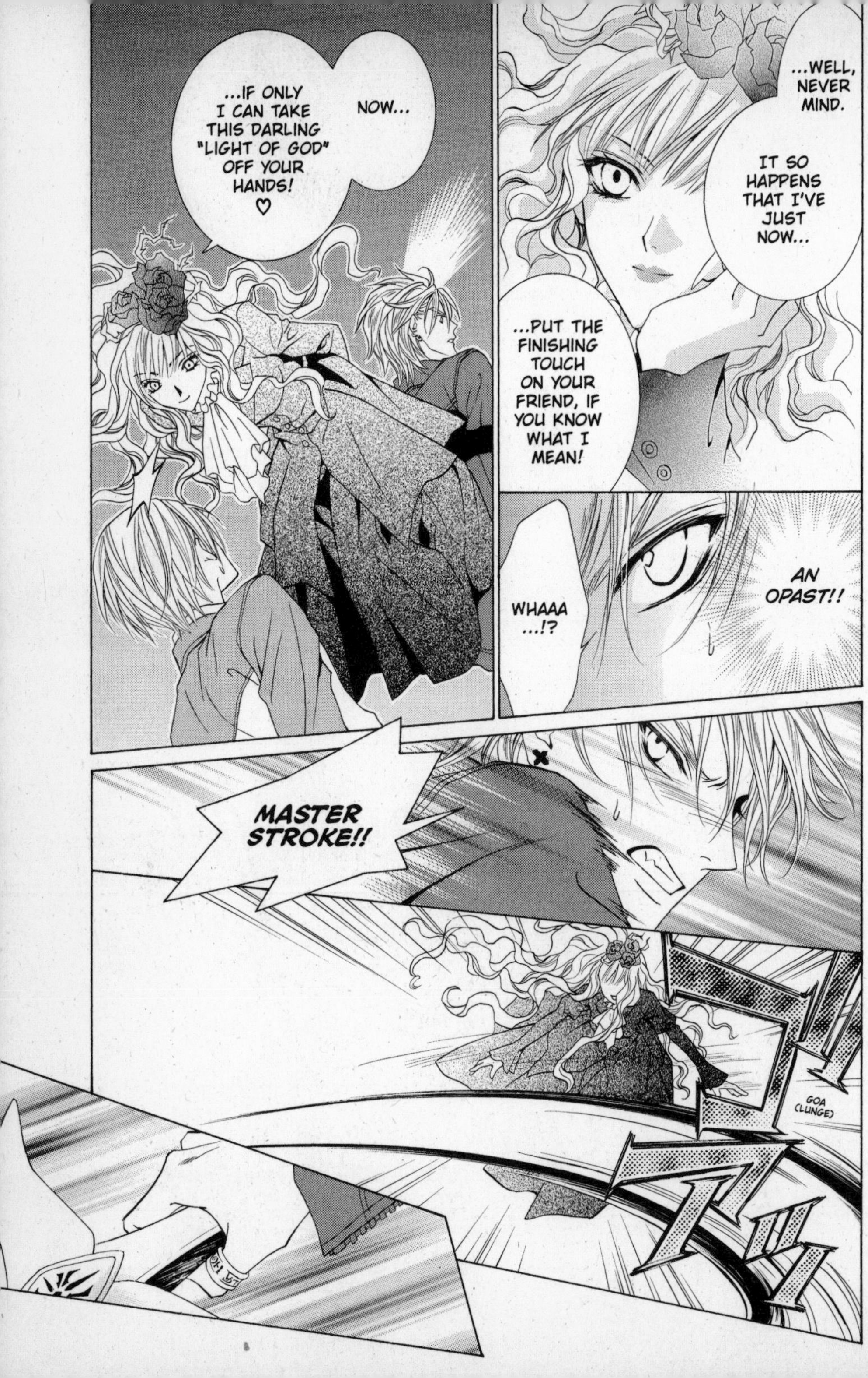
NOW...
...IF ONLY I CAN TAKE THIS DARLING "LIGHT OF GOD" OFF YOUR HANDS! ♡
...WELL, NEVER MIND.
IT SO HAPPENS THAT I'VE JUST NOW...
...PUT THE FINISHING TOUCH ON YOUR FRIEND, IF YOU KNOW WHAT I MEAN!
WHAAA ...!?
AN OPAST!!
MASTER STROKE!!
GOA (LUNGE)

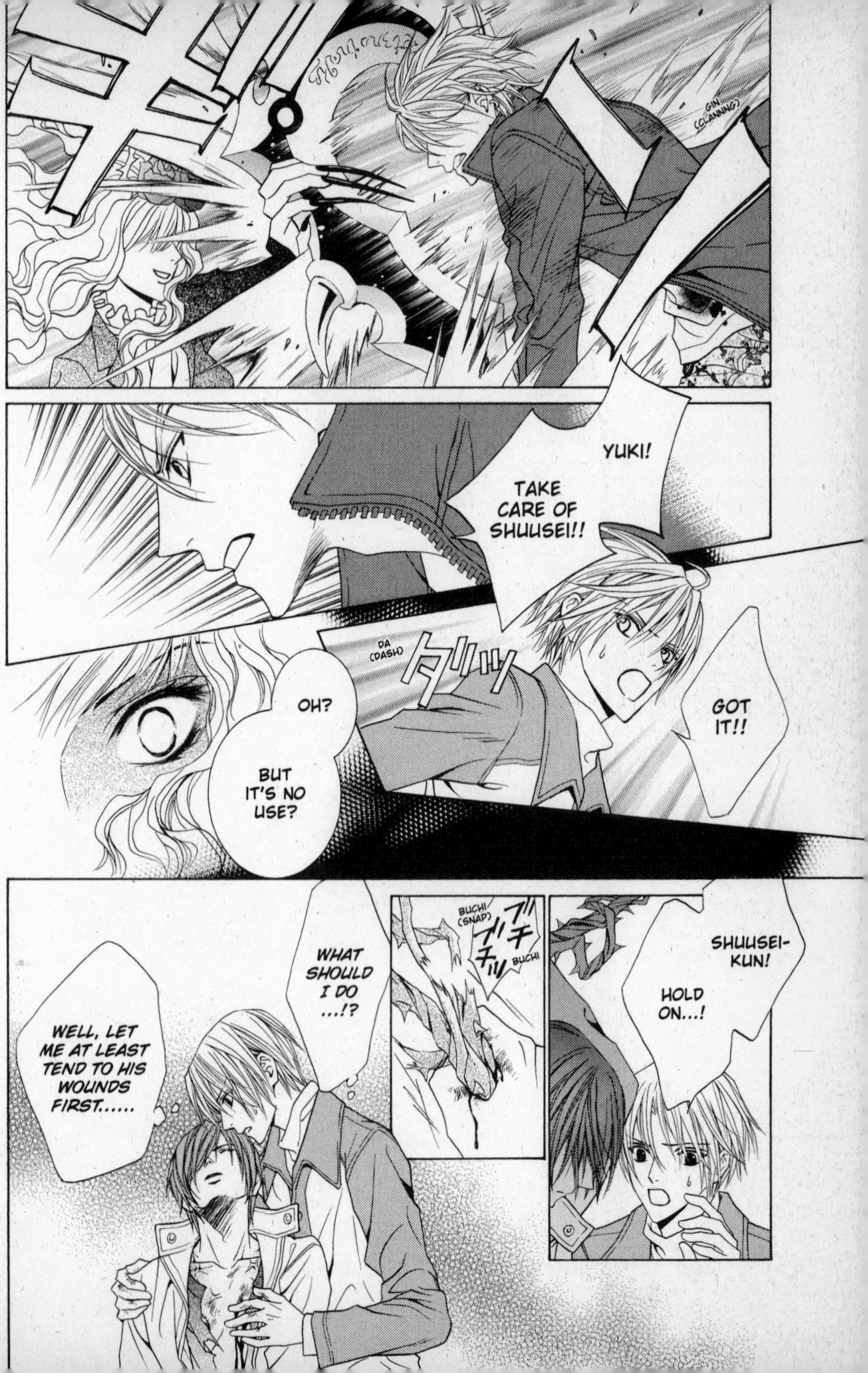
GIN (CLANNNG)
YUKI!
TAKE CARE OF SHUUSEI!!
GOT IT!!
DA (DASH)
OH?
BUT IT'S NO USE?
SHUUSEI-KUN!
HOLD ON...!
BUCHI (SNAP)
BUCHI
WHAT SHOULD I DO ...!?
WELL, LET ME AT LEAST TEND TO HIS WOUNDS FIRST......

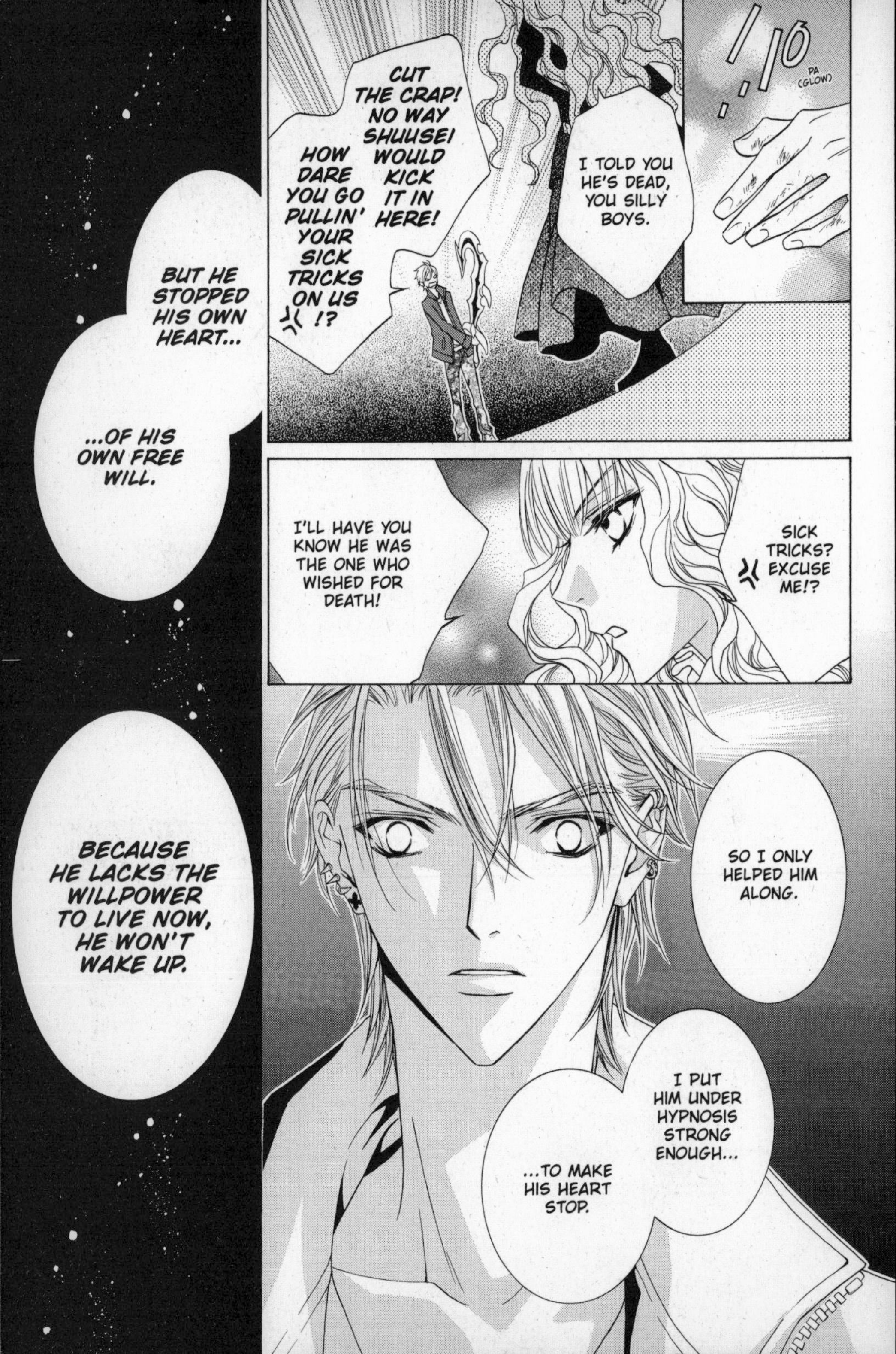
PA (GLOW)
I TOLD YOU HE'S DEAD, YOU SILLY BOYS.
CUT THE CRAP! NO WAY SHUUSEI WOULD KICK IT IN HERE!
HOW DARE YOU GO PULLIN' YOUR SICK TRICKS ON US !?
SICK TRICKS? EXCUSE ME!?
I'LL HAVE YOU KNOW HE WAS THE ONE WHO WISHED FOR DEATH!
SO I ONLY HELPED HIM ALONG.
I PUT HIM UNDER HYPNOSIS STRONG ENOUGH...
...TO MAKE HIS HEART STOP.
BUT HE STOPPED HIS OWN HEART...
...OF HIS OWN FREE WILL.
BECAUSE HE LACKS THE WILLPOWER TO LIVE NOW, HE WON'T WAKE UP.

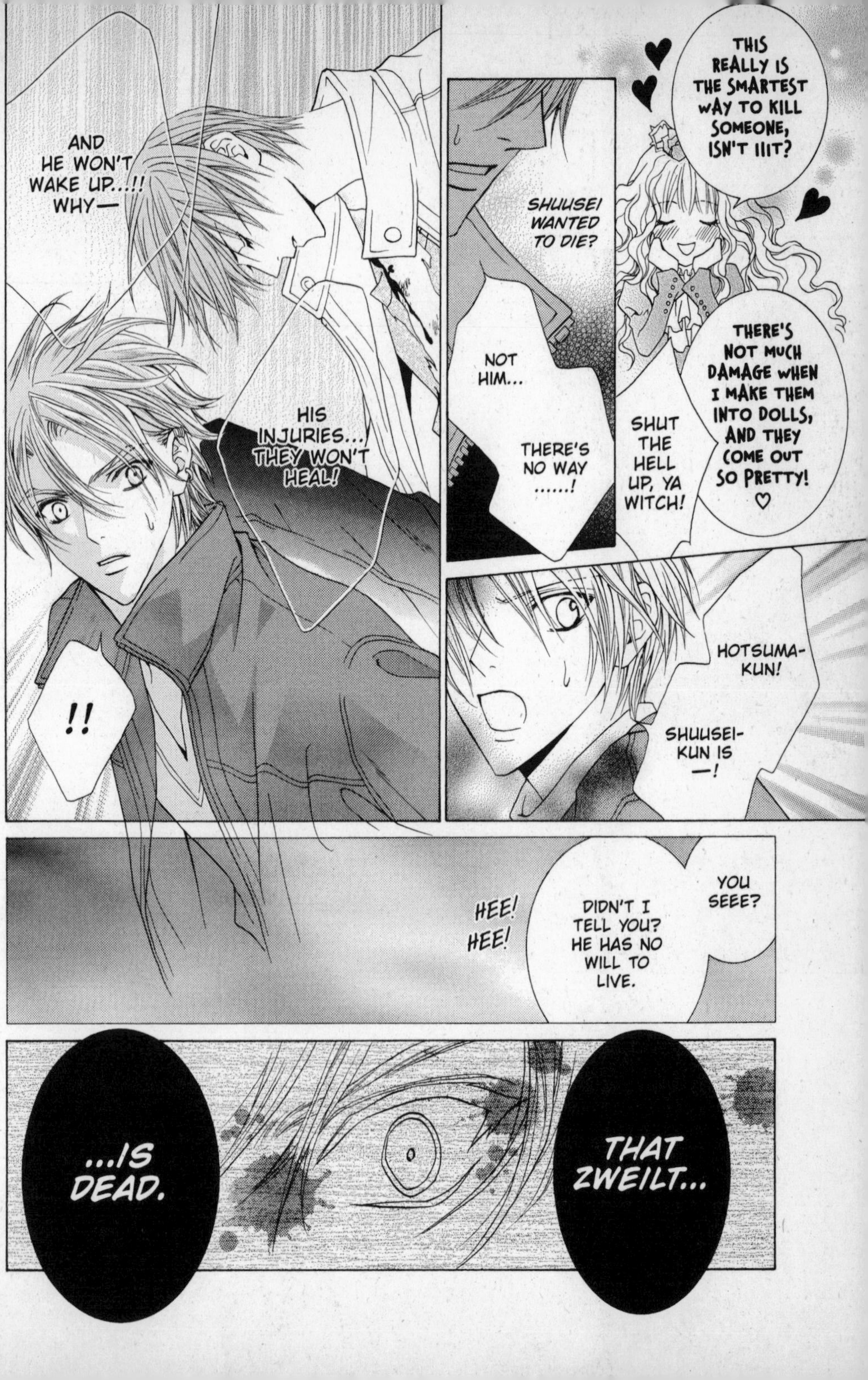

THIS REALLY IS THE SMARTEST WAY TO KILL SOMEONE, ISN'T IIIT?
THERE'S NOT MUCH DAMAGE WHEN I MAKE THEM INTO DOLLS, AND THEY COME OUT SO PRETTY! ♡
SHUUSEI WANTED TO DIE?
NOT HIM...
THERE'S NO WAY ......!
SHUT THE HELL UP, YA WITCH!
HOTSUMA-KUN!
SHUUSEI-KUN IS —!
AND HE WON'T WAKE UP...!! WHY—
HIS INJURIES... THEY WON'T HEAL!
!!
YOU SEEE?
DIDN'T I TELL YOU? HE HAS NO WILL TO LIVE.
HEE! HEE!
THAT ZWEILT...
...IS DEAD.

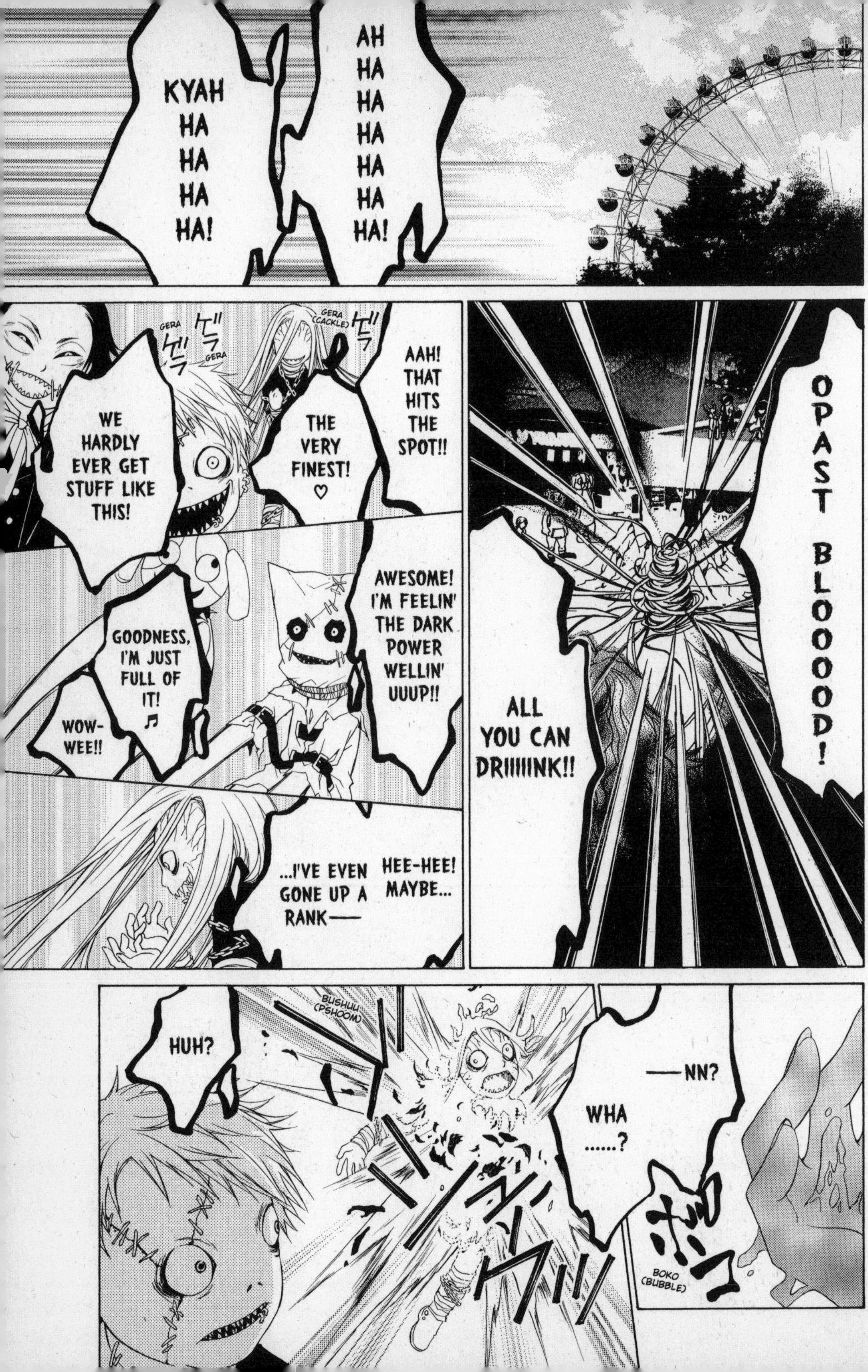
AH HA HA HA HA HA HA!
KYAH HA HA HA HA!
OPAST BLOOOOOD!
ALL YOU CAN DRIIIIINK!!
AAH! THAT HITS THE SPOT!!
GERA (CACKLE)
GERA
GERA
THE VERY FINEST! ♡
WE HARDLY EVER GET STUFF LIKE THIS!
AWESOME! I'M FEELIN' THE DARK POWER WELLIN' UUUP!!
GOODNESS, I'M JUST FULL OF IT! ♪
WOW-WEE!!
HEE-HEE! MAYBE...
...I'VE EVEN GONE UP A RANK——
——NN?
WHA ......?
BOKO (BUBBLE)
BUSHUU (PSHOOM)
HUH?

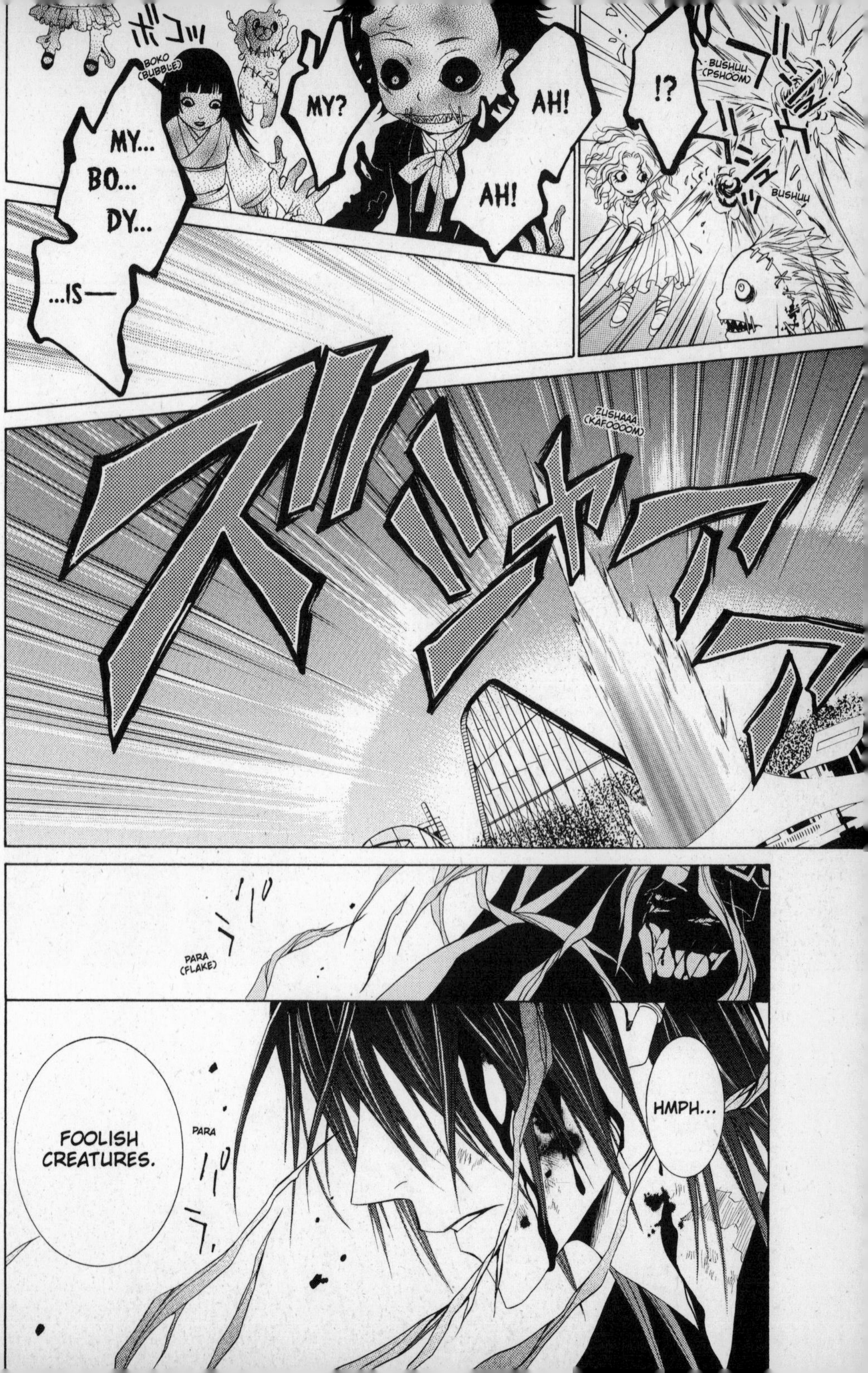
!?
BUSHUU (PSHOOM)
BUSHUU
AH!
AH!
MY?
ボコッ
BOKO (BUBBLE)
MY... BO... DY... ...IS—
ZUSHAAA (KAFOOOOM)
PARA (FLAKE)
HMPH...
PARA
FOOLISH CREATURES.

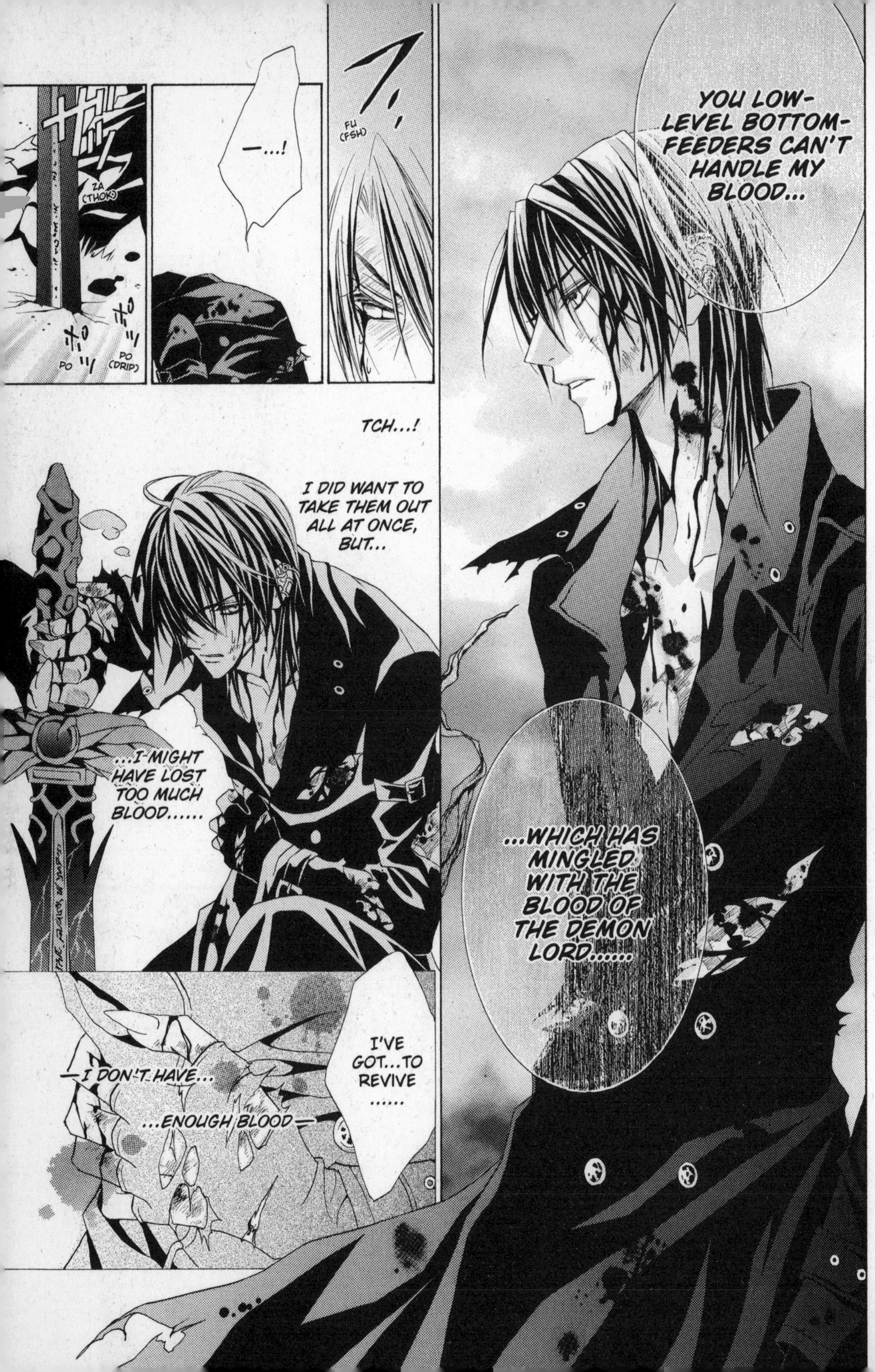

YOU LOW-LEVEL BOTTOM-FEEDERS CAN'T HANDLE MY BLOOD...
...WHICH HAS MINGLED WITH THE BLOOD OF THE DEMON LORD......
FU (FSH)
—...!
PO (DRIP)
ZA (THOK)
PO
TCH...!
I DID WANT TO TAKE THEM OUT ALL AT ONCE, BUT...
...I-MIGHT HAVE LOST TOO MUCH BLOOD......
I'VE GOT...TO REVIVE ......
—I DON'T HAVE...
...ENOUGH BLOOD—

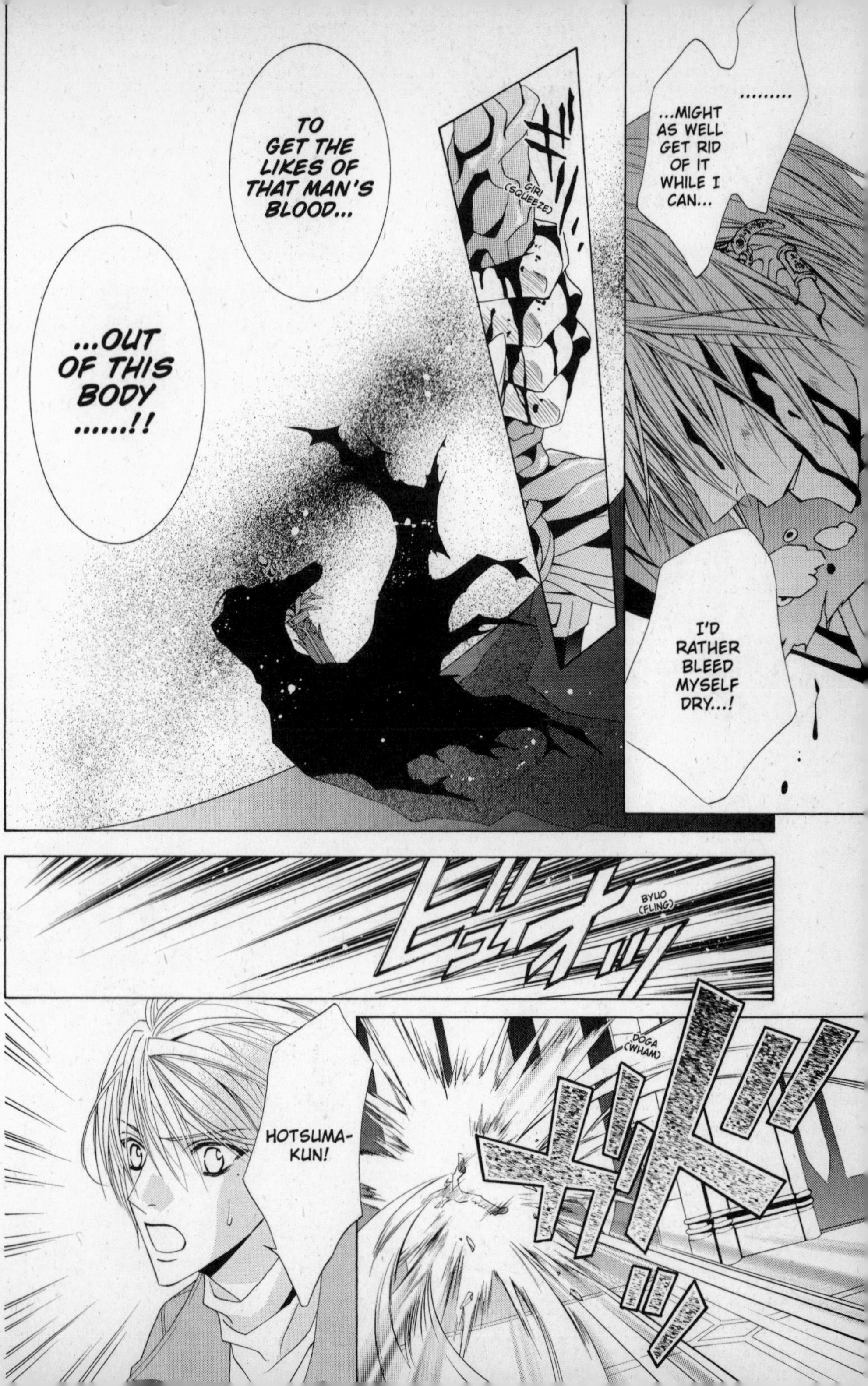
....
...MIGHT AS WELL GET RID OF IT WHILE I CAN...
I'D RATHER BLEED MYSELF DRY...!
GIRI (SQUEEZE)
TO GET THE LIKES OF THAT MAN'S BLOOD...
...OUT OF THIS BODY ......!!
BYUO (FLING)
DOGA (WHAM)
HOTSUMA-KUN!

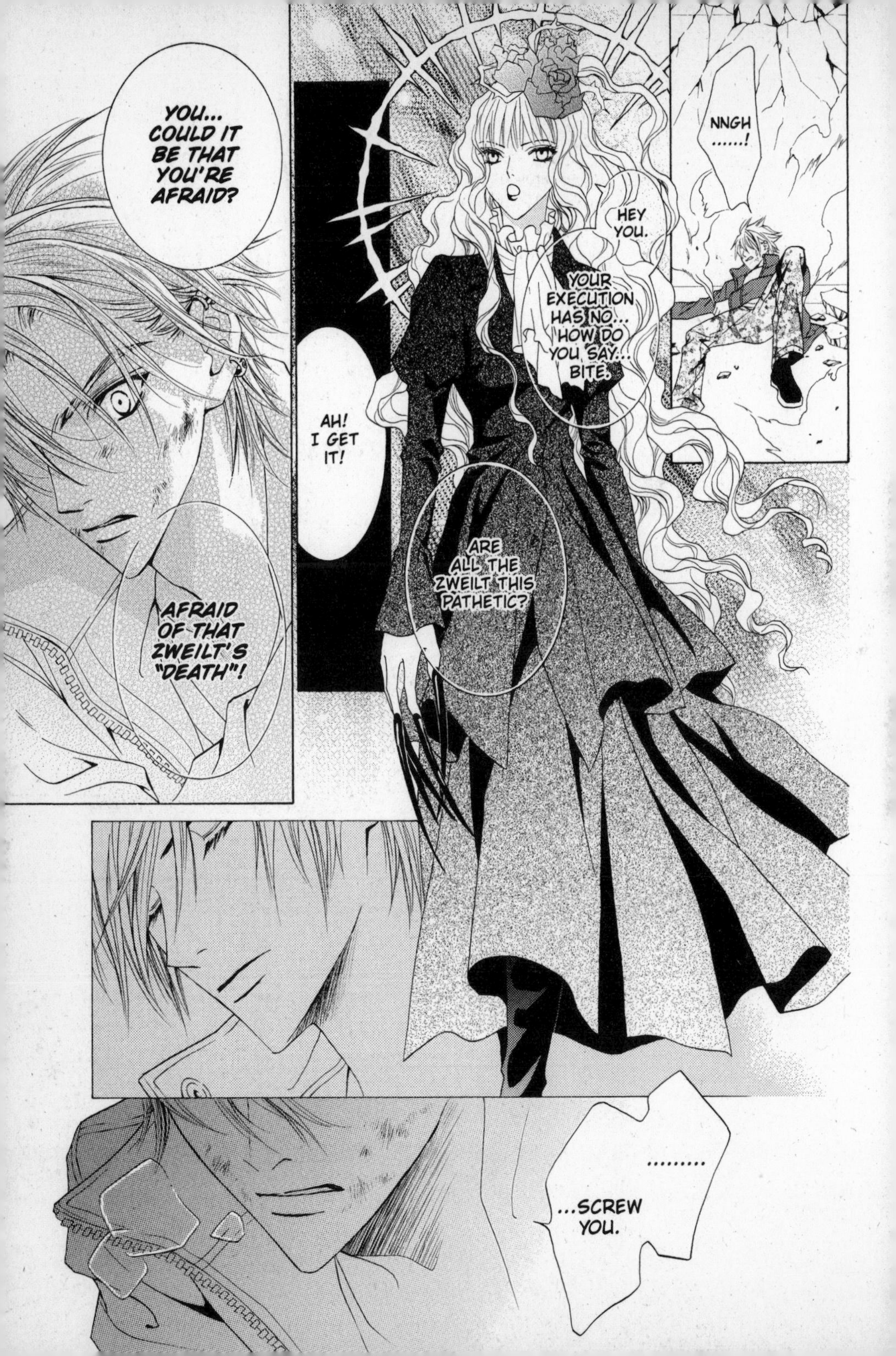
NNGH ......!
HEY YOU.
YOUR EXECUTION HAS NO... HOW DO YOU SAY... BITE.
ARE ALL THE ZWEILT THIS PATHETIC?
AH! I GET IT!
YOU... COULD IT BE THAT YOU'RE AFRAID?
AFRAID OF THAT ZWEILT'S "DEATH"!
....
...SCREW YOU.

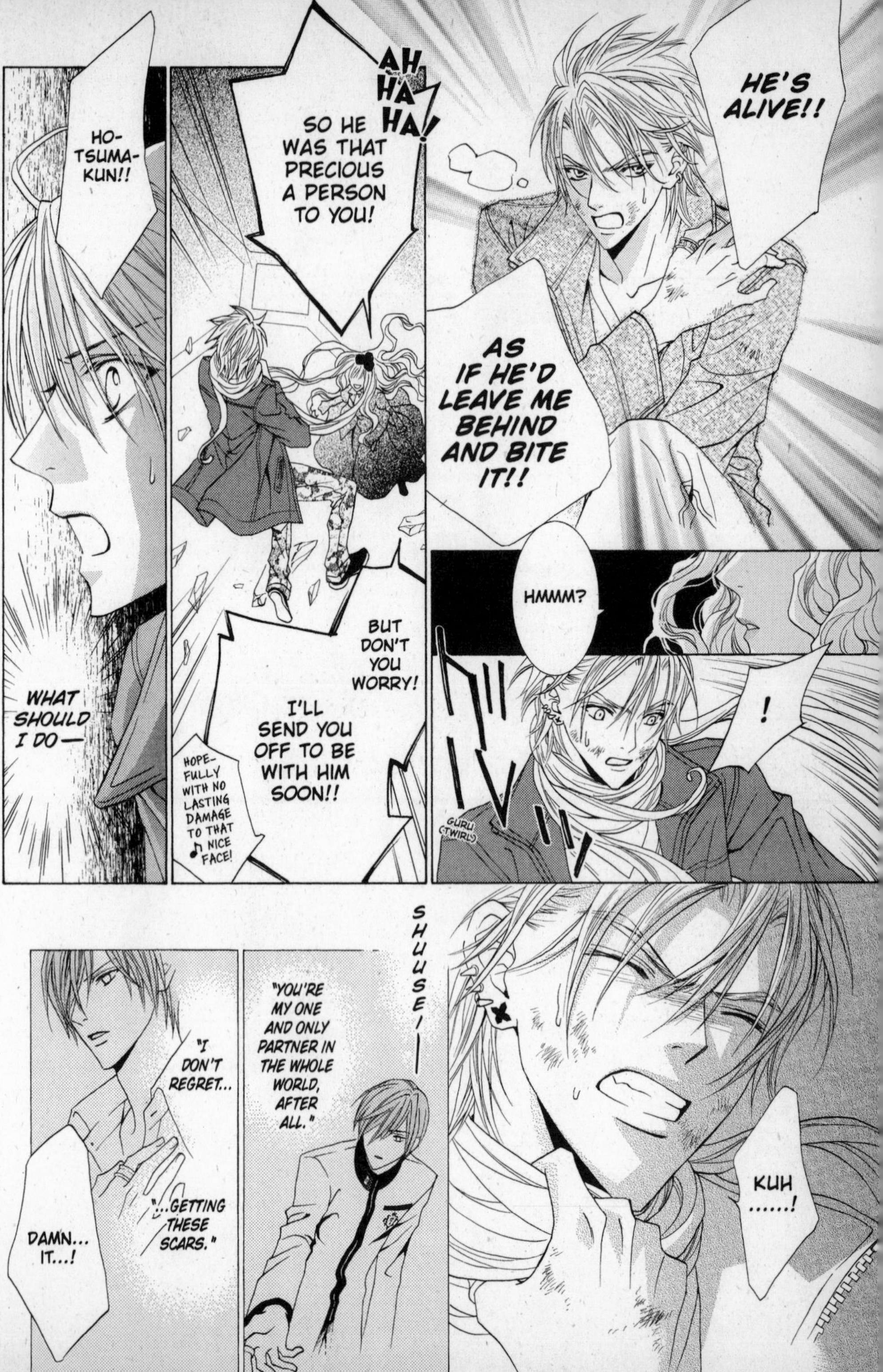
HE'S ALIVE!!
AS IF HE'D LEAVE ME BEHIND AND BITE IT!!
HMMM?
!
GURU (TWIRL)
AH HA HA!
SO HE WAS THAT PRECIOUS A PERSON TO YOU!
BUT DON'T YOU WORRY!
I'LL SEND YOU OFF TO BE WITH HIM SOON!!
HOPE-FULLY WITH NO LASTING DAMAGE TO THAT NICE FACE! ♪
HO-TSUMA-KUN!!
WHAT SHOULD I DO—
SHUUSEI—
KUH ......!
"YOU'RE MY ONE AND ONLY PARTNER IN THE WHOLE WORLD, AFTER ALL."
"I DON'T REGRET...
"...GETTING THESE SCARS."
DAMN... IT...!

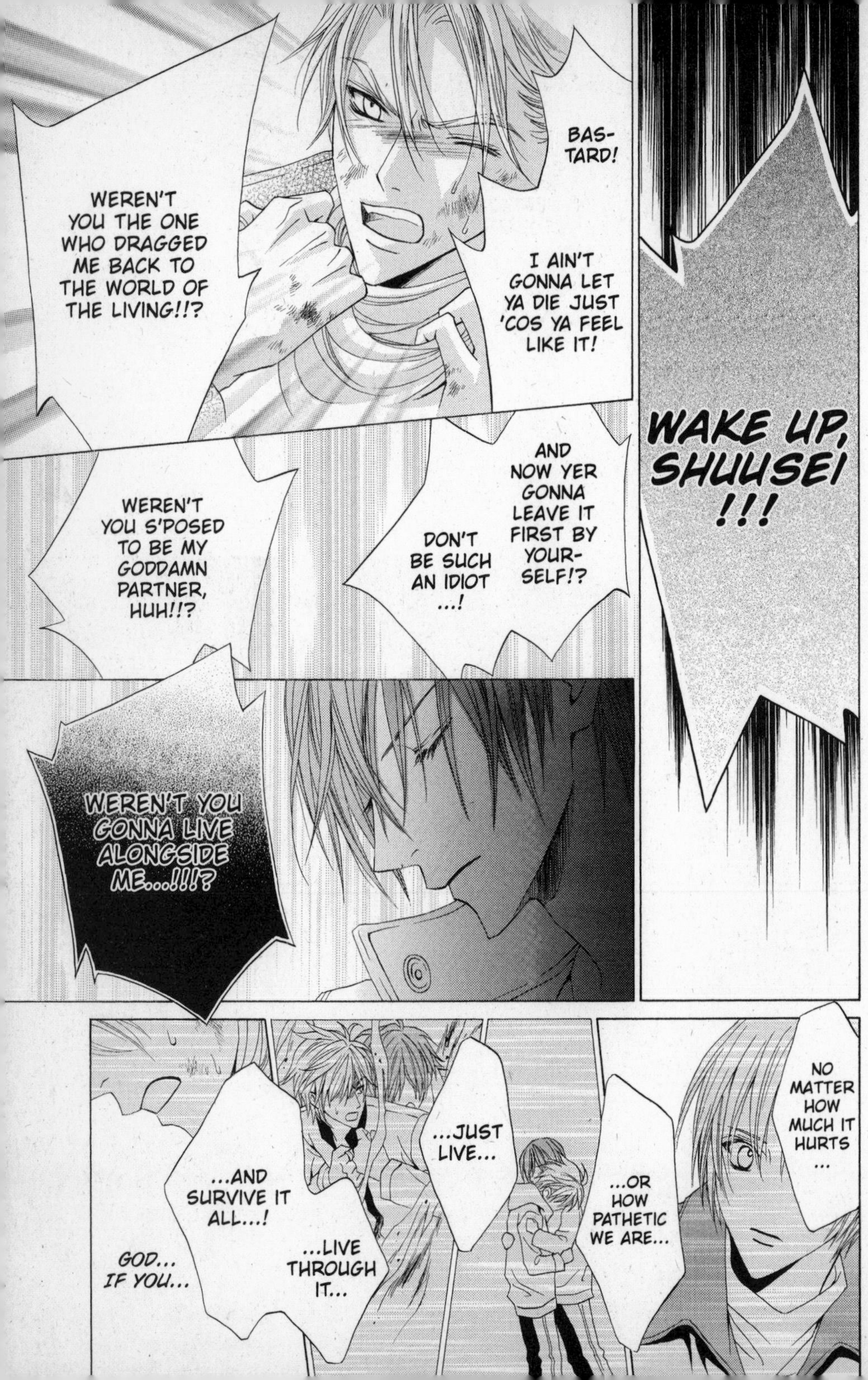
WAKE UP, SHUUSEI !!!
BAS-TARD!
I AIN'T GONNA LET YA DIE JUST 'COS YA FEEL LIKE IT!
WEREN'T YOU THE ONE WHO DRAGGED ME BACK TO THE WORLD OF THE LIVING!!?
AND NOW YER GONNA LEAVE IT FIRST BY YOUR-SELF!?
DON'T BE SUCH AN IDIOT ...!
WEREN'T YOU S'POSED TO BE MY GODDAMN PARTNER, HUH!!?
WEREN'T YOU GONNA LIVE ALONGSIDE ME...!!!?
NO MATTER HOW MUCH IT HURTS ...
...OR HOW PATHETIC WE ARE...
...JUST LIVE...
...LIVE THROUGH IT...
...AND SURVIVE IT ALL...!
GOD... IF YOU...

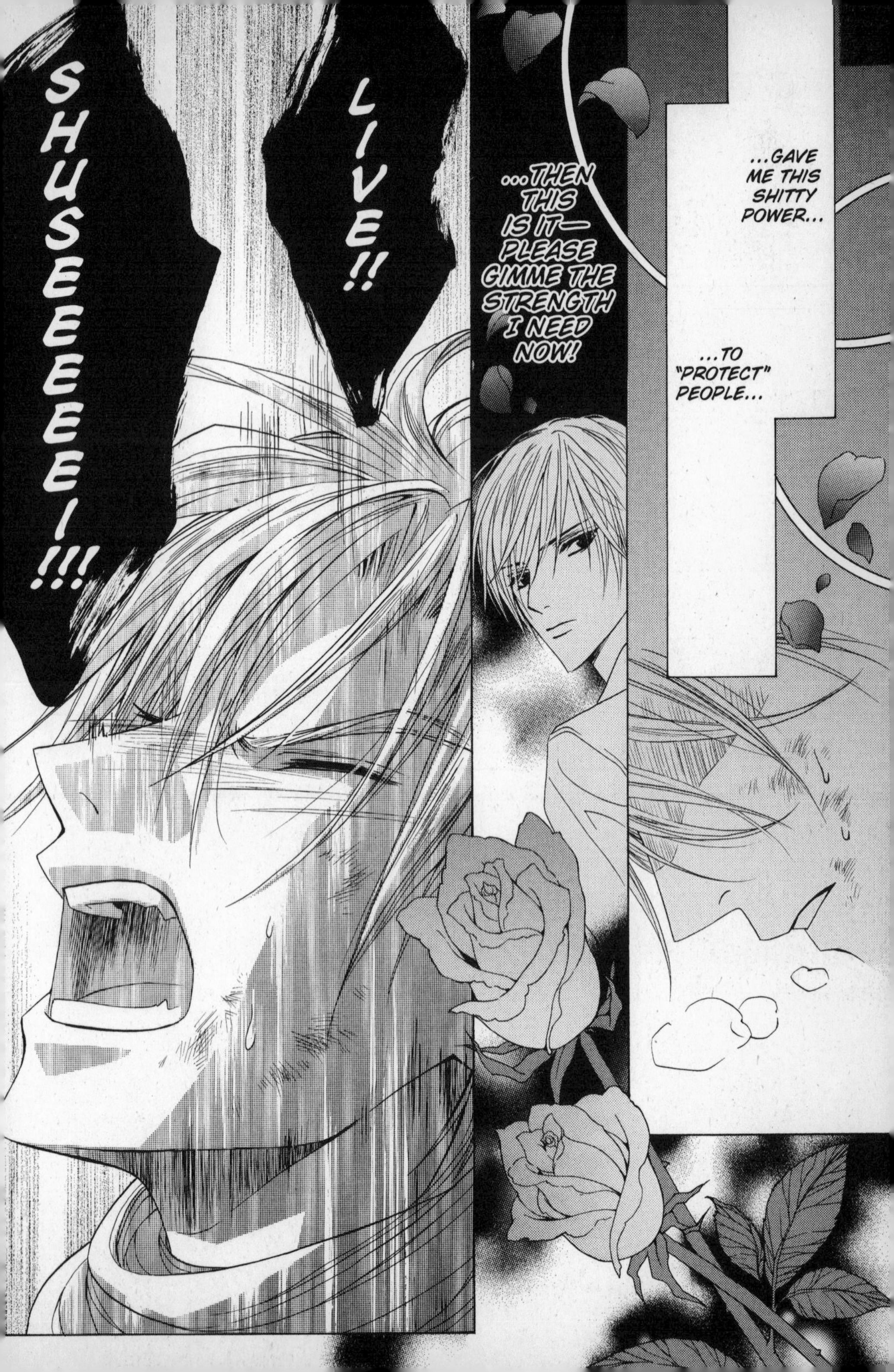
...GAVE ME THIS SHITTY POWER...
...TO "PROTECT" PEOPLE...
...THEN THIS IS IT—PLEASE GIMME THE STRENGTH I NEED NOW!
LIVE!!
SHUSEEEEEI!!!

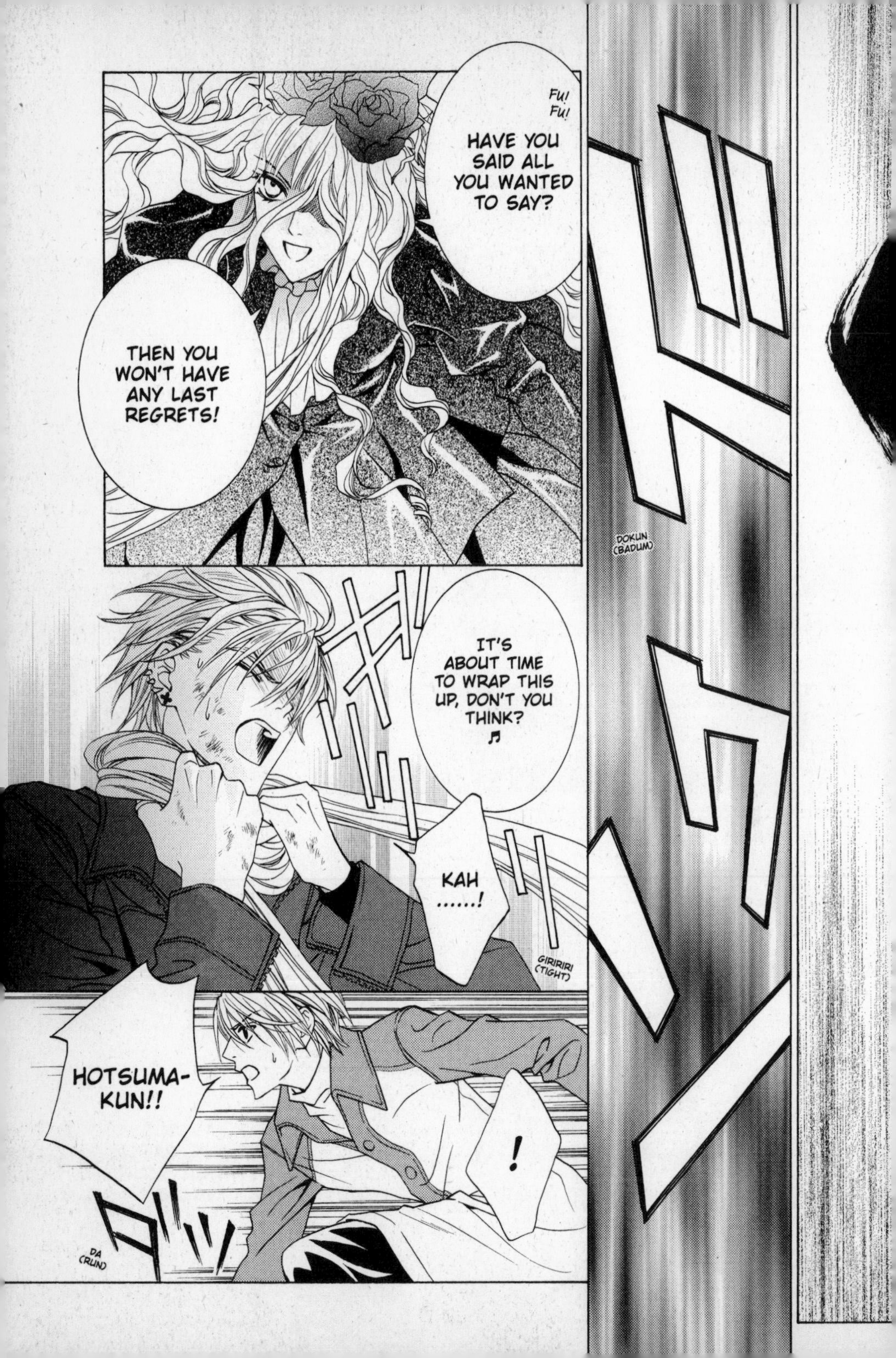
DOKUN (BADUM)
FU! FU!
HAVE YOU SAID ALL YOU WANTED TO SAY?
THEN YOU WON'T HAVE ANY LAST REGRETS!
IT'S ABOUT TIME TO WRAP THIS UP, DON'T YOU THINK? ♫
KAH ......!
GIRIRIRI (TIGHT)
HOTSUMA-KUN!!
!
DA (RUN)

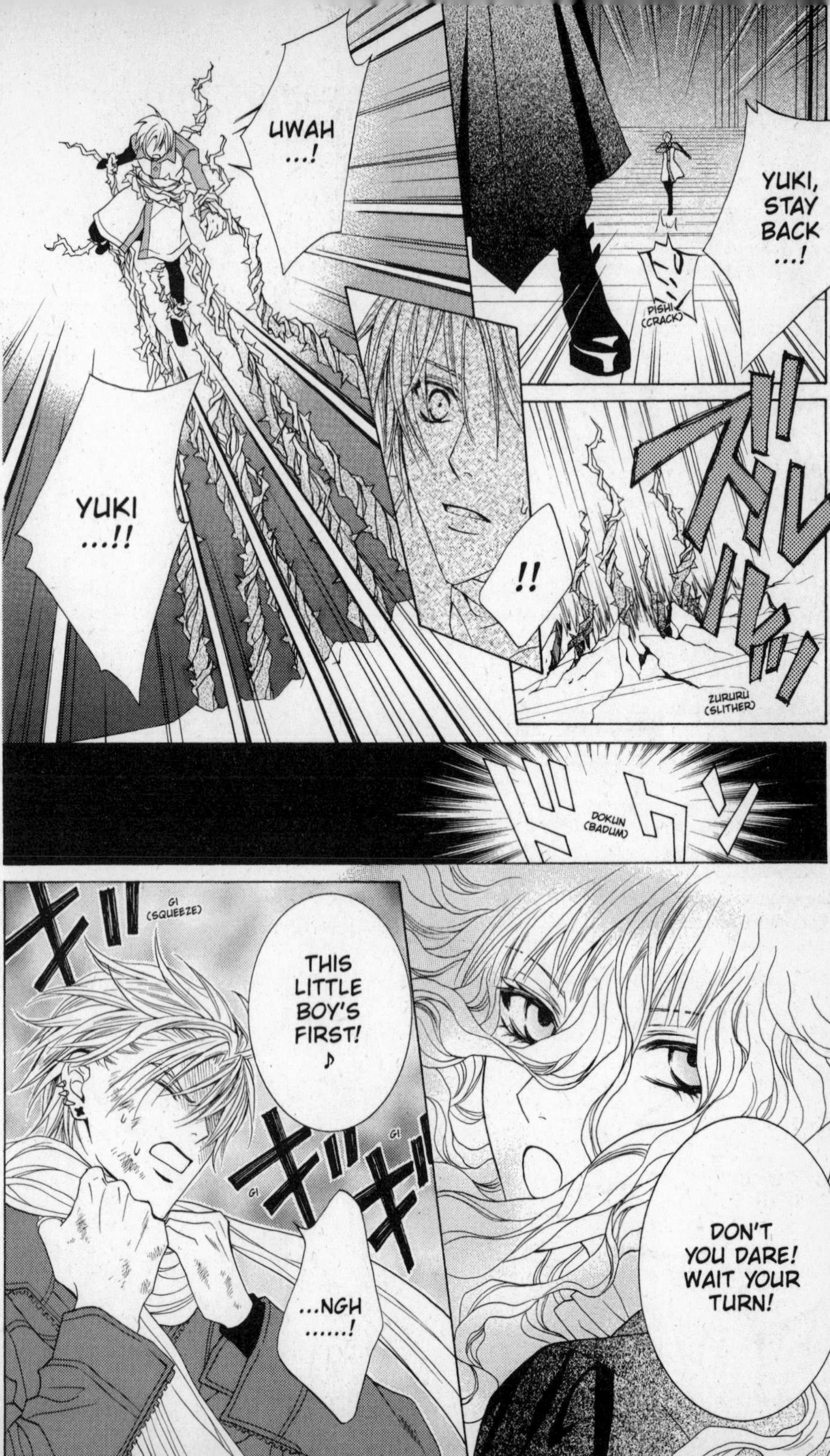
YUKI, STAY BACK ...!
PISHI (CRACK)
ZURURU (SLITHER)
!!
UWAH ...!
YUKI ...!!
DOKUN (BADUM)
DON'T YOU DARE! WAIT YOUR TURN!
THIS LITTLE BOY'S FIRST! ♪
GI (SQUEEZE)
GI
GI
...NGH ......!

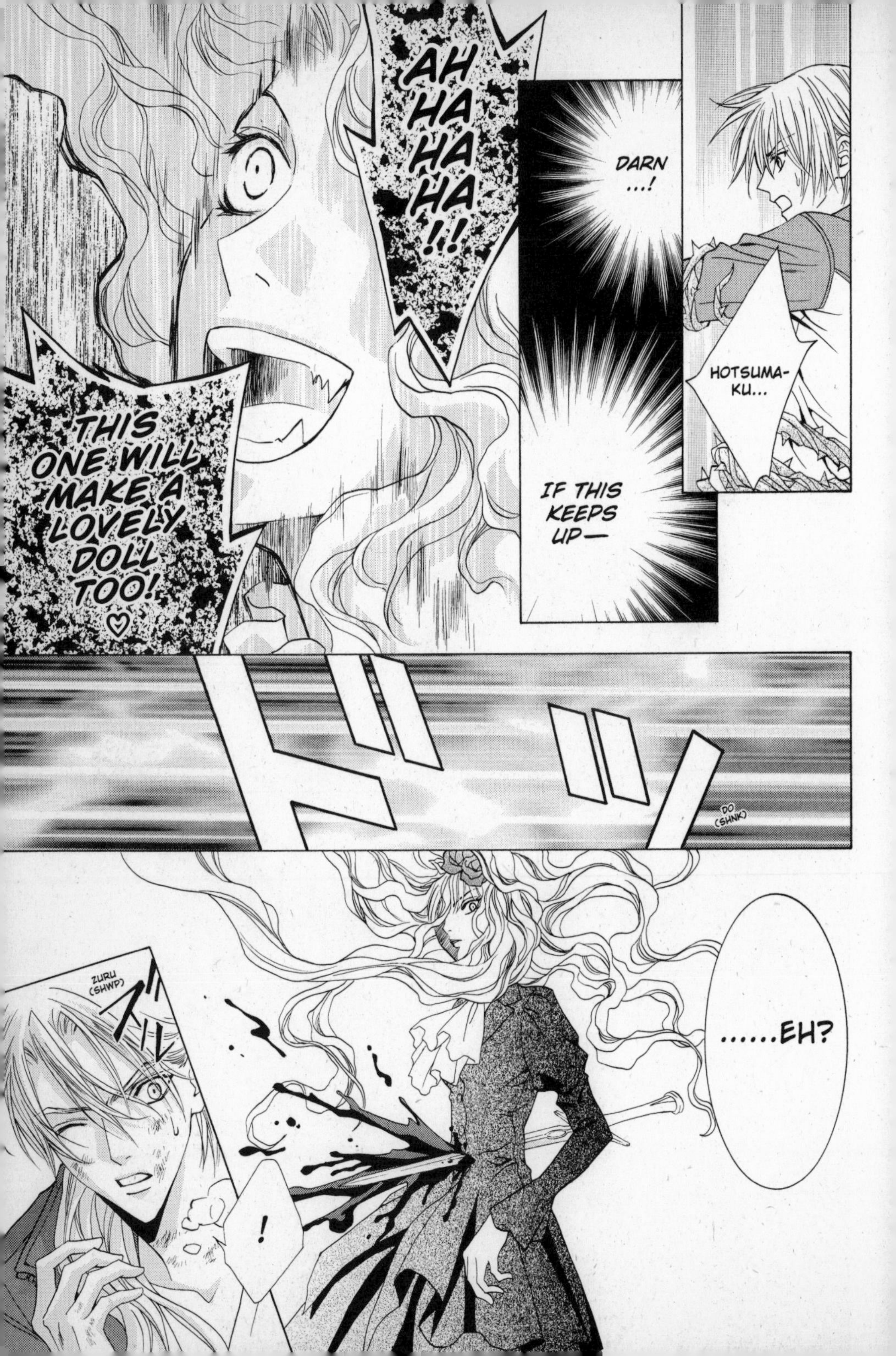
HOTSUMA-KU...
DARN ...!
IF THIS KEEPS UP—
AH HA HA HA!!
THIS ONE WILL MAKE A LOVELY DOLL TOO! ♡
DO (SHNK)
......EH?
!
ZURU (SHWP)

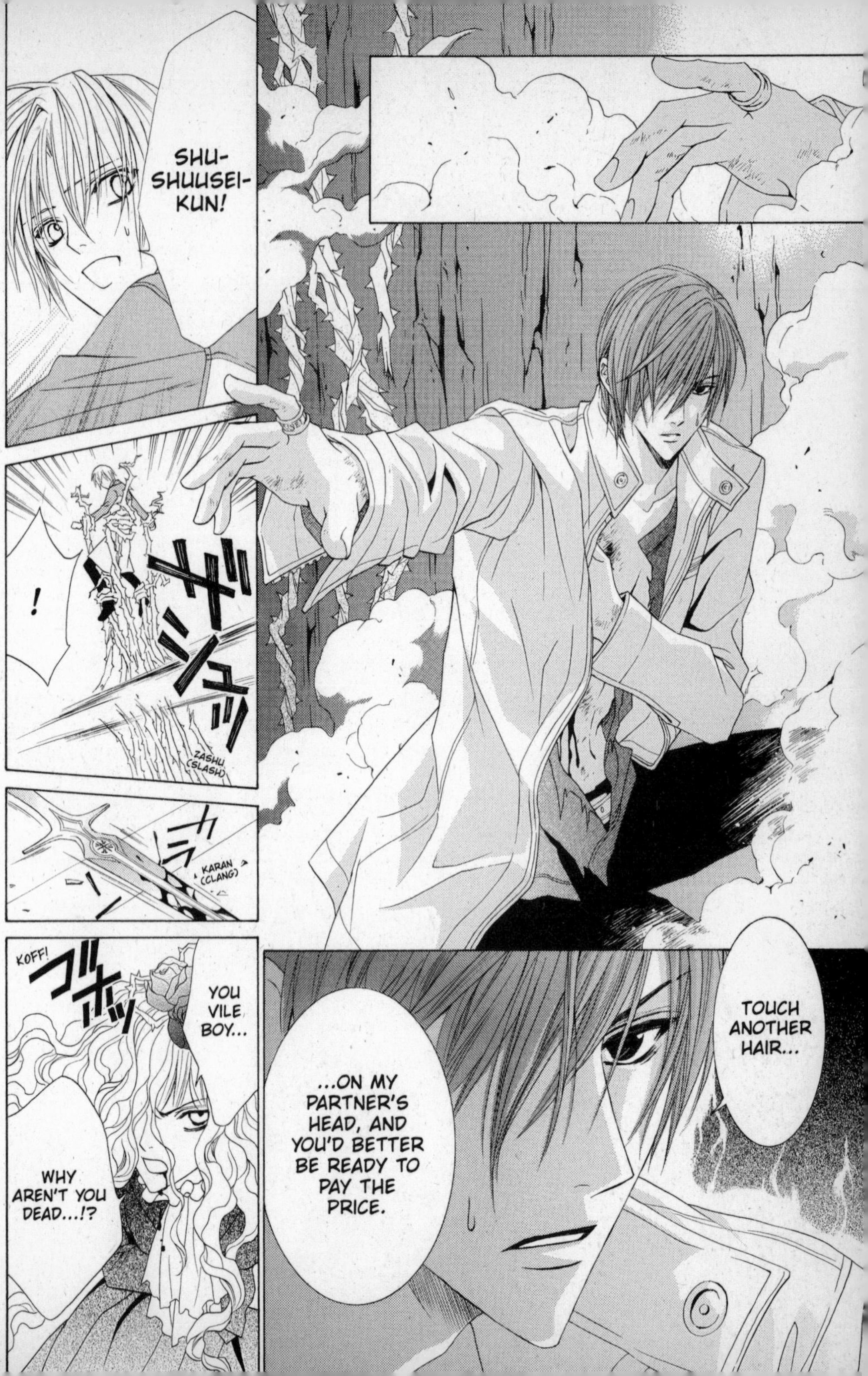
SHU-SHUUSEI-KUN!
!
ザシュッ
ZASHU (SLASH)
カラン
KARAN (CLANG)
TOUCH ANOTHER HAIR...
...ON MY PARTNER'S HEAD, AND YOU'D BETTER BE READY TO PAY THE PRICE.
ゴホッ
KOFF!
YOU VILE BOY...
WHY AREN'T YOU DEAD...!?

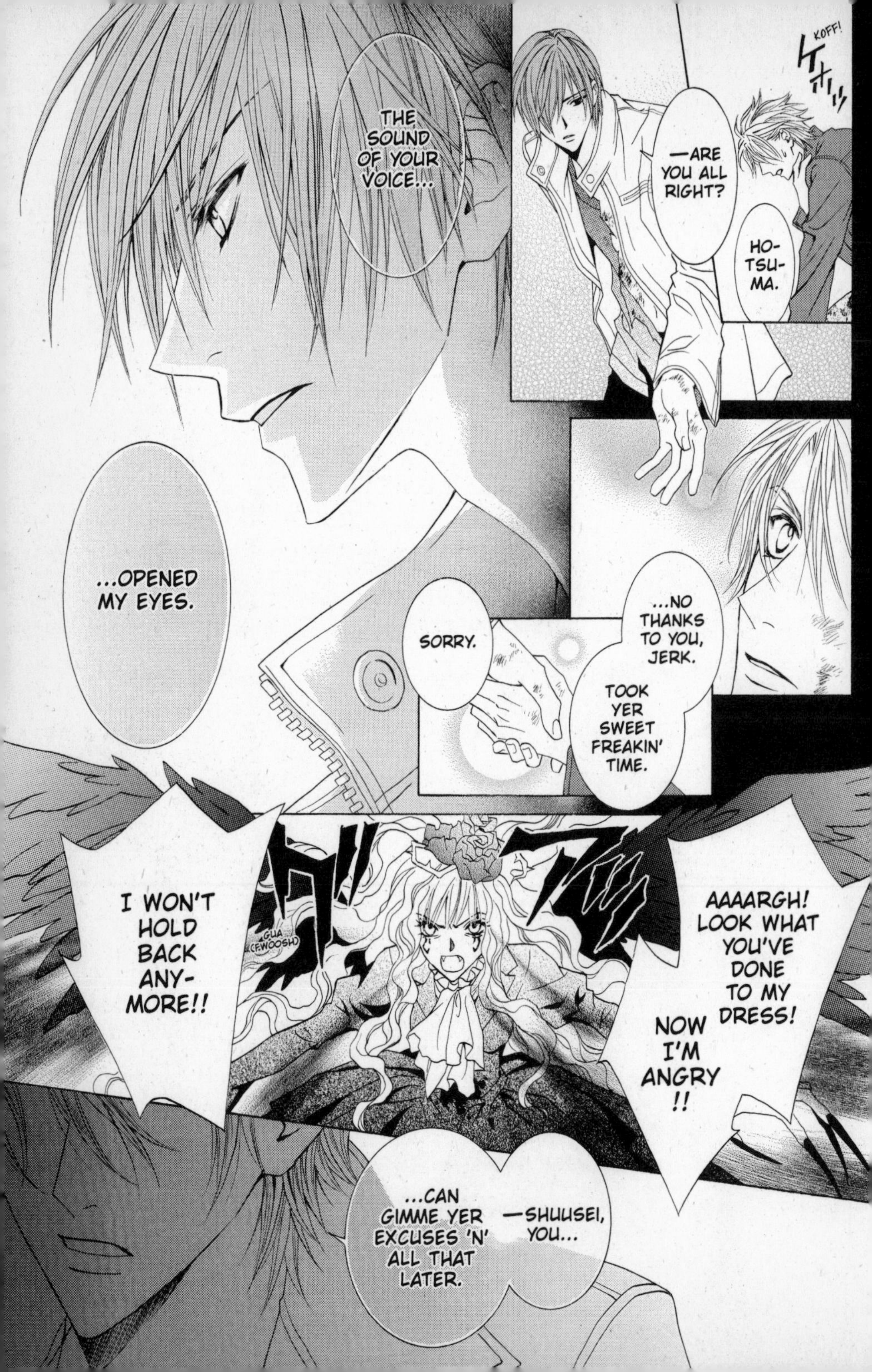
KOFF!
—ARE YOU ALL RIGHT?
HO-TSU-MA.
...NO THANKS TO YOU, JERK.
TOOK YER SWEET FREAKIN' TIME.
SORRY.
THE SOUND OF YOUR VOICE...
...OPENED MY EYES.
AAAARGH! LOOK WHAT YOU'VE DONE TO MY DRESS!
NOW I'M ANGRY!!
GUA (FWOOSH)
I WON'T HOLD BACK ANY-MORE!!
—SHUUSEI, YOU...
...CAN GIMME YER EXCUSES 'N' ALL THAT LATER.

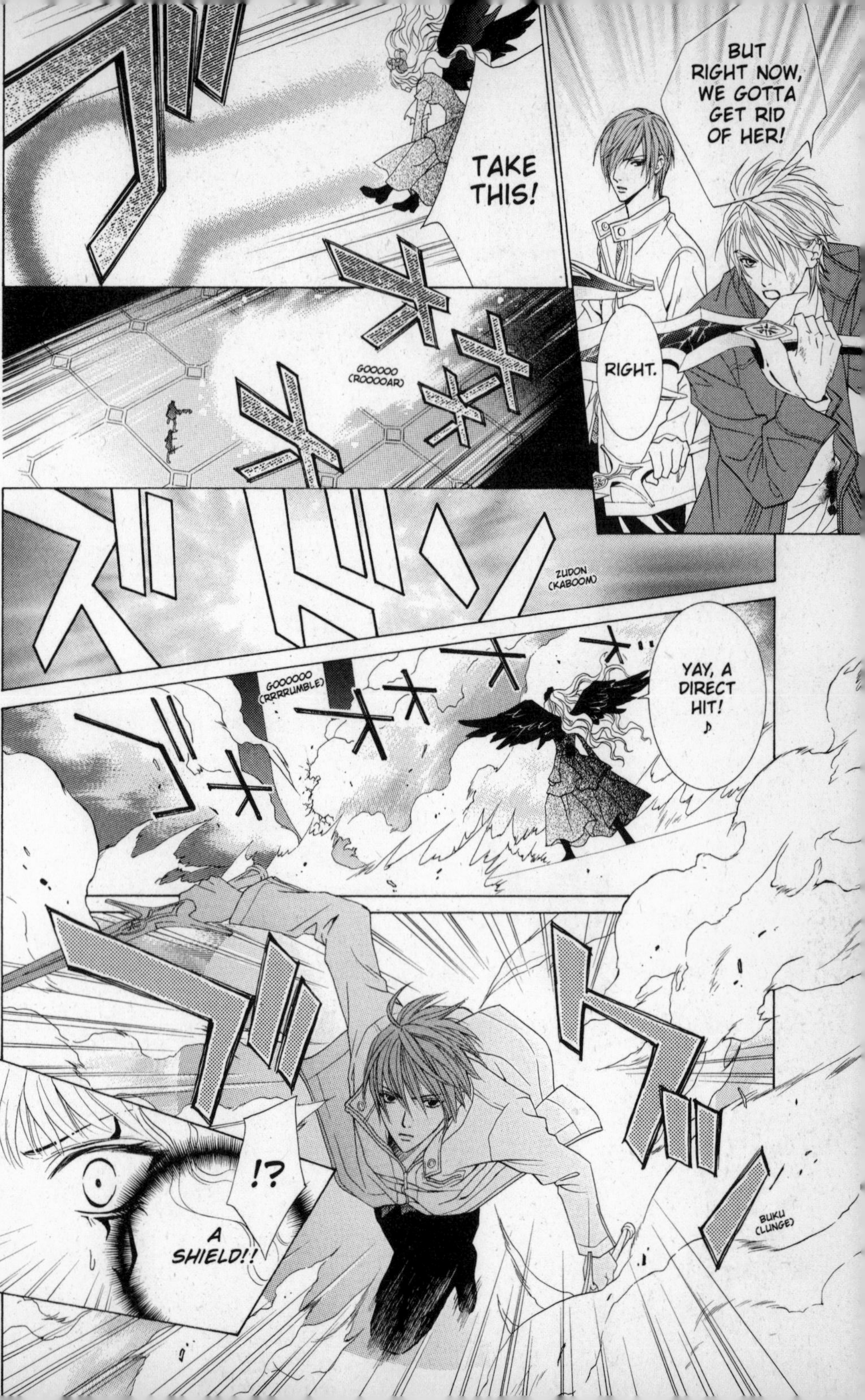

BUT RIGHT NOW, WE GOTTA GET RID OF HER!
RIGHT.
TAKE THIS!
GOOOOO (ROOOOAR)
ZUDON (KABOOM)
YAY, A DIRECT HIT! ♪
GOOOOOO (RRRRUMBLE)
BUKU (LUNGE)
!?
A SHIELD!!

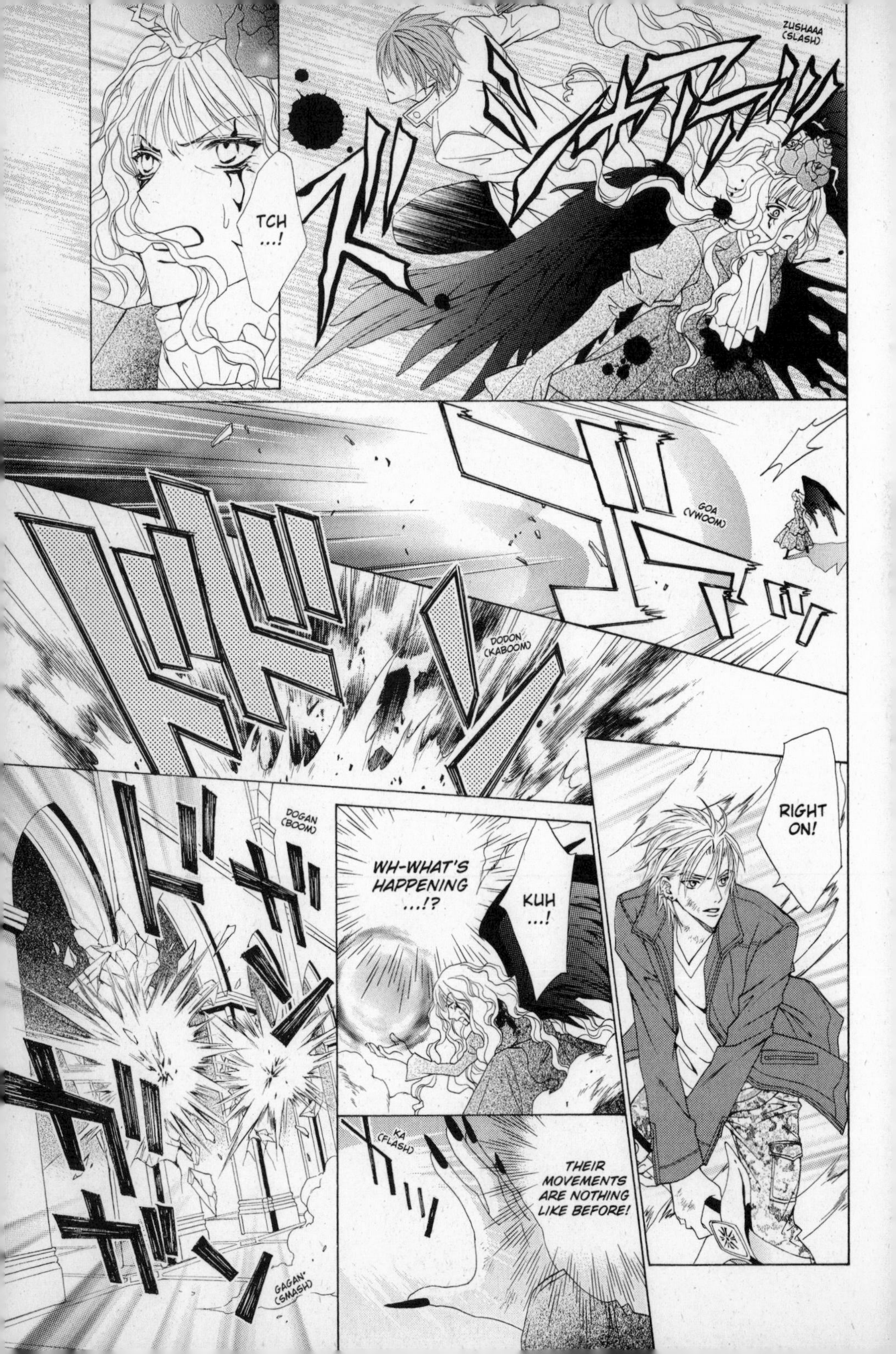
ZUSHAAA (SLASH)
TCH ...!
GOA (VWOOM)
DODON (KABOOM)
RIGHT ON!
WH-WHAT'S HAPPENING ...!?
KUH ...!
KA (FLASH)
THEIR MOVEMENTS ARE NOTHING LIKE BEFORE!
DOGAN (BOOM)
GAGAN (SMASH)

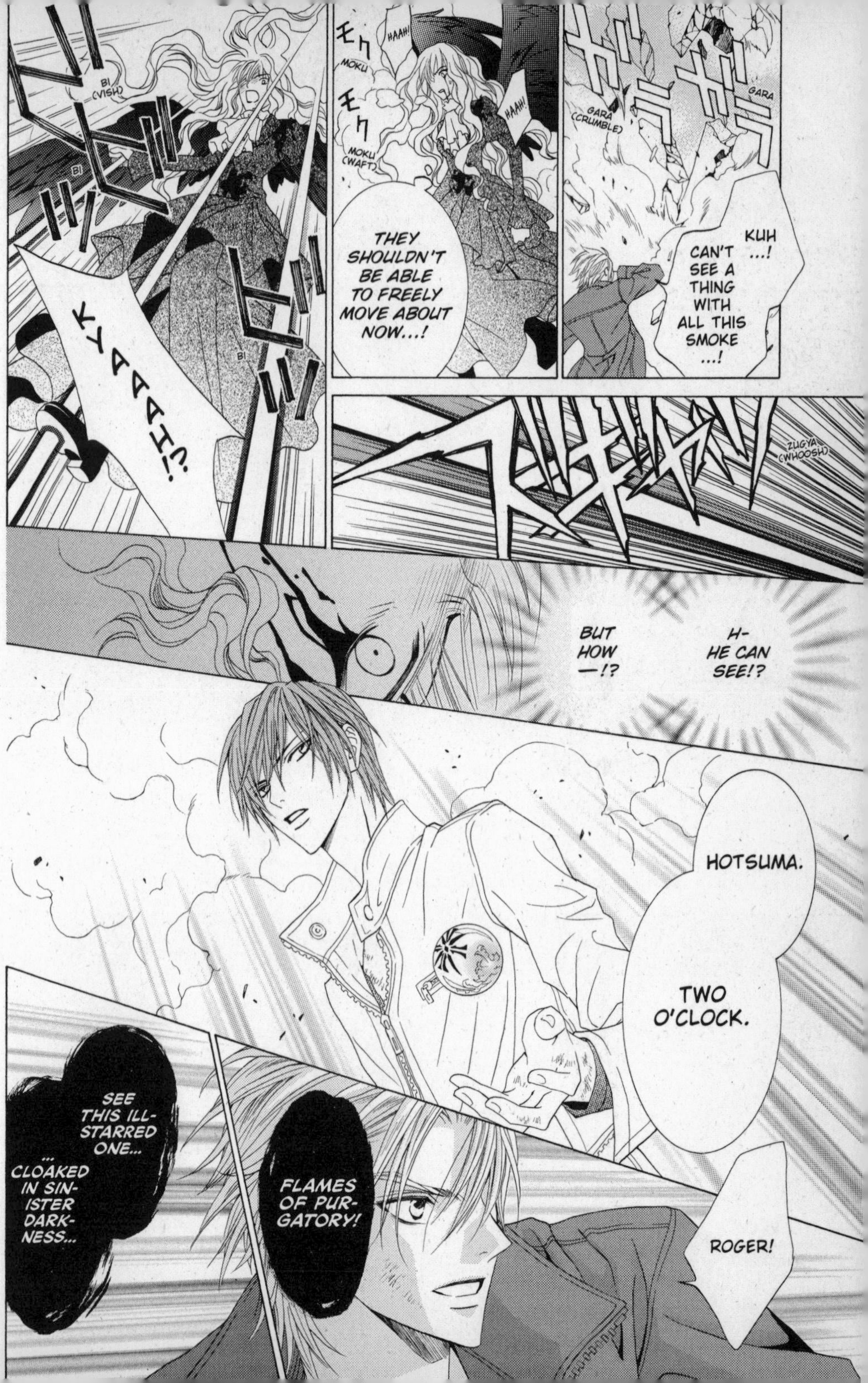
GARA
GARA (CRUMBLE)
KUH ...!
CAN'T SEE A THING WITH ALL THIS SMOKE ...!
HAAH!
MOKU
MOKU (WAFT)
HAAH!
THEY SHOULDN'T BE ABLE TO FREELY MOVE ABOUT NOW...!
ZUGYA (WHOOSH)
BI (VISH)
BI
BI
KYAAAAH!?
H-HE CAN SEE!?
BUT HOW—!?
HOTSUMA.
TWO O'CLOCK.
ROGER!
FLAMES OF PURGATORY!
SEE THIS ILL-STARRED ONE...
... CLOAKED IN SINISTER DARKNESS...

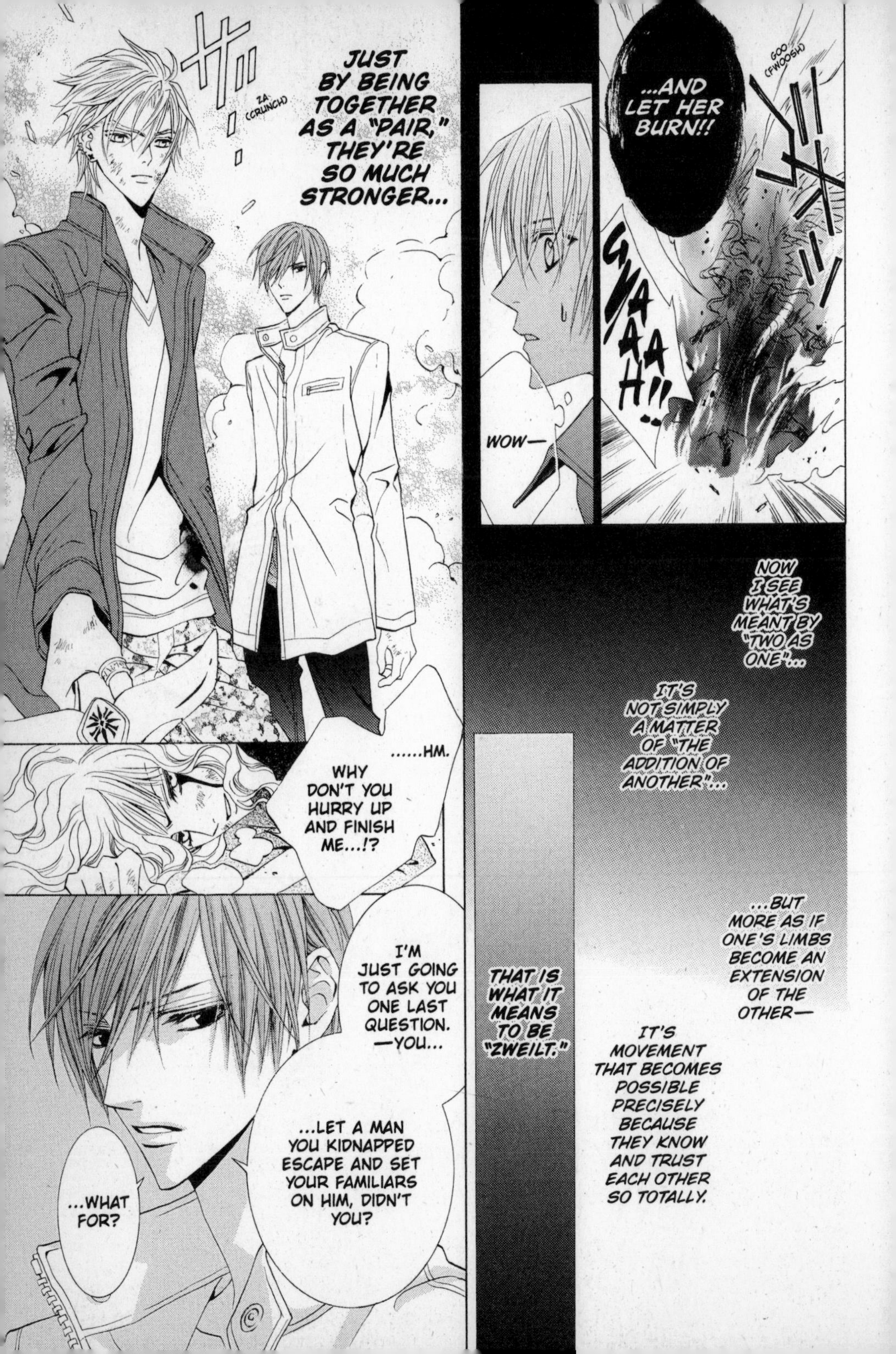
GOO (FWOOSH)
...AND LET HER BURN!!
UWAAAAH!!...
WOW—
NOW I SEE WHAT'S MEANT BY "TWO AS ONE"...
IT'S NOT SIMPLY A MATTER OF "THE ADDITION OF ANOTHER"...
...BUT MORE AS IF ONE'S LIMBS BECOME AN EXTENSION OF THE OTHER—
IT'S MOVEMENT THAT BECOMES POSSIBLE PRECISELY BECAUSE THEY KNOW AND TRUST EACH OTHER SO TOTALLY.
THAT IS WHAT IT MEANS TO BE "ZWEILT."
JUST BY BEING TOGETHER AS A "PAIR," THEY'RE SO MUCH STRONGER...
ZA (CRUNCH)
......HM.
WHY DON'T YOU HURRY UP AND FINISH ME...!?
I'M JUST GOING TO ASK YOU ONE LAST QUESTION. —YOU...
...LET A MAN YOU KIDNAPPED ESCAPE AND SET YOUR FAMILIARS ON HIM, DIDN'T YOU?
...WHAT FOR?

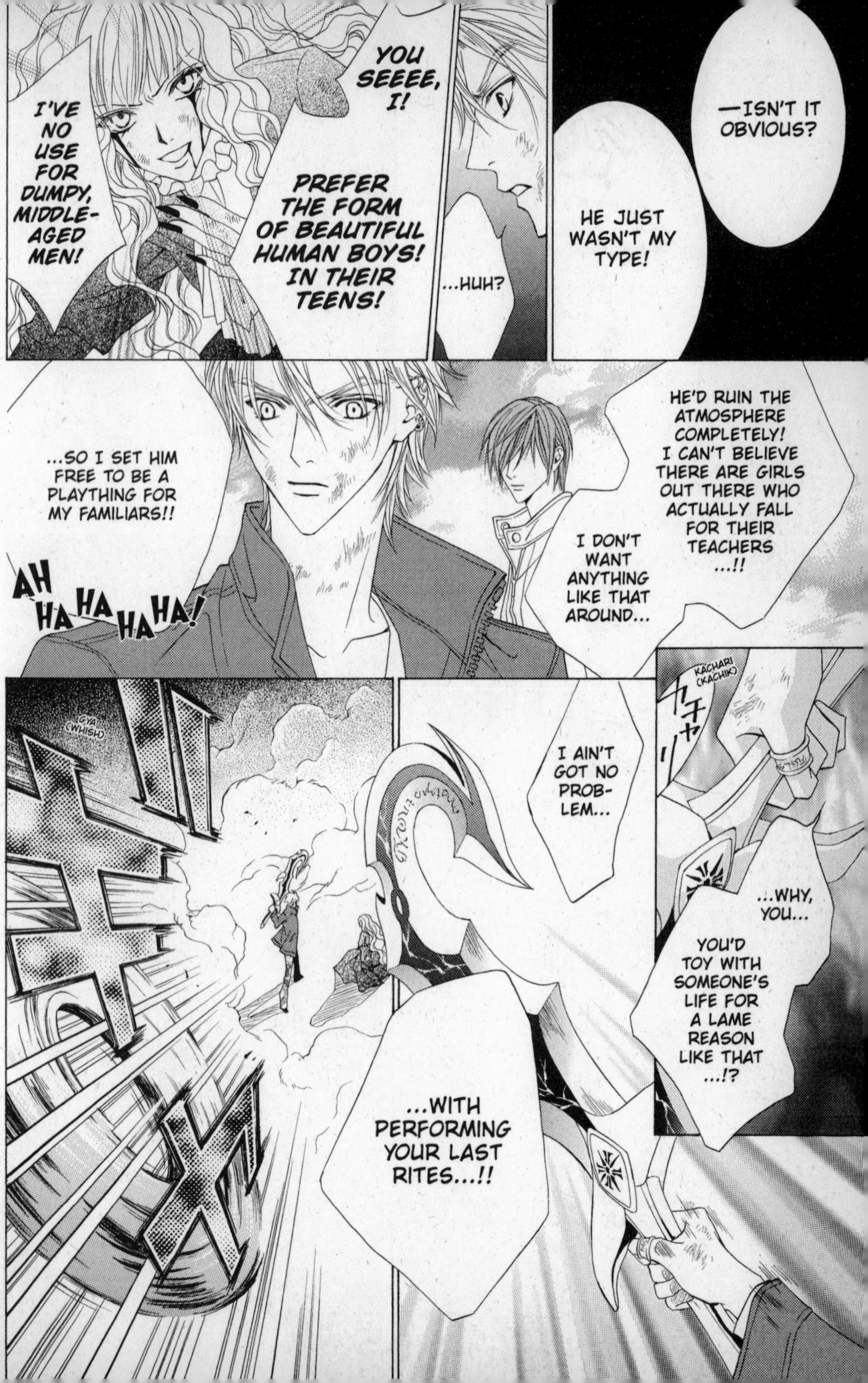
—ISN'T IT OBVIOUS?
HE JUST WASN'T MY TYPE!
...HUH?
YOU SEEEE, I!
PREFER THE FORM OF BEAUTIFUL HUMAN BOYS! IN THEIR TEENS!
I'VE NO USE FOR DUMPY, MIDDLE-AGED MEN!
HE'D RUIN THE ATMOSPHERE COMPLETELY! I CAN'T BELIEVE THERE ARE GIRLS OUT THERE WHO ACTUALLY FALL FOR THEIR TEACHERS ...!!
I DON'T WANT ANYTHING LIKE THAT AROUND...
...SO I SET HIM FREE TO BE A PLAYTHING FOR MY FAMILIARS!!
AH HA HA HA HA!
KACHARI (KACHIK)
...WHY, YOU...
YOU'D TOY WITH SOMEONE'S LIFE FOR A LAME REASON LIKE THAT ...!?
I AIN'T GOT NO PROB-LEM...
...WITH PERFORMING YOUR LAST RITES...!!
GYA (WHISH)

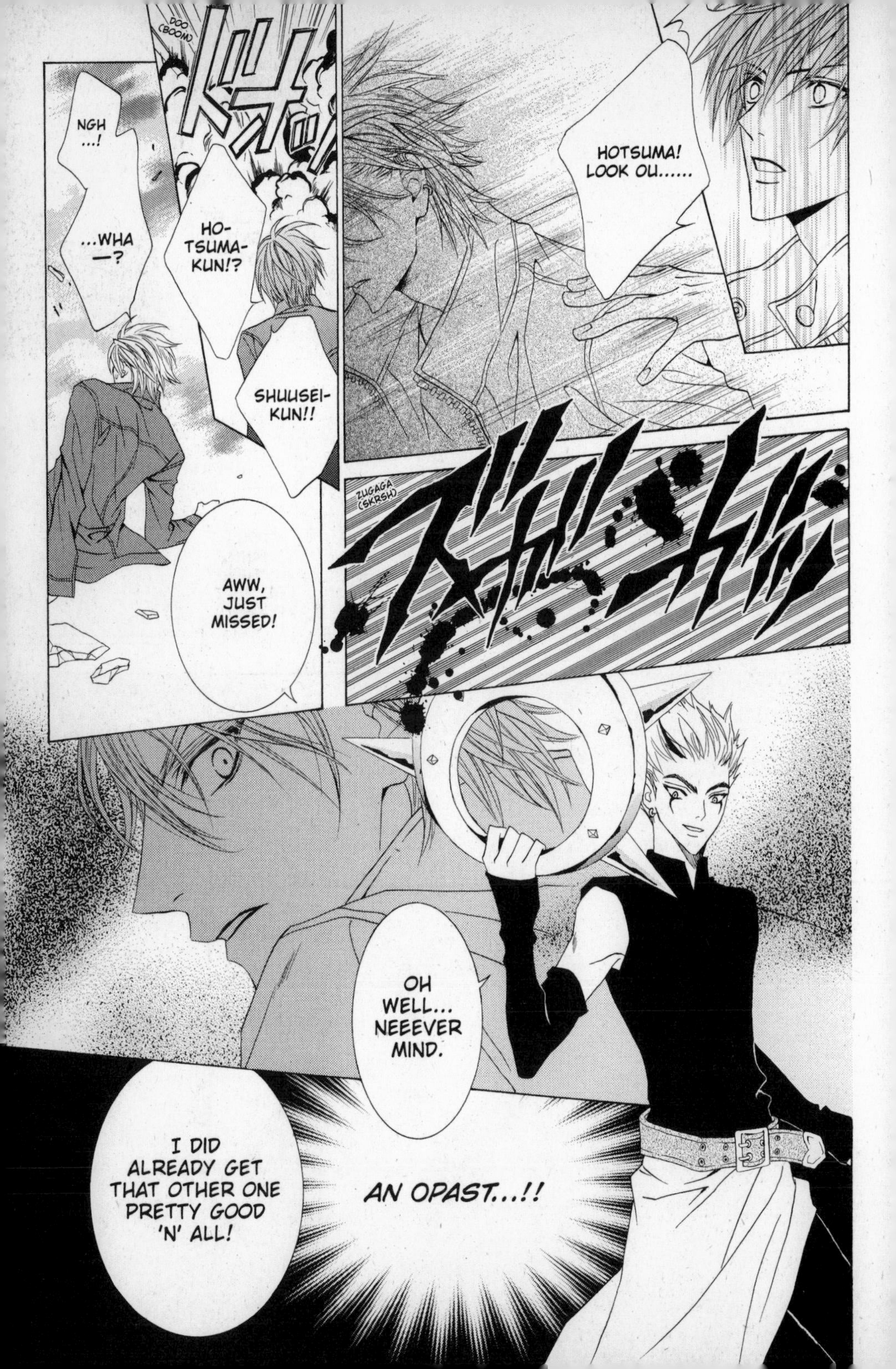
HOTSUMA! LOOK OU......
ZUGAGA (SKRSH)
DOO (BOOM)
HO-TSUMA-KUN!?
SHUUSEI-KUN!!
NGH ...!
...WHA—?
AWW, JUST MISSED!
OH WELL... NEEEVER MIND.
I DID ALREADY GET THAT OTHER ONE PRETTY GOOD 'N' ALL!
AN OPAST...!!

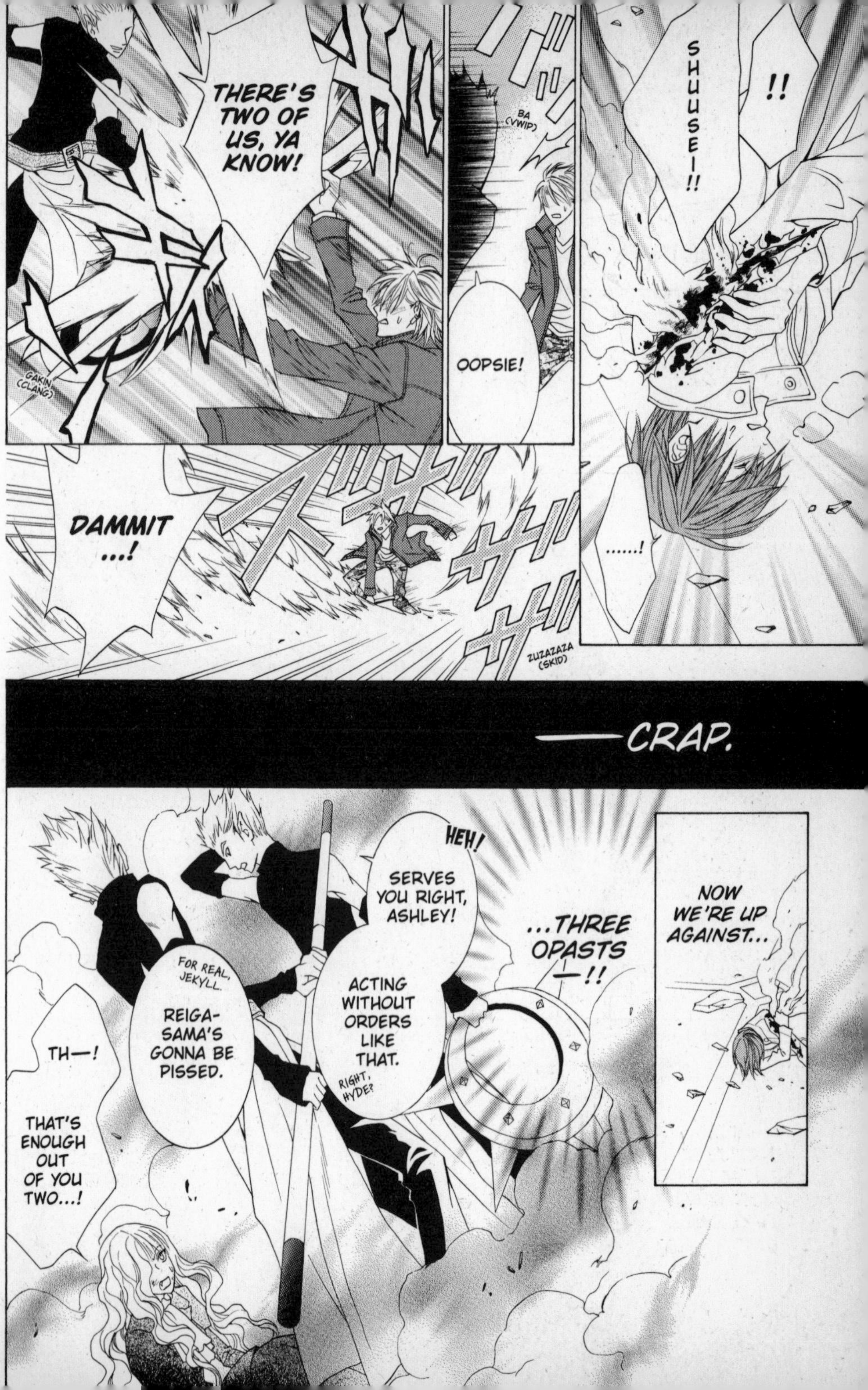
!!
SHUUSEI!!
......!
BA (VWIP)
OOPSIE!
THERE'S TWO OF US, YA KNOW!
GAKIN (CLANG)
DAMMIT ...!
ZUZAZAZA (SKID)
——CRAP.
NOW WE'RE UP AGAINST...
...THREE OPASTS—!!
HEH!
SERVES YOU RIGHT, ASHLEY!
ACTING WITHOUT ORDERS LIKE THAT.
RIGHT, HYDE?
FOR REAL, JEKYLL.
REIGA-SAMA'S GONNA BE PISSED.
TH—!
THAT'S ENOUGH OUT OF YOU TWO...!

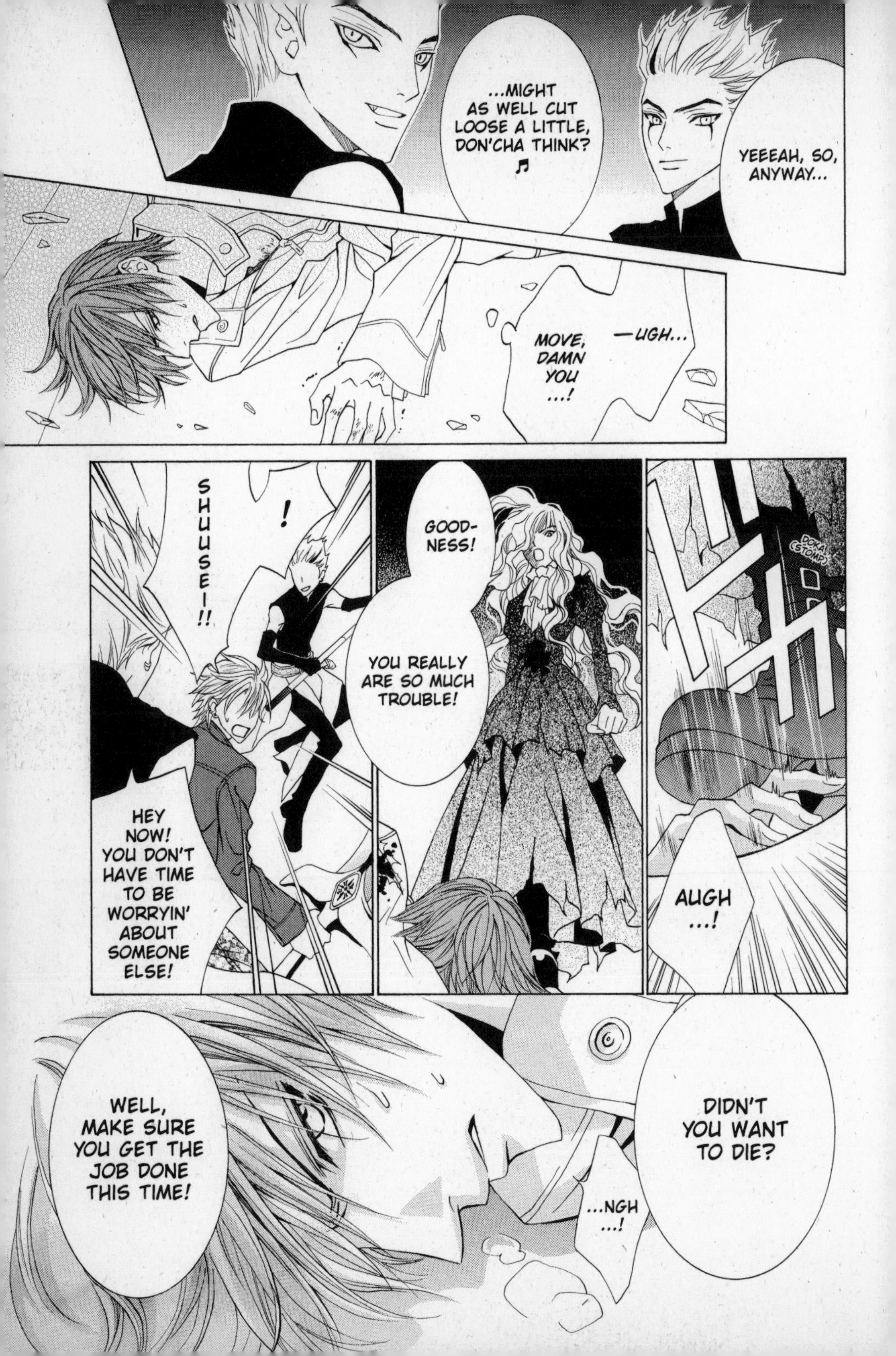
YEEEAH, SO, ANYWAY...
...MIGHT AS WELL CUT LOOSE A LITTLE, DON'CHA THINK? ♪
—UGH...
MOVE, DAMN YOU ...!
DOKA (STOMP)
AUGH ...!
GOOD-NESS!
YOU REALLY ARE SO MUCH TROUBLE!
!
SHUUSEI!!
HEY NOW! YOU DON'T HAVE TIME TO BE WORRYIN' ABOUT SOMEONE ELSE!
DIDN'T YOU WANT TO DIE?
...NGH ...!
WELL, MAKE SURE YOU GET THE JOB DONE THIS TIME!

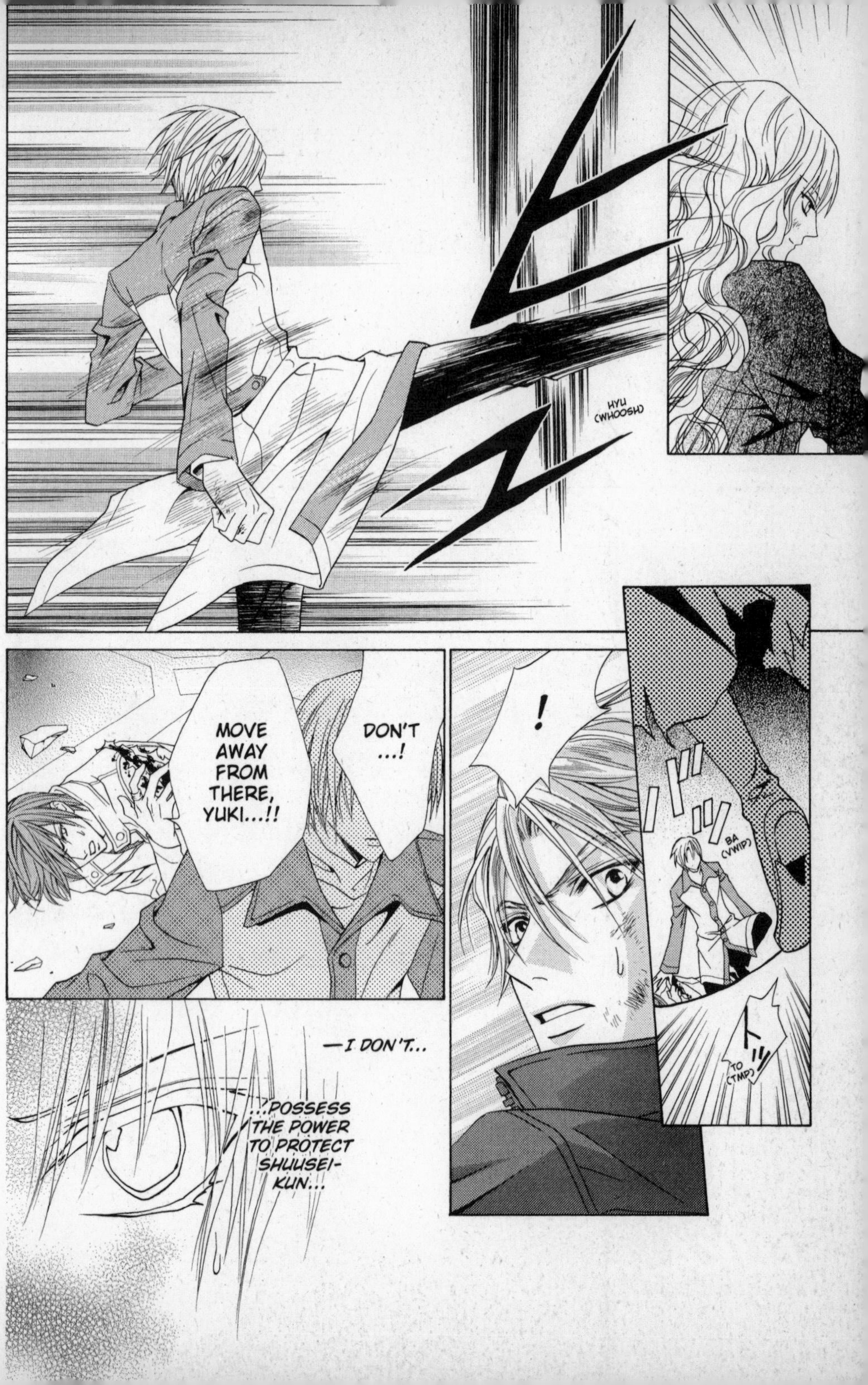
HYU
(WHOOSH)
BA
(VWIP)
TO
(TMP)
!
DON'T ...!
MOVE AWAY FROM THERE, YUKI...!!
—I DON'T...
...POSSESS THE POWER TO PROTECT SHUUSEI-KUN...

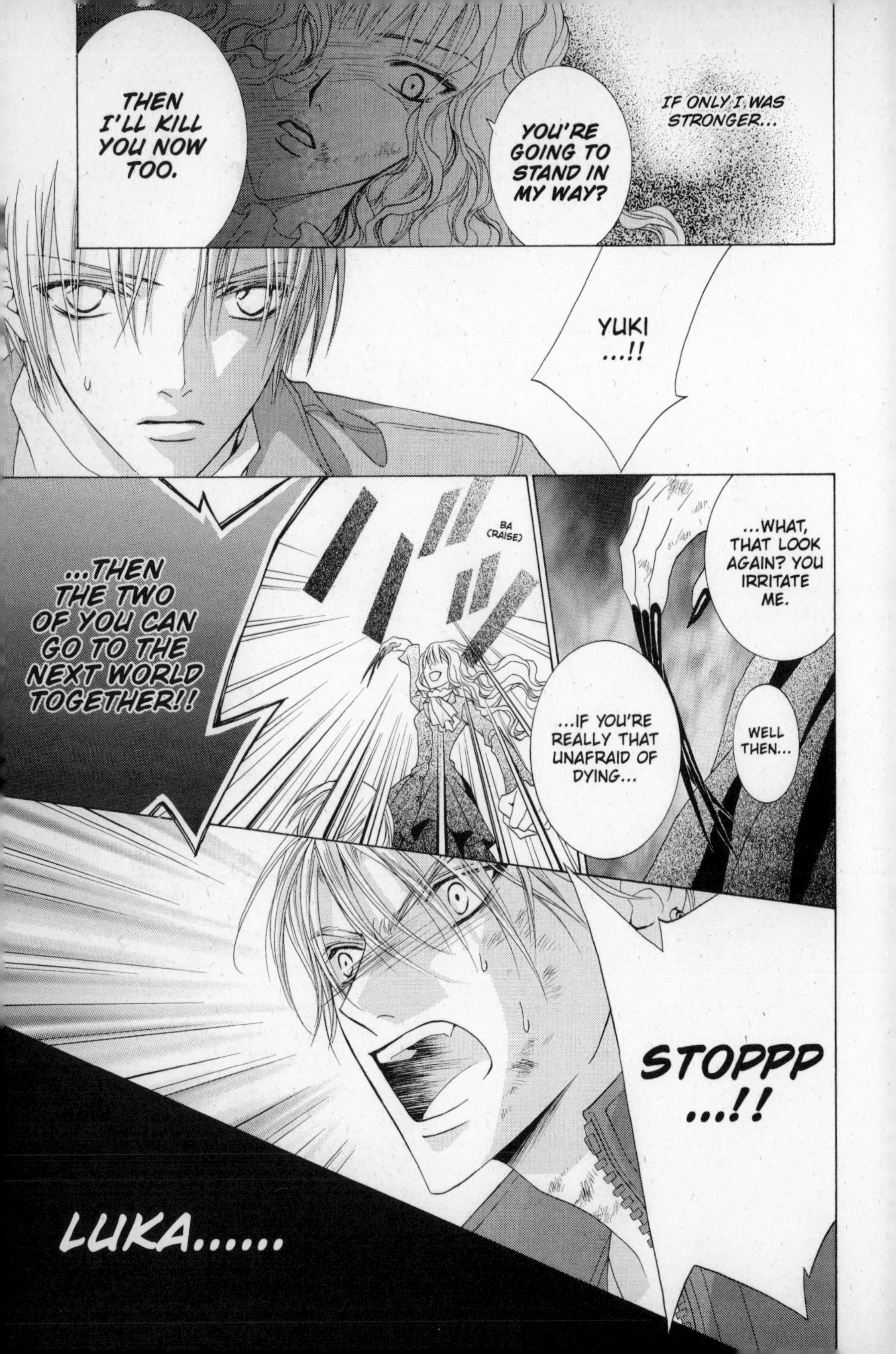
IF ONLY I WAS STRONGER...
YOU'RE GOING TO STAND IN MY WAY?
THEN I'LL KILL YOU NOW TOO.
YUKI ...!!
...WHAT, THAT LOOK AGAIN? YOU IRRITATE ME.
WELL THEN...
...IF YOU'RE REALLY THAT UNAFRAID OF DYING...
BA (RAISE)
...THEN THE TWO OF YOU CAN GO TO THE NEXT WORLD TOGETHER!!
STOPPP ...!!
LUKA......

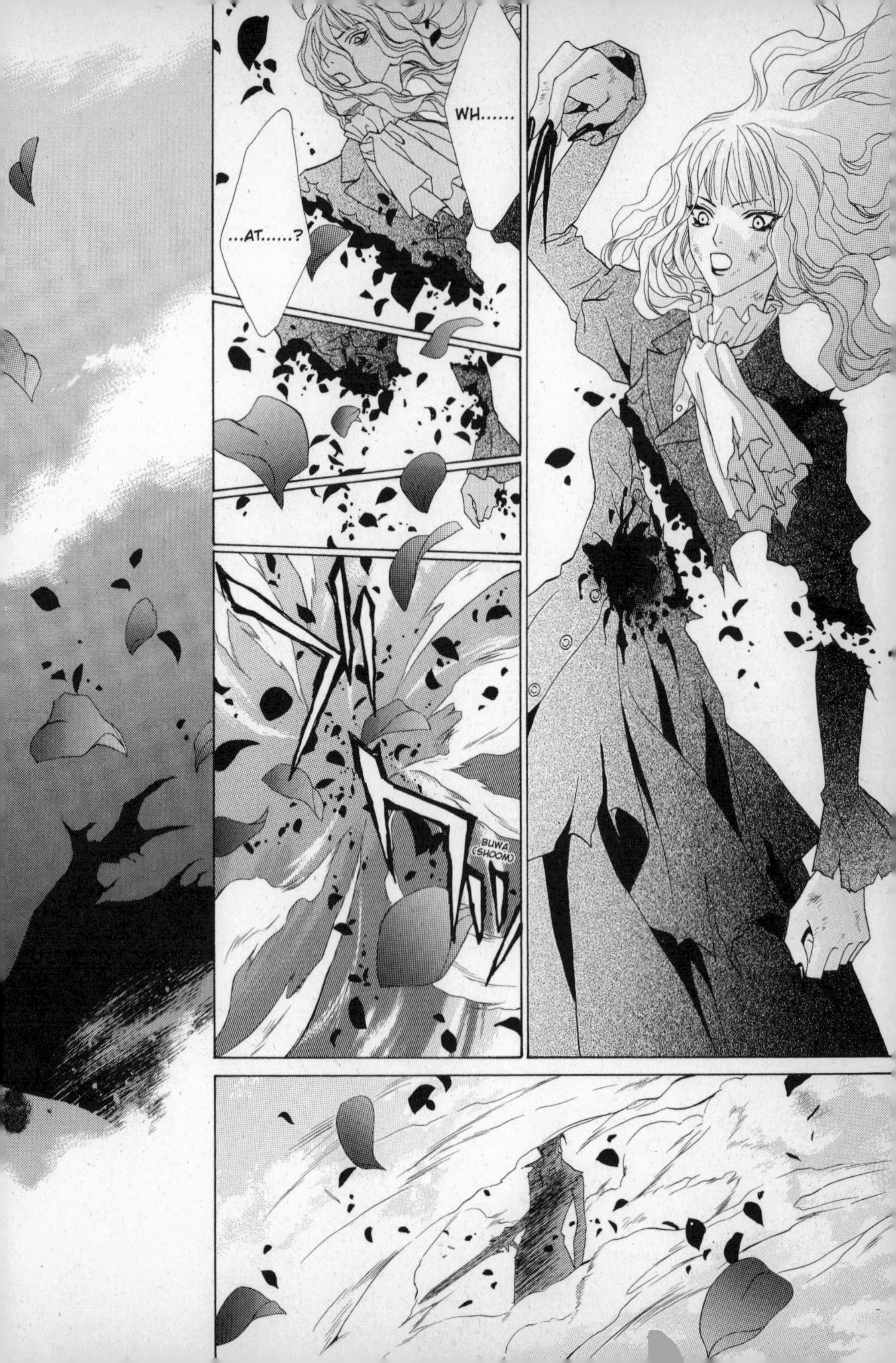
WH......
...AT......?
BUWA (SHOOM)

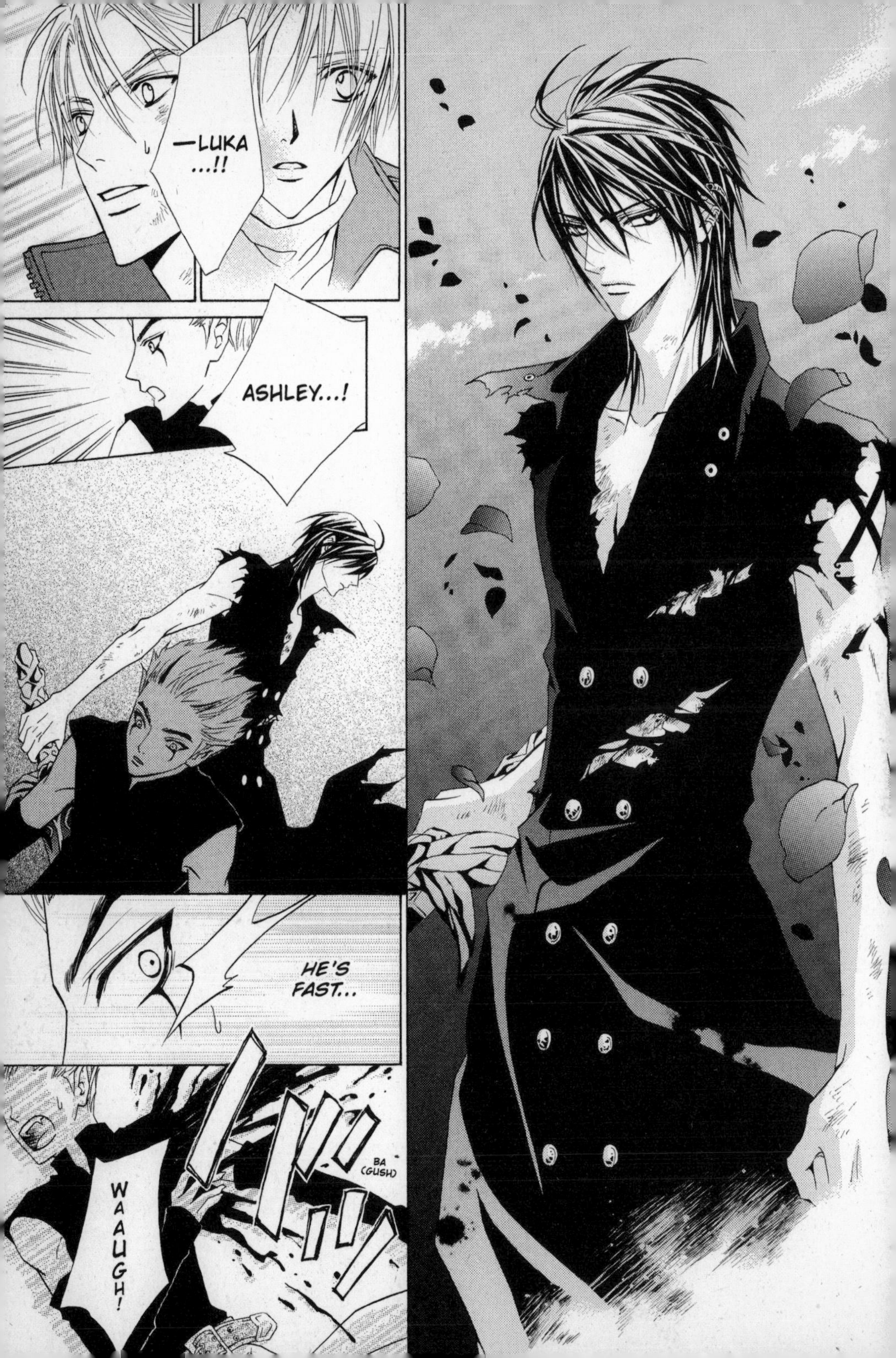
—LUKA ...!!
ASHLEY...!
HE'S FAST...
BA (GUSH)
WAAUGH!

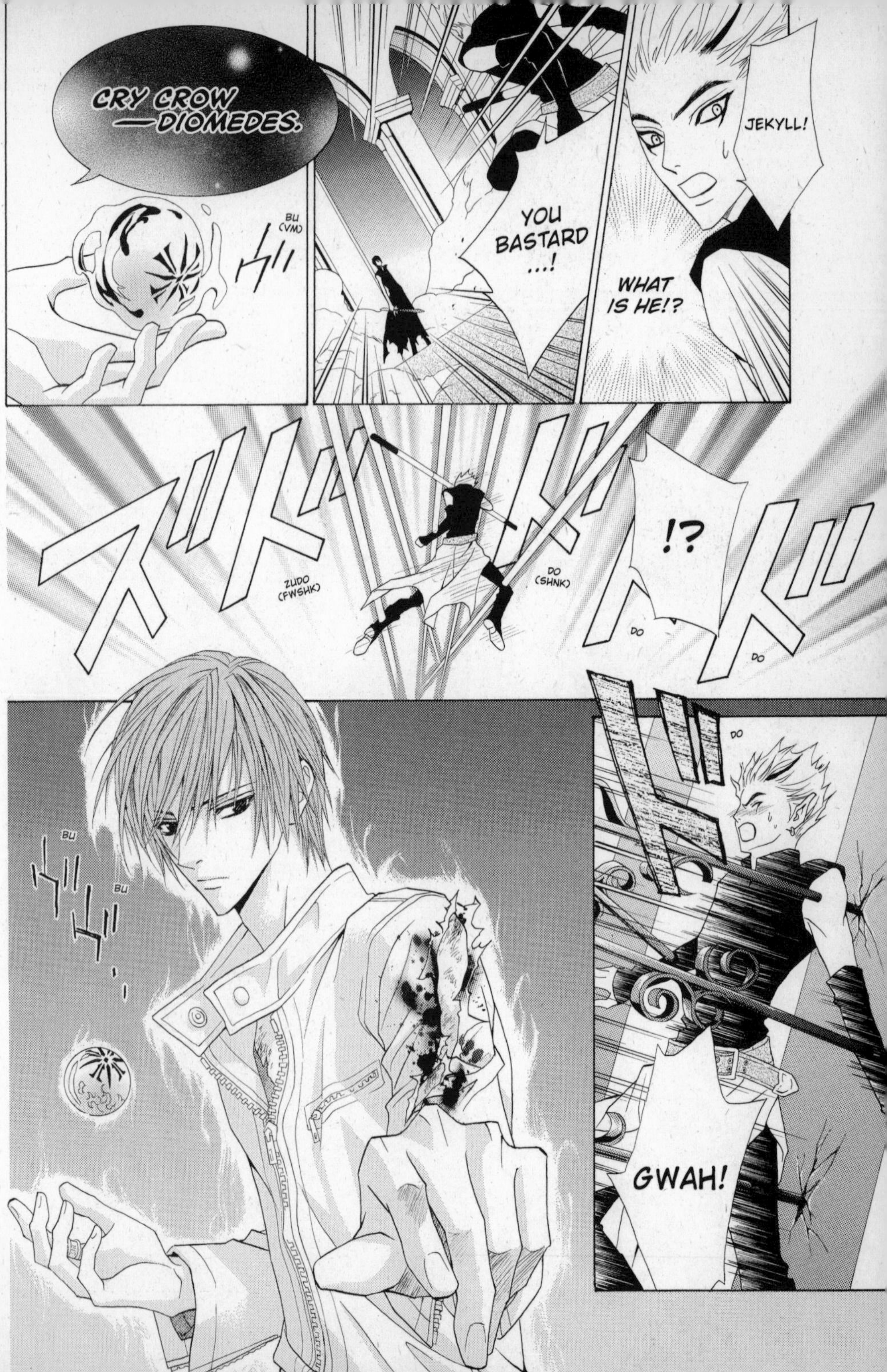
JEKYLL!
WHAT IS HE!?
YOU BASTARD ...!
CRY CROW —DIOMEDES.
BU (VM)
DO
DO
!?
DO (SHNK)
ZUDO (FWSHK)
DO
GWAH!
BU
BU

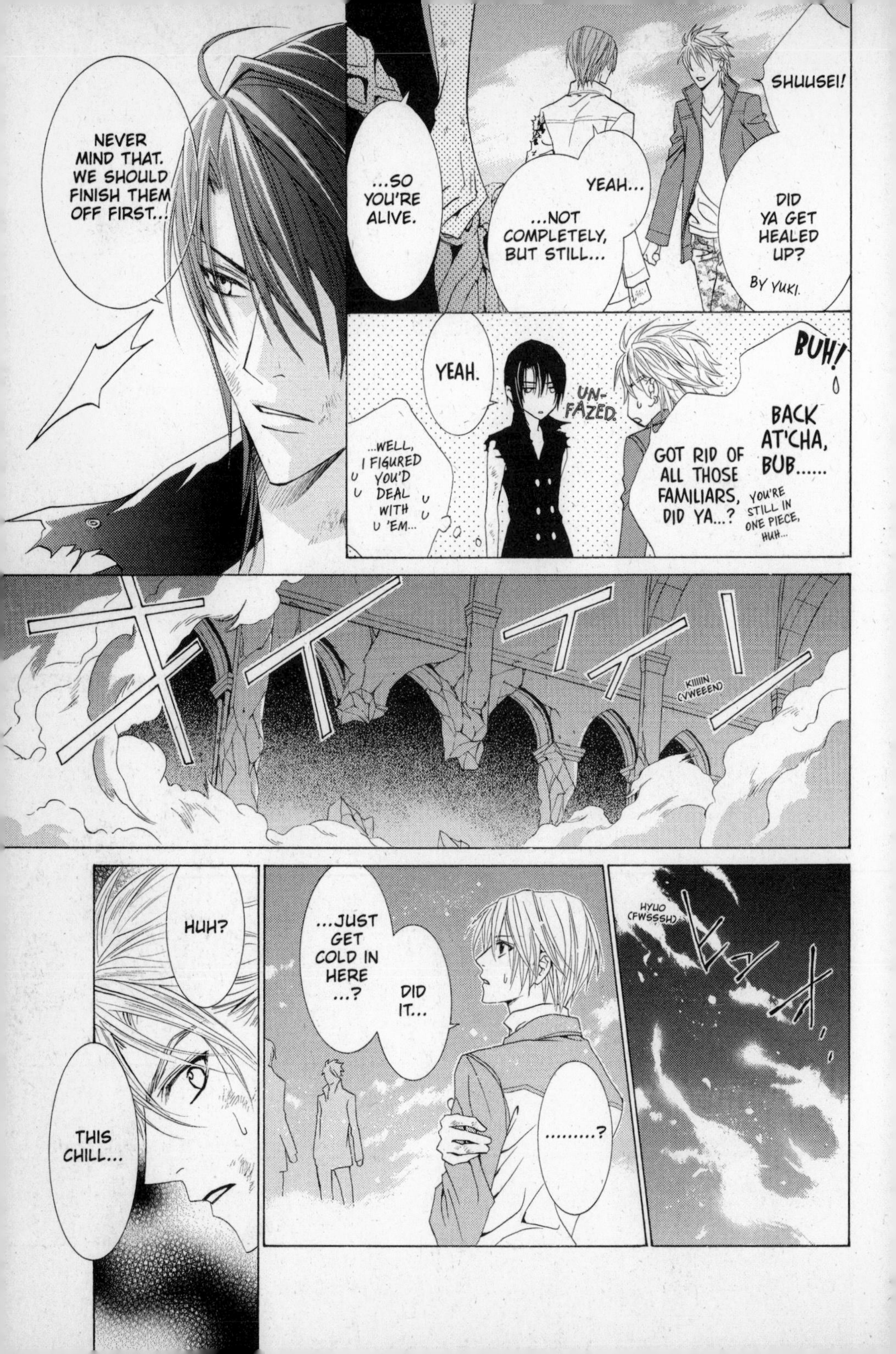
SHUUSEI!
DID YA GET HEALED UP?
BY YUKI.
YEAH...
...NOT COMPLETELY, BUT STILL...
...SO YOU'RE ALIVE.
BUH!
BACK AT'CHA, BUB......
YOU'RE STILL IN ONE PIECE, HUH...
GOT RID OF ALL THOSE FAMILIARS, DID YA...?
UN-FAZED.
YEAH.
...WELL, I FIGURED YOU'D DEAL WITH 'EM...
NEVER MIND THAT. WE SHOULD FINISH THEM OFF FIRST...!
KIIIIN (VWEEEN)
HYUO (FWSSSH)
DID IT...
...JUST GET COLD IN HERE...?
.........?
HUH?
THIS CHILL...

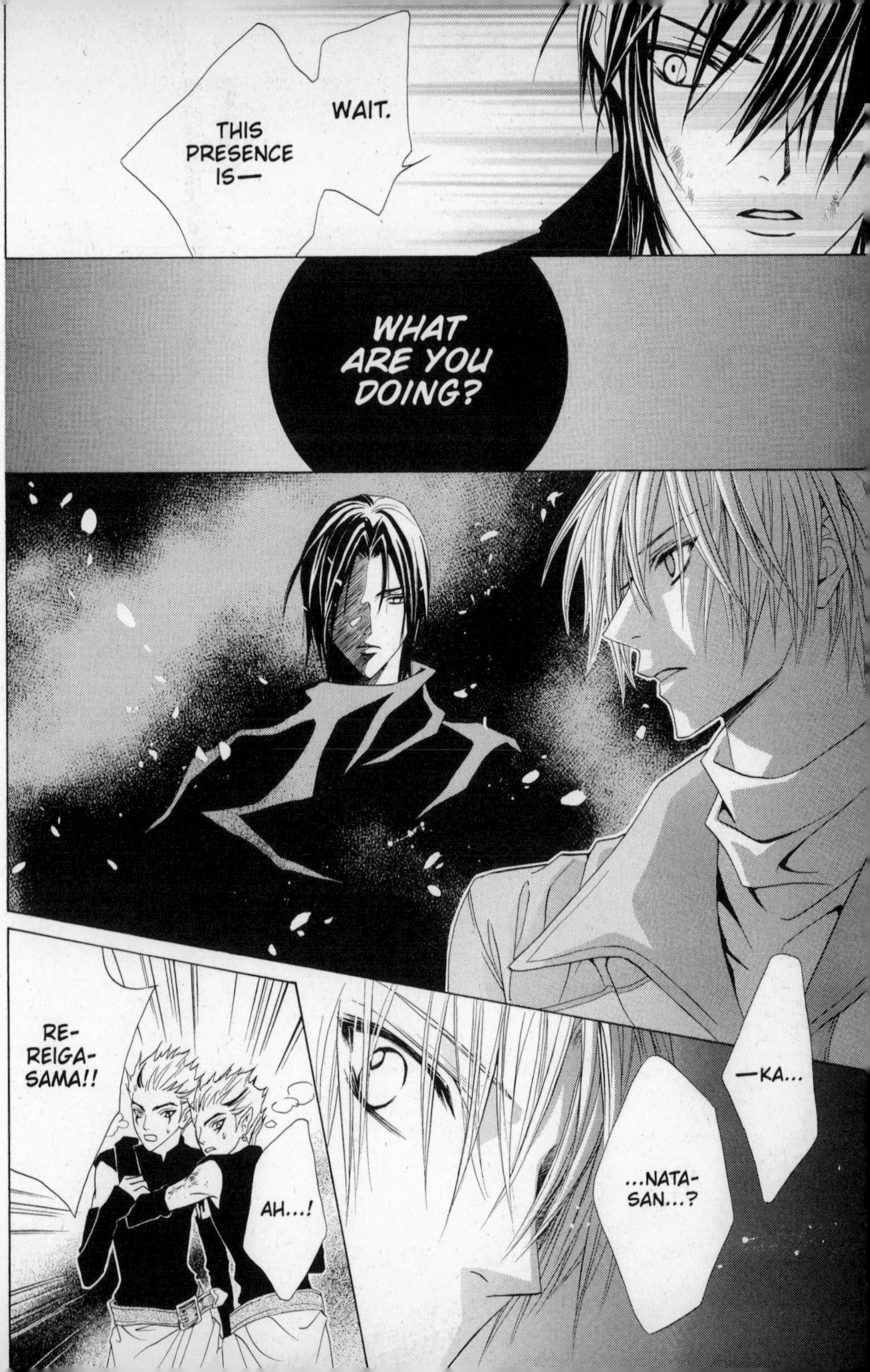
WAIT.
THIS PRESENCE IS—
WHAT ARE YOU DOING?
—KA...
...NATA-SAN...?
RE-REIGA-SAMA!!
AH...!

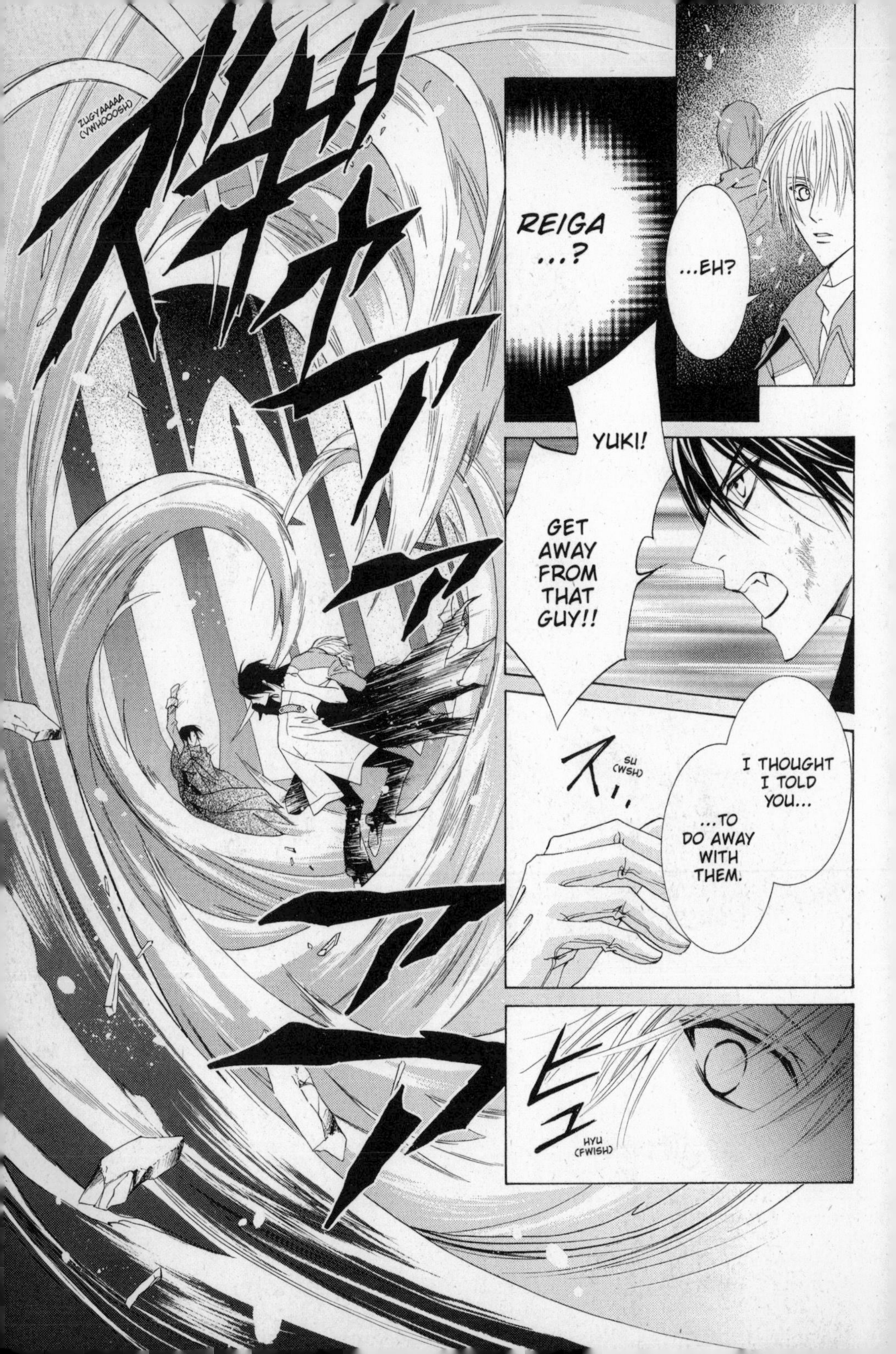
...EH?
REIGA ...?
YUKI!
GET AWAY FROM THAT GUY!!
I THOUGHT I TOLD YOU...
...TO DO AWAY WITH THEM.
SU (WSH)
HYU (FWISH)
ZUGYAAAAA (VWHOOOSH)

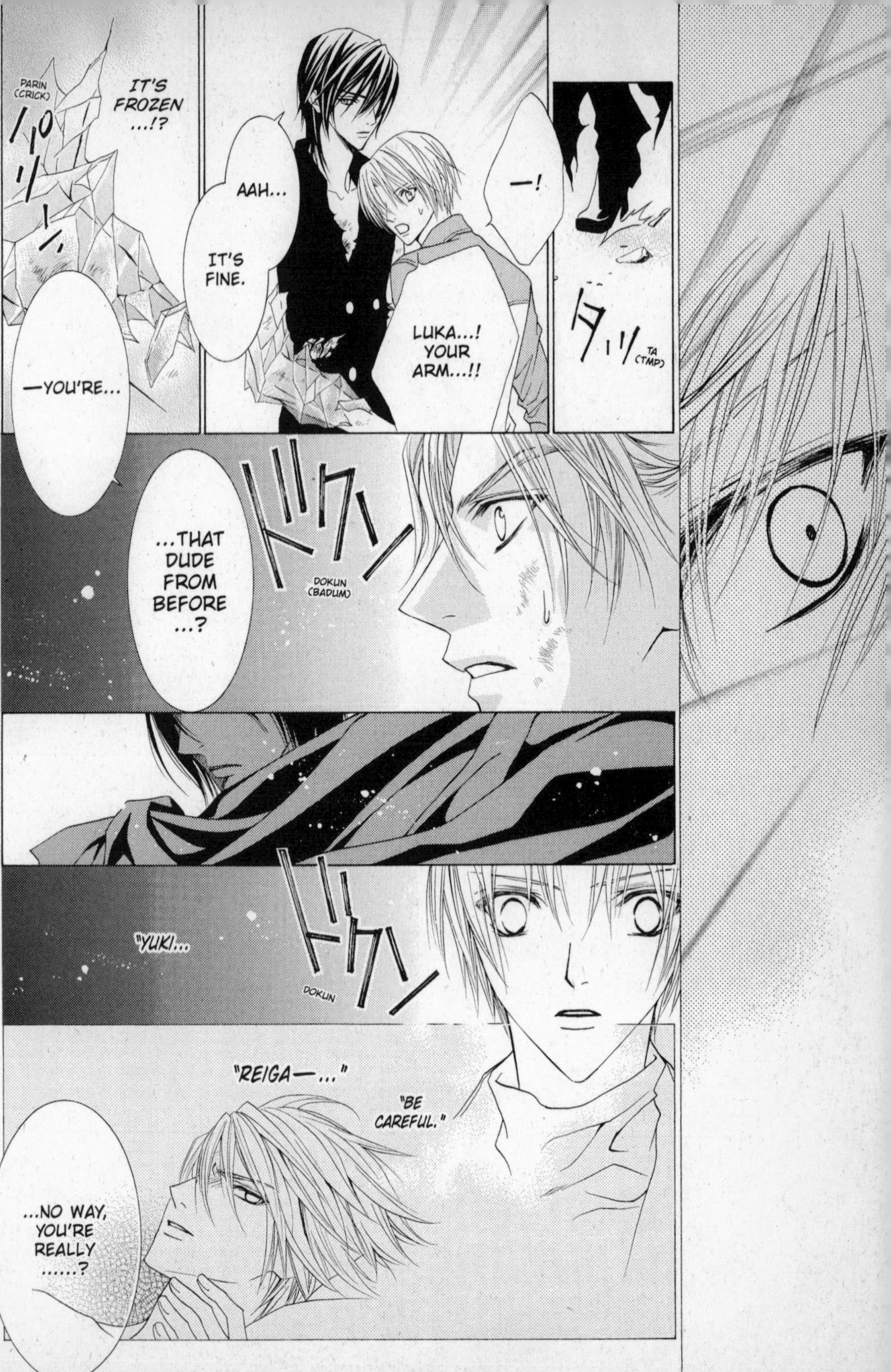
—!
TA (TMP)
LUKA...! YOUR ARM...!!
AAH...
IT'S FINE.
IT'S FROZEN ...!?
PARIN (CRICK)
—YOU'RE...
...THAT DUDE FROM BEFORE ...?
DOKUN (BADUM)
"YUKI...
DOKUN
"REIGA—..."
"BE CAREFUL."
...NO WAY, YOU'RE REALLY ......?

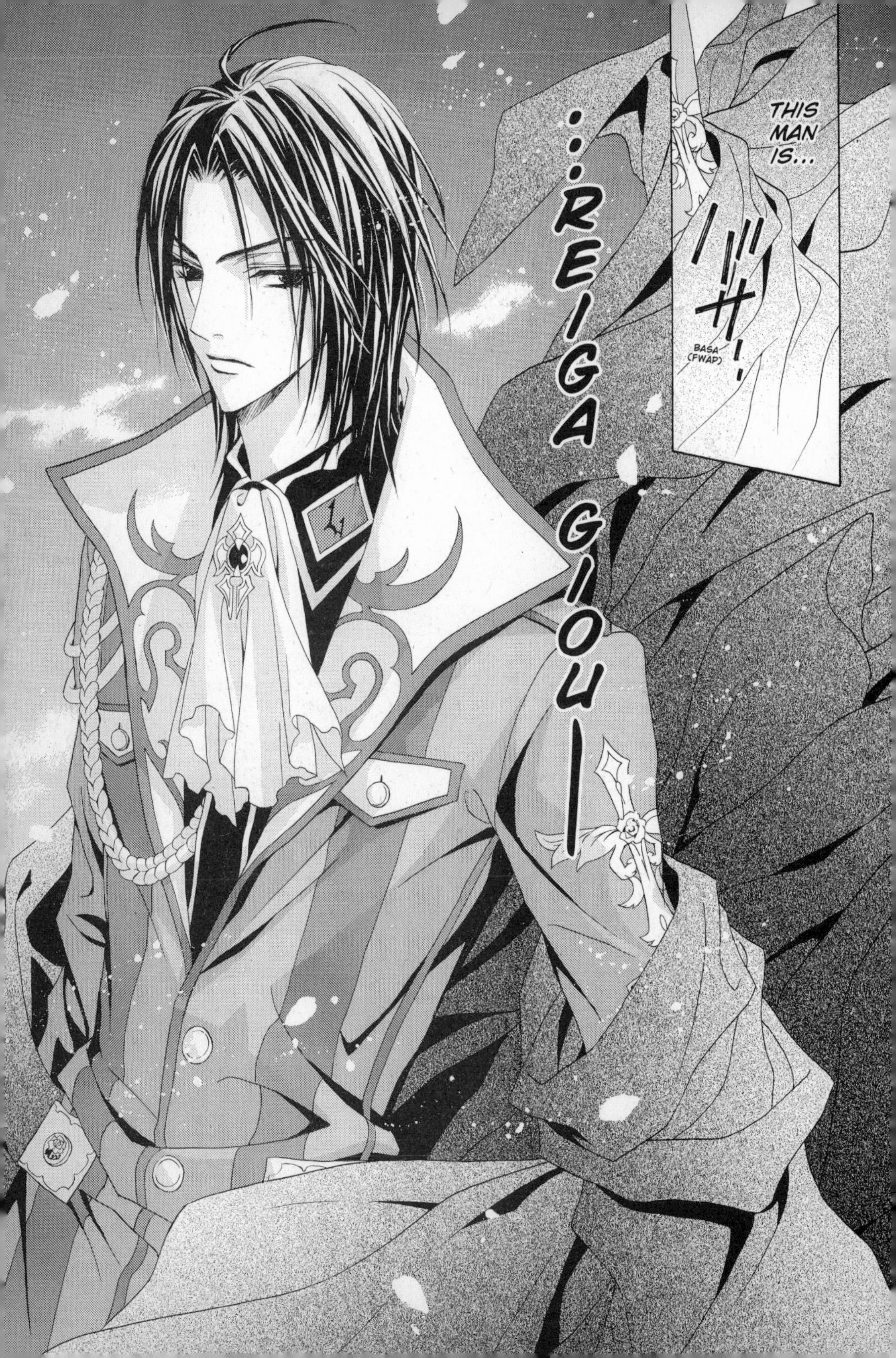
THIS MAN IS...
BASA (FWAP)
...REIGA GIOU!

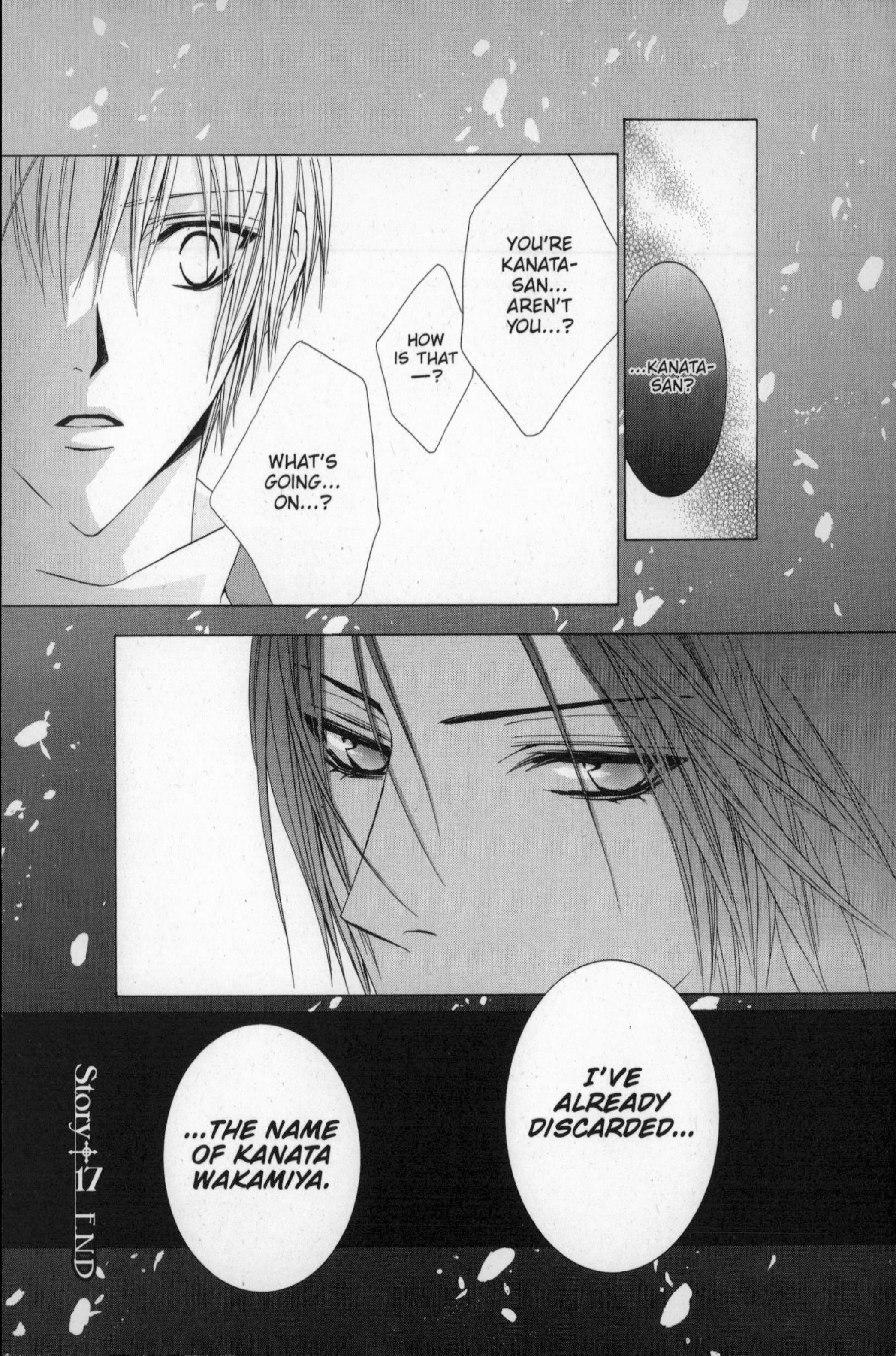
...KANATA-SAN?
YOU'RE KANATA-SAN... AREN'T YOU...?
HOW IS THAT —?
WHAT'S GOING... ON...?
I'VE ALREADY DISCARDED...
...THE NAME OF KANATA WAKAMIYA.
Story 17 END

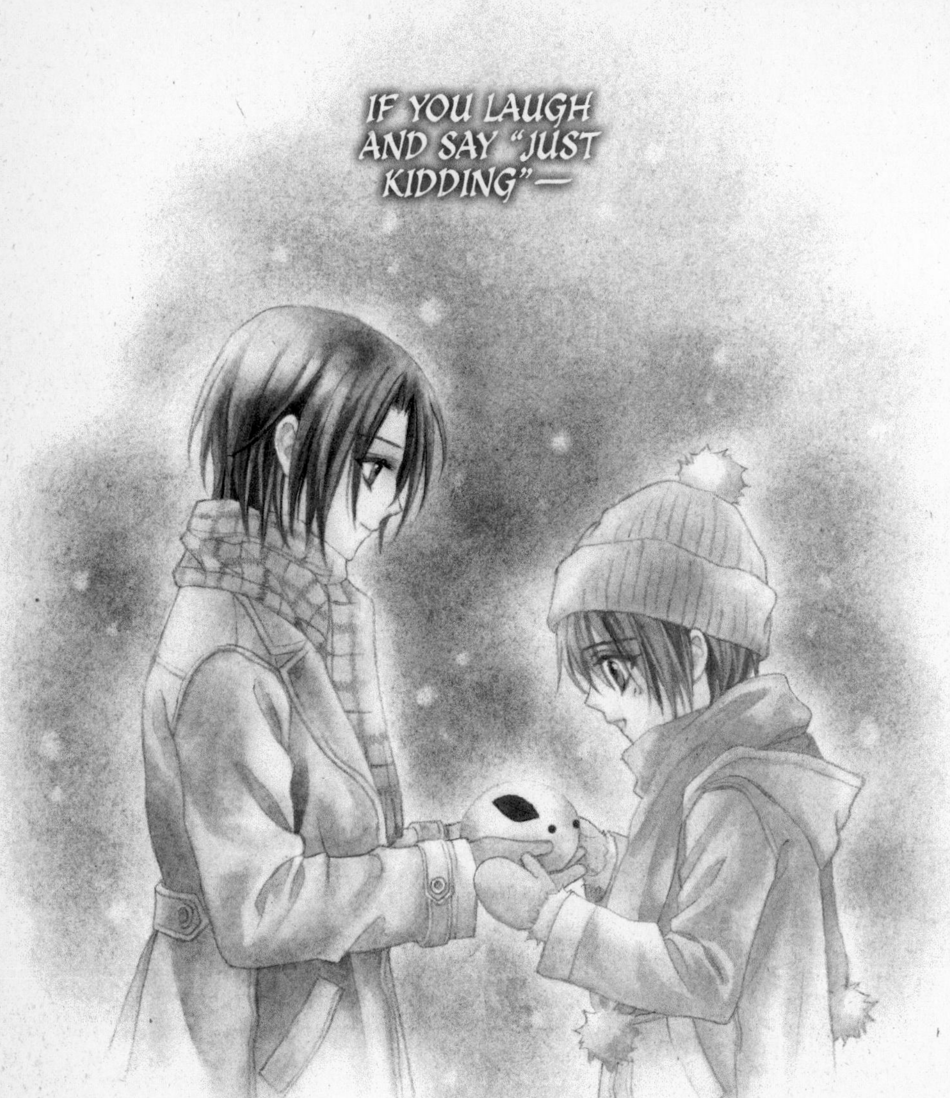
IF YOU LAUGH AND SAY "JUST KIDDING"—

Story 18

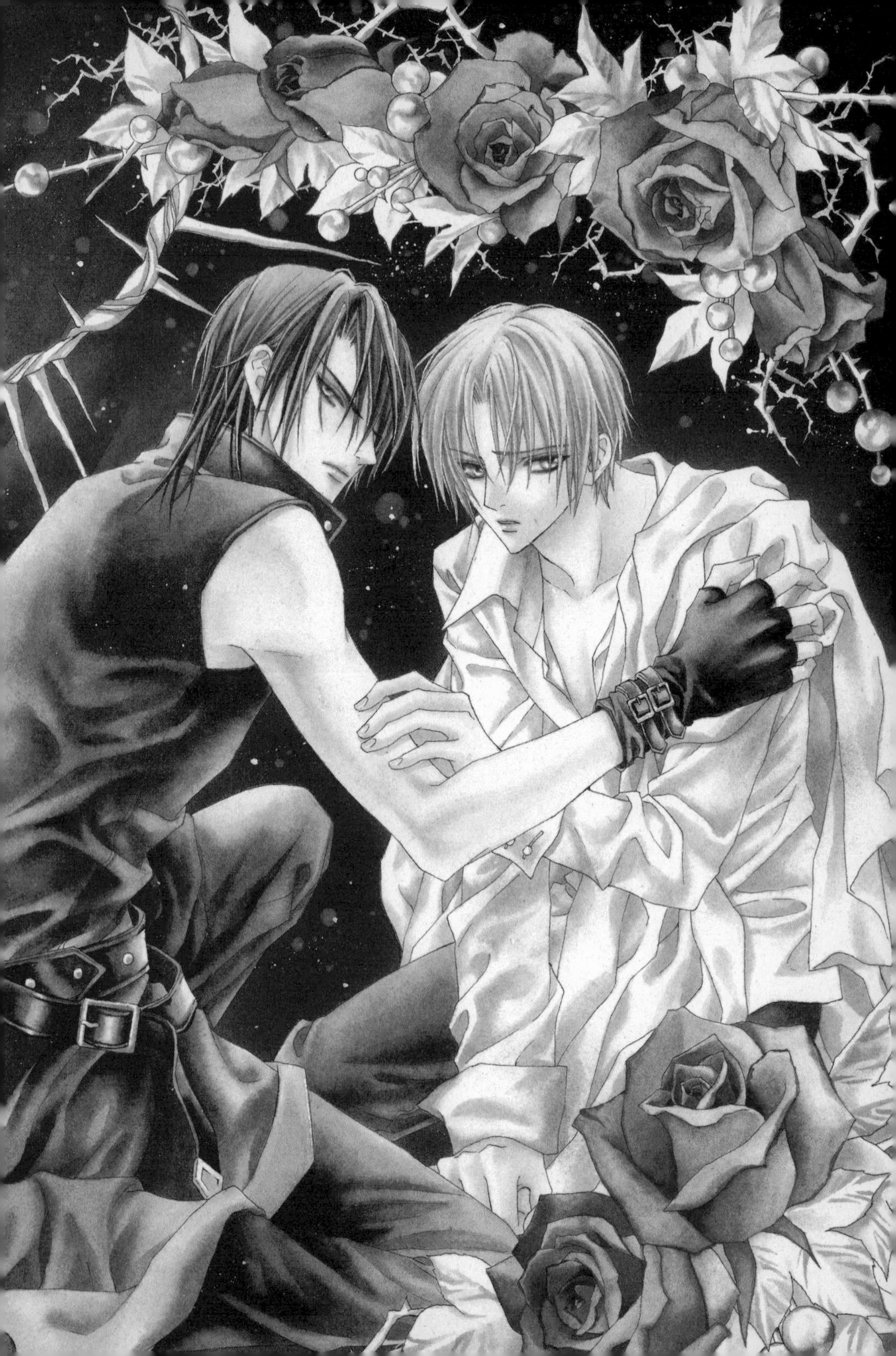

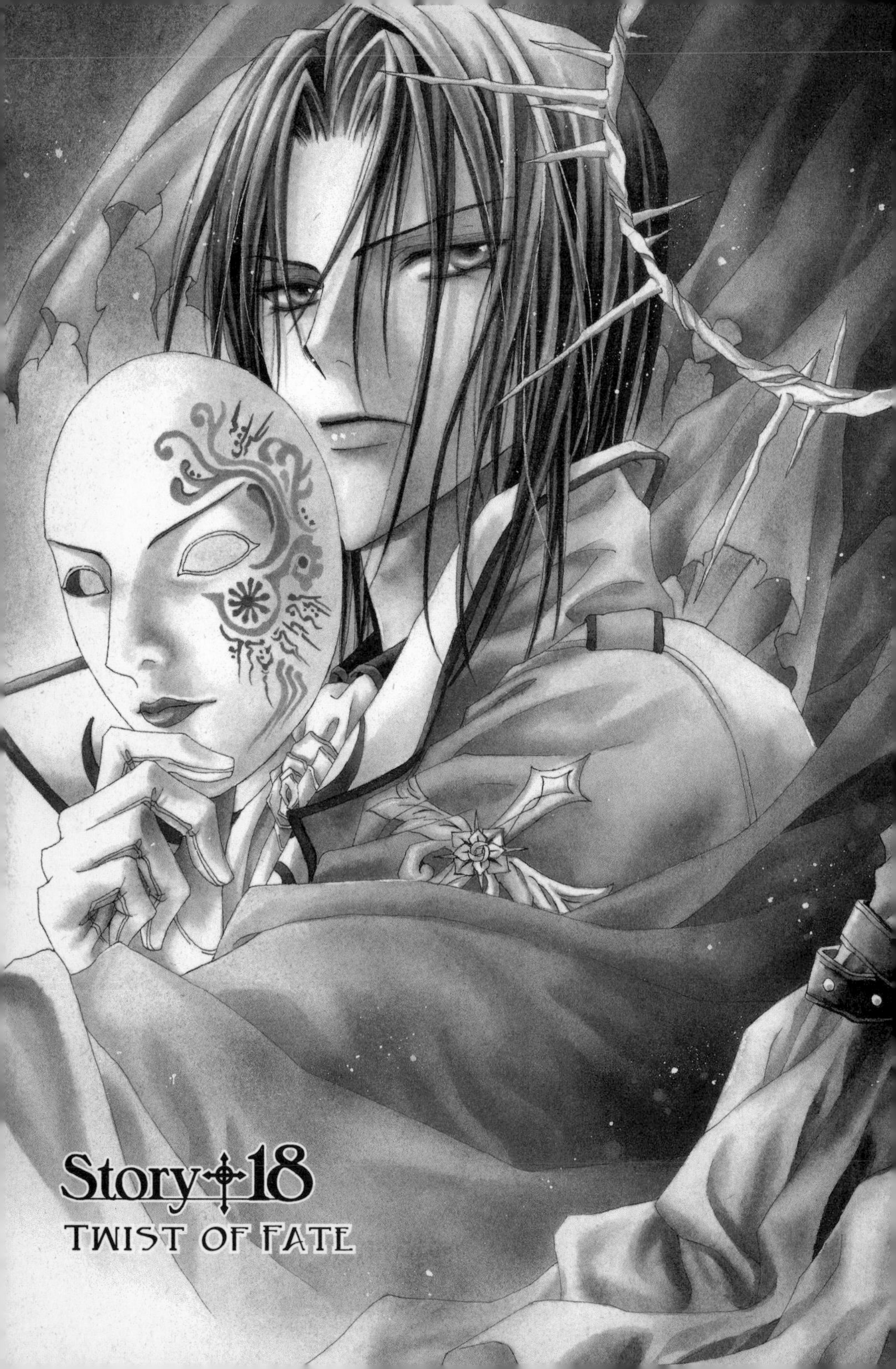

Story 18
TWIST OF FATE

The Betrayal Knows My Name

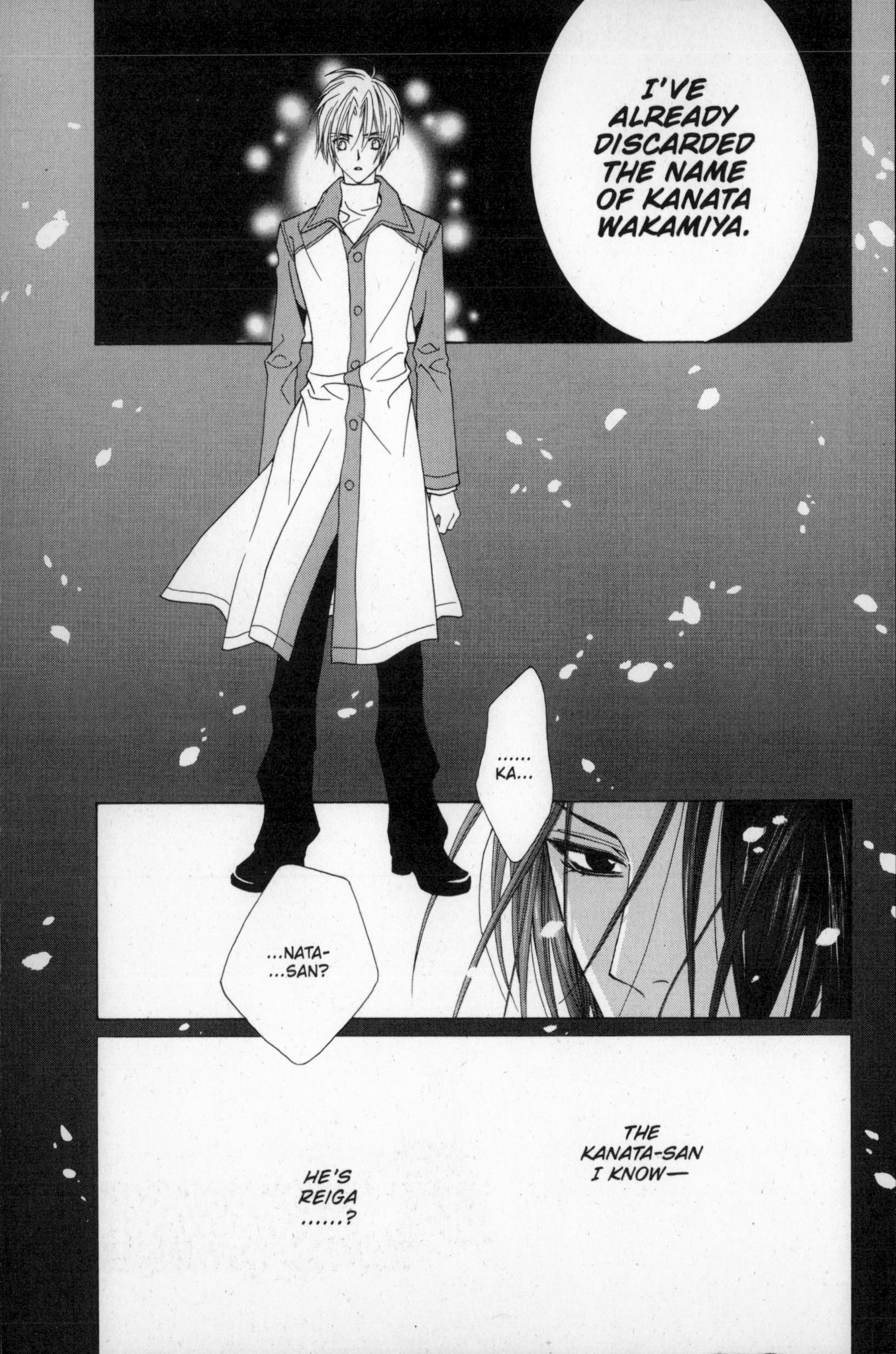
I'VE ALREADY DISCARDED THE NAME OF KANATA WAKAMIYA.
......KA...
...NATA-...SAN?
THE KANATA-SAN I KNOW—
HE'S REIGA ......?

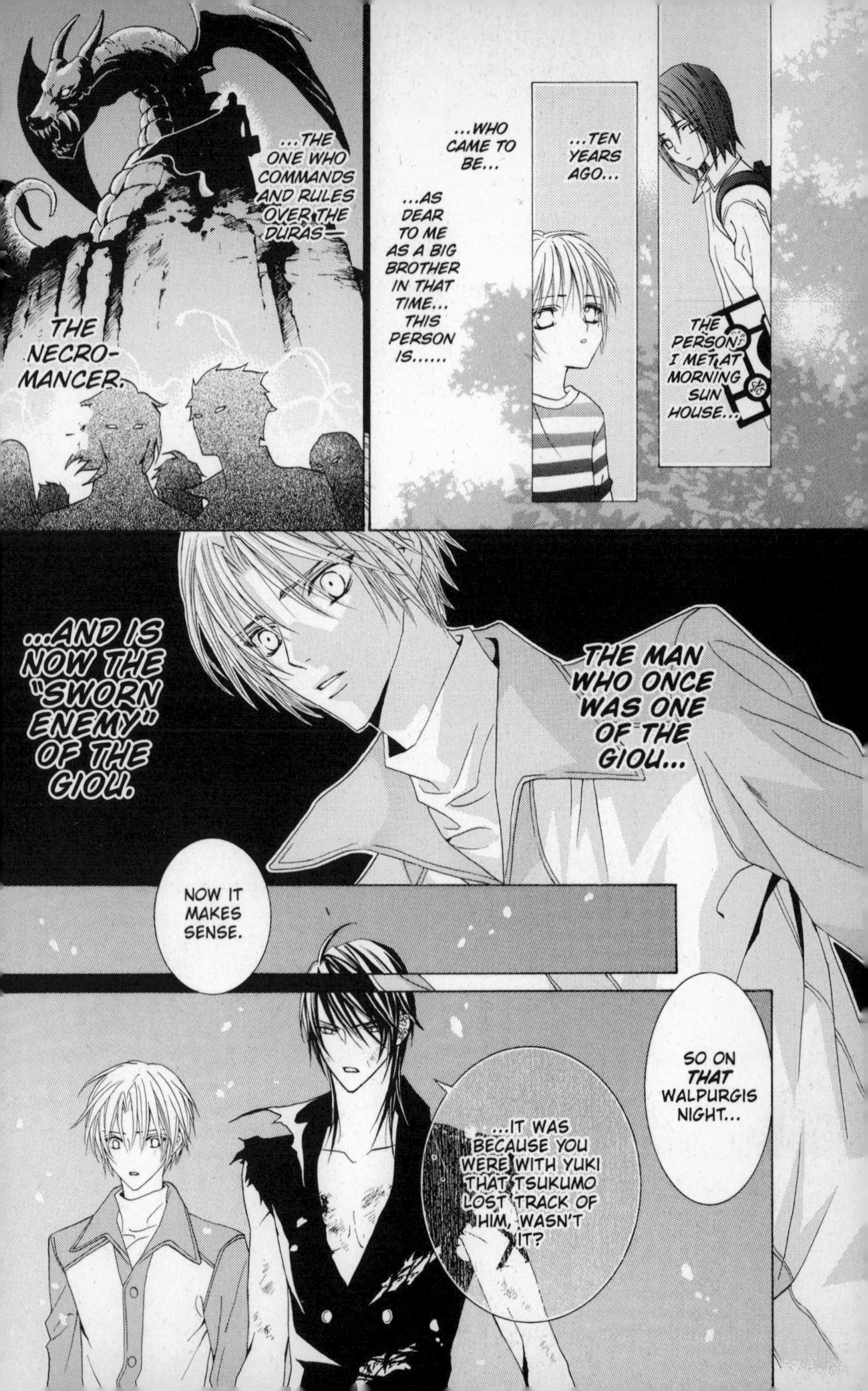
THE PERSON I MET AT MORNING SUN HOUSE...
...TEN YEARS AGO...
...WHO CAME TO BE...
...AS DEAR TO ME AS A BIG BROTHER IN THAT TIME... THIS PERSON IS......
...THE ONE WHO COMMANDS AND RULES OVER THE DURAS—
THE NECROMANCER.
THE MAN WHO ONCE WAS ONE OF THE GIOU...
...AND IS NOW THE "SWORN ENEMY" OF THE GIOU.
NOW IT MAKES SENSE.
SO ON *THAT* WALPURGIS NIGHT...
...IT WAS BECAUSE YOU WERE WITH YUKI THAT TSUKUMO LOST TRACK OF HIM, WASN'T IT?

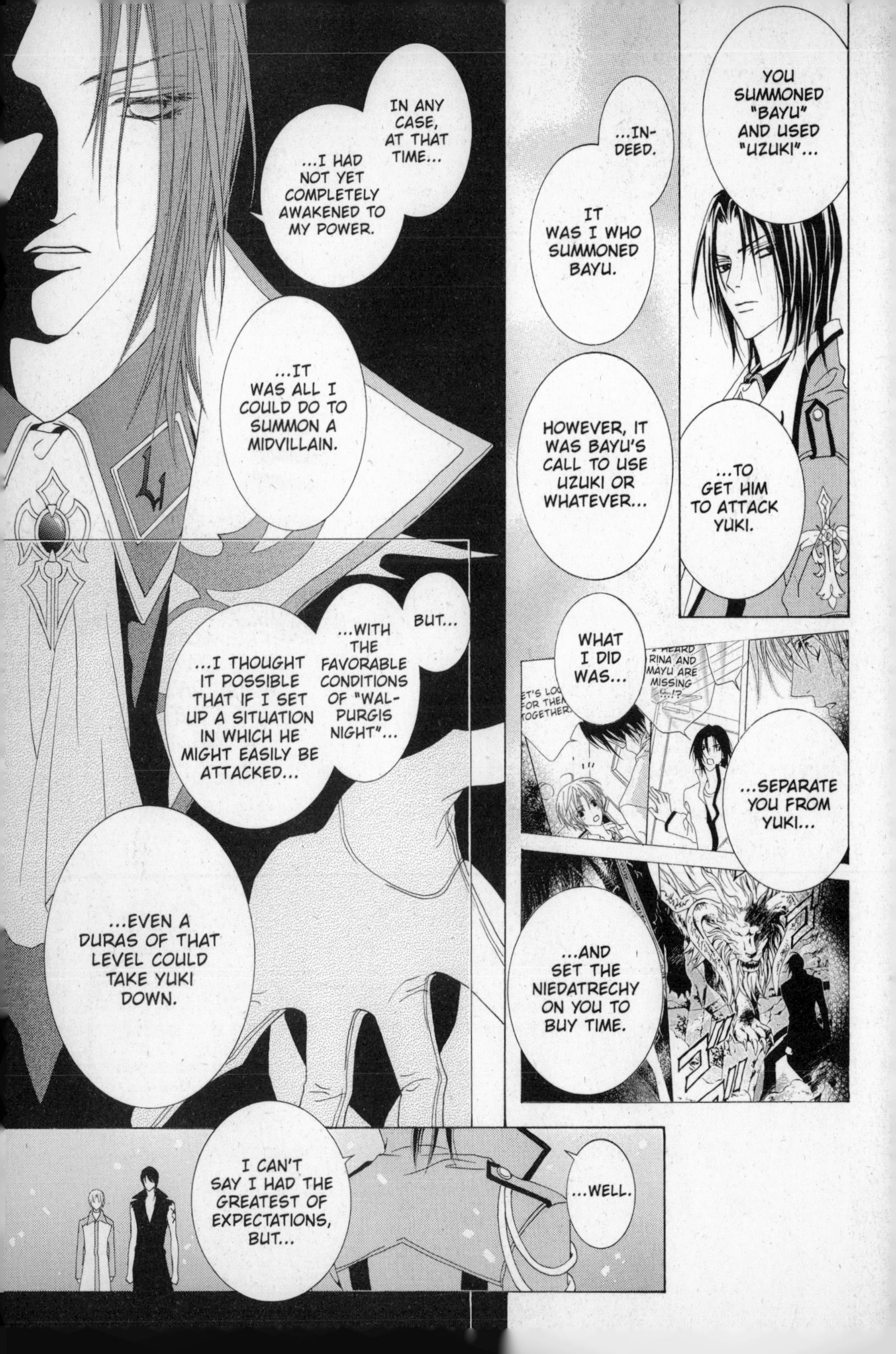
YOU SUMMONED "BAYU" AND USED "UZUKI"...
...TO GET HIM TO ATTACK YUKI.
...IN-DEED.
IT WAS I WHO SUMMONED BAYU.
HOWEVER, IT WAS BAYU'S CALL TO USE UZUKI OR WHATEVER...
WHAT I DID WAS...
I HEARD RINA AND MAYU ARE MISSING ...!?
...SEPARATE YOU FROM YUKI...
...AND SET THE NIEDATRECHY ON YOU TO BUY TIME.
IN ANY CASE, AT THAT TIME...
...I HAD NOT YET COMPLETELY AWAKENED TO MY POWER.
...IT WAS ALL I COULD DO TO SUMMON A MIDVILLAIN.
BUT...
...WITH THE FAVORABLE CONDITIONS OF "WAL-PURGIS NIGHT"...
...I THOUGHT IT POSSIBLE THAT IF I SET UP A SITUATION IN WHICH HE MIGHT EASILY BE ATTACKED...
...EVEN A DURAS OF THAT LEVEL COULD TAKE YUKI DOWN.
...WELL.
I CAN'T SAY I HAD THE GREATEST OF EXPECTATIONS, BUT...

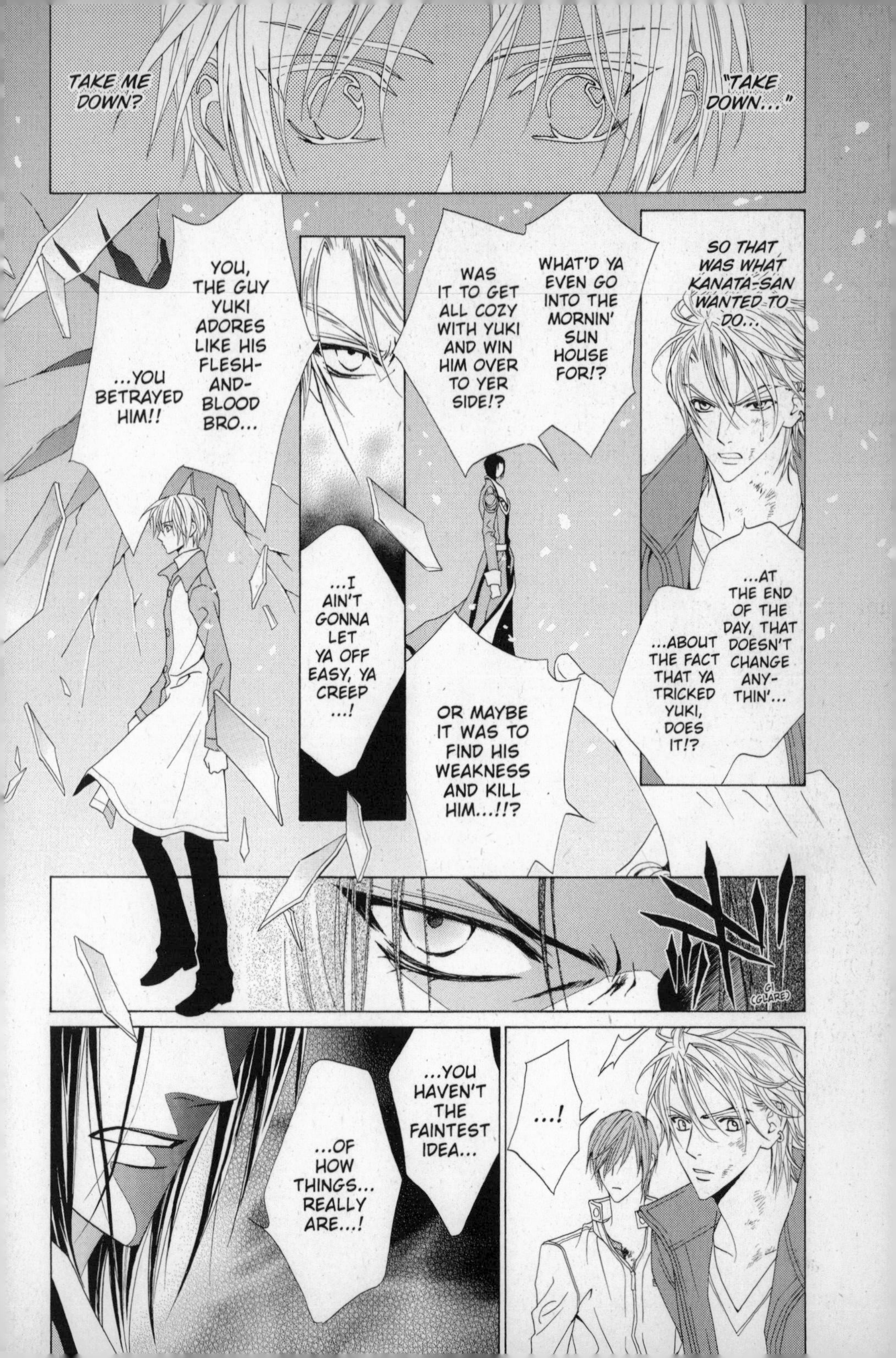
"TAKE DOWN..."
TAKE ME DOWN?
SO THAT WAS WHAT KANATA-SAN WANTED TO DO...
WHAT'D YA EVEN GO INTO THE MORNIN' SUN HOUSE FOR!?
WAS IT TO GET ALL COZY WITH YUKI AND WIN HIM OVER TO YER SIDE!?
OR MAYBE IT WAS TO FIND HIS WEAKNESS AND KILL HIM...!!?
...AT THE END OF THE DAY, THAT DOESN'T CHANGE ANY-THIN'...
...ABOUT THE FACT THAT YA TRICKED YUKI, DOES IT!?
YOU, THE GUY YUKI ADORES LIKE HIS FLESH-AND-BLOOD BRO...
...YOU BETRAYED HIM!!
...I AIN'T GONNA LET YA OFF EASY, YA CREEP...!
GI (GLARE)
...!
...YOU HAVEN'T THE FAINTEST IDEA...
...OF HOW THINGS... REALLY ARE...!

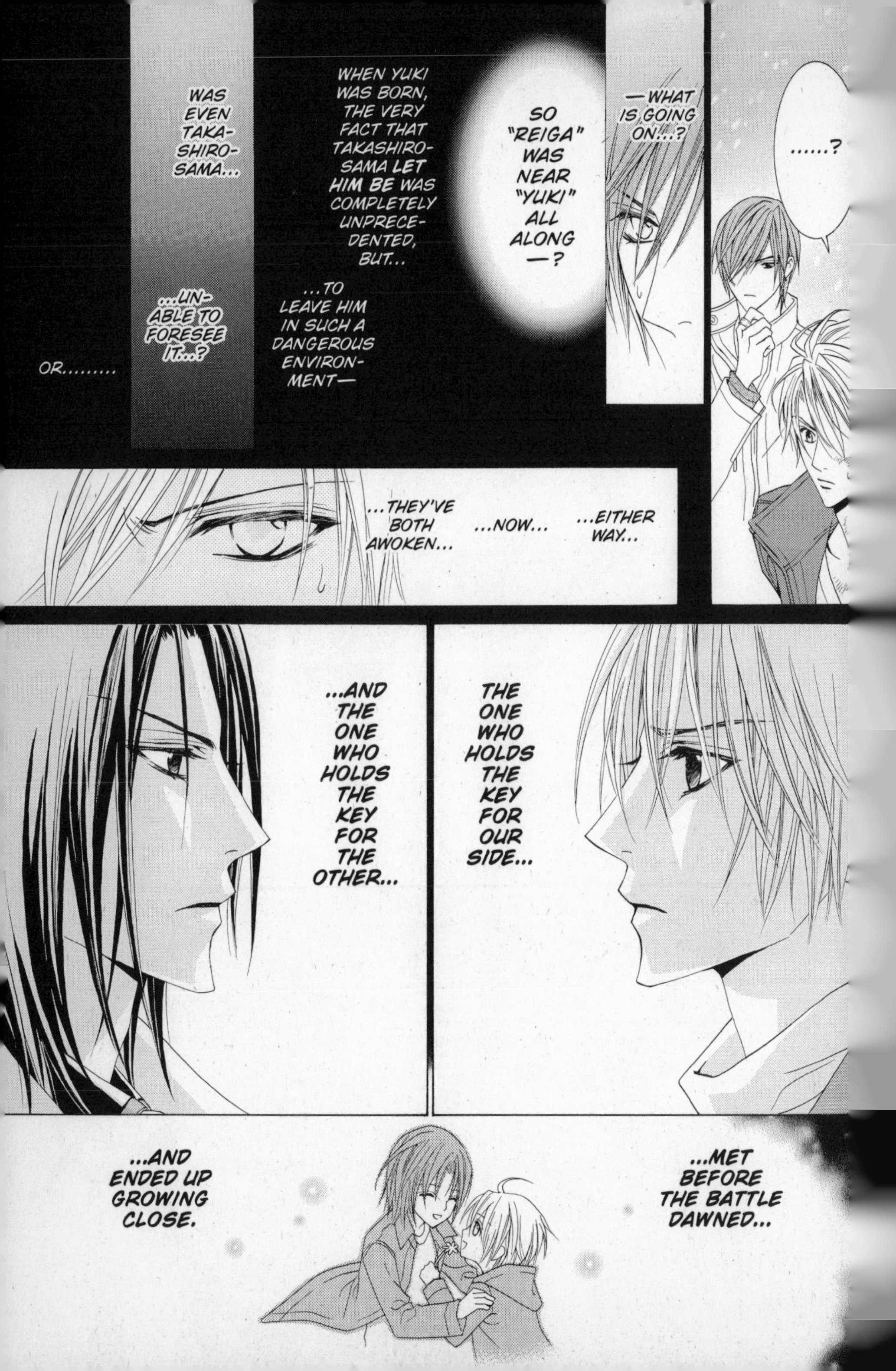
......?
—WHAT IS GOING ON...?
SO "REIGA" WAS NEAR "YUKI" ALL ALONG—?
WHEN YUKI WAS BORN, THE VERY FACT THAT TAKASHIRO-SAMA LET HIM BE WAS COMPLETELY UNPRECEDENTED, BUT...
...TO LEAVE HIM IN SUCH A DANGEROUS ENVIRONMENT—
OR.........
WAS EVEN TAKASHIRO-SAMA...
...UNABLE TO FORESEE IT...?
...EITHER WAY...
...NOW...
...THEY'VE BOTH AWOKEN...
THE ONE WHO HOLDS THE KEY FOR OUR SIDE...
...AND THE ONE WHO HOLDS THE KEY FOR THE OTHER...
...MET BEFORE THE BATTLE DAWNED...
...AND ENDED UP GROWING CLOSE.

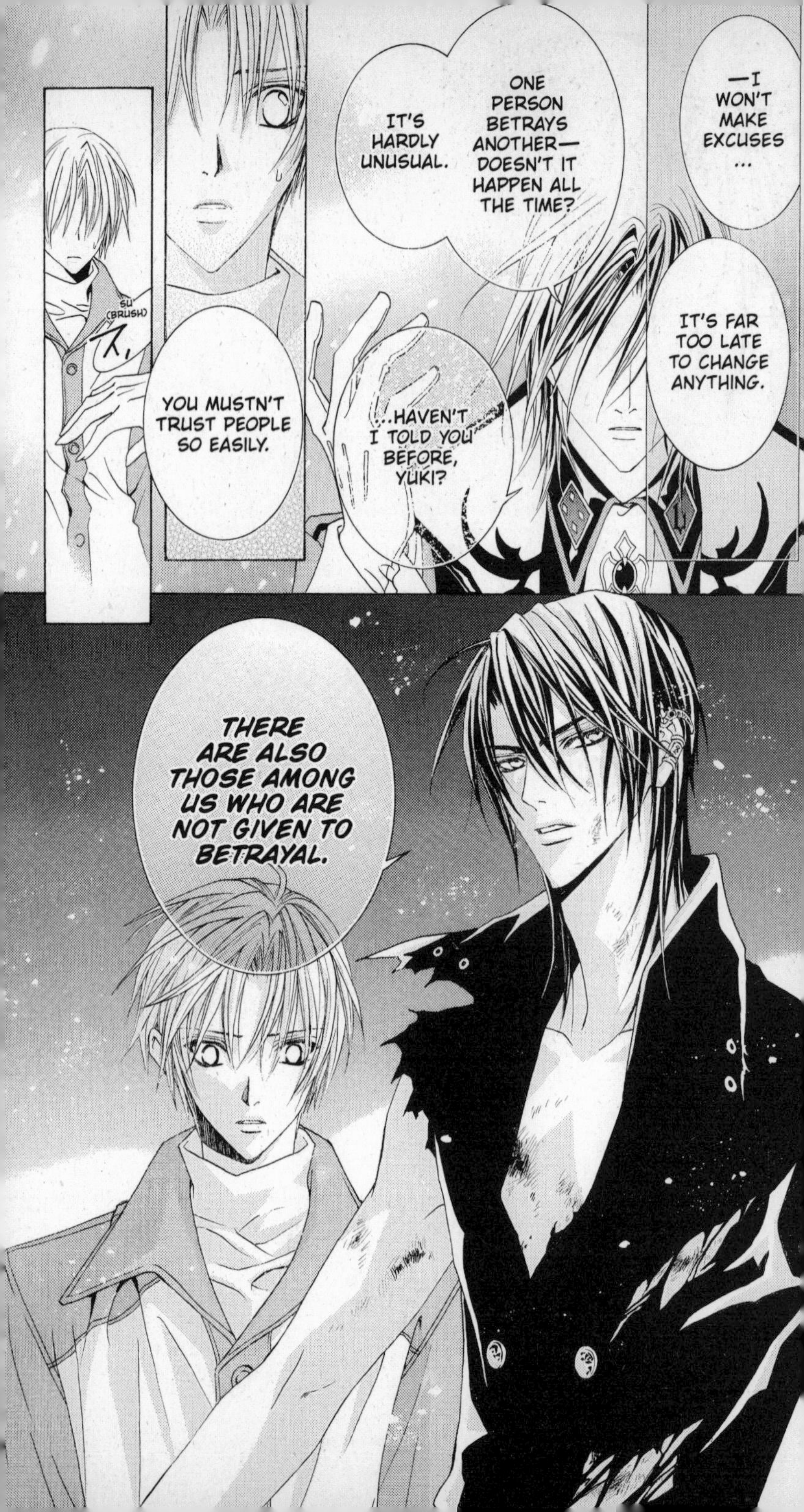
—I WON'T MAKE EXCUSES ...
IT'S FAR TOO LATE TO CHANGE ANYTHING.
ONE PERSON BETRAYS ANOTHER—DOESN'T IT HAPPEN ALL THE TIME?
IT'S HARDLY UNUSUAL.
...HAVEN'T I TOLD YOU BEFORE, YUKI?
YOU MUSTN'T TRUST PEOPLE SO EASILY.
SU (BRUSH)
THERE ARE ALSO THOSE AMONG US WHO ARE NOT GIVEN TO BETRAYAL.

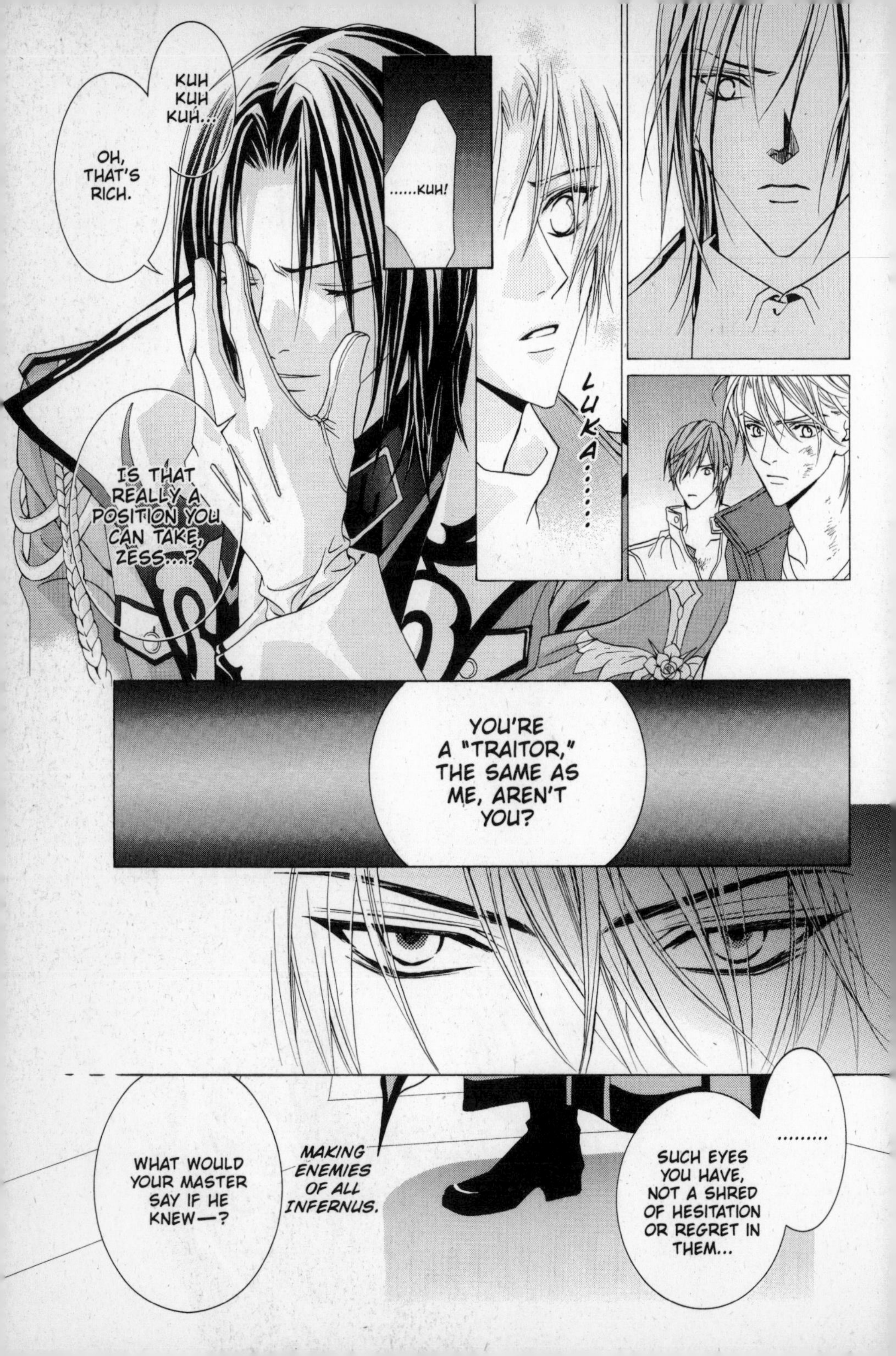
......KUH!
LUKA......
KUH KUH KUH...
OH, THAT'S RICH.
IS THAT REALLY A POSITION YOU CAN TAKE, ZESS...?
YOU'RE A "TRAITOR," THE SAME AS ME, AREN'T YOU?
....
SUCH EYES YOU HAVE, NOT A SHRED OF HESITATION OR REGRET IN THEM...
MAKING ENEMIES OF ALL INFERNUS.
WHAT WOULD YOUR MASTER SAY IF HE KNEW—?

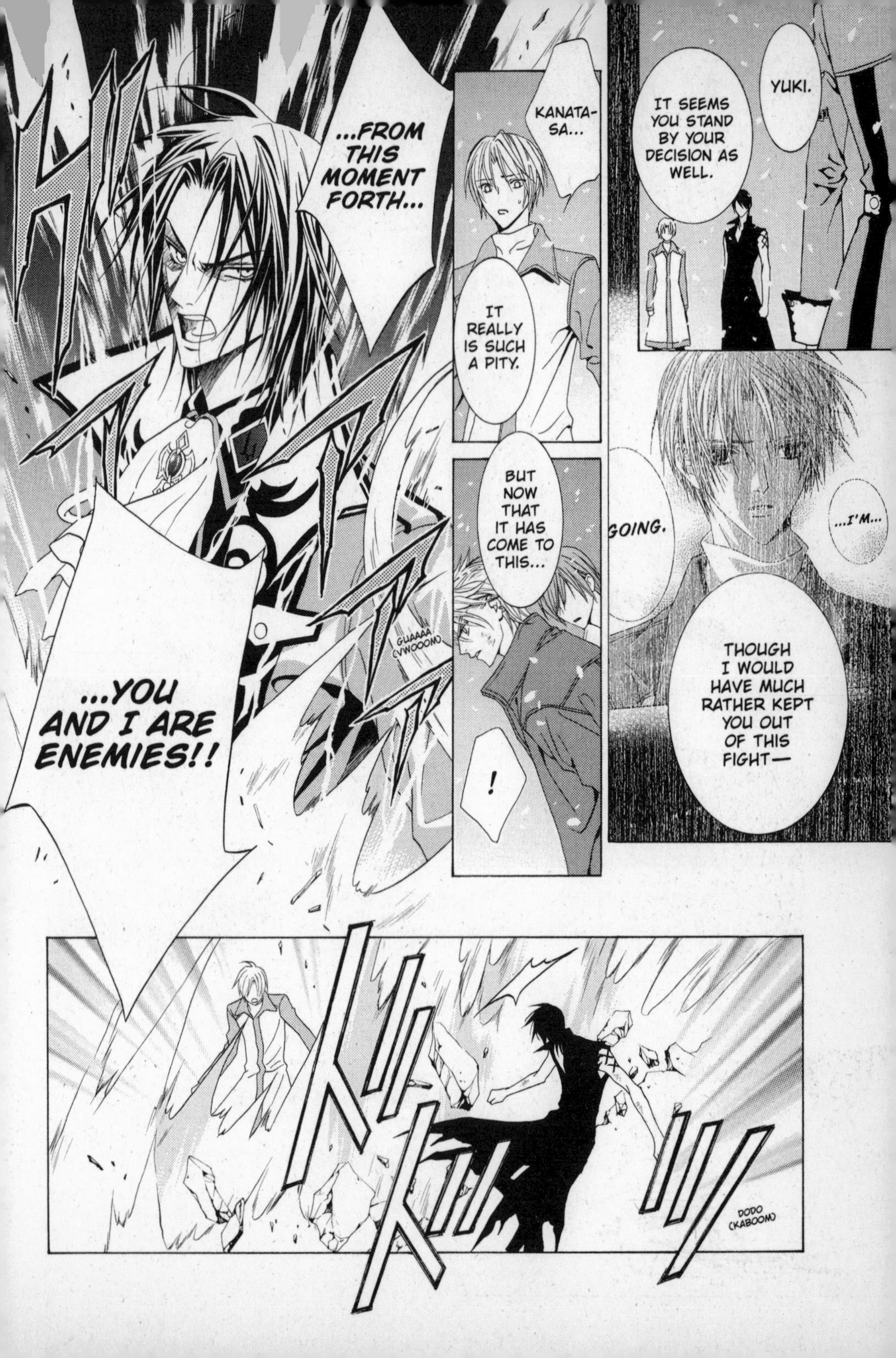

YUKI.
IT SEEMS YOU STAND BY YOUR DECISION AS WELL.
...I'M...
GOING.
THOUGH I WOULD HAVE MUCH RATHER KEPT YOU OUT OF THIS FIGHT—
KANATA-SA...
IT REALLY IS SUCH A PITY.
BUT NOW THAT IT HAS COME TO THIS...
!
GUAAAA (VWOOOM)
...FROM THIS MOMENT FORTH...
...YOU AND I ARE ENEMIES!!
DODO (KABOOM)

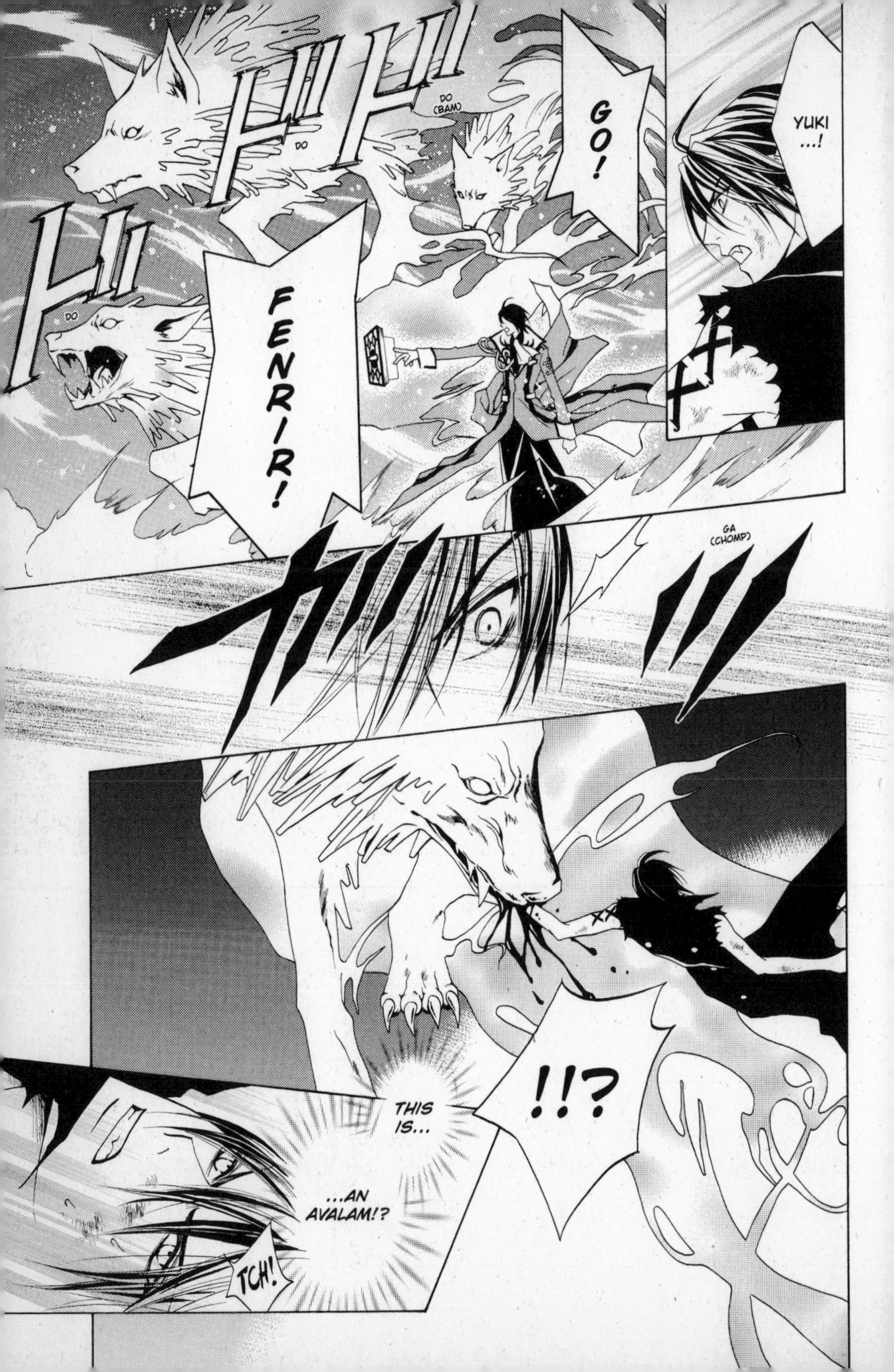
YUKI ...!
GO!
DO (BAM)
DO
DO
FENRIR!
GA (CHOMP)
!!?
THIS IS...
...AN AVALAM!?
TCH!

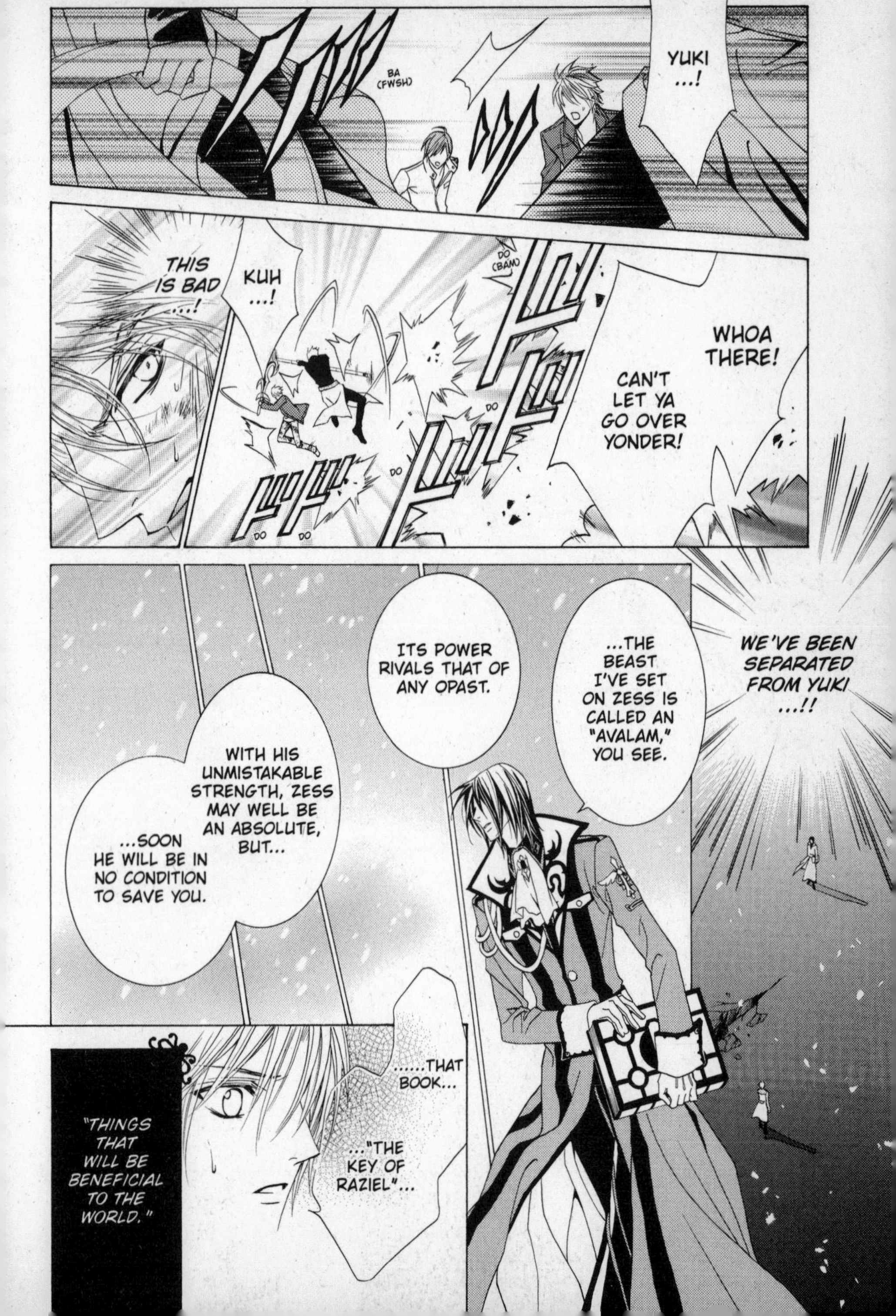
YUKI ...!
BA (FWSH)
WHOA THERE!
CAN'T LET YA GO OVER YONDER!
DO (BAM)
DO
DO
DO
DO
KUH ...!
THIS IS BAD ...!
WE'VE BEEN SEPARATED FROM YUKI ...!!
...THE BEAST I'VE SET ON ZESS IS CALLED AN "AVALAM," YOU SEE.
ITS POWER RIVALS THAT OF ANY OPAST.
WITH HIS UNMISTAKABLE STRENGTH, ZESS MAY WELL BE AN ABSOLUTE, BUT...
...SOON HE WILL BE IN NO CONDITION TO SAVE YOU.
......THAT BOOK...
..."THE KEY OF RAZIEL"...
"THINGS THAT WILL BE BENEFICIAL TO THE WORLD."

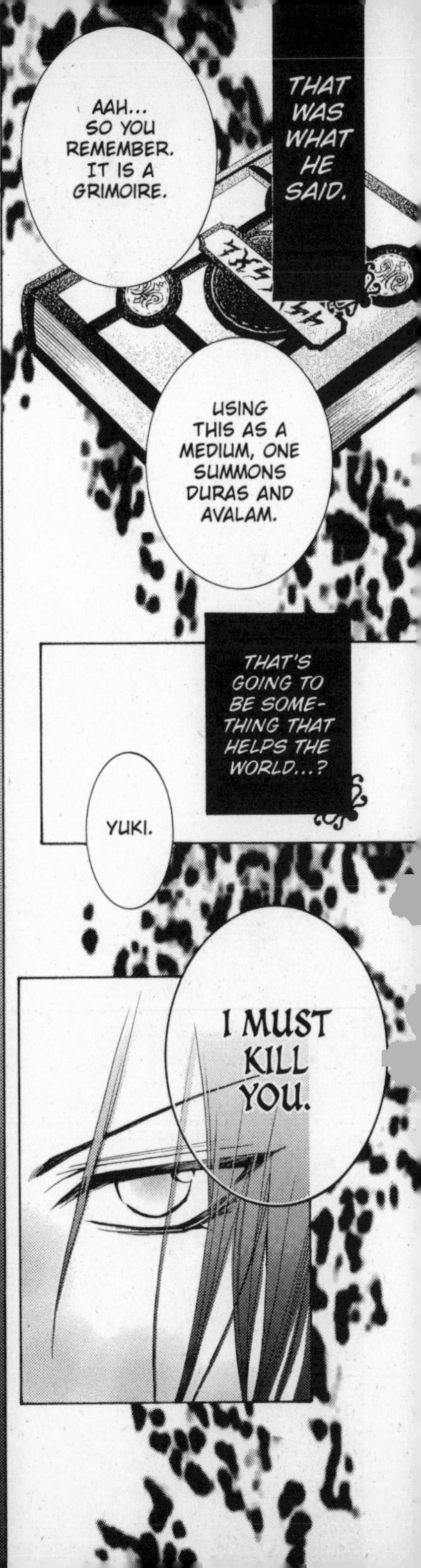
THAT WAS WHAT HE SAID.
AAH... SO YOU REMEMBER. IT IS A GRIMOIRE.
USING THIS AS A MEDIUM, ONE SUMMONS DURAS AND AVALAM.
THAT'S GOING TO BE SOMETHING THAT HELPS THE WORLD...?
YUKI.
I MUST KILL YOU.
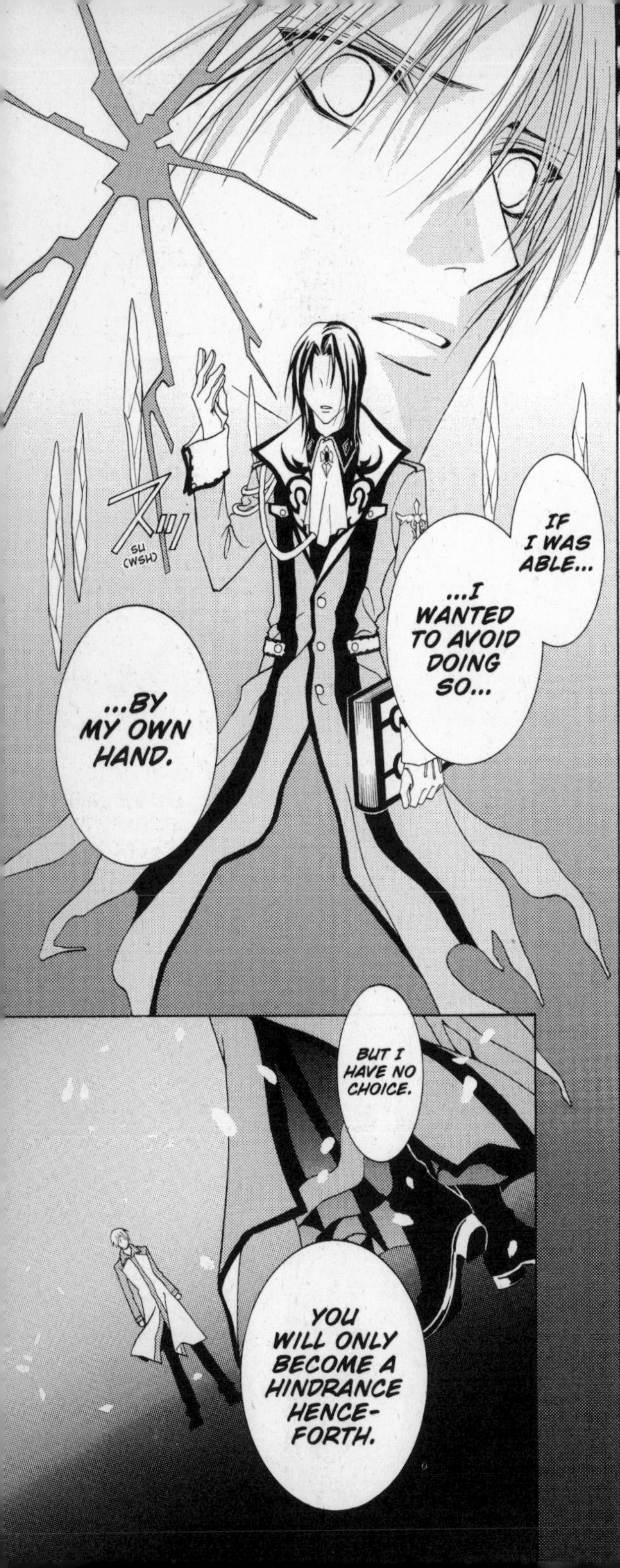
IF I WAS ABLE...
...I WANTED TO AVOID DOING SO...
スッ
SU (WSH)
...BY MY OWN HAND.
BUT I HAVE NO CHOICE.
YOU WILL ONLY BECOME A HINDRANCE HENCE-FORTH.

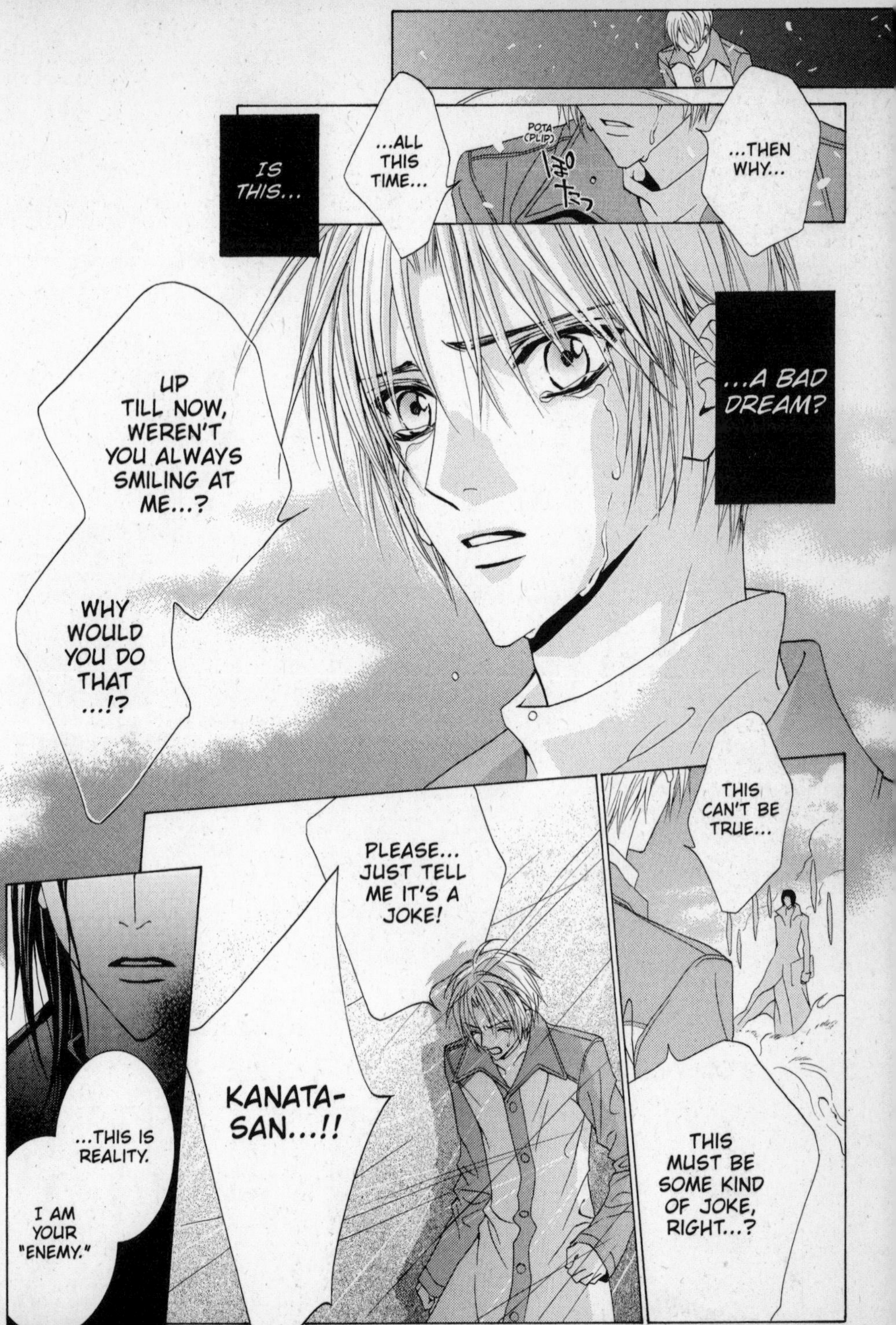
...ALL THIS TIME...
...THEN WHY...
POTA (PLIP)
IS THIS...
...A BAD DREAM?
UP TILL NOW, WEREN'T YOU ALWAYS SMILING AT ME...?
WHY WOULD YOU DO THAT ...!?
THIS CAN'T BE TRUE...
THIS MUST BE SOME KIND OF JOKE, RIGHT...?
PLEASE... JUST TELL ME IT'S A JOKE!
KANATA-SAN...!!
...THIS IS REALITY.
I AM YOUR "ENEMY."

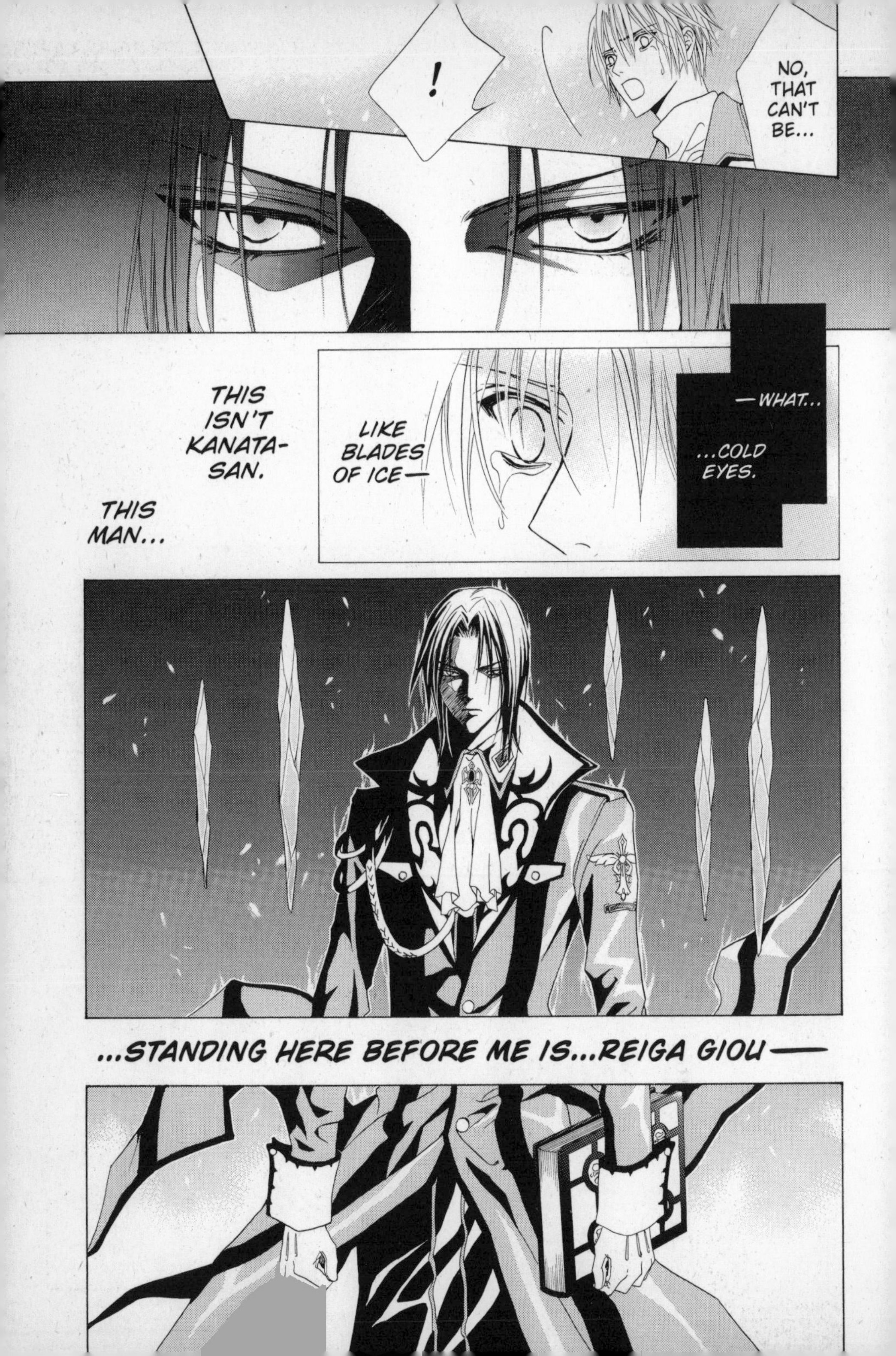
NO, THAT CAN'T BE...
!
—WHAT...
...COLD EYES.
LIKE BLADES OF ICE—
THIS ISN'T KANATA-SAN.
THIS MAN...
...STANDING HERE BEFORE ME IS...REIGA GIOU—

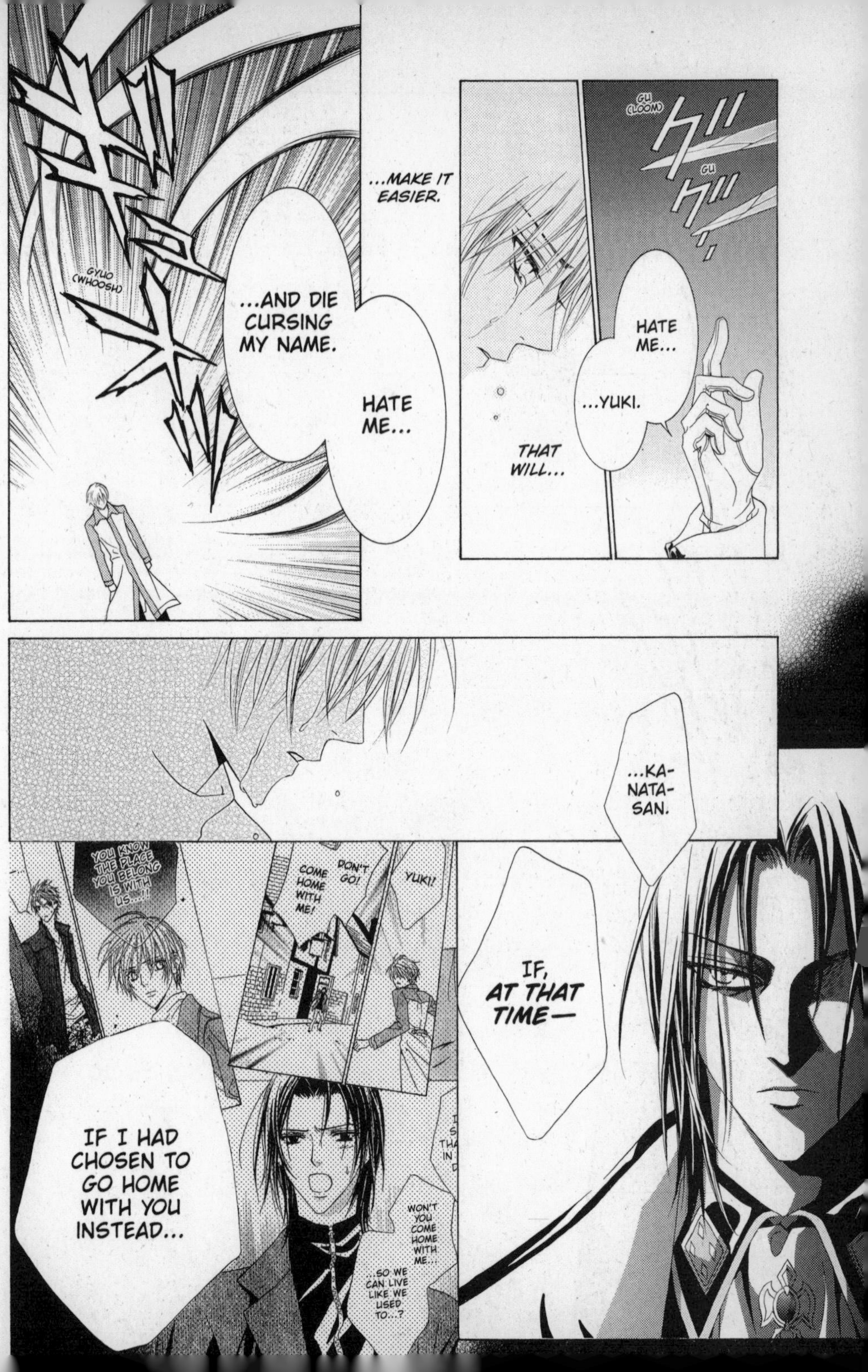
GU (LOOM)
GU
HATE ME...
...YUKI.
THAT WILL...
...MAKE IT EASIER.
HATE ME...
...AND DIE CURSING MY NAME.
GYUO (WHOOSH)
...KA-NATA-SAN.
IF, AT THAT TIME—
YUKI!
DON'T GO!
COME HOME WITH ME!
YOU KNOW THE PLACE YOU BELONG IS WITH US...!!
IF I HAD CHOSEN TO GO HOME WITH YOU INSTEAD...
WON'T YOU COME HOME WITH ME...
...SO WE CAN LIVE LIKE WE USED TO...?

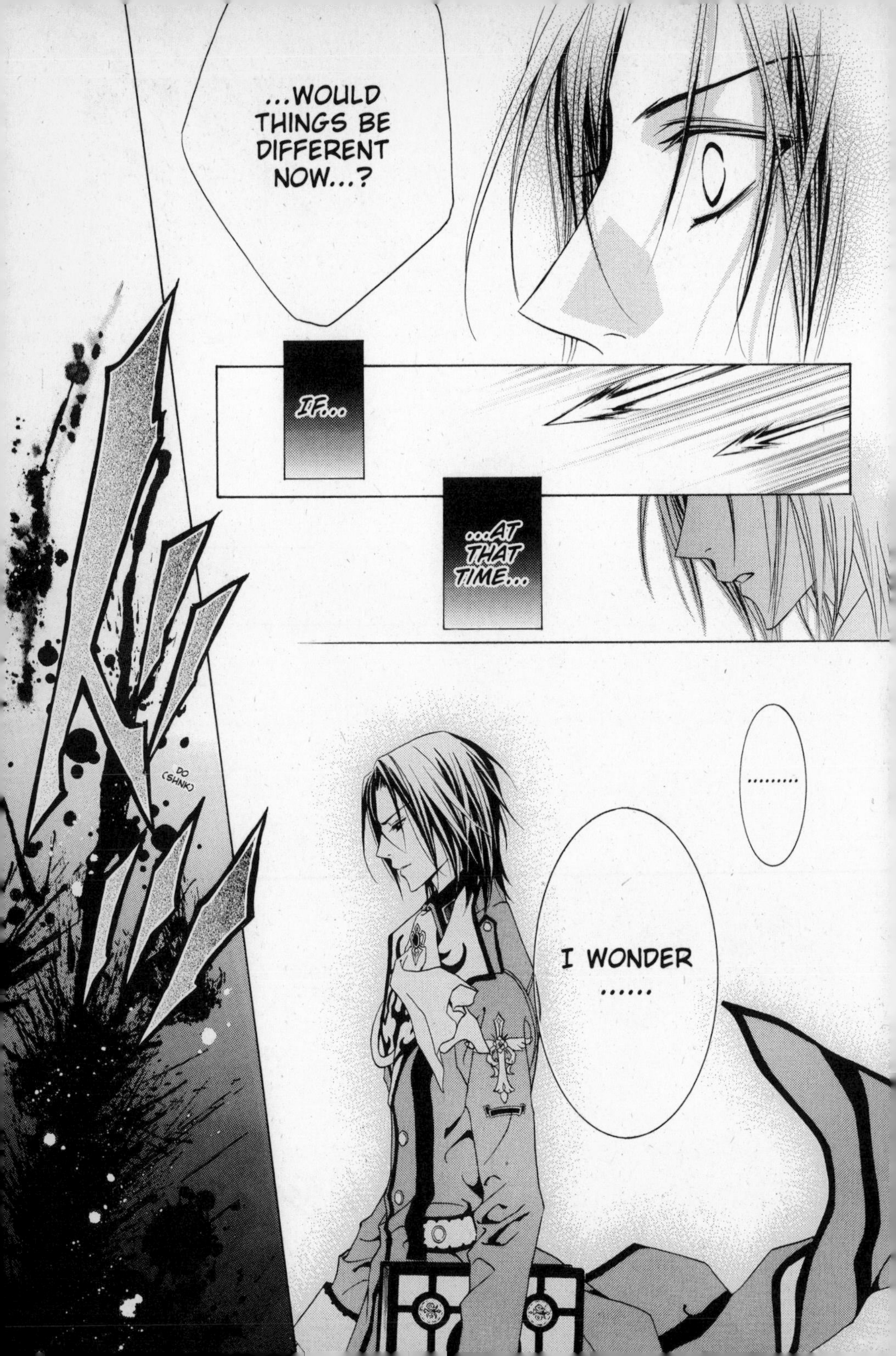
...WOULD THINGS BE DIFFERENT NOW...?
IF...
...AT THAT TIME...
....
I WONDER ......
DO (SHNK)

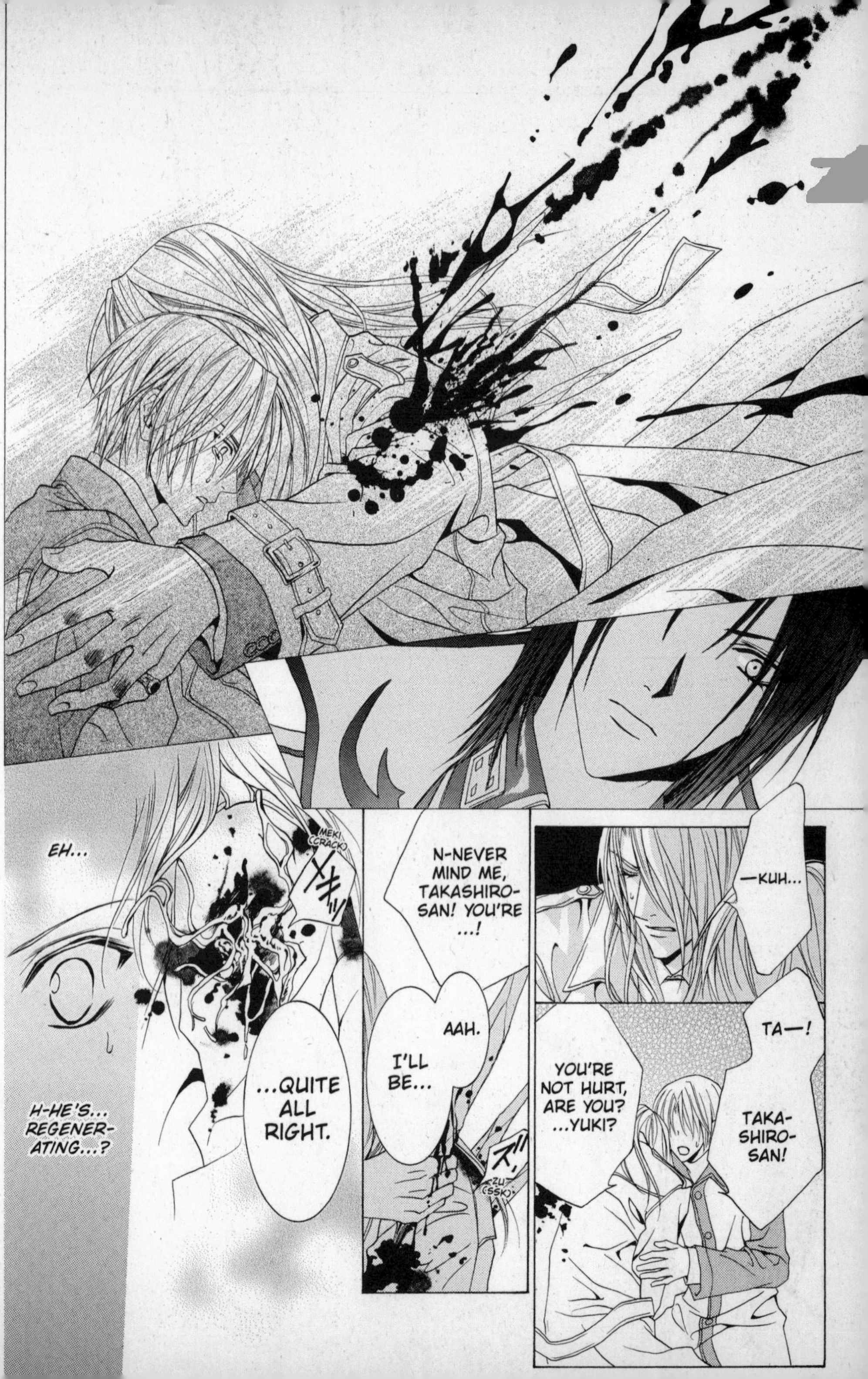
—KUH...
TA—!
TAKA-SHIRO-SAN!
YOU'RE NOT HURT, ARE YOU? ...YUKI?
N-NEVER MIND ME, TAKASHIRO-SAN! YOU'RE ...!
AAH.
I'LL BE...
ZU (SSK)
MEKI (CRACK)
EH...
...QUITE ALL RIGHT.
H-HE'S... REGENER-ATING...?

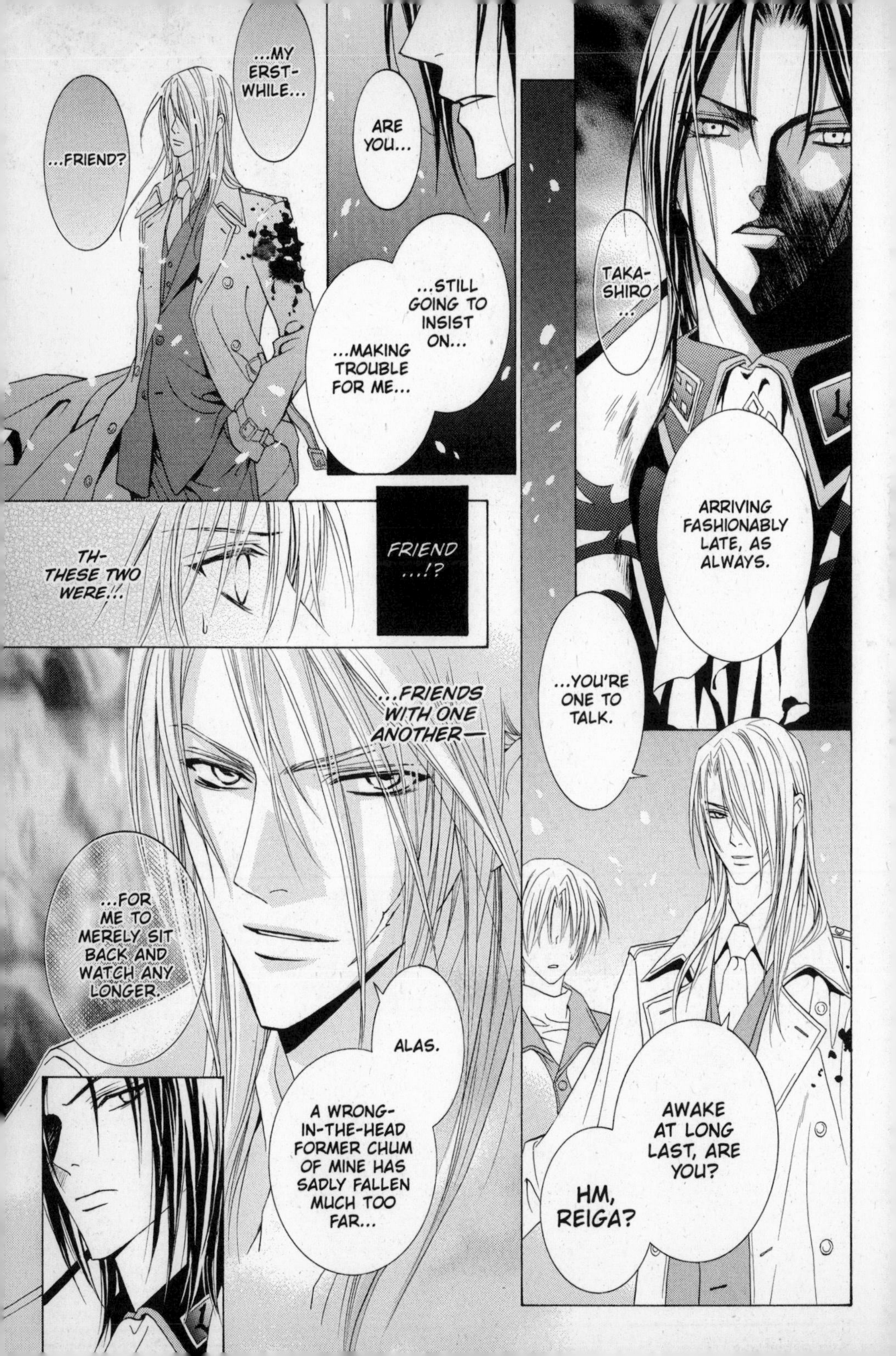

TAKA-SHIRO...
ARRIVING FASHIONABLY LATE, AS ALWAYS.
...YOU'RE ONE TO TALK.
AWAKE AT LONG LAST, ARE YOU?
HM, REIGA?
ARE YOU...
...STILL GOING TO INSIST ON...
...MAKING TROUBLE FOR ME...
...MY ERST-WHILE...
...FRIEND?
FRIEND ...!?
TH-THESE TWO WERE...
...FRIENDS WITH ONE ANOTHER—
ALAS.
A WRONG-IN-THE-HEAD FORMER CHUM OF MINE HAS SADLY FALLEN MUCH TOO FAR...
...FOR ME TO MERELY SIT BACK AND WATCH ANY LONGER.

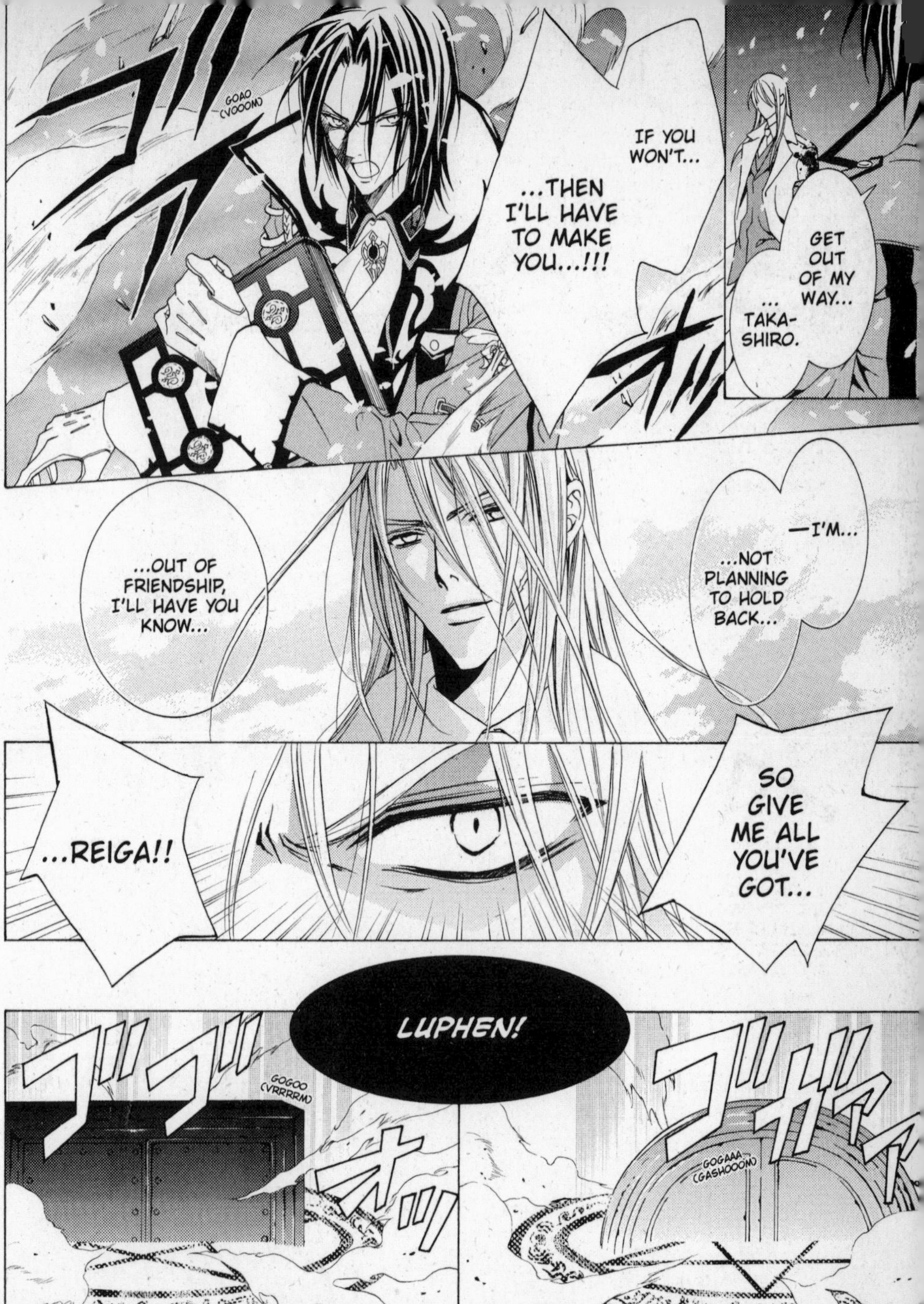
GET OUT OF MY WAY...
...TAKA-SHIRO.
IF YOU WON'T...
...THEN I'LL HAVE TO MAKE YOU...!!!
GOAO (VOOOM)
—I'M...
...NOT PLANNING TO HOLD BACK...
...OUT OF FRIENDSHIP, I'LL HAVE YOU KNOW...
SO GIVE ME ALL YOU'VE GOT...
...REIGA!!
LUPHEN!
GOGAAA (GASHOOOM)
GOGOO (VRRRRM)

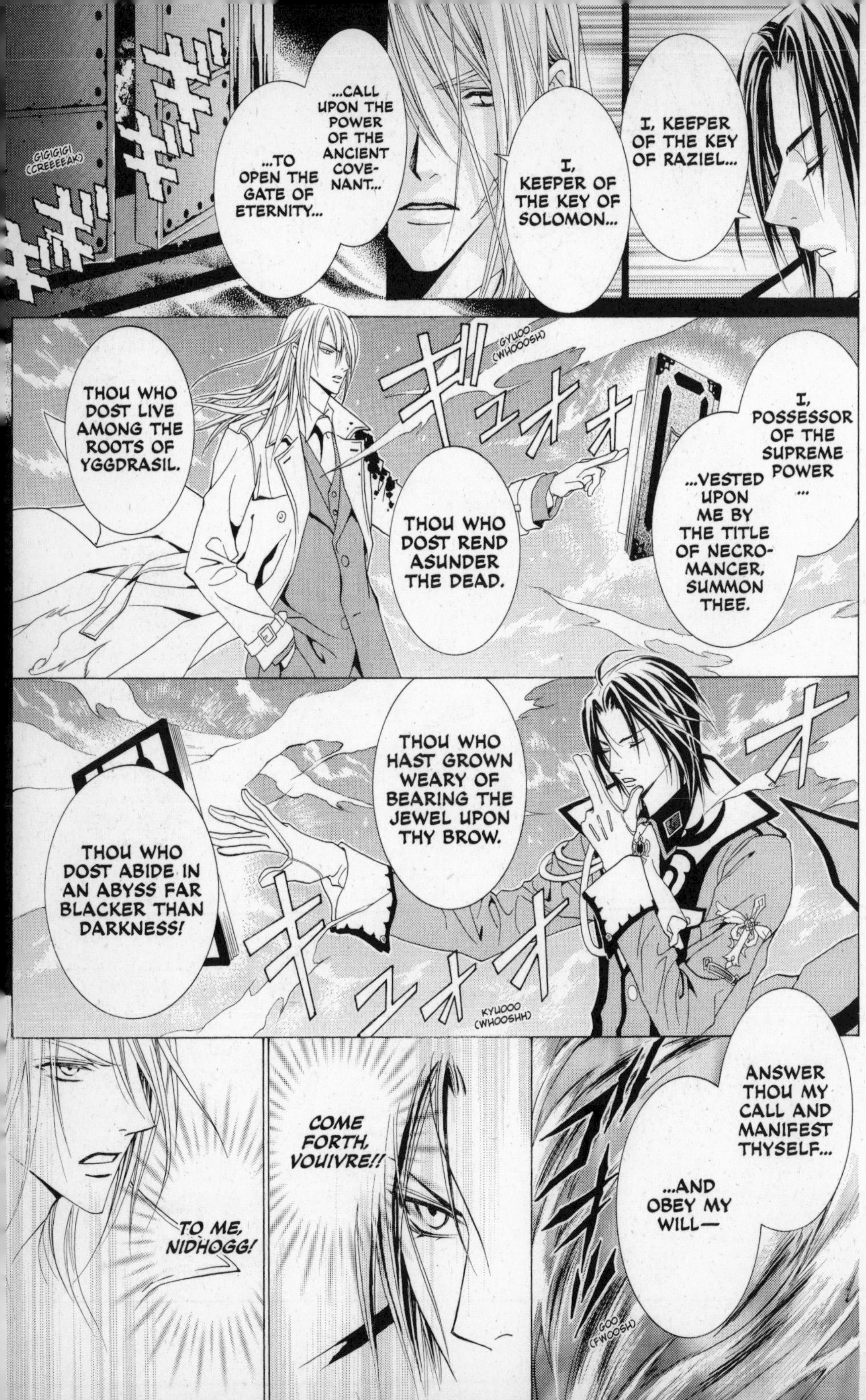
I, KEEPER OF THE KEY OF RAZIEL...
I, KEEPER OF THE KEY OF SOLOMON...
...CALL UPON THE POWER OF THE ANCIENT COVENANT...
...TO OPEN THE GATE OF ETERNITY...
GIGIGIGI (CREEEEAK)
I, POSSESSOR OF THE SUPREME POWER...
...VESTED UPON ME BY THE TITLE OF NECROMANCER, SUMMON THEE.
GYUOO (WHOOOSH)
THOU WHO DOST REND ASUNDER THE DEAD.
THOU WHO DOST LIVE AMONG THE ROOTS OF YGGDRASIL.
THOU WHO HAST GROWN WEARY OF BEARING THE JEWEL UPON THY BROW.
THOU WHO DOST ABIDE IN AN ABYSS FAR BLACKER THAN DARKNESS!
KYUOOO (WHOOSHH)
ANSWER THOU MY CALL AND MANIFEST THYSELF...
...AND OBEY MY WILL—
GOO (FWOOSH)
COME FORTH, VOUIVRE!!
TO ME, NIDHOGG!

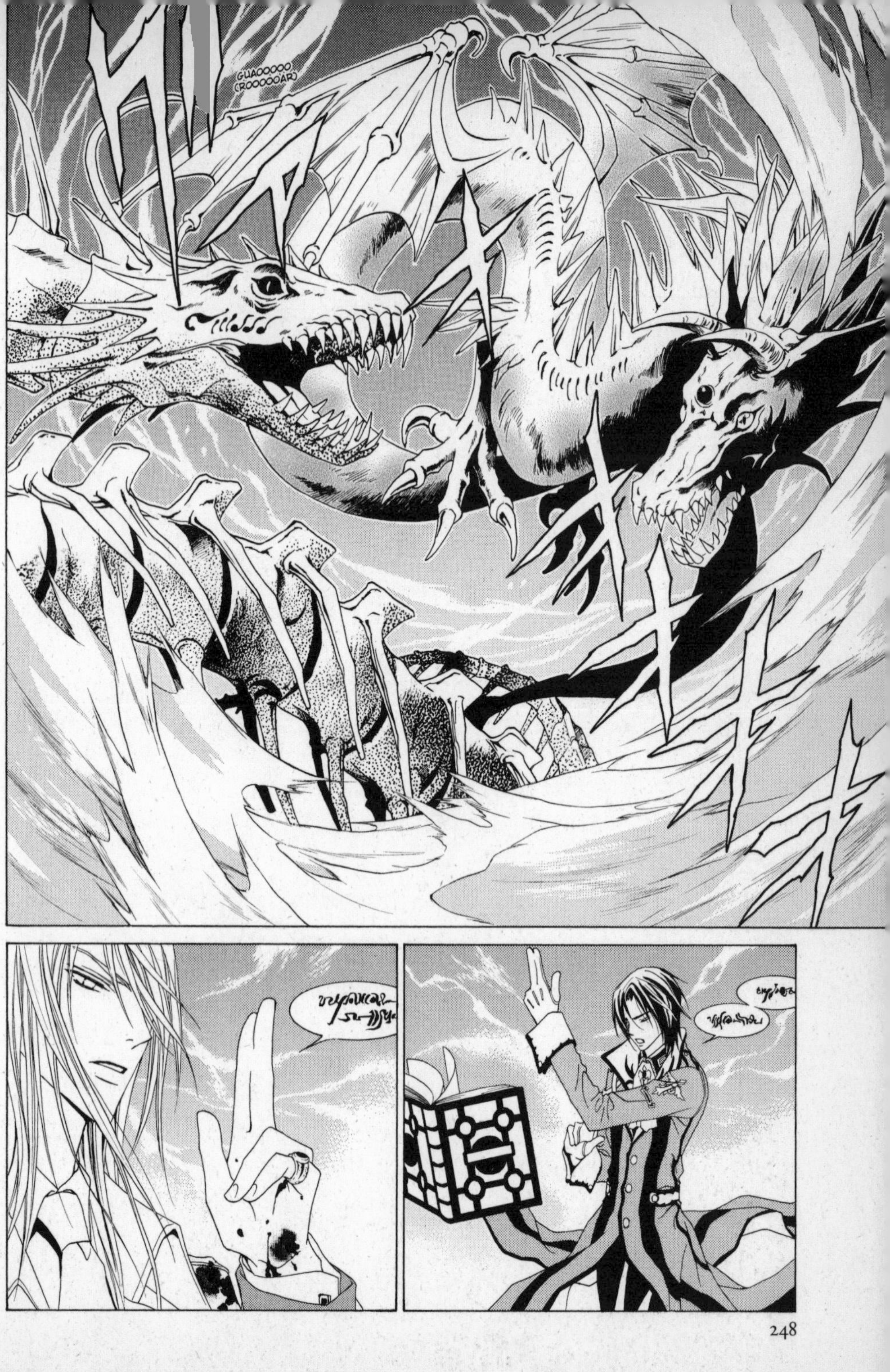
GUAOOOOO
(ROOOOOAR)

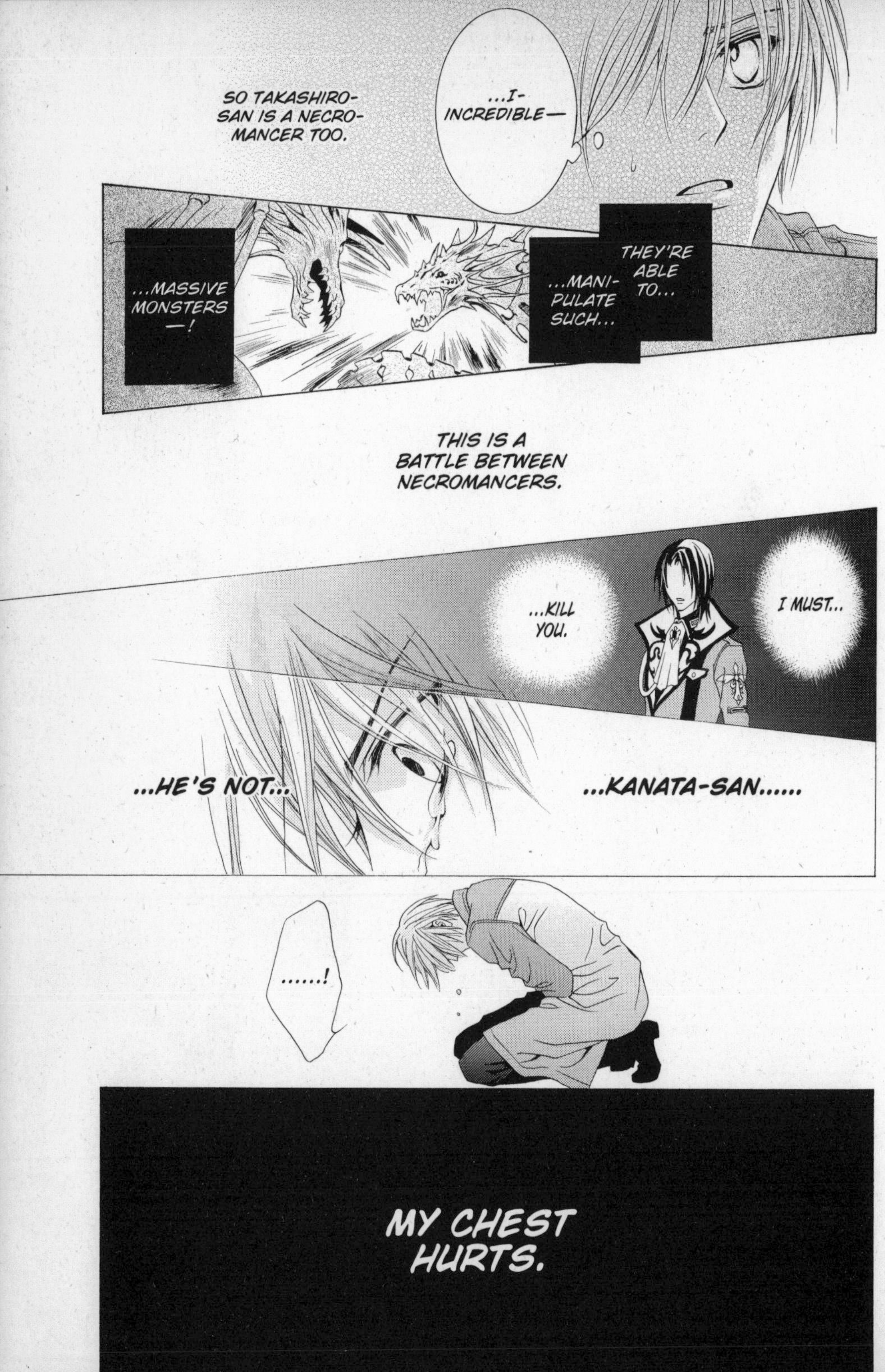
...I- INCREDIBLE—
SO TAKASHIRO-SAN IS A NECROMANCER TOO.
THEY'RE ABLE TO...
...MANIPULATE SUCH...
...MASSIVE MONSTERS—!
THIS IS A BATTLE BETWEEN NECROMANCERS.
I MUST...
...KILL YOU.
...KANATA-SAN......
...HE'S NOT...
......!
MY CHEST HURTS.

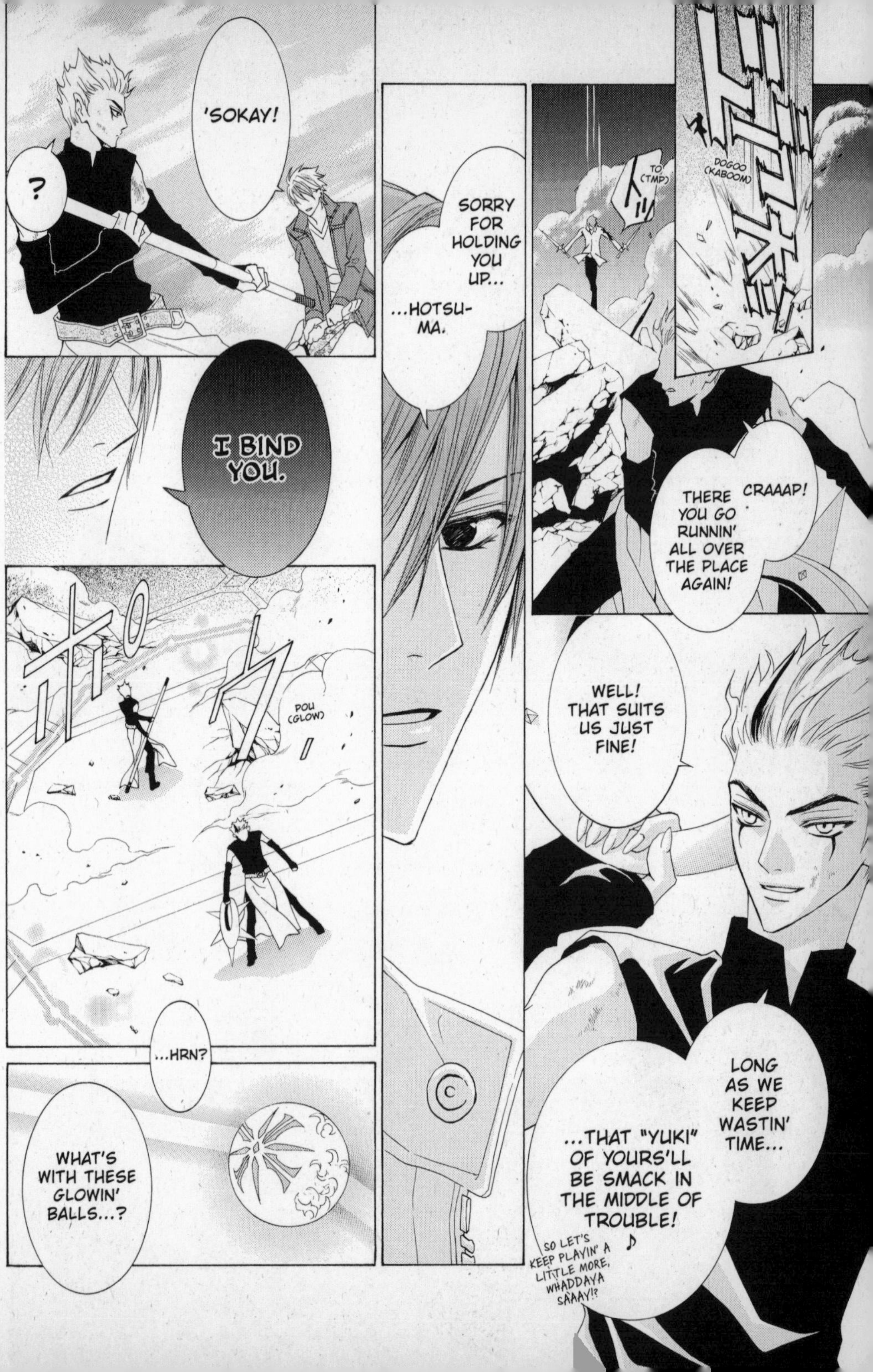
DOGOO (KABOOM)
TO (TMP)
CRAAAP!
THERE YOU GO RUNNIN' ALL OVER THE PLACE AGAIN!
WELL! THAT SUITS US JUST FINE!
LONG AS WE KEEP WASTIN' TIME...
...THAT "YUKI" OF YOURS'LL BE SMACK IN THE MIDDLE OF TROUBLE!
SO LET'S KEEP PLAYIN' A LITTLE MORE, WHADDAYA SAAAY!? ♪
SORRY FOR HOLDING YOU UP...
...HOTSU-MA.
'SOKAY!
?
I BIND YOU.
POU (GLOW)
...HRN?
WHAT'S WITH THESE GLOWIN' BALLS...?

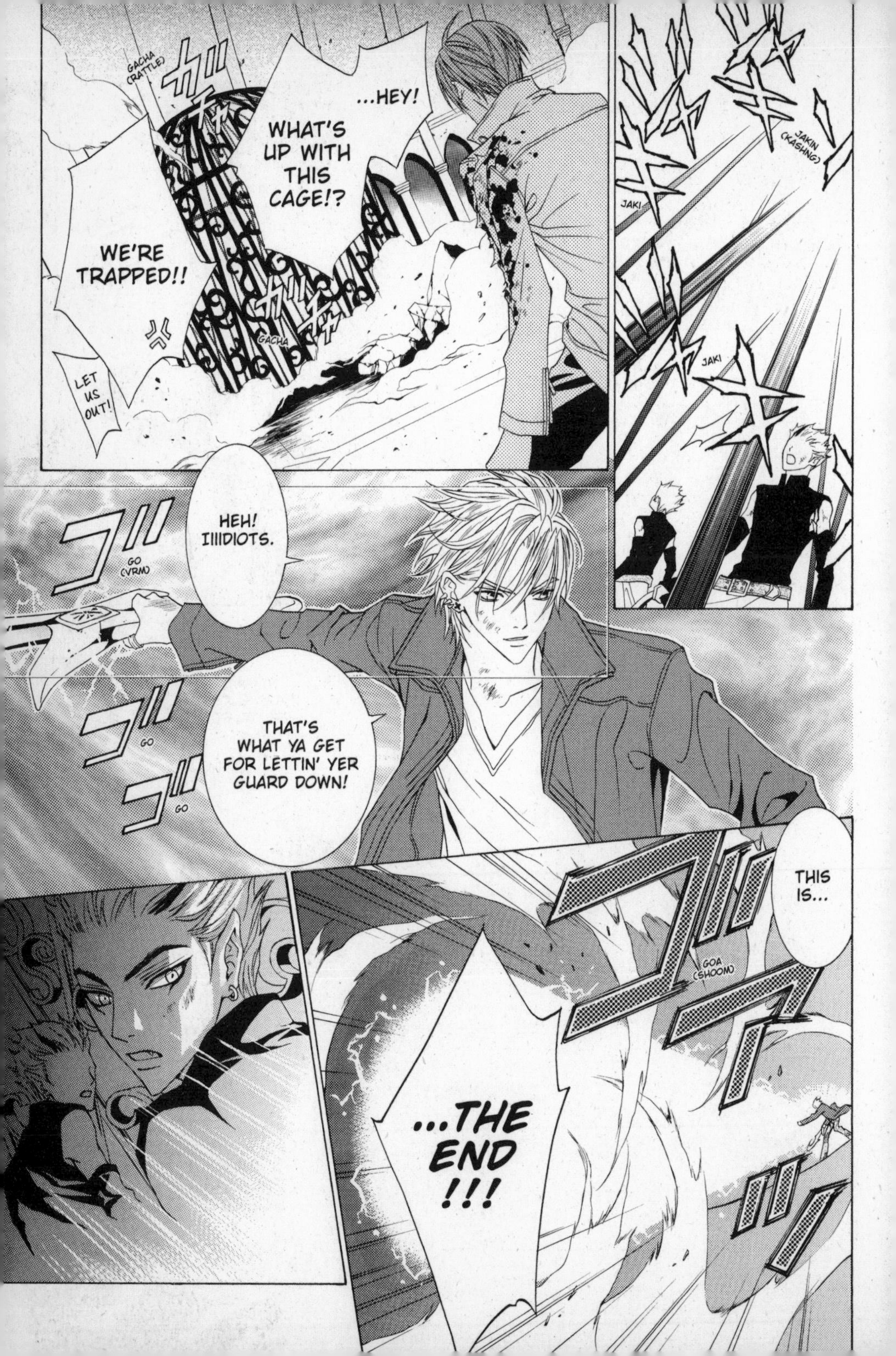
JAKIN (KASHNG)
JAKI
JAKI
...HEY!
WHAT'S UP WITH THIS CAGE!?
GACHA (RATTLE)
WE'RE TRAPPED!!
GACHA
LET US OUT!
HEH! IIIIDIOTS.
GO (VRM)
THAT'S WHAT YA GET FOR LETTIN' YER GUARD DOWN!
GO
GO
THIS IS...
GOA (SHOOM)
...THE END!!!

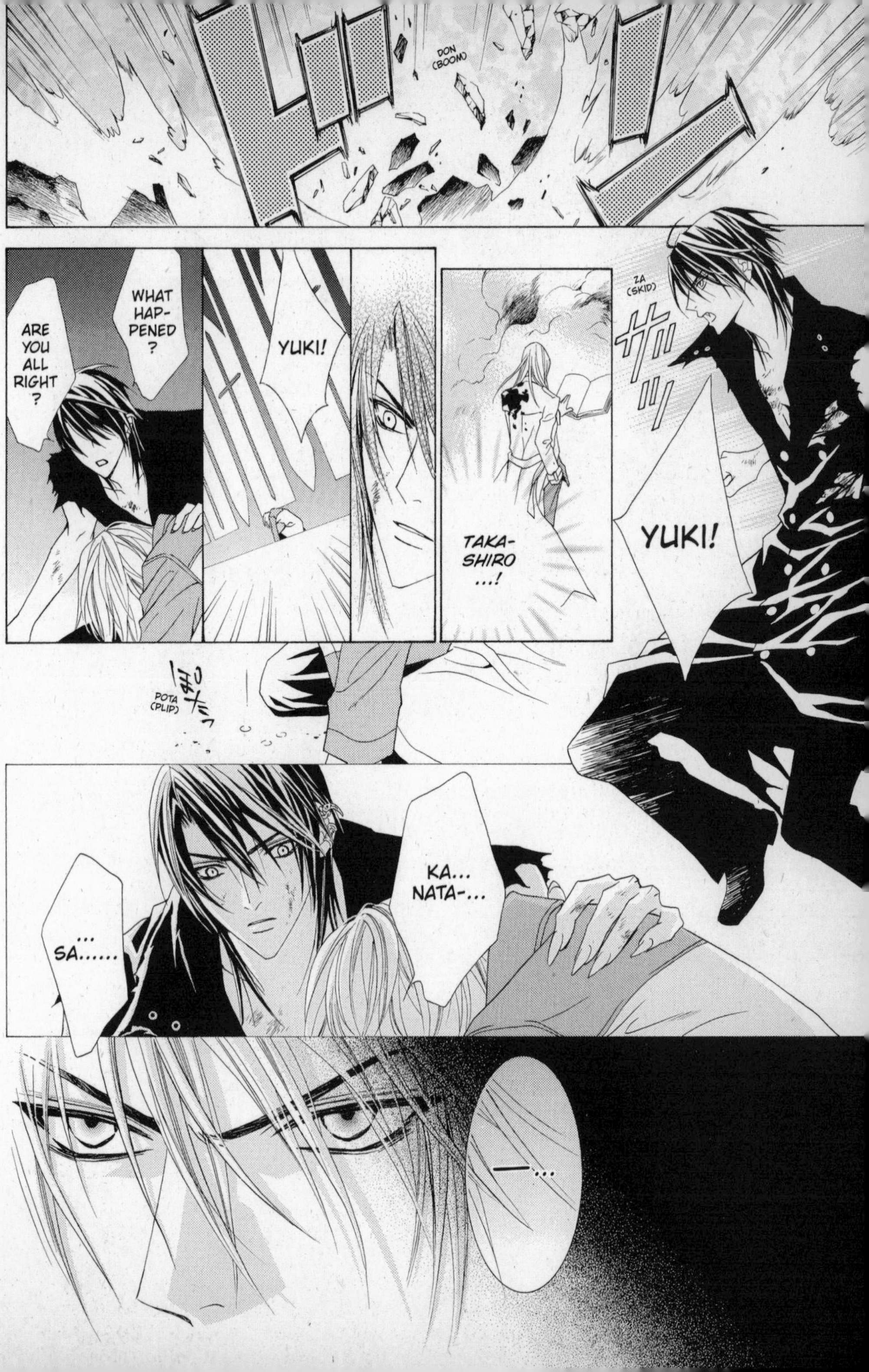
DON (BOOM)
ZA (SKID)
YUKI!
TAKA-SHIRO ...!
YUKI!
WHAT HAP-PENED ?
ARE YOU ALL RIGHT ?
POTA (PLIP)
KA... NATA-...
... SA......
—...

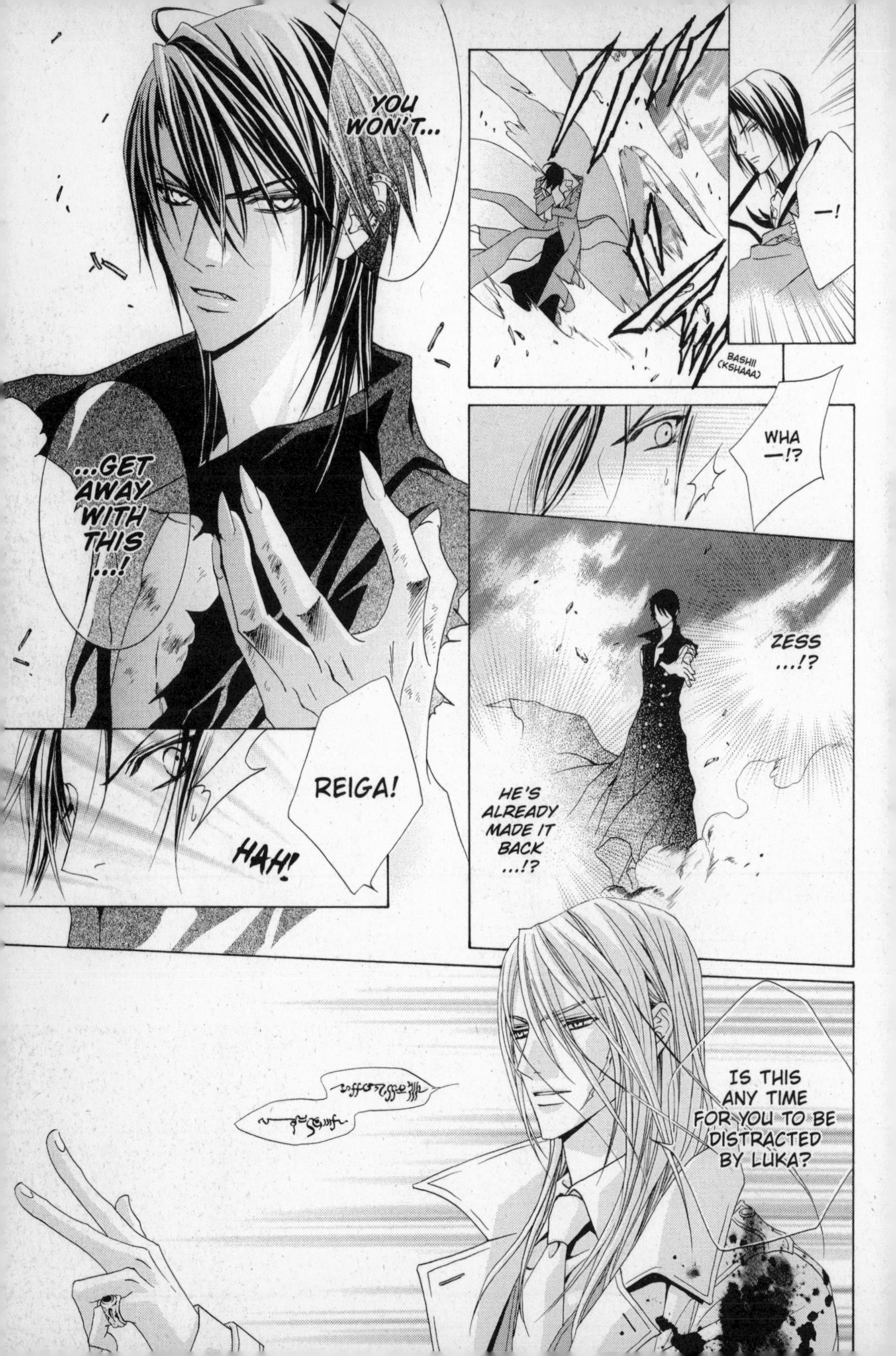
—!
BASHII (KSHAAA)
WHA—!?
ZESS ...!?
HE'S ALREADY MADE IT BACK ...!?
YOU WON'T...
...GET AWAY WITH THIS ...!
REIGA!
HAH!
IS THIS ANY TIME FOR YOU TO BE DISTRACTED BY LUKA?

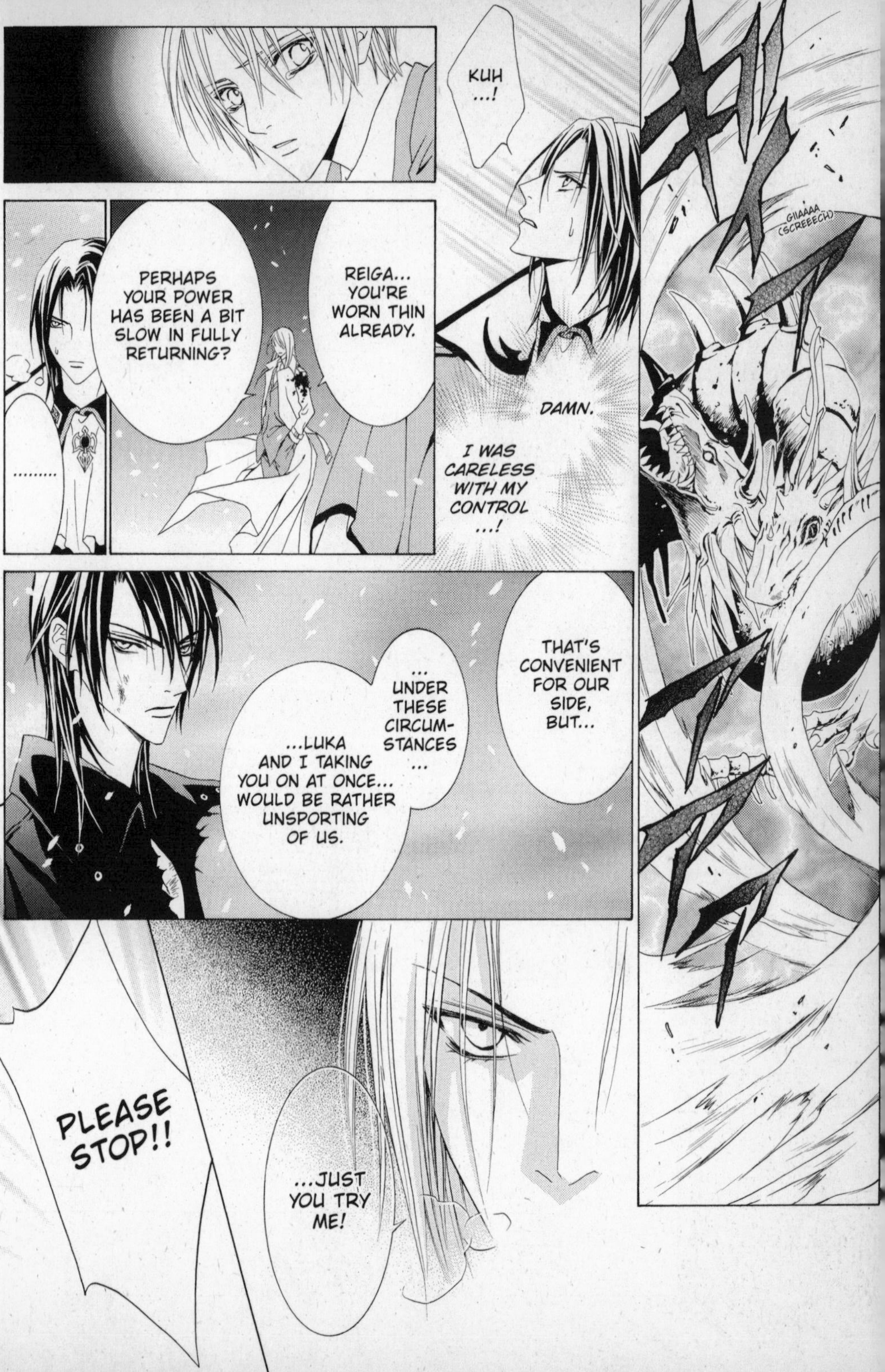
GIIAAAA (SCREEECH)
KUH ...!
DAMN.
I WAS CARELESS WITH MY CONTROL ...!
REIGA... YOU'RE WORN THIN ALREADY.
PERHAPS YOUR POWER HAS BEEN A BIT SLOW IN FULLY RETURNING?
....
THAT'S CONVENIENT FOR OUR SIDE, BUT...
... UNDER THESE CIRCUM-STANCES ...
...LUKA AND I TAKING YOU ON AT ONCE... WOULD BE RATHER UNSPORTING OF US.
...JUST YOU TRY ME!
PLEASE STOP!!

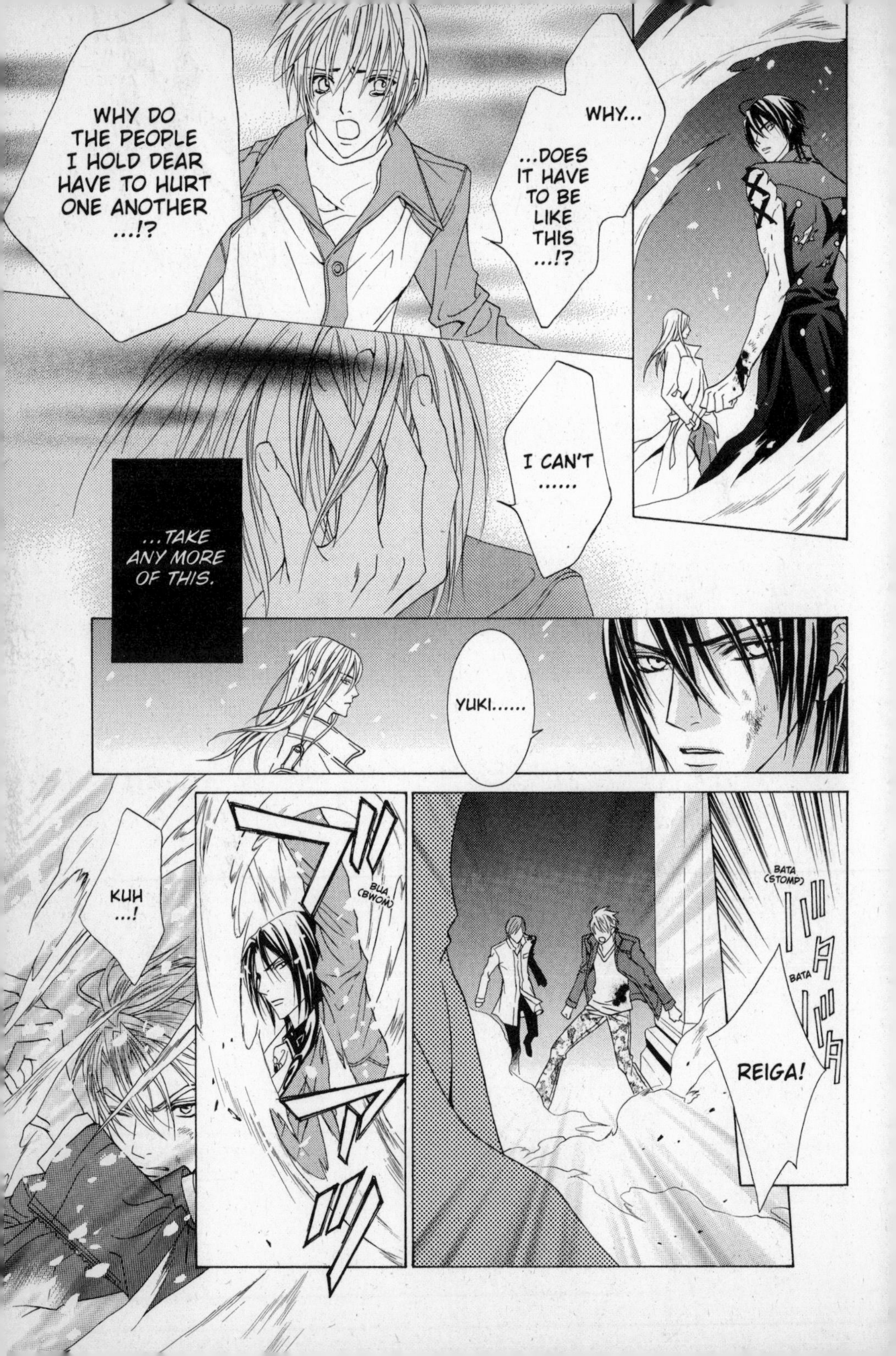
WHY...
...DOES IT HAVE TO BE LIKE THIS ...!?
WHY DO THE PEOPLE I HOLD DEAR HAVE TO HURT ONE ANOTHER ...!?
I CAN'T ......
...TAKE ANY MORE OF THIS.
YUKI......
BATA (STOMP)
BATA
REIGA!
BUA (BWOM)
KUH ...!

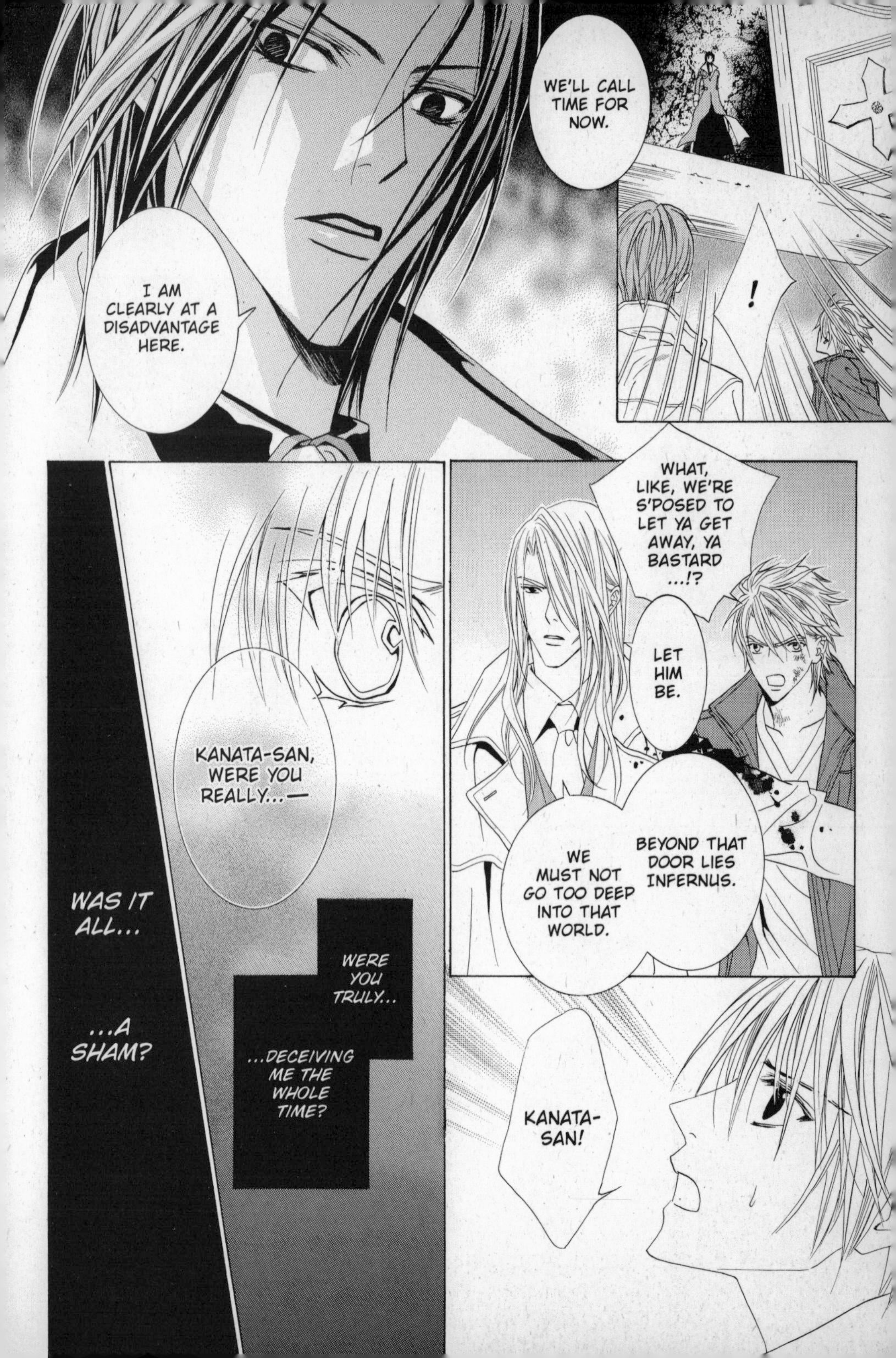
!
WE'LL CALL TIME FOR NOW.
I AM CLEARLY AT A DISADVANTAGE HERE.
WHAT, LIKE, WE'RE S'POSED TO LET YA GET AWAY, YA BASTARD ...!?
LET HIM BE.
BEYOND THAT DOOR LIES INFERNUS.
WE MUST NOT GO TOO DEEP INTO THAT WORLD.
KANATA-SAN!
KANATA-SAN, WERE YOU REALLY...—
WERE YOU TRULY...
...DECEIVING ME THE WHOLE TIME?
WAS IT ALL...
...A SHAM?

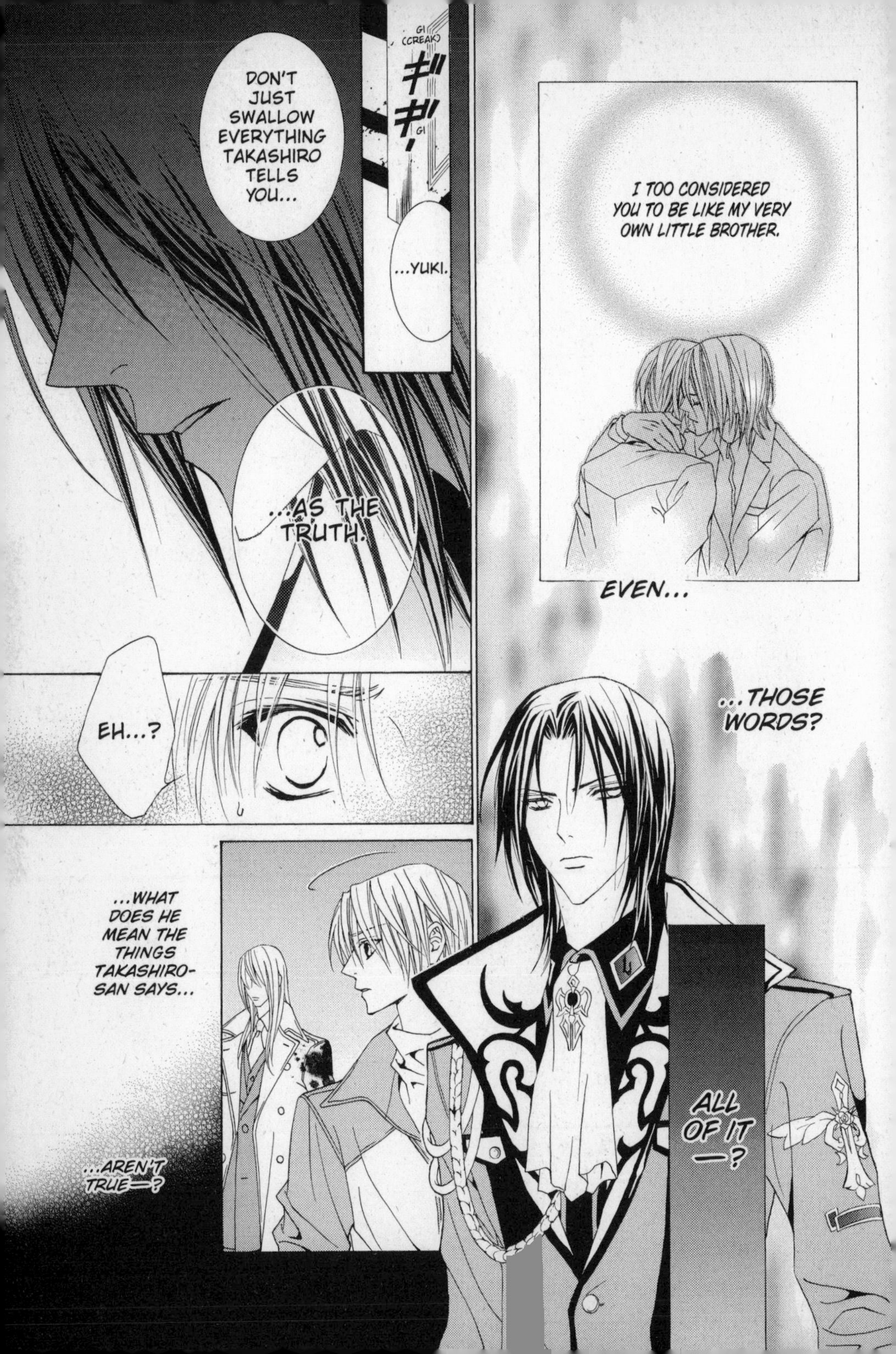
GI (CREAK)
GI
...YUKI.
DON'T JUST SWALLOW EVERYTHING TAKASHIRO TELLS YOU...
...AS THE TRUTH.
EH...?
...WHAT DOES HE MEAN THE THINGS TAKASHIRO-SAN SAYS...
...AREN'T TRUE—?
I TOO CONSIDERED YOU TO BE LIKE MY VERY OWN LITTLE BROTHER.
EVEN...
...THOSE WORDS?
ALL OF IT—?

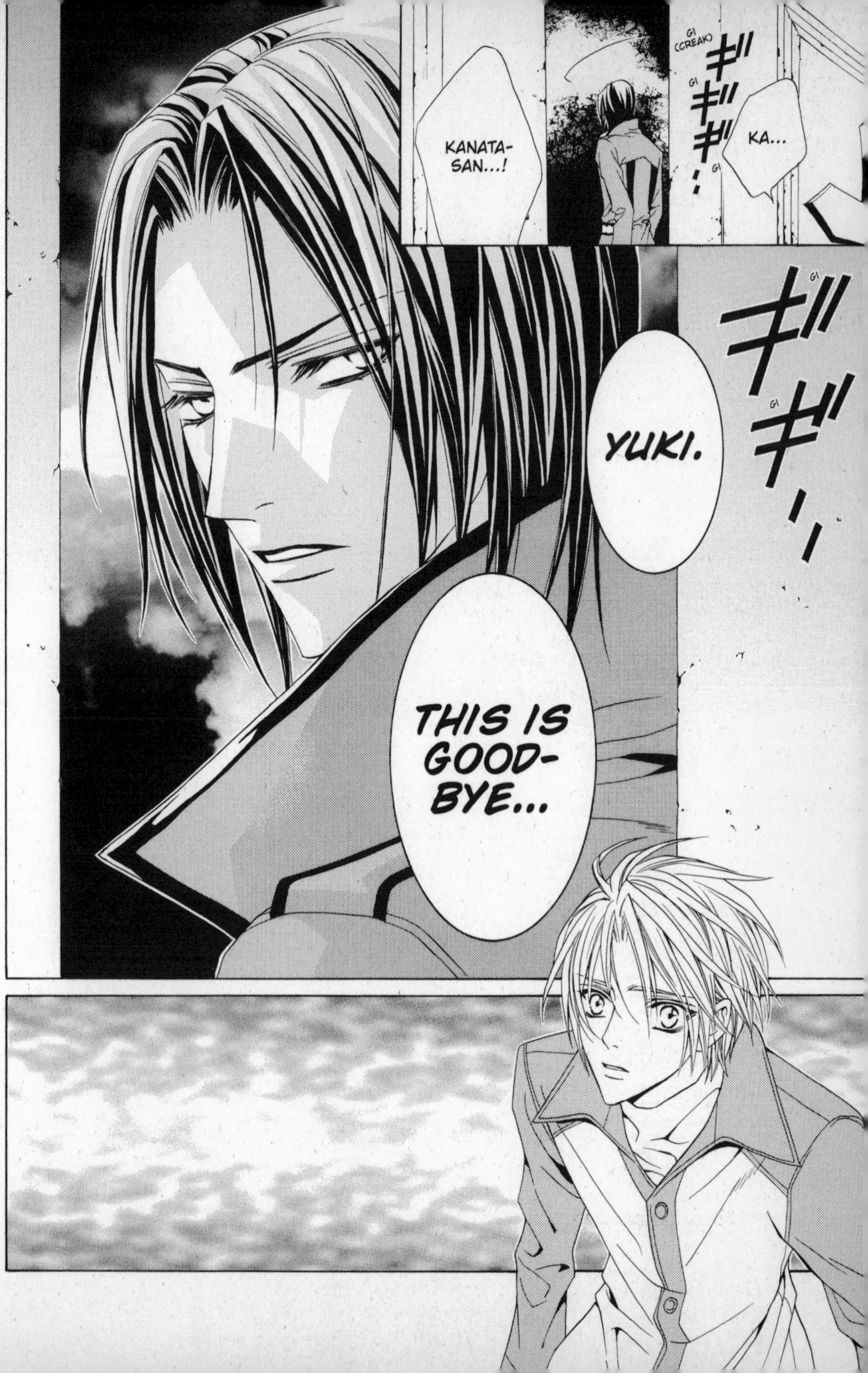

GI (CREAK)
ギ
GI
ギ
GI
ギ
KA...
KANATA-SAN...!
GI
ギ
GI
ギ
YUKI.
THIS IS GOOD-BYE...

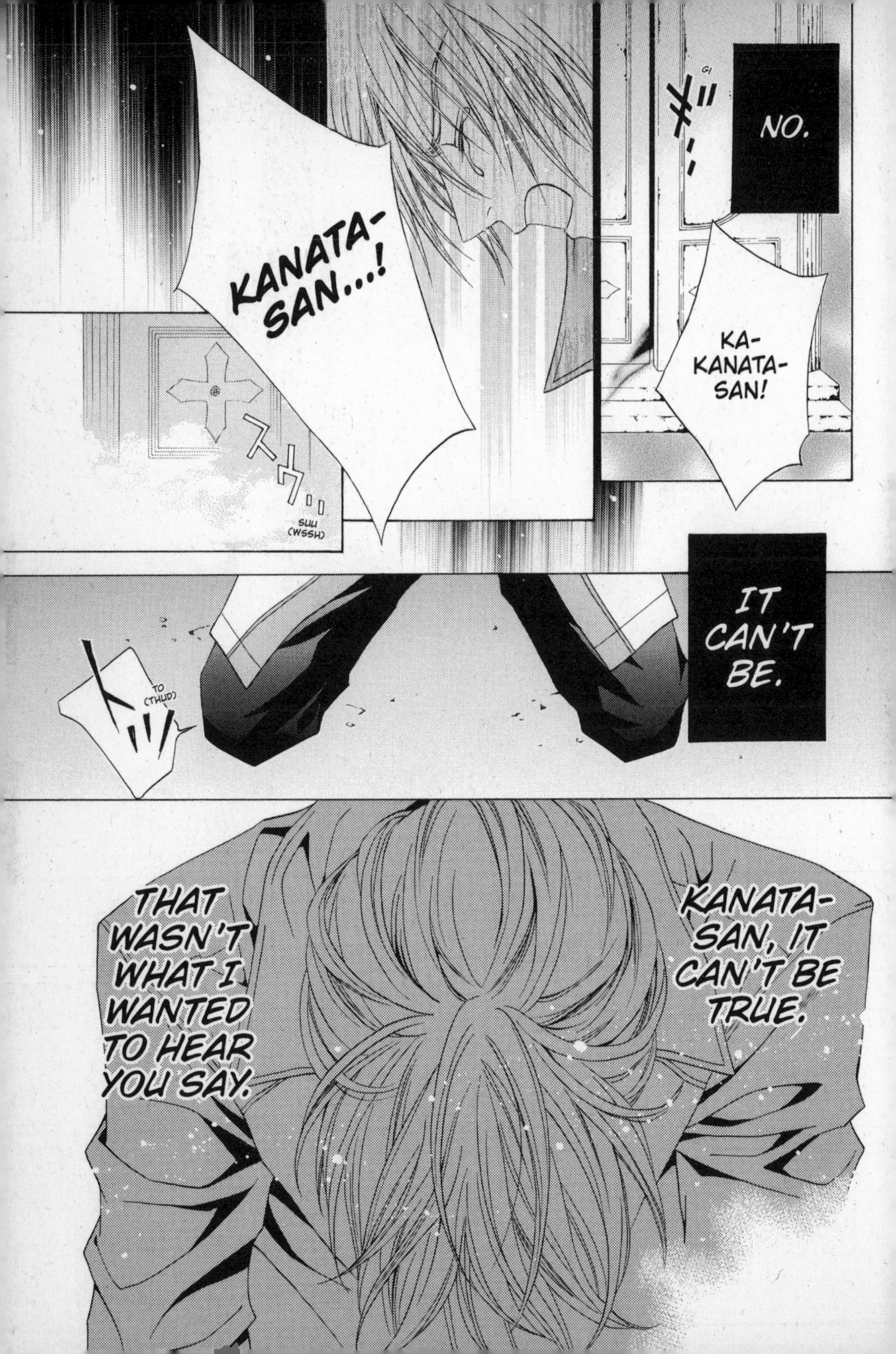
GI
NO.
KA-KANATA-SAN!
KANATA-SAN...!
SUU (WSSH)
IT CAN'T BE.
TO (THUD)
KANATA-SAN, IT CAN'T BE TRUE.
THAT WASN'T WHAT I WANTED TO HEAR YOU SAY.

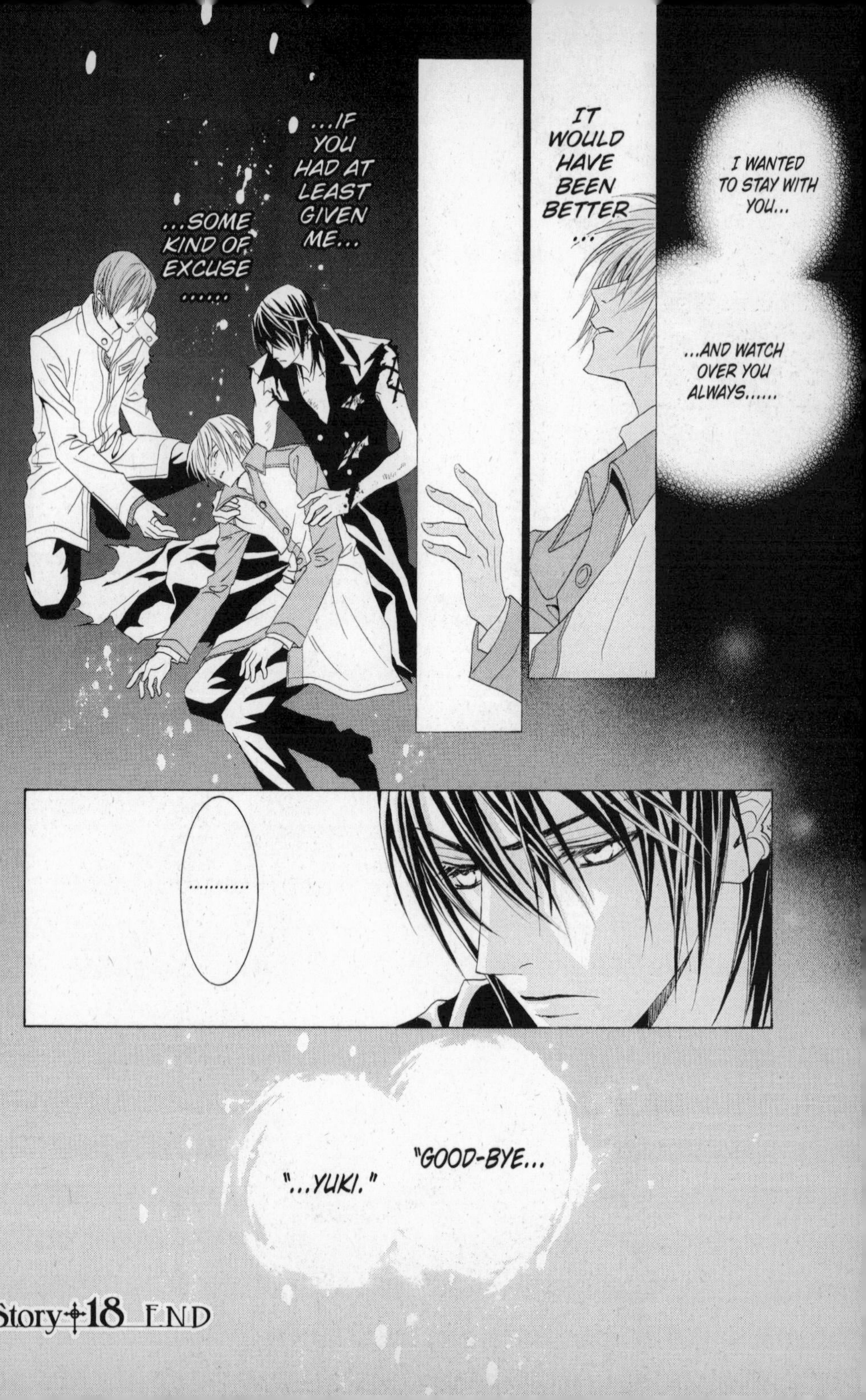
I WANTED TO STAY WITH YOU...
...AND WATCH OVER YOU ALWAYS......
IT WOULD HAVE BEEN BETTER...
...IF YOU HAD AT LEAST GIVEN ME...
...SOME KIND OF EXCUSE......
....
"GOOD-BYE...
"...YUKI."

Story 18 END

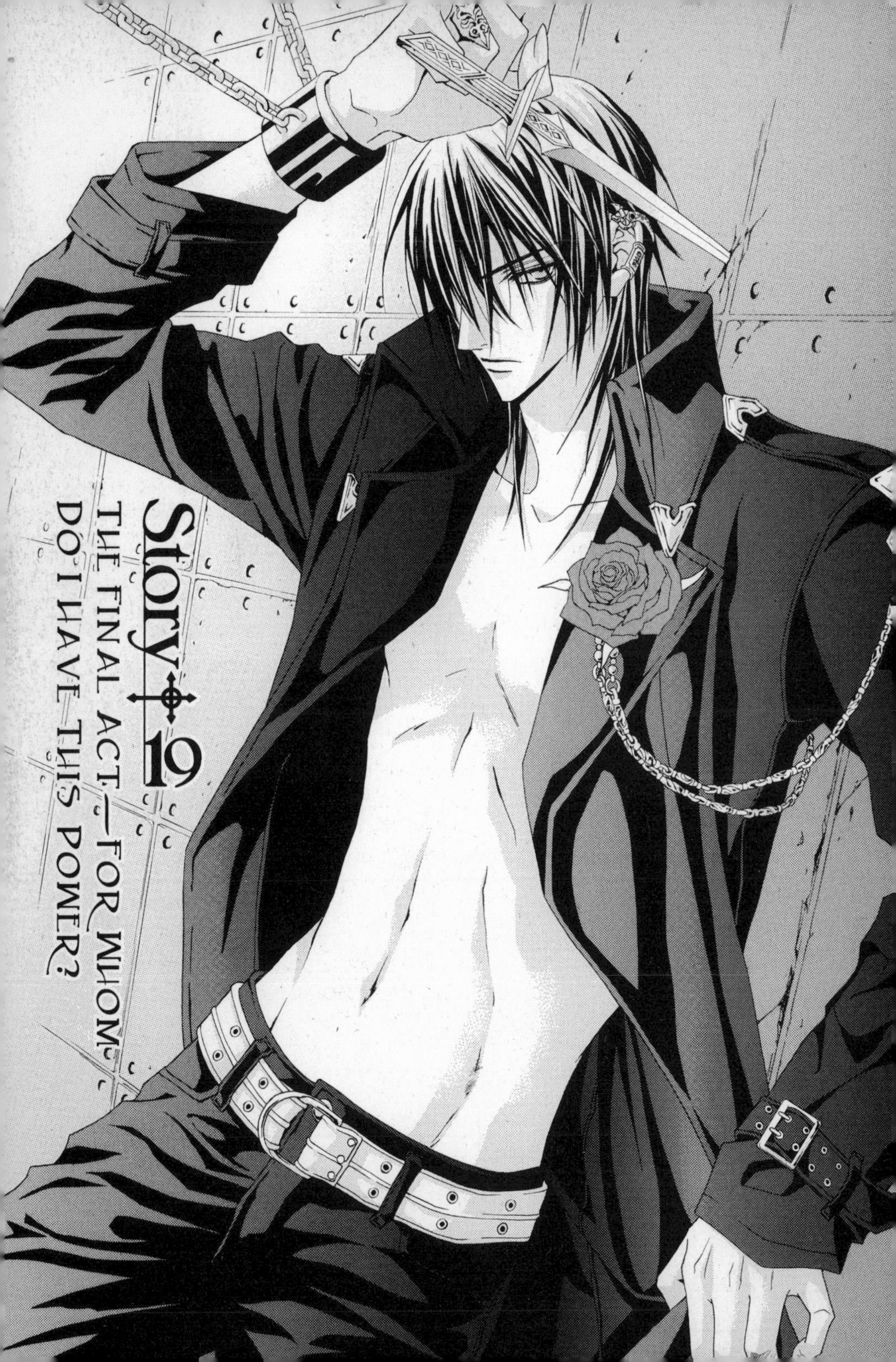
Story 19
The Final Act—For Whom
Do I Have This Power?

I WAS DREAMING.
IN THE DREAM, I WAS IN COLLEGE...
...AND I WAS...
...WALKING AROUND CAMPUS ALONGSIDE KANATA-SAN, WHO WAS A GRAD STUDENT.
IT WAS A SAD DREAM.
AND THEN...
...THE TWO OF US WENT TO VISIT THE MORNING SUN HOUSE...
WE PLAYED WITH THE CHILDREN...
...AND LAUGHED...
WE TALKED THE NIGHT AWAY...
...ABOUT OUR DREAMS FOR THE FUTURE AND SO ON—
JUST...
...SILLY EVERYDAY SCENES LIKE THAT...

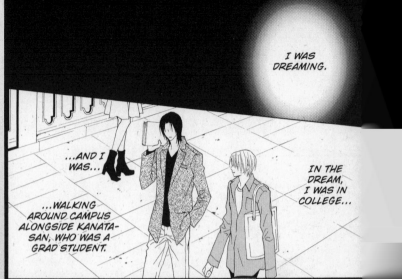

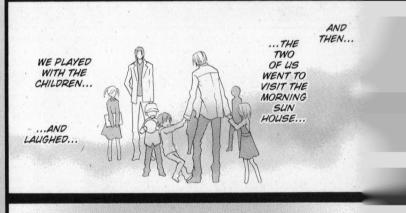

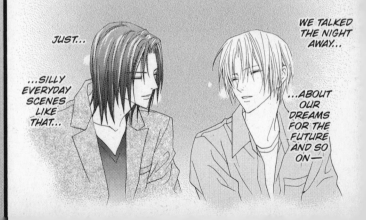

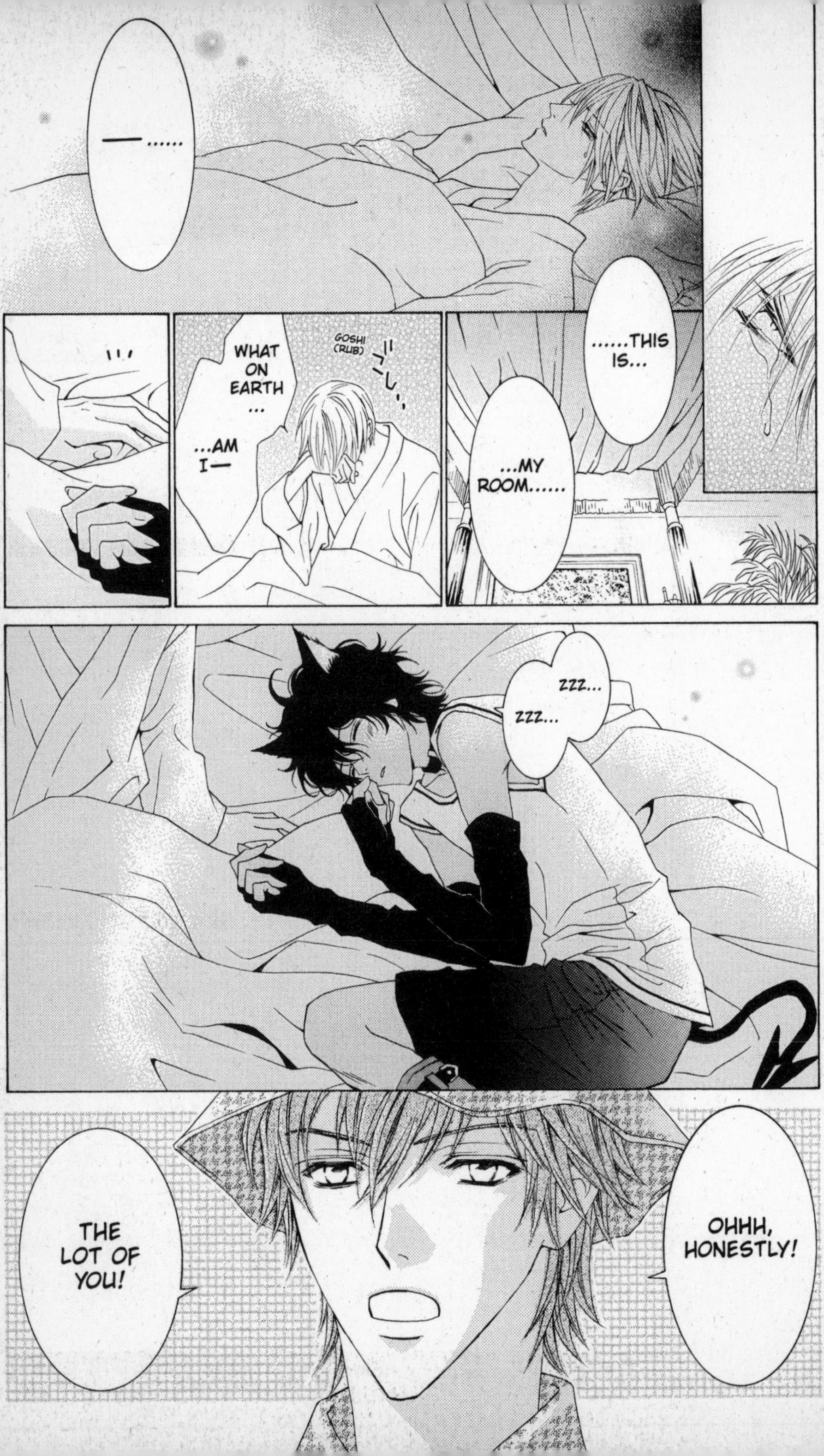
—......
......THIS IS...
...MY ROOM......
GOSHI (RUB)
WHAT ON EARTH ...
...AM I—
zzz... zzz...
OHHH, HONESTLY!
THE LOT OF YOU!

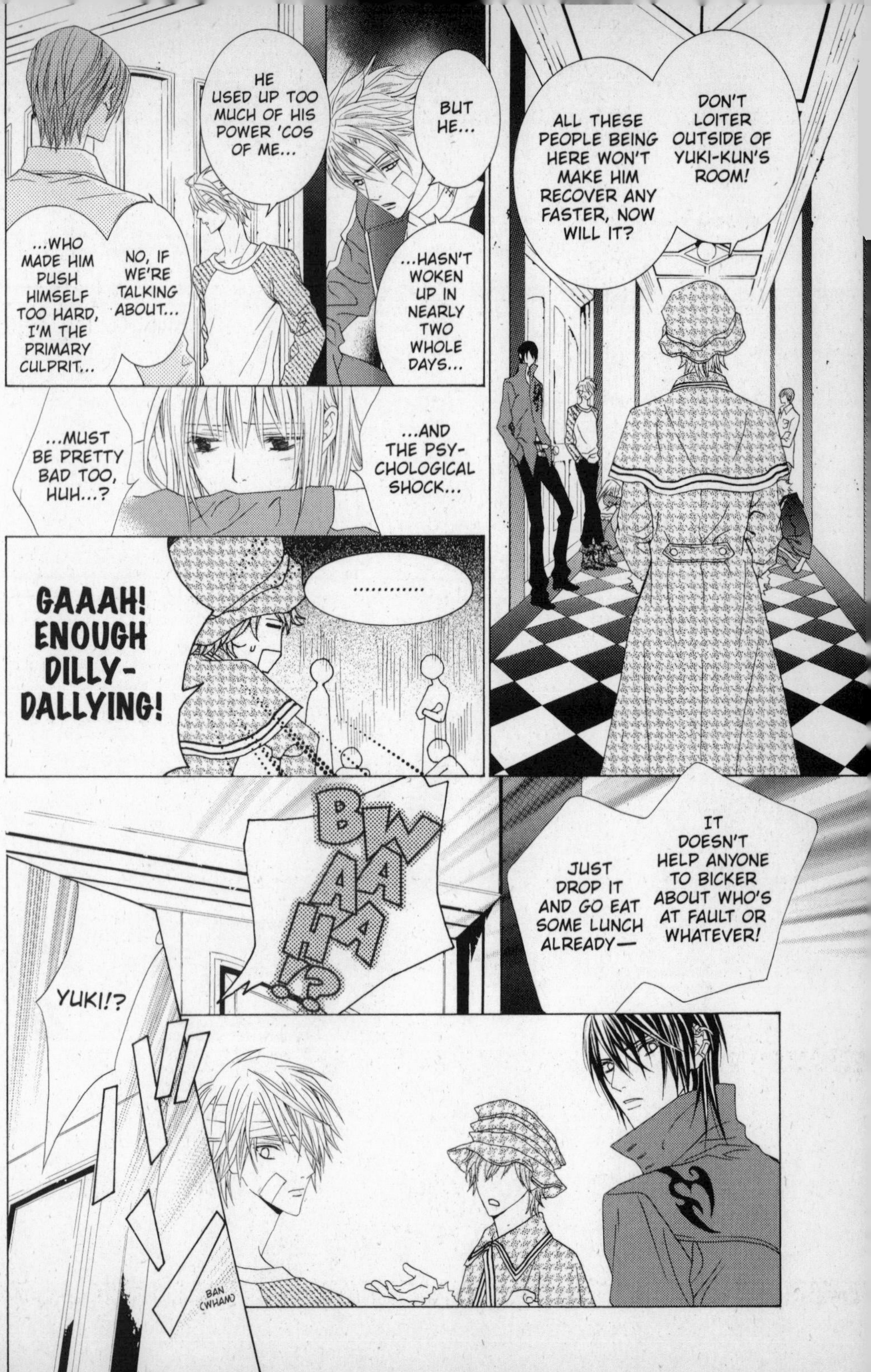
DON'T LOITER OUTSIDE OF YUKI-KUN'S ROOM!
ALL THESE PEOPLE BEING HERE WON'T MAKE HIM RECOVER ANY FASTER, NOW WILL IT?
HE USED UP TOO MUCH OF HIS POWER 'COS OF ME...
BUT HE...
...HASN'T WOKEN UP IN NEARLY TWO WHOLE DAYS...
NO, IF WE'RE TALKING ABOUT...
...WHO MADE HIM PUSH HIMSELF TOO HARD, I'M THE PRIMARY CULPRIT...
...AND THE PSY-CHOLOGICAL SHOCK...
...MUST BE PRETTY BAD TOO, HUH...?
....
GAAAH! ENOUGH DILLY-DALLYING!
IT DOESN'T HELP ANYONE TO BICKER ABOUT WHO'S AT FAULT OR WHATEVER!
JUST DROP IT AND GO EAT SOME LUNCH ALREADY—
BWAAAHA!?
YUKI!?
BAN (WHAM)

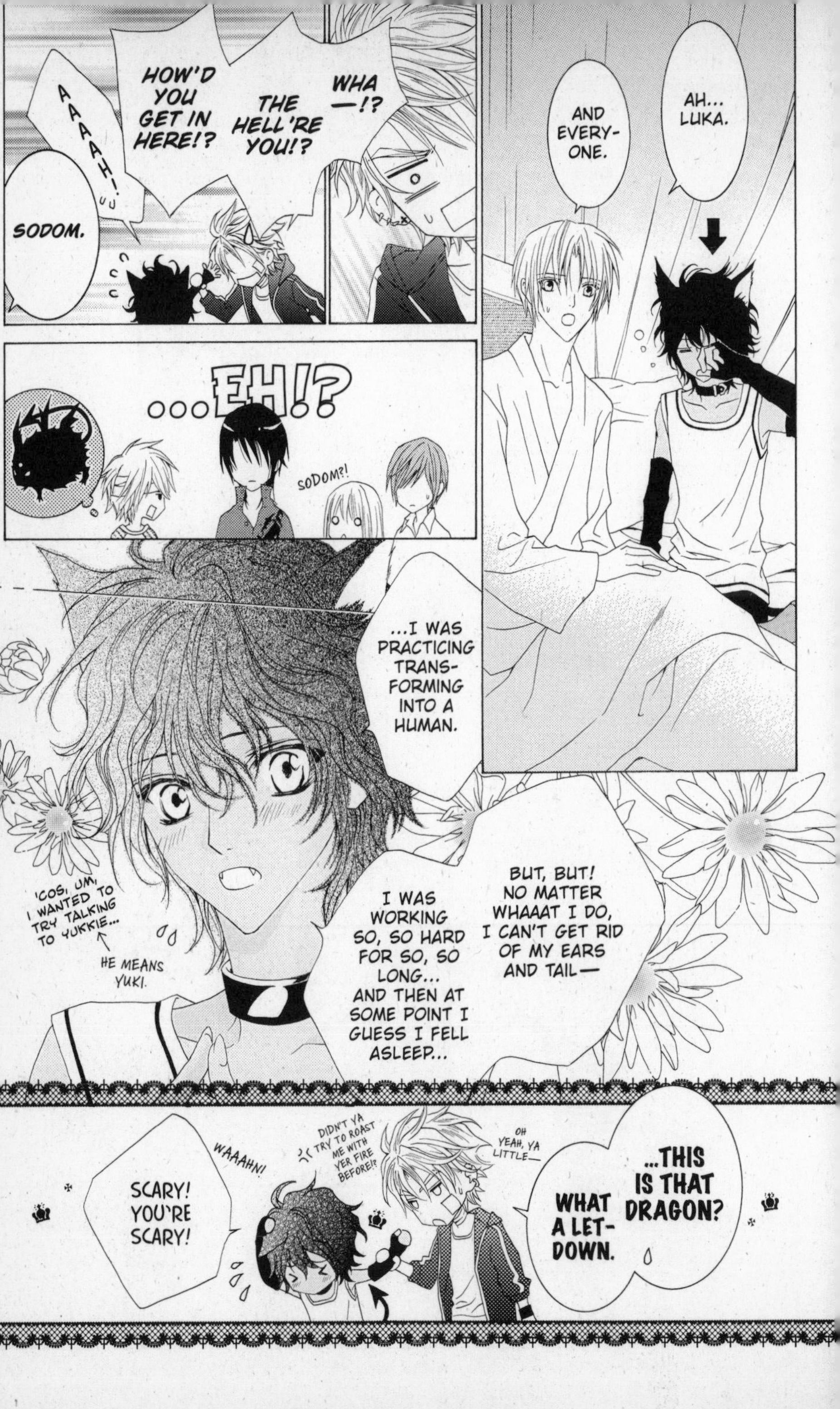
AH... LUKA.
AND EVERY-ONE.
WHA—!?
THE HELL'RE YOU!?
HOW'D YOU GET IN HERE!?
AAAAAH!
SODOM.
...EH!?
SODOM?!
...I WAS PRACTICING TRANS-FORMING INTO A HUMAN.
BUT, BUT! NO MATTER WHAAAT I DO, I CAN'T GET RID OF MY EARS AND TAIL—
I WAS WORKING SO, SO HARD FOR SO, SO LONG... AND THEN AT SOME POINT I GUESS I FELL ASLEEP...
'COS, UM, I WANTED TO TRY TALKING TO YUKKIE...
HE MEANS YUKI.
...THIS IS THAT DRAGON?
WHAT A LET-DOWN.
OH YEAH, YA LITTLE—
DIDN'T YA TRY TO ROAST ME WITH YER FIRE BEFORE!?
WAAAAHN!
SCARY! YOU'RE SCARY!

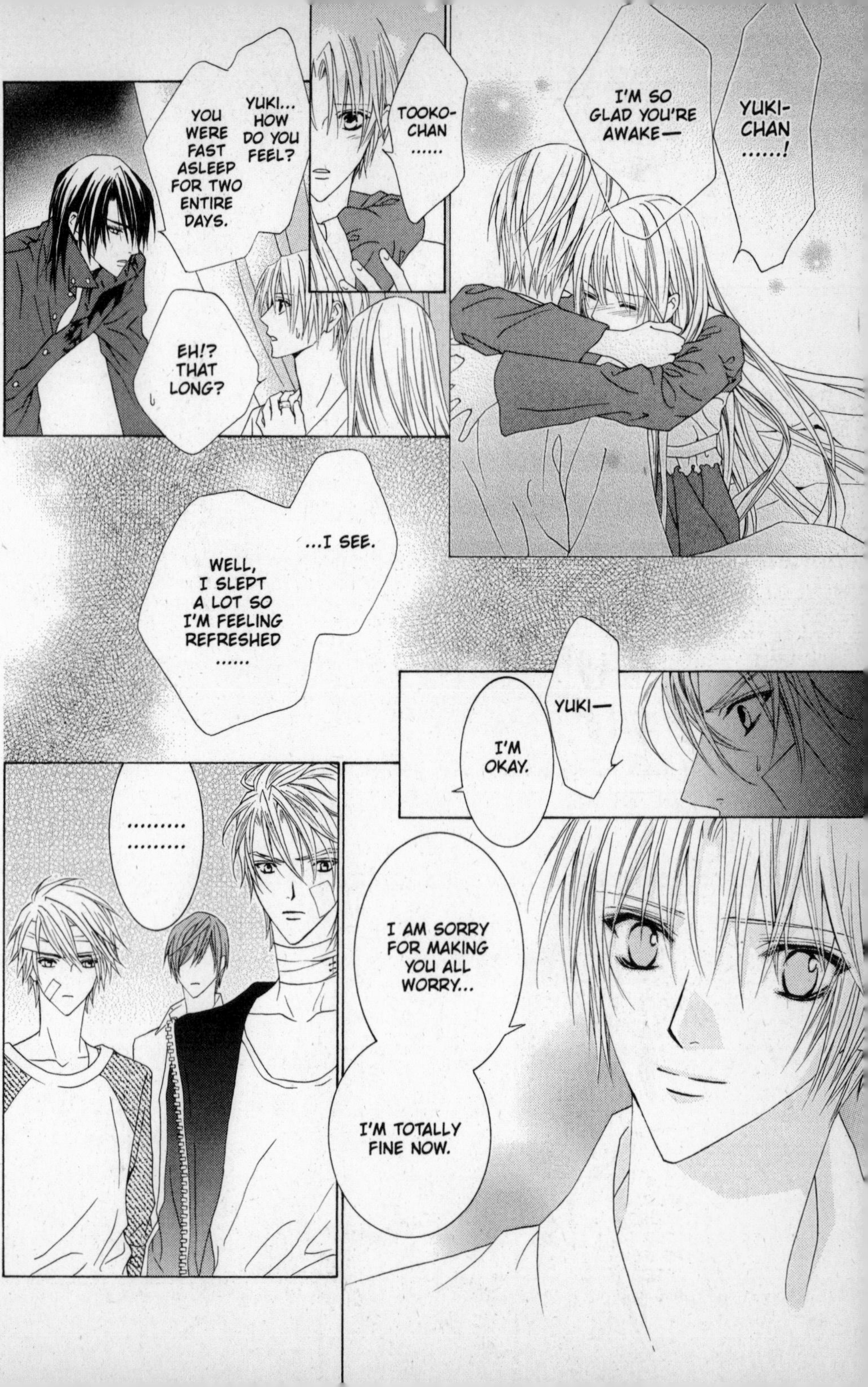
YUKI-CHAN ......!
I'M SO GLAD YOU'RE AWAKE—
TOOKO-CHAN ......
YUKI... HOW DO YOU FEEL?
YOU WERE FAST ASLEEP FOR TWO ENTIRE DAYS.
EH!? THAT LONG?
...I SEE.
WELL, I SLEPT A LOT SO I'M FEELING REFRESHED ......
YUKI—
I'M OKAY.
I AM SORRY FOR MAKING YOU ALL WORRY...
I'M TOTALLY FINE NOW.
....

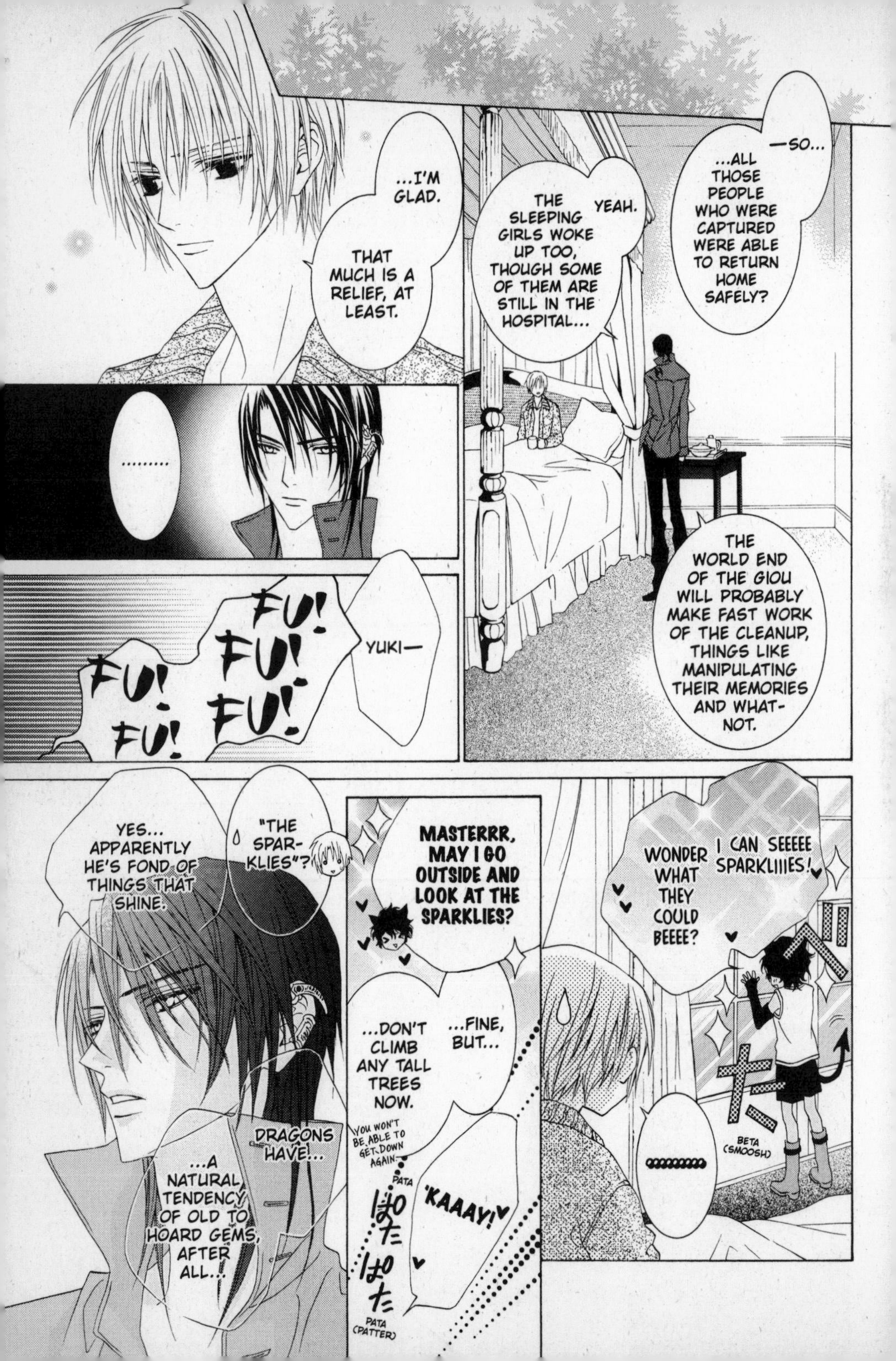

—SO...
...ALL THOSE PEOPLE WHO WERE CAPTURED WERE ABLE TO RETURN HOME SAFELY?
YEAH.
THE SLEEPING GIRLS WOKE UP TOO, THOUGH SOME OF THEM ARE STILL IN THE HOSPITAL...
THE WORLD END OF THE GIOU WILL PROBABLY MAKE FAST WORK OF THE CLEANUP, THINGS LIKE MANIPULATING THEIR MEMORIES AND WHAT-NOT.
...I'M GLAD.
THAT MUCH IS A RELIEF, AT LEAST.
....
YUKI—
FU! FU! FU! FU! FU! FU!
I CAN SEEEEE SPARKLIIIES!
WONDER WHAT THEY COULD BEEEE?
....
BETA (SMOOSH)
MASTERRR, MAY I GO OUTSIDE AND LOOK AT THE SPARKLIES?
...FINE, BUT...
...DON'T CLIMB ANY TALL TREES NOW.
YOU WON'T BE ABLE TO GET DOWN AGAIN.
'KAAAY!
PATA
ぱた
ぱた
PATA (PATTER)
"THE SPARKLIES"?
YES... APPARENTLY HE'S FOND OF THINGS THAT SHINE.
DRAGONS HAVE...
...A NATURAL TENDENCY OF OLD TO HOARD GEMS, AFTER ALL...

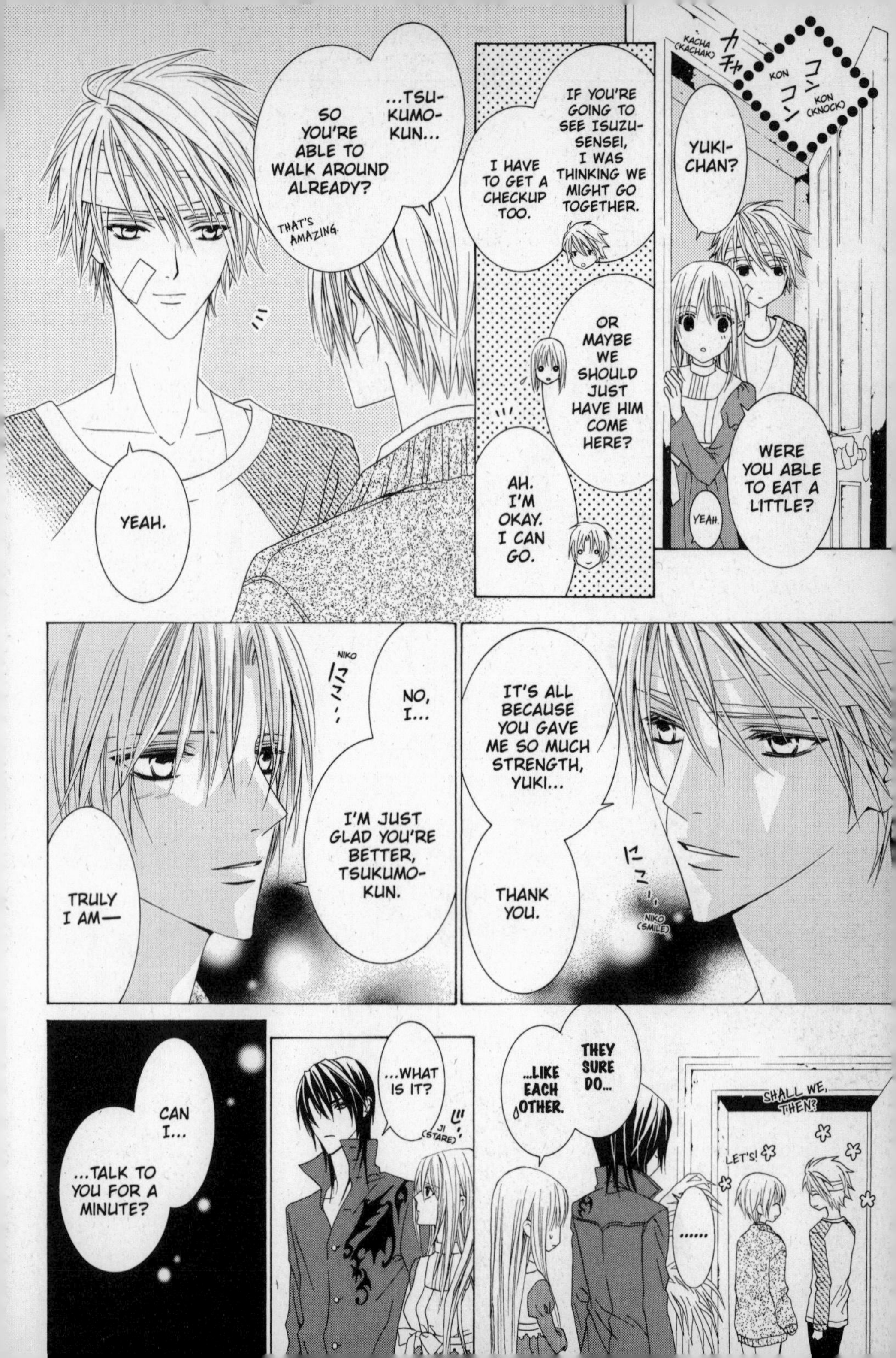
KACHA (KACHAK)
カチャ
コンコン
KON KON (KNOCK)
YUKI-CHAN?
WERE YOU ABLE TO EAT A LITTLE?
YEAH.
IF YOU'RE GOING TO SEE ISUZU-SENSEI, I WAS THINKING WE MIGHT GO TOGETHER.
I HAVE TO GET A CHECKUP TOO.
OR MAYBE WE SHOULD JUST HAVE HIM COME HERE?
AH. I'M OKAY. I CAN GO.
...TSUKUMO-KUN...
SO YOU'RE ABLE TO WALK AROUND ALREADY?
THAT'S AMAZING.
YEAH.
IT'S ALL BECAUSE YOU GAVE ME SO MUCH STRENGTH, YUKI...
THANK YOU.
NIKO (SMILE)
NIKO
NO, I...
I'M JUST GLAD YOU'RE BETTER, TSUKUMO-KUN.
TRULY I AM—
SHALL WE, THEN?
LET'S!
THEY SURE DO...
...LIKE EACH OTHER.
......
...WHAT IS IT?
JI (STARE)
CAN I...
...TALK TO YOU FOR A MINUTE?

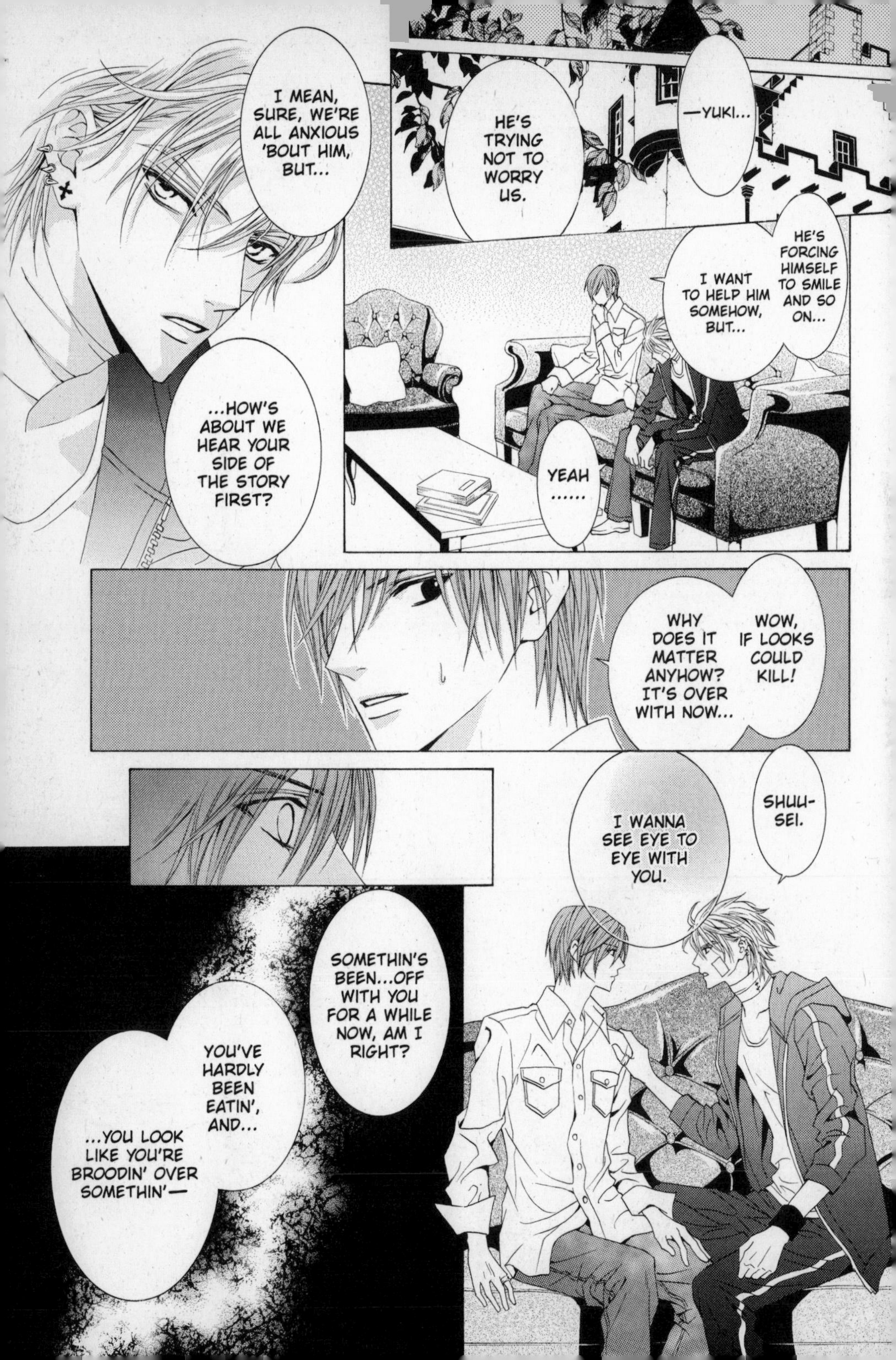
—YUKI...
HE'S TRYING NOT TO WORRY US.
HE'S FORCING HIMSELF TO SMILE AND SO ON...
I WANT TO HELP HIM SOMEHOW, BUT...
YEAH ......
I MEAN, SURE, WE'RE ALL ANXIOUS 'BOUT HIM, BUT...
...HOW'S ABOUT WE HEAR YOUR SIDE OF THE STORY FIRST?
WOW, IF LOOKS COULD KILL!
WHY DOES IT MATTER ANYHOW? IT'S OVER WITH NOW...
SHUU-SEI.
I WANNA SEE EYE TO EYE WITH YOU.
SOMETHIN'S BEEN...OFF WITH YOU FOR A WHILE NOW, AM I RIGHT?
YOU'VE HARDLY BEEN EATIN', AND...
...YOU LOOK LIKE YOU'RE BROODIN' OVER SOMETHIN'—

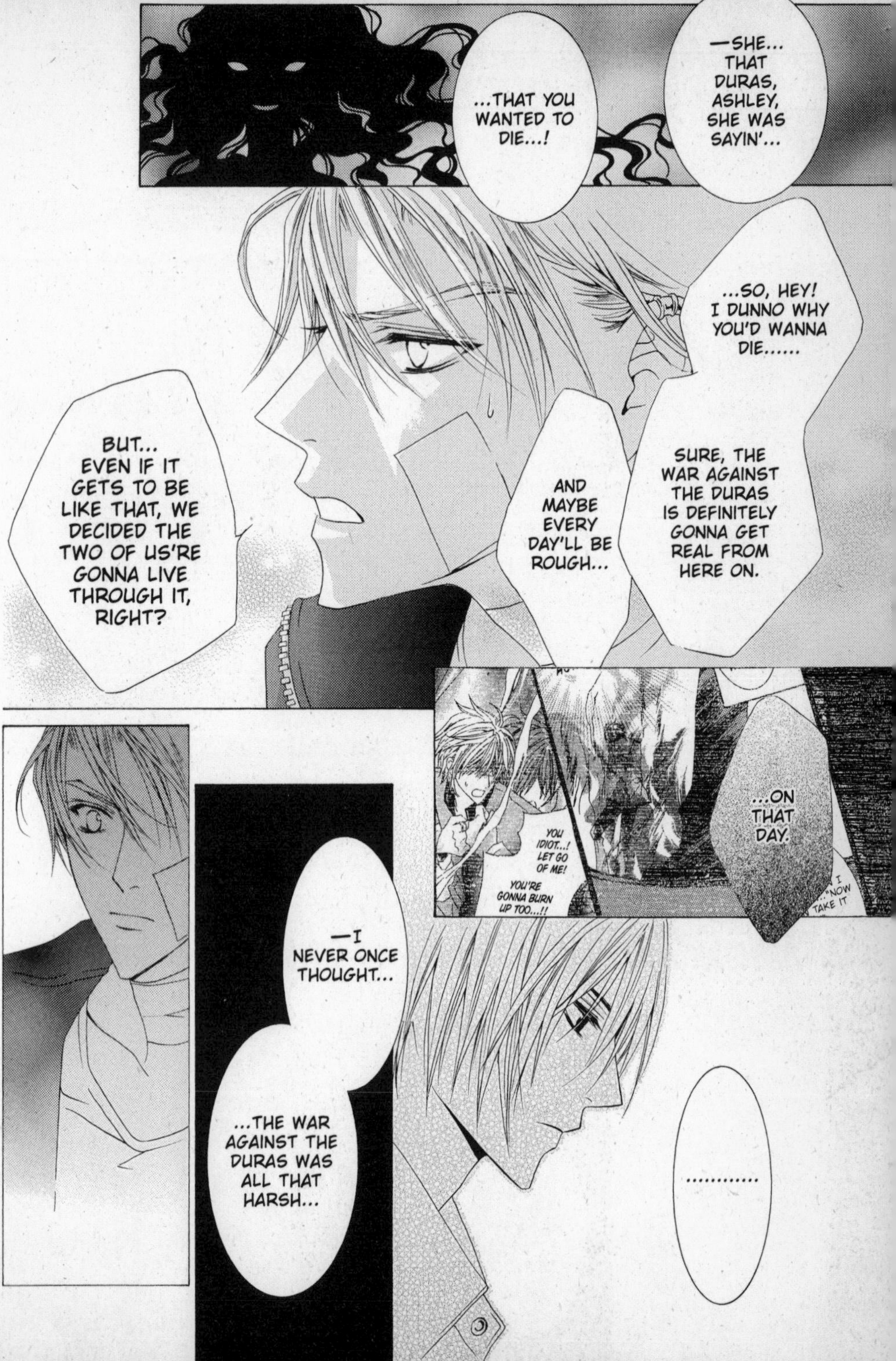
—SHE... THAT DURAS, ASHLEY, SHE WAS SAYIN'...
...THAT YOU WANTED TO DIE...!
...SO, HEY! I DUNNO WHY YOU'D WANNA DIE......
SURE, THE WAR AGAINST THE DURAS IS DEFINITELY GONNA GET REAL FROM HERE ON.
AND MAYBE EVERY DAY'LL BE ROUGH...
BUT... EVEN IF IT GETS TO BE LIKE THAT, WE DECIDED THE TWO OF US'RE GONNA LIVE THROUGH IT, RIGHT?
...ON THAT DAY.
YOU IDIOT...! LET GO OF ME!
YOU'RE GONNA BURN UP TOO...!!
....
—I NEVER ONCE THOUGHT...
...THE WAR AGAINST THE DURAS WAS ALL THAT HARSH...

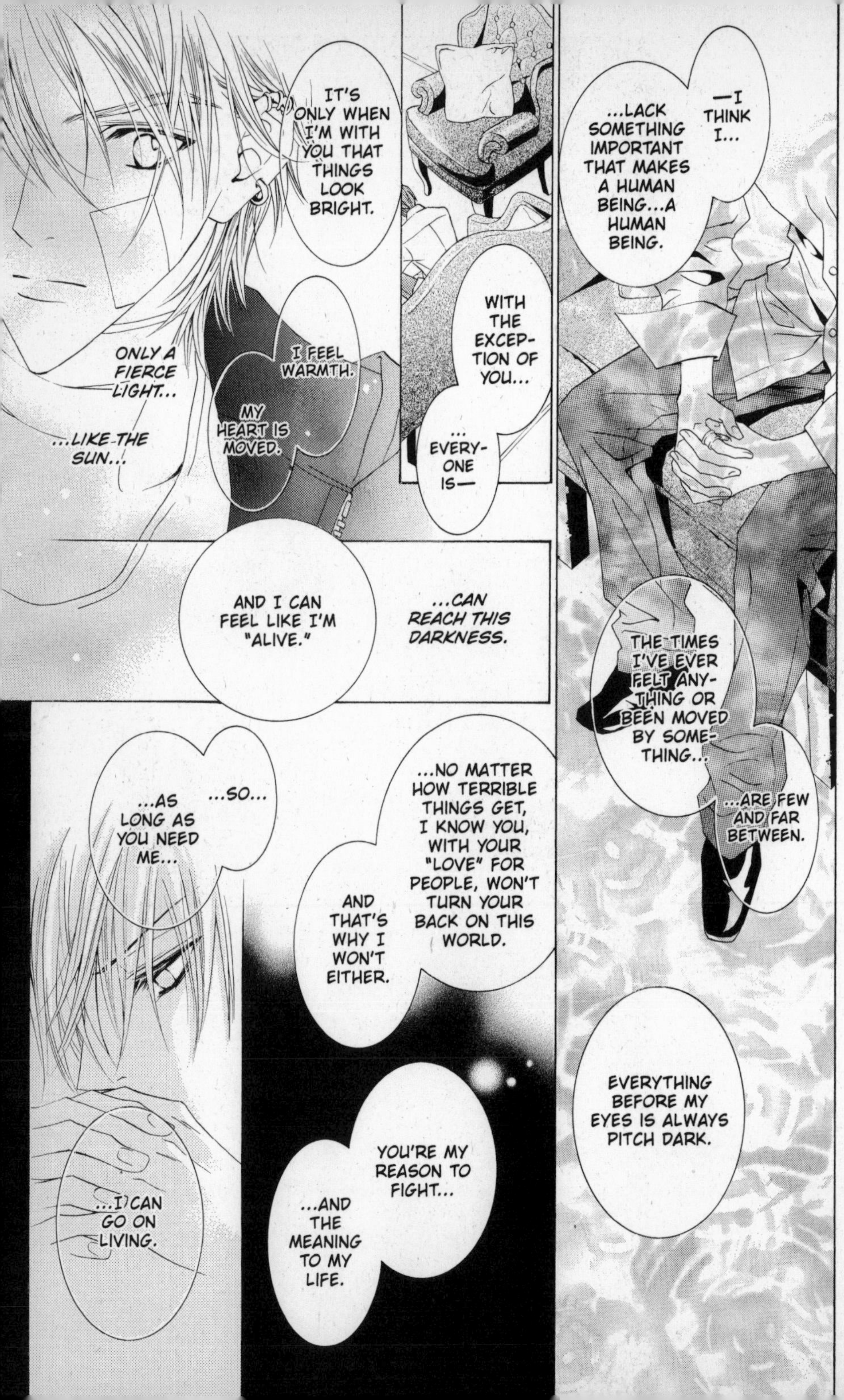

—I THINK I...
...LACK SOMETHING IMPORTANT THAT MAKES A HUMAN BEING...A HUMAN BEING.
THE TIMES I'VE EVER FELT ANYTHING OR BEEN MOVED BY SOMETHING...
...ARE FEW AND FAR BETWEEN.
EVERYTHING BEFORE MY EYES IS ALWAYS PITCH DARK.
WITH THE EXCEPTION OF YOU...
...EVERYONE IS—
IT'S ONLY WHEN I'M WITH YOU THAT THINGS LOOK BRIGHT.
I FEEL WARMTH.
MY HEART IS MOVED.
ONLY A FIERCE LIGHT...
...LIKE THE SUN...
...CAN REACH THIS DARKNESS.
AND I CAN FEEL LIKE I'M "ALIVE."
...NO MATTER HOW TERRIBLE THINGS GET, I KNOW YOU, WITH YOUR "LOVE" FOR PEOPLE, WON'T TURN YOUR BACK ON THIS WORLD.
AND THAT'S WHY I WON'T EITHER.
YOU'RE MY REASON TO FIGHT...
...AND THE MEANING TO MY LIFE.
...SO...
...AS LONG AS YOU NEED ME...
...I CAN GO ON LIVING.

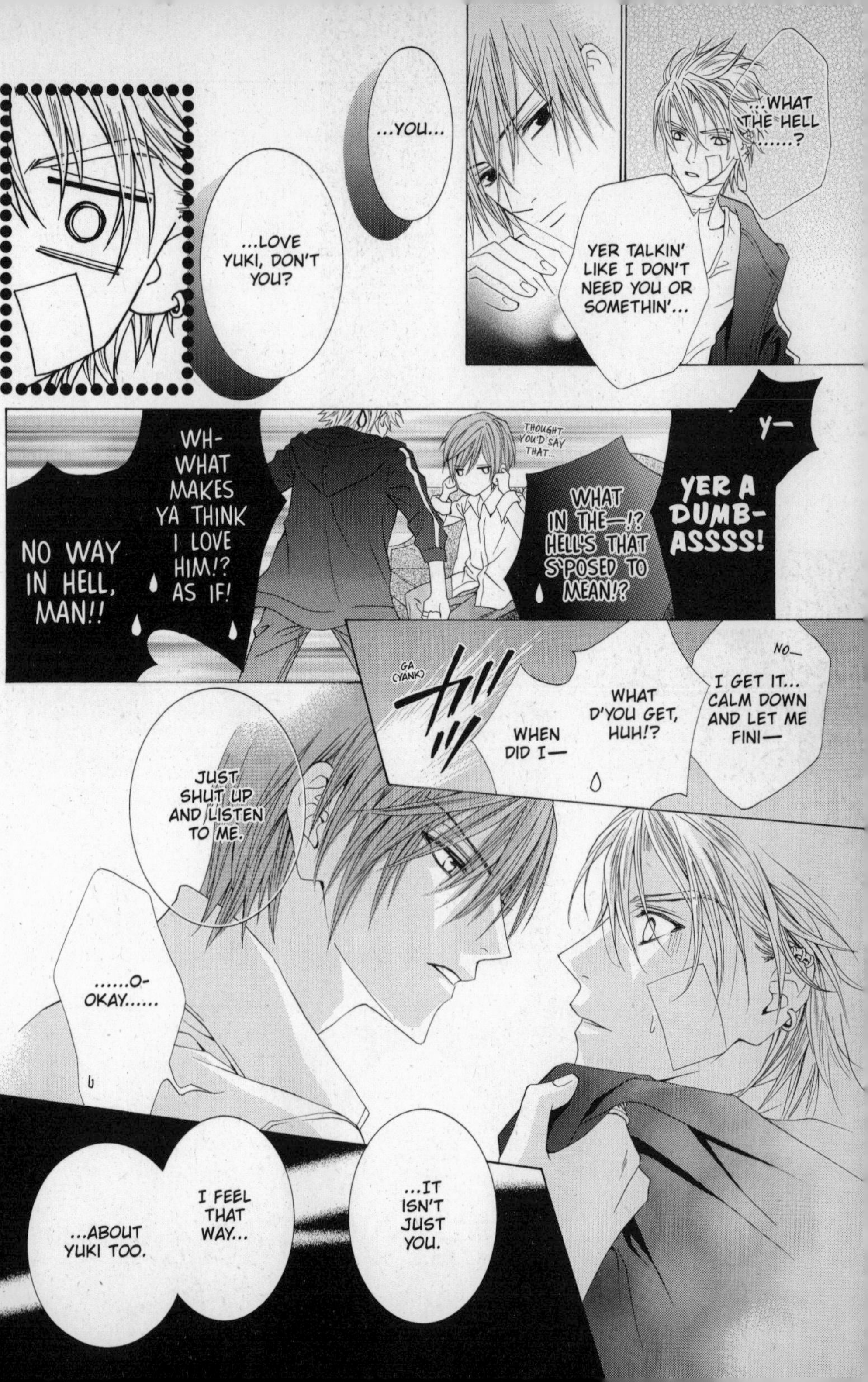
...WHAT THE HELL ......?
YER TALKIN' LIKE I DON'T NEED YOU OR SOMETHIN'...
...YOU...
...LOVE YUKI, DON'T YOU?
Y—
YER A DUMB-ASSSS!
WHAT IN THE—!? HELL'S THAT S'POSED TO MEAN!?
THOUGHT YOU'D SAY THAT...
WH-WHAT MAKES YA THINK I LOVE HIM!? AS IF!
NO WAY IN HELL, MAN!!
NO—
I GET IT... CALM DOWN AND LET ME FINI—
WHAT D'YOU GET, HUH!?
WHEN DID I—
GA (YANK)
JUST SHUT UP AND LISTEN TO ME.
......O-OKAY......
...IT ISN'T JUST YOU.
I FEEL THAT WAY...
...ABOUT YUKI TOO.

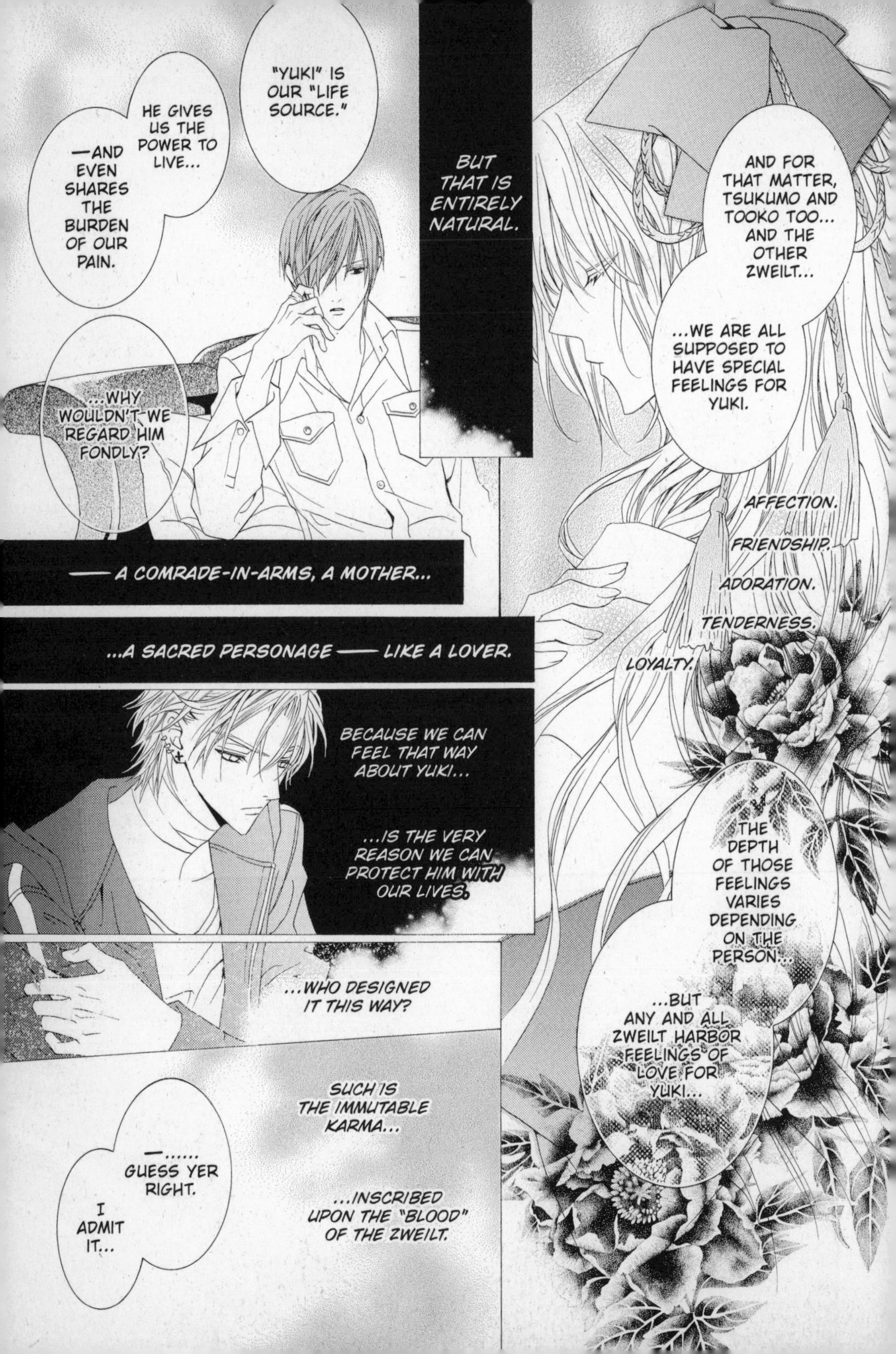
AND FOR THAT MATTER, TSUKUMO AND TOOKO TOO... AND THE OTHER ZWEILT...
...WE ARE ALL SUPPOSED TO HAVE SPECIAL FEELINGS FOR YUKI.
AFFECTION.
FRIENDSHIP.
ADORATION.
TENDERNESS.
LOYALTY.
THE DEPTH OF THOSE FEELINGS VARIES DEPENDING ON THE PERSON...
...BUT ANY AND ALL ZWEILT HARBOR FEELINGS OF LOVE FOR YUKI...
BUT THAT IS ENTIRELY NATURAL.
"YUKI" IS OUR "LIFE SOURCE."
HE GIVES US THE POWER TO LIVE...
—AND EVEN SHARES THE BURDEN OF OUR PAIN.
...WHY WOULDN'T WE REGARD HIM FONDLY?
—A COMRADE-IN-ARMS, A MOTHER...
...A SACRED PERSONAGE—LIKE A LOVER.
BECAUSE WE CAN FEEL THAT WAY ABOUT YUKI...
...IS THE VERY REASON WE CAN PROTECT HIM WITH OUR LIVES.
...WHO DESIGNED IT THIS WAY?
SUCH IS THE IMMUTABLE KARMA...
...INSCRIBED UPON THE "BLOOD" OF THE ZWEILT.
—...... GUESS YER RIGHT.
I ADMIT IT...

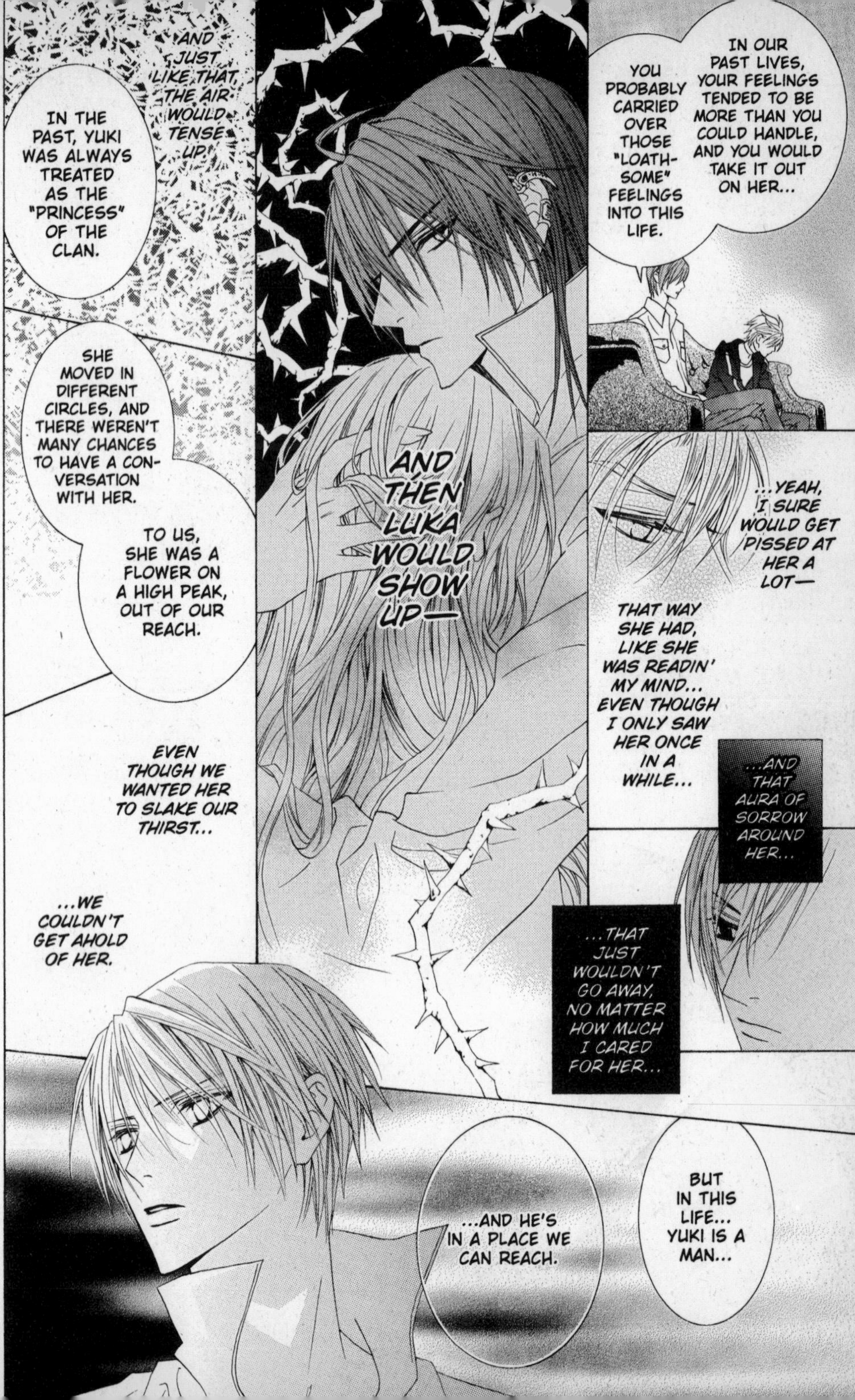
IN OUR PAST LIVES, YOUR FEELINGS TENDED TO BE MORE THAN YOU COULD HANDLE, AND YOU WOULD TAKE IT OUT ON HER...
YOU PROBABLY CARRIED OVER THOSE "LOATH-SOME" FEELINGS INTO THIS LIFE.
...YEAH, I SURE WOULD GET PISSED AT HER A LOT—
THAT WAY SHE HAD, LIKE SHE WAS READIN' MY MIND... EVEN THOUGH I ONLY SAW HER ONCE IN A WHILE...
...AND THAT AURA OF SORROW AROUND HER...
...THAT JUST WOULDN'T GO AWAY, NO MATTER HOW MUCH I CARED FOR HER...
AND THEN LUKA WOULD SHOW UP—
AND JUST LIKE THAT, THE AIR WOULD TENSE UP.
IN THE PAST, YUKI WAS ALWAYS TREATED AS THE "PRINCESS" OF THE CLAN.
SHE MOVED IN DIFFERENT CIRCLES, AND THERE WEREN'T MANY CHANCES TO HAVE A CON-VERSATION WITH HER.
TO US, SHE WAS A FLOWER ON A HIGH PEAK, OUT OF OUR REACH.
EVEN THOUGH WE WANTED HER TO SLAKE OUR THIRST...
...WE COULDN'T GET AHOLD OF HER.
BUT IN THIS LIFE... YUKI IS A MAN...
...AND HE'S IN A PLACE WE CAN REACH.

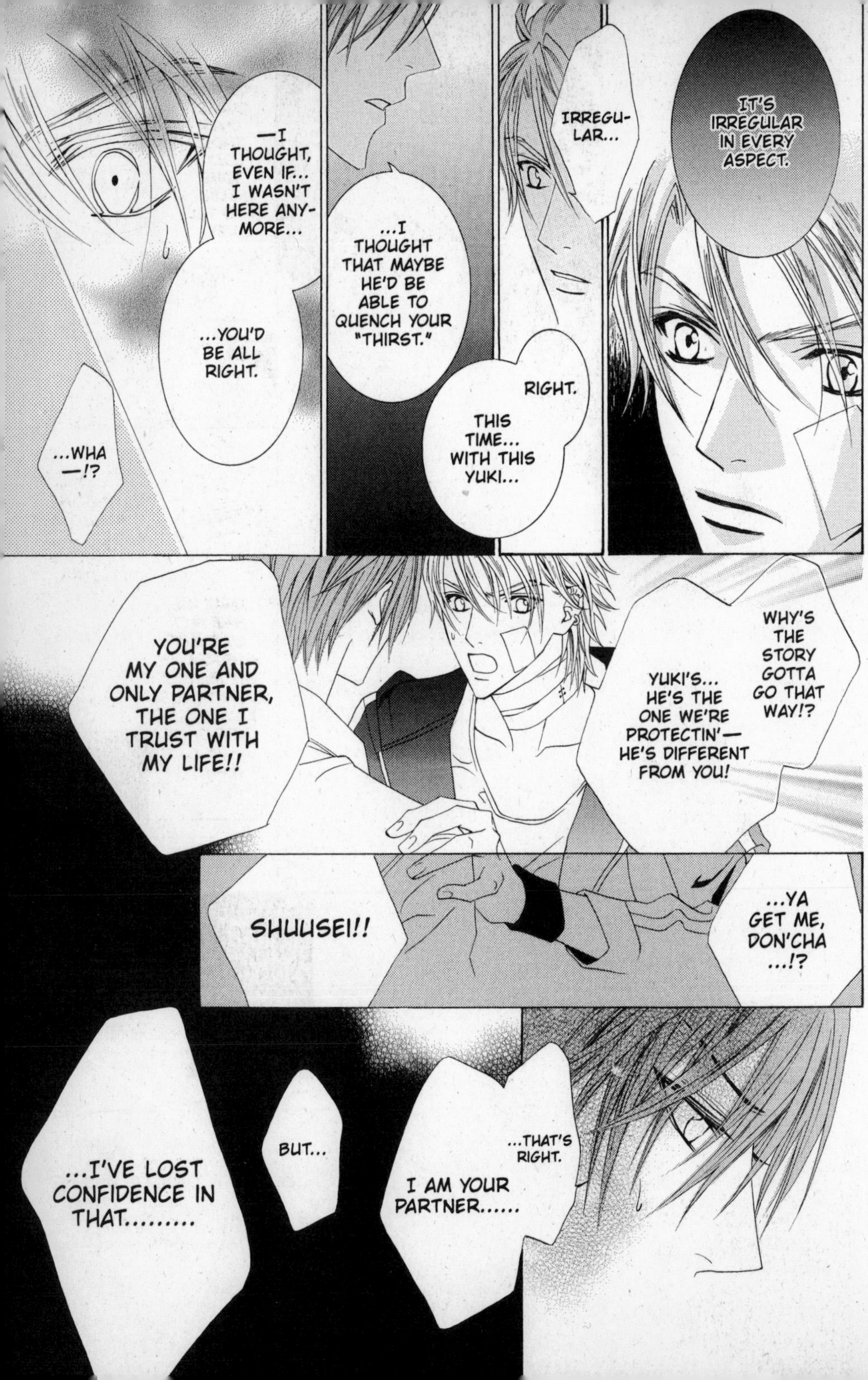
IT'S IRREGULAR IN EVERY ASPECT.
IRREGU-LAR...
RIGHT.
THIS TIME... WITH THIS YUKI...
...I THOUGHT THAT MAYBE HE'D BE ABLE TO QUENCH YOUR "THIRST."
—I THOUGHT, EVEN IF... I WASN'T HERE ANY-MORE...
...YOU'D BE ALL RIGHT.
...WHA—!?
WHY'S THE STORY GOTTA GO THAT WAY!?
YUKI'S... HE'S THE ONE WE'RE PROTECTIN'— HE'S DIFFERENT FROM YOU!
YOU'RE MY ONE AND ONLY PARTNER, THE ONE I TRUST WITH MY LIFE!!
...YA GET ME, DON'CHA ...!?
SHUUSEI!!
...THAT'S RIGHT.
I AM YOUR PARTNER......
BUT...
...I'VE LOST CONFIDENCE IN THAT.........

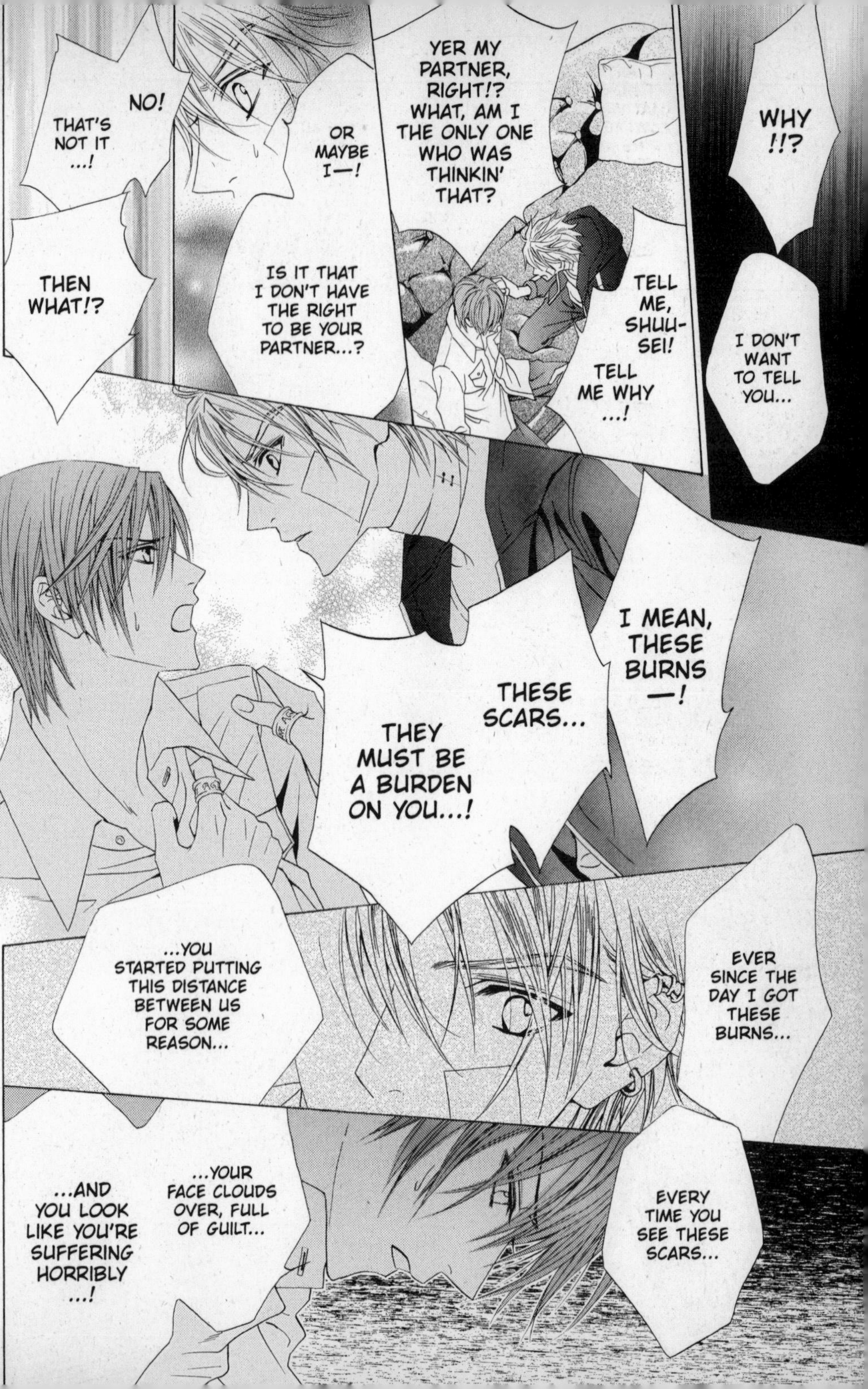
WHY!!?
I DON'T WANT TO TELL YOU...
YER MY PARTNER, RIGHT!? WHAT, AM I THE ONLY ONE WHO WAS THINKIN' THAT?
TELL ME, SHUU-SEI!
TELL ME WHY...!
OR MAYBE I—!
IS IT THAT I DON'T HAVE THE RIGHT TO BE YOUR PARTNER...?
NO!
THAT'S NOT IT...!
THEN WHAT!?
I MEAN, THESE BURNS—!
THESE SCARS...
THEY MUST BE A BURDEN ON YOU...!
EVER SINCE THE DAY I GOT THESE BURNS...
...YOU STARTED PUTTING THIS DISTANCE BETWEEN US FOR SOME REASON...
EVERY TIME YOU SEE THESE SCARS...
...YOUR FACE CLOUDS OVER, FULL OF GUILT...
...AND YOU LOOK LIKE YOU'RE SUFFERING HORRIBLY...!

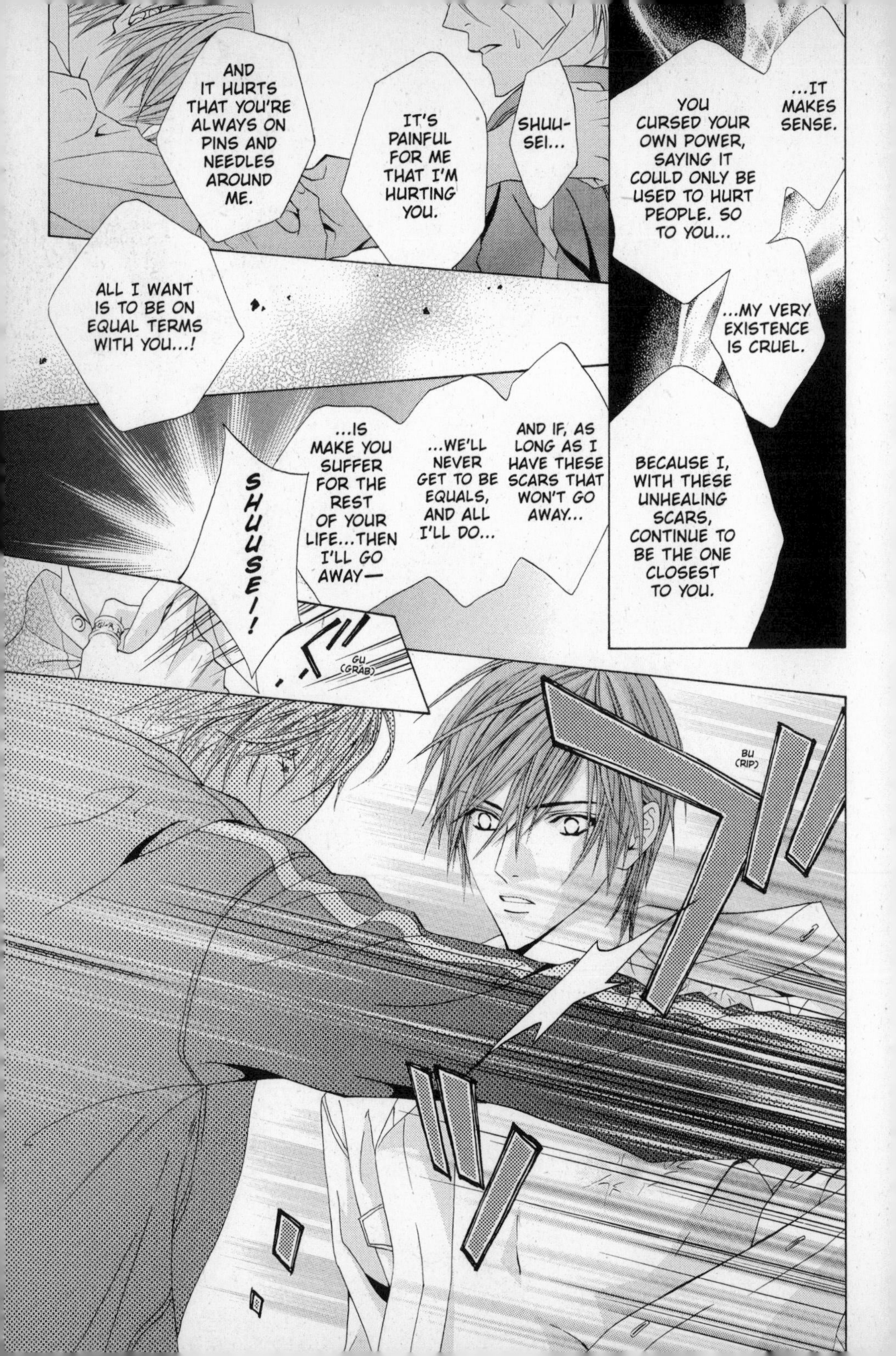
...IT MAKES SENSE.
YOU CURSED YOUR OWN POWER, SAYING IT COULD ONLY BE USED TO HURT PEOPLE. SO TO YOU...
...MY VERY EXISTENCE IS CRUEL.
BECAUSE I, WITH THESE UNHEALING SCARS, CONTINUE TO BE THE ONE CLOSEST TO YOU.
SHUU-SEI...
IT'S PAINFUL FOR ME THAT I'M HURTING YOU.
AND IT HURTS THAT YOU'RE ALWAYS ON PINS AND NEEDLES AROUND ME.
ALL I WANT IS TO BE ON EQUAL TERMS WITH YOU...!
AND IF, AS LONG AS I HAVE THESE SCARS THAT WON'T GO AWAY...
...WE'LL NEVER GET TO BE EQUALS, AND ALL I'LL DO...
...IS MAKE YOU SUFFER FOR THE REST OF YOUR LIFE...THEN I'LL GO AWAY—
SHUUSEI!
GU (GRAB)
BU (RIP)

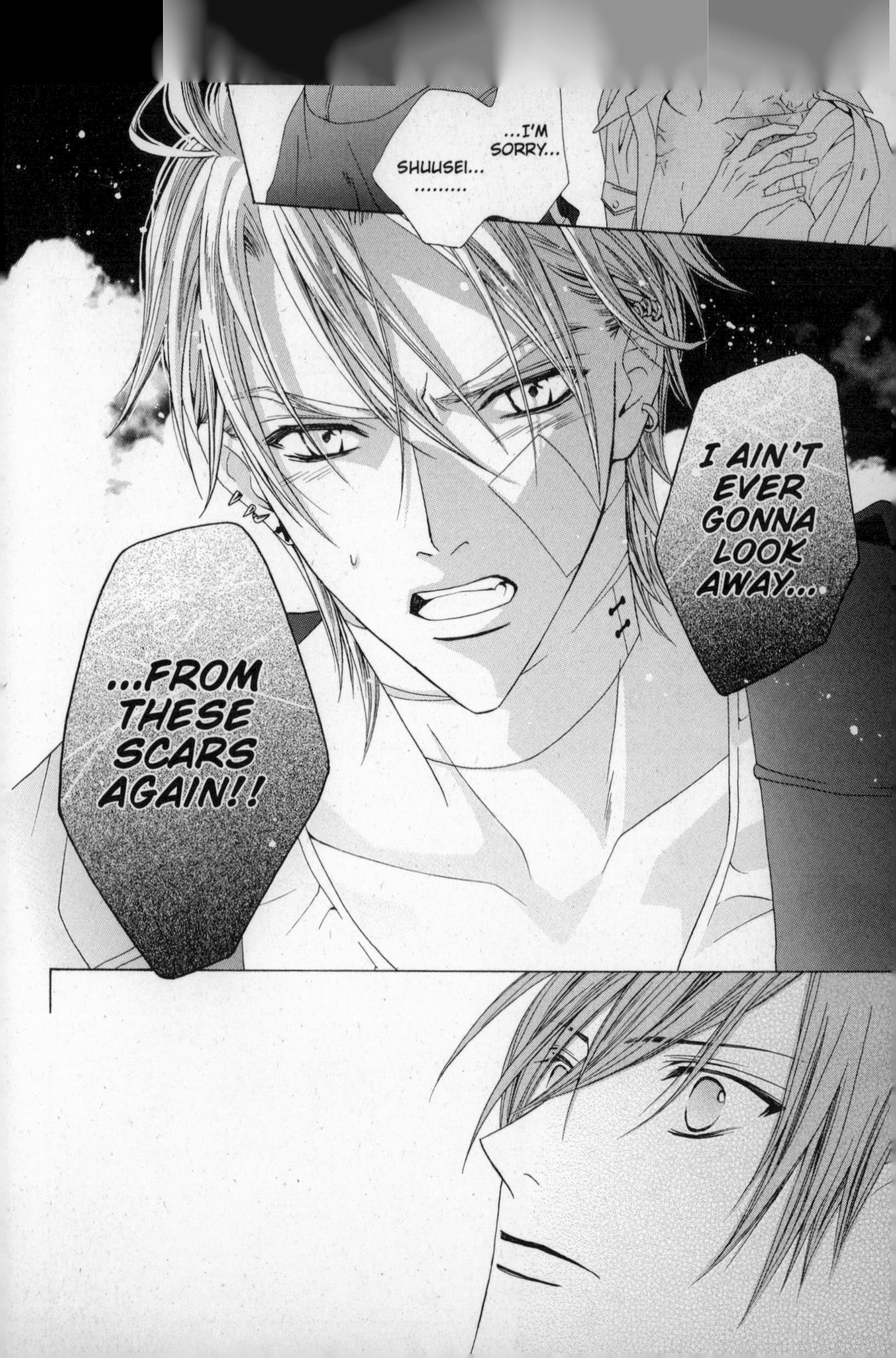
...I'M SORRY... SHUUSEI... ....
I AIN'T EVER GONNA LOOK AWAY...
...FROM THESE SCARS AGAIN!!

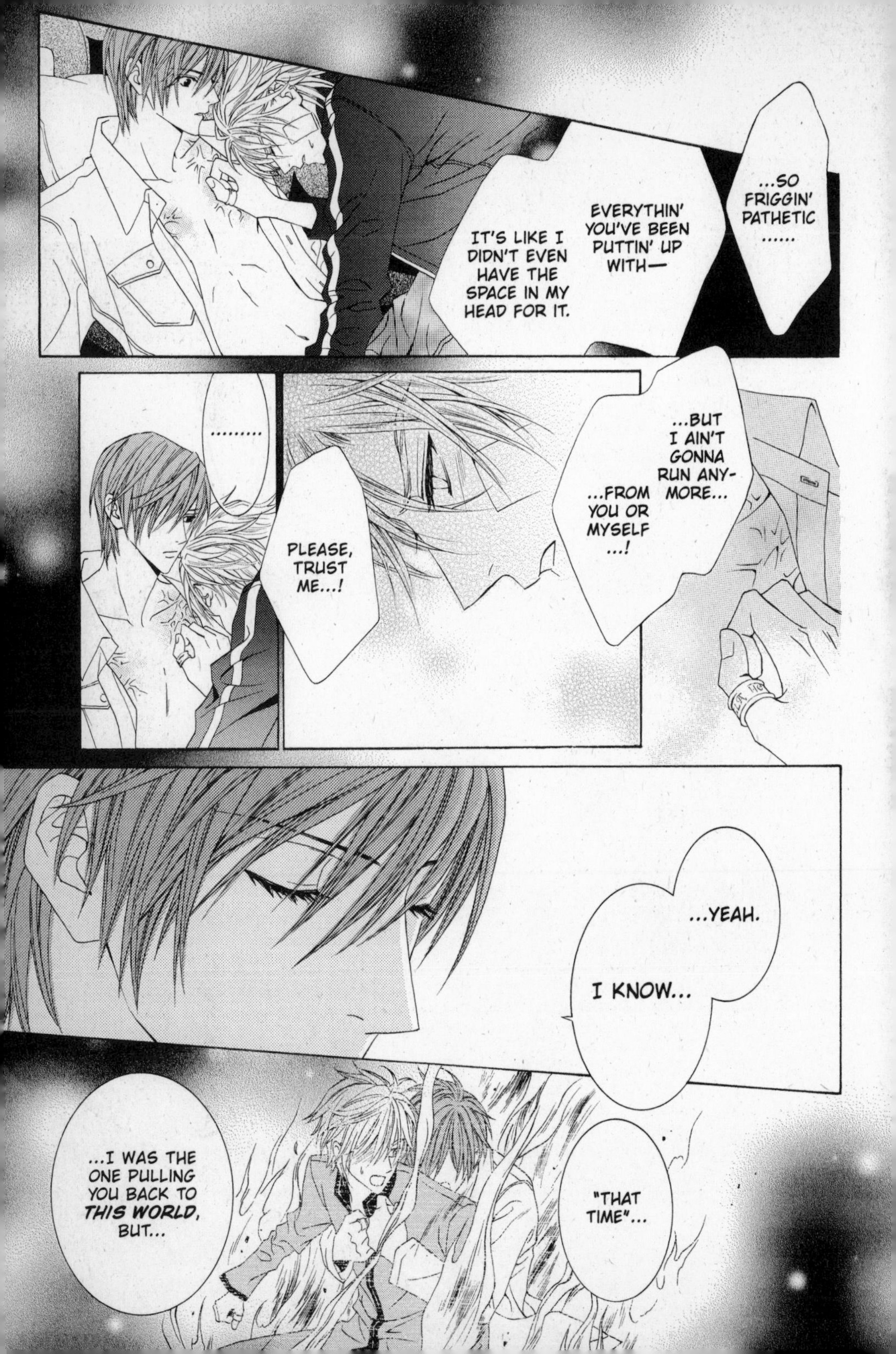
...SO FRIGGIN' PATHETIC ......
EVERYTHIN' YOU'VE BEEN PUTTIN' UP WITH—
IT'S LIKE I DIDN'T EVEN HAVE THE SPACE IN MY HEAD FOR IT.
...BUT I AIN'T GONNA RUN ANY-MORE...
...FROM YOU OR MYSELF ...!
PLEASE, TRUST ME...!
....
...YEAH.
I KNOW...
"THAT TIME"...
...I WAS THE ONE PULLING YOU BACK TO *THIS WORLD*, BUT...

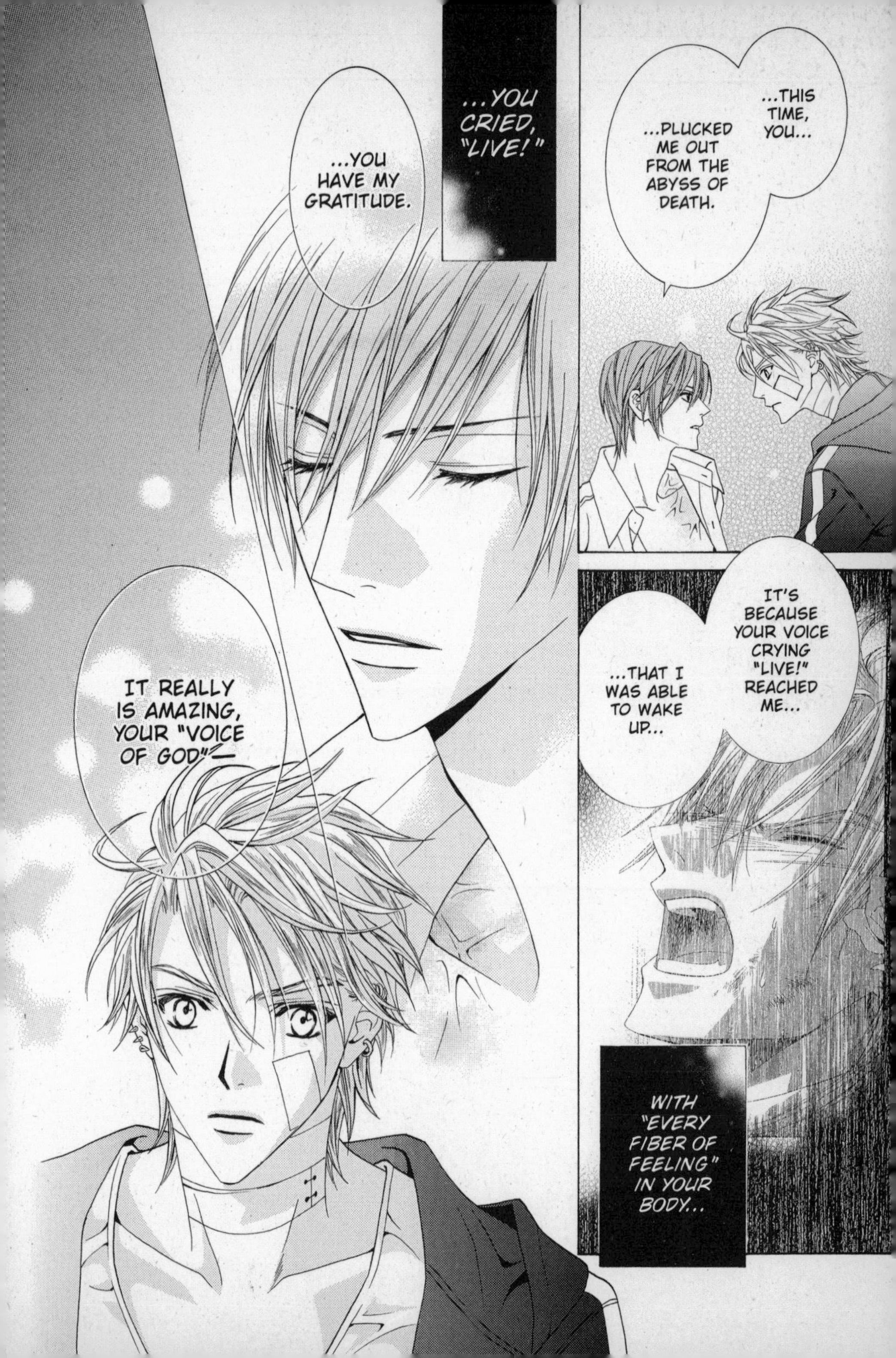
...THIS TIME, YOU...
...PLUCKED ME OUT FROM THE ABYSS OF DEATH.
IT'S BECAUSE YOUR VOICE CRYING "LIVE!" REACHED ME...
...THAT I WAS ABLE TO WAKE UP...
WITH "EVERY FIBER OF FEELING" IN YOUR BODY...
...YOU CRIED, "LIVE!"
...YOU HAVE MY GRATITUDE.
IT REALLY IS AMAZING, YOUR "VOICE OF GOD"—

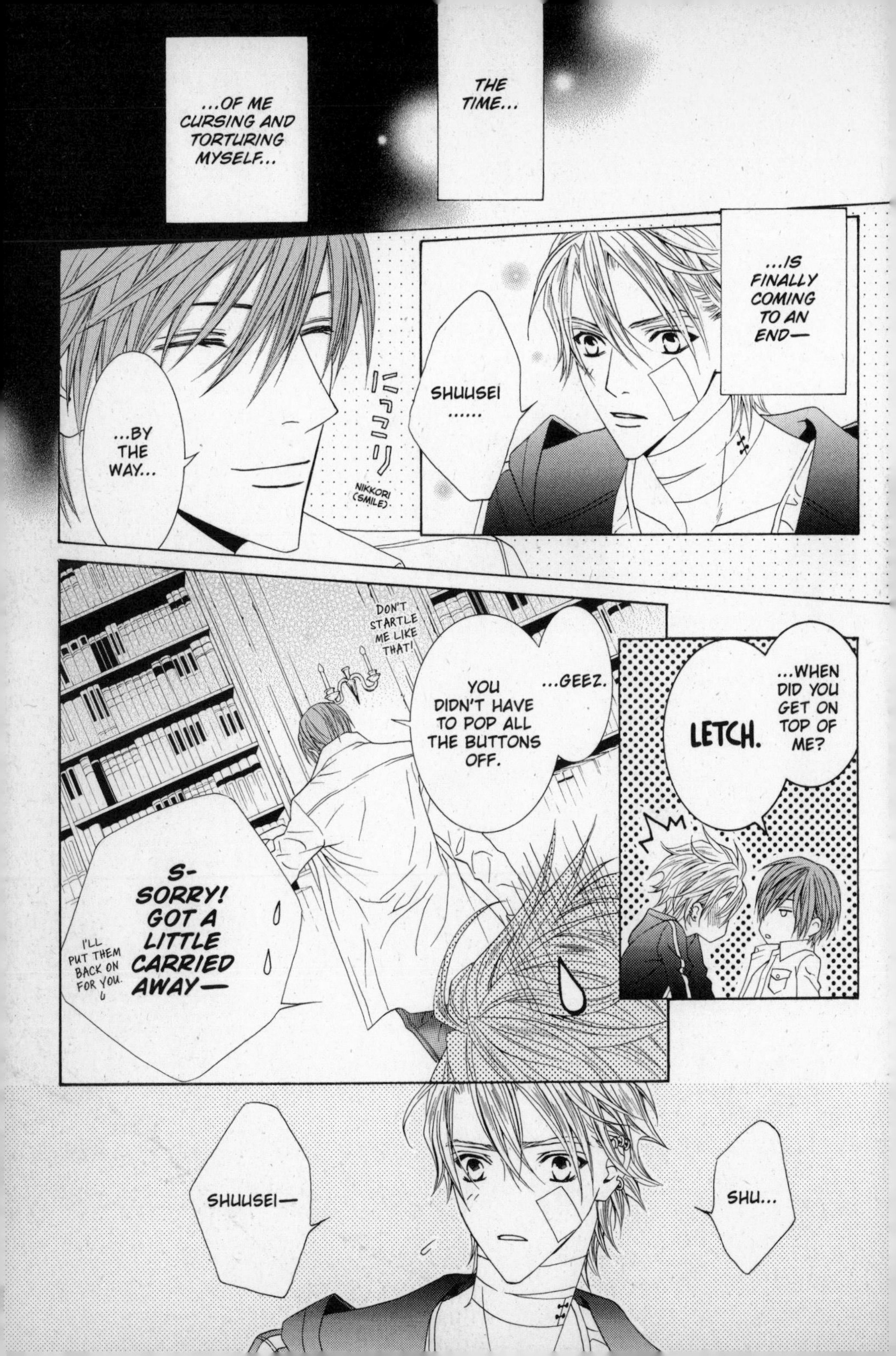
THE TIME...
...OF ME CURSING AND TORTURING MYSELF...
...IS FINALLY COMING TO AN END—
SHUUSEI ......
...BY THE WAY...
NIKKORI (SMILE)
...WHEN DID YOU GET ON TOP OF ME?
LETCH.
...GEEZ.
YOU DIDN'T HAVE TO POP ALL THE BUTTONS OFF.
DON'T STARTLE ME LIKE THAT!
S-SORRY! GOT A LITTLE CARRIED AWAY—
I'LL PUT THEM BACK ON FOR YOU.
SHU...
SHUUSEI—

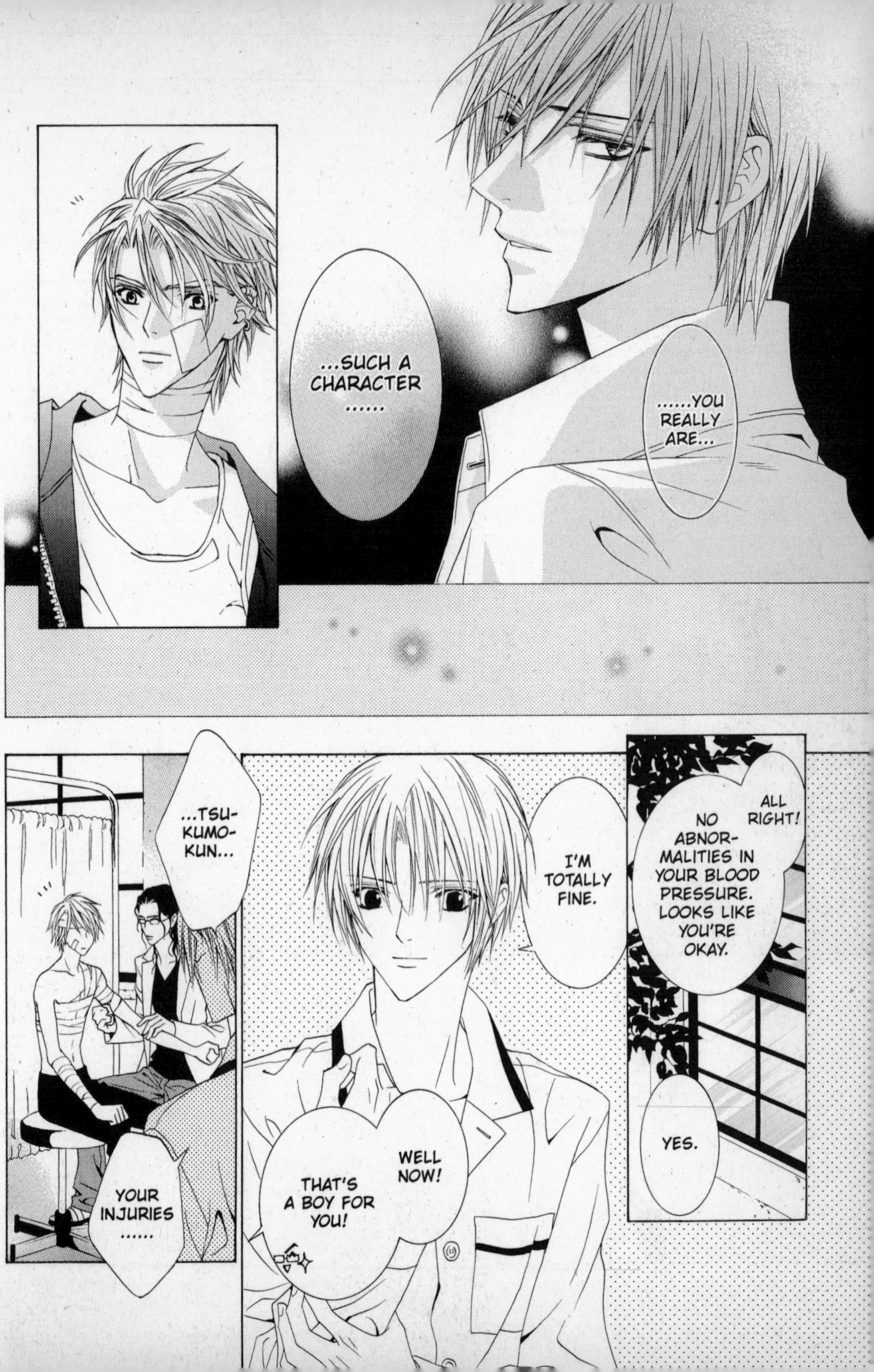
......YOU REALLY ARE...
...SUCH A CHARACTER ......
ALL RIGHT! NO ABNOR-MALITIES IN YOUR BLOOD PRESSURE. LOOKS LIKE YOU'RE OKAY.
YES.
I'M TOTALLY FINE.
WELL NOW! THAT'S A BOY FOR YOU!
...TSU-KUMO-KUN...
YOUR INJURIES ......

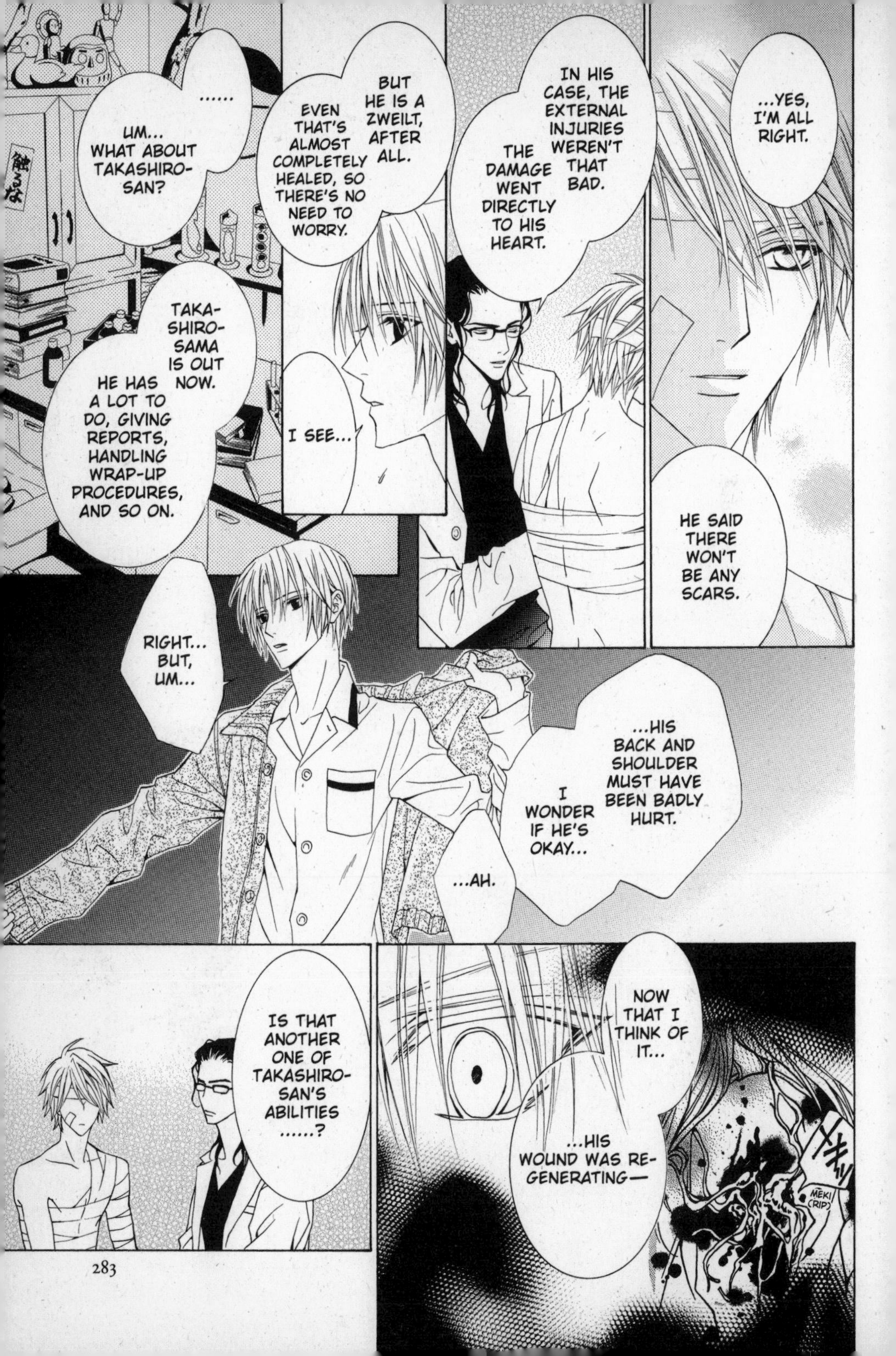
...YES, I'M ALL RIGHT.
HE SAID THERE WON'T BE ANY SCARS.
IN HIS CASE, THE EXTERNAL INJURIES WEREN'T THAT BAD.
THE DAMAGE WENT DIRECTLY TO HIS HEART.
BUT HE IS A ZWEILT, AFTER ALL.
EVEN THAT'S ALMOST COMPLETELY HEALED, SO THERE'S NO NEED TO WORRY.
I SEE...
......
UM... WHAT ABOUT TAKASHIRO-SAN?
TAKA-SHIRO-SAMA IS OUT NOW.
HE HAS A LOT TO DO, GIVING REPORTS, HANDLING WRAP-UP PROCEDURES, AND SO ON.
RIGHT... BUT, UM...
...HIS BACK AND SHOULDER MUST HAVE BEEN BADLY HURT.
I WONDER IF HE'S OKAY...
...AH.
NOW THAT I THINK OF IT...
...HIS WOUND WAS RE-GENERATING—
MEKI (RIP)
IS THAT ANOTHER ONE OF TAKASHIRO-SAN'S ABILITIES ......?

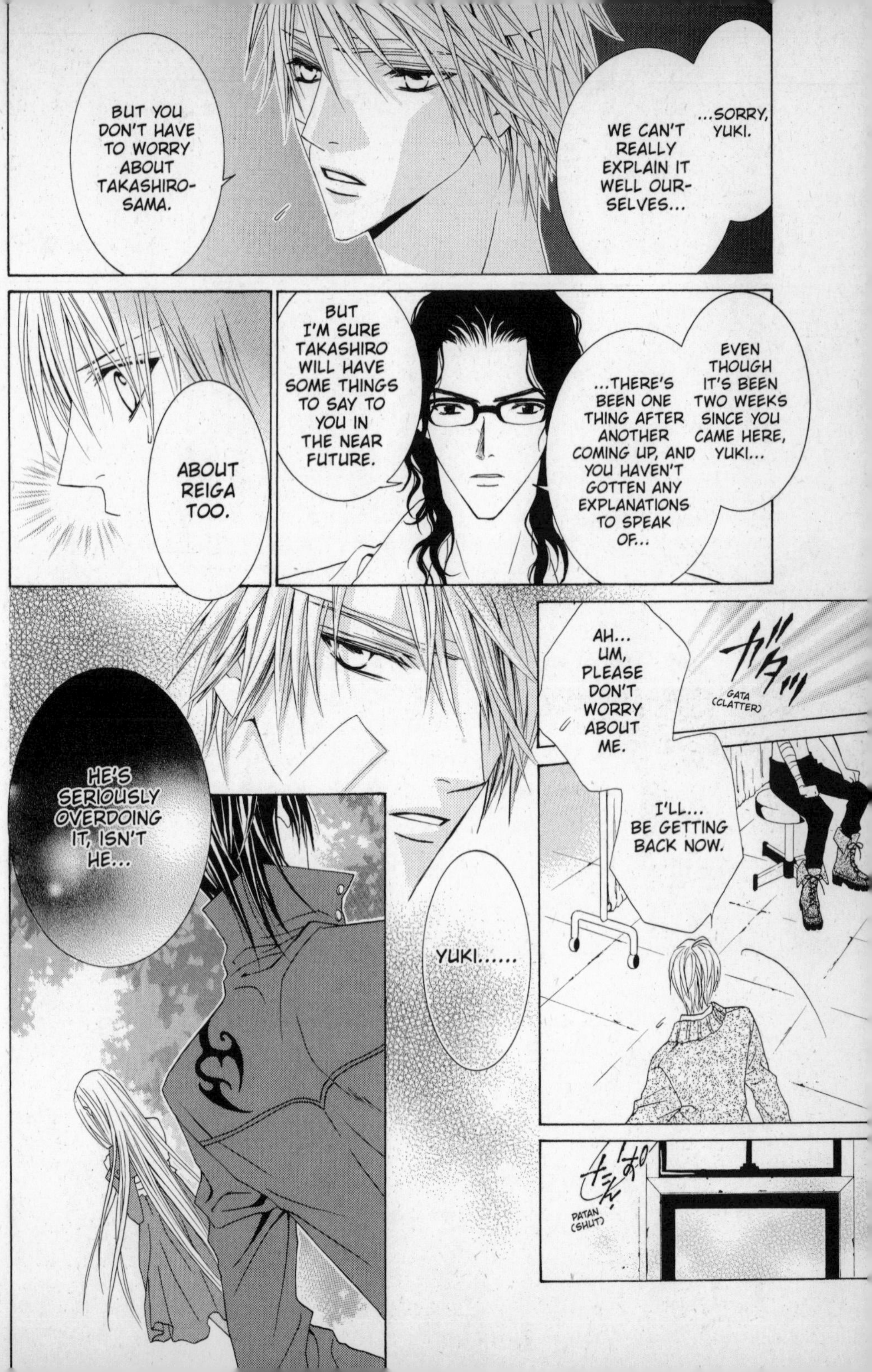
...SORRY, YUKI.
WE CAN'T REALLY EXPLAIN IT WELL OURSELVES...
BUT YOU DON'T HAVE TO WORRY ABOUT TAKASHIRO-SAMA.
EVEN THOUGH IT'S BEEN TWO WEEKS SINCE YOU CAME HERE, YUKI...
...THERE'S BEEN ONE THING AFTER ANOTHER COMING UP, AND YOU HAVEN'T GOTTEN ANY EXPLANATIONS TO SPEAK OF...
BUT I'M SURE TAKASHIRO WILL HAVE SOME THINGS TO SAY TO YOU IN THE NEAR FUTURE.
ABOUT REIGA TOO.
ガタッ
GATA (CLATTER)
AH... UM, PLEASE DON'T WORRY ABOUT ME.
I'LL... BE GETTING BACK NOW.
PATAN (SHUT)
YUKI......
HE'S SERIOUSLY OVERDOING IT, ISN'T HE...

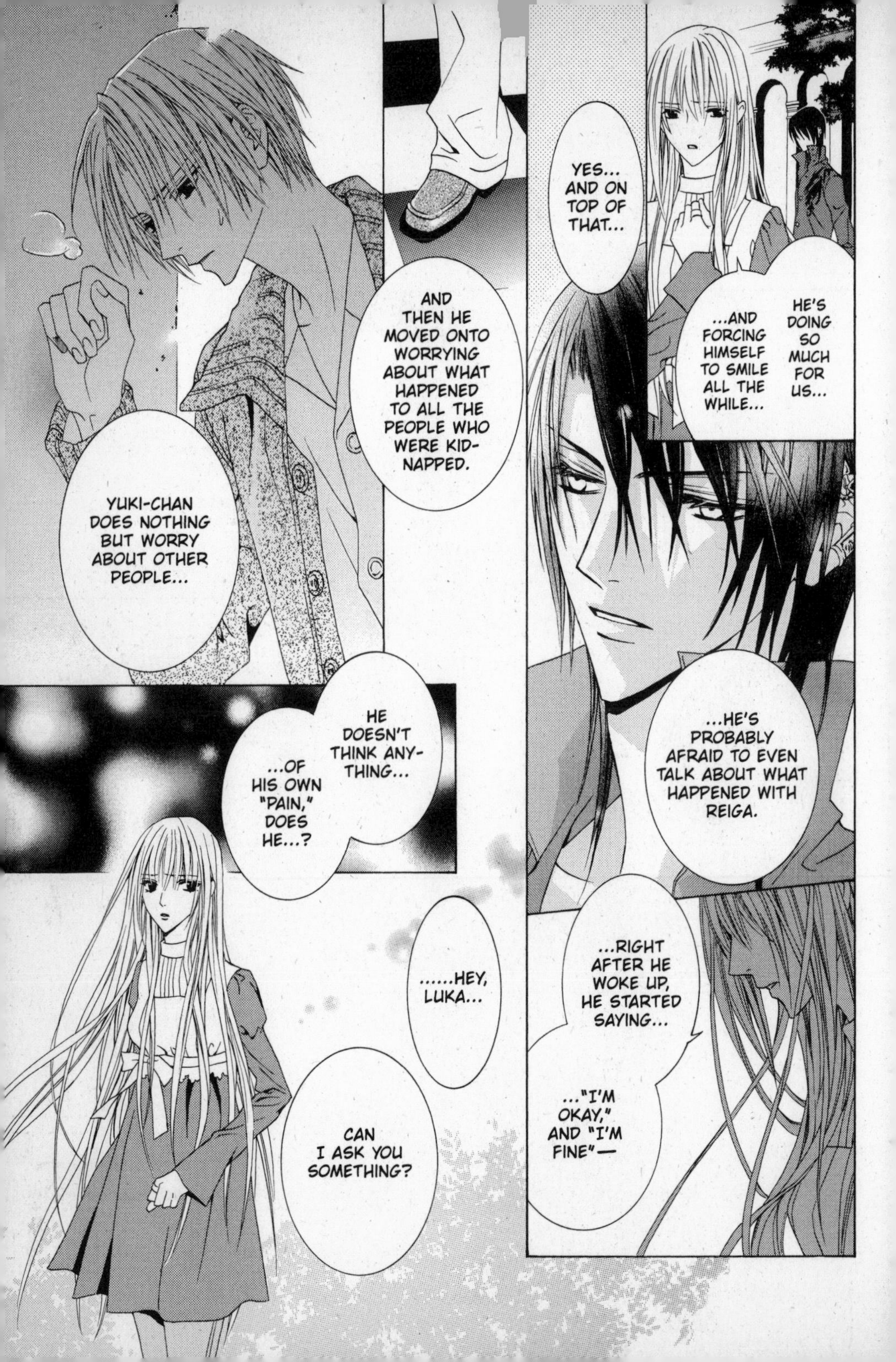
YES... AND ON TOP OF THAT...
HE'S DOING SO MUCH FOR US...
...AND FORCING HIMSELF TO SMILE ALL THE WHILE...
...HE'S PROBABLY AFRAID TO EVEN TALK ABOUT WHAT HAPPENED WITH REIGA.
...RIGHT AFTER HE WOKE UP, HE STARTED SAYING...
..."I'M OKAY," AND "I'M FINE"—
AND THEN HE MOVED ONTO WORRYING ABOUT WHAT HAPPENED TO ALL THE PEOPLE WHO WERE KID-NAPPED.
YUKI-CHAN DOES NOTHING BUT WORRY ABOUT OTHER PEOPLE...
HE DOESN'T THINK ANY-THING...
...OF HIS OWN "PAIN," DOES HE...?
......HEY, LUKA...
CAN I ASK YOU SOMETHING?

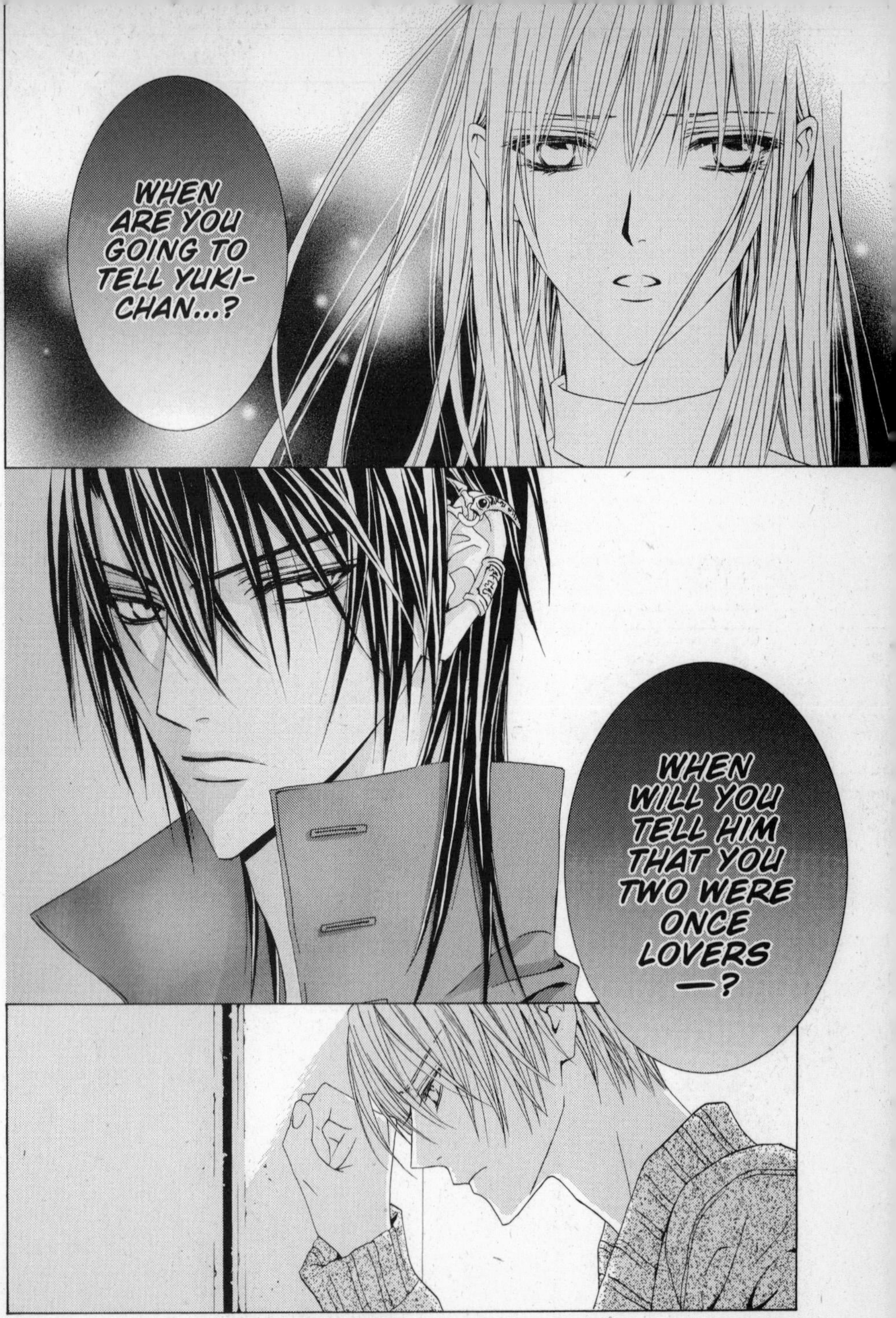
WHEN ARE YOU GOING TO TELL YUKI-CHAN...?
WHEN WILL YOU TELL HIM THAT YOU TWO WERE ONCE LOVERS—?

Story 19 END

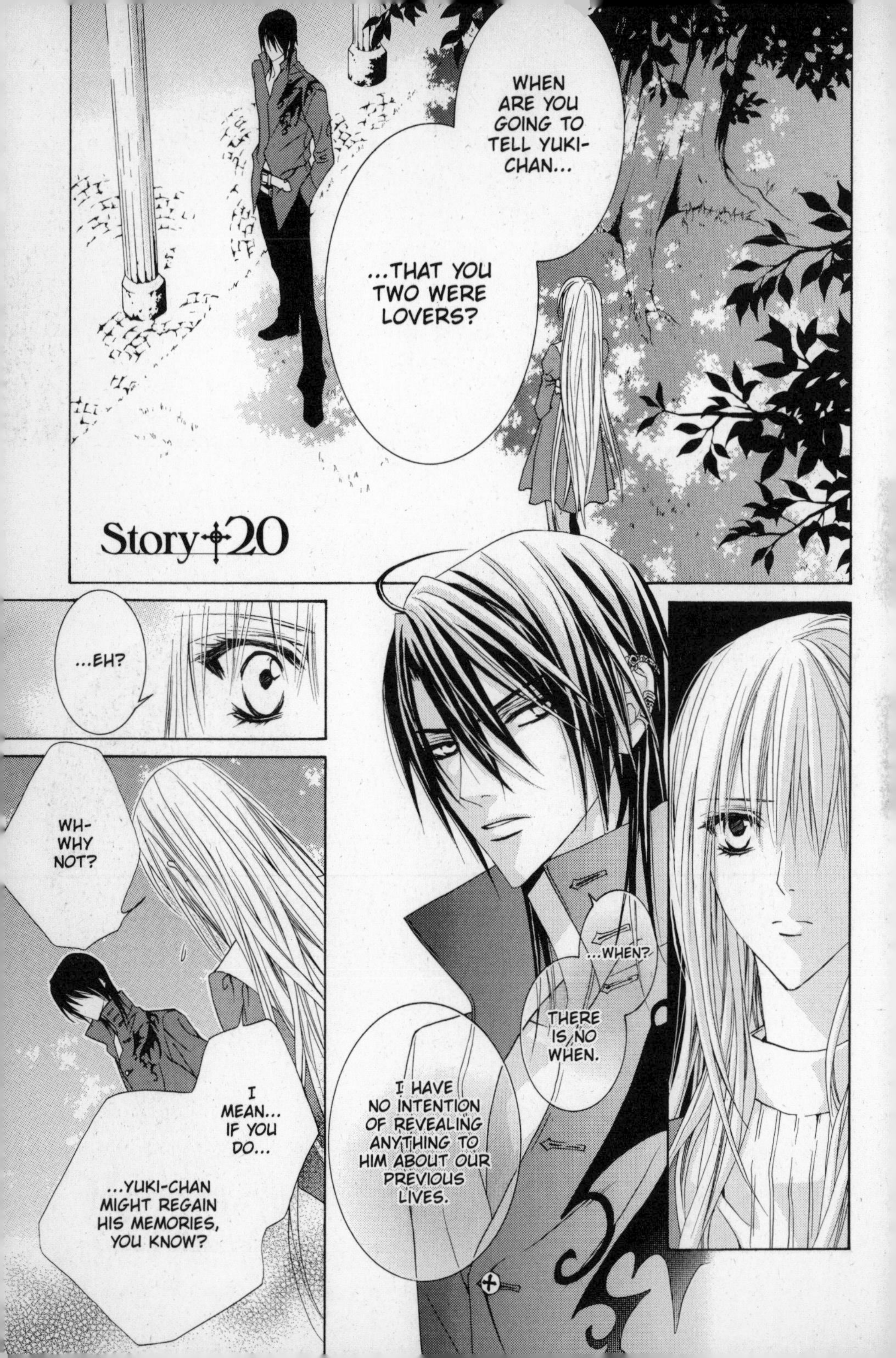
WHEN ARE YOU GOING TO TELL YUKI-CHAN...
...THAT YOU TWO WERE LOVERS?
Story 20
...WHEN?
THERE IS NO WHEN.
I HAVE NO INTENTION OF REVEALING ANYTHING TO HIM ABOUT OUR PREVIOUS LIVES.
...EH?
WH-WHY NOT?
I MEAN... IF YOU DO...
...YUKI-CHAN MIGHT REGAIN HIS MEMORIES, YOU KNOW?

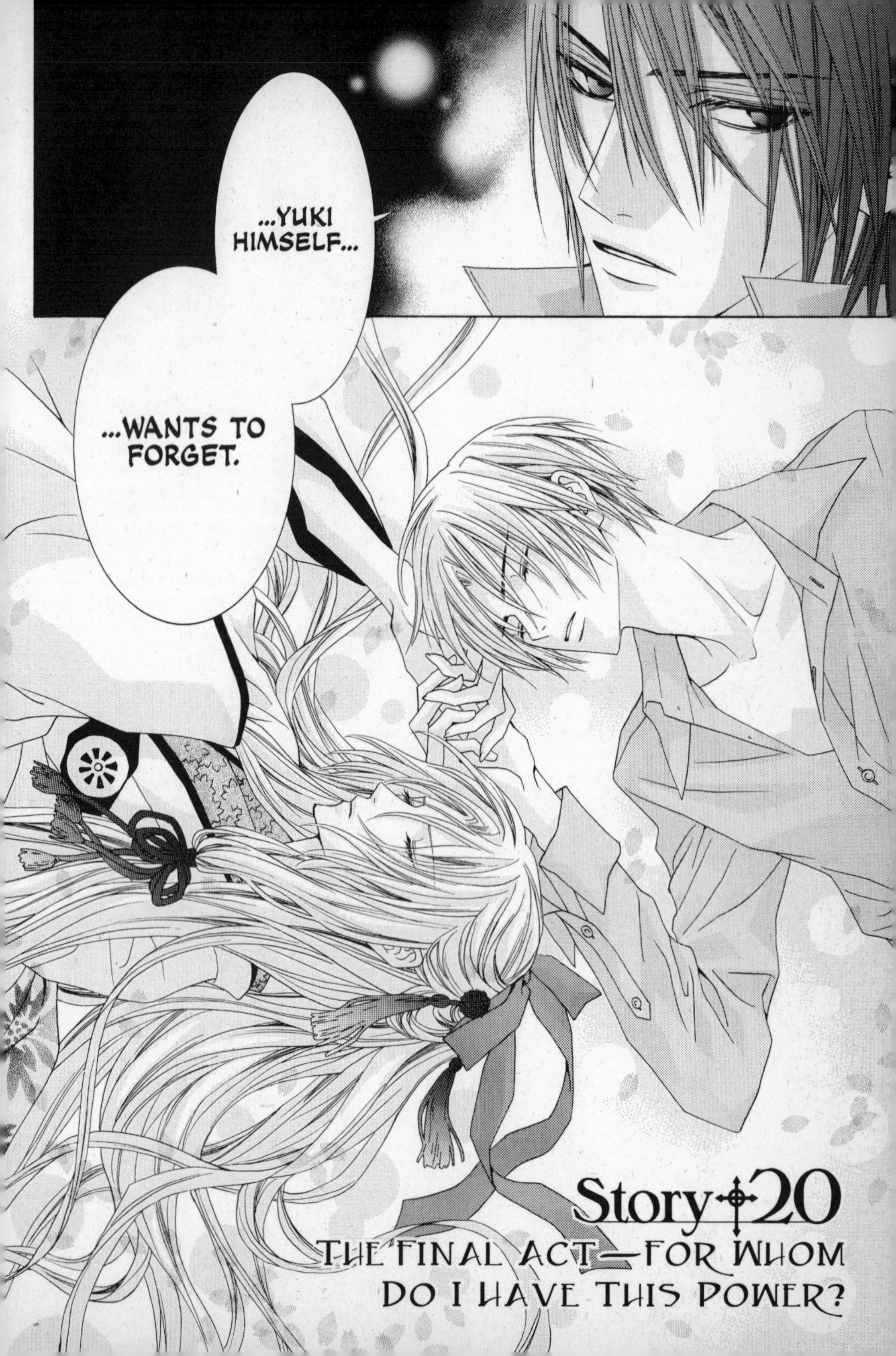
...YUKI HIMSELF...
...WANTS TO FORGET.
Story 20
THE FINAL ACT—FOR WHOM DO I HAVE THIS POWER?

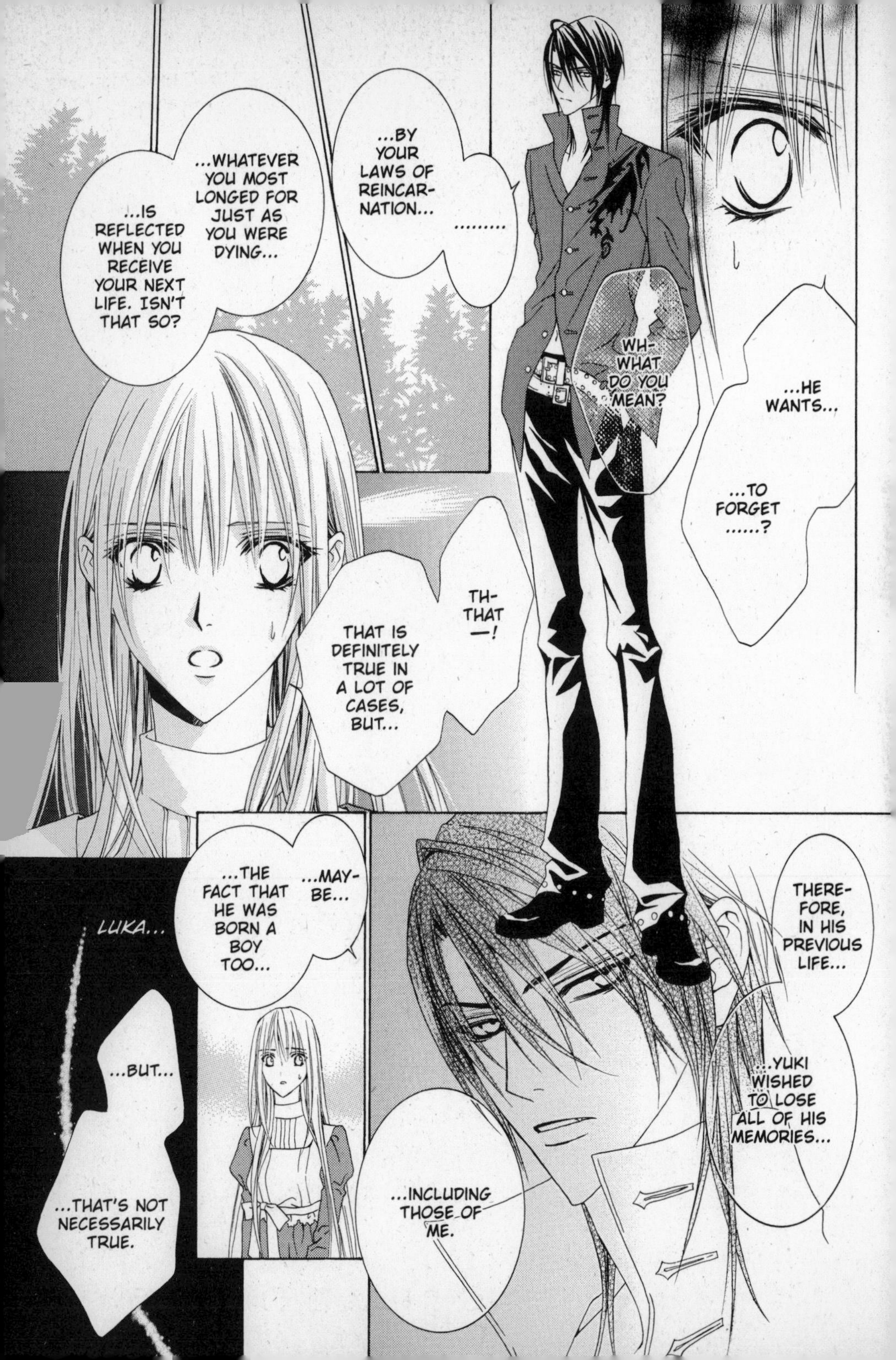
...HE WANTS...
...TO FORGET ......?
WH-WHAT DO YOU MEAN?
...BY YOUR LAWS OF REINCARNATION...
....
...WHATEVER YOU MOST LONGED FOR JUST AS YOU WERE DYING...
...IS REFLECTED WHEN YOU RECEIVE YOUR NEXT LIFE. ISN'T THAT SO?
TH-THAT—!
THAT IS DEFINITELY TRUE IN A LOT OF CASES, BUT...
THEREFORE, IN HIS PREVIOUS LIFE...
...YUKI WISHED TO LOSE ALL OF HIS MEMORIES...
...INCLUDING THOSE OF ME.
...MAY-BE...
...THE FACT THAT HE WAS BORN A BOY TOO...
LUKA...
...BUT...
...THAT'S NOT NECESSARILY TRUE.

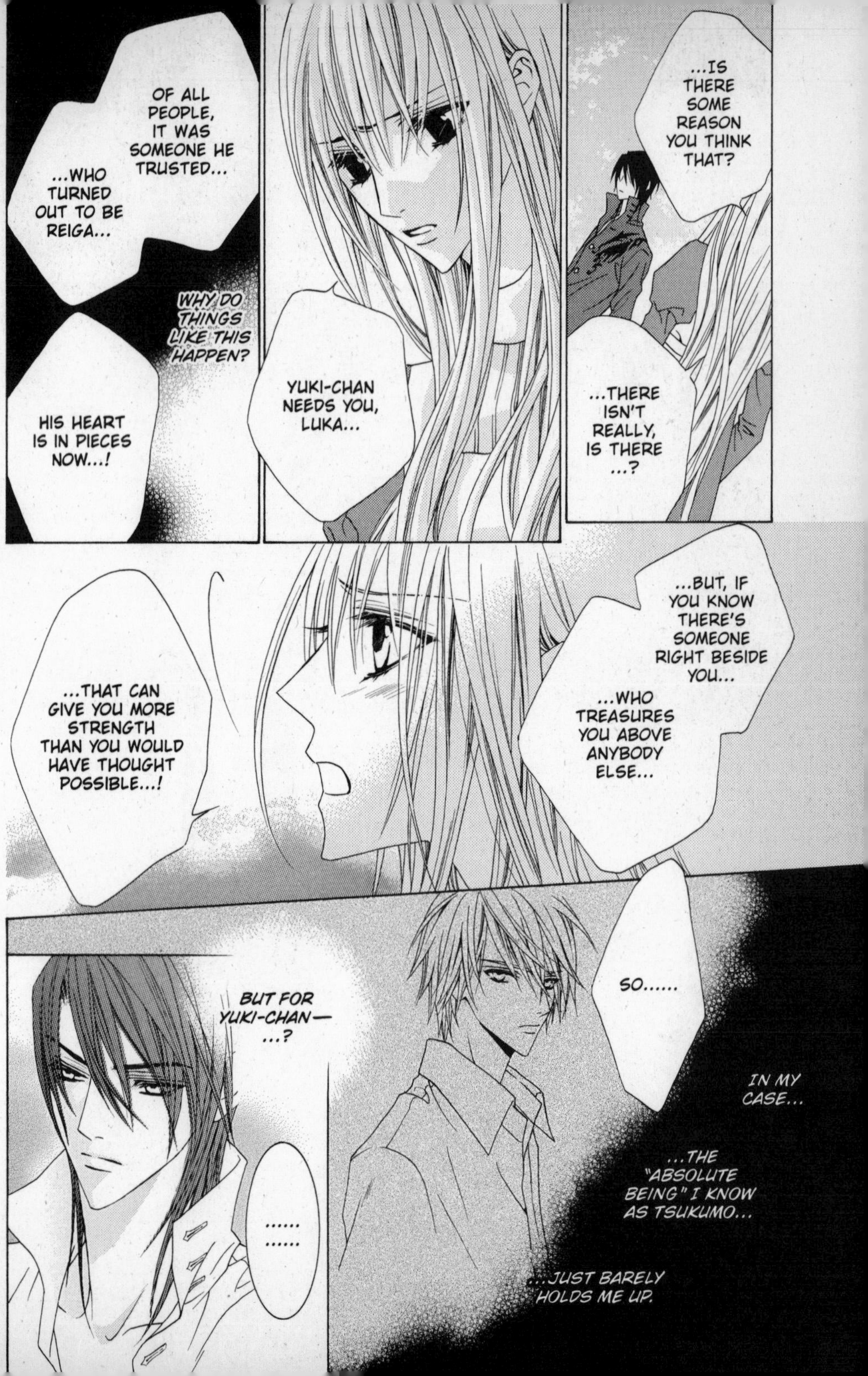
...IS THERE SOME REASON YOU THINK THAT?
...THERE ISN'T REALLY, IS THERE ...?
YUKI-CHAN NEEDS YOU, LUKA...
OF ALL PEOPLE, IT WAS SOMEONE HE TRUSTED...
...WHO TURNED OUT TO BE REIGA...
WHY DO THINGS LIKE THIS HAPPEN?
HIS HEART IS IN PIECES NOW...!
...BUT, IF YOU KNOW THERE'S SOMEONE RIGHT BESIDE YOU...
...WHO TREASURES YOU ABOVE ANYBODY ELSE...
...THAT CAN GIVE YOU MORE STRENGTH THAN YOU WOULD HAVE THOUGHT POSSIBLE...!
SO......
IN MY CASE...
...THE "ABSOLUTE BEING" I KNOW AS TSUKUMO...
...JUST BARELY HOLDS ME UP.
BUT FOR YUKI-CHAN—...?
....

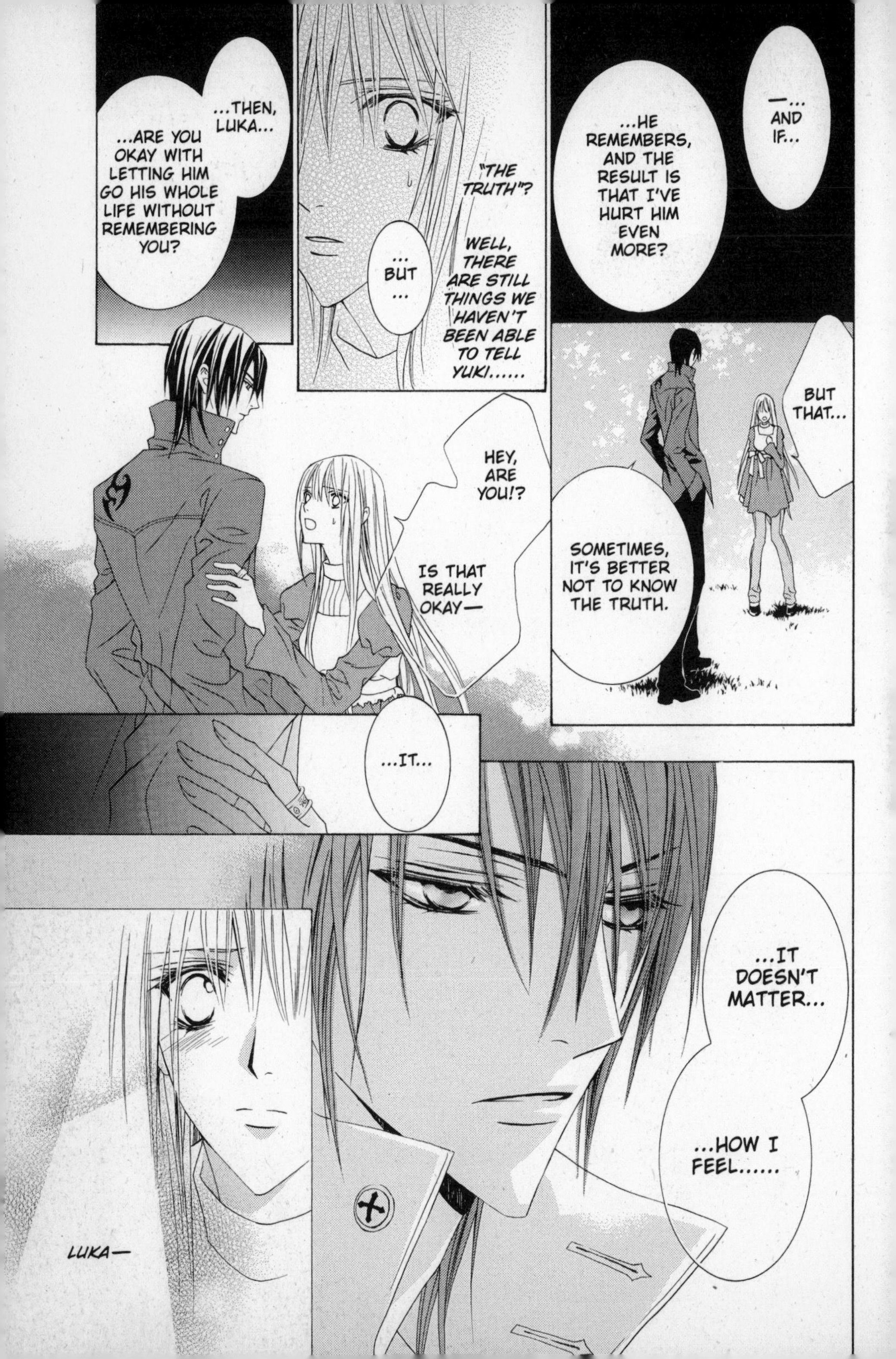
—... AND IF...
...HE REMEMBERS, AND THE RESULT IS THAT I'VE HURT HIM EVEN MORE?
... BUT ...
"THE TRUTH"?
WELL, THERE ARE STILL THINGS WE HAVEN'T BEEN ABLE TO TELL YUKI......
...THEN, LUKA...
...ARE YOU OKAY WITH LETTING HIM GO HIS WHOLE LIFE WITHOUT REMEMBERING YOU?
BUT THAT...
SOMETIMES, IT'S BETTER NOT TO KNOW THE TRUTH.
HEY, ARE YOU!?
IS THAT REALLY OKAY—
...IT...
...IT DOESN'T MATTER...
...HOW I FEEL......
LUKA—

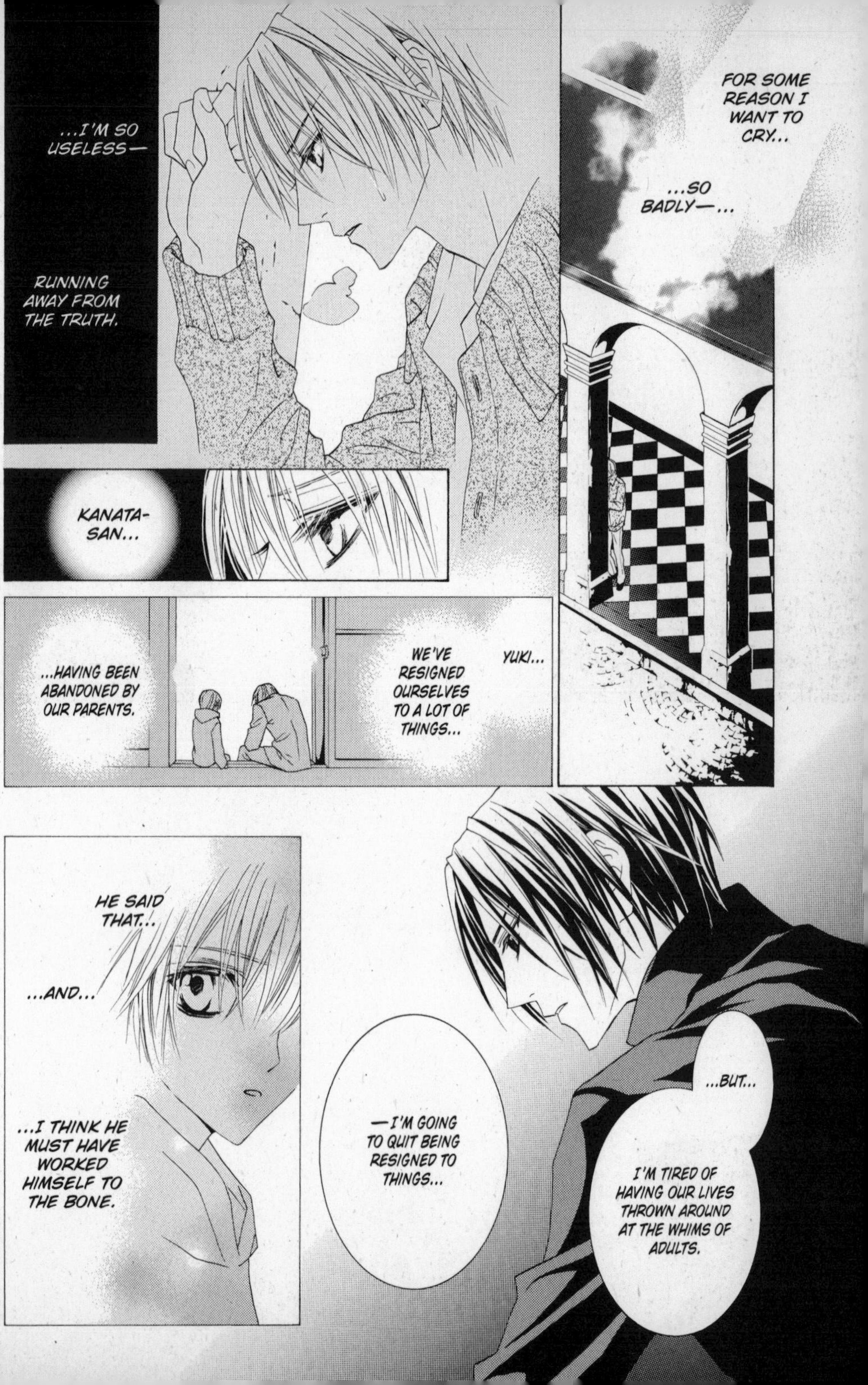
FOR SOME REASON I WANT TO CRY...
...SO BADLY—...
...I'M SO USELESS—
RUNNING AWAY FROM THE TRUTH.
KANATA-SAN...
YUKI...
WE'VE RESIGNED OURSELVES TO A LOT OF THINGS...
...HAVING BEEN ABANDONED BY OUR PARENTS.
...BUT...
I'M TIRED OF HAVING OUR LIVES THROWN AROUND AT THE WHIMS OF ADULTS.
—I'M GOING TO QUIT BEING RESIGNED TO THINGS...
HE SAID THAT...
...AND...
...I THINK HE MUST HAVE WORKED HIMSELF TO THE BONE.

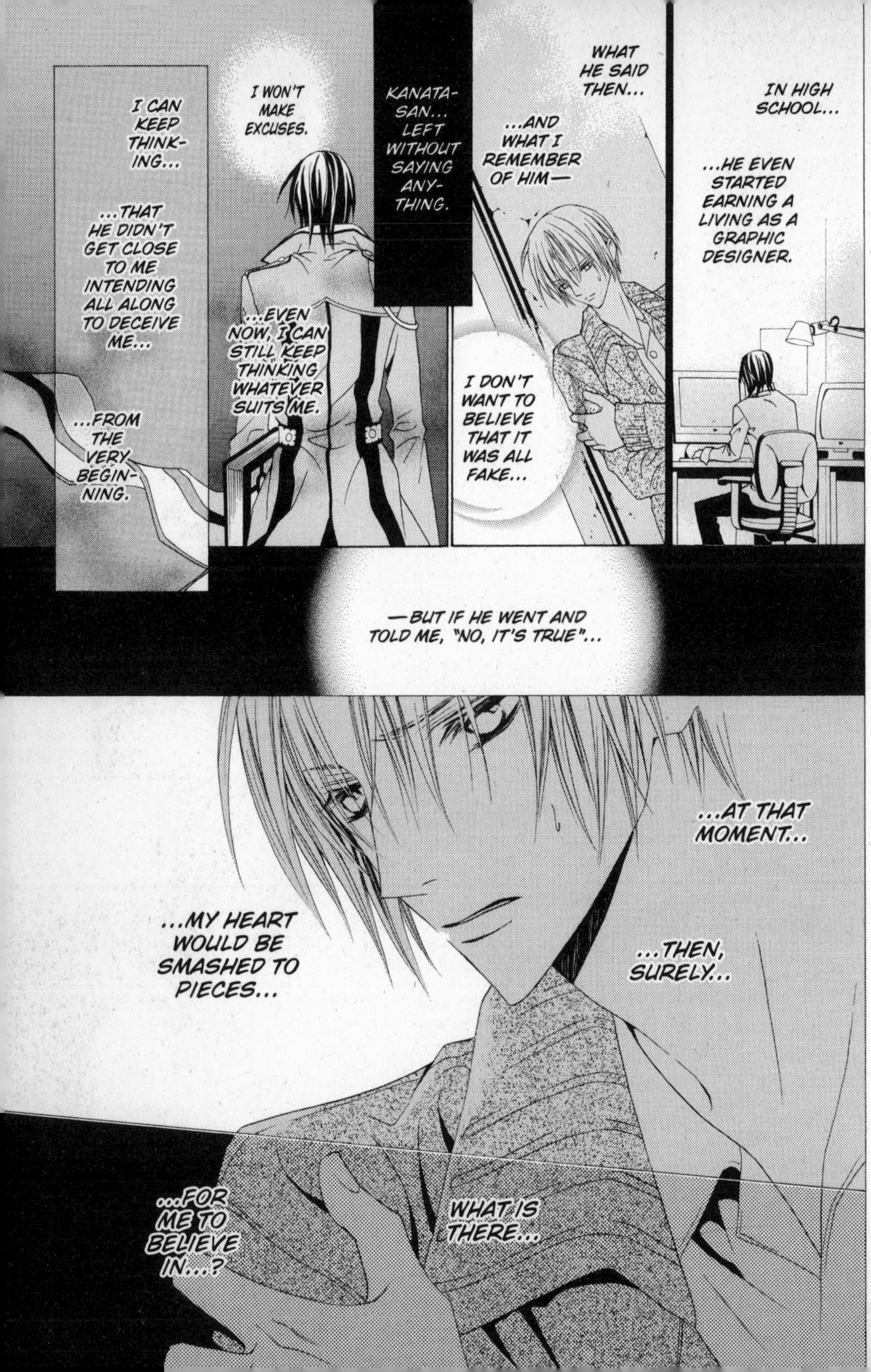
IN HIGH SCHOOL...
...HE EVEN STARTED EARNING A LIVING AS A GRAPHIC DESIGNER.
WHAT HE SAID THEN...
...AND WHAT I REMEMBER OF HIM—
I DON'T WANT TO BELIEVE THAT IT WAS ALL FAKE...
KANATA-SAN... LEFT WITHOUT SAYING ANYTHING.
I WON'T MAKE EXCUSES.
...EVEN NOW, I CAN STILL KEEP THINKING WHATEVER SUITS ME.
I CAN KEEP THINKING...
...THAT HE DIDN'T GET CLOSE TO ME INTENDING ALL ALONG TO DECEIVE ME...
...FROM THE VERY BEGINNING.
—BUT IF HE WENT AND TOLD ME, "NO, IT'S TRUE"...
...AT THAT MOMENT...
...THEN, SURELY...
...MY HEART WOULD BE SMASHED TO PIECES...
WHAT IS THERE...
...FOR ME TO BELIEVE IN...?

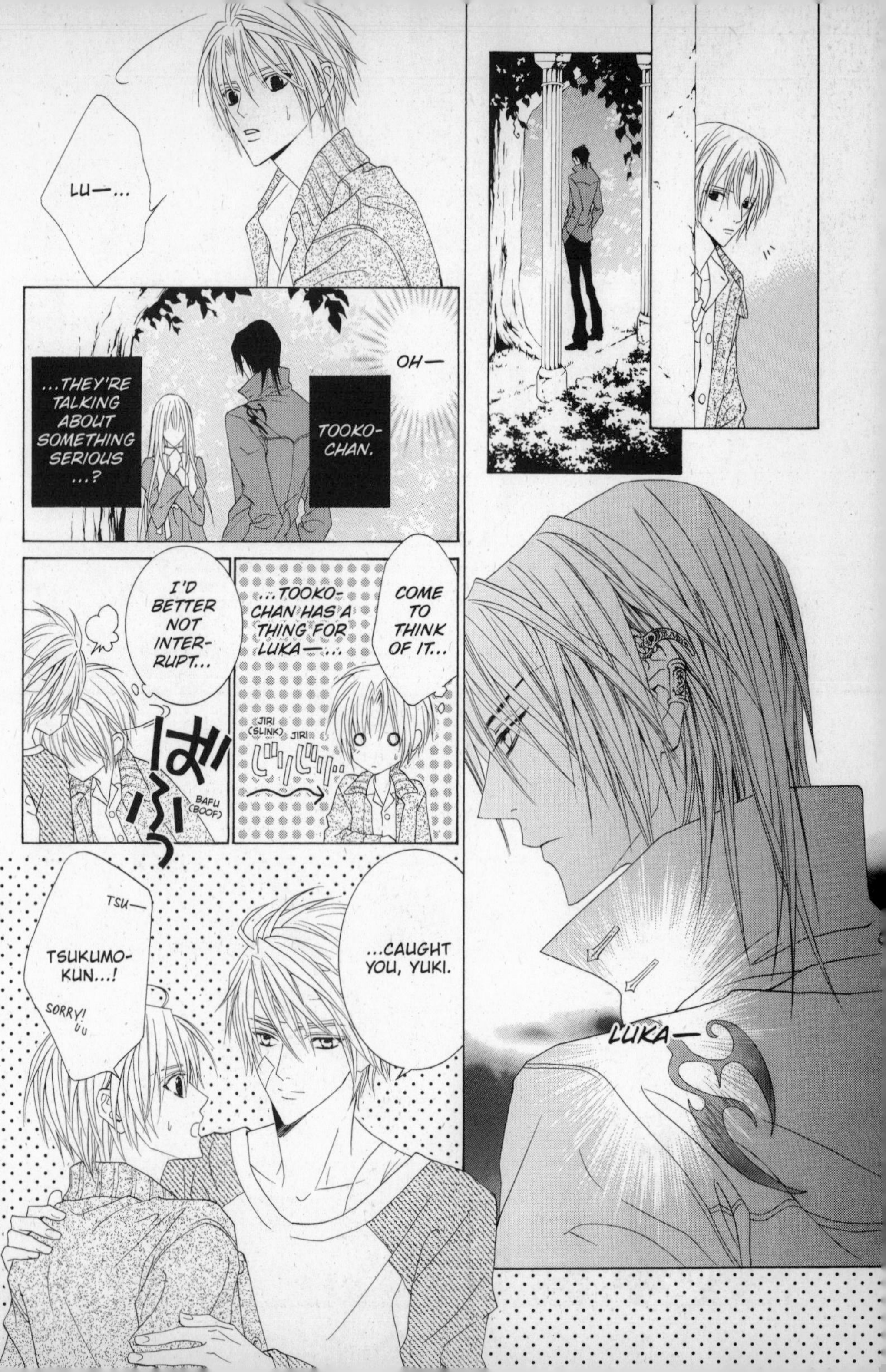
LU—...
OH—
TOOKO-CHAN.
...THEY'RE TALKING ABOUT SOMETHING SERIOUS ...?
LUKA—
COME TO THINK OF IT...
...TOOKO-CHAN HAS A THING FOR LUKA—...
JIRI (SLINK) JIRI
I'D BETTER NOT INTER-RUPT...
BAFU (BOOF)
...CAUGHT YOU, YUKI.
TSU—
TSUKUMO-KUN...!
SORRY!

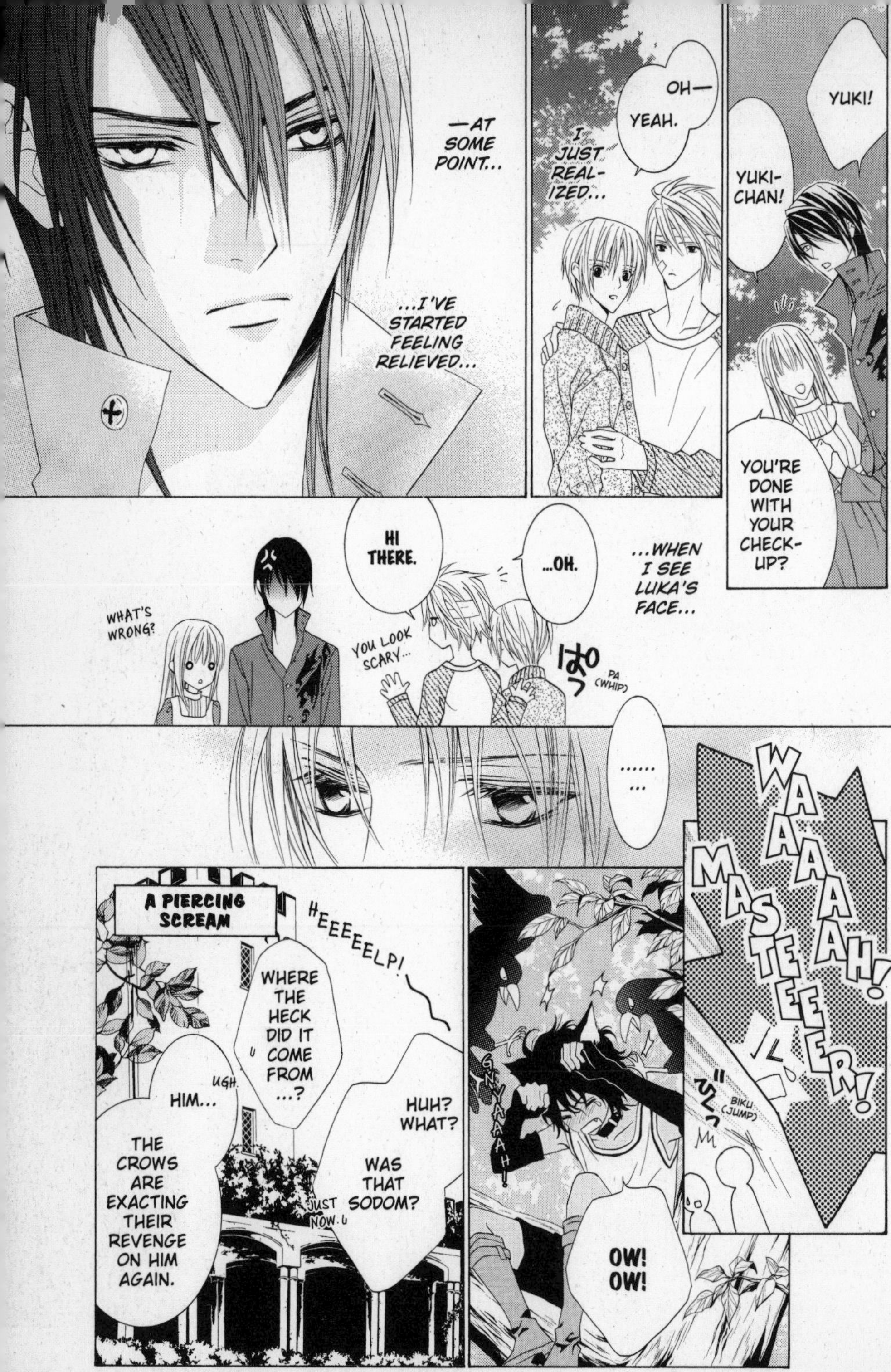

YUKI!
YUKI-CHAN!
YOU'RE DONE WITH YOUR CHECK-UP?
OH— YEAH.
I JUST REAL-IZED...
—AT SOME POINT...
...I'VE STARTED FEELING RELIEVED...
...WHEN I SEE LUKA'S FACE...
...OH.
HI THERE.
YOU LOOK SCARY...
PA (WHIP)
WHAT'S WRONG?
....
WAAAAAAH!
MASTEEEER!
BIKU (JUMP)
GNYAAAH!
OW! OW!
A PIERCING SCREAM
HEEEEELP!
WHERE THE HECK DID IT COME FROM ...?
HUH? WHAT?
WAS THAT SODOM?
JUST NOW.
HIM... UGH.
THE CROWS ARE EXACTING THEIR REVENGE ON HIM AGAIN.

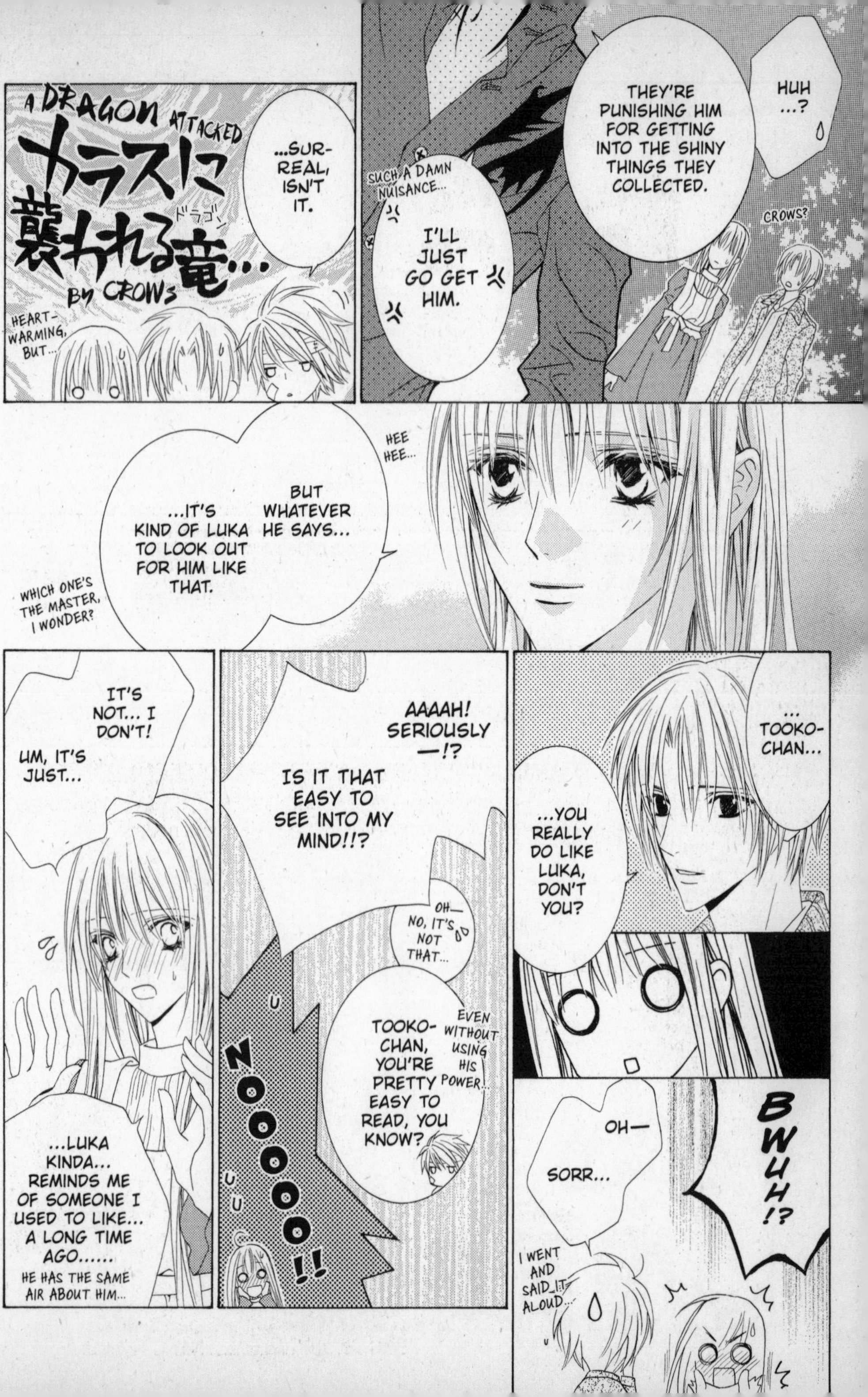
THEY'RE PUNISHING HIM FOR GETTING INTO THE SHINY THINGS THEY COLLECTED.
HUH ...?
CROWS?
SUCH A DAMN NUISANCE...
I'LL JUST GO GET HIM.
A DRAGON ATTACKED BY CROWS
カラスに襲われる竜(ドラゴン)…
...SUR-REAL, ISN'T IT.
HEART-WARMING, BUT...
HEE HEE...
BUT WHATEVER HE SAYS...
...IT'S KIND OF LUKA TO LOOK OUT FOR HIM LIKE THAT.
WHICH ONE'S THE MASTER, I WONDER?
... TOOKO-CHAN...
...YOU REALLY DO LIKE LUKA, DON'T YOU?
BWUH!?
OH— SORR...
I WENT AND SAID IT ALOUD...
AAAAH! SERIOUSLY—!?
IS IT THAT EASY TO SEE INTO MY MIND!!?
OH— NO, IT'S NOT THAT...
TOOKO-CHAN, YOU'RE PRETTY EASY TO READ, YOU KNOW?
EVEN WITHOUT USING HIS POWER...
NOOOOOO!!
IT'S NOT... I DON'T!
UM, IT'S JUST...
...LUKA KINDA... REMINDS ME OF SOMEONE I USED TO LIKE... A LONG TIME AGO......
HE HAS THE SAME AIR ABOUT HIM...

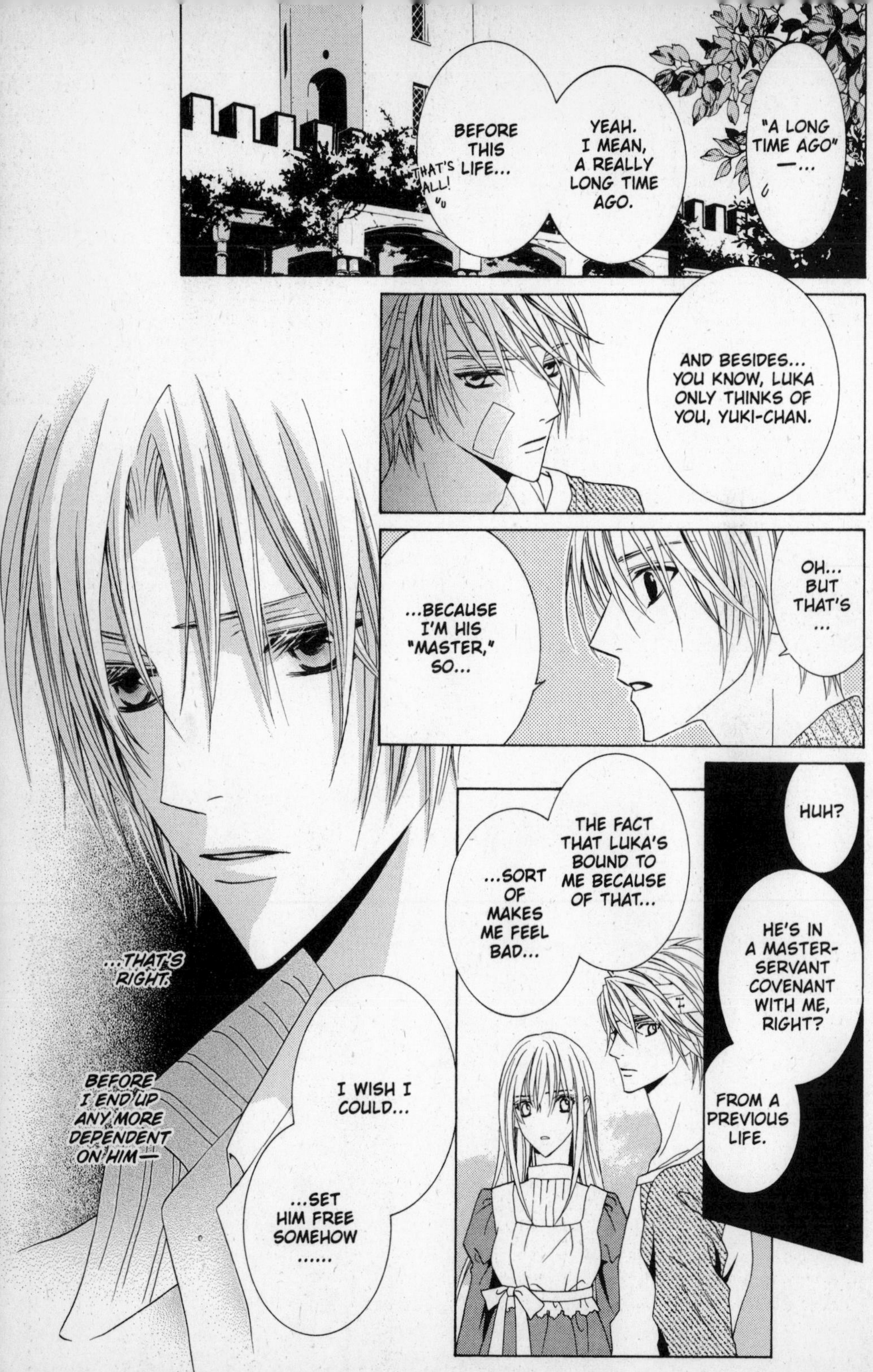
"A LONG TIME AGO"—...
YEAH. I MEAN, A REALLY LONG TIME AGO.
BEFORE THIS LIFE...
THAT'S ALL!
AND BESIDES... YOU KNOW, LUKA ONLY THINKS OF YOU, YUKI-CHAN.
OH... BUT THAT'S...
...BECAUSE I'M HIS "MASTER," SO...
HUH?
HE'S IN A MASTER-SERVANT COVENANT WITH ME, RIGHT?
FROM A PREVIOUS LIFE.
THE FACT THAT LUKA'S BOUND TO ME BECAUSE OF THAT...
...SORT OF MAKES ME FEEL BAD...
I WISH I COULD...
...SET HIM FREE SOMEHOW......
...THAT'S RIGHT.
BEFORE I END UP ANY MORE DEPENDENT ON HIM—

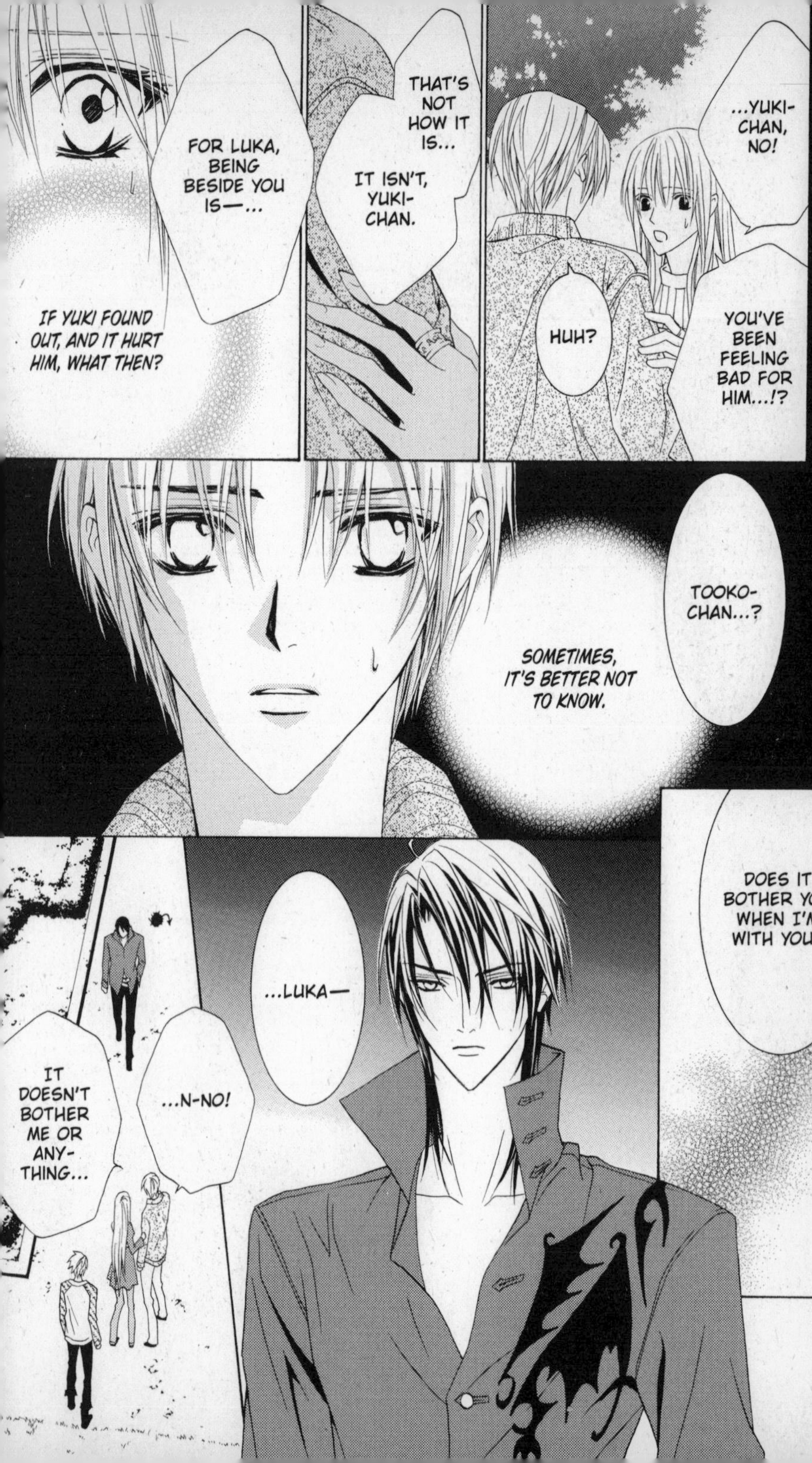
...YUKI-CHAN, NO!
YOU'VE BEEN FEELING BAD FOR HIM...!?
HUH?
THAT'S NOT HOW IT IS...
IT ISN'T, YUKI-CHAN.
FOR LUKA, BEING BESIDE YOU IS—...
IF YUKI FOUND OUT, AND IT HURT HIM, WHAT THEN?
TOOKO-CHAN...?
SOMETIMES, IT'S BETTER NOT TO KNOW.
DOES IT BOTHER YOU WHEN I'M WITH YOU?
...LUKA—
...N-NO!
IT DOESN'T BOTHER ME OR ANYTHING...

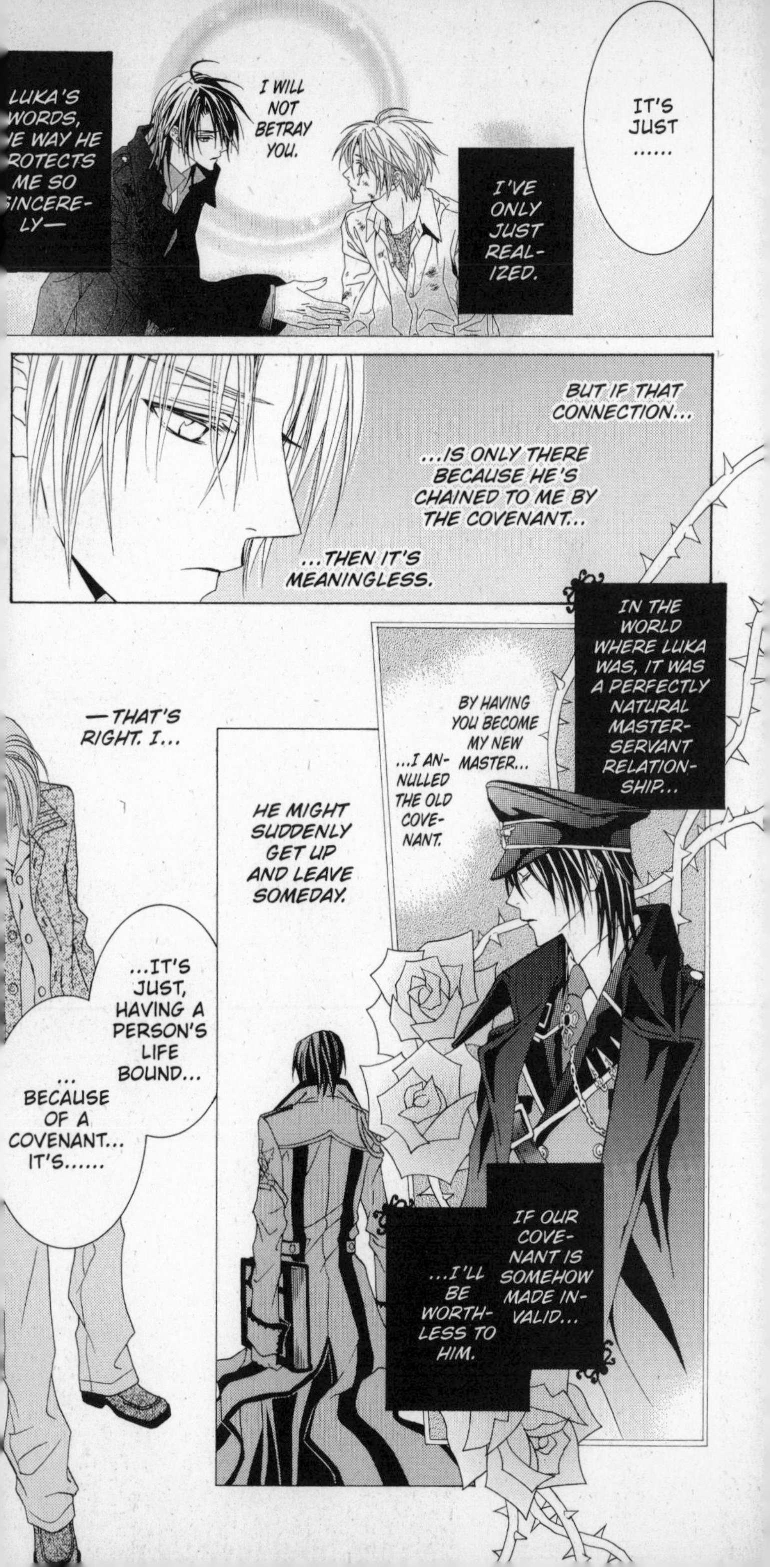
IT'S JUST ......
I'VE ONLY JUST REALIZED.
I WILL NOT BETRAY YOU.
LUKA'S WORDS, E WAY HE ROTECTS ME SO INCERE-LY—
BUT IF THAT CONNECTION...
...IS ONLY THERE BECAUSE HE'S CHAINED TO ME BY THE COVENANT...
...THEN IT'S MEANINGLESS.
IN THE WORLD WHERE LUKA WAS, IT WAS A PERFECTLY NATURAL MASTER-SERVANT RELATIONSHIP...
BY HAVING YOU BECOME MY NEW MASTER...
...I ANNULLED THE OLD COVENANT.
IF OUR COVENANT IS SOMEHOW MADE INVALID...
...I'LL BE WORTHLESS TO HIM.
HE MIGHT SUDDENLY GET UP AND LEAVE SOMEDAY.
—THAT'S RIGHT. I...
...IT'S JUST, HAVING A PERSON'S LIFE BOUND...
...BECAUSE OF A COVENANT... IT'S......

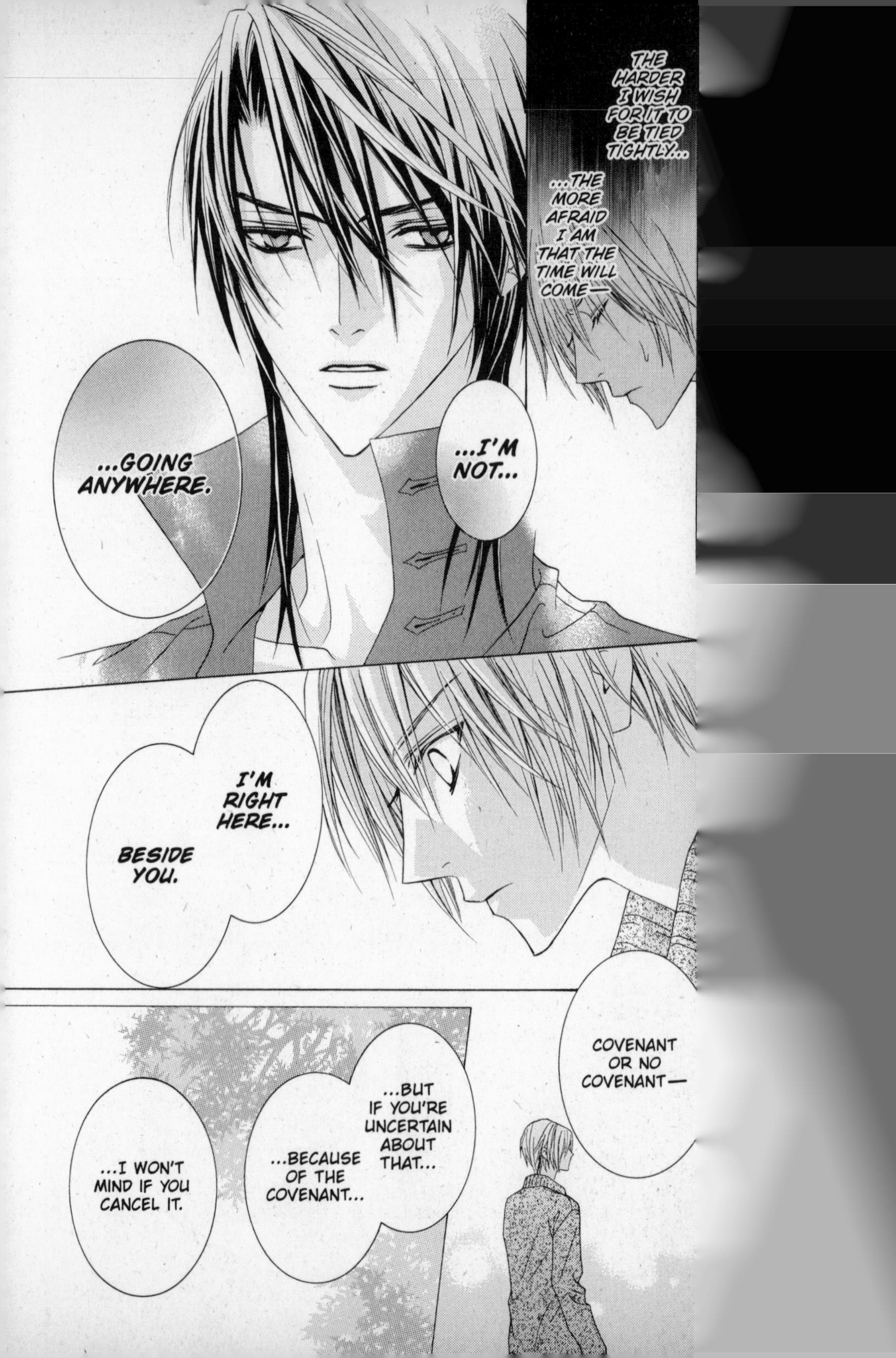
THE HARDER I WISH FOR IT TO BE TIED TIGHTLY...
...THE MORE AFRAID I AM THAT THE TIME WILL COME—
...I'M NOT...
...GOING ANYWHERE.
I'M RIGHT HERE...
BESIDE YOU.
COVENANT OR NO COVENANT—
...BUT IF YOU'RE UNCERTAIN ABOUT THAT...
...BECAUSE OF THE COVENANT...
...I WON'T MIND IF YOU CANCEL IT.

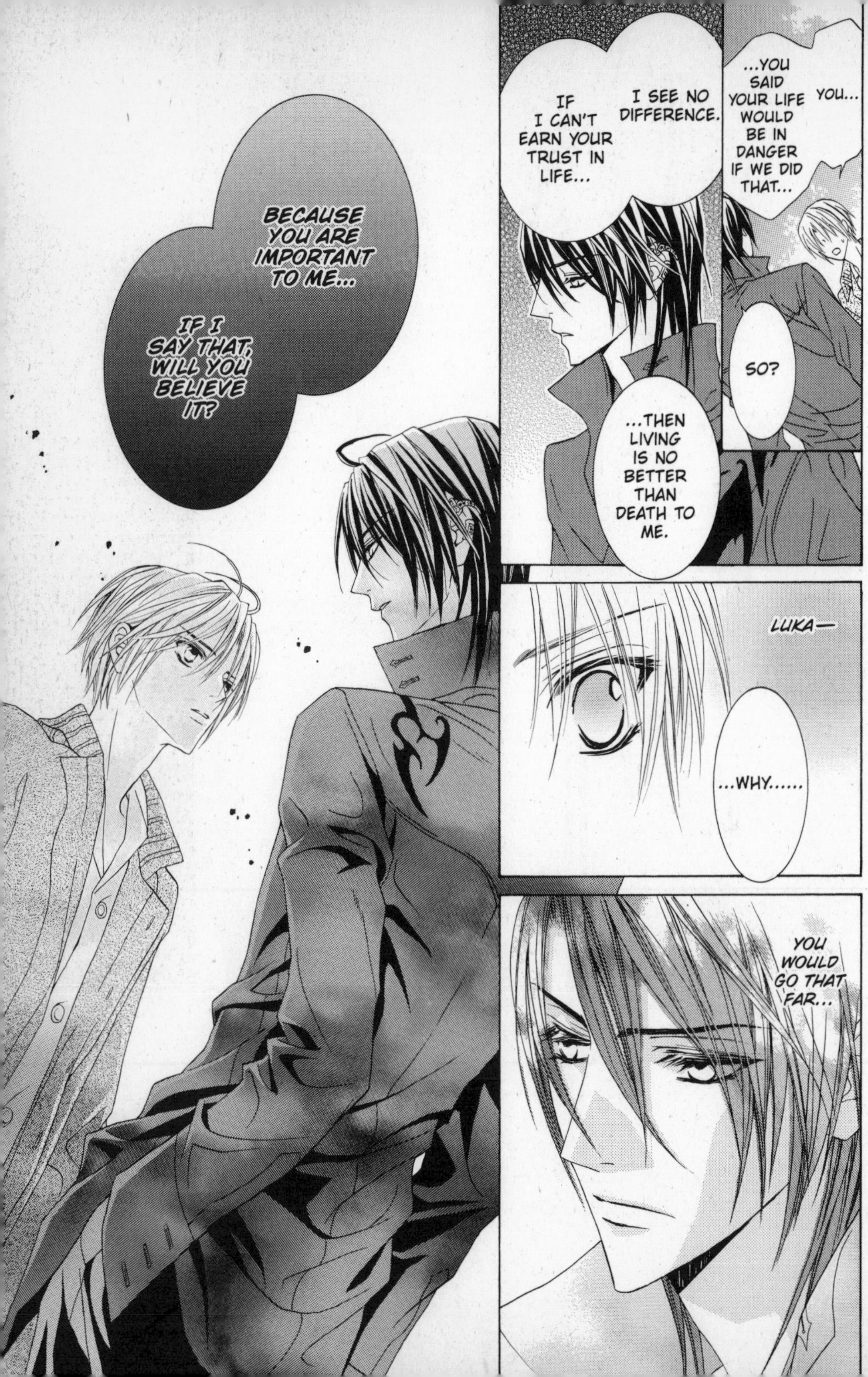
YOU...
...YOU SAID YOUR LIFE WOULD BE IN DANGER IF WE DID THAT...
SO?
I SEE NO DIFFERENCE.
IF I CAN'T EARN YOUR TRUST IN LIFE...
...THEN LIVING IS NO BETTER THAN DEATH TO ME.
LUKA—
...WHY......
YOU WOULD GO THAT FAR...
BECAUSE YOU ARE IMPORTANT TO ME...
IF I SAY THAT, WILL YOU BELIEVE IT?

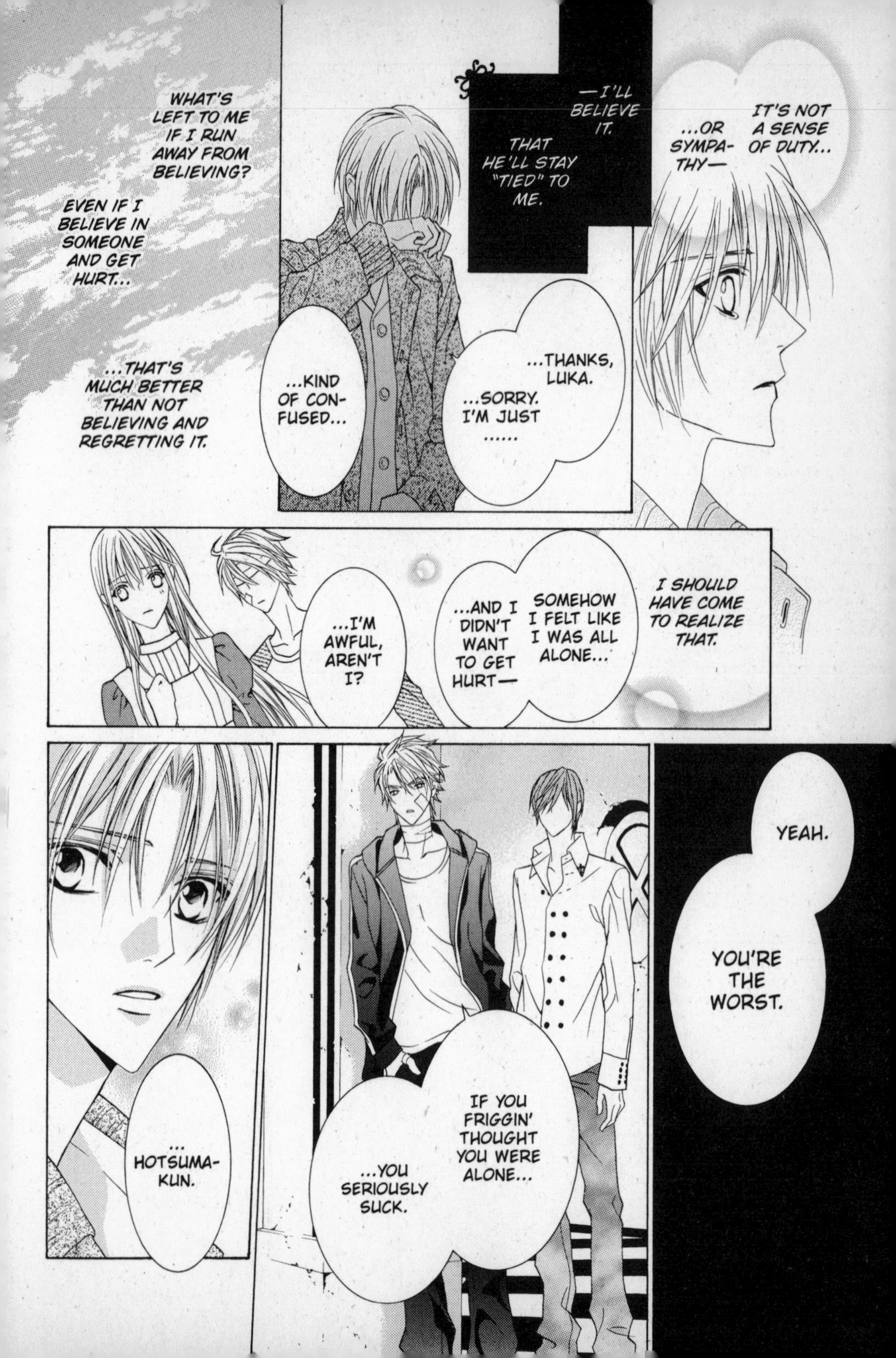
IT'S NOT A SENSE OF DUTY...
...OR SYMPA-THY—
—I'LL BELIEVE IT.
THAT HE'LL STAY "TIED" TO ME.
...THANKS, LUKA.
...SORRY. I'M JUST ......
...KIND OF CON-FUSED...
WHAT'S LEFT TO ME IF I RUN AWAY FROM BELIEVING?
EVEN IF I BELIEVE IN SOMEONE AND GET HURT...
...THAT'S MUCH BETTER THAN NOT BELIEVING AND REGRETTING IT.
I SHOULD HAVE COME TO REALIZE THAT.
SOMEHOW I FELT LIKE I WAS ALL ALONE...
...AND I DIDN'T WANT TO GET HURT—
...I'M AWFUL, AREN'T I?
YEAH.
YOU'RE THE WORST.
IF YOU FRIGGIN' THOUGHT YOU WERE ALONE...
...YOU SERIOUSLY SUCK.
... HOTSUMA-KUN.

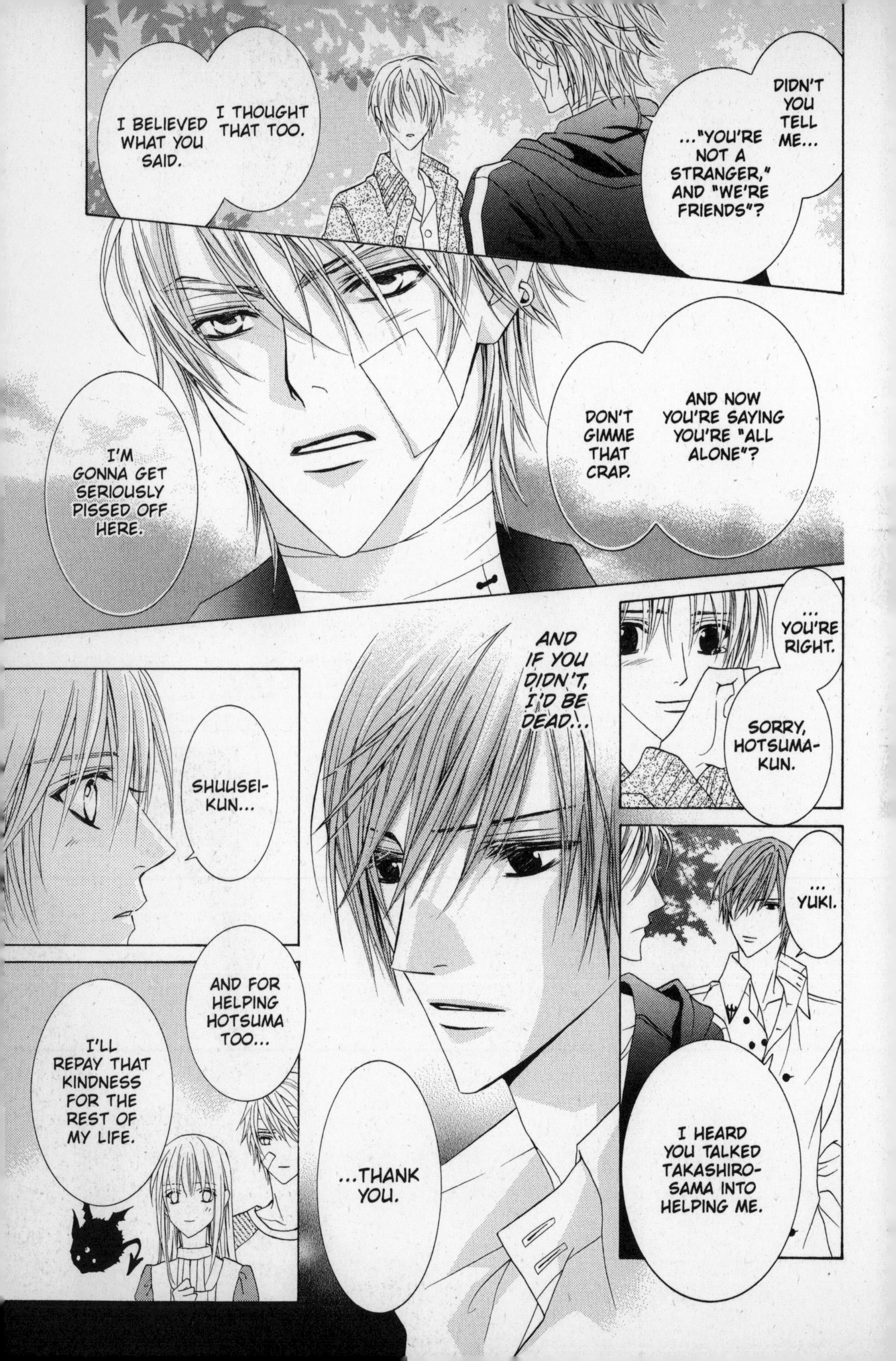
DIDN'T YOU TELL ME...
..."YOU'RE NOT A STRANGER," AND "WE'RE FRIENDS"?
I THOUGHT THAT TOO.
I BELIEVED WHAT YOU SAID.
AND NOW YOU'RE SAYING YOU'RE "ALL ALONE"?
DON'T GIMME THAT CRAP.
I'M GONNA GET SERIOUSLY PISSED OFF HERE.
...YOU'RE RIGHT.
SORRY, HOTSUMA-KUN.
...YUKI.
I HEARD YOU TALKED TAKASHIRO-SAMA INTO HELPING ME.
AND IF YOU DIDN'T, I'D BE DEAD...
...THANK YOU.
SHUUSEI-KUN...
AND FOR HELPING HOTSUMA TOO...
I'LL REPAY THAT KINDNESS FOR THE REST OF MY LIFE.

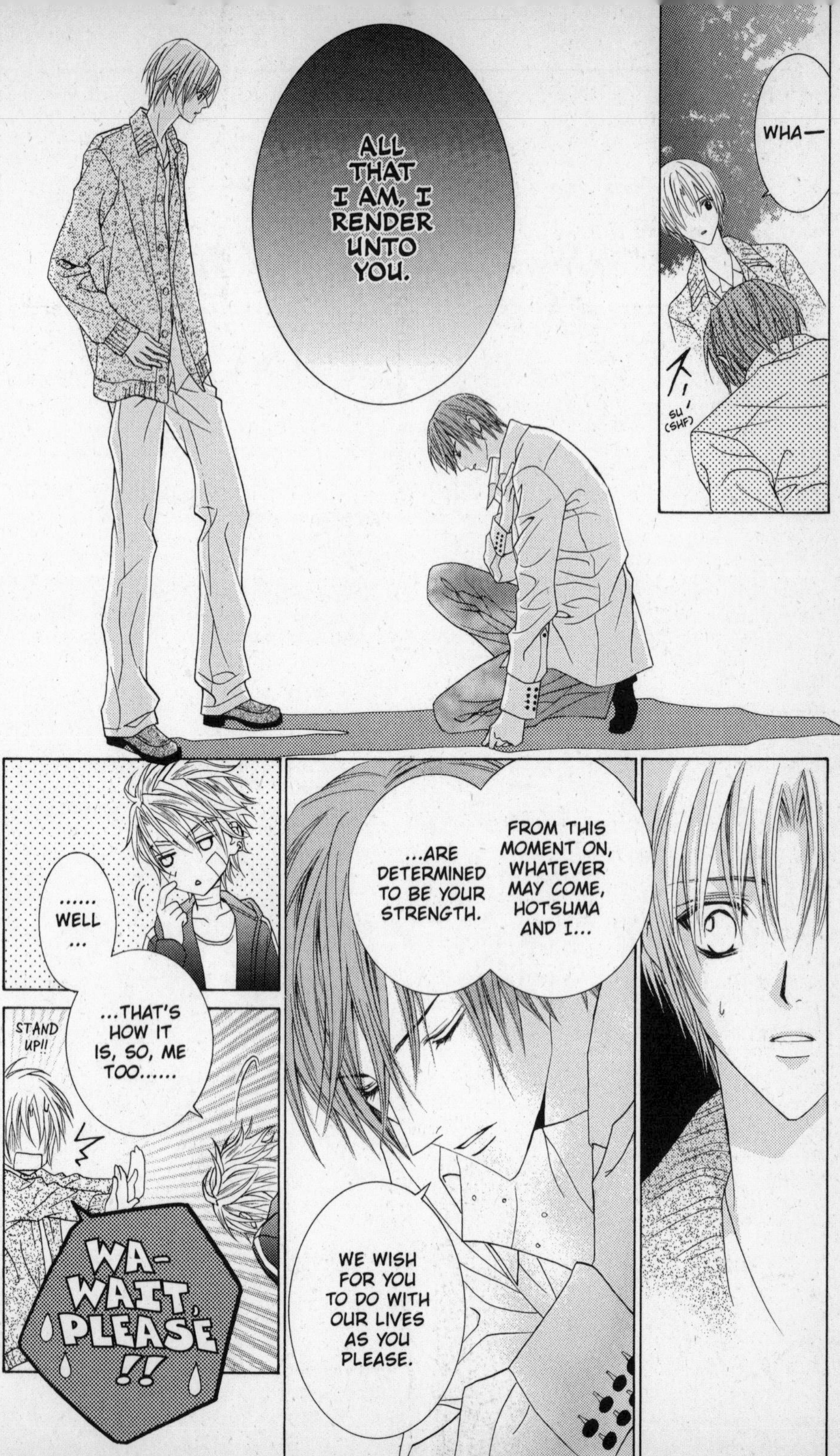
WHA—
SU (SHF)
ALL THAT I AM, I RENDER UNTO YOU.
FROM THIS MOMENT ON, WHATEVER MAY COME, HOTSUMA AND I...
...ARE DETERMINED TO BE YOUR STRENGTH.
WE WISH FOR YOU TO DO WITH OUR LIVES AS YOU PLEASE.
......WELL...
...THAT'S HOW IT IS, SO, ME TOO......
STAND UP!!
WA-WAIT, PLEASE!!

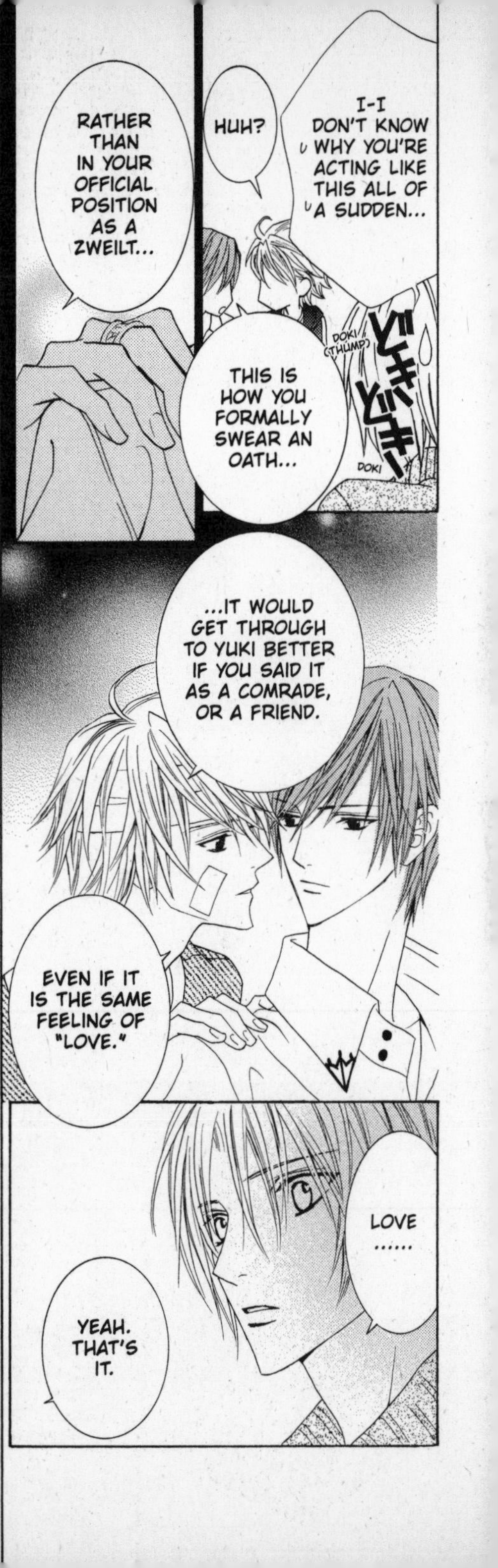
I-I DON'T KNOW WHY YOU'RE ACTING LIKE THIS ALL OF A SUDDEN...
HUH?
DOKI (THUMP) DOKI
THIS IS HOW YOU FORMALLY SWEAR AN OATH...
RATHER THAN IN YOUR OFFICIAL POSITION AS A ZWEILT...
...IT WOULD GET THROUGH TO YUKI BETTER IF YOU SAID IT AS A COMRADE, OR A FRIEND.
EVEN IF IT IS THE SAME FEELING OF "LOVE."
LOVE ......
YEAH. THAT'S IT.
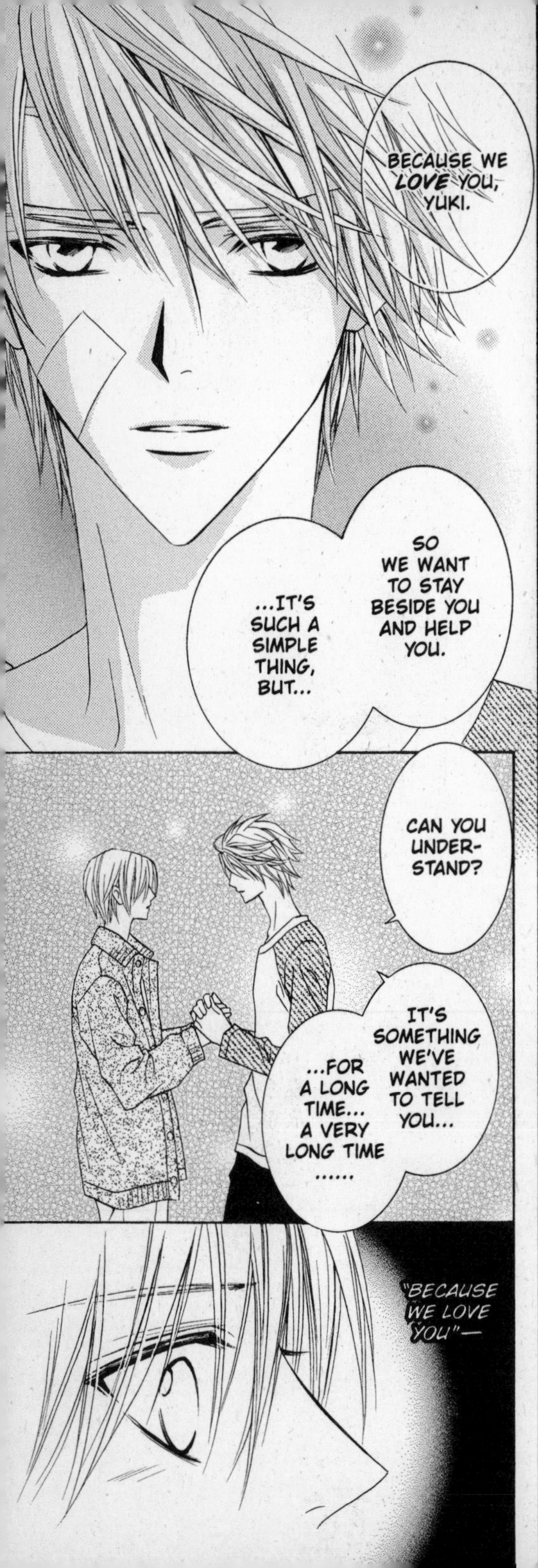
BECAUSE WE *LOVE* YOU, YUKI.
SO WE WANT TO STAY BESIDE YOU AND HELP YOU.
...IT'S SUCH A SIMPLE THING, BUT...
CAN YOU UNDERSTAND?
IT'S SOMETHING WE'VE WANTED TO TELL YOU...
...FOR A LONG TIME... A VERY LONG TIME ......
"BECAUSE WE LOVE YOU"—

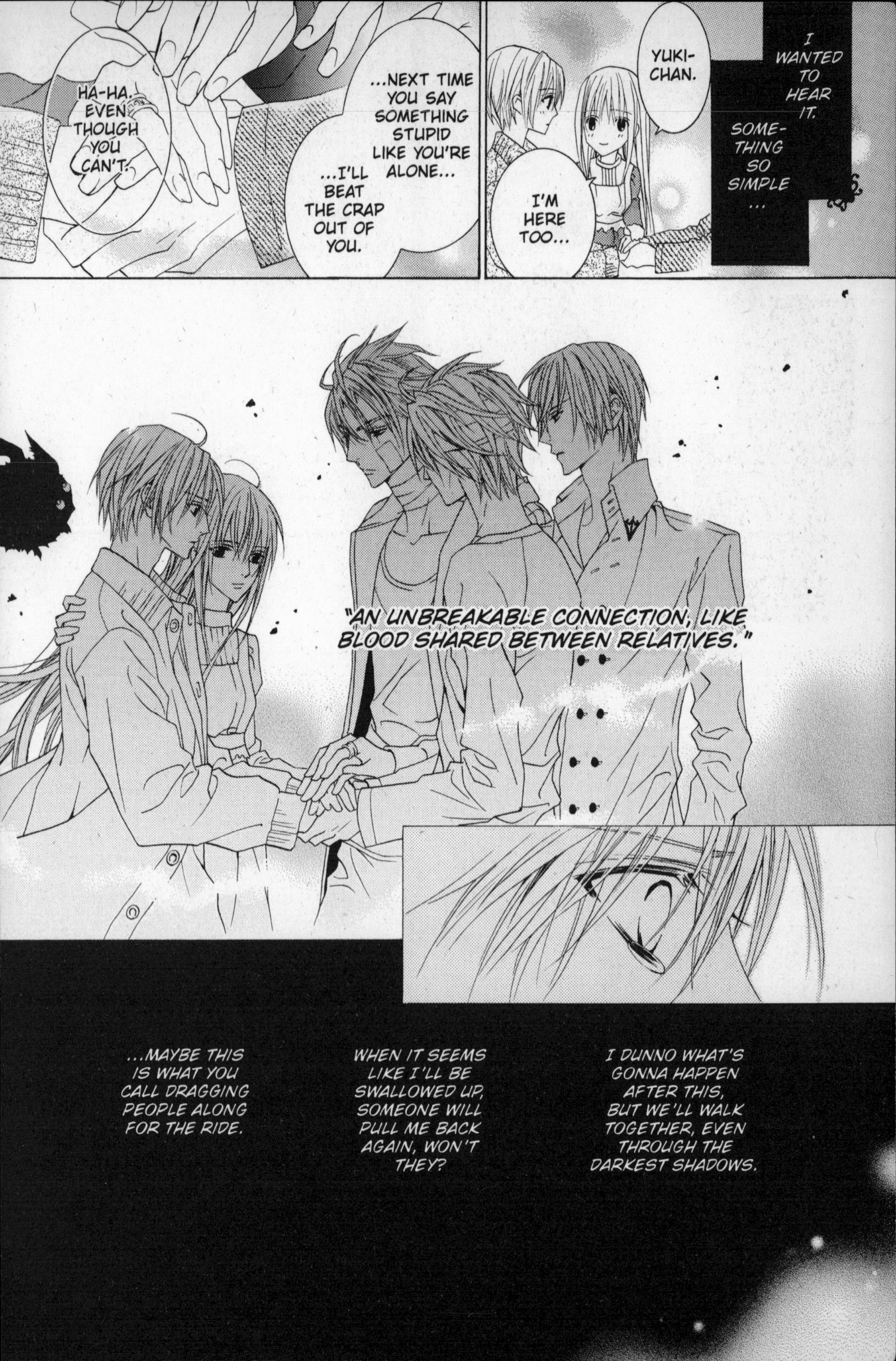
YUKI-CHAN.
I'M HERE TOO...
I WANTED TO HEAR IT.
SOMETHING SO SIMPLE...
...NEXT TIME YOU SAY SOMETHING STUPID LIKE YOU'RE ALONE...
...I'LL BEAT THE CRAP OUT OF YOU.
HA-HA. EVEN THOUGH YOU CAN'T.
"AN UNBREAKABLE CONNECTION, LIKE BLOOD SHARED BETWEEN RELATIVES."
I DUNNO WHAT'S GONNA HAPPEN AFTER THIS, BUT WE'LL WALK TOGETHER, EVEN THROUGH THE DARKEST SHADOWS.
WHEN IT SEEMS LIKE I'LL BE SWALLOWED UP, SOMEONE WILL PULL ME BACK AGAIN, WON'T THEY?
...MAYBE THIS IS WHAT YOU CALL DRAGGING PEOPLE ALONG FOR THE RIDE.

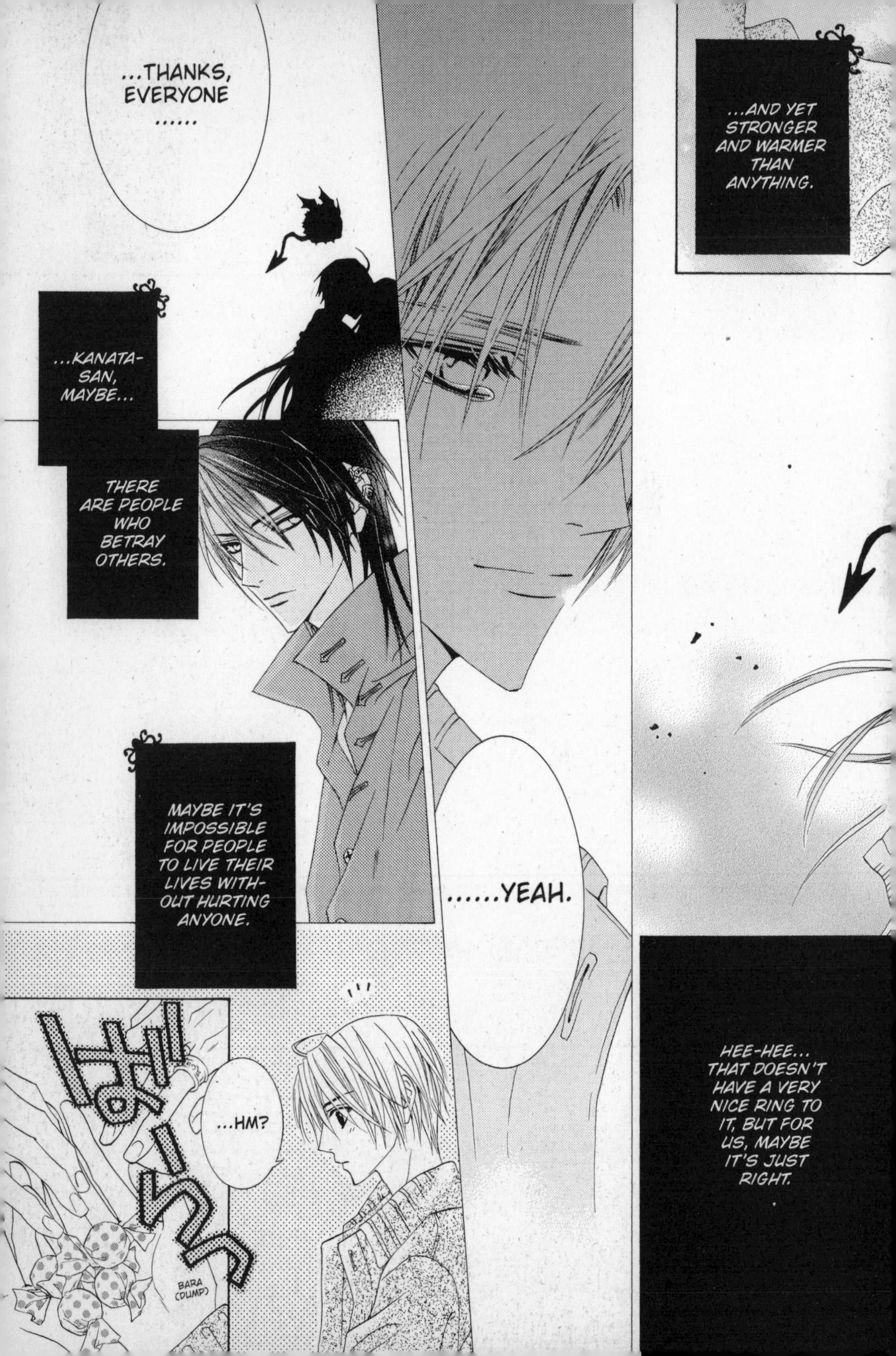
...AND YET STRONGER AND WARMER THAN ANYTHING.
...THANKS, EVERYONE ......
...KANATA-SAN, MAYBE...
THERE ARE PEOPLE WHO BETRAY OTHERS.
MAYBE IT'S IMPOSSIBLE FOR PEOPLE TO LIVE THEIR LIVES WITH-OUT HURTING ANYONE.
......YEAH.
...HM?
BARA (DUMP)
HEE-HEE... THAT DOESN'T HAVE A VERY NICE RING TO IT, BUT FOR US, MAYBE IT'S JUST RIGHT.

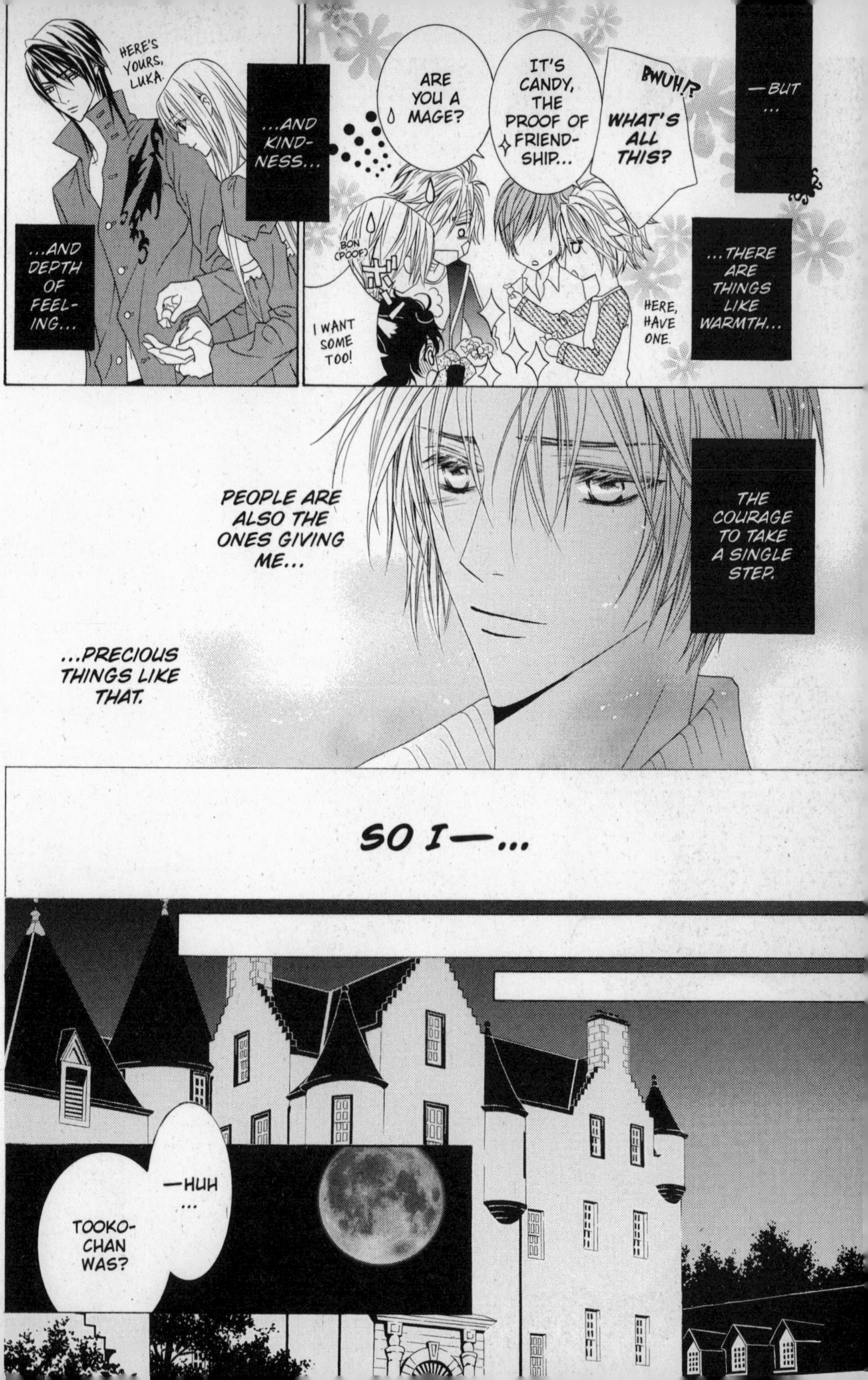
—BUT ...
BWUH!?
WHAT'S ALL THIS?
IT'S CANDY, THE PROOF OF FRIENDSHIP...
ARE YOU A MAGE?
...THERE ARE THINGS LIKE WARMTH...
HERE, HAVE ONE.
BON (POOF)
I WANT SOME TOO!
...AND KINDNESS...
HERE'S YOURS, LUKA.
...AND DEPTH OF FEELING...
THE COURAGE TO TAKE A SINGLE STEP.
PEOPLE ARE ALSO THE ONES GIVING ME...
...PRECIOUS THINGS LIKE THAT.
SO I—...
—HUH ...
TOOKO-CHAN WAS?

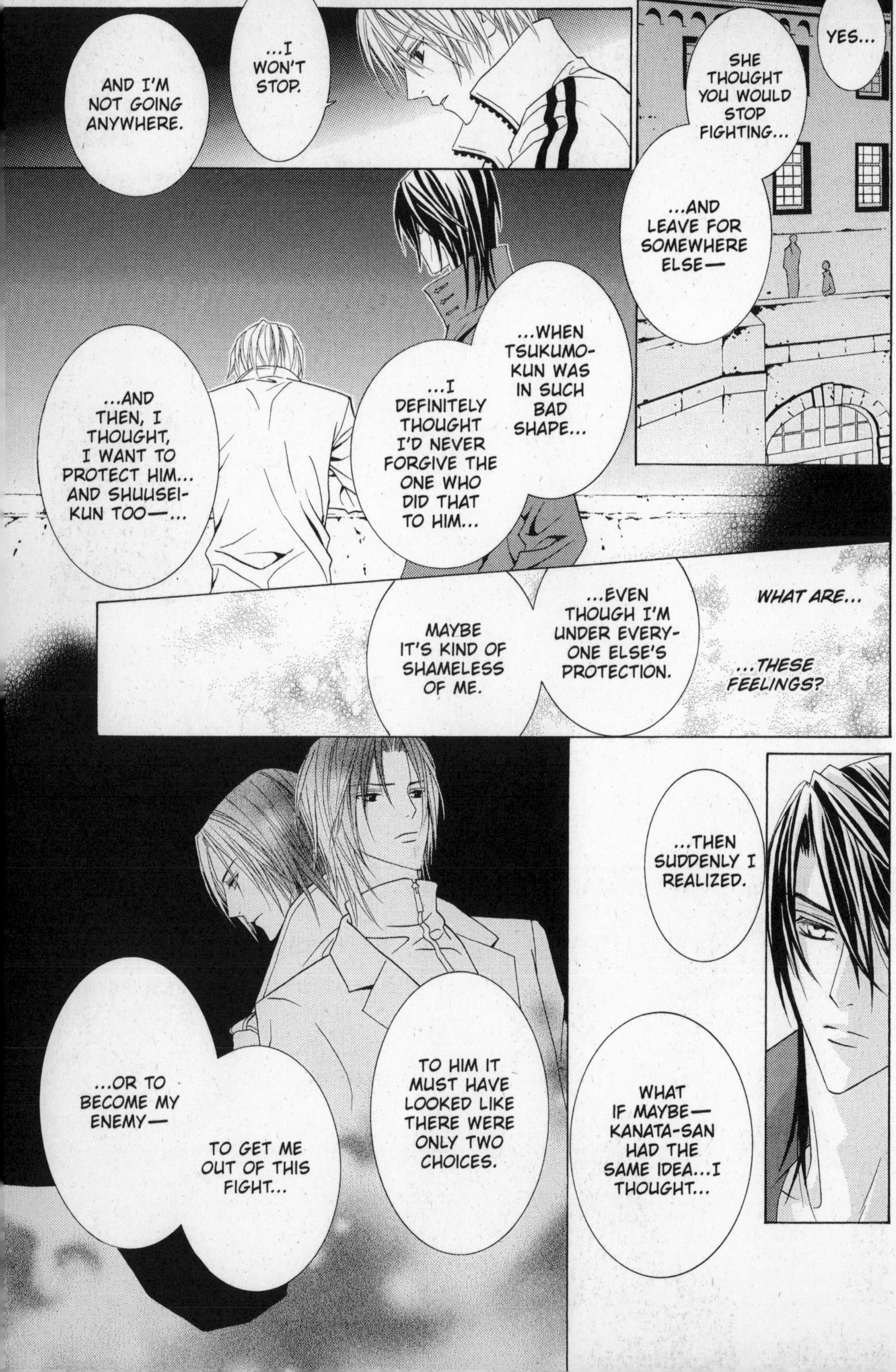
YES...
SHE THOUGHT YOU WOULD STOP FIGHTING...
...AND LEAVE FOR SOMEWHERE ELSE—
...I WON'T STOP.
AND I'M NOT GOING ANYWHERE.
...WHEN TSUKUMO-KUN WAS IN SUCH BAD SHAPE...
...I DEFINITELY THOUGHT I'D NEVER FORGIVE THE ONE WHO DID THAT TO HIM...
...AND THEN, I THOUGHT, I WANT TO PROTECT HIM... AND SHUUSEI-KUN TOO—...
WHAT ARE...
...THESE FEELINGS?
...EVEN THOUGH I'M UNDER EVERY-ONE ELSE'S PROTECTION.
MAYBE IT'S KIND OF SHAMELESS OF ME.
...THEN SUDDENLY I REALIZED.
WHAT IF MAYBE— KANATA-SAN HAD THE SAME IDEA...I THOUGHT...
TO HIM IT MUST HAVE LOOKED LIKE THERE WERE ONLY TWO CHOICES.
TO GET ME OUT OF THIS FIGHT...
...OR TO BECOME MY ENEMY—

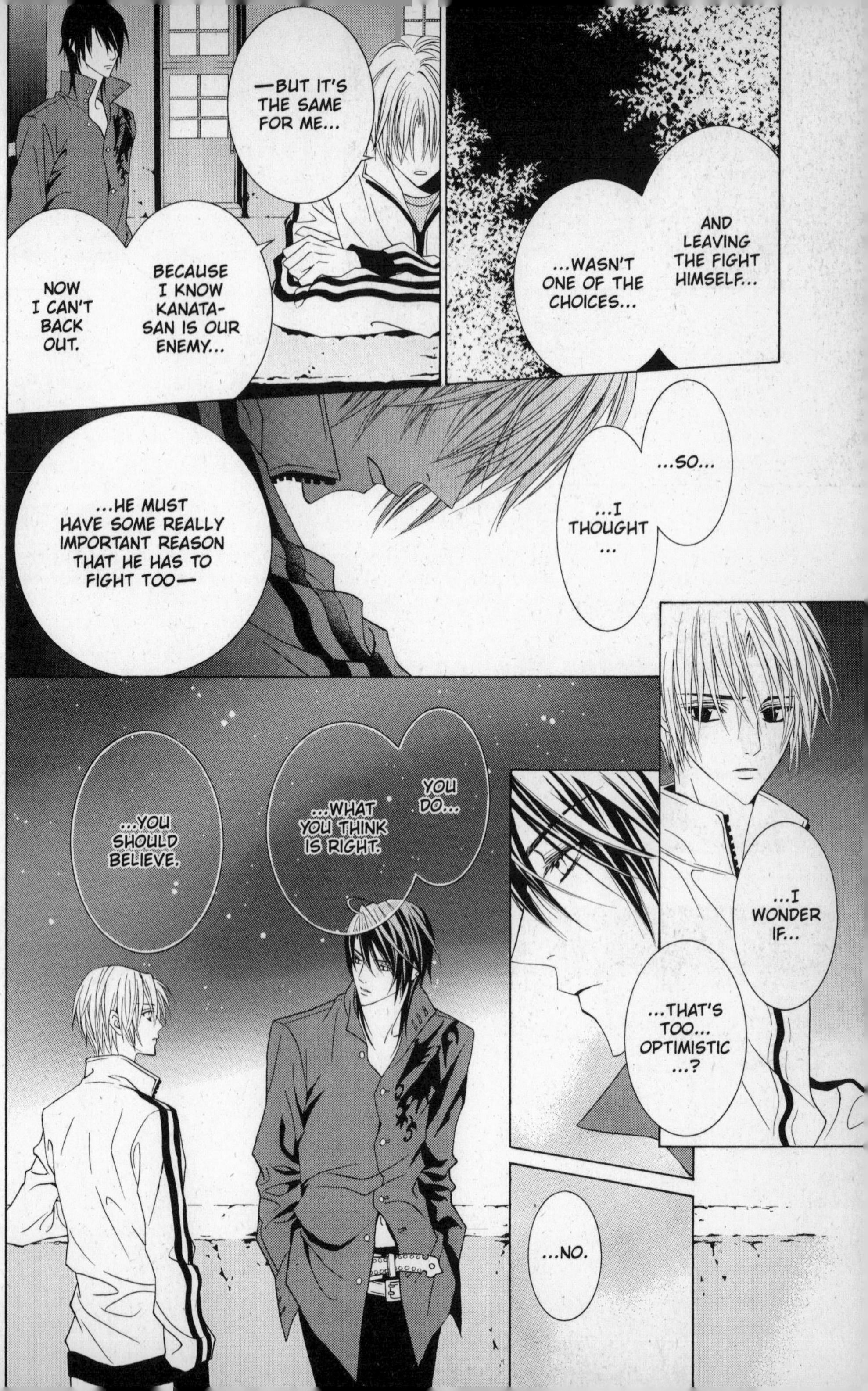

AND LEAVING THE FIGHT HIMSELF...
...WASN'T ONE OF THE CHOICES...
—BUT IT'S THE SAME FOR ME...
BECAUSE I KNOW KANATA-SAN IS OUR ENEMY...
NOW I CAN'T BACK OUT.
...SO...
...I THOUGHT...
...HE MUST HAVE SOME REALLY IMPORTANT REASON THAT HE HAS TO FIGHT TOO—
...I WONDER IF...
...THAT'S TOO... OPTIMISTIC ...?
...NO.
YOU DO...
...WHAT YOU THINK IS RIGHT.
...YOU SHOULD BELIEVE.

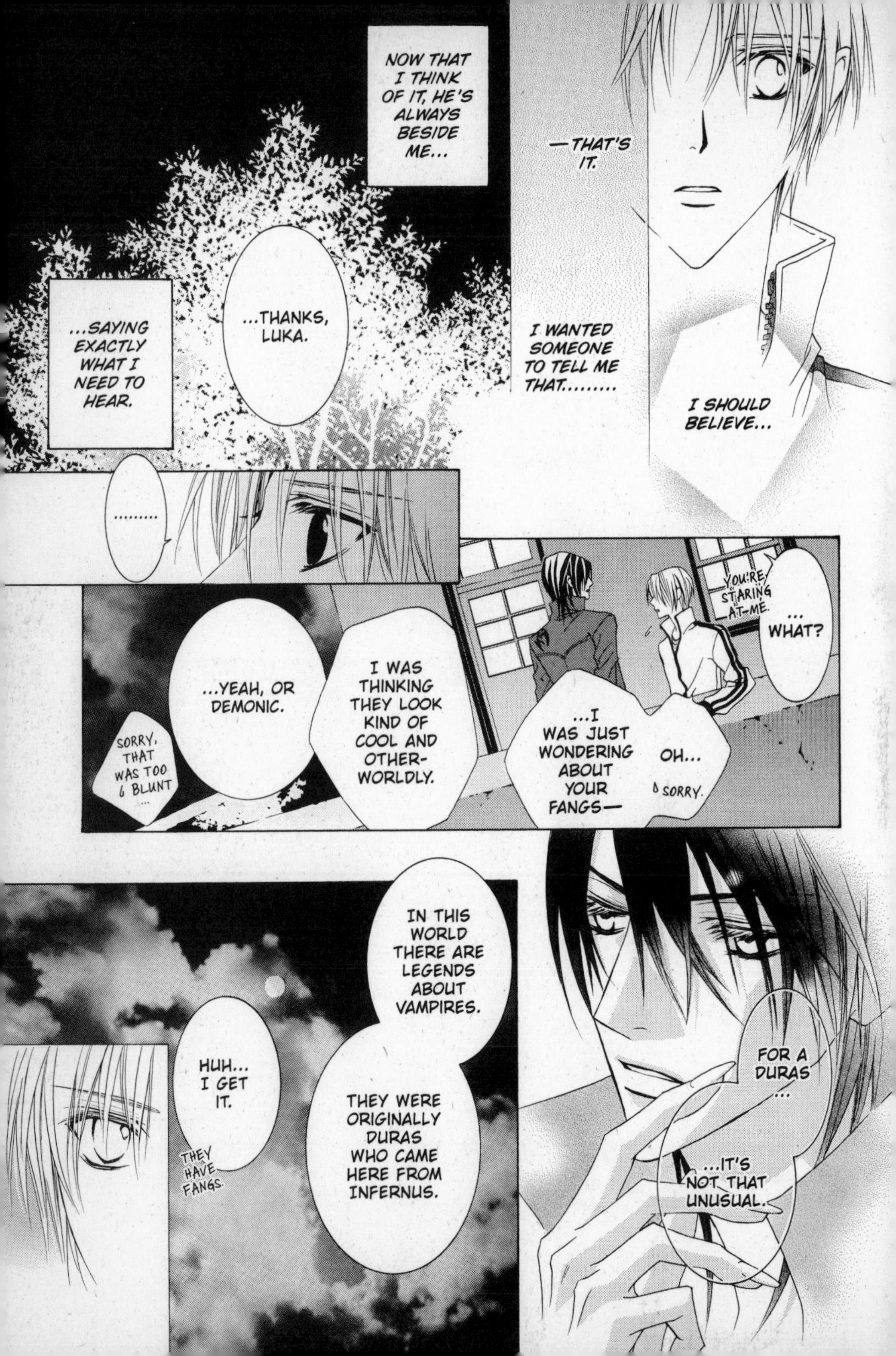

—THAT'S IT.
I WANTED SOMEONE TO TELL ME THAT........
I SHOULD BELIEVE...
NOW THAT I THINK OF IT, HE'S ALWAYS BESIDE ME...
...THANKS, LUKA.
...SAYING EXACTLY WHAT I NEED TO HEAR.
....
...WHAT?
YOU'RE STARING AT ME.
...I WAS JUST WONDERING ABOUT YOUR FANGS—
OH... SORRY.
I WAS THINKING THEY LOOK KIND OF COOL AND OTHER-WORLDLY.
...YEAH, OR DEMONIC.
SORRY, THAT WAS TOO BLUNT...
FOR A DURAS...
...IT'S NOT THAT UNUSUAL.
IN THIS WORLD THERE ARE LEGENDS ABOUT VAMPIRES.
THEY WERE ORIGINALLY DURAS WHO CAME HERE FROM INFERNUS.
HUH... I GET IT.
THEY HAVE FANGS.

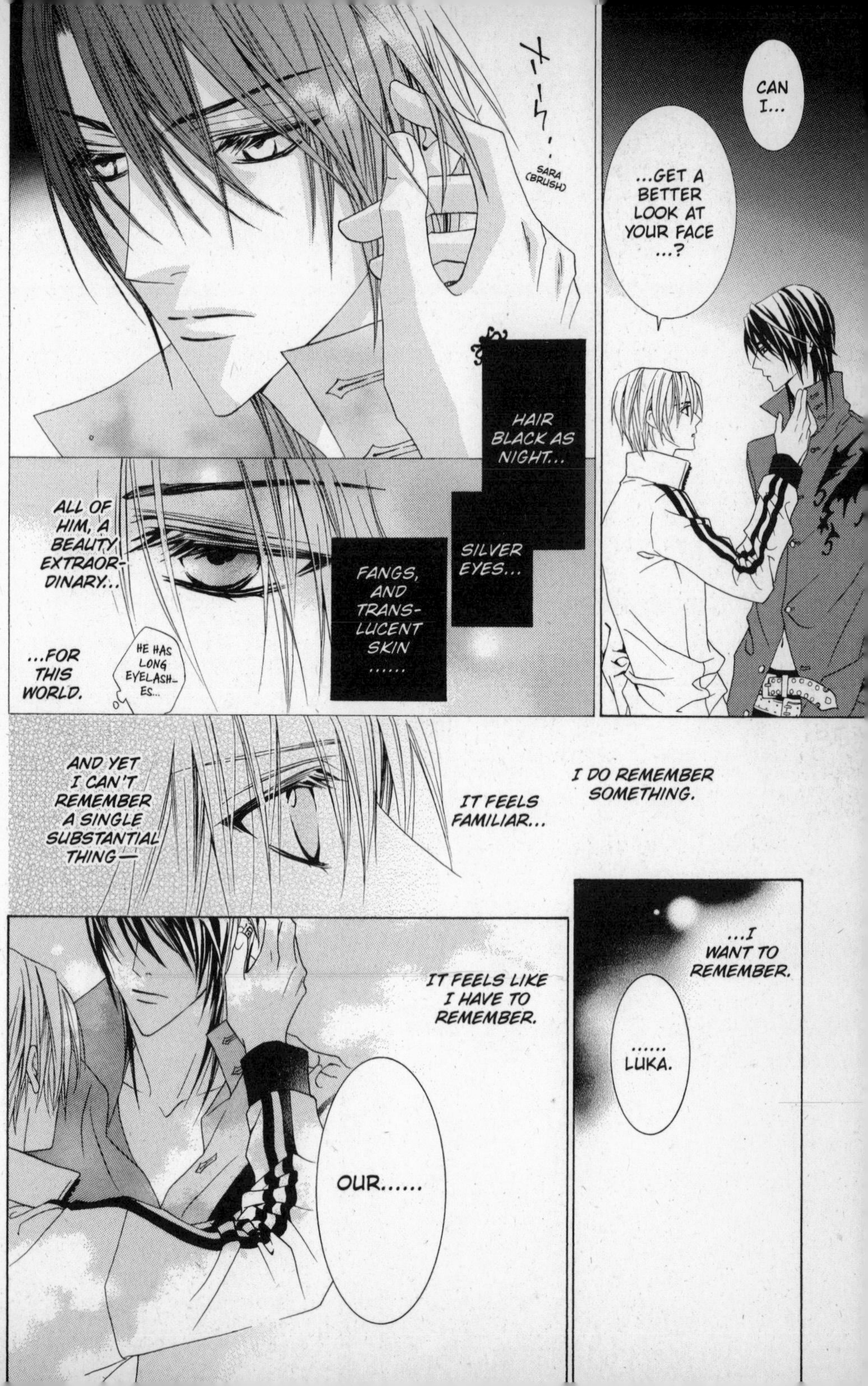
CAN I...
...GET A BETTER LOOK AT YOUR FACE ...?
SARA (BRUSH)
HAIR BLACK AS NIGHT...
SILVER EYES...
FANGS, AND TRANS-LUCENT SKIN ......
ALL OF HIM, A BEAUTY EXTRAOR-DINARY...
...FOR THIS WORLD.
HE HAS LONG EYELASH-ES...
I DO REMEMBER SOMETHING.
IT FEELS FAMILIAR...
AND YET I CAN'T REMEMBER A SINGLE SUBSTANTIAL THING—
...I WANT TO REMEMBER.
...... LUKA.
IT FEELS LIKE I HAVE TO REMEMBER.
OUR......

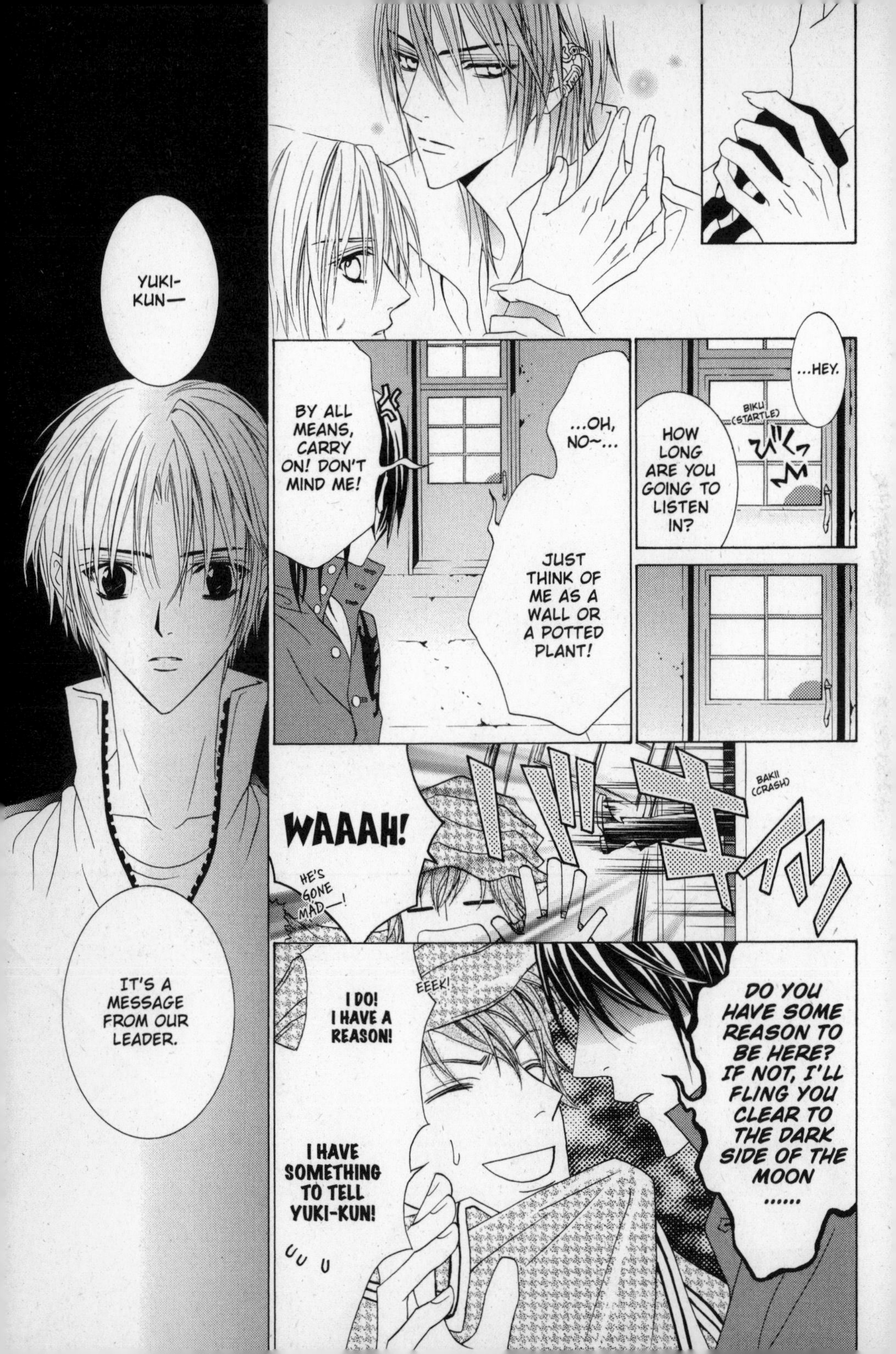
...HEY.
HOW LONG ARE YOU GOING TO LISTEN IN?
BIKU (STARTLE)
...OH, NO~...
BY ALL MEANS, CARRY ON! DON'T MIND ME!
JUST THINK OF ME AS A WALL OR A POTTED PLANT!
BAKII (CRASH)
WAAAH!
HE'S GONE MAD—!
DO YOU HAVE SOME REASON TO BE HERE? IF NOT, I'LL FLING YOU CLEAR TO THE DARK SIDE OF THE MOON ......
EEEK!
I DO! I HAVE A REASON!
I HAVE SOMETHING TO TELL YUKI-KUN!
U U U
YUKI-KUN—
IT'S A MESSAGE FROM OUR LEADER.

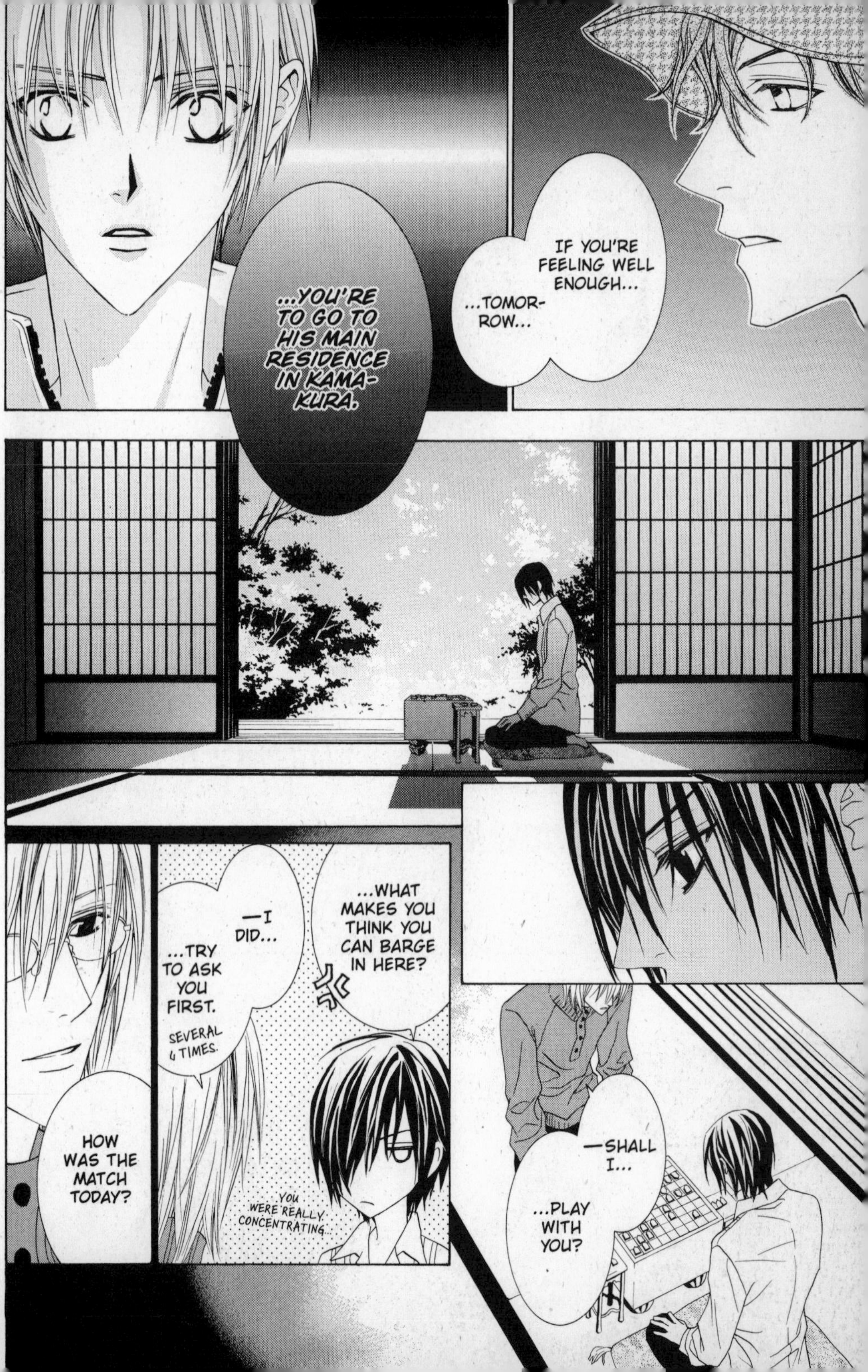
IF YOU'RE FEELING WELL ENOUGH...
...TOMOR-ROW...
...YOU'RE TO GO TO HIS MAIN RESIDENCE IN KAMA-KURA.
—SHALL I...
...PLAY WITH YOU?
...WHAT MAKES YOU THINK YOU CAN BARGE IN HERE?
—I DID...
...TRY TO ASK YOU FIRST.
SEVERAL TIMES.
YOU WERE REALLY CONCENTRATING...
HOW WAS THE MATCH TODAY?

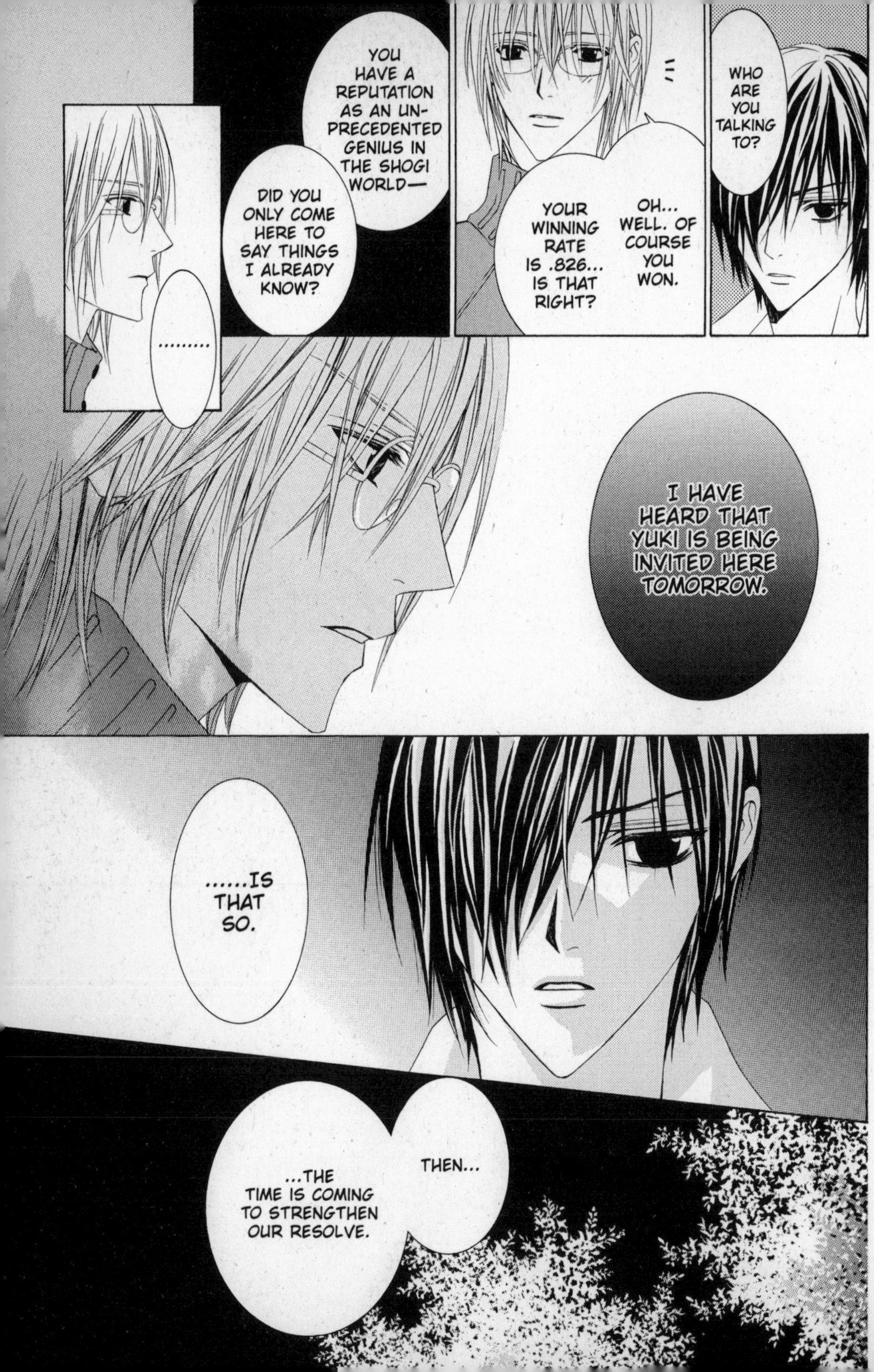
WHO ARE YOU TALKING TO?
OH... WELL. OF COURSE YOU WON.
YOUR WINNING RATE IS .826... IS THAT RIGHT?
YOU HAVE A REPUTATION AS AN UN-PRECEDENTED GENIUS IN THE SHOGI WORLD—
DID YOU ONLY COME HERE TO SAY THINGS I ALREADY KNOW?
....
I HAVE HEARD THAT YUKI IS BEING INVITED HERE TOMORROW.
......IS THAT SO.
THEN...
...THE TIME IS COMING TO STRENGTHEN OUR RESOLVE.

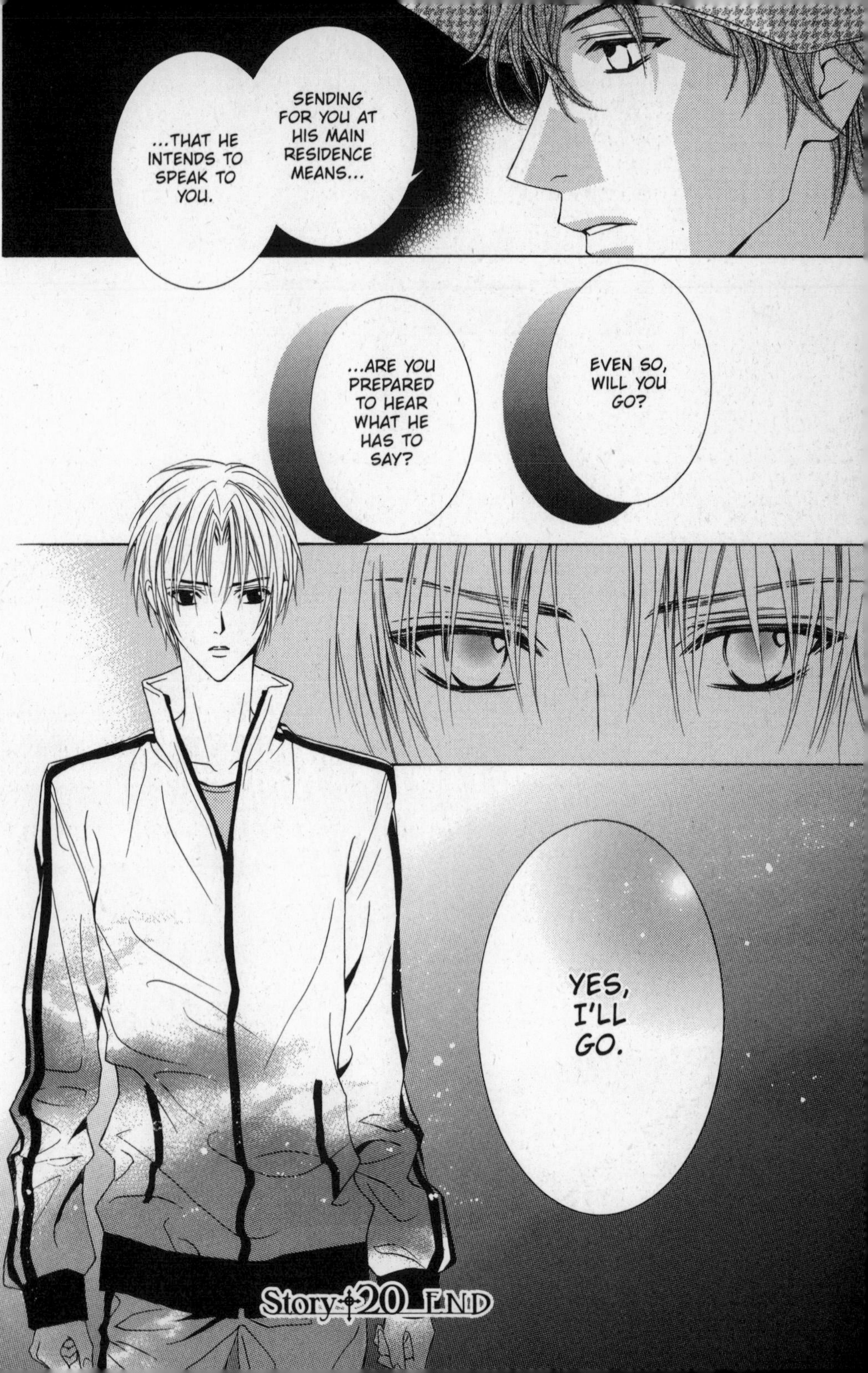
SENDING FOR YOU AT HIS MAIN RESIDENCE MEANS...
...THAT HE INTENDS TO SPEAK TO YOU.
EVEN SO, WILL YOU GO?
...ARE YOU PREPARED TO HEAR WHAT HE HAS TO SAY?
YES, I'LL GO.
Story 20_END

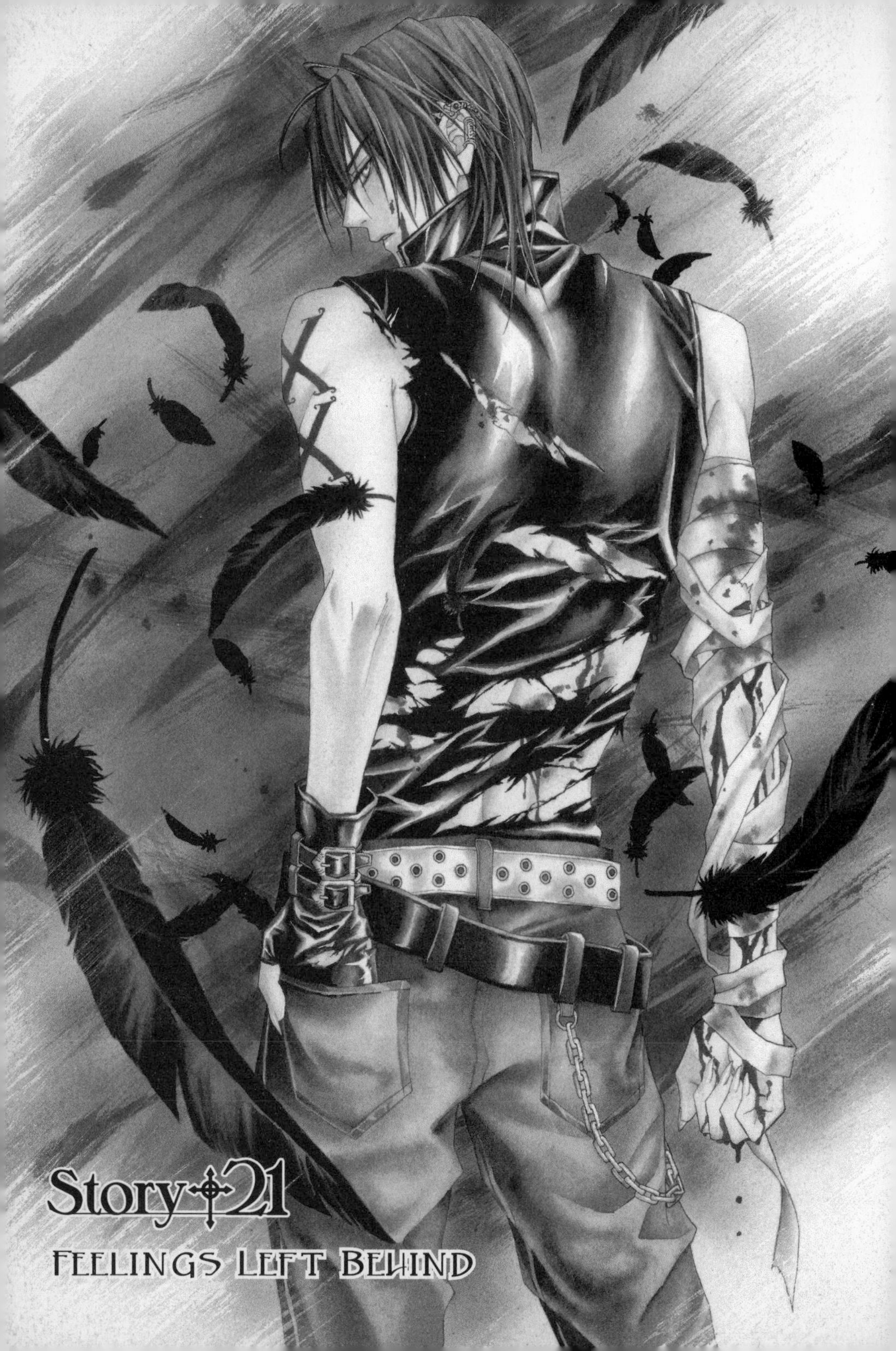
Story 21
Feelings Left Behind

THE BUTTONS... LATER

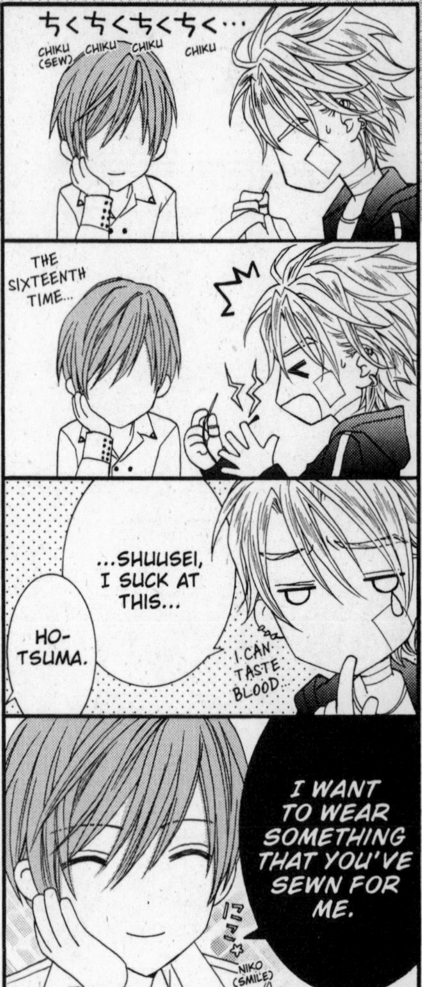
ちくちくちくちく…
CHIKU (SEW) CHIKU CHIKU CHIKU
THE SIXTEENTH TIME...
...SHUUSEI, I SUCK AT THIS...
I CAN TASTE BLOOD.
HO-TSUMA.
I WANT TO WEAR SOMETHING THAT YOU'VE SEWN FOR ME.
NIKO (SMILE)
ちくちくちくちくちくちく
ちく
CHIKU CHIKU CHIKU CHIKU CHIKU CHIKU CHIKU

—IN RESPONSE TO THE REQUESTS BY THOSE WHO SAID THEY'RE INTERESTED IN WHAT HAPPENS LATER—APPARENTLY HE FINISHED SEWING IT. (LOL)

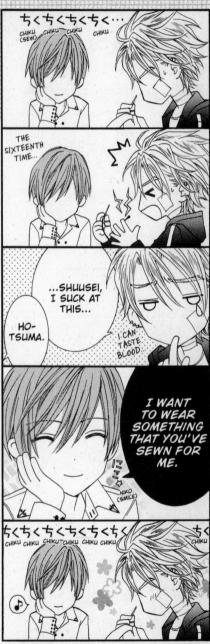

▸THIS IS THE FOURTH VOLUME OF URABOKU. SOMEHOW, I'M KEEPING IT GOING (LOL). IT'S A PRETTY SMOOTH PACE FOR ME...I GUESS? OR MAYBE IT'S FAST, OR MAYBE IT'S SLOW... HOWEVER IT IS, IT'S ALL THANKS TO MY READERS. THANK YOU~~~!!

▸AS DETERMINED BY MAJORITY VOTE, THE OFF-SHOT CARD THIS TIME (THE ONE THAT COMES WITH THE FIRST EDITION), IS TSU-KUN! ♪ IT'S TSU-KUN AND SMALL ANIMALS AFTER SCHOOL...A FLUFF SCENE! ♥ BUT THESE CARDS—I DIDN'T THINK THIS WOULD BECOME SUCH A SERIES, SO I WONDER HOW LONG THEY'LL CONTINUE? I HAVE SOME DOUBTS. (OF COURSE, I'M NOT THE ONE WHO DECIDES!) STILL, AS LONG AS THERE ARE REQUESTS FOR THEM, I INTEND TO WORK HARD ON THEM!

▸AND AT LAST REIGA'S TRUE IDENTITY HAS BEEN REVEALED. IT'S ABOUT A SIXTY-FORTY SPLIT BETWEEN THOSE WHO SAW IT COMING AND FELT LIKE "FINALLY!" AND THOSE WHO WERE SURPRISED AND FELT LIKE "WHAT A TWIST!" AS FOR MYSELF, MORE PEOPLE WERE SURPRISED THAN I THOUGHT WOULD BE, SO I'M SURPRISED. AT ANY RATE, I'VE MADE THE BIG REVEAL...AND I HAD PLANNED TO MAKE IT CLEAR IN VOLUME 1 (HOW RECKLESS! LOL). SO I WROTE KANATA-SAN TO BE PRETTY SUSPICIOUS FROM THE BEGINNING, AND I WAS THINKING ALMOST EVERYONE WOULD PICK UP ON IT. ...AND, SADLY, NOW YUKI'S FANS TOTALLY HATE HIM... OH KANATA-SAN (÷CRIES÷). ALTHOUGH I GUESS THAT'S ONLY NATURAL. YOU'RE ALL WORRYING SO MUCH ABOUT YUKI—PLEASE KEEP WATCHING OVER HIM!

▸RECENTLY THERE'S BEEN A TREND IN EVERYONE'S LETTERS (I'M EXAGGERATING...LOL). THAT IS, PEOPLE ARE MAKING SUBTLE CRACKS PLAYING ON LUKA'S CATCHPHRASE "I WILL NOT BETRAY YOU." FOR EXAMPLE: "I WILL NOT BETRAY YOU, ODAGIRI-SENSEI!" OR "ODAGIRI-SAN HAS NOT BETRAYED US READERS!" (LOL) COME TO THINK OF IT, JUN FUKUYAMA, WHO PLAYED TSU-KUN ON THE DRAMA CD, EVEN USED IT IN AN INTERVIEW, SAYING "I WILL NOT BETRAY EVERYONE'S EXPECTATIONS!" ...COULD HE HAVE BEEN INFLUENCED BY IT? ANYWAY, AS THE CREATOR, I APPRECIATE IT.

✿I THINK THEY'RE DOING A CHARACTER POPULARITY POLL RIGHT NOW IN THE URABOKU FC IN ASUKA. SO GO AHEAD AND PUT IN A VOTE FOR YOUR FAVORITE! ♡ THERE'S A PRESENT TOO! ~~

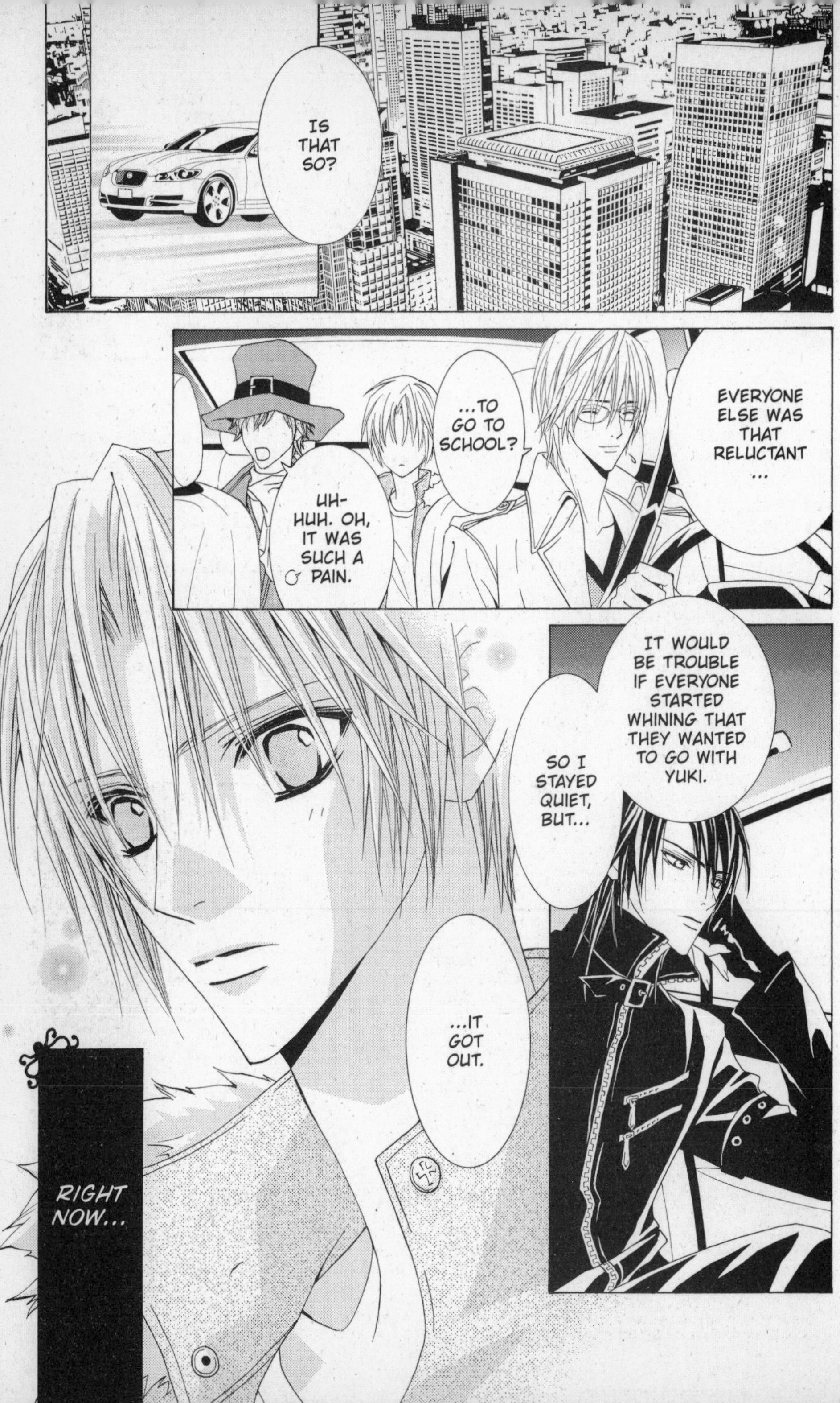
IS THAT SO?
EVERYONE ELSE WAS THAT RELUCTANT ...
...TO GO TO SCHOOL?
UH-HUH. OH, IT WAS SUCH A PAIN.
IT WOULD BE TROUBLE IF EVERYONE STARTED WHINING THAT THEY WANTED TO GO WITH YUKI.
SO I STAYED QUIET, BUT...
...IT GOT OUT.
RIGHT NOW...

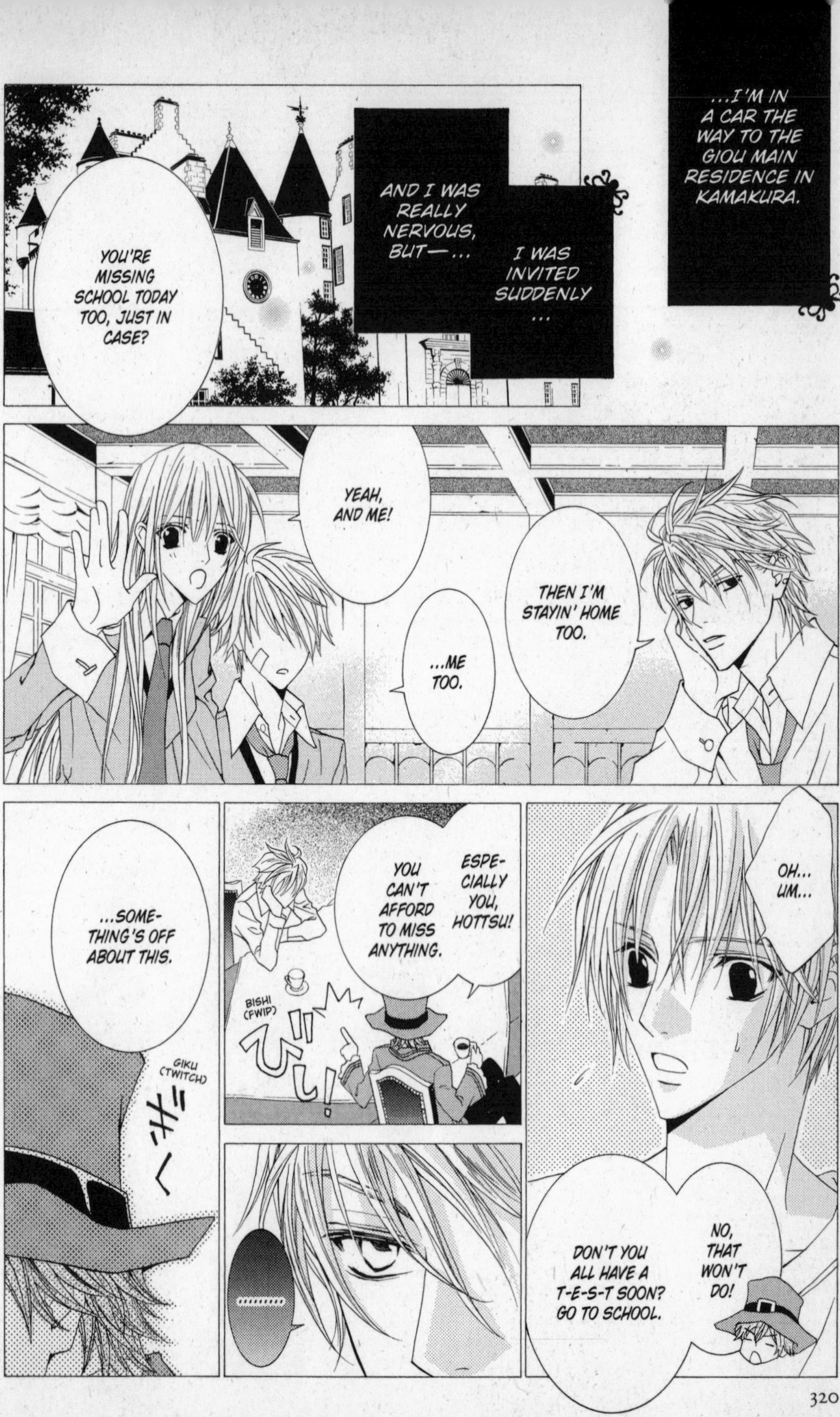
...I'M IN A CAR THE WAY TO THE GIOU MAIN RESIDENCE IN KAMAKURA.
I WAS INVITED SUDDENLY ...
AND I WAS REALLY NERVOUS, BUT—...
YOU'RE MISSING SCHOOL TODAY TOO, JUST IN CASE?
THEN I'M STAYIN' HOME TOO.
YEAH, AND ME!
...ME TOO.
OH... UM...
NO, THAT WON'T DO!
DON'T YOU ALL HAVE A T-E-S-T SOON? GO TO SCHOOL.
ESPE-CIALLY YOU, HOTTSU!
YOU CAN'T AFFORD TO MISS ANYTHING.
BISHI (FWIP)
びし!
......
...SOME-THING'S OFF ABOUT THIS.
GIKU (TWITCH)
ギく

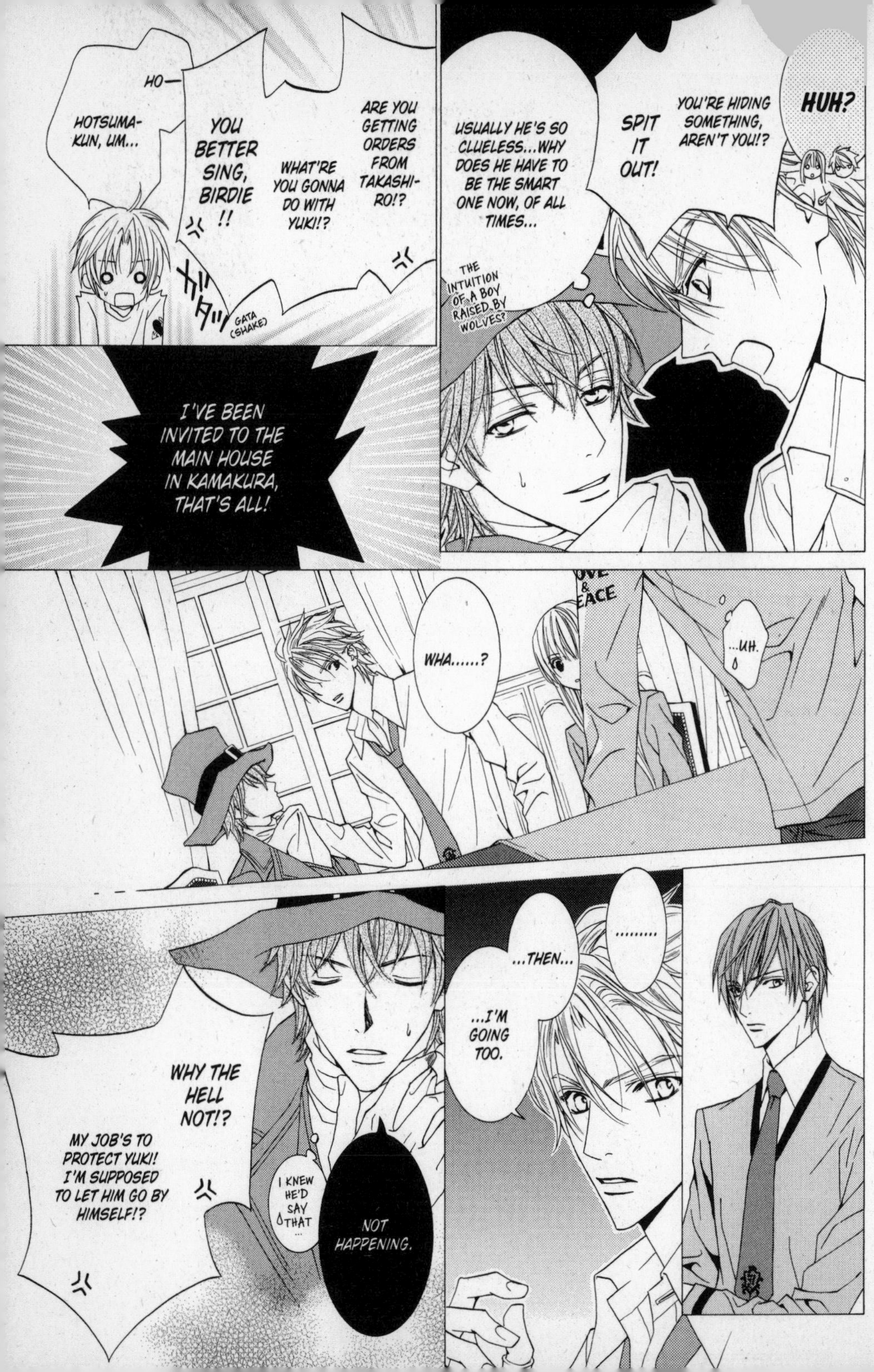
HUH?
YOU'RE HIDING SOMETHING, AREN'T YOU!?
SPIT IT OUT!
USUALLY HE'S SO CLUELESS...WHY DOES HE HAVE TO BE THE SMART ONE NOW, OF ALL TIMES...
THE INTUITION OF A BOY RAISED BY WOLVES?
ARE YOU GETTING ORDERS FROM TAKASHIRO!?
WHAT'RE YOU GONNA DO WITH YUKI!?
YOU BETTER SING, BIRDIE!!
HO—
HOTSUMA-KUN, UM...
GATA (SHAKE)
I'VE BEEN INVITED TO THE MAIN HOUSE IN KAMAKURA, THAT'S ALL!
...UH.
WHA......?
....
...THEN...
...I'M GOING TOO.
NOT HAPPENING.
I KNEW HE'D SAY THAT...
WHY THE HELL NOT!?
MY JOB'S TO PROTECT YUKI! I'M SUPPOSED TO LET HIM GO BY HIMSELF!?

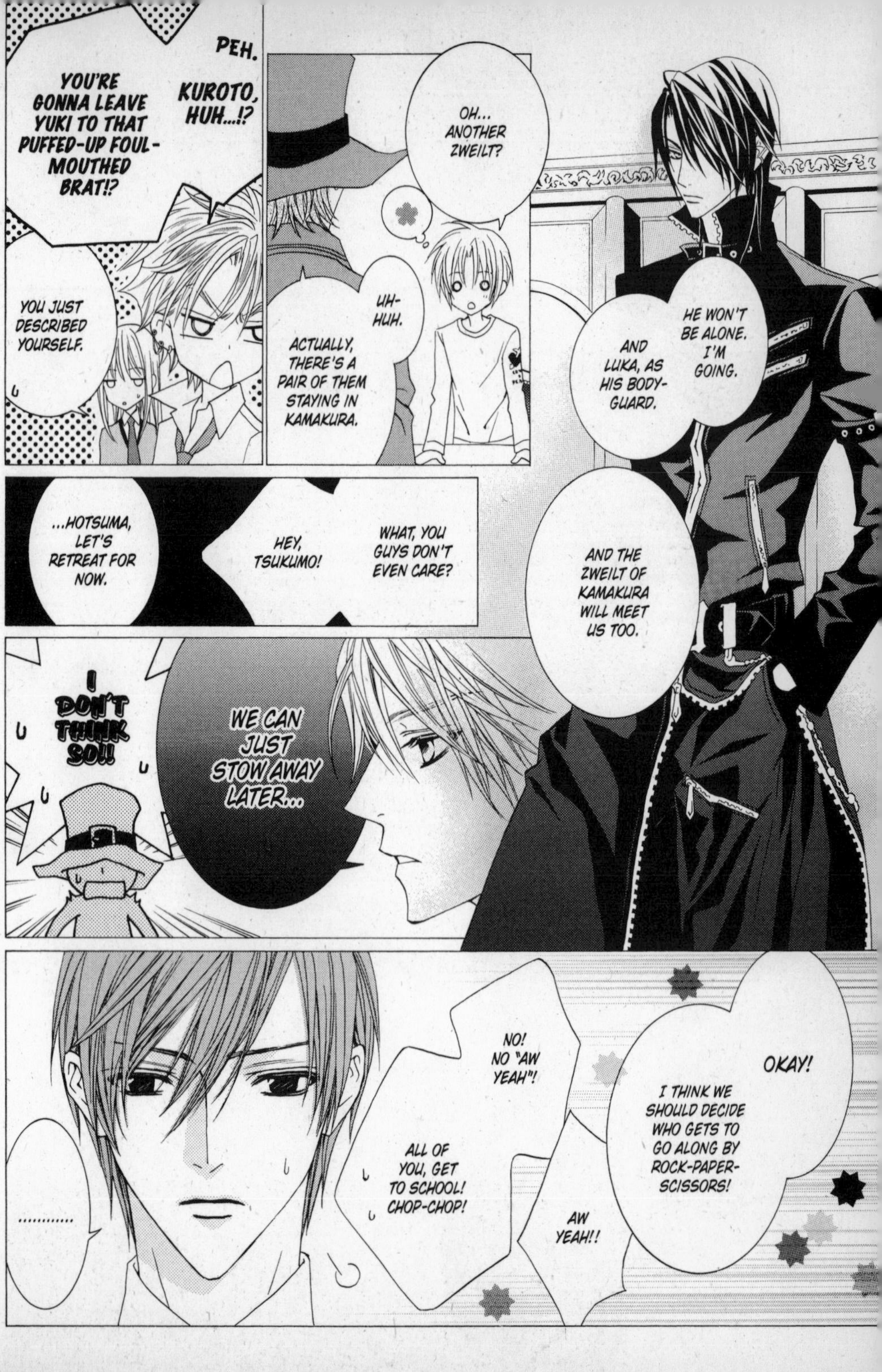
HE WON'T BE ALONE. I'M GOING.
AND LUKA, AS HIS BODY-GUARD.
AND THE ZWEILT OF KAMAKURA WILL MEET US TOO.
OH... ANOTHER ZWEILT?
UH-HUH.
ACTUALLY, THERE'S A PAIR OF THEM STAYING IN KAMAKURA.
PEH.
KUROTO, HUH...!?
YOU'RE GONNA LEAVE YUKI TO THAT PUFFED-UP FOUL-MOUTHED BRAT!?
YOU JUST DESCRIBED YOURSELF.
WHAT, YOU GUYS DON'T EVEN CARE?
HEY, TSUKUMO!
...HOTSUMA, LET'S RETREAT FOR NOW.
WE CAN JUST STOW AWAY LATER...
I DON'T THINK SO!!
OKAY!
I THINK WE SHOULD DECIDE WHO GETS TO GO ALONG BY ROCK-PAPER-SCISSORS!
AW YEAH!!
NO! NO "AW YEAH"!
ALL OF YOU, GET TO SCHOOL! CHOP-CHOP!
....

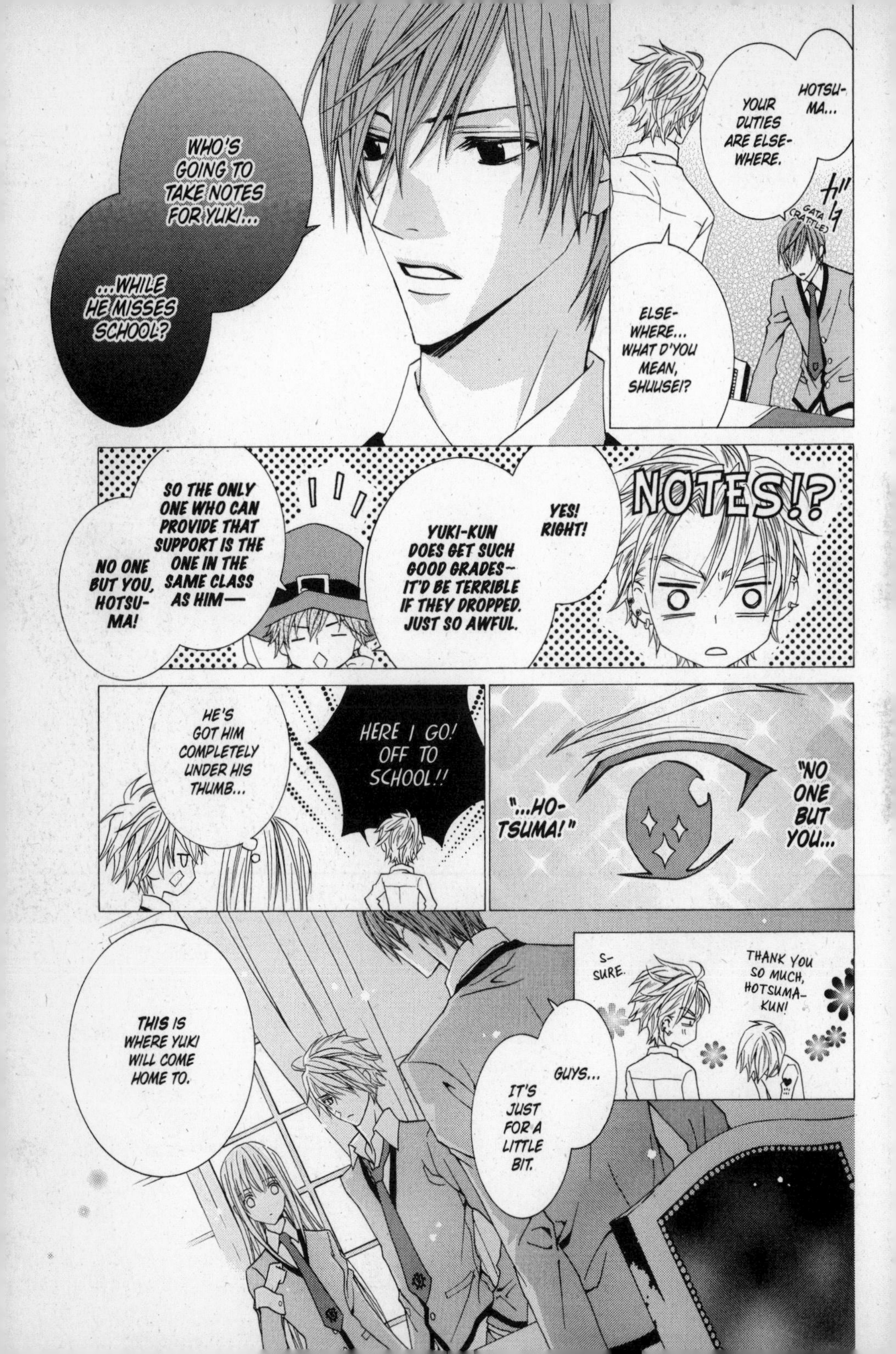
HOTSUMA... YOUR DUTIES ARE ELSEWHERE.
ガタ GATA (RATTLE)
ELSEWHERE... WHAT D'YOU MEAN, SHUUSEI?
WHO'S GOING TO TAKE NOTES FOR YUKI...
...WHILE HE MISSES SCHOOL?
NOTES!?
YES! RIGHT!
YUKI-KUN DOES GET SUCH GOOD GRADES— IT'D BE TERRIBLE IF THEY DROPPED. JUST SO AWFUL.
SO THE ONLY ONE WHO CAN PROVIDE THAT SUPPORT IS THE ONE IN THE SAME CLASS AS HIM—
NO ONE BUT YOU, HOTSUMA!
"NO ONE BUT YOU...
...HOTSUMA!"
HERE I GO! OFF TO SCHOOL!!
HE'S GOT HIM COMPLETELY UNDER HIS THUMB...
THANK YOU SO MUCH, HOTSUMA-KUN!
S-SURE.
GUYS... IT'S JUST FOR A LITTLE BIT.
THIS IS WHERE YUKI WILL COME HOME TO.

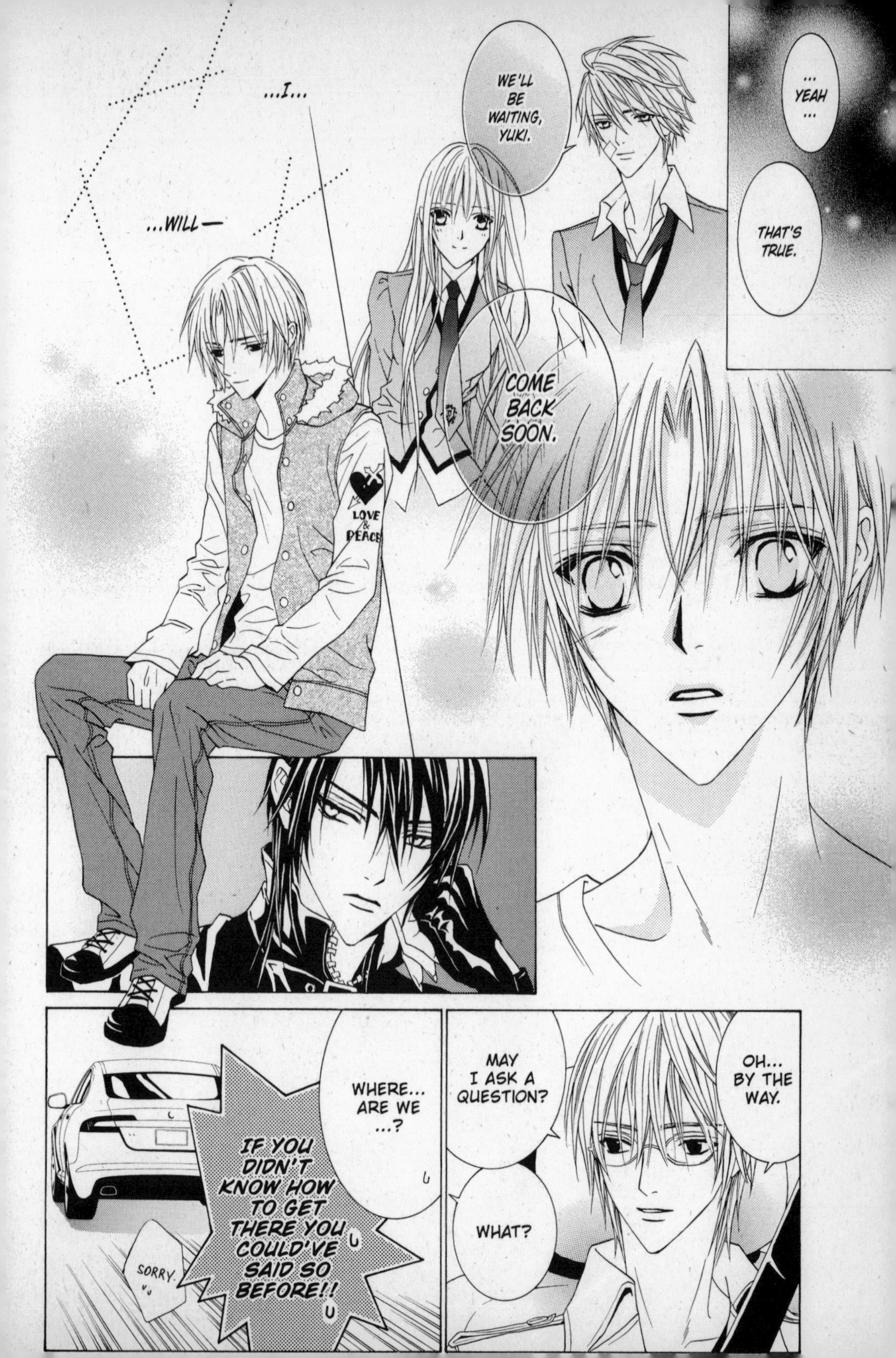

... YEAH ...
THAT'S TRUE.
WE'LL BE WAITING, YUKI.
COME BACK SOON.
...I...
...WILL—
OH... BY THE WAY.
MAY I ASK A QUESTION?
WHAT?
WHERE... ARE WE ...?
IF YOU DIDN'T KNOW HOW TO GET THERE YOU COULD'VE SAID SO BEFORE!!
SORRY.

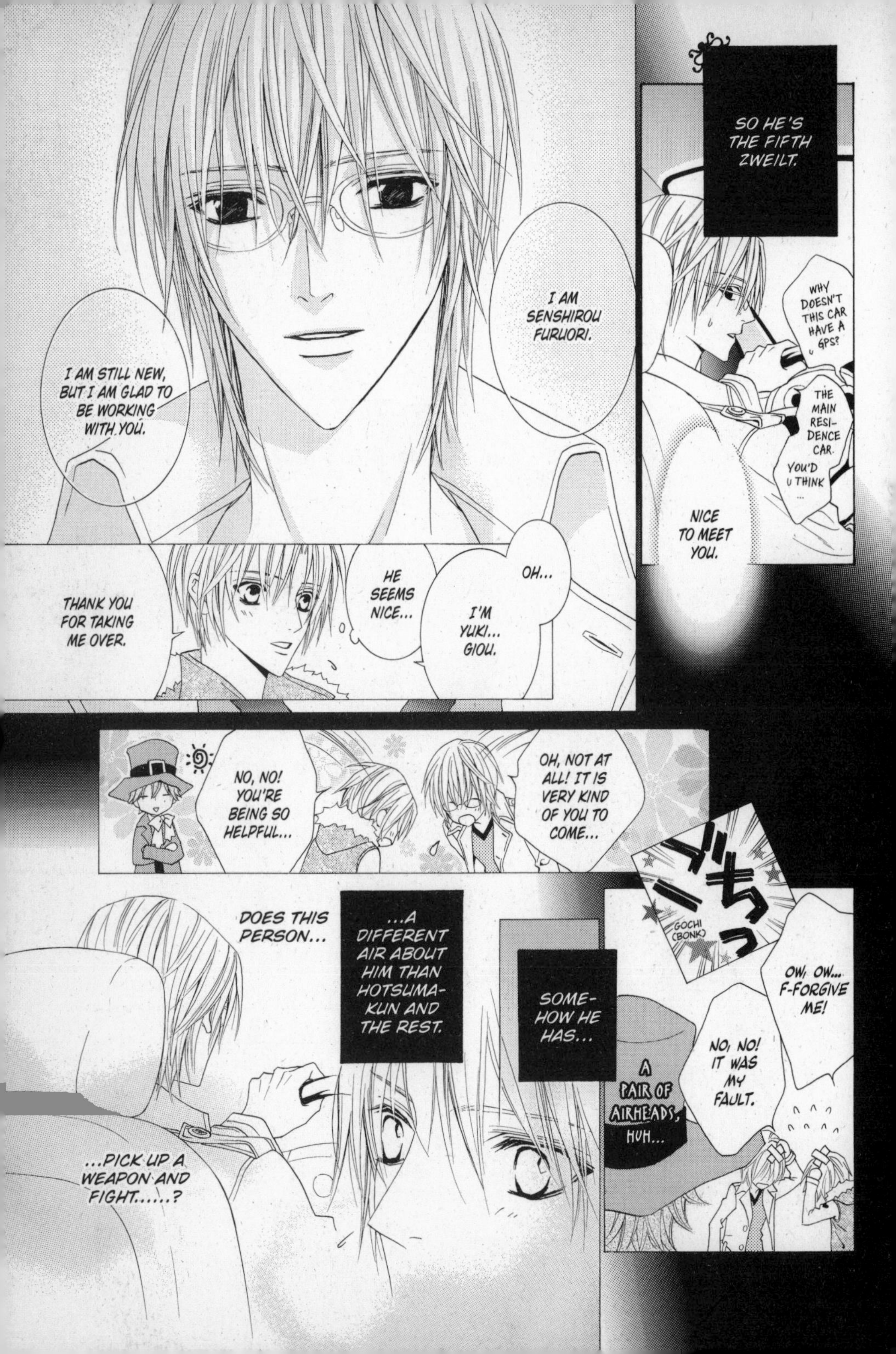
SO HE'S THE FIFTH ZWEILT.
WHY DOESN'T THIS CAR HAVE A GPS?
THE MAIN RESI-DENCE CAR.
YOU'D THINK...
NICE TO MEET YOU.
I AM SENSHIROU FURUORI.
I AM STILL NEW, BUT I AM GLAD TO BE WORKING WITH YOU.
OH...
I'M YUKI... GIOU.
HE SEEMS NICE...
THANK YOU FOR TAKING ME OVER.
OH, NOT AT ALL! IT IS VERY KIND OF YOU TO COME...
NO, NO! YOU'RE BEING SO HELPFUL...
GOCHI (BONK)
OW, OW... F-FORGIVE ME!
NO, NO! IT WAS MY FAULT.
A PAIR OF AIRHEADS, HUH...
SOME-HOW HE HAS...
...A DIFFERENT AIR ABOUT HIM THAN HOTSUMA-KUN AND THE REST.
DOES THIS PERSON...
...PICK UP A WEAPON AND FIGHT......?

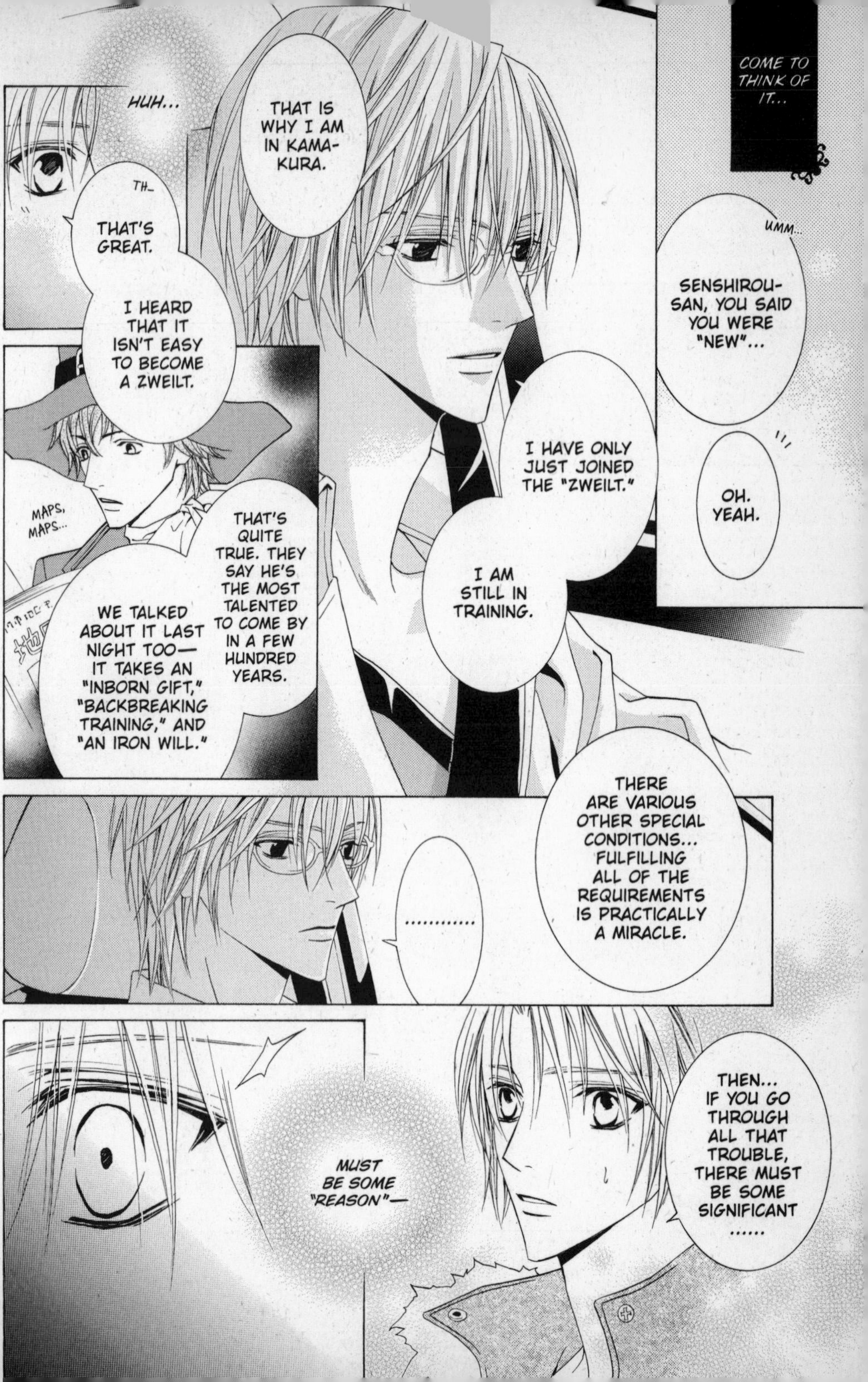
COME TO THINK OF IT...
UMM...
SENSHIROU-SAN, YOU SAID YOU WERE "NEW"...
OH. YEAH.
I HAVE ONLY JUST JOINED THE "ZWEILT."
I AM STILL IN TRAINING.
THAT IS WHY I AM IN KAMA-KURA.
HUH...
TH_ THAT'S GREAT.
I HEARD THAT IT ISN'T EASY TO BECOME A ZWEILT.
THAT'S QUITE TRUE. THEY SAY HE'S THE MOST TALENTED TO COME BY IN A FEW HUNDRED YEARS.
MAPS, MAPS...
WE TALKED ABOUT IT LAST NIGHT TOO—IT TAKES AN "INBORN GIFT," "BACKBREAKING TRAINING," AND "AN IRON WILL."
THERE ARE VARIOUS OTHER SPECIAL CONDITIONS... FULFILLING ALL OF THE REQUIREMENTS IS PRACTICALLY A MIRACLE.
....
THEN... IF YOU GO THROUGH ALL THAT TROUBLE, THERE MUST BE SOME SIGNIFICANT ......
MUST BE SOME "REASON"—

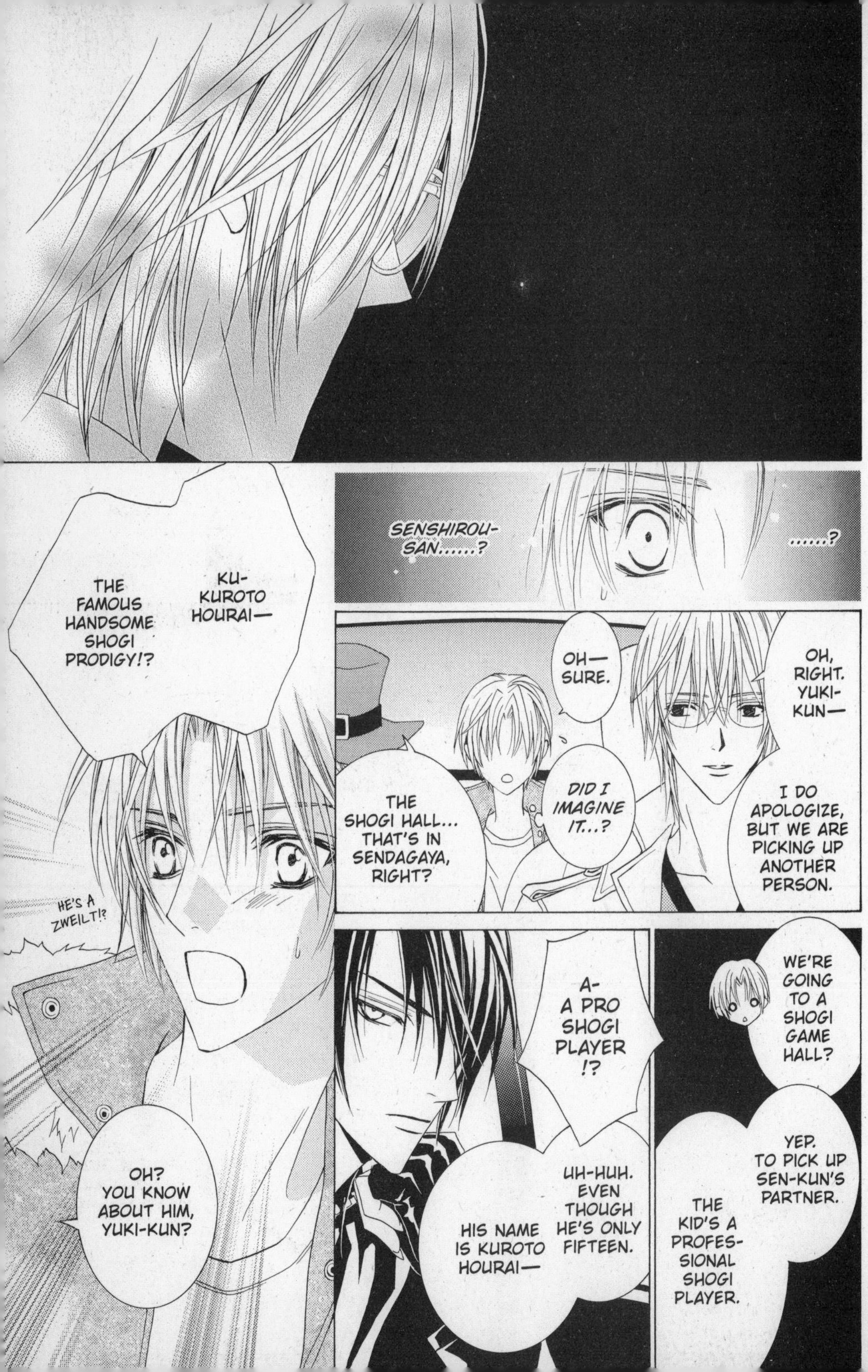

......?
SENSHIROU-SAN......?
OH, RIGHT. YUKI-KUN—
I DO APOLOGIZE, BUT WE ARE PICKING UP ANOTHER PERSON.
OH— SURE.
DID I IMAGINE IT...?
THE SHOGI HALL... THAT'S IN SENDAGAYA, RIGHT?
WE'RE GOING TO A SHOGI GAME HALL?
YEP. TO PICK UP SEN-KUN'S PARTNER.
THE KID'S A PROFES-SIONAL SHOGI PLAYER.
A- A PRO SHOGI PLAYER !?
UH-HUH. EVEN THOUGH HE'S ONLY FIFTEEN.
HIS NAME IS KUROTO HOURAI—
KU-KUROTO HOURAI—
THE FAMOUS HANDSOME SHOGI PRODIGY!?
HE'S A ZWEILT!?
OH? YOU KNOW ABOUT HIM, YUKI-KUN?

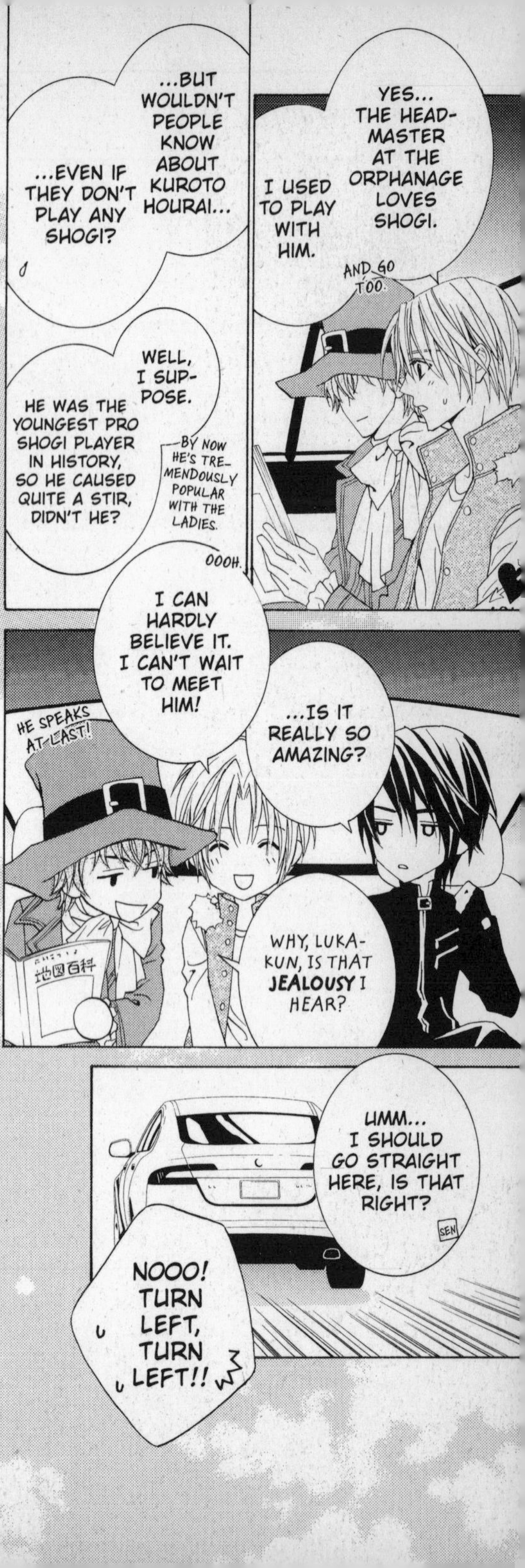
YES... THE HEAD-MASTER AT THE ORPHANAGE LOVES SHOGI.
I USED TO PLAY WITH HIM.
AND GO TOO.
...BUT WOULDN'T PEOPLE KNOW ABOUT KUROTO HOURAI...
...EVEN IF THEY DON'T PLAY ANY SHOGI?
WELL, I SUP-POSE.
HE WAS THE YOUNGEST PRO SHOGI PLAYER IN HISTORY, SO HE CAUSED QUITE A STIR, DIDN'T HE?
BY NOW HE'S TRE-MENDOUSLY POPULAR WITH THE LADIES.
OOOH.
I CAN HARDLY BELIEVE IT. I CAN'T WAIT TO MEET HIM!
...IS IT REALLY SO AMAZING?
HE SPEAKS AT LAST!
WHY, LUKA-KUN, IS THAT JEALOUSY I HEAR?
地図百科
UMM... I SHOULD GO STRAIGHT HERE, IS THAT RIGHT?
SEN
NOOO! TURN LEFT, TURN LEFT!!
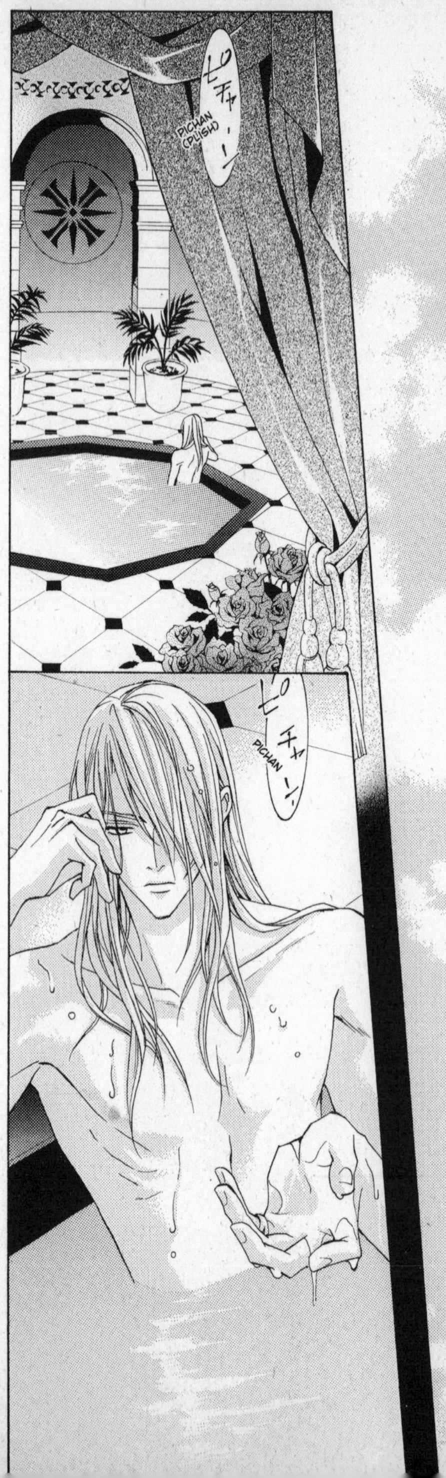
PICHAN (PLISH)
PICHAN

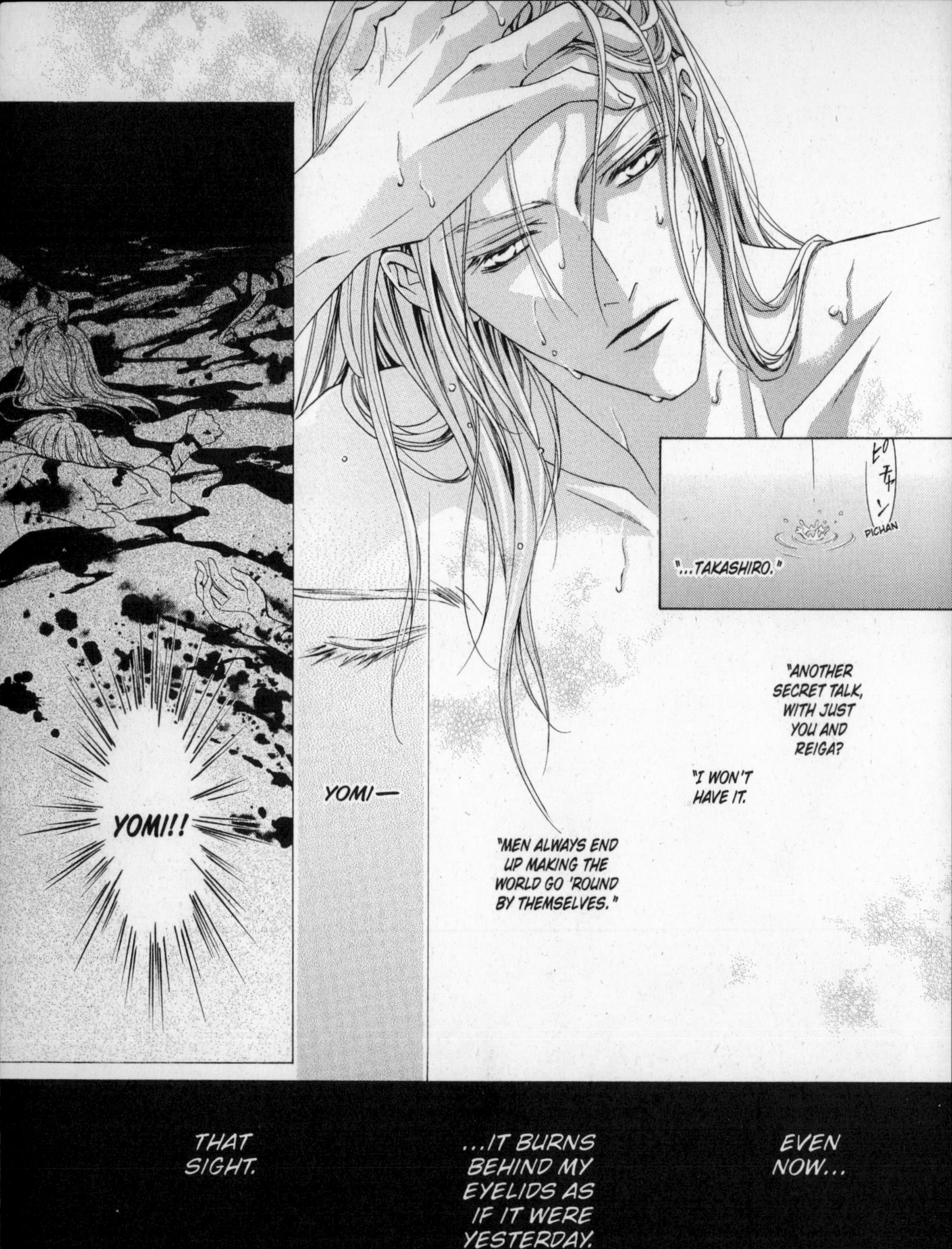
ピチャン
PICHAN
"...TAKASHIRO."
"ANOTHER SECRET TALK, WITH JUST YOU AND REIGA?
"I WON'T HAVE IT.
"MEN ALWAYS END UP MAKING THE WORLD GO 'ROUND BY THEMSELVES."
YOMI—
YOMI!!
EVEN NOW...
...IT BURNS BEHIND MY EYELIDS AS IF IT WERE YESTERDAY.
THAT SIGHT.

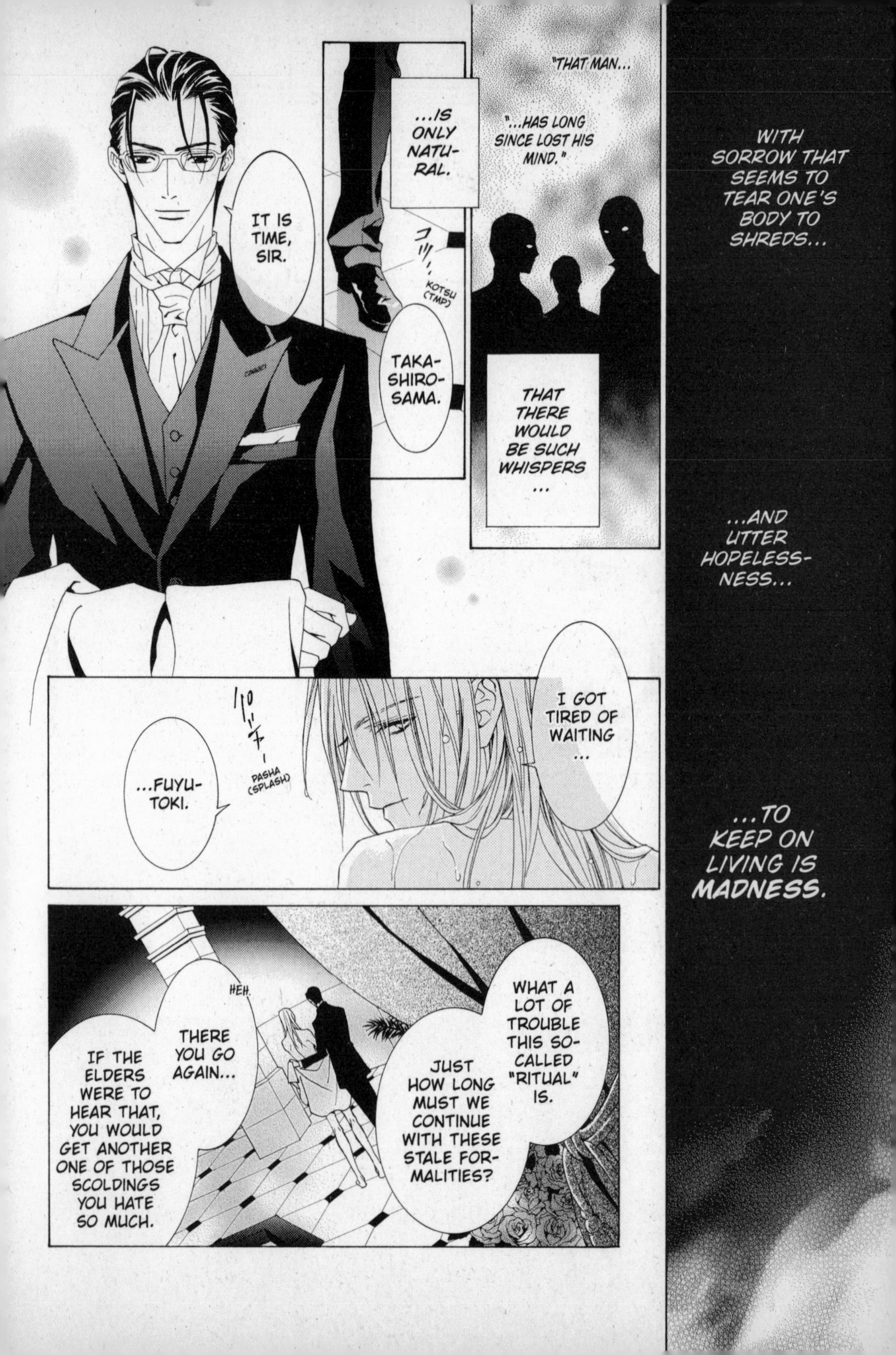
WITH SORROW THAT SEEMS TO TEAR ONE'S BODY TO SHREDS...
...AND UTTER HOPELESSNESS...
...TO KEEP ON LIVING IS MADNESS.
"THAT MAN...
"...HAS LONG SINCE LOST HIS MIND."
THAT THERE WOULD BE SUCH WHISPERS...
...IS ONLY NATURAL.
KOTSU (TMP)
TAKASHIRO-SAMA.
IT IS TIME, SIR.
I GOT TIRED OF WAITING...
PASHA (SPLASH)
...FUYUTOKI.
WHAT A LOT OF TROUBLE THIS SO-CALLED "RITUAL" IS.
JUST HOW LONG MUST WE CONTINUE WITH THESE STALE FORMALITIES?
HEH.
THERE YOU GO AGAIN...
IF THE ELDERS WERE TO HEAR THAT, YOU WOULD GET ANOTHER ONE OF THOSE SCOLDINGS YOU HATE SO MUCH.

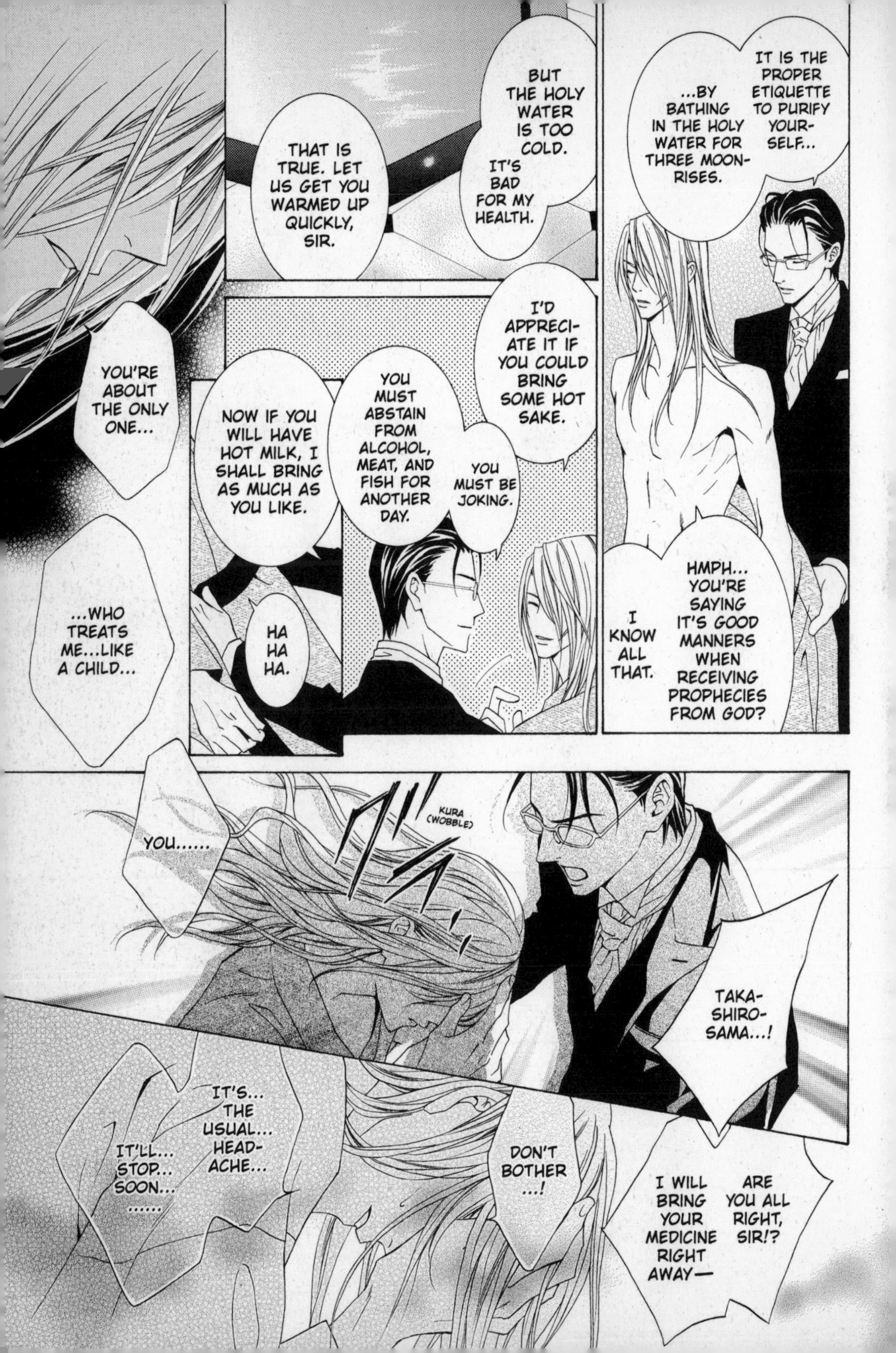
IT IS THE PROPER ETIQUETTE TO PURIFY YOURSELF...
...BY BATHING IN THE HOLY WATER FOR THREE MOONRISES.
HMPH... YOU'RE SAYING IT'S GOOD MANNERS WHEN RECEIVING PROPHECIES FROM GOD?
I KNOW ALL THAT.
BUT THE HOLY WATER IS TOO COLD.
IT'S BAD FOR MY HEALTH.
THAT IS TRUE. LET US GET YOU WARMED UP QUICKLY, SIR.
I'D APPRECIATE IT IF YOU COULD BRING SOME HOT SAKE.
YOU MUST BE JOKING.
YOU MUST ABSTAIN FROM ALCOHOL, MEAT, AND FISH FOR ANOTHER DAY.
NOW IF YOU WILL HAVE HOT MILK, I SHALL BRING AS MUCH AS YOU LIKE.
HA HA HA.
YOU'RE ABOUT THE ONLY ONE...
...WHO TREATS ME...LIKE A CHILD...
KURA (WOBBLE)
TAKA-SHIRO-SAMA...!
YOU......
ARE YOU ALL RIGHT, SIR!?
I WILL BRING YOUR MEDICINE RIGHT AWAY—
DON'T BOTHER ...!
IT'S... THE USUAL... HEADACHE...
IT'LL... STOP... SOON... ......

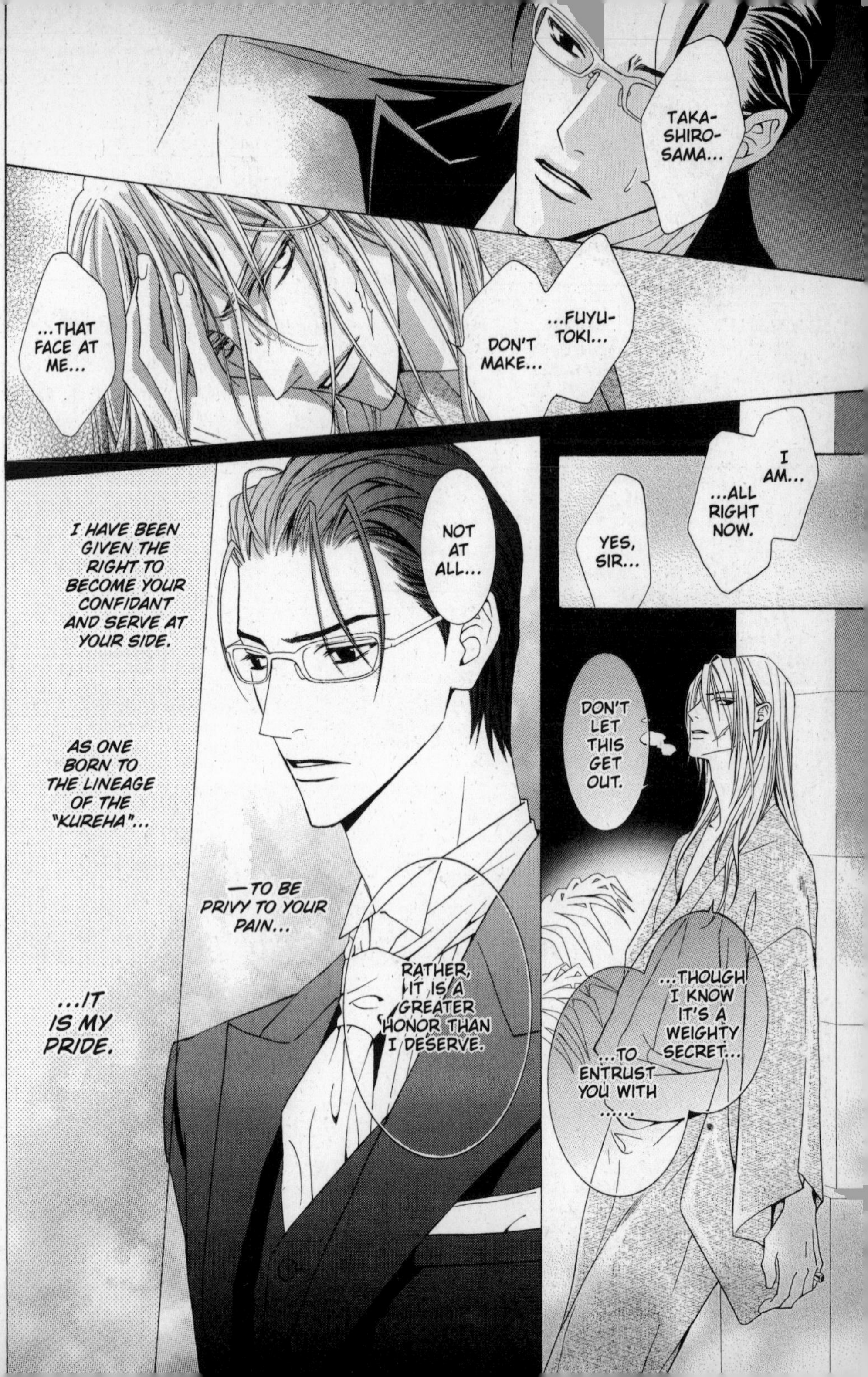
TAKA-SHIRO-SAMA...
...FUYU-TOKI...
DON'T MAKE...
...THAT FACE AT ME...
I AM... ...ALL RIGHT NOW.
YES, SIR...
DON'T LET THIS GET OUT.
...THOUGH I KNOW IT'S A WEIGHTY SECRET...
...TO ENTRUST YOU WITH ......
NOT AT ALL...
RATHER, IT IS A GREATER HONOR THAN I DESERVE.
I HAVE BEEN GIVEN THE RIGHT TO BECOME YOUR CONFIDANT AND SERVE AT YOUR SIDE.
AS ONE BORN TO THE LINEAGE OF THE "KUREHA"...
—TO BE PRIVY TO YOUR PAIN...
...IT IS MY PRIDE.

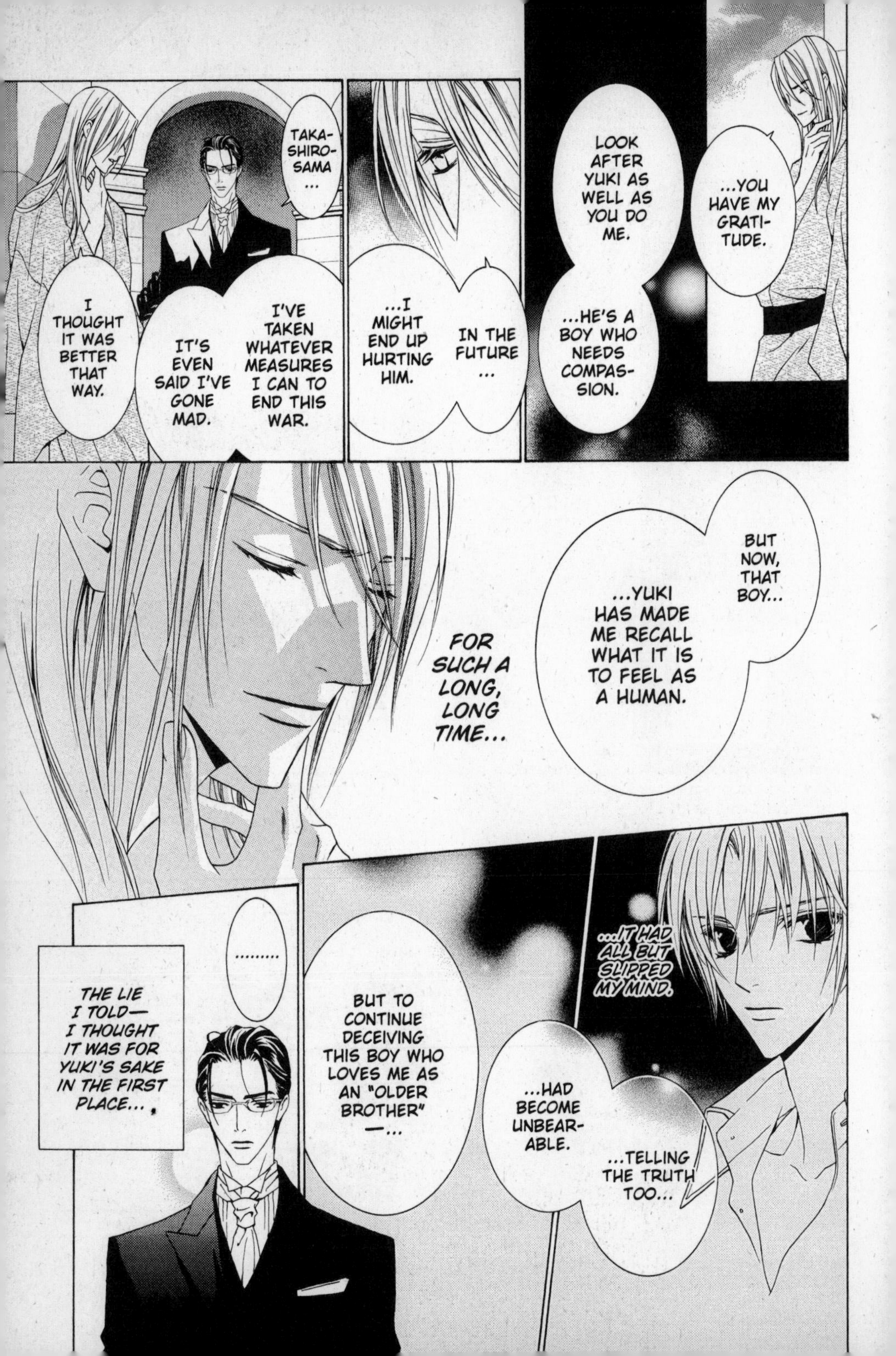
...YOU HAVE MY GRATITUDE.
LOOK AFTER YUKI AS WELL AS YOU DO ME.
...HE'S A BOY WHO NEEDS COMPASSION.
IN THE FUTURE...
...I MIGHT END UP HURTING HIM.
TAKA-SHIRO-SAMA...
I'VE TAKEN WHATEVER MEASURES I CAN TO END THIS WAR.
IT'S EVEN SAID I'VE GONE MAD.
I THOUGHT IT WAS BETTER THAT WAY.
BUT NOW, THAT BOY...
...YUKI HAS MADE ME RECALL WHAT IT IS TO FEEL AS A HUMAN.
FOR SUCH A LONG, LONG TIME...
...IT HAD ALL BUT SLIPPED MY MIND.
...HAD BECOME UNBEARABLE.
...TELLING THE TRUTH TOO...
....
BUT TO CONTINUE DECEIVING THIS BOY WHO LOVES ME AS AN "OLDER BROTHER"—...
THE LIE I TOLD—I THOUGHT IT WAS FOR YUKI'S SAKE IN THE FIRST PLACE...

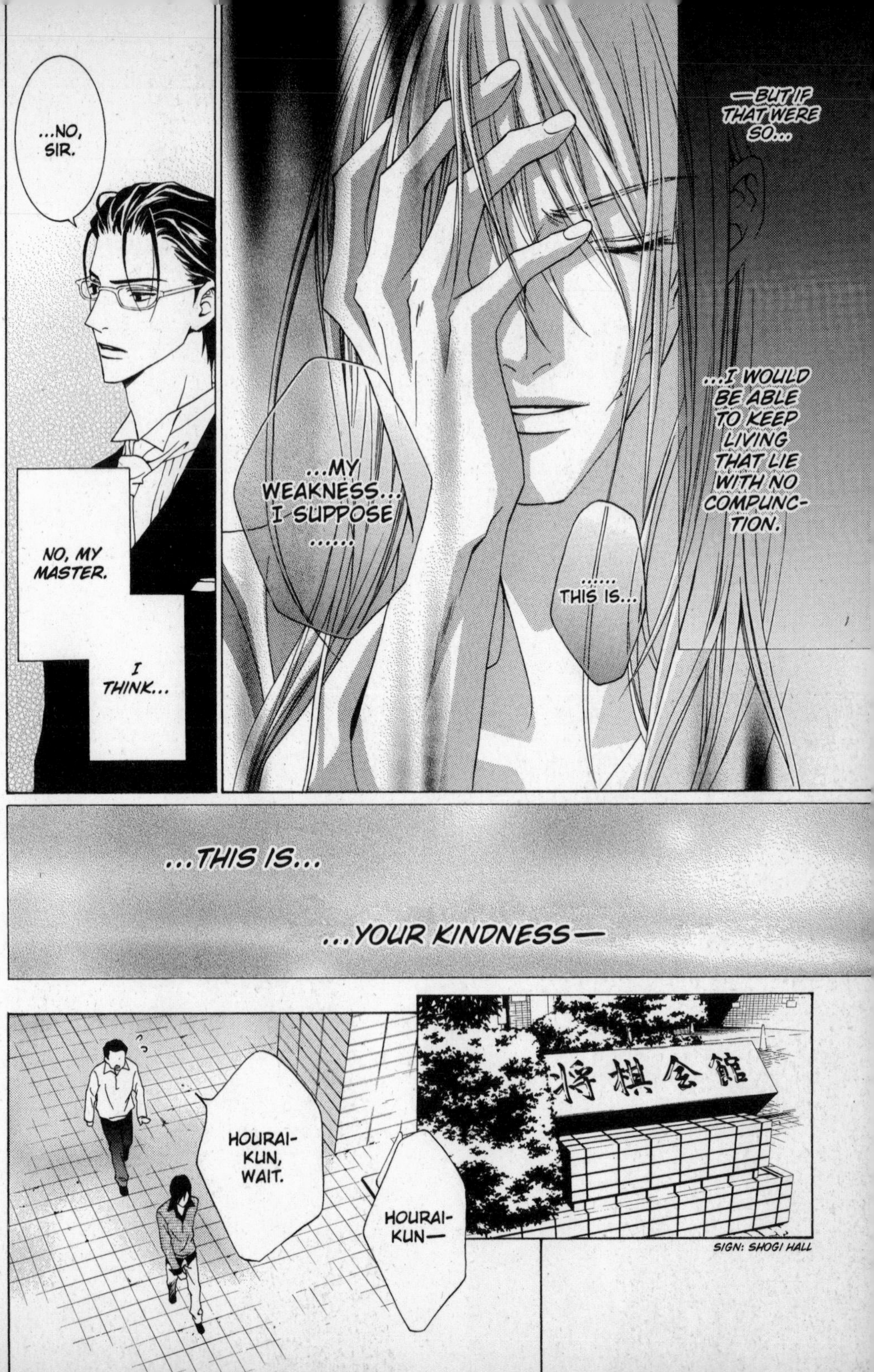
—BUT IF THAT WERE SO...
...I WOULD BE ABLE TO KEEP LIVING THAT LIE WITH NO COMPUNCTION.
......THIS IS...
...MY WEAKNESS... I SUPPOSE ......
...NO, SIR.
NO, MY MASTER.
I THINK...
...THIS IS...
...YOUR KINDNESS—
将棋会館
SIGN: SHOGI HALL
HOURAI-KUN—
HOURAI-KUN, WAIT.

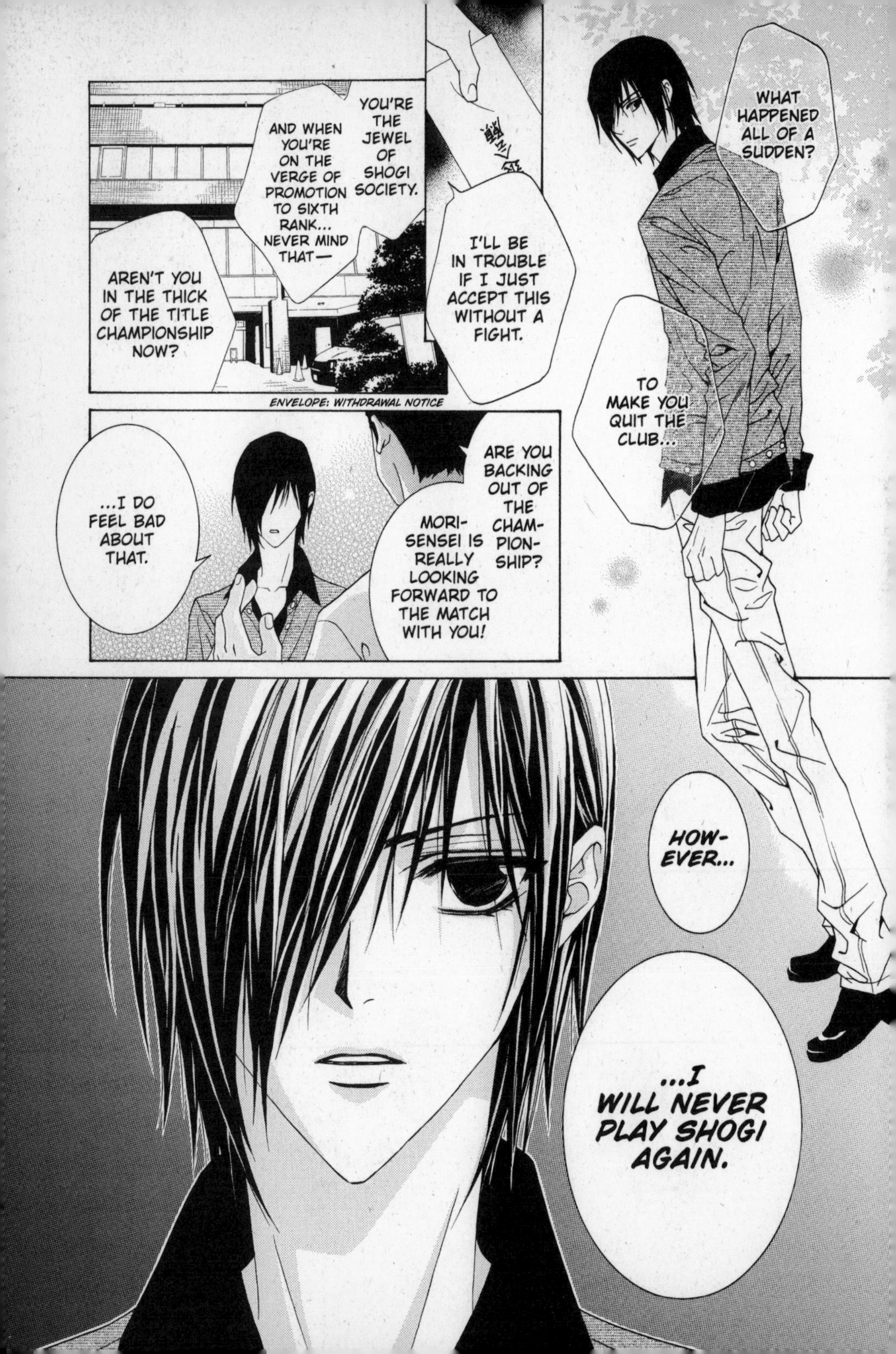
WHAT HAPPENED ALL OF A SUDDEN?
TO MAKE YOU QUIT THE CLUB...
I'LL BE IN TROUBLE IF I JUST ACCEPT THIS WITHOUT A FIGHT.
ENVELOPE: WITHDRAWAL NOTICE
YOU'RE THE JEWEL OF SHOGI SOCIETY.
AND WHEN YOU'RE ON THE VERGE OF PROMOTION TO SIXTH RANK... NEVER MIND THAT—
AREN'T YOU IN THE THICK OF THE TITLE CHAMPIONSHIP NOW?
ARE YOU BACKING OUT OF THE CHAMPIONSHIP?
MORI-SENSEI IS REALLY LOOKING FORWARD TO THE MATCH WITH YOU!
...I DO FEEL BAD ABOUT THAT.
HOWEVER...
...I WILL NEVER PLAY SHOGI AGAIN.

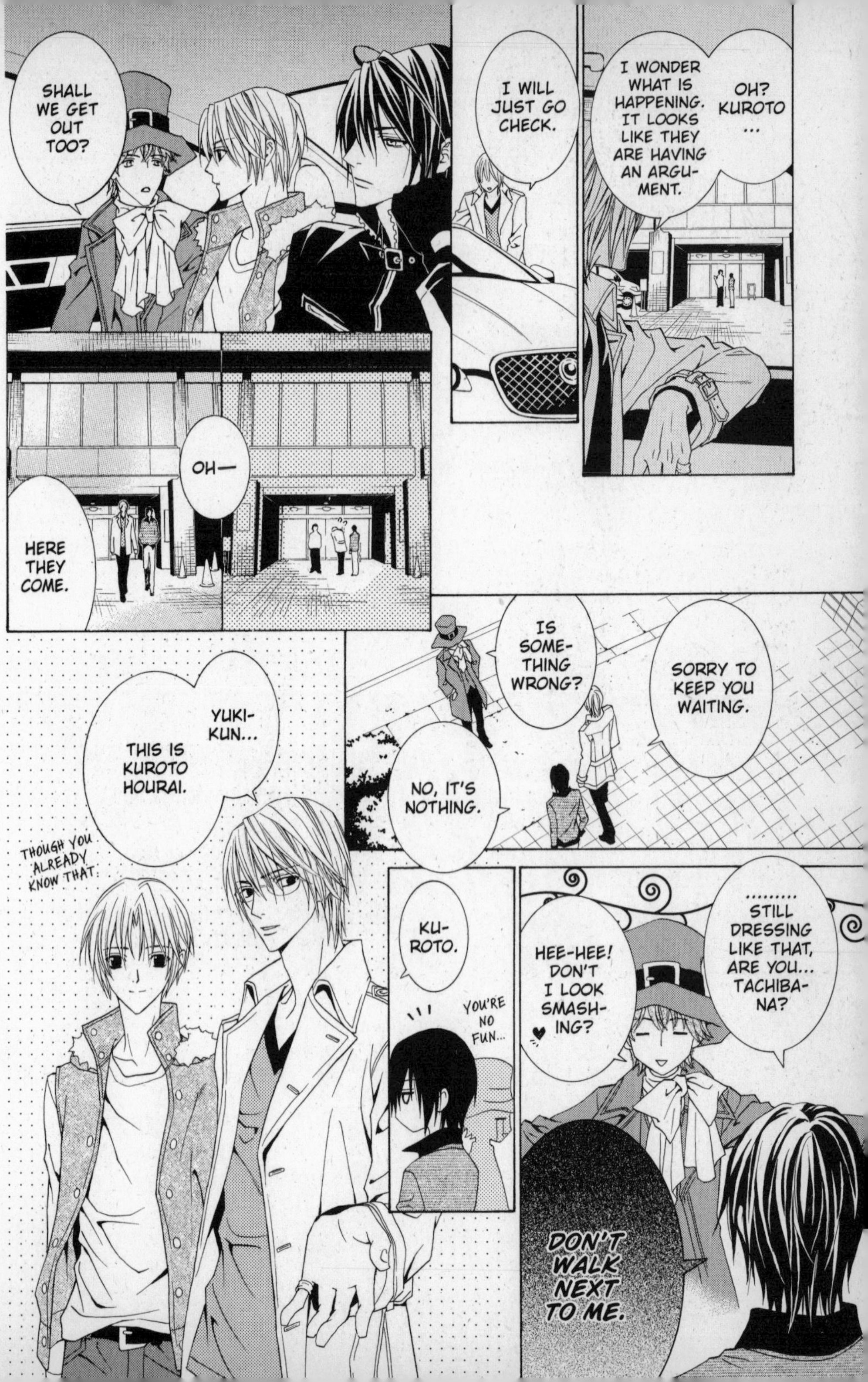
OH? KUROTO ...
I WONDER WHAT IS HAPPENING. IT LOOKS LIKE THEY ARE HAVING AN ARGUMENT.
I WILL JUST GO CHECK.
SHALL WE GET OUT TOO?
OH—
HERE THEY COME.
SORRY TO KEEP YOU WAITING.
IS SOMETHING WRONG?
NO, IT'S NOTHING.
.... STILL DRESSING LIKE THAT, ARE YOU... TACHIBANA?
HEE-HEE! DON'T I LOOK SMASHING?
DON'T WALK NEXT TO ME.
KU-ROTO.
YOU'RE NO FUN...
YUKI-KUN... THIS IS KUROTO HOURAI.
THOUGH YOU ALREADY KNOW THAT.

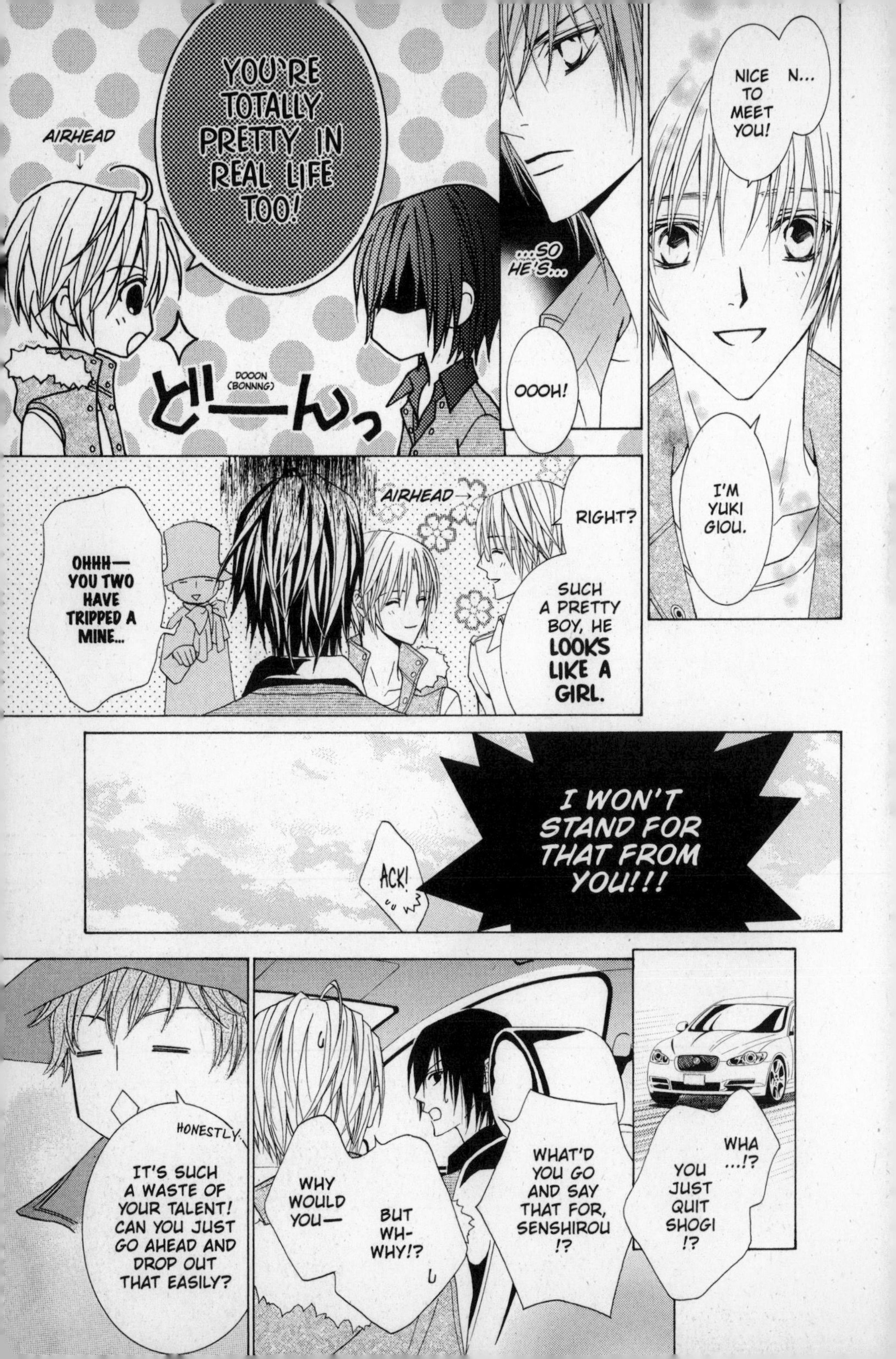
N...
NICE TO MEET YOU!
I'M YUKI GIOU.
...SO HE'S...
OOOH!
YOU'RE TOTALLY PRETTY IN REAL LIFE TOO!
AIRHEAD
どーんっ
DOOON (BONNNG)
RIGHT?
SUCH A PRETTY BOY, HE LOOKS LIKE A GIRL.
AIRHEAD
OHHH— YOU TWO HAVE TRIPPED A MINE...
I WON'T STAND FOR THAT FROM YOU!!!
ACK!
WHA ...!?
YOU JUST QUIT SHOGI!?
WHAT'D YOU GO AND SAY THAT FOR, SENSHIROU!?
BUT WH-WHY!?
WHY WOULD YOU—
HONESTLY.
IT'S SUCH A WASTE OF YOUR TALENT! CAN YOU JUST GO AHEAD AND DROP OUT THAT EASILY?

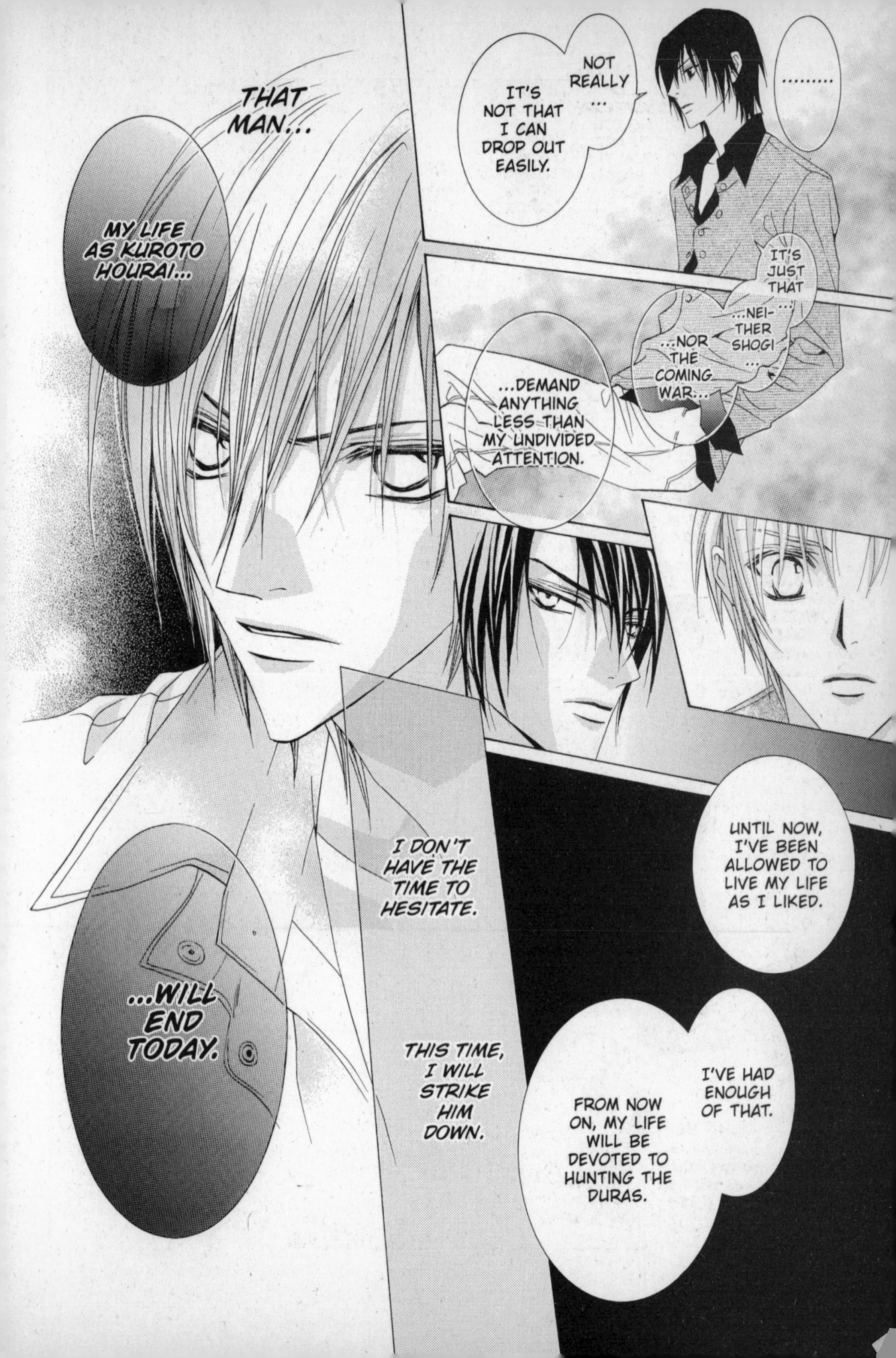

....
NOT REALLY...
IT'S NOT THAT I CAN DROP OUT EASILY.
IT'S JUST THAT...
...NEITHER SHOGI...
...NOR THE COMING WAR...
...DEMAND ANYTHING LESS THAN MY UNDIVIDED ATTENTION.
UNTIL NOW, I'VE BEEN ALLOWED TO LIVE MY LIFE AS I LIKED.
I'VE HAD ENOUGH OF THAT.
FROM NOW ON, MY LIFE WILL BE DEVOTED TO HUNTING THE DURAS.
I DON'T HAVE THE TIME TO HESITATE.
THIS TIME, I WILL STRIKE HIM DOWN.
THAT MAN...
MY LIFE AS KUROTO HOURAI...
...WILL END TODAY.

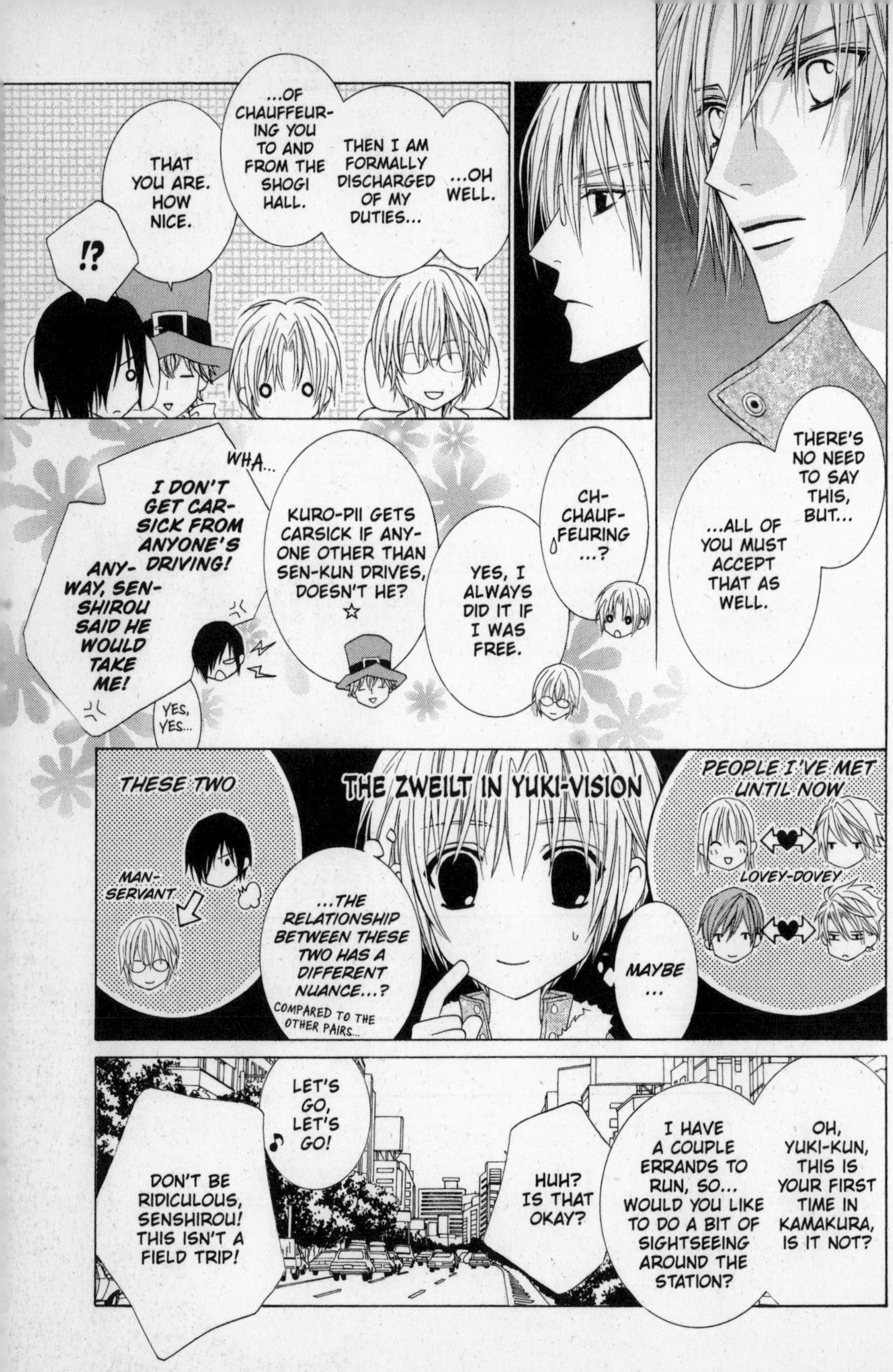
THERE'S NO NEED TO SAY THIS, BUT...
...ALL OF YOU MUST ACCEPT THAT AS WELL.
...OH WELL.
THEN I AM FORMALLY DISCHARGED OF MY DUTIES...
...OF CHAUFFEURING YOU TO AND FROM THE SHOGI HALL.
THAT YOU ARE. HOW NICE.
!?
CH-CHAUFFEURING ...?
YES, I ALWAYS DID IT IF I WAS FREE.
KURO-PII GETS CARSICK IF ANYONE OTHER THAN SEN-KUN DRIVES, DOESN'T HE? ☆
WHA...
I DON'T GET CARSICK FROM ANYONE'S DRIVING!
ANYWAY, SENSHIROU SAID HE WOULD TAKE ME!
YES, YES...
THE ZWEILT IN YUKI-VISION
PEOPLE I'VE MET UNTIL NOW
LOVEY-DOVEY
MAYBE ...
...THE RELATIONSHIP BETWEEN THESE TWO HAS A DIFFERENT NUANCE...?
COMPARED TO THE OTHER PAIRS...
THESE TWO
MAN-SERVANT
OH, YUKI-KUN, THIS IS YOUR FIRST TIME IN KAMAKURA, IS IT NOT?
I HAVE A COUPLE ERRANDS TO RUN, SO... WOULD YOU LIKE TO DO A BIT OF SIGHTSEEING AROUND THE STATION?
HUH? IS THAT OKAY?
LET'S GO, LET'S GO!
DON'T BE RIDICULOUS, SENSHIROU! THIS ISN'T A FIELD TRIP!

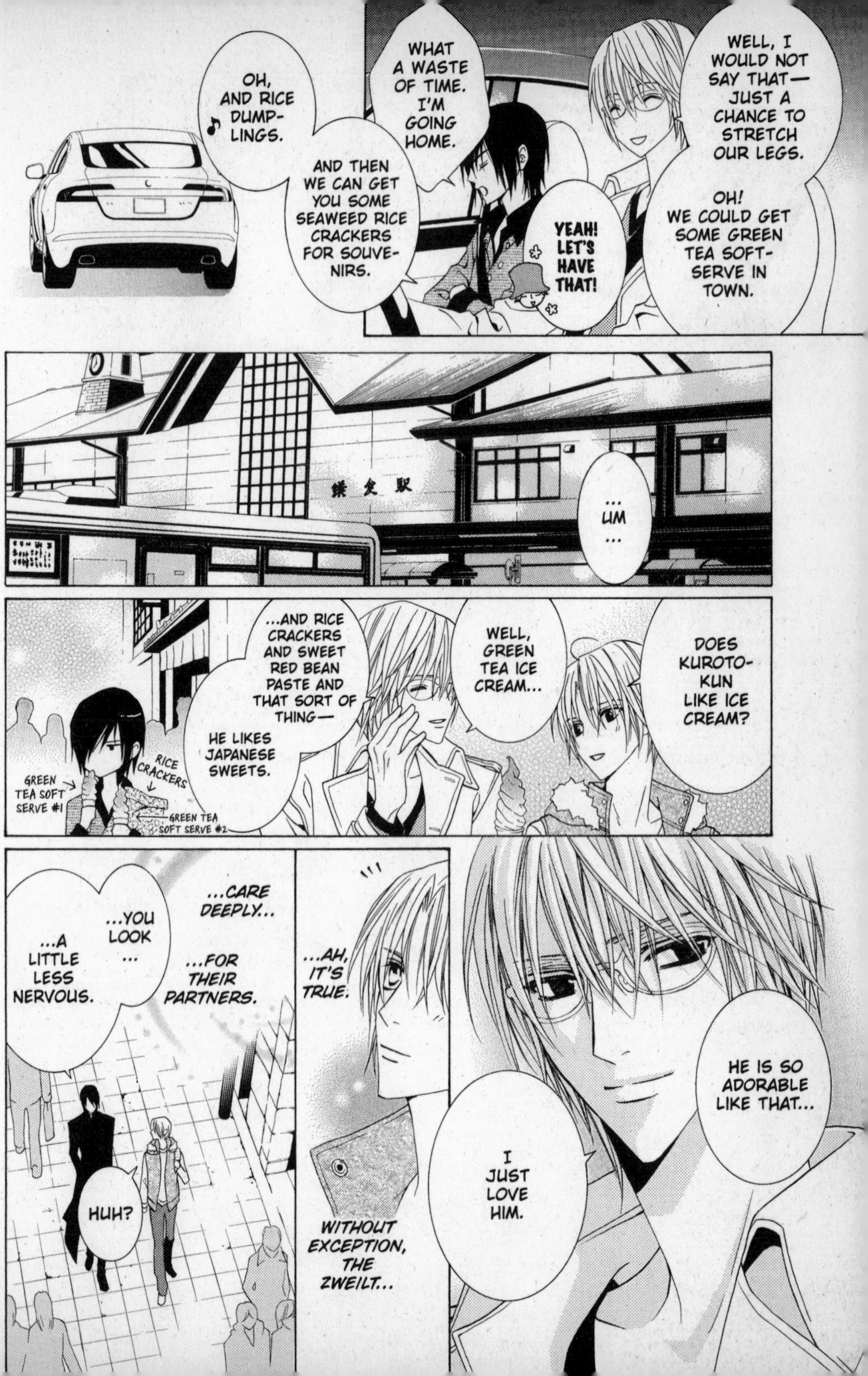
WELL, I WOULD NOT SAY THAT—JUST A CHANCE TO STRETCH OUR LEGS.
OH! WE COULD GET SOME GREEN TEA SOFT-SERVE IN TOWN.
YEAH! LET'S HAVE THAT!
WHAT A WASTE OF TIME. I'M GOING HOME.
AND THEN WE CAN GET YOU SOME SEAWEED RICE CRACKERS FOR SOUVENIRS.
OH, AND RICE DUMPLINGS.
... UM ...
DOES KUROTO-KUN LIKE ICE CREAM?
WELL, GREEN TEA ICE CREAM...
...AND RICE CRACKERS AND SWEET RED BEAN PASTE AND THAT SORT OF THING—
HE LIKES JAPANESE SWEETS.
RICE CRACKERS
GREEN TEA SOFT SERVE #1
GREEN TEA SOFT SERVE #2
HE IS SO ADORABLE LIKE THAT...
I JUST LOVE HIM.
...AH, IT'S TRUE.
WITHOUT EXCEPTION, THE ZWEILT...
...CARE DEEPLY...
...FOR THEIR PARTNERS.
...YOU LOOK ...
...A LITTLE LESS NERVOUS.
HUH?

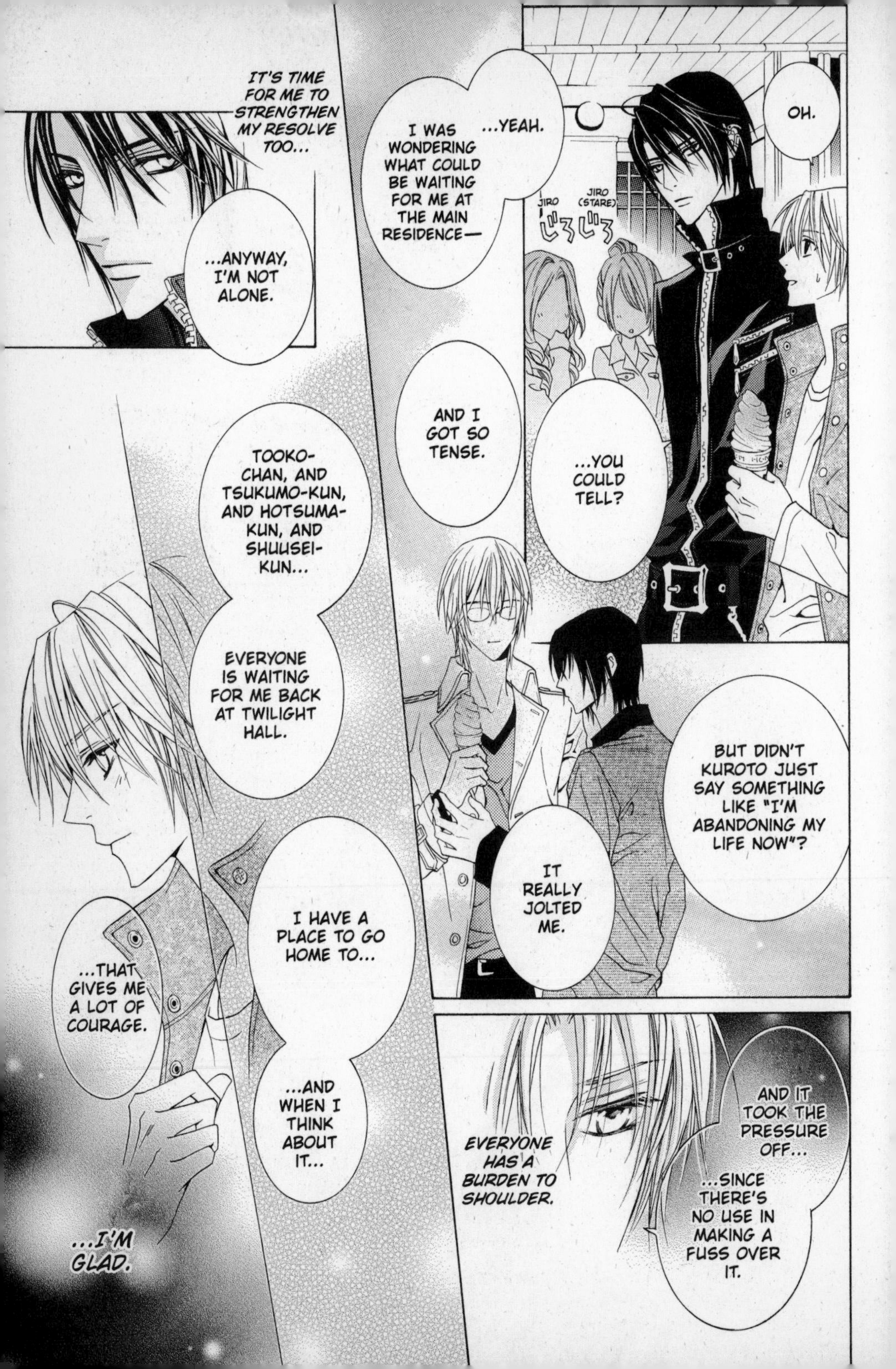
OH.
...YEAH.
I WAS WONDERING WHAT COULD BE WAITING FOR ME AT THE MAIN RESIDENCE—
AND I GOT SO TENSE.
...YOU COULD TELL?
JIRO JIRO (STARE)
じろじろ
BUT DIDN'T KUROTO JUST SAY SOMETHING LIKE "I'M ABANDONING MY LIFE NOW"?
IT REALLY JOLTED ME.
AND IT TOOK THE PRESSURE OFF...
...SINCE THERE'S NO USE IN MAKING A FUSS OVER IT.
EVERYONE HAS A BURDEN TO SHOULDER.
IT'S TIME FOR ME TO STRENGTHEN MY RESOLVE TOO...
...ANYWAY, I'M NOT ALONE.
TOOKO-CHAN, AND TSUKUMO-KUN, AND HOTSUMA-KUN, AND SHUUSEI-KUN...
EVERYONE IS WAITING FOR ME BACK AT TWILIGHT HALL.
I HAVE A PLACE TO GO HOME TO...
...AND WHEN I THINK ABOUT IT...
...THAT GIVES ME A LOT OF COURAGE.
...I'M GLAD.

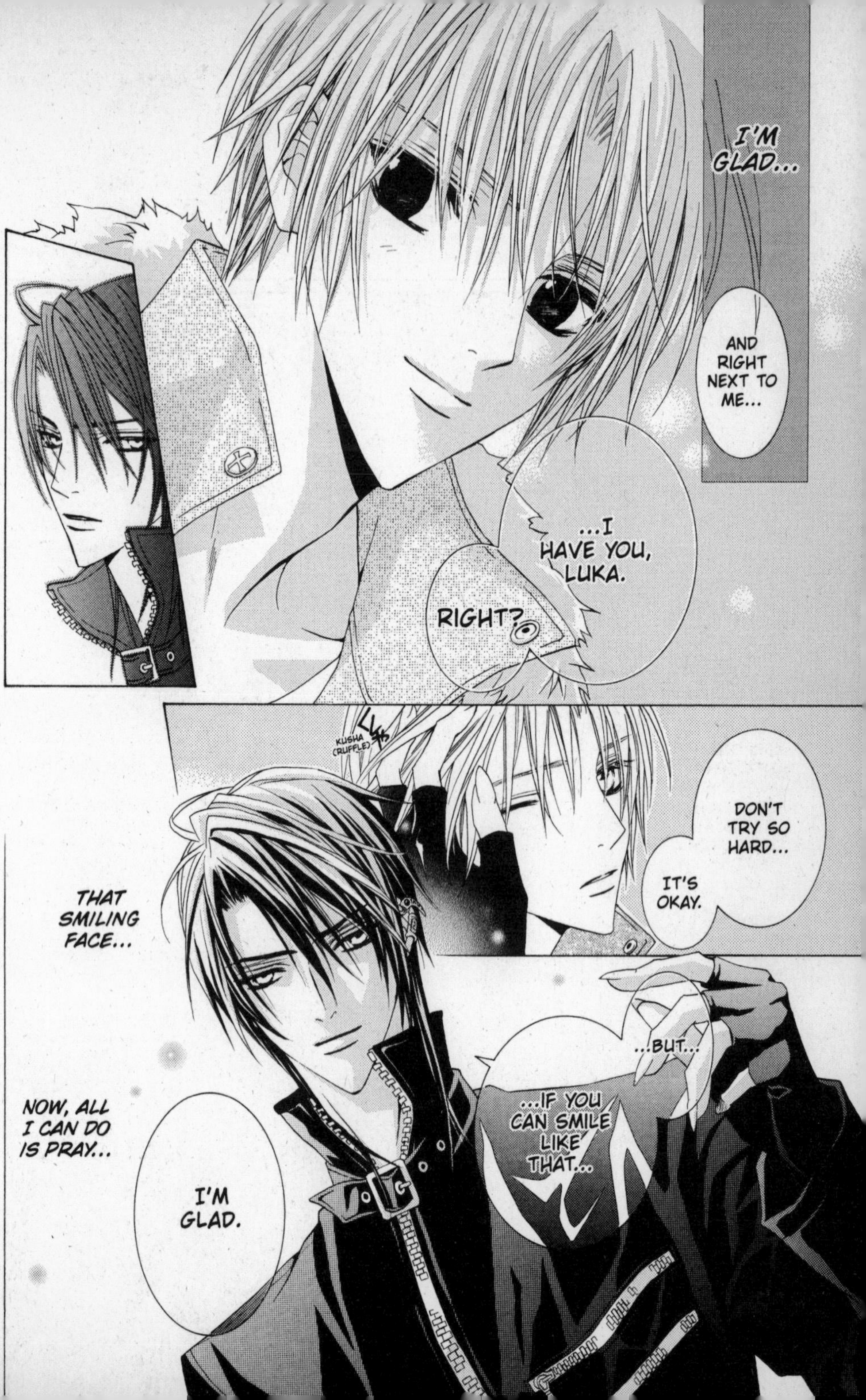
I'M GLAD...
AND RIGHT NEXT TO ME...
...I HAVE YOU, LUKA.
RIGHT?
KUSHA (RUFFLE)
DON'T TRY SO HARD...
IT'S OKAY.
THAT SMILING FACE...
...BUT...
...IF YOU CAN SMILE LIKE THAT...
I'M GLAD.
NOW, ALL I CAN DO IS PRAY...

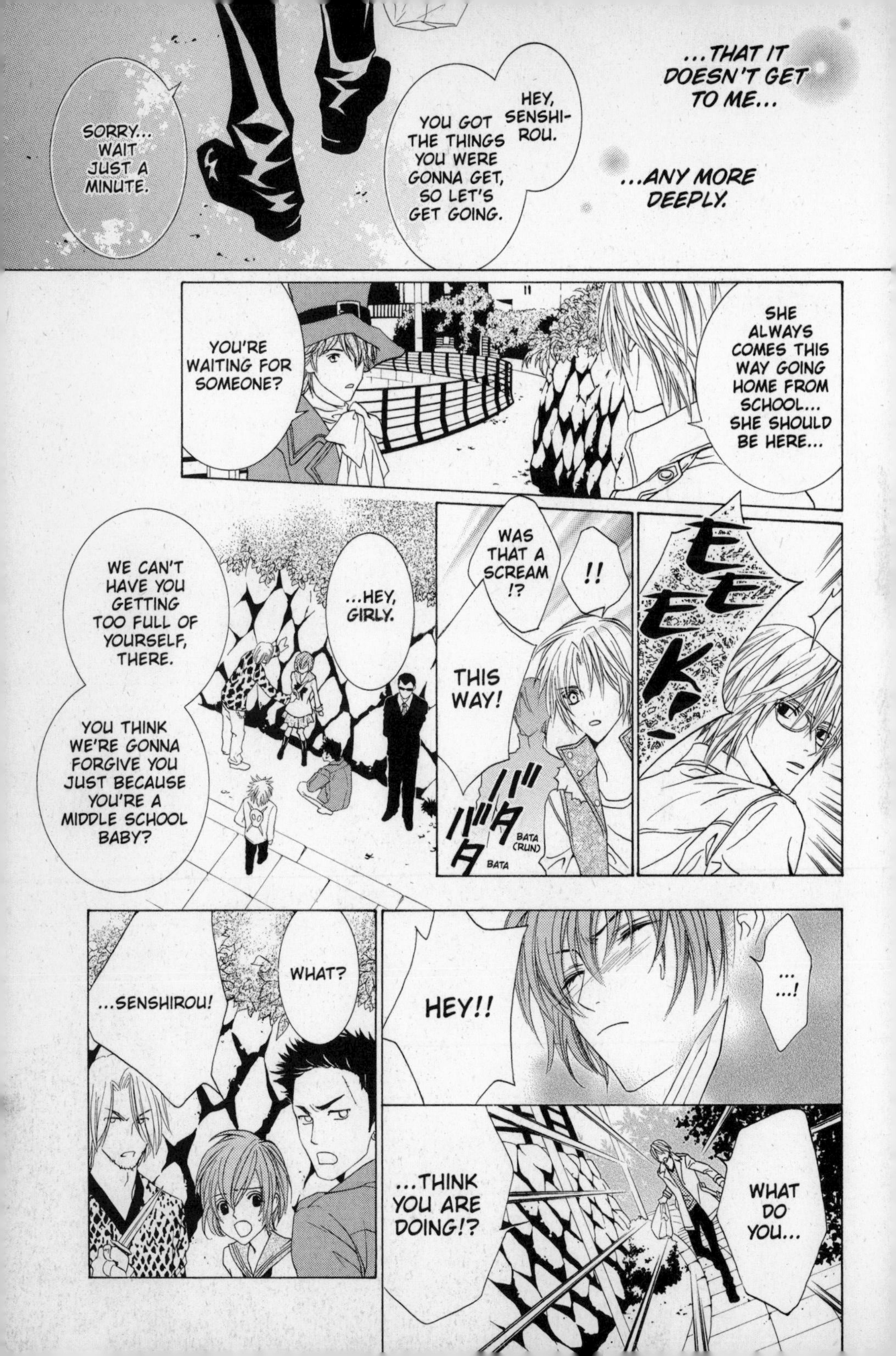
...THAT IT DOESN'T GET TO ME...
...ANY MORE DEEPLY.
HEY, SENSHIROU.
YOU GOT THE THINGS YOU WERE GONNA GET, SO LET'S GET GOING.
SORRY... WAIT JUST A MINUTE.
SHE ALWAYS COMES THIS WAY GOING HOME FROM SCHOOL... SHE SHOULD BE HERE...
YOU'RE WAITING FOR SOMEONE?
EEEK–
WAS THAT A SCREAM!?
!!
THIS WAY!
BATA (RUN)
BATA
...HEY, GIRLY.
WE CAN'T HAVE YOU GETTING TOO FULL OF YOURSELF, THERE.
YOU THINK WE'RE GONNA FORGIVE YOU JUST BECAUSE YOU'RE A MIDDLE SCHOOL BABY?
... ...!
HEY!!
WHAT DO YOU...
...THINK YOU ARE DOING!?
WHAT?
...SENSHIROU!

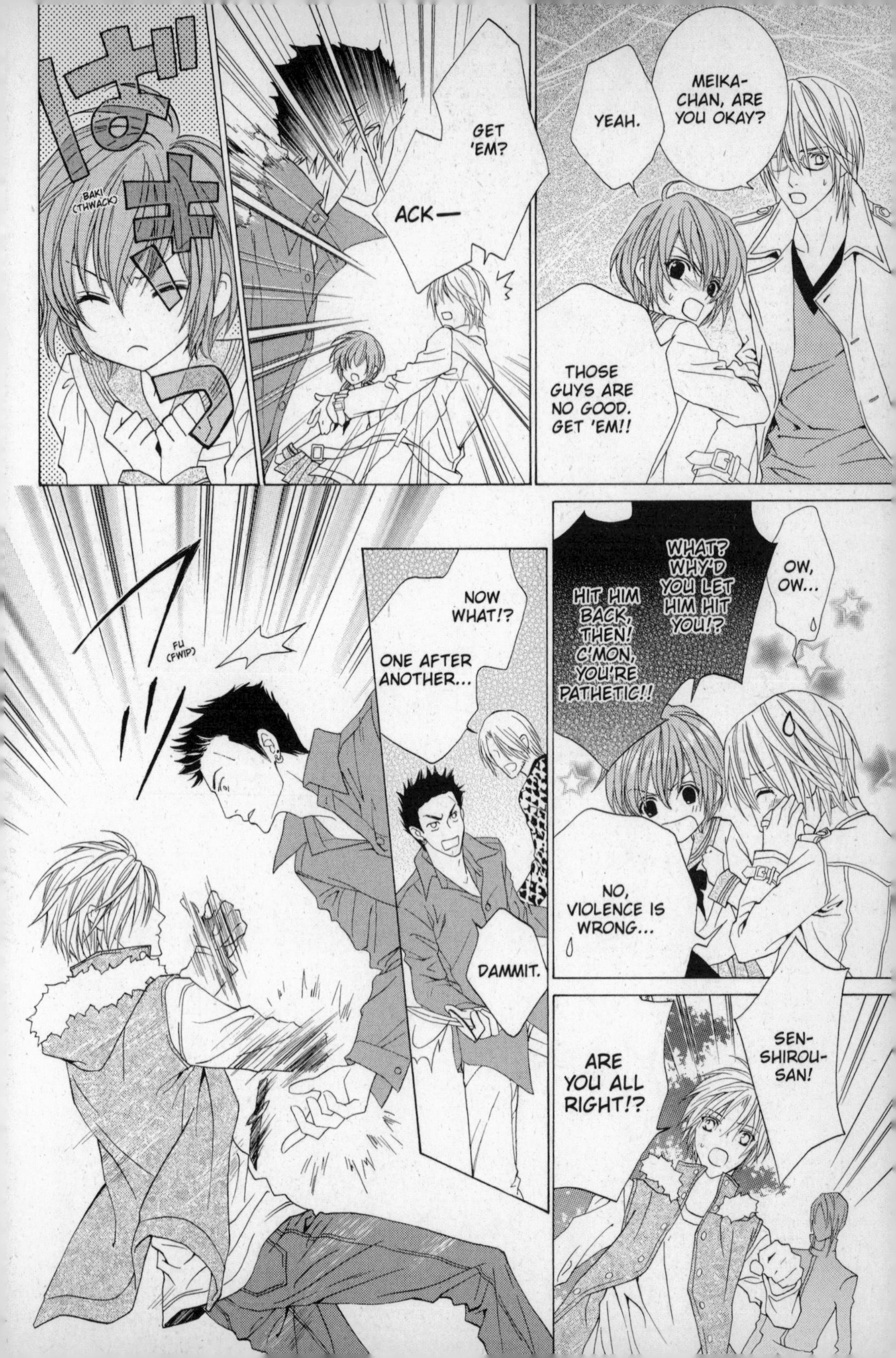
MEIKA-CHAN, ARE YOU OKAY?
YEAH.
THOSE GUYS ARE NO GOOD. GET 'EM!!
GET 'EM?
ACK—
BAKI (THWACK)
OW, OW...
WHAT? WHY'D YOU LET HIM HIT YOU!?
HIT HIM BACK, THEN! C'MON, YOU'RE PATHETIC!!
NO, VIOLENCE IS WRONG...
SEN-SHIROU-SAN!
ARE YOU ALL RIGHT!?
NOW WHAT!?
ONE AFTER ANOTHER...
DAMMIT.
FU (FWIP)

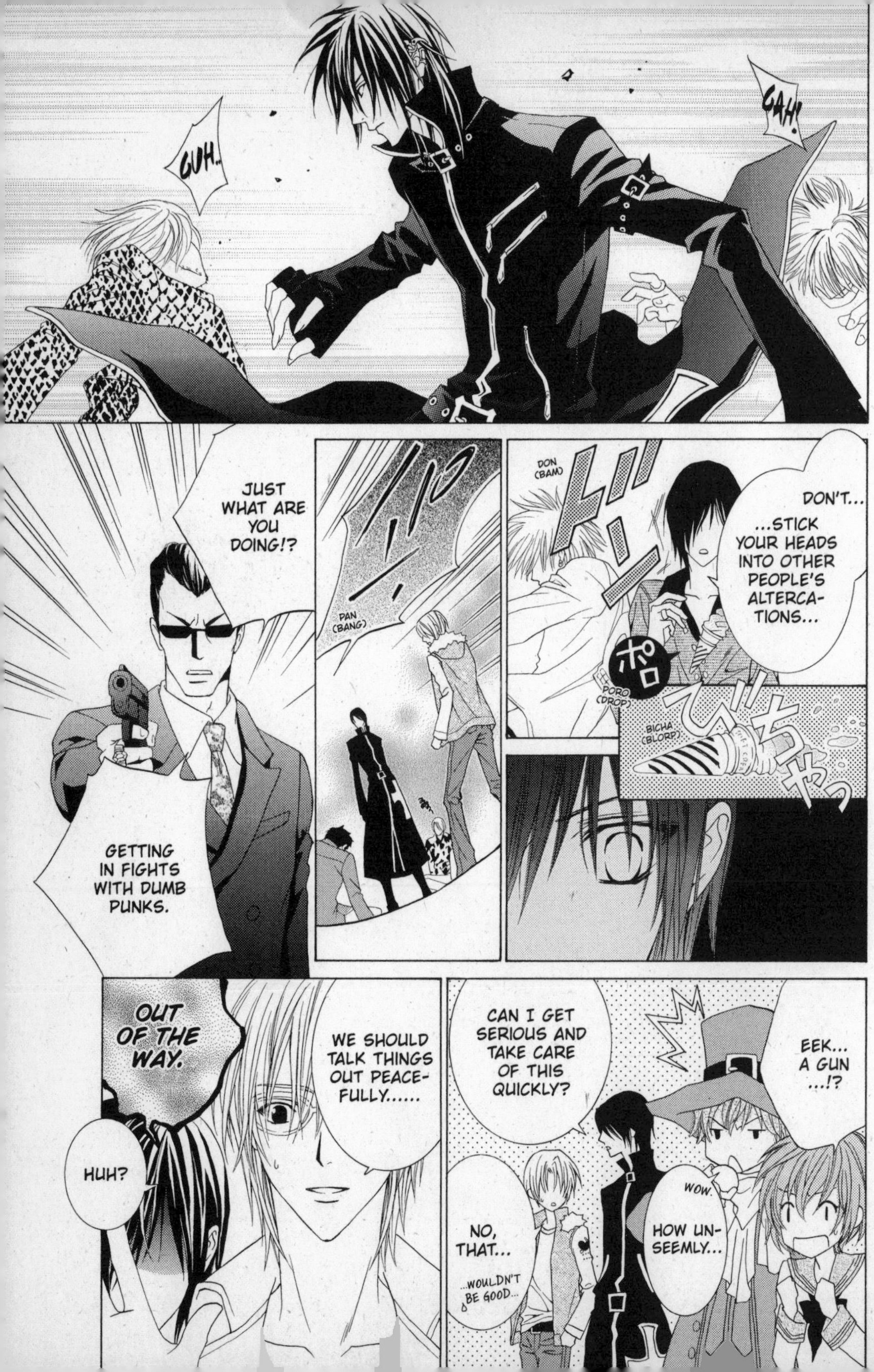
GAH!
GUH...
DON'T...
...STICK YOUR HEADS INTO OTHER PEOPLE'S ALTERCA-TIONS...
DON (BAM)
ポロ
PORO (DROP)
BICHA (BLORP)
PAN (BANG)
JUST WHAT ARE YOU DOING!?
GETTING IN FIGHTS WITH DUMB PUNKS.
EEK... A GUN ...!?
CAN I GET SERIOUS AND TAKE CARE OF THIS QUICKLY?
WOW.
HOW UN-SEEMLY...
NO, THAT...
...WOULDN'T BE GOOD...
WE SHOULD TALK THINGS OUT PEACE-FULLY......
OUT OF THE WAY.
HUH?

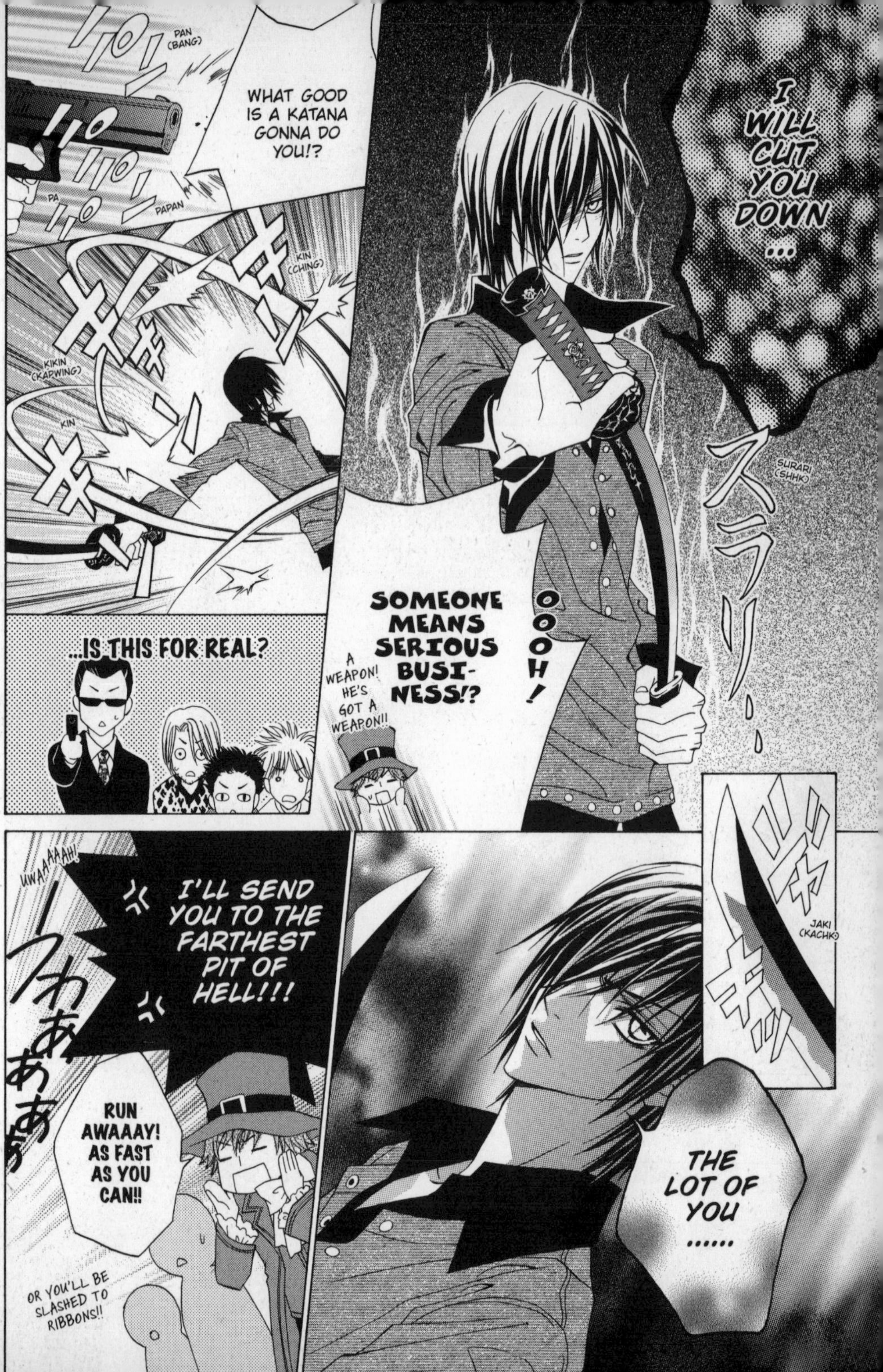
I WILL CUT YOU DOWN ...
SURARI (SHHK)
OOOOH!
SOMEONE MEANS SERIOUS BUSINESS!?
PAN (BANG)
WHAT GOOD IS A KATANA GONNA DO YOU!?
PA
PAPAN
KIN (CHING)
KIKIN (KAPWING)
KIN
...IS THIS FOR REAL?
A WEAPON! HE'S GOT A WEAPON!!
JAKI (KACHK)
THE LOT OF YOU ......
UWAAAAAH!
I'LL SEND YOU TO THE FARTHEST PIT OF HELL!!!
RUN AWAAAY! AS FAST AS YOU CAN!!
OR YOU'LL BE SLASHED TO RIBBONS!!

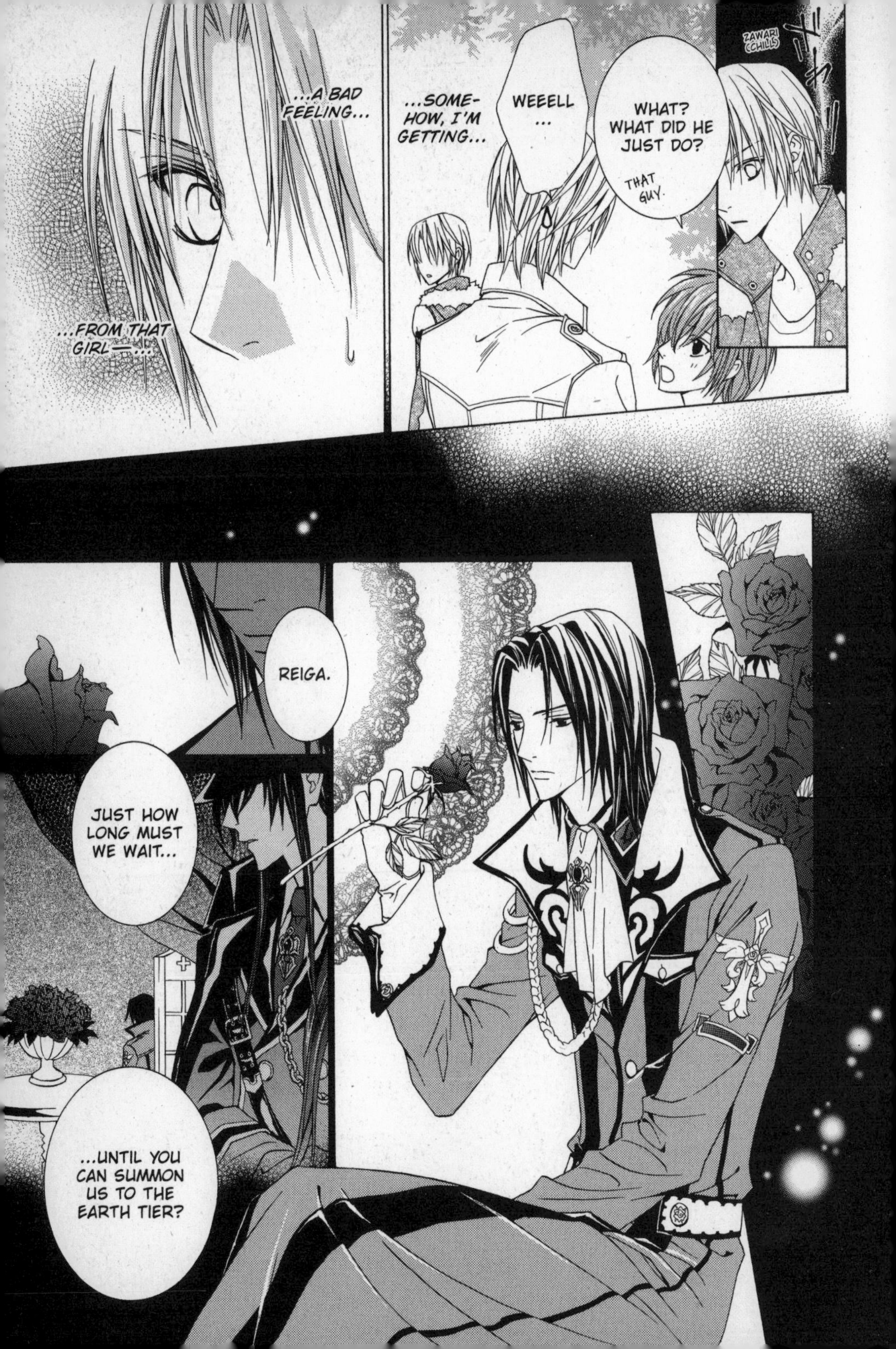
ZAWARI (CHILLS)
WHAT? WHAT DID HE JUST DO?
THAT GUY.
WEEELL ...
...SOME-HOW, I'M GETTING...
...A BAD FEELING...
...FROM THAT GIRL—...
REIGA.
JUST HOW LONG MUST WE WAIT...
...UNTIL YOU CAN SUMMON US TO THE EARTH TIER?

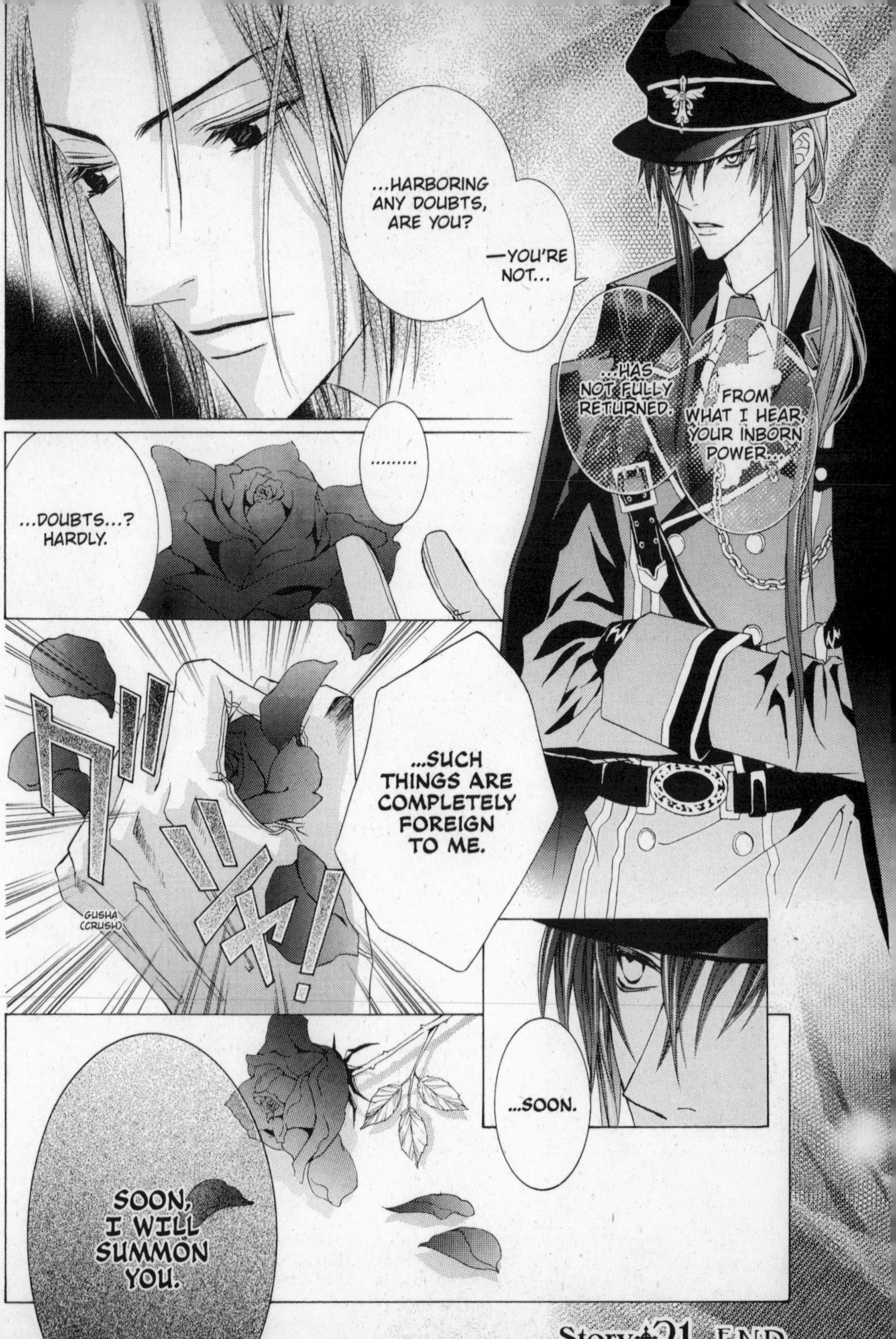
FROM WHAT I HEAR YOUR INBORN POWER...
...HAS NOT FULLY RETURNED.
—YOU'RE NOT...
...HARBORING ANY DOUBTS, ARE YOU?
....
...DOUBTS...? HARDLY.
...SUCH THINGS ARE COMPLETELY FOREIGN TO ME.
GUSHA (CRUSH)
...SOON.
SOON, I WILL SUMMON YOU.

Story 21 END

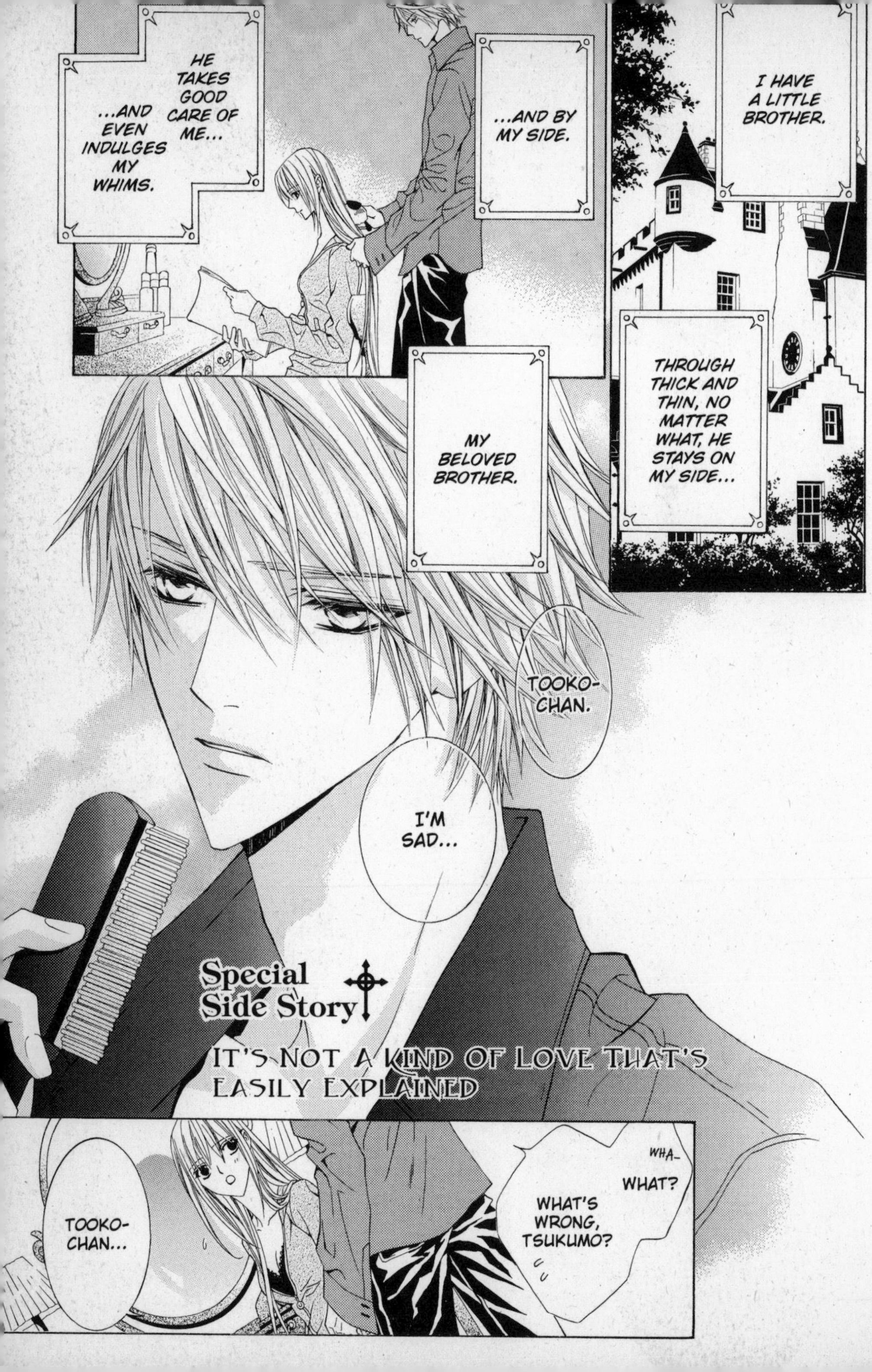
I HAVE A LITTLE BROTHER.
THROUGH THICK AND THIN, NO MATTER WHAT, HE STAYS ON MY SIDE...
...AND BY MY SIDE.
HE TAKES GOOD CARE OF ME...
...AND EVEN INDULGES MY WHIMS.
MY BELOVED BROTHER.
TOOKO-CHAN.
I'M SAD...
Special Side Story
IT'S NOT A KIND OF LOVE THAT'S EASILY EXPLAINED
WHA- WHAT?
WHAT'S WRONG, TSUKUMO?
TOOKO-CHAN...

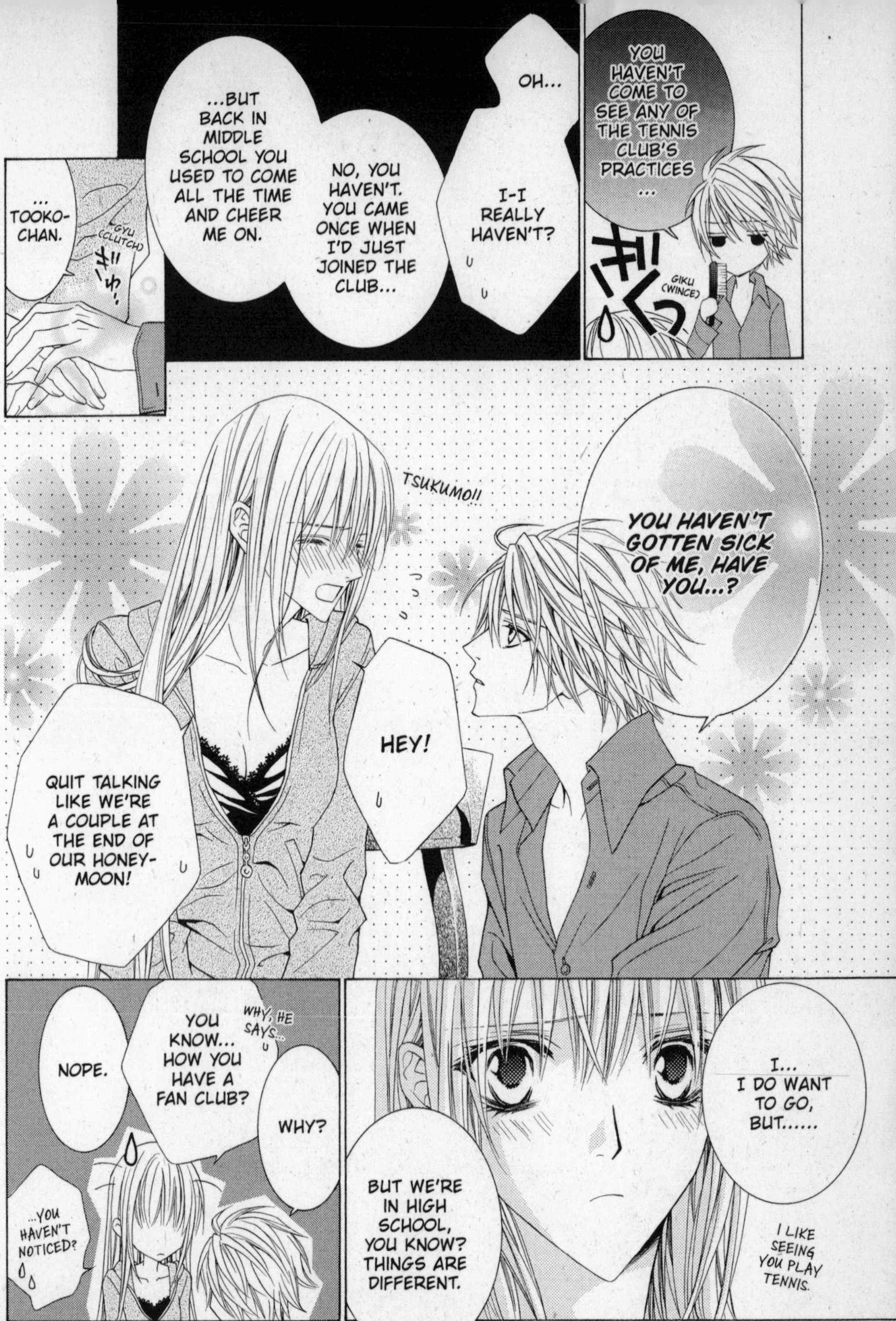
YOU HAVEN'T COME TO SEE ANY OF THE TENNIS CLUB'S PRACTICES ...
GIKU (WINCE)
OH...
I-I REALLY HAVEN'T?
NO, YOU HAVEN'T. YOU CAME ONCE WHEN I'D JUST JOINED THE CLUB...
...BUT BACK IN MIDDLE SCHOOL YOU USED TO COME ALL THE TIME AND CHEER ME ON.
... TOOKO-CHAN.
GYU (CLUTCH)
YOU HAVEN'T GOTTEN SICK OF ME, HAVE YOU...?
TSUKUMO!!
HEY!
QUIT TALKING LIKE WE'RE A COUPLE AT THE END OF OUR HONEY-MOON!
I... I DO WANT TO GO, BUT......
I LIKE SEEING YOU PLAY TENNIS.
BUT WE'RE IN HIGH SCHOOL, YOU KNOW? THINGS ARE DIFFERENT.
WHY?
WHY, HE SAYS...
YOU KNOW... HOW YOU HAVE A FAN CLUB?
NOPE.
...YOU HAVEN'T NOTICED?

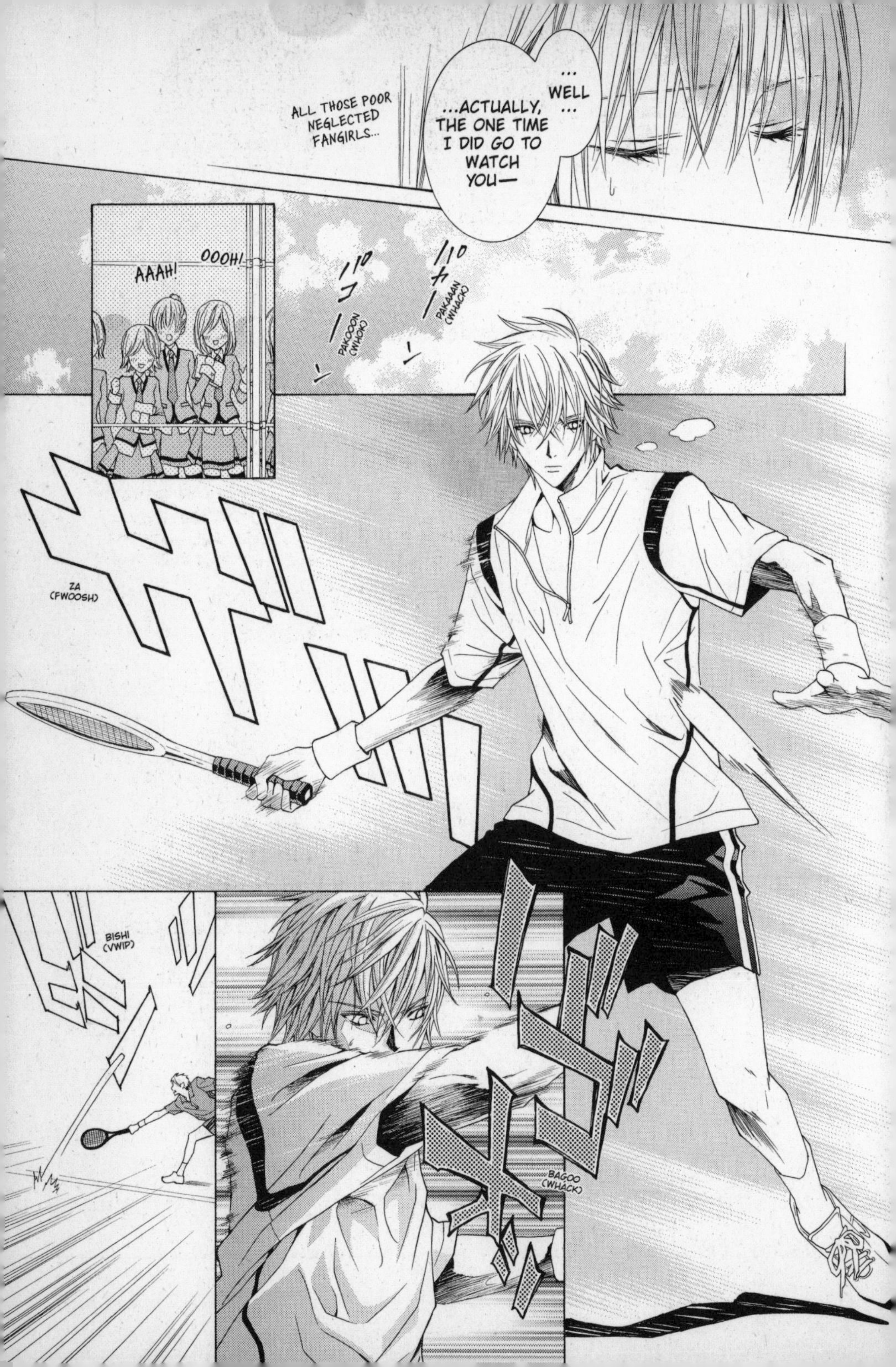

... WELL ...
...ACTUALLY, THE ONE TIME I DID GO TO WATCH YOU—
ALL THOSE POOR NEGLECTED FANGIRLS...
PAKAAAN (WHACK)
PAKOOON (WHOK)
OOOH!
AAAH!
ZA (FWOOSH)
BAGOO (WHACK)
BISHI (VWIP)

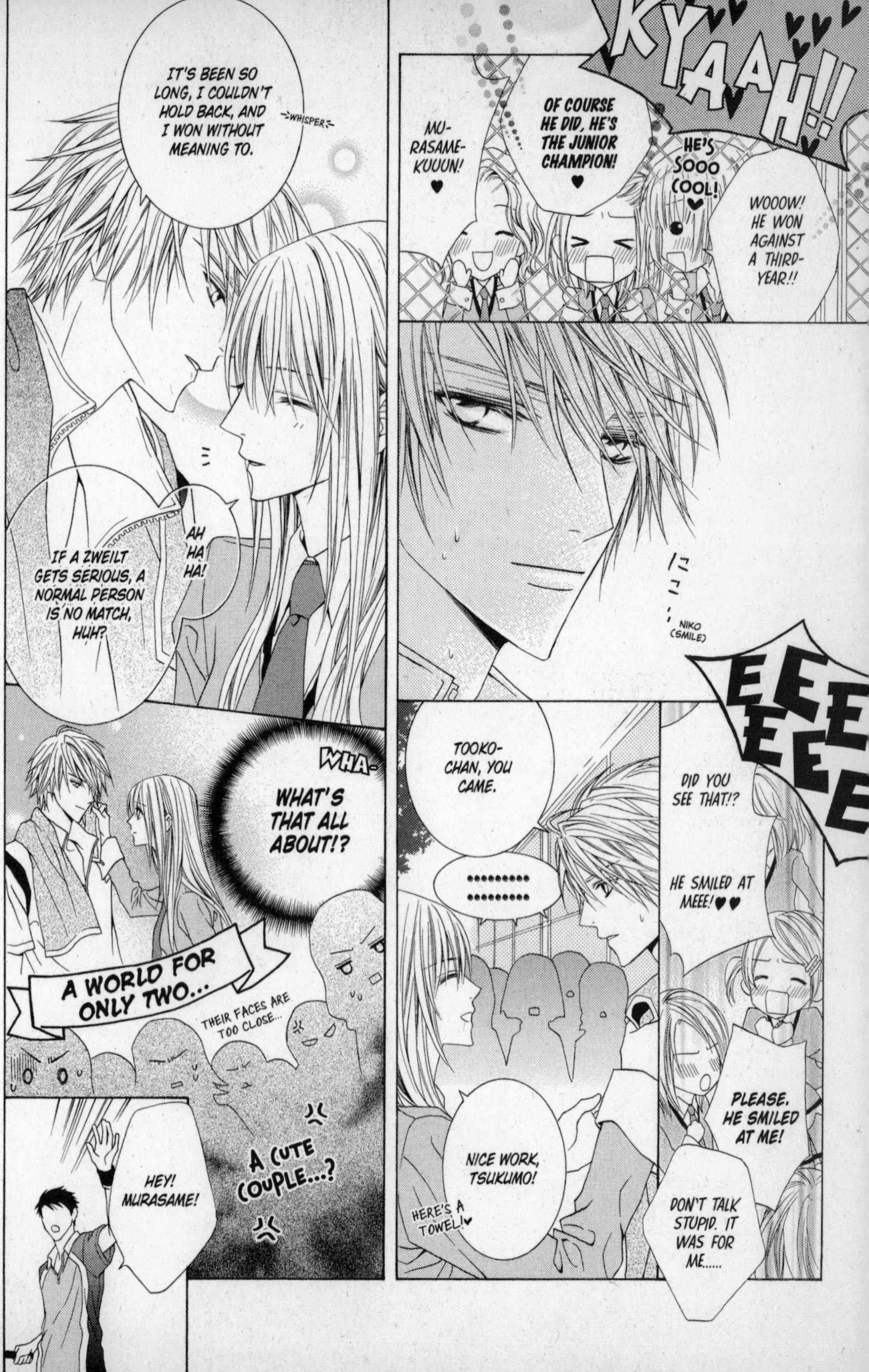
KYAAH!!
WOOOW! HE WON AGAINST A THIRD-YEAR!!
HE'S SOOO COOL!
OF COURSE HE DID, HE'S THE JUNIOR CHAMPION!
MU-RASAME-KUUUN!
にこ…
NIKO (SMILE)
EEEEEE
IT'S BEEN SO LONG, I COULDN'T HOLD BACK, AND I WON WITHOUT MEANING TO.
WHISPER
AH HA HA!
IF A ZWEILT GETS SERIOUS, A NORMAL PERSON IS NO MATCH, HUH?
DID YOU SEE THAT!?
HE SMILED AT MEEE!
PLEASE. HE SMILED AT ME!
DON'T TALK STUPID. IT WAS FOR ME.....
TOOKO-CHAN, YOU CAME.
....
....
NICE WORK, TSUKUMO!
HERE'S A TOWEL!
WHA-
WHAT'S THAT ALL ABOUT!?
A WORLD FOR ONLY TWO...
THEIR FACES ARE TOO CLOSE...
A CUTE COUPLE...?
HEY! MURASAME!

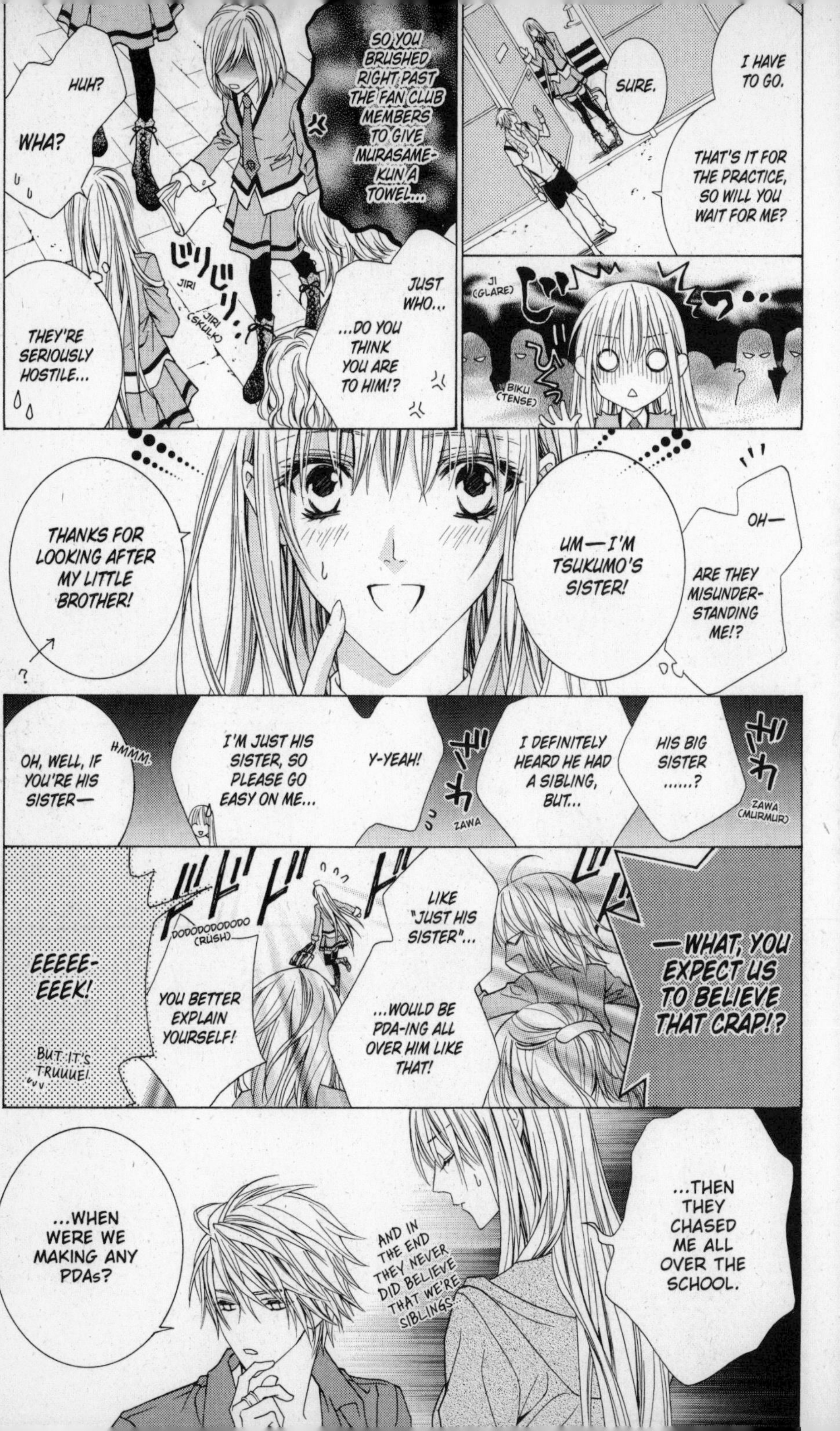
I HAVE TO GO.
THAT'S IT FOR THE PRACTICE, SO WILL YOU WAIT FOR ME?
SURE.
JI (GLARE)
BIKU (TENSE)
SO YOU BRUSHED RIGHT PAST THE FAN CLUB MEMBERS TO GIVE MURASAME-KUN A TOWEL...
JUST WHO...
...DO YOU THINK YOU ARE TO HIM!?
JIRI JIRI (SKULK)
HUH?
WHA?
THEY'RE SERIOUSLY HOSTILE...
OH—
ARE THEY MISUNDERSTANDING ME!?
UM—I'M TSUKUMO'S SISTER!
THANKS FOR LOOKING AFTER MY LITTLE BROTHER!
ZAWA (MURMUR)
HIS BIG SISTER ......?
I DEFINITELY HEARD HE HAD A SIBLING, BUT...
ZAWA
Y-YEAH!
I'M JUST HIS SISTER, SO PLEASE GO EASY ON ME...
HMMM.
OH, WELL, IF YOU'RE HIS SISTER—
—WHAT, YOU EXPECT US TO BELIEVE THAT CRAP!?
LIKE "JUST HIS SISTER"...
...WOULD BE PDA-ING ALL OVER HIM LIKE THAT!
DODODODODODO (RUSH)
YOU BETTER EXPLAIN YOURSELF!
EEEEE-EEEK!
BUT IT'S TRUUUE!
...THEN THEY CHASED ME ALL OVER THE SCHOOL.
AND IN THE END THEY NEVER DID BELIEVE THAT WE'RE SIBLINGS.
...WHEN WERE WE MAKING ANY PDAs?

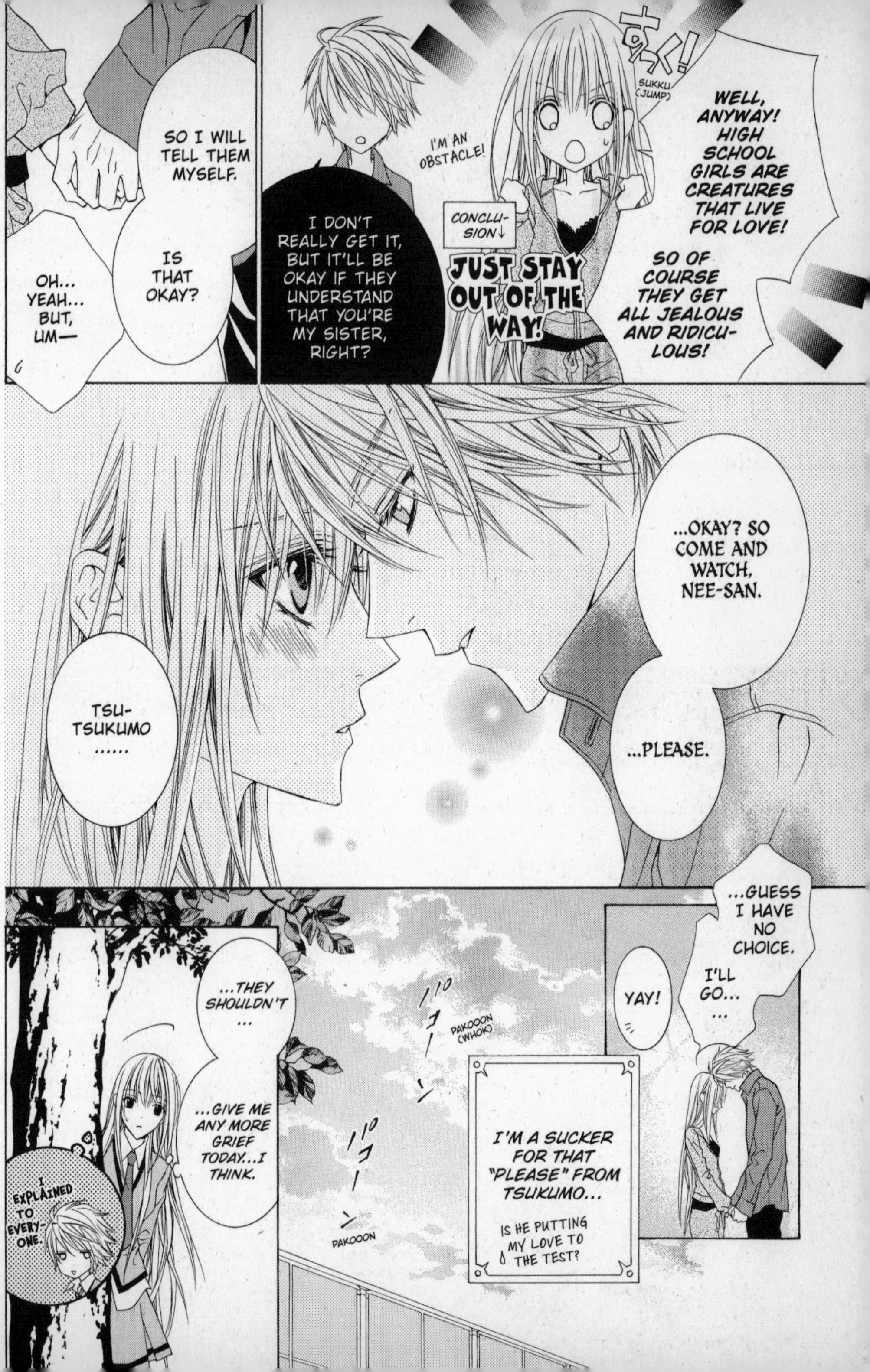
すっく!
SUKKU (JUMP)
WELL, ANYWAY! HIGH SCHOOL GIRLS ARE CREATURES THAT LIVE FOR LOVE!
SO OF COURSE THEY GET ALL JEALOUS AND RIDICULOUS!
I'M AN OBSTACLE!
CONCLU-SION↓
JUST STAY OUT OF THE WAY!
I DON'T REALLY GET IT, BUT IT'LL BE OKAY IF THEY UNDERSTAND THAT YOU'RE MY SISTER, RIGHT?
SO I WILL TELL THEM MYSELF.
IS THAT OKAY?
OH... YEAH... BUT, UM—
...OKAY? SO COME AND WATCH, NEE-SAN.
...PLEASE.
TSU-TSUKUMO ......
...GUESS I HAVE NO CHOICE.
I'LL GO... ...
YAY!
I'M A SUCKER FOR THAT "PLEASE" FROM TSUKUMO...
IS HE PUTTING MY LOVE TO THE TEST?
パコーン
PAKOOON (WHOK)
パコーン
PAKOOON
...THEY SHOULDN'T ...
...GIVE ME ANY MORE GRIEF TODAY...I THINK.
I EXPLAINED TO EVERYONE.

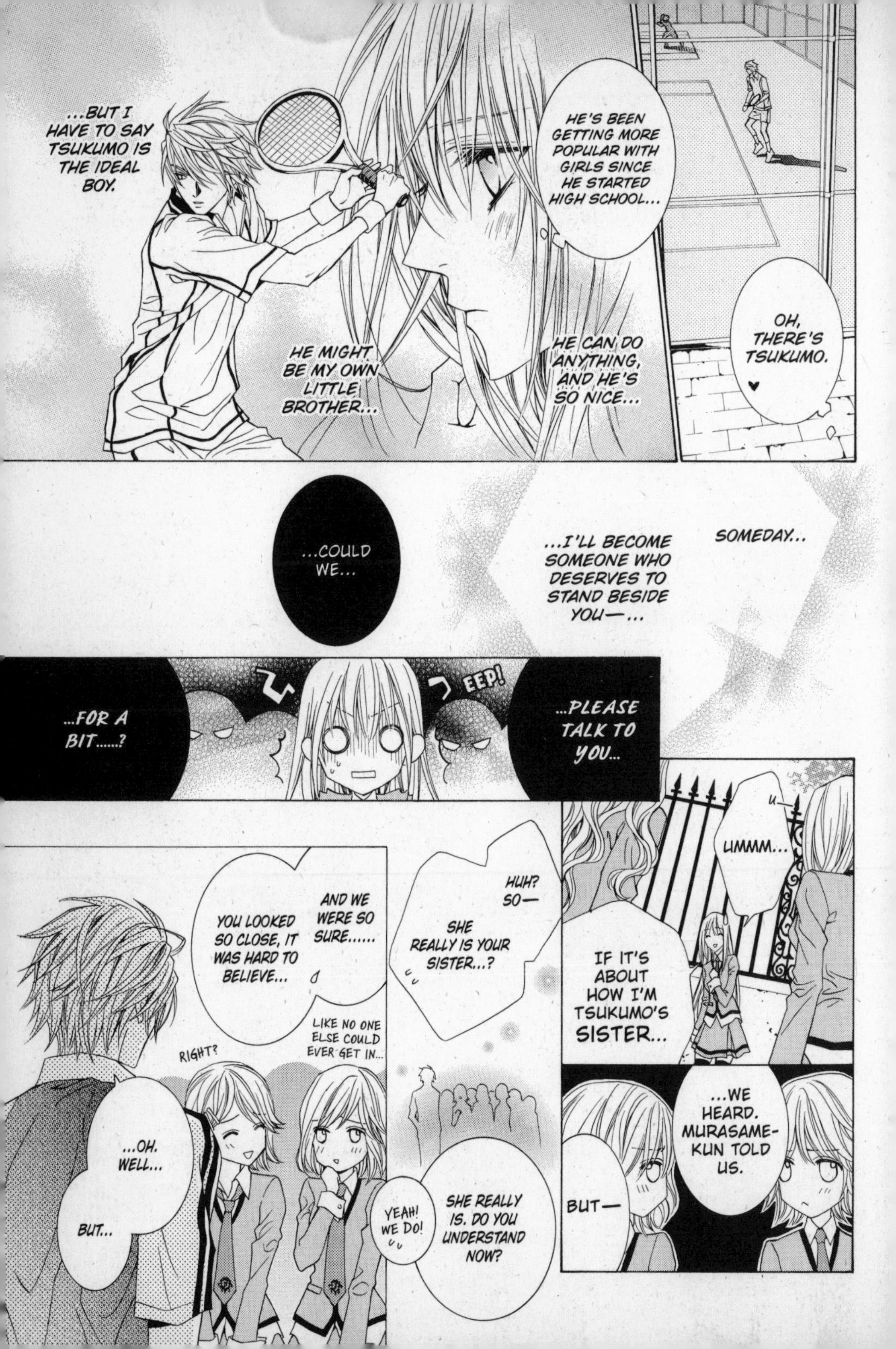
OH, THERE'S TSUKUMO.
HE'S BEEN GETTING MORE POPULAR WITH GIRLS SINCE HE STARTED HIGH SCHOOL...
HE CAN DO ANYTHING, AND HE'S SO NICE...
HE MIGHT BE MY OWN LITTLE BROTHER...
...BUT I HAVE TO SAY TSUKUMO IS THE IDEAL BOY.
SOMEDAY...
...I'LL BECOME SOMEONE WHO DESERVES TO STAND BESIDE YOU—...
...COULD WE...
...PLEASE TALK TO YOU...
EEP!
...FOR A BIT......?
U—
UMMM...
IF IT'S ABOUT HOW I'M TSUKUMO'S SISTER...
...WE HEARD. MURASAME-KUN TOLD US.
BUT—
HUH? SO—
SHE REALLY IS YOUR SISTER...?
SHE REALLY IS. DO YOU UNDERSTAND NOW?
YEAH! WE DO!
AND WE WERE SO SURE......
YOU LOOKED SO CLOSE, IT WAS HARD TO BELIEVE...
LIKE NO ONE ELSE COULD EVER GET IN...
RIGHT?
...OH. WELL...
BUT...

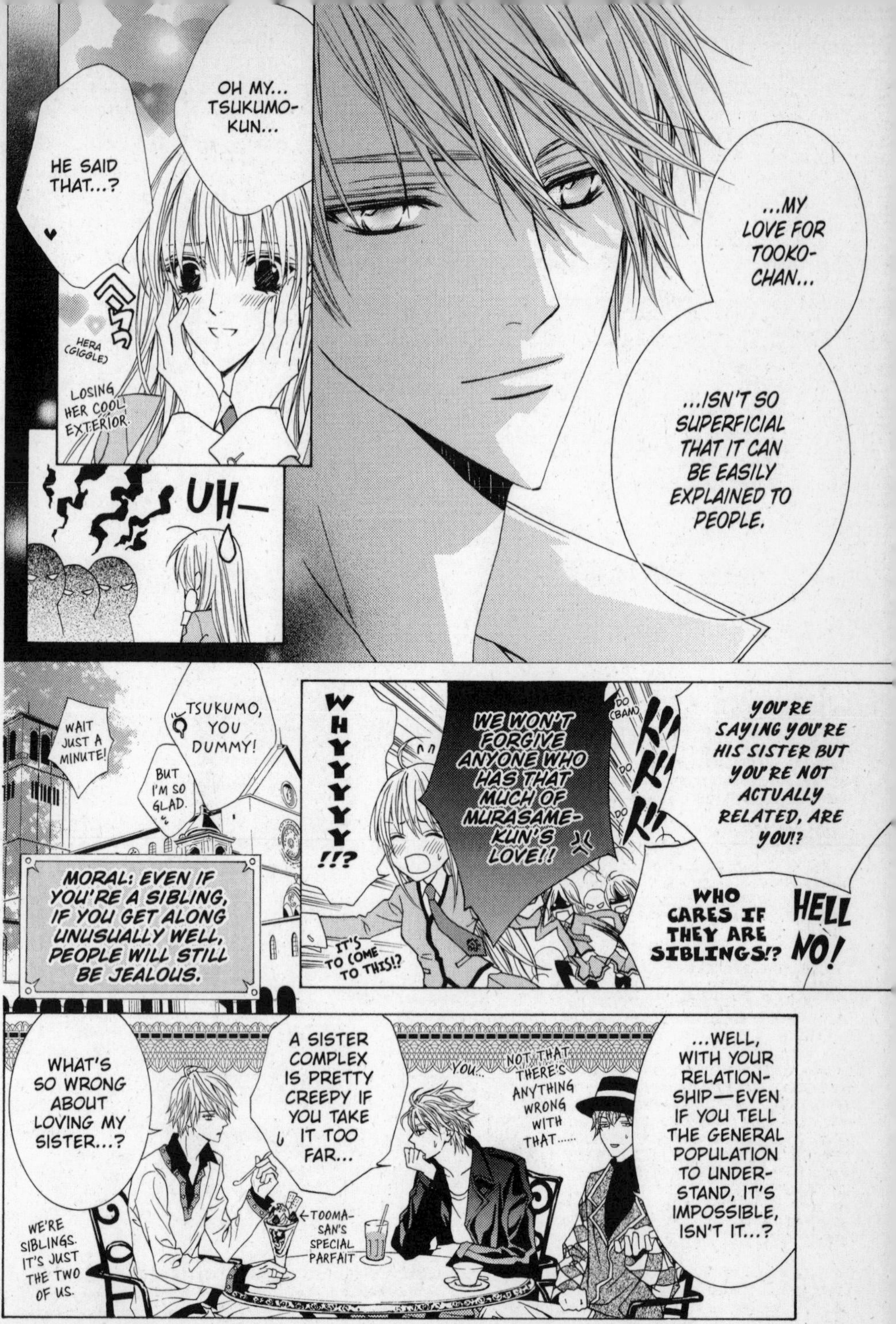
...MY LOVE FOR TOOKO-CHAN...
...ISN'T SO SUPERFICIAL THAT IT CAN BE EASILY EXPLAINED TO PEOPLE.
OH MY... TSUKUMO-KUN...
HE SAID THAT...?
HERA (GIGGLE)
LOSING HER COOL EXTERIOR.
UH—
YOU'RE SAYING YOU'RE HIS SISTER BUT YOU'RE NOT ACTUALLY RELATED, ARE YOU!?
DO (BAM) DO DO
WE WON'T FORGIVE ANYONE WHO HAS THAT MUCH OF MURASAME-KUN'S LOVE!!
WHYYYYYY!!?
WHO CARES IF THEY ARE SIBLINGS!?
HELL NO!
IT'S TO COME TO THIS!?
TSUKUMO, YOU DUMMY!
WAIT JUST A MINUTE!
BUT I'M SO GLAD.
MORAL: EVEN IF YOU'RE A SIBLING, IF YOU GET ALONG UNUSUALLY WELL, PEOPLE WILL STILL BE JEALOUS.
...WELL, WITH YOUR RELATIONSHIP—EVEN IF YOU TELL THE GENERAL POPULATION TO UNDERSTAND, IT'S IMPOSSIBLE, ISN'T IT...?
YOU...
NOT THAT THERE'S ANYTHING WRONG WITH THAT......
A SISTER COMPLEX IS PRETTY CREEPY IF YOU TAKE IT TOO FAR...
WHAT'S SO WRONG ABOUT LOVING MY SISTER...?
←TOOMA-SAN'S SPECIAL PARFAIT
WE'RE SIBLINGS. IT'S JUST THE TWO OF US.

Special Side Story END

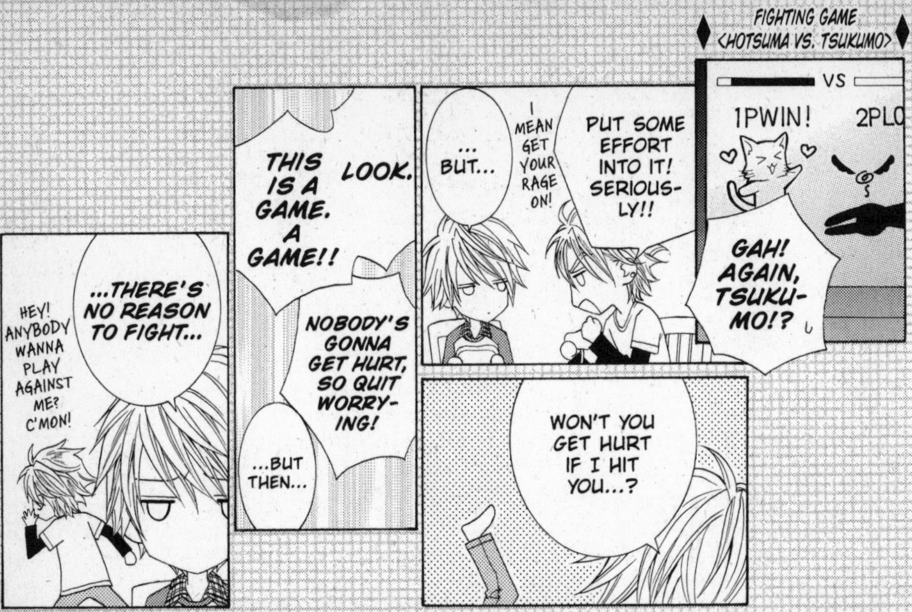
FIGHTING GAME
<HOTSUMA VS. TSUKUMO>
VS
1PWIN!
2PLO
GAH! AGAIN, TSUKUMO!?
PUT SOME EFFORT INTO IT! SERIOUSLY!!
I MEAN GET YOUR RAGE ON!
... BUT...
WON'T YOU GET HURT IF I HIT YOU...?
LOOK.
THIS IS A GAME. A GAME!!
NOBODY'S GONNA GET HURT, SO QUIT WORRYING!
...BUT THEN...
...THERE'S NO REASON TO FIGHT...
HEY! ANYBODY WANNA PLAY AGAINST ME? C'MON!

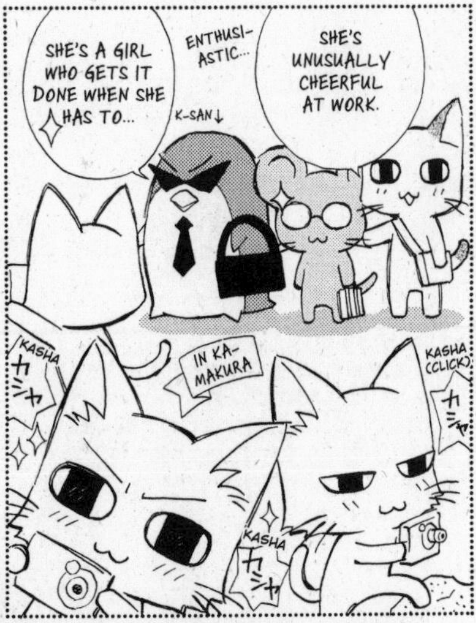
SHE'S UNUSUALLY CHEERFUL AT WORK.
ENTHUSIASTIC...
SHE'S A GIRL WHO GETS IT DONE WHEN SHE HAS TO...
K-SAN↓
KASHA (CLICK)
IN KAMAKURA
KASHA
KASHA

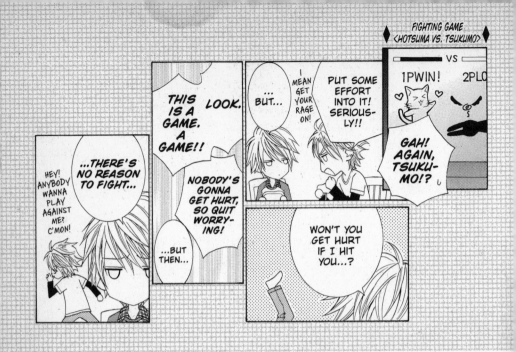

▸SO I WAS FINALLY ABLE TO INTRODUCE SOME NEW CHARACTERS! ♪ WHEN THEY GET TO THE MAIN RESIDENCE IN VOLUME 5 THERE WILL BE EVEN MORE NEW CHARACTERS MAKING THEIR DEBUTS. AND TAKASHIRO-SAN'S STORY WILL BE IN VOLUME 5 TOO, SO—UNTIL NEXT TIME! ANYWAY, I WENT TO KAMAKURA TO GATHER REFERENCE MATERIAL! ♪ IT WAS THE FIRST TIME I'D BEEN THERE, BUT THERE WERE SO MANY LOCATIONS THAT MATCHED UP WITH THE IDEAS IN MY HEAD, I WAS THRILLED! ♪ THE WEATHER WAS NICE TOO, AND DESPITE FORCING MY SLEEP-DEPRIVED SELF ON AN EXPEDITION, I WAS ABLE TO MOVE AROUND FULL OF ENERGY, SO THAT WAS GOOD. ONE COULD SAY IT REALLY AGREED WITH ME... IT'S SUCH A NICE PLACE, I'D LIKE TO GO AGAIN. THANK YOU TO EVERYONE WHO SHOWED ME AROUND! ♥

▸THIS TIME, BECAUSE OF PAGE SPACE REASONS, I WROTE LESS IN MY ASIDES. TO THOSE WHO WERE LOOKING FORWARD TO THEM, I APOLOGIZE. (I DID EDIT A LOT, THOUGH...PAINFUL.) BUT I WANT TO KEEP WRITING ASIDES WHEREVER I GET BLANK SPACE! ☆

▸THANK YOU FOR THE LETTERS, AND THE BIRTHDAY PRESENTS AND CARDS AND GIFTS AND NEW YEAR GREETINGS...THEY'RE MY ENCOURAGEMENT. OH—AND THE VALENTINE'S DAY CHOCOLATE TOO! ♥ MY EDITOR GIVES ME CHOCOLATE EVERY YEAR, BUT EACH TIME I END UP THINKING, THAT MUST SUCK FOR THE EMPLOYEES (BECAUSE I'M ALWAYS FORGETTING)... AND THEN I FORGET WHITE DAY TOO, SO I ALWAYS END UP RECEIVING AND NEVER RECIPROCATING... (I MUST REPENT). BUT I HAVEN'T FORGOTTEN ABOUT REPLYING TO YOUR LETTERS! JUDGING FROM THE MEETINGS WITH MY EDITOR, THOUGH, IT DOESN'T LOOK LIKE I'LL BE GETTING A LONG VACATION... I REALLY NEED TO PLAN MY SCHEDULE PRECISELY IF I'M ABLE TO DO ANYTHING AT ALL. BUT I SHAN'T GIVE UP! I CAN'T SAY WHEN FOR CERTAIN, BUT PLEASE KEEP WAITING. (OH, AND I DON'T NEED STAMPS.)

▸AND LASTLY, TO ALL THE STAFF WHO HELPED ME, INCLUDING K-SAN, TO MY EDITOR AND THE ASUKA EDITING DEPARTMENT WHOM I'VE WORRIED AND HARASSED SO, TO EVERYONE KINDLY WORKING WITH ME...AND ABOVE ALL, TO EVERYONE READING URABOKU, MY HEARTFELT THANKS. I'M TRULY GRATEFUL. STAY WITH ME FOR VOLUME 5...!

➡ To be continued.

Translation Notes

Page 92
Tsukumo's spell is written with the kanji for "Black Gun."

Page 131
Kamakura is a historical area near Tokyo in Kanagawa prefecture. It was the seat of the shogunate government (during the Kamakura Period, from 1185 to 1333) as well as a powerful religious center. It is now famous for its temples and the Great Buddha statue.

Page 140
Shuusei's spell is written with the kanji for "Crime and Punishment."

Page 177
Yakiniku is marinated grilled meat, often Korean barbecue style.

Page 181
Tsundere is a term for a certain type of character who is mean and off-putting at first (*tsun-tsun*), then turns sweet and lovey-dovey (*dere-dere*).

Page 181
The kanji characters for "Hotsuma" and "Shuusei" are so difficult that Odagiri-sensei printed the names beside the in-character autographs in simpler phonetic script, or hiragana.

Page 218
"Diomedes" is written with the characters for "Crucifixion."

Page 237
"Avalam" is written with characters meaning "Mythical Beast."

Page 315
Shogi is a strategic board game, also known as Japanese chess. Like Western chess, it has a long history and was played in its present form as early as the sixteenth century and also boasts a similar game culture.

Page 357
In Japan, it is customary (practically mandatory) to give chocolate on Valentine's Day to the person you like, or, when you grow up, the people you work with. White Day, set a month later on March 14, is a chance to reciprocate the Valentine's Day gift, because in Japan it is a cardinal sin to leave a gift or favor unreciprocated (which is why this forgetful artist must repent).

The Betrayal
Knows My Name

HoTaru oDagiri

Yuki and the
gang are fighting
demons, but here
in the studio, we're
fighting Luka. He takes
three times as much work
as the other characters...
"Luka, go away already-
yyy~!" (◂···As if.) Those
anguished cries are
ringing out again
today...

Message from Volume 3
(Japanese edition)

HoTaru oDagiri

I've become such a
shut-in that the list of
"Vehicles That Don't Give
Me Motion Sickness" has
been reduced to bullet
trains and airplanes. But
the thing is, I never have
any reason to travel
by bullet train or
airplane...

**MESSAGE FROM
VOLUME 4**
(Japanese edition)

Can't wait for the next volume? You don't have to!

Keep up with the latest chapters of some of your favorite manga every month online in the pages of YEN PLUS!

WITCH & WIZARD

MAXIMUM RIDE

DANIEL X

SOULLESS

K-ON!

Visit us at
www.yenplus.com
for details!

Maximum Ride © James Patterson, Illustrations © Hachette Book Group • Witch & Wizard © James Patterson, Illustrations © Hachette Book Group, • Daniel X © James Patterson,
Illustrations © Hachette Book Group • Soulless © Tofa Borregaard, Illustrations © Hachette Book Group • K-ON! © Kakifly / HOUBUNSHA

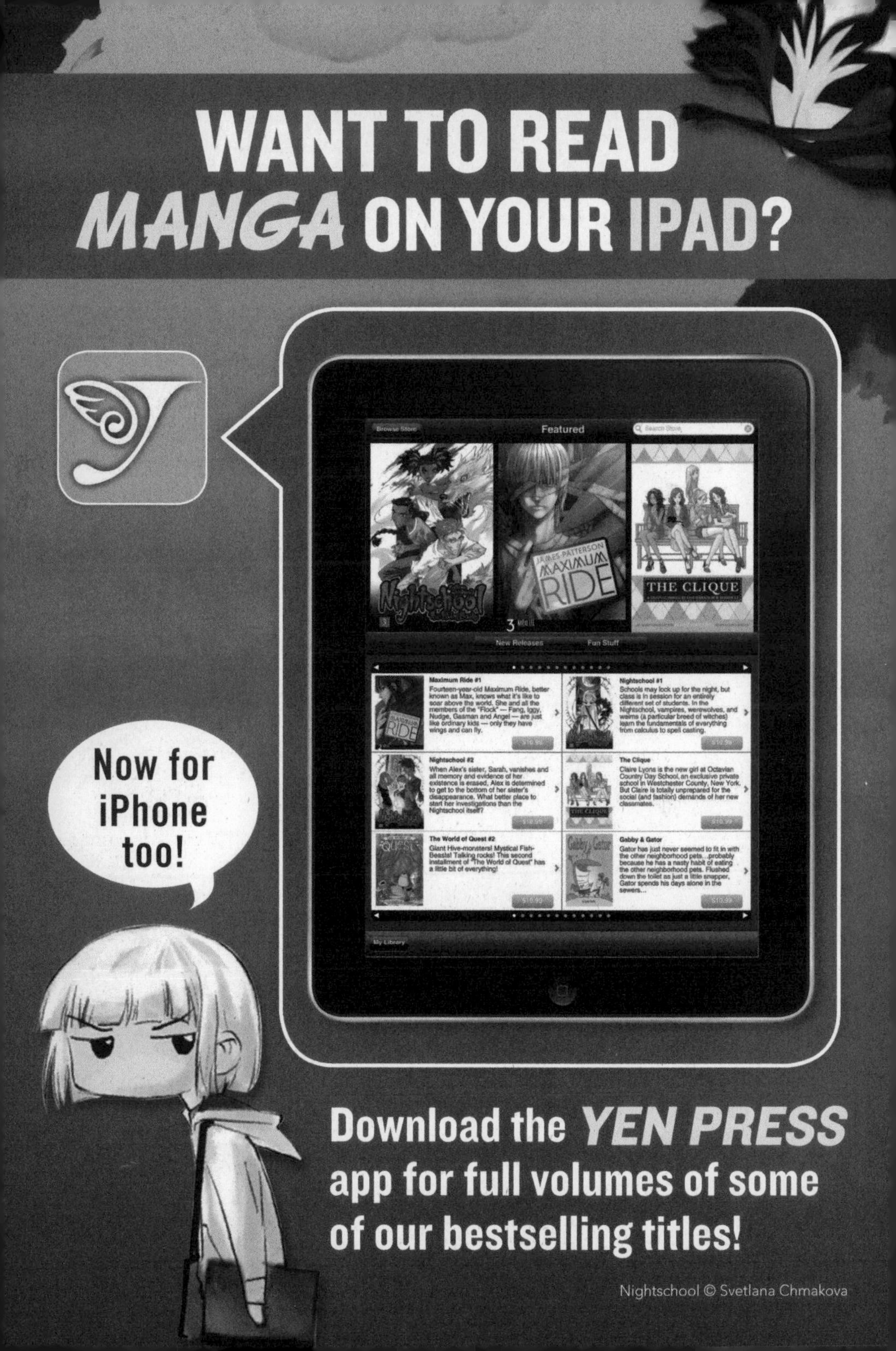
WANT TO READ MANGA ON YOUR IPAD?
Now for iPhone too!
Featured
Download the YEN PRESS app for full volumes of some of our bestselling titles!
Nightschool © Svetlana Chmakova

The Phantomhive family has a butler who's almost too good to be true...

...or maybe he's just too good to be human.

Black Butler

YANA TOBOSO

VOLUMES 1-7 IN STORES NOW!

Yen Press
www.yenpress.com

BLACK BUTLER © Yana Toboso / SQUARE ENIX
Yen Press is an imprint of Hachette Book Group, Inc.

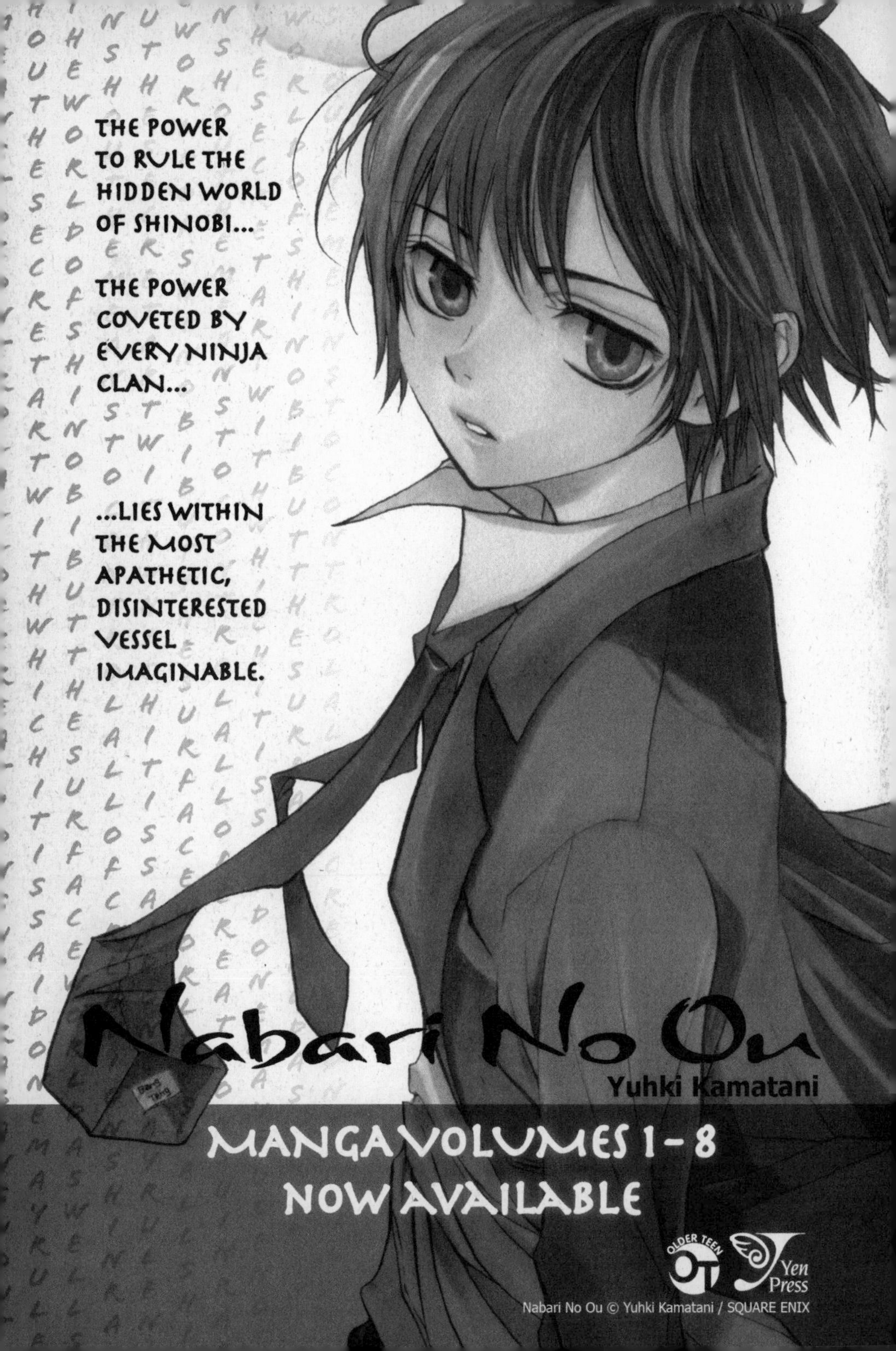
THE POWER TO RULE THE HIDDEN WORLD OF SHINOBI...
THE POWER COVETED BY EVERY NINJA CLAN...
...LIES WITHIN THE MOST APATHETIC, DISINTERESTED VESSEL IMAGINABLE.
Nabari No Ou
Yuhki Kamatani
MANGA VOLUMES 1-8
NOW AVAILABLE
OLDER TEEN OT
Yen Press
Nabari No Ou © Yuhki Kamatani / SQUARE ENIX

To become the ultimate weapon, one boy must eat the souls of 99 humans...

...and one witch.

Maka is a scythe meister, working to perfect her demon scythe until it is good enough to become Death's Weapon—the weapon used by Shinigami-sama, the spirit of Death himself. And if that isn't strange enough, her scythe also has the power to change form—into a human-looking boy!

Yen Press

Yen Press is an imprint of Hachette Book Group

www.yenpress.com

VOLUME 7 IN STORES NOW!!

Soul Eater ©Atsushi Ohkubo/SQUARE ENIX

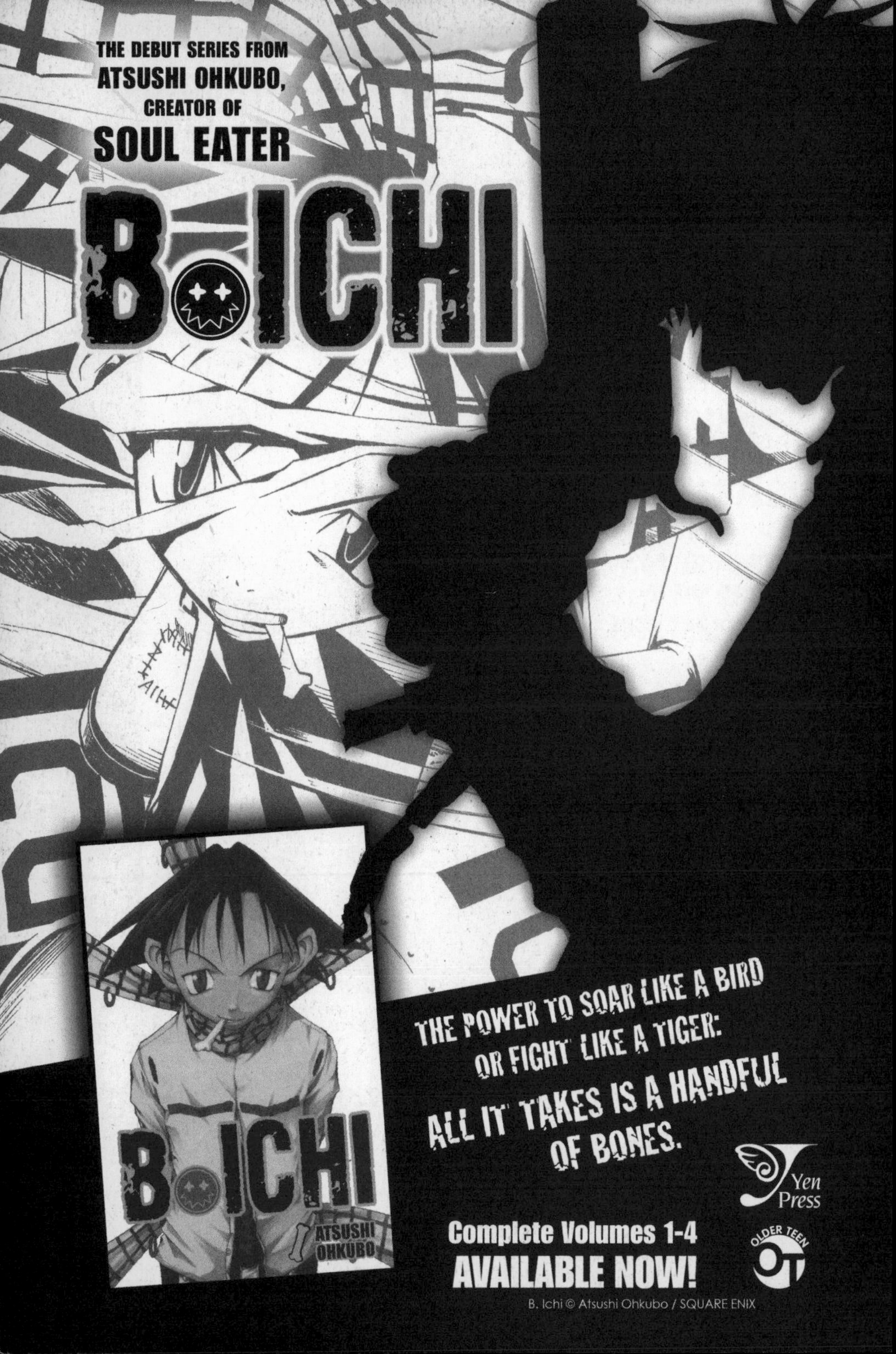
THE DEBUT SERIES FROM
ATSUSHI OHKUBO,
CREATOR OF
SOUL EATER
B. ICHI
THE POWER TO SOAR LIKE A BIRD
OR FIGHT LIKE A TIGER:
ALL IT TAKES IS A HANDFUL
OF BONES.
B. ICHI
ATSUSHI OHKUBO
Yen Press
Complete Volumes 1-4
AVAILABLE NOW!
OLDER TEEN
OT
B. Ichi © Atsushi Ohkubo / SQUARE ENIX

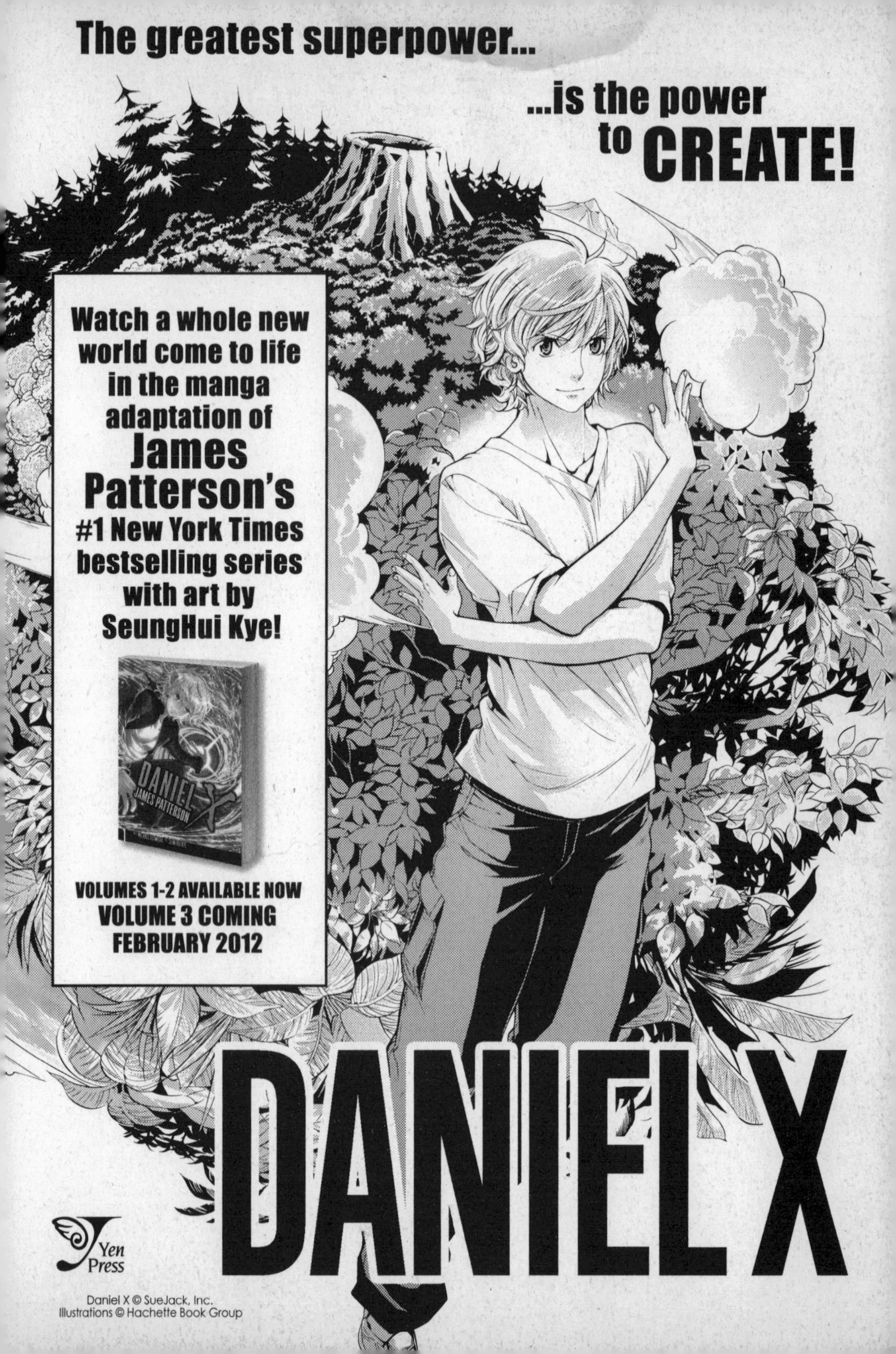
The greatest superpower...
...is the power to CREATE!
Watch a whole new world come to life in the manga adaptation of James Patterson's #1 New York Times bestselling series with art by SeungHui Kye!
DANIEL X
JAMES PATTERSON
VOLUMES 1-2 AVAILABLE NOW
VOLUME 3 COMING
FEBRUARY 2012
DANIEL X
Yen Press
Daniel X © SueJack, Inc.
Illustrations © Hachette Book Group

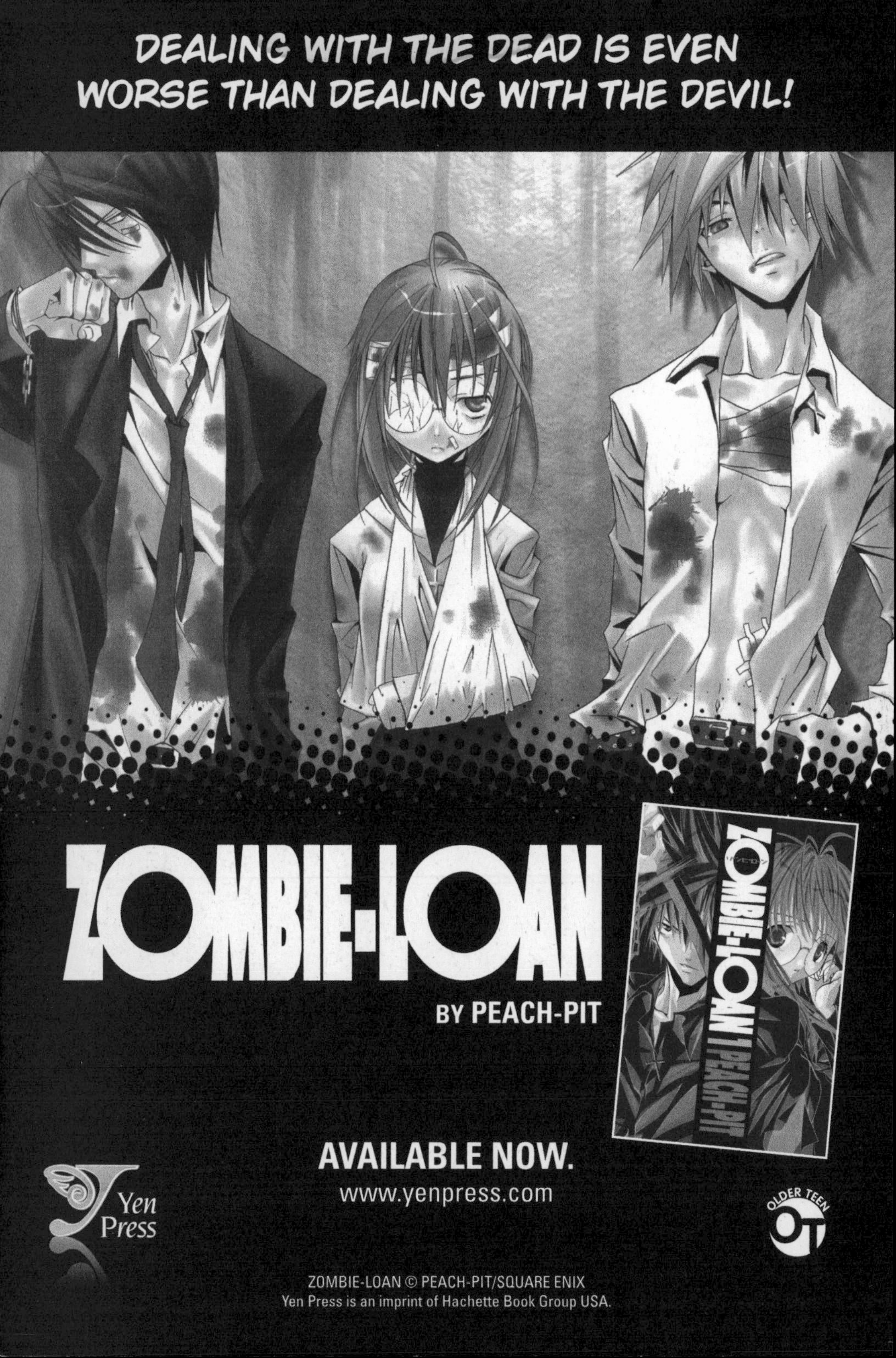
DEALING WITH THE DEAD IS EVEN WORSE THAN DEALING WITH THE DEVIL!
ZOMBIE-LOAN
BY PEACH-PIT
ZOMBIE-LOAN 1 PEACH-PIT
AVAILABLE NOW.
www.yenpress.com
Yen Press
OLDER TEEN OT
ZOMBIE-LOAN © PEACH-PIT/SQUARE ENIX
Yen Press is an imprint of Hachette Book Group USA.

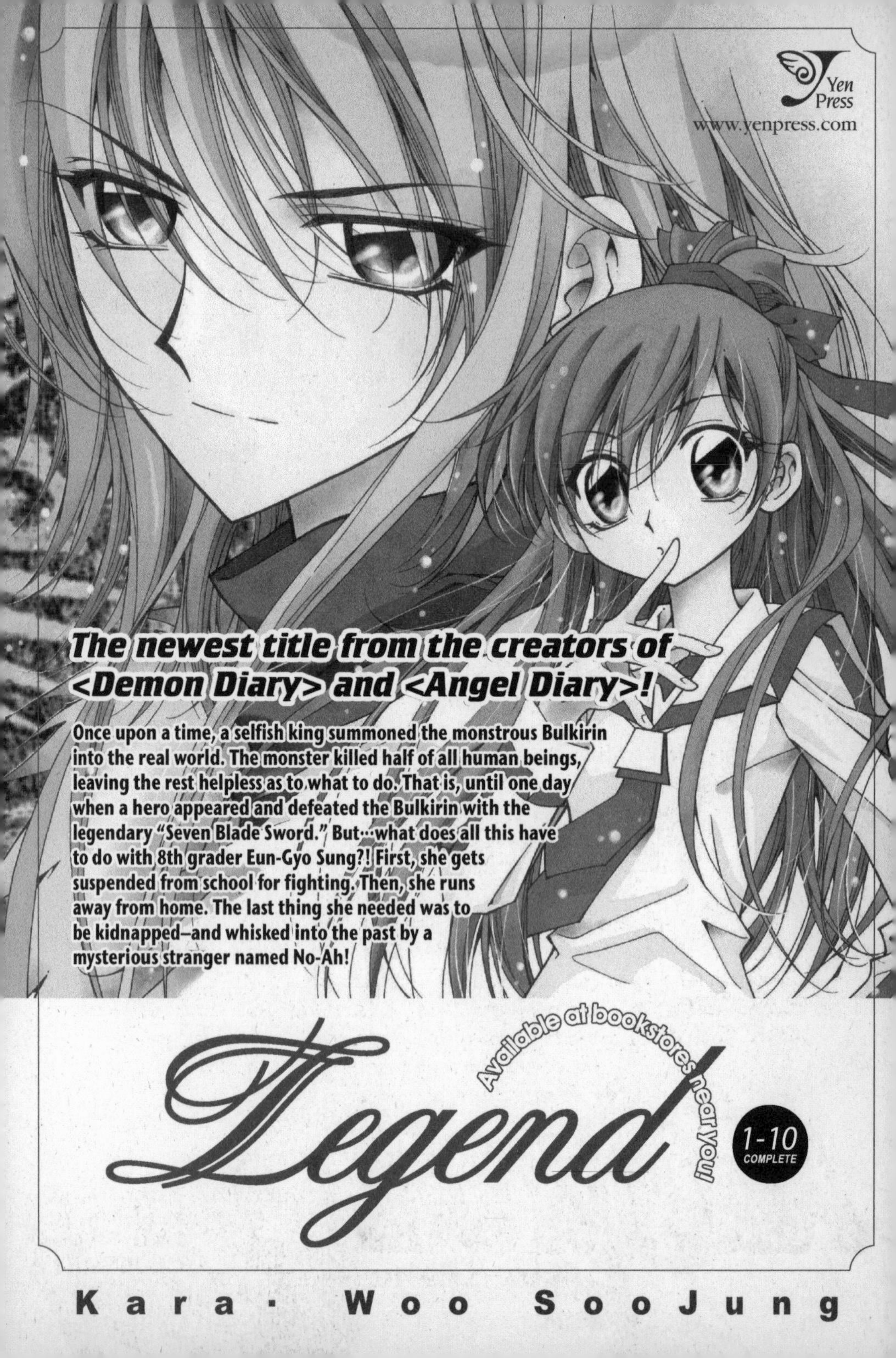
Yen Press
www.yenpress.com
The newest title from the creators of <Demon Diary> and <Angel Diary>!
Once upon a time, a selfish king summoned the monstrous Bulkirin into the real world. The monster killed half of all human beings, leaving the rest helpless as to what to do. That is, until one day when a hero appeared and defeated the Bulkirin with the legendary "Seven Blade Sword." But…what does all this have to do with 8th grader Eun-Gyo Sung?! First, she gets suspended from school for fighting. Then, she runs away from home. The last thing she needed was to be kidnapped–and whisked into the past by a mysterious stranger named No-Ah!
Legend
Available at bookstores near you!
1-10
COMPLETE
Kara · Woo SooJung

www.yenpress.com

THE HIGHLY ANTICIPATED NEW TITLE FROM THE CREATORS OF <DEMON DIARY>!

Dong-Young is a royal daughter of Heaven, betrothed to the King of Hell. Determined to escape her fate, she runs away before the wedding. The four Guardians of Heaven are ordered to find the angel princess while she's hiding out on planet Earth – disguised as a boy! Will she be able to escape from her destiny?! This is a cute gender-bending tale, a romantic comedy/fantasy series about an angel, the King of Hell, and four super-powered chaperones...

AVAILABLE AT A BOOKSTORE NEAR YOU!

Angel Diary

1~13 COMPLETE

Kara · Lee YunHee

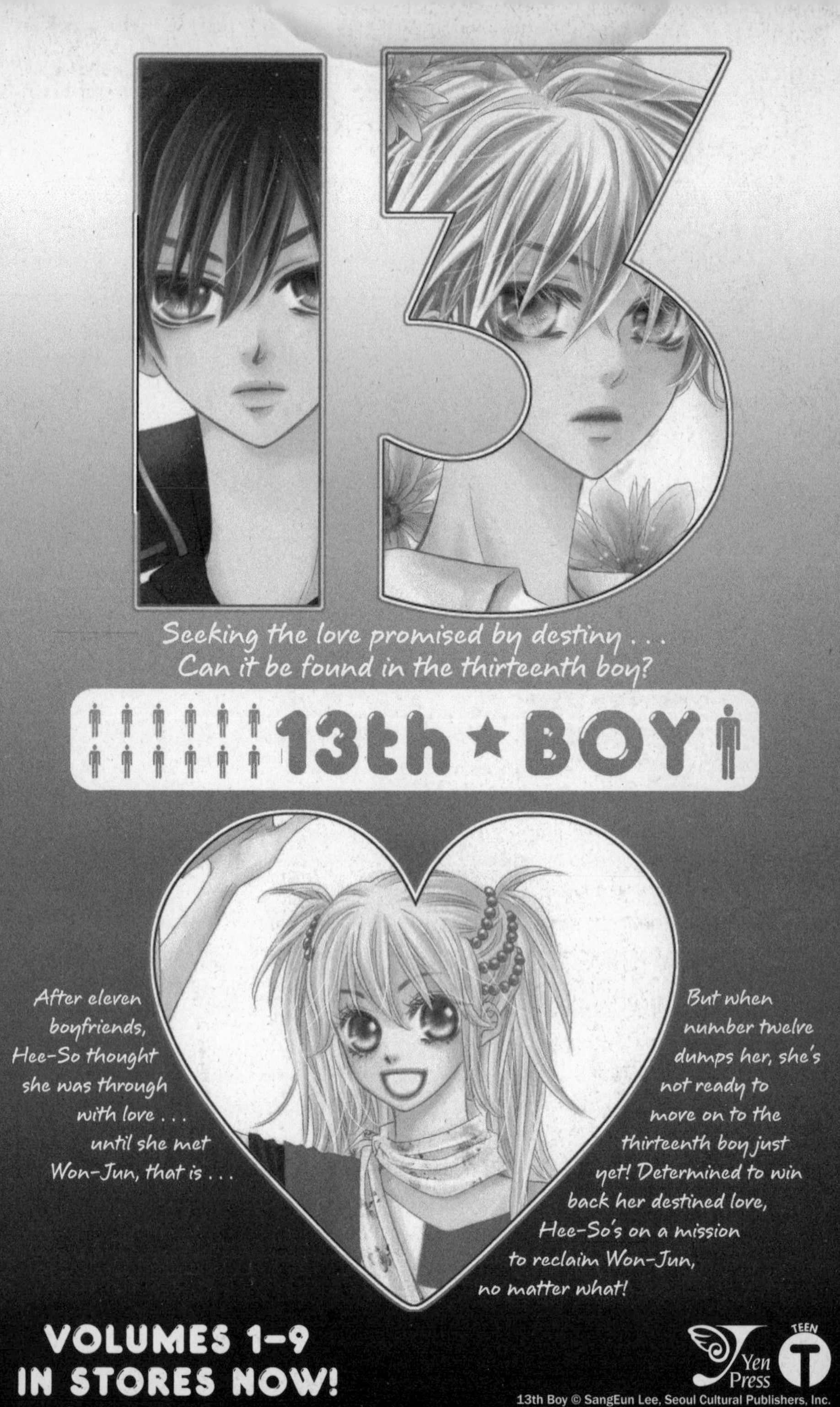
Seeking the love promised by destiny . . .
Can it be found in the thirteenth boy?
13th ★ BOY
After eleven boyfriends, Hee-So thought she was through with love . . . until she met Won-Jun, that is . . .
But when number twelve dumps her, she's not ready to move on to the thirteenth boy just yet! Determined to win back her destined love, Hee-So's on a mission to reclaim Won-Jun, no matter what!
VOLUMES 1–9 IN STORES NOW!
Yen Press
TEEN T
13th Boy © SangEun Lee, Seoul Cultural Publishers, Inc.

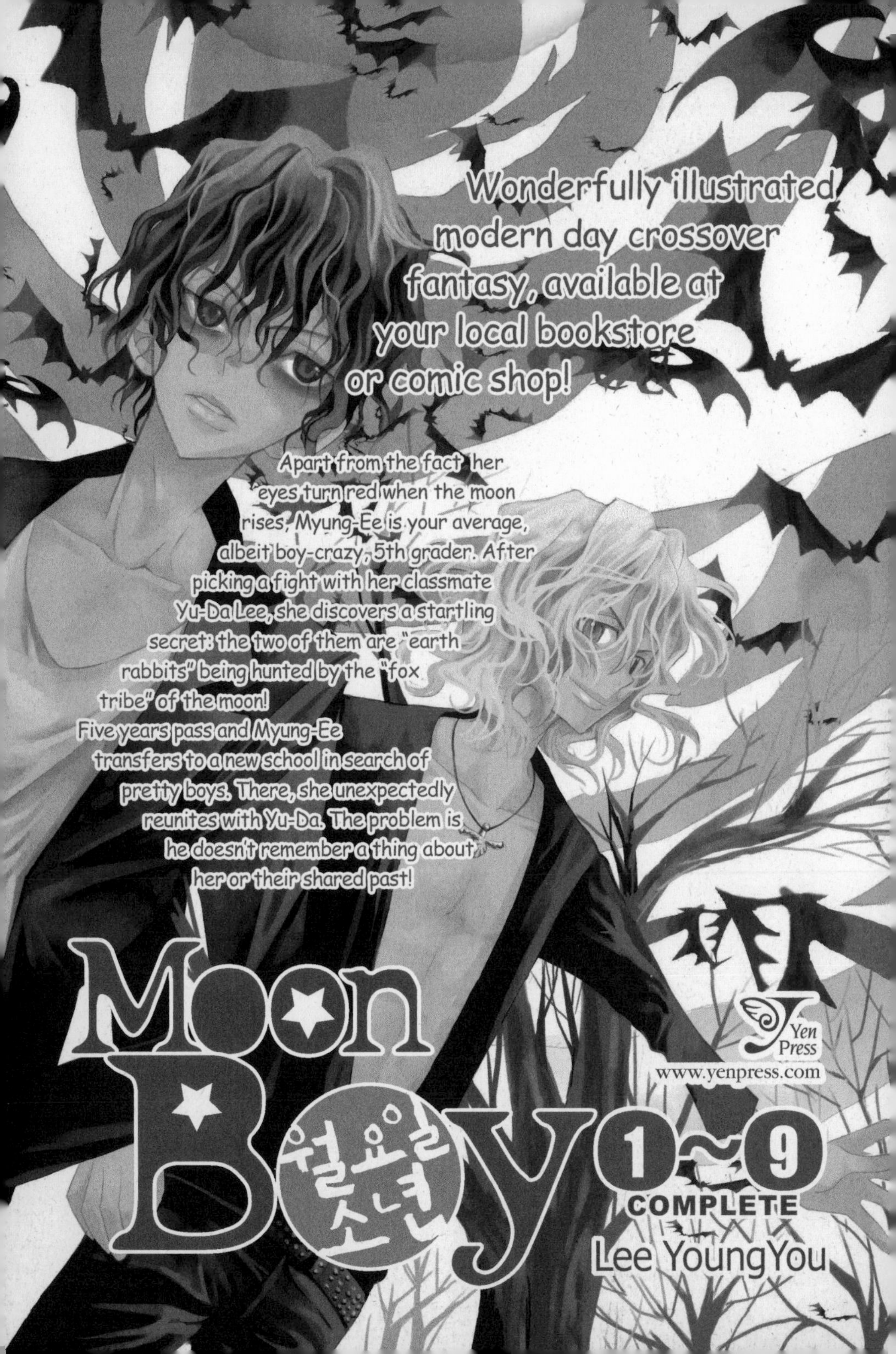

Wonderfully illustrated modern day crossover fantasy, available at your local bookstore or comic shop!
Apart from the fact her eyes turn red when the moon rises, Myung-Ee is your average, albeit boy-crazy, 5th grader. After picking a fight with her classmate Yu-Da Lee, she discovers a startling secret: the two of them are "earth rabbits" being hunted by the "fox tribe" of the moon!
Five years pass and Myung-Ee transfers to a new school in search of pretty boys. There, she unexpectedly reunites with Yu-Da. The problem is, he doesn't remember a thing about her or their shared past!
Moon Boy
월요일 소년
1~9
COMPLETE
Lee YoungYou
Yen Press
www.yenpress.com

A totally new Arabian nights, where Scheherazade is a guy!

Everyone knows the story of Scheherazade and her wonderful tales from the Arabian Nights. For one thousand and one nights, the stories that she created entertained the mad Sultan and eventually saved her life. In this version, Scheherazade is a guy who disguises himself as a woman to save his sister from the mad Sultan. When he puts his life on the line, what kind of strange and unique stories will he tell? This new twist on one of the greatest classical tales might just keep you awake for another ONE THOUSAND AND ONE NIGHTS!

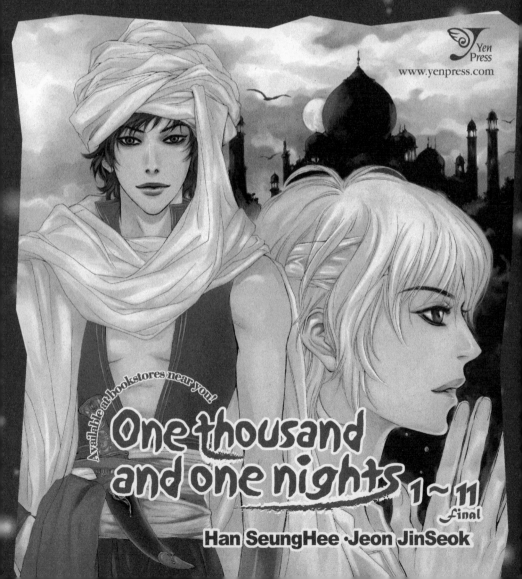

Yen Press

www.yenpress.com

Available at bookstores near you!

One thousand and one nights 1~11 final

Han SeungHee Jeon JinSeok

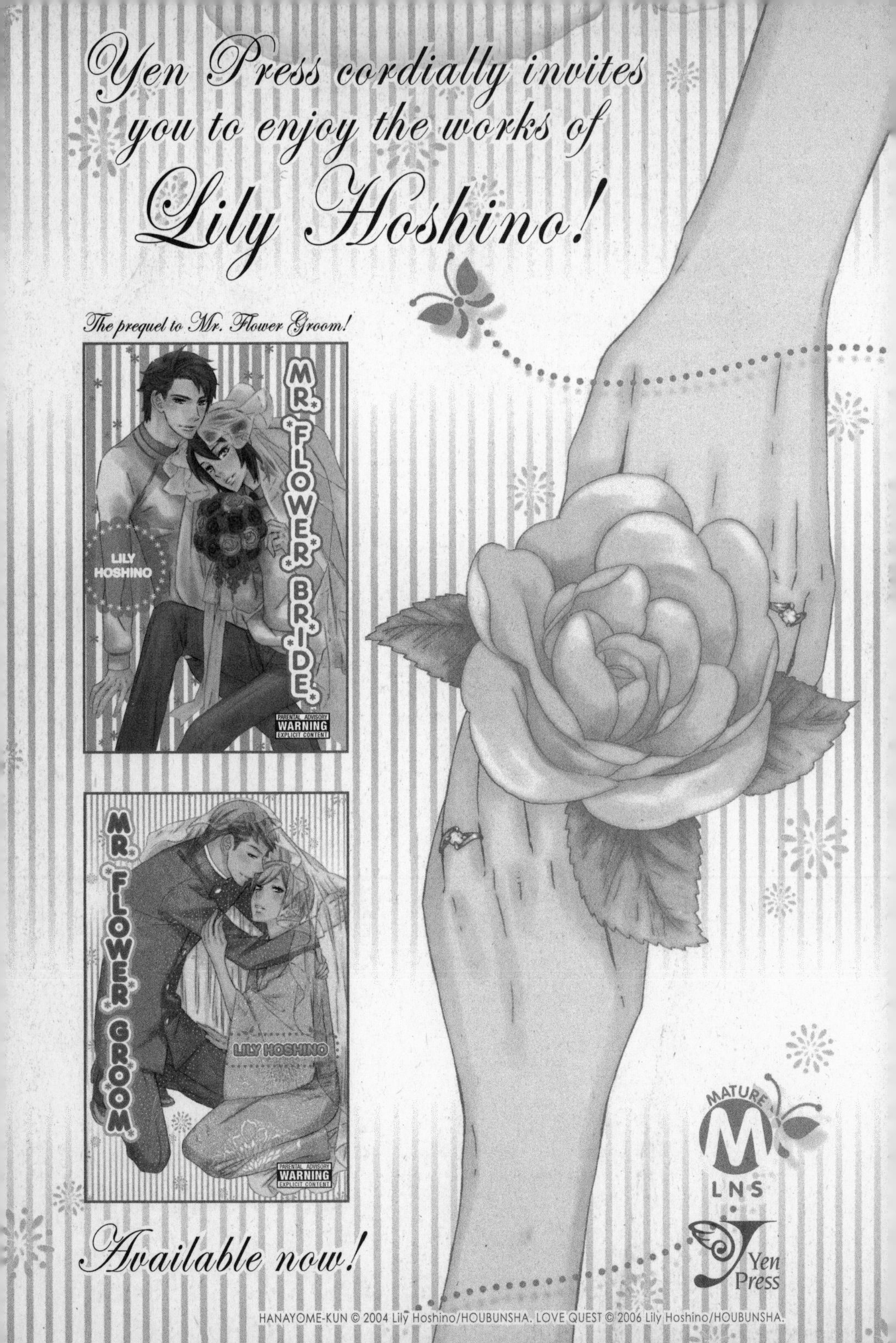

THE BETRAYAL

kNoWS MY NAME

HOTARU ODAGIRI

Translation: Melissa Tanaka † Lettering: Lys Blakeslee

URAGIRI WA BOKU NO NAMAE WO SHITTEIRU Volumes 3 and 4 © Hotaru ODAGIRI 2007, 2008. First published in Japan in 2007, 2008 by KADOKAWA SHOTEN Co., Ltd., Tokyo. English translation rights arranged with KADOKAWA SHOTEN Co., Ltd., Tokyo through TUTTLE MORI AGENCY, INC., Tokyo.

Translation © 2011 by Hachette Book Group, Inc.

All rights reserved. Except as permitted under the U.S. Copyright Act of 1976, no part of this publication may be reproduced, distributed, or transmitted in any form or by any means, or stored in a database or retrieval system, without the prior written permission of the publisher. The characters and events in this book are fictitious. Any similarity to real persons, living or dead, is coincidental and not intended by the author.

Yen Press
Hachette Book Group
237 Park Avenue, New York, NY 10017

www.HachetteBookGroup.com
www.YenPress.com

Yen Press is an imprint of Hachette Book Group, Inc. The Yen Press name and logo are trademarks of Hachette Book Group, Inc.

First Yen Press Edition: December 2011

ISBN: 978-0-316-11942-9

10 9 8 7 6 5 4 3 2

BVG

Printed in the
United States of America